Expert One-on-One
Microsoft® Access Application Development

Expert One-on-One
Microsoft® Access Application Development

Helen Feddema

WILEY

Wiley Publishing, Inc.

Expert One-on-One
Microsoft® Access Application Development

Published by
Wiley Publishing, Inc.
10475 Crosspoint Boulevard
Indianapolis, IN 46256

Library of Congress Cataloging-in-Publication Data:

ISBN: 0-7645-5904-4

Feddema, Helen Bell.
  Expert one-on-one Microsoft access application development / Helen Feddema.
    p. cm.
  Includes index.
  ISBN 0-7645-5904-4 (paper/website)
  1. Microsoft Access. 2. Database management. 3. Computer software—Development. I. Title.
  QA76.9.D3F4365 2004
  005.75'65—dc22

                    2004001551

Printed in the United States of America

10 9 8 7 6 5 4 3 2 1

1B/RU/QU/QU/IN

Credits

Vice President and Executive Group Publisher
Richard Swadley

Vice President and Executive Publisher
Robert Ipsen

Vice President and Publisher
Joseph B. Wikert

Executive Editorial Director
Mary Bednarek

Executive Editor
Robert M. Elliott

Editorial Manager
Kathryn A. Malm

Technical Editor
Mary Hardy

Senior Production Editor
Fred Bernardi

Development Editor
Emilie Herman

Production Editor
Pamela Hanley

Project Coordinator
Erin Smith

Text Design & Composition
Wiley Composition Services

Proofreading and Indexing
TECHBOOKS Production Services

Dedication

To all the developers who have posted their code on the Internet (and its predecessors) for others to use—you may not have been paid, but your work is appreciated!

Contents

Contents

Contents

Contents

Contents

Acknowledgments

As always, thanks to my agent, Claudette Moore, for her work on this book project. Much thanks to my editors at Wiley, Bob Elliott and Emilie Herman, and to production editor Pamela Hanley and all the production staff who worked on this book. I am very grateful to my tech editor, Mary Hardy, who has greatly improved the quality of the sample databases by reviewing them in many versions, spotting problems and suggesting improvements.

About the Author

Helen Feddema grew up in New York City. She was ready for computers when she was 12, but personal computers were still in the future, so she got a B.S. in Philosophy from Columbia and an M.T.S. in Theological Studies from Harvard Divinity School, while working at various office jobs. It was at HDS that she got her first computer, an Osborne, and soon computers were her primary interest. She started with word processing and spreadsheets, went on to learn dBASE, and did dBASE development for six years, part of this time as a corporate developer. After being laid off in a flurry of corporate downsizing in the 1980's, she started doing independent consulting and development, using dBASE, ObjectVision, WordPerfect and Paradox.

Always looking for something new and better, Helen beta tested Access 1.0, and soon recognized that this was the database she had been looking for ever since Windows 3.0 was introduced and she saw the gap waiting to be filled by a great Windows database. Since then she has worked as a developer of Microsoft Office applications, concentrating on Access, Word and Outlook.

Helen co-authored *Inside Microsoft Access 1.0* (New Riders, 1992), and wrote two books for Pinnacle's "The Pros Talk Access" series, *Power Forms* and *Power Reports* (1994). She also co-authored *Access How-Tos* for the Waite Group Press (1995), and contributed to *The Microsoft Outlook Handbook* (Osborne-McGraw-Hill), Que's *Special Edition: Using Microsoft Outlook 97* (1997), *Office Annoyances* (O'Reilly, 1997), and *Outlook Annoyances* (O'Reilly, 1998). She also contributed chapters to Que's *Special Edition: Using Microsoft Project 98* (1997) and Sams' *Teach Yourself Project* (1998).

Helen co-authored Sybex' *MCSD: Access 95 Study Guide* (1998), and contributed chapters on Outlook programming to Que's *Special Edition: Using Microsoft Outlook 2000* (1999), and wrote *DAO Object Model: The Definitive Reference* for O'Reilly (2000), and *Access 2002 Inside-Out* for Microsoft Press.

Helen has been a regular contributor to Pinnacle's *Smart Access* and *Office Developer* journals, *Woody's Underground Office* newsletter, *PC Magazine's Undocumented Office* and the *MS Office and VBA Journal* (now *OfficePro*). She is the editor of the *Woody's Access Watch* ezine, and writes its Access Archon column.

Helen is a big-time beta tester, sometimes having 7 or 8 betas running at once, mostly Microsoft, but with some from other vendors as well. She has participated in every Access beta from 1.0 to 2003, and is a member of the Access Insiders group.

She lives in the mid-Hudson valley area of New York state, with varying numbers of cats and computers.

Helen maintains a Web page (www.helenfeddema.com) with a large selection of code samples concentrating on connecting Access, Outlook, Word and Excel (including several Access add-ins), and all her Access Archon articles.

Introduction

If you are developing databases for your own use, you may not mind opening forms or printing reports directly from the database window, and you know what query to run before printing which report or exporting data to Word. However, if you are planning to create applications for the use of others, particularly for clients who aren't familiar with Access, and don't understand databases in general, you have to do a lot more work, mostly in the form of writing VBA code to automate the application's processes. As a rule of thumb, it's generally true that the easier the application is for the end user, the harder (and more time-consuming) it is to develop. In this book I concentrate on teaching you how to set up your tables and relationships to ensure that the database is properly normalized, and write VBA code to create the connective tissue that turns a bunch of tables, queries, forms and reports into a complete and coherent application.

Over the last eight years, I have created several Access add-ins, to save time while creating applications. I use these add-ins to create a main menu for an application, automatically apply a naming convention to database objects, and ensure a consistent and professional appearance of the application's forms. I'll discuss the use of my add-ins to help construct an application in the appropriate chapters of this book.

You won't find excruciatingly detailed step-by-step explanations of how to create a table, or lists of all the properties of a textbox—I assume that an experienced Access user either already knows how to do these things, or can look them up in Help or the Object Browser. But this book isn't aimed at the advanced developer either, such as those who want to create their own custom objects and controls, use Windows API calls, or delve into the mysteries of the PrtMip property of the Print dialog (when you reach that point, I recommend the Access Developers Handbook, by Getz, Litwin and Gilbert).

Instead, this book concentrates on writing VBA code to connect the components of a database into a functioning, coherent application, with special attention to the very important but inadequately documented area of Automation code, which is used to communicate with other Office applications, since sometimes the best way to add a requested feature to an Access application is to use a built-in feature of Word or Outlook.

Audience

I wrote this book for experienced Access users, who know how to create tables, queries, forms and other Access objects, and have some familiarity with writing Access VBA code, but need help in making the transition from an experienced and competent Access user who can create databases for personal use, to an Access developer who can make a living developing applications for clients.

How This Book is Organized

Part One of this book, Creating an Access Application, covers the basics—creating tables, forms, and other database objects as part of an application, with chapters on creating a database (including tables and relationships), forms, controls, queries, PivotTables and PivotCharts, reports, and modules.

Part Two, Modifying, Updating, and Maintaining Access Applications, covers the techniques you need to use over the course of an application's life cycle, including reworking applications created by non-developers, moving old data into a new database, and upgrading to a new Office version.

Part Three, Working with Other Office Components (and More), deals with using Automation code to exchange data among Office components, and even a few non-Office programs, with separate chapters for exchanging data with Word, Outlook, and Excel, and a chapter for communicating with non-Office applications, including Symantec WinFax. If you need to write Access data to Word letters or Excel worksheets, you can go right to the relevant chapter.

Access Versions

The book covers Access versions from Office 2000 to Office 2003, and most of the book's material applies to all of these versions. Where a specific element (such as PivotCharts, introduced in Access 2002) requires a higher version of Access, this will be noted in the text.

With the exception of the ActiveX controls discussed in Chapter 3 (Selecting the Right Controls for Forms), all you need to work through the examples in this book is Access 2000 or higher; if you want to use the ActiveX controls, however, you need the Developer edition of Access (which includes these controls) or another program that includes them, such as Visual Basic.

Conventions

To help you get the most from the text and keep track of what's happening, we've used a number of conventions throughout the book.

> **Boxes like this one hold important, not-to-be forgotten information that is directly relevant to the surrounding text.**

Tips, hints, tricks, and asides to the current discussion are offset and placed in italics like this.

As for styles in the text:

❑   We *highlight* important words when we introduce them

❑   We show keyboard strokes like this: Ctrl+A

❑   We show file names, URLs, and code within the text like so: `persistence.properties`

❑   We present code in two different ways:

```
In code examples we highlight new and important code with a gray background.
```

The gray highlighting is not used for code that's less important in the present context, or has been shown before.

Source Code

As you work through the examples in this book, you may choose either to type in all the code manually (this is practical if you just need to add a few lines of code to an existing procedure), or you can use the sample databases that accompany the book, or import forms, reports, or modules from the sample databases into your own databases. All of the sample databases used in this book are available for download at http://www.wrox.com. Once at the site, simply locate the book's title (either by using the Search box or by using one of the title lists) and click the Download Files link on the book's detail page to obtain all the sample files for the book. There is a zip file for each part of the book, containing the sample databases, add-ins and other files needed for the chapters in that part.

> *Because many books have similar titles, you may find it easiest to search by ISBN; for this book the ISBN is 0-764-55904-4.*

Once you download the zip file, just decompress it with your favorite compression tool. Alternately, you can go to the main Wrox code download page at http://www.wrox.com/dynamic/books/download.aspx to see the sample databases and/or code available for this book and all other Wrox books.

Sample Files

A number of sample databases are used as illustrations for various chapters; and three of my add-ins are also used to enhance database functionality; the chapters where the sample databases and add-ins are used are listed in the table below. In the case of add-ins, they may also be mentioned briefly in other chapters; the listed chapters are the ones where the use of the add-in is described in detail.

Zip File	Contents	Chapter(s)
Part One.zip	Design Schemes.zip	2 (Forms)
	Menu Manager Add-in.zip	6 (Reports)
	PivotTables and PivotCharts.mdb	5 (PivotTables and PivotCharts)
	Query Expressions.mdb	4 (Queries)
	Toy Workshop (*).mdb	1 (Creating a Database for an Application), 2 (Forms), 3 (Controls), 4 (Queries), 6 (Reports), and 7 (Modules) (Start and Finish versions)

Table continued on following page

Zip File	Contents	Chapter(s)
Part Two.zip	EBook Companion.mdb	9 (Reworking an Existing Application)
	LNC Rename Add-in.zip	9 (Reworking an Existing Application)
	Original EBook Companion.mdb	9 (Reworking an Existing Application)
	Test References.mdb	8 (Managing The Application Life Cycle)
	Toy Workshop (*).mdb	10 (Moving Data) (Start and Finish versions)
Part Three.zip	Categories.xls	13 (Working with Excel)
	Customers.xls	13 (Working with Excel)
	Excel Data Exchange.mdb	13 (Working with Excel)
	Non-Office Data Exchange.mdb	14 (Working outside of Office)
	Outlook Data Exchange with Redemption.mdb	12 (Working with Outlook)
	Outlook Data Exchange.mdb	12 (Working with Outlook)
	Word Data Exchange.mdb	11 (Working with Word)
	Word Docs.zip	11 (Working with Word)

Errata

We make every effort to ensure that there are no errors in the text or in the code. However, no one is perfect, and mistakes do occur. If you find an error in one of our books, like a spelling mistake or faulty piece of code, we would be very grateful for your feedback. By sending in errata you may save another reader hours of frustration and at the same time you will be helping us provide even higher quality information.

To find the errata page for this book, go to `http://www.wrox.com` and locate the title using the Search box or one of the title lists. Then, on the book details page, click the Book Errata link. On this page you can view all errata that has been submitted for this book and posted by Wrox editors. A complete book list including links to each's book's errata is also available at `www.wrox.com/misc-pages/booklist.shtml`.

If you don't spot "your" error on the Book Errata page, go to `www.wrox.com/contact/techsupport.shtml` and complete the form there to send us the error you have found. We'll check the information and, if appropriate, post a message to the book's errata page and fix the problem in subsequent editions of the book.

p2p.wrox.com

For author and peer discussion, join the P2P forums at p2p.wrox.com. The forums are a Web-based system for you to post messages relating to Wrox books and related technologies and interact with other readers and technology users. The forums offer a subscription feature to e-mail you topics of interest of your choosing when new posts are made to the forums. Wrox authors, editors, other industry experts, and your fellow readers are present on these forums.

At http://p2p.wrox.com you will find a number of different forums that will help you not only as you read this book, but also as you develop your own applications. To join the forums, just follow these steps:

1. Go to p2p.wrox.com and click the Register link.
2. Read the terms of use and click Agree.
3. Complete the required information to join as well as any optional information you wish to provide and click Submit.
4. You will receive an e-mail with information describing how to verify your account and complete the joining process.

> *You can read messages in the forums without joining P2P but in order to post your own messages, you must join.*

Once you join, you can post new messages and respond to messages other users post. You can read messages at any time on the Web. If you would like to have new messages from a particular forum e-mailed to you, click the Subscribe to this Forum icon by the forum name in the forum listing.

For more information about how to use the Wrox P2P, be sure to read the P2P FAQs for answers to questions about how the forum software works as well as many common questions specific to P2P and Wrox books. To read the FAQs, click the FAQ link on any P2P page.

Part 1: Creating an Access Application

Creating a Database
for an Application

An application is more than just a database. Anybody with Access can create a database, but a database with a bunch of disconnected tables, queries, forms, and reports is not an application. An application consists of a database—or possibly several databases—containing normalized tables with appropriate relationships between them; queries that filter and sort data; forms to add and edit data; reports to display the data; and possibly PivotTables or PivotCharts to analyze the data, with all of these components connected into an efficiently functioning and coherent whole by *Visual Basic for Applications* (VBA) code. This chapter covers preparation for creating an application (getting and analyzing the information you need from the client), and creating tables to hold the application's data.

Most Access books give you lots of information about Access database tables (and other database objects), but don't necessarily tell you the stuff you really need to know: how to divide up the raw data you receive from a client into separate tables, how to decide what field type to use for each field in a table, and what relationships to set up between tables to create an efficient and well-integrated application. Through a series of developer-client Q&A sessions, I'll show you how to extract the information you need to create the right tables for your application and link them into appropriate relationships.

I have always found it easier to understand a process by watching somebody do it, as opposed to reading abstract technical information about it, so in this chapter, I will explain what I am doing as I walk you through the preparation for creating an application and then the creation of its tables. Succeeding chapters will deal with creating the application's forms, queries, and reports. Some technical information is necessary, of course, but it will be interspersed with demonstrations of what you need to do, and the explanations will tend to follow the actions, rather than precede them. Sometimes, if you can see how something is done correctly, that is all you need to know in order to do it right yourself, while an abstract technical explanation by itself is rarely adequate to teach you how to do something correctly.

There won't be lots of step-by-step walk-throughs illustrating how to create database objects in this book, or long lists of properties and other attributes. I am assuming that you already know how to create tables, forms, and other database objects (and if you need detailed information, you know how to get it from Help), and that instead, what you need is help in making decisions on what kind of data goes into which table, how the tables should be related, and what types of forms, queries, and reports are best for working with the data in your application.

Although code is crucial to binding an application into a coherent whole, there won't be any code in this chapter, because in Access, code runs from event procedures, and tables don't have event procedures. Before writing event procedures, we need to create tables to hold the data, and that is what this chapter covers.

Gathering Data

To start creating an Access application, you need two things: a clear idea of what tasks the application should perform and the output it should produce, and an adequate quantity of realistic data. Rather than just asking the client for a list of the tasks the application needs to perform, I usually ask a series of questions designed to elicit the required information. A typical Q&A session is presented in the next section of this chapter. However, if there is already a functioning database, printouts of its reports and screen shots of its forms can be helpful as an indication of what tasks are currently being done.

For best results, there is no substitute for large quantities of real data, such as the ebook data in the sample EBook Companion database used in Chapter 9, *Reworking an Existing Application*. But if you have a reasonable quantity of representative data and a client who is willing to answer your questions, that should be sufficient to set up tables with the correct fields. With this information, you can create tables with the necessary fields; set up relationships between them; and proceed to create the queries, forms, reports, and VBA code that will let you create an application that does what the client wants.

Curiously, I'm often asked to start working on an application for a client without any data at all. It may be difficult to convey this concept to a client, but it is important to get real-life data (either in electronic or paper form) in order to set up tables and fields correctly. If you (the developer) have to create dummy data to have something to work with when creating tables and other database objects, you will probably end up having to make changes—possibly major changes—to tables later on, and find that further changes are needed to other database components; so, it really helps to have a substantial amount of representative data to work with.

However, realistically there are cases where you won't be able to get data from the client. There are two cases where data isn't available: a brand-new business (or other enterprise) that doesn't have any data yet, and a business whose data is confidential. In these cases, you just have to do the best you can, creating dummy data after questioning the client about what data needs to be stored in the application's tables.

Once you have obtained the data in electronic or paper form, it's best to just use it as raw material to help you determine what fields you need when designing tables and other components, rather than as ready-made components to plug into your application. Looking at real data, you can see (for example) whether or not there are unique IDs for products. If there is a unique Product ID, that field should be the key field of the Products table; otherwise, you will need to create an AutoNumber field. If you see multiple addresses for customers or clients, you will need to create linked tables for address data, for purposes of normalization; if there is only one address per customer or client, address data can be stored directly in the Customers or Clients table. In most cases, even if you are given a database with Access tables, you will need to make some modifications for purposes of normalization, and create a number of supporting tables as well as lookup tables to use as the row sources of comboboxes used to select values or records.

Figuring Out Business Tasks and Objects

When designing an application for a client, after obtaining a reasonable quantity of representative data, you need to discuss the processes to be modeled in the application—not just how they are done currently, but how they could be done better and more efficiently. For example, users may have been typing data into textboxes; if the data is limited in nature (for example, sales regions or phone number types) a combobox with a lookup table as its row source will ensure that users don't mistype an entry, which would cause problems when sorting or filtering data later on.

A client may give you piles of paper documentation, or descriptions of business processes, which again may or may not be helpful, depending on how well thought out these processes are. Often, real-world business practices develop bit by bit over the years, with new procedures not being integrated with older processes as well as they might be. When designing an application, it's a good idea to review the existing procedures and consider whether they should be streamlined for greater efficiency when setting up the database.

Don't just attempt to duplicate existing business processes in your database—at least not without examining them closely. Upon examination, you will often find that there are serious gaps in procedures that need to be remedied in the database. Just because users have been manually typing customer letters in Word and typing the customer address off the screen from a database record doesn't mean that you shouldn't generate Word letters automatically. (See Chapter 11, *Working with Word,* for information about generating Word letters from an Access database.)

You may also see that your application could do some tasks that aren't being done at all, but that would be very useful, such as generating email to clients, or analyzing data in PivotTables or PivotCharts. See Chapter 12, *Working with Outlook,* for information on sending email messages from Access. But the application first needs tables to store data, so the initial task is to set up the database's tables.

Determining Your Entities

The first task in setting up a database is determining what things it works with and how they work with each other. (The technical term often used in database literature is *entity,* but as far as I am concerned, *thing* works just as well.) If you are developing an application for a client, there may be an existing database. Depending on the skills of the person who created the database, this may be more of a problem than a helpful first step.

As an example of how to figure out the things your application needs to work with, following is a hypothetical example of a client who wants an application to manage his business, called the Toy Workshop. Let's start by asking the client some basic questions:

Q: What does the business do?

A: We sell toys.

We need a Toys table.

Q: Do you have an ID or product number for each toy?

A: Yes, a combination of letters and numbers.

We need a text ToyID field as a key field in tblToys.

Q: Do you make the toys or purchase them from vendors and resell them?

A: Both.

We need a table of materials used in manufacturing toys. We might need two tables for toys—one for toys purchased for resale and one for toys manufactured in-house. We need to determine whether the two types of toys are different enough to require different tables or whether they can be stored in one table, with different values in a few fields, and a Materials table, for toy-making materials.

Q: What are the differences between manufactured and purchased toys?

A: For purchased toys we need to record the vendor name, vendor product number, purchase price and purchase date; for manufactured toys we need to know how much of each component is used, the labor costs, and when they were manufactured.

Sounds like we could use a single Toys table, with a Yes/No Purchased field to indicate whether the toy is purchased or manufactured; that field could then be used to enable or disable various controls on forms. We also need a Vendors table, to use when selecting a value for the VendorName field, and a Materials table, for toy-making materials.

Q: Are raw materials purchased from different vendors than toys to resell, or could one vendor sell you both materials and finished toys?

A: Most of the vendors we use sell only finished toys; some sell only materials, and just a few sell both materials and finished toys.

Then all the vendors could be stored in one table, with Yes/No fields to indicate whether they sell finished toys, materials, or both.

Q: When you make the toys, is this done in your own workshop or factory, or contracted out?

A: Done in our workshop.

No need for a Contractors table.

Q: Do you have just one workshop, or several?

A: Just one.

Don't need a lookup table for workshops.

Q: Do you do anything else other than selling toys?

A: Yes, we also repair broken toys.

Need a Repairs table.

Q: Just the ones you sell, or others too?

A: Our own and other similar toys.

We can't just identify the repaired toys by ToyID; we'll need an AutoNumber field to uniquely identify toys made or purchased elsewhere that come in for repair.

Q: Are the repairs done in-house, or contracted out?

A: In-house only.

We need a table of employees, with a field to identify those who do the repairs.

Q: Do you send out catalogs or other promotional materials?

A: Yes.

We need a table of customers, and also a table of potential customers or leads.

Q: By mail, email, or both?

A: Both.

The Mailing List table(s) should have both the mailing address and email address.

Q: Do you sell toys in a store, by mail, or over the Internet?

A: From a factory store and by mail or phone. No Internet sales yet, but maybe in the future that will be added.

We need an Orders table, with a field for sale type. Customers should be selected from a Customers table, with a provision for entering a new customer on the fly when taking an order. Since mail or phone orders will require both a shipping and a billing address, we need a linked table of shipping addresses.

From these answers, we know that the application needs primary tables for the following things (these are the application's entities):

❑   Toys

❑   Categories

❑   Vendors

❑   Customers

❑   Shipping addresses

❑   Mailing list

❑   Materials

❑   Repairs

❑   Employees

❑   Orders

Additionally, a number of linked tables will be needed, to store data linked to records in the main tables, and some lookup tables will be needed to store data for selection from comboboxes, to ensure data accuracy.

Creating Tables for an Application

Now that you have some information from the client, you can start creating tables and setting up relationships between them, turning a mass of inchoate data into a set of normalized tables representing the things (entities) the database works with. Using the list of tables obtained from the Q&A session with the client, let's start creating tables for the Toy Workshop application. First, though, a note on naming objects: applying a naming convention right from the start when creating a database will make it much easier to work with. I use the Leszynski Naming Convention (LNC), which is described more fully in Chapter 9, *Reworking an Existing Application*. For tables, the LNC tag is *tbl*, so all table names will start with that tag.

Table Creation Methods

To create a new table, click the New button in the Database window with the Tables object selected in the object bar. You have several choices in the New Table dialog, as shown in Figure 1.1.

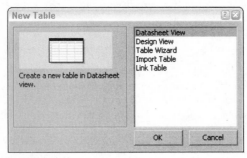

Figure 1.1

In many cases, it's best to just select the Design view choice and go ahead with creating the table fields, but some of the other choices are useful in certain cases. The primary consideration is whether your table is a standard table type (in which case the Table Wizard is a useful shortcut) or not (Design view is best). All the choices are discussed more fully in later sections:

❑   **Datasheet view.** This choice doesn't have much to offer. The new table opens in Datasheet view, and you can enter data into the first row. To name the fields in Datasheet view, you need to click several times on the Field*n* field name (until it is highlighted), then type the new name over it—much less convenient than just entering the field name on a new row in Design view. Access guesses at the field data type according to the data entered into the first row, not always accurately, so you will have to modify data types in Design view in any case. In the sample table shown in Figures 1.2 and 1.3, for example, when you switch to Design view you will see that the ToyID field is not identified as the key field, and the two price fields are Long Integer rather than Currency.

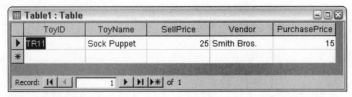

Figure 1.2

When creating a new table in Datasheet view, if you enter text into a field, a Text field is created; if you enter a number alone, a Long Integer field is created; if you enter a number with a dollar sign, a Currency field is created; and if you enter a recognizable date, a Date field is created. If you need any other data types (such as a Double numeric field, a Yes/No field, a Memo field, or an OLE Object field), you will have to create them in Design view.

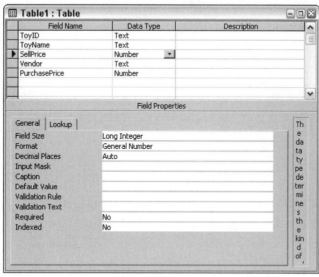

Figure 1.3

❏ **Design view.** The best choice for nonstandard tables you need to create from scratch. The table opens in Design view, letting you enter each field name on its own row and select the appropriate data type from the Data Type drop-down list (see Figure 1.4).

❏ **Table Wizard.** Useful as a shortcut when creating standard tables, such as a table of customer name and address data. However, these tables should be used with caution, because they are not always normalized. For example, the Contacts table shown in Figure 1.5 has a number of phone number fields (perhaps to match Outlook contacts), which (depending on the contact) could either provide too many or too few phone fields. With rare exceptions, phone and ID data should be stored in a linked table, which lets you enter exactly as many items as are needed for each contact.

❏ **ImportTable.** Lets you import data from an external source into an Access table. If you import outside data as a starter, you will need to examine the fields to make sure that they have the correct data type, and possibly break up the table into several linked, normalized tables.

❏ **LinkTable.** Links an Access table to data in another program, such as Excel. Linked tables aren't as useful as other tables because you can't modify their structure; use linked tables only when you need a quick view of current data maintained in an outside program.

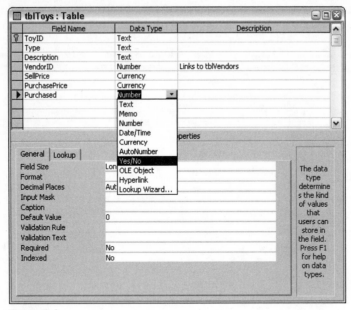

Figure 1.4

In the Database window, linked tables have an arrow to the left of the table name, and a distinctive icon for each data type, as shown in Figure 1.6, where you can see three linked tables—one a comma-delimited text file, one a dBASE file, and one an Excel worksheet. I use the tag *tcsv* for a linked comma-delimited text file, *tdbf* for a linked dBASE file, and *txls* for a linked Excel worksheet, so that I will know what type of linked file I am dealing with when I can't see the icons in the Database window.

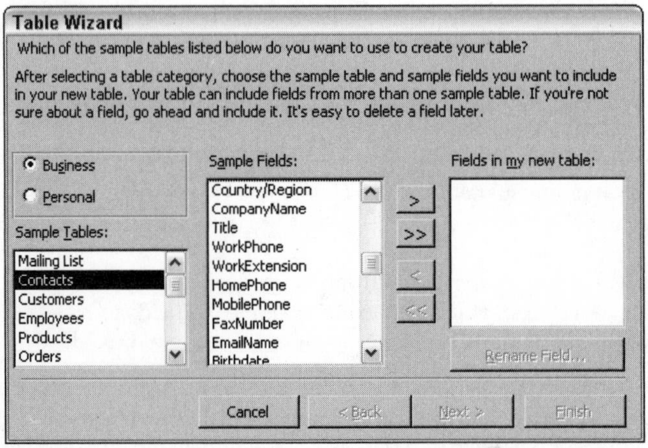

Figure 1.5

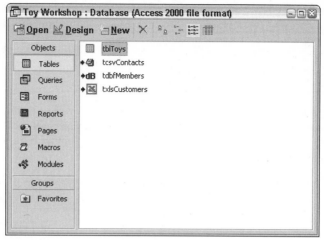

Figure 1.6

A *native* table is a table that contains data within Access; the great majority of tables you will work with in Access are native tables. When you create a table in Access, it is a native table, and when you import data from an outside program, the imported data is placed into a native table. In addition to native tables, you can also work with *linked* tables, which let you work with data in other programs, such as Excel or dBASE.

Creating the Tables

I'll start with tblToys, which is the database's main table, containing information about the toys sold (and in some cases, manufactured) by the client. Since the Table Wizard offers a Products table, let's start with that, and modify it as needed. Figure 1.7 shows the Products table in the Table Wizard; I selected most of the standard fields to get a head start on creating tblToys.

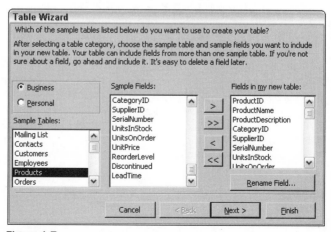

Figure 1.7

There is a button on the Table Wizard screen that lets you rename a field; you can either rename fields as desired in the wizard, or wait until the table opens in Design view and rename fields as needed there. After selecting and (optionally) renaming fields as desired, click the Next button to go to the next page of the wizard, where you give the table a name (tblToys in this case), and select the option to have Access set the primary key, or do it yourself; select *No, I'll set the primary key*, because you want to have control over the selection of the key field.

After clicking Next again, the wizard correctly assumes that the ToyID field should be the key field, and gives you three choices (shown in Figure 1.8). Select the third, because in this case the ToyID field contains a combination of letters and numbers. (If you need an AutoNumber ID, select the first option; for a numeric ID, the second option is appropriate.)

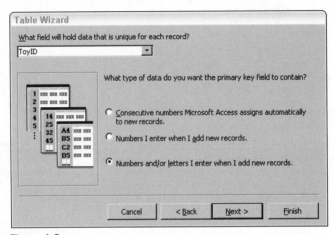

Figure 1.8

After clicking Next again, you are asked if you want to link the new table to any other tables in the database; because this is a new table, just click Next again. On the final screen, select *Modify the table design* to open the new table in Design view, where you can finalize its structure.

If you don't set table relationships in the Table Wizard, you can always set them later in the Relationships window—in fact, you may prefer to create all your relationships there, using its more intuitive visual interface.

The first step is to set up an input mask for the ToyID key field, to ensure that data entry into this field meets the client's specifications for this field. To create the input mask, you can either click the Build button to the right of the Input Mask property for the ToyID field to open the Input Mask Wizard, or just type in the input mask. Since the Input Mask Wizard doesn't have a standard selection of the appropriate type, we'll need to type it directly. The table below lists the characters you can use in input masks, to restrict data entry into the field.

Mask Character	Entries Allowed.
0	Required digit from 0 through 9; plus and minus signs not allowed.
9	Optional digit from 9 through 9, or space; plus and minus signs not allowed.
#	Optional digit or space; blanks converted to spaces; plus and minus signs allowed.
L	Required letter A through Z or a through z.
?	Optional letter A through Z or a through z.
A	Required letter or digit.
a	Optional letter or digit.
&	Required character or space.
C	Optional character or space.
. , : ; - /	Decimal placeholder and thousands, date, and time separators—the character used depends on the Regional settings in the Control Panel.
<	Converts following characters to lowercase.
>	Converts following characters to uppercase.
!	Causes the input mask to be displayed from right to left, instead of the standard left to right. In some versions of Office, this switch does not work correctly. See the Microsoft Knowledge Base (KB) article 209049, Input Mask Character (!) Does Not Work as Expected" for a discussion of the problem in Access 2000. KB articles can be viewed or downloaded from the Microsoft support Web site at http://support.microsoft.com/
\	Marks the next character as a literal character.
Password	Creates a password entry textbox—characters typed into the textbox are stored as entered, but displayed as asterisks, for security.

For the sample table's key field, the client says that the ToyID consists of two uppercase letters and three numbers, so we'll need the > character to make entered letters uppercase, then two L's and three zeroes entered into the InputMask property of this field:

```
>LL000
```

In addition to the standard fields from the Table Wizard, we'll need a few more fields to hold data related to manufactured toys. Figure 1.9 shows the table with the extra fields. There is another product ID field in the table, VendorProductID, but I won't put an input mask on this field, because vendors have their own ID formats.

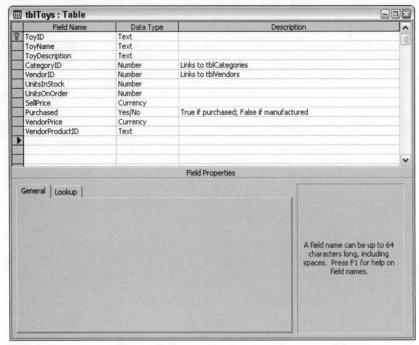

Figure 1.9

Information on materials isn't stored in this table, but in another table that will be created later.

Next, we need to create tblVendors and tblCategories, which will be linked to tblToys. After selecting the standard Categories table in the Table Wizard, click the Relationships button to set up a relationship with the CategoryID field in tblToys, as shown in Figure 1.10.

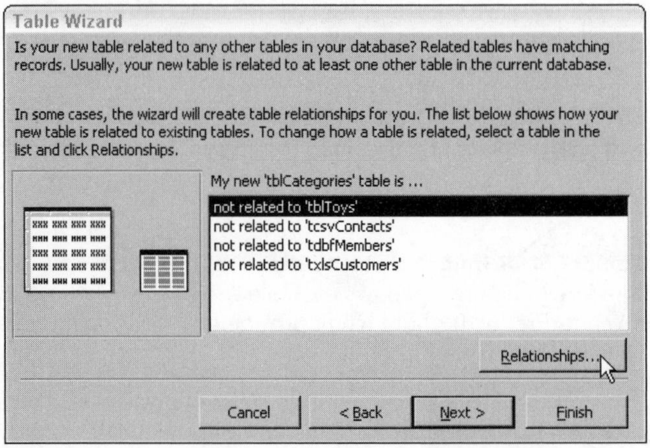

Figure 1.10

Select the middle choice on the next wizard screen (shown in Figure 1.11), because one toy category will be selected for many records in tblToys.

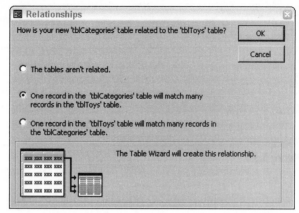

Figure 1.11

Now the wizard screen shows that tblCategories is related to tblToys (see Figure 1.12).

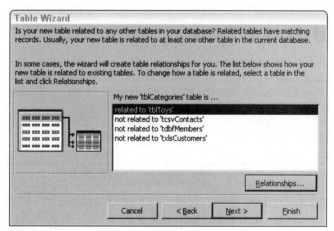

Figure 1.12

There is now a relationship between tblToys and tblCategories, which you can see in the Relationships window in Figure 1.13.

Note that although we selected *One record in the 'tblCategories' table will match many records in the 'tblToys' table,* in the Relationships page of the Table Wizard, the relationship between these two tables is not set up as a one-to-many relationship—although it should be one (another reason you may prefer to not create relationships in the wizard, and just set up all relationships in the Relationships window). See the Relationships section later in this chapter for information on modifying the relation types set up by the Table Wizard.

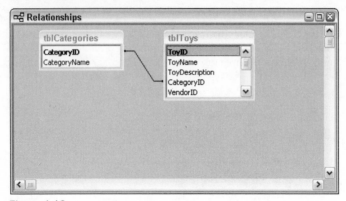

Figure 1.13

Continuing with table creation, tblVendors can be created using the Table Wizard, selecting the standard Suppliers table as the source, and linking it to tblToys on the VendorID field. The Table Wizard doesn't do all you need to link these tables, though. If you want to set up tblCategories or tblVendors as the row source of a lookup field, so the value can be selected from the linked table, you will need to do this yourself (see the lookup field information in the "Table Field Data Types" section in this chapter).

Table Field Data Types

When creating table fields, it's important to select the correct data type for each field, so that you can enter data into the field (you can't enter text into a numeric field!), and also use the data for sorting and filtering as needed. The table below lists the field data types available in Access tables, with comments. The primary data type is what you see in the drop-down Data Type list when creating or editing a field; some fields (Numeric and AutoNumber) also have subtypes, which are selected from the Field Size property in the field properties sheet.

Primary Data Type	Subtypes	Description	Comments
Text		Text data up to 255 characters in length.	Use for text data, and numbers (such as IDs) that are not used for calculations.
Memo		Blocks of text up to 65,535 characters in length.	Use for long text; only limited sorting is available on this field (just the first 255 characters are used).
Number	Byte	Whole numbers from 0 through 255.	Small numbers with no decimal points.
	Integer	Whole numbers from −32,768 through 32,767.	Medium-sized numbers with no decimal points.

Primary Data Type	Subtypes	Description	Comments
	Long Integer	Whole numbers from –2,147,483,648 through 2,147,483,647.	Long numbers with no decimal points. This is the default value. Matches AutoNumber fields when linking tables.
	Single	Numbers from –3.402823E38 through –1.401298E–45 for negative values and from 1.401298E–45 to 3.402823E38 for positive values.	Accurate to 7 decimal points.
	Double	Numbers from –1.79769313486231E308 through –4.94065645841247E–324 for negative values and from 4.94065645841247E–324 through 1.79769313486231E308 for positive values.	Accurate to 15 decimal points.
	Replication ID	Globally unique identifier (GUID), a 16-byte field used as a unique identifier for database replication.	Only used in replicated databases.
	Decimal	Numbers from $-10^{28}-1$ through $10^{28}-1$.	Accurate to 28 decimal points.
Date/Time		Dates or times.	Always store dates in a Date/Time field, so you can do date and time calculations on them.
Currency		Currency values, or numbers that need great accuracy in calculations.	Use a Currency field to prevent rounding off during calculations. A Currency field is accurate to 15 digits to the left of the decimal point and 4 digits to the right.
AutoNumber	Long Integer	Incrementing sequential numbers used as unique record IDs.	Same data type as Long Integer for linking purposes. There may be gaps in the numbering sequence, if records are created and later deleted.
	Replication ID	Random numbers used as unique record IDs.	This is a very long and strange looking string.
Yes/No		Data that is either True or False.	Null values are not allowed.

Table continued on following page

Primary Data Type	Subtypes	Description	Comments
OLE Object		Documents created in programs that support OLE (such as Word or Excel).	You can't see the object in the table; use a form or report control to display it. Can't sort or index on this field.
Hyperlink		URLs or UNC paths.	You can click on a value in this field to open a Web site (if it is a valid link).
Lookup Wizard		Not a separate field type, but a wizard that lets you select a table or value list for selecting a value for a field.	Once a field is set up as a lookup field, you won't see the value stored in the field in table Datasheet view.

Whether they are created by the Table Wizard or manually in Design view, I prefer not to use lookup fields in tables, but instead select the lookup table in a combobox or listbox's RowSource property on a form. The reason for this is that if you set up a field (such as VendorID) as a lookup field, then you won't see the VendorID when you look at the table in Datasheet view—just the vendor name from the lookup table. If you need to see the actual VendorID, you will have to convert the field back to a standard field. Also, a lookup field will always be placed on a form as a combobox, while you may prefer to have the field displayed in a textbox, for example on a read-only form.

The tblVendors table as created by the Table Wizard is shown in Figure 1.14.

Figure 1.14

> You can use the F6 function key as a shortcut for moving between a field in table Design view, and its properties sheet. This hot key is especially handy when setting the FieldSize property of numeric fields.

Because the client said that vendors could sell either finished toys or raw materials, the table needs two Yes/No fields to indicate whether the vendor sells finished toys, materials, or both, so I added these fields, setting the default value of the SellsToys field to True (since the client said that the majority of his vendors sell toys), and the default value of the SellsMaterials field to False.

Although Access lets you use spaces (and most punctuation marks) in field names—note the slash in the Country/Region field in tblVendors—I prefer not to use spaces or punctuation marks other than underscores in field names, to prevent problems when referencing fields in code and SQL statements, or when exporting table data to other applications that may not support spaces or punctuation marks.

As is often the case, on examining the table I realized that I needed to ask the client some more questions. It is rare to find all of the information you need to create tables at one time, right at the beginning. You will need to confer with your client from time to time while creating the application, asking more specific questions in order to refine table structure as needed. The question here is whether the vendors are all in the United States, or if there are some non-U.S. ones. If all the vendors are in the United States, we can eliminate the Country/Region field, and put input masks for U.S. state abbreviations or zip codes on the PostalCode and StateOrProvince fields; otherwise, the CountryRegion field is needed (I removed the slash in the field name), and we have to either leave the PostalCode and StateOrProvince fields without input masks, or take care of formatting by swapping input masks on a form or running event procedures to check that the correct data is entered into these fields.

Q: Are the vendors are all in the United States, or are there some non-U.S. ones?

A: There are some vendors outside of the United States.

Leave the table's fields as they are.

Now some more questions arise:

Q: Do you need just one phone number and one fax number, or could vendors have more than one phone number? Also, is one email address enough?

A: Some vendors have cell phone numbers too, and multiple email addresses.

We need to remove the phone and email fields from tblVendors, and create separate linked tables to hold this data.

Q: Do you need to send Word letters to vendor contacts?

A: No, the name is just so we know whom to ask for when we call the vendor.

Then we don't need to break up the contact name into its components, as would be required if we were going to create letters to them.

Figure 1.15 shows the final tblVendors.

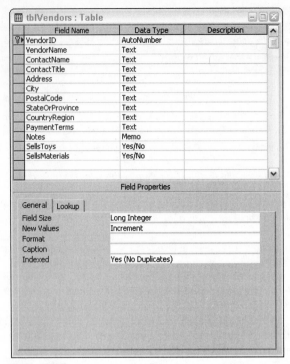

Figure 1.15

The linked tables require only the VendorID field and fields for (respectively) phone descriptions and numbers, and email addresses; the VendorID field in the linked tables is a Long Integer, to match the AutoNumber VendorID in tblVendors. When saving the new tables, don't create a key field; VendorID is a foreign key in tblVendorPhones and tblVendorEMails. (See the "Relationships" section later in this chapter for a definition of *foreign key*.) Since the vendors could be outside the United States, there is no need to create an input mask for the VendorPhone field. Figure 1.16 shows the two tables of vendor phone and email data; they will be linked to tblVendors in the Relationships window later in this chapter. tblVendorPhones has a phone number field and another field for the description (work, home, fax, and so forth), which allows you to enter as many different phone numbers as are needed for each vendor, each with its own description.

Continuing with table creation for the Toy Workshop application, tblCustomers can be created using the Table Wizard Customers table template, using all the fields to start with (just changing CompanyOrDepartment to Department), and setting up no relationships. The starter tblCustomers is shown in Figure 1.17.

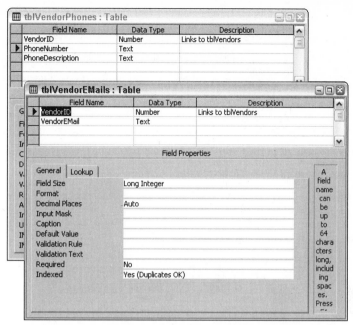

Figure 1.16

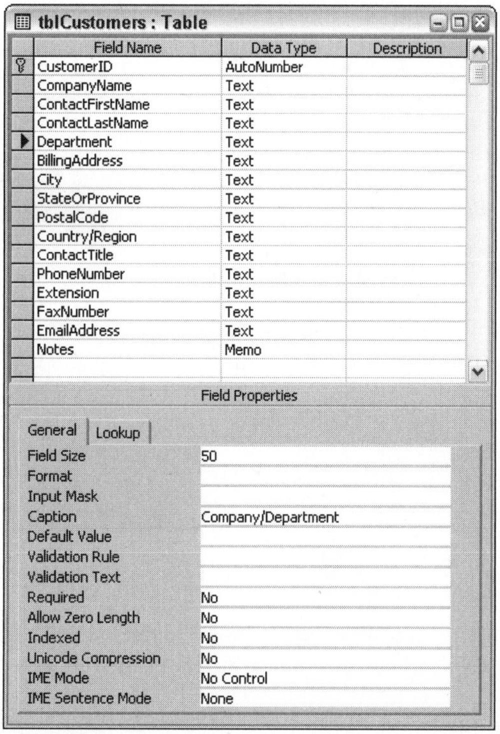

Figure 1.17

As with tblVendors, we have a few questions for the client:

Q: Do you need just one phone number and one fax number for customers, or could customers have more phone numbers? Also, is one email address enough?

A: Some customers have cell phone numbers too, and multiple email addresses. Come to think of it, some of them have Web sites, too.

We need to remove the phone and email fields from tblCustomers, and create separate linked tables to hold this data. And we need to add a WebSite Hyperlink field.

Q: Are the customers all in the United States, or do you have foreign customers too?

A: The customers are all in the United States.

We can remove the Country/Region field, and put appropriate input masks on the StateOrProvince and PostalCode fields.

The finished tblCustomers is shown in Figure 1.18.

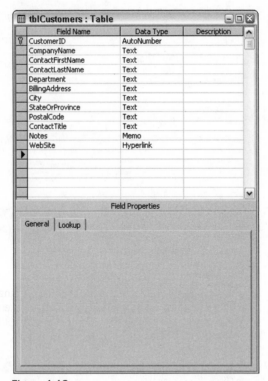

Figure 1.18

tblCustomerPhones and tblCustomerEmails are similar to tblVendorPhones and tblVendorEmails. We also need another linked table, to hold shipping addresses (this was determined in the initial Q&A

session). The billing address can be stored directly in tblCustomers, because there is only one billing address per customer, although there could be multiple shipping addresses. tblShippingAddresses has an AutoNumber ShipAddressID field, the linking CustomerID field, an address identifier field (for selecting a shipping address from a combobox on a form), and a set of address fields. Although the address fields could have the same names as the corresponding fields in tblCustomers, I like to prefix their names with "Shipping" or "Ship" so that if the billing and shipping addresses are combined in a query, we won't need to use the table name prefix to distinguish between them. tblShippingAddresses is shown in Figure 1.19.

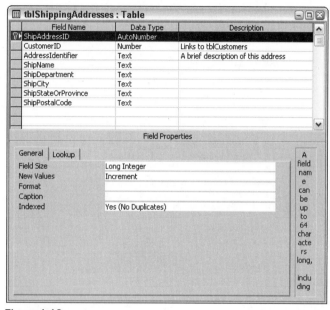

Figure 1.19

The next table is tblMailingList, which is created from the Mailing List template in the Table Wizard, omitting all fields except name, address, and email fields, plus DateUpdated and Notes. The tblMailingList table is shown in Figure 1.20.

On examining the initial version of this table, it occurs to me that the mailing list could contain several persons at the same company, so the company information should be broken out into a separate table, linked by CompanyID. However, some people on the mailing list might not be affiliated with companies, so we'll leave the address fields in the table, for entering personal address data, and add a CompanyID field to link to a separate tblMailingListCompanies table, for records that need it. The modified tblMailingList and tblMailingListCompanies tables are shown in Figure 1.21. When a mailing list record is entered on a form, the tblMailingList address fields will be enabled only if no company is selected for the CompanyID field; if a company is selected, its address will be used for mailings to that person.

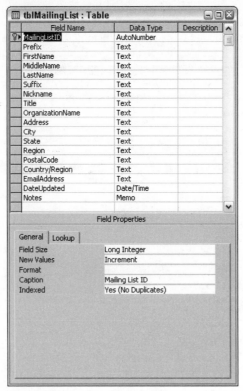

Figure 1.20

Customers will presumably get mailings too, but this doesn't mean that the whole mailing list needs to be in the tblCustomers table—we can combine data from tblCustomers and tblMailingList with a union query, when sending out mailings (See Chapter 4, *Sorting and Filtering Data with Queries*, for information on union queries.)

For date fields, I recommend selecting a date format that will display four digits for years, to avoid twentieth century/twenty-first century confusion. For an individual field, you can either select one of the standard formats from the Format property of a date field, or enter a format directly, such as m/d/yyyy. See the *Format Property—Date/Time Data Type* Help topic for full information on date and time formatting (you can locate this Help topic by entering *date format* in the Answer Box or Answer Wizard). Additionally, you can turn on 4-digit date formatting globally, overriding the Format property of fields and controls, by opening the Options dialog box from the Tools menu to the General page, and checking one of the checkboxes in the *Use four-digit year formatting* section, as shown in Figure 1.22. While you are on this page, take the opportunity to turn off Name AutoCorrect, which is nothing but trouble, because it doesn't make all the changes needed and sometimes makes changes when it shouldn't. Chapter 9, *Reworking an Existing Application*, lists better ways to rename database objects, using my LNC Rename add-in.

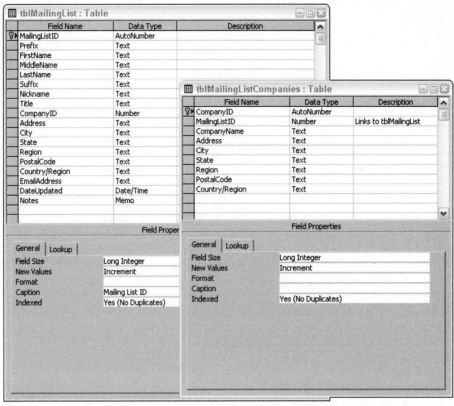

Figure 1.21

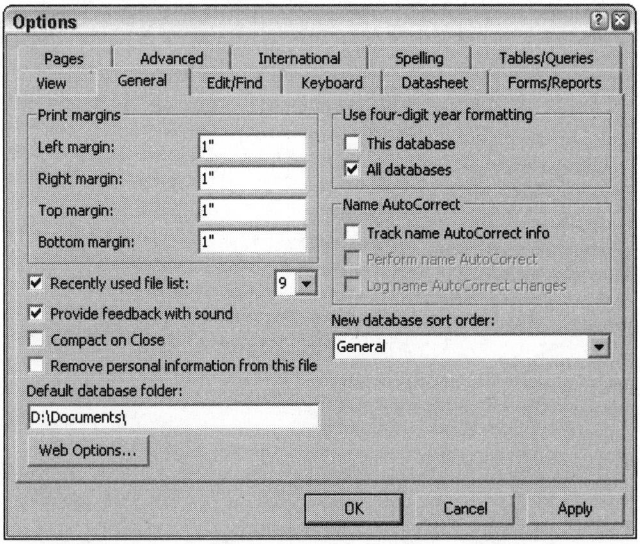

Figure 1.22

The next table to create is tblMaterials, which lists the materials used to make toys. The Table Wizard Products template is a good starter, omitting the fields that aren't needed and changing a few field names. The table is related to tblVendors on VendorID. tblMaterials is shown in Figure 1.23.

Figure 1.23

Since a material could be used for many toys, and a toy could use many materials, we need a many-to-many relationship between tblToys and tblMaterials; this is done by means of a linking table containing just the key fields; this linking table (tblToyMaterials) is shown in Figure 1.24.

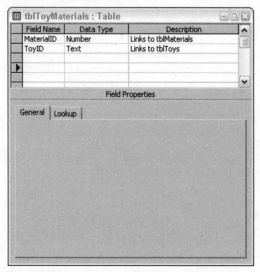

Figure 1.24

There is no suitable table template for tblRepairs, so I created this table directly in Design view, with just a few fields, as shown in Figure 1.25.

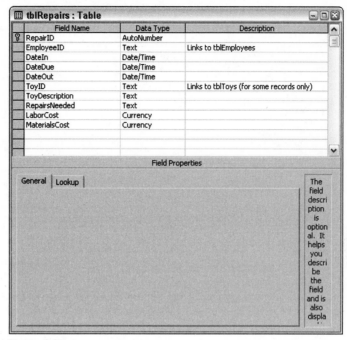

Figure 1.25

Following are some names you shouldn't use for fields: **Name, Date, Month, Year, Value, Number, Sub. In general, any word that is a built-in Access function, property, or key word should be avoided, because it is highly likely to cause problems in VBA code and elsewhere. Just add another word to the field name (CustomerName, OrderDate), and you can avoid these problems.**

Because repairs also use materials, we need a linked table, tblRepairMaterials, which lists the materials used to do repairs, and the quantity of each material. This table is shown in Figure 1.26.

The tblEmployees table is based on the default Employees table in the Table Wizard, with some unnecessary fields deleted. The client's company uses a numeric Employee ID, but since employees in this company already have IDs, we can't use an AutoNumber field; instead, EmployeeID is a text field, and it will be filled with existing employee numbers, with an incrementing number for new employees created by a procedure run from a form. tblEmployees is shown in Figure 1.27.

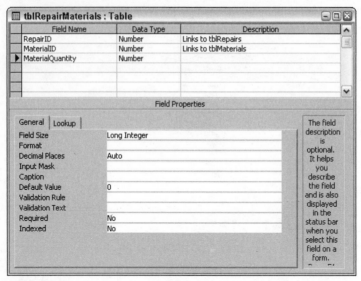

Figure 1.26

The last main table is tblOrders; it is also based on a template (Orders) in the Table Wizard, skipping the shipping address fields, and replacing them with a field (ShipAddressID) that links to tblShippingAddresses. We also need to add ToyID, to identify the toy that was purchased, and ToyQuantity (a curious omission from the Orders table template). tblOrders is shown in Figure 1.29.

The SupervisorID field takes an EmployeeID value that will be picked from a combobox on a form.

Some employee information should remain confidential, so the Social Security number (SSN) and salary are stored in a separate table, tblEmployeesConfidential, which is shown in Figure 1.28. (The input mask on the SSN field is one of the standard input masks, selected from the Input Mask Wizard.) Placing this information in a separate table lets you restrict its use to certain employees, using Access object-level permissions in a secured database. Even if you don't want to secure your database, there is a certain measure of confidentiality in just placing the information in another table so that it isn't visible when doing routine work on the main Employees form.

One default field in this table (ShippingMethodID) requires a lookup table of shipping methods; I created this table manually, and tblShippingMethods is shown in Figure 1.30.

Using an AutoNumber ShippingMethodID lets you select the shipper from an option group on a form (Access option group buttons have Integer values), and the selected value links to the shipper name in tblShippingMethods.

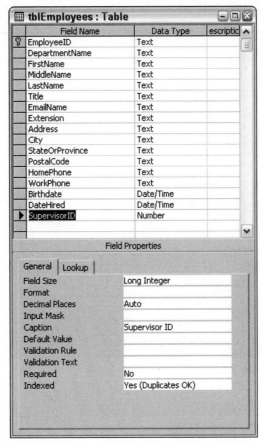

Figure 1.27

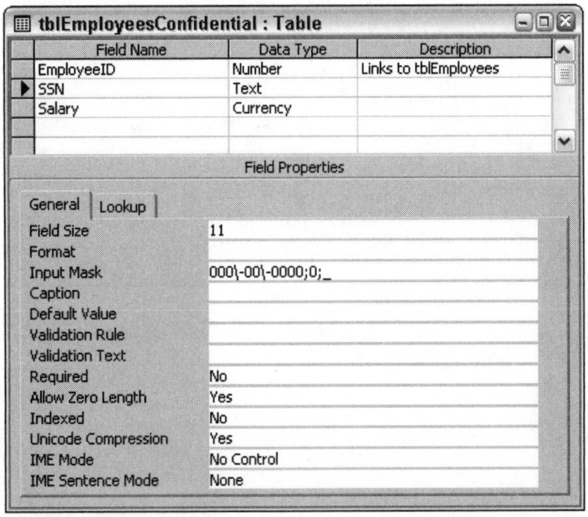

Figure 1.28

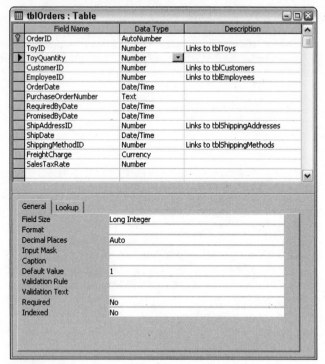

Figure 1.29

Figure 1.30

Normalization

Up to this point in the chapter, we have been *normalizing* tables—though without using that term. Database normalization can be (and often is) discussed in a very complex and opaque manner, bristling with technical terms, but this isn't necessary. When designing Access databases, normalization boils down to eliminating duplication of data in different tables, and using key fields to link tables so you can get the data you need from other tables through the links. There are five levels of database normalization (*first normal form* through the *fifth normal form*); generally, only the first three are used in Access databases. I define the five normal forms below, first in technospeak, then in regular English.

First Normal Form: Eliminate Repeating Groups

This means that you shouldn't have multiple fields for the same type of information in a table, such as multiple phone numbers or addresses for a customer. In some cases (generally only in tables imported from flat-file databases) the repeating data may be in a single field, such as a list of graduate degrees for faculty members, separated by commas. The problem with putting separate bits of information into a single field is obvious: If you wanted to create a query to view all the faculty with Ph.Ds, this would be a difficult task, requiring the creation of complex expressions to extract the different degrees for each faculty member, and you would probably not get all the records you need, because of differences in punctuation when the data was entered.

Several of the table templates in the Table Wizard violate the first normal form, such as the Contacts table with its multiple phone numbers. Instead of keeping multiple phone fields in tblVendors and tblCustomers, I created separate tables to hold phone numbers and email addresses for vendors and customers: tblCustomerPhones, tblCustomerEmails, tblVendorPhones, and tblVendorEmails. Breaking out this information into separate tables serves two practical purposes: It guarantees that you will always be able to enter another phone number or email address for a client (if you have just phone and fax fields, how are you going to enter the customer's cell phone number?), and it also makes it easier to use the information elsewhere in the database—you can pick up the phone numbers belonging to a customer by linking to tblCustomerPhones by CustomerID, instead of having to reference each of a set of named phone fields separately.

Repeating data in a single field (as in the faculty degrees example mentioned previously) should also be broken out into a separate table, both for accuracy of data entry (users should select degrees from a lookup table, rather than typing them into a field), and to allow entry of as many degrees as are needed for a faculty member.

Second Normal Form: Eliminate Redundant Data

There are two ways that redundant data can get into a database: One is by entering the same data into different records of a table. This could happen if you use the Table Wizard's Orders table template, with its address fields, and enter several orders from the same customer. If you enter that customer's shipping address into three different records, that is duplicate data. I avoided this situation by breaking out shipping address data into its own table, tblShippingAddresses, and placing a ShipAddressID field in tblOrders. This field links to the key field of the same name in tblShippingAddresses, which avoids the need to enter the same data into many records, and also guarantees that if there is a change in the shipping address, it needs to be made only once, not in every order record using that address.

You can also have redundant data when the same information is entered into two different tables. For example, if you have a Customers table and an Orders table, you should not put customer billing address fields in both tables. Either place the billing address fields in a separate table, linked one-to-one with tblCustomers by CustomerID, or place them in the Customers table and remove them from the Orders table. Shipping address fields should also not be duplicated in two tables; in this case, they should definitely be moved to a separate table (as I do in the sample database), because there can be multiple shipping addresses per customer.

In some cases, for recordkeeping purposes, it might be desirable to keep a record of the shipping address used at the time an order is shipped—even if that address changes later on. In that case, the shipping address fields could be retained in tblOrders, along with the ShipAddressID field, and when a shipping address is selected on a form, data from the selected shipping address could be pulled from tblShippingAddresses and written to the shipping address fields in tblOrders. This method eliminates the need to type the shipping address into every record, but preserves the shipping address data for each order even if the customer's shipping address is changed later on.

Third Normal Form: Eliminate Columns Not Dependent on Key

This means that any fields that don't belong to the record should be moved into a separate table. For example, the initial version of tblMailingList, made from the Table Wizard Mailing List table template, contains both information about the person receiving the mailings (name information, title, and so forth) and information about the company (company name and address). Because the company information doesn't belong to the person, I created a separate tblMailingListCompanies table linked by a CompanyID field to store mailing list company data. However, I left the address fields in tblMailingList, so they could be used for personal addresses for persons on the mailing list who are using their own addresses rather than company addresses.

Fourth Normal Form: Isolate Independent Multiple Relationships

In a database with many-to-many relationships, don't add irrelevant fields to the linking table that connects the two "many" tables. In a student records database, for example, using a many-to-many relationship between Students and Classes, with a linking table tblStudentClasses, you might have a Semester and Year field, indicating that a particular student took a particular class in a specific semester and year. That would be appropriate, but if you were to add a phone number field to the linking table, that would violate the fourth normal form because that field doesn't belong to the combined student-class record, but to the student record, so it should be placed in the Student table.

In the Toy Workshop sample database, there is a many-to-many relationship between Toys and Materials. For example, a toy can use multiple materials, and a material can be used for multiple toys. tblToyMaterials is the linking table for this many-to-many relationship. As is typical of such tables, it contains only the two foreign key fields that link to the key fields in the two "many" tables. If you add any extra fields other than the two key fields to such a table, they should be related to the combination of the two linked records, to avoid violation of the fourth normal form.

It is unlikely that you will have to worry about violating the fourth normal form because (unlike the first through third normal forms) it isn't likely that you'll be inclined to set up tables that violate it, or even have to rework tables that violate this form.

Fifth Normal Form: Isolate Semantically Related Multiple Relationships

Violation of this normal form requires a complex and unlikely scenario, and frankly there is a minimal chance that you will ever have to worry about it. In some circumstances, this form requires the separation of even related fields into a separate table. For example, in a many-to-many Students-Classes relationship, although semester and year information could appropriately be added to the linking tblStudentsClasses table, in some cases it would be preferable to maintain that information in a separate table, with information linking classes to specific Semester-Year combinations.

Setting Up Relationships

The Table Wizard gives you a start at setting up relationships between tables, but it doesn't do all the work. Even though you specify that a record in one table can match many records in another table, the relationship is not set up as a one-to-many relationship; you need to do this manually, in the Relationships window. I'll describe the three types of relationships you can create in an Access database, and show you how to set them up in the Relationships window.

Let's start with some definitions of terms used in creating relationships between tables:

❑ **Primary key.** A field (or, less commonly, a set of fields) with a different value (or value combination) for each record in a table. The key field must be unique and can't be Null.

❑ **Foreign key.** A nonunique field in a table that links to the primary key field in another table. In a one-to-many relationships, the primary key is in the "one" table, and the foreign key in the "many" table.

❑ **Cascading update.** When referential integrity is enforced, if you change the primary key value in a record in the primary table (for example, EmployeeID in tblEmployees), that value will be changed to match in all the matching records in any related tables. This is generally a good idea.

❑ **Cascading delete.** When referential integrity is enforced, if you delete a field in a primary table, all matching records in any related tables are also deleted. This is dangerous, and generally should be avoided.

❑ **Inner join.** There must be a matching value in the linked fields of both tables. With an inner join between tblCustomers and tblOrders, for example, you will see only records for customers with orders.

❑ **Left outer join.** All records from the left side of the LEFT JOIN operation in a query's SQL statement are included in the results, even if there are no matching records in the other table. A left outer join between tblCustomers and tblOrders includes all the Customer records, even those with no orders.

❑ **Right outer join.** All records from the right side of the RIGHT JOIN operation in a query's SQL statement are included in the results, even if there are no matching records in the other table. A right outer join between tblMailingListCompanies and tblMailingList includes all the tblMailingList records, even those with no company selected (they won't have matching records in tblMailingListCompanies).

❑ **Referential integrity.** A set of rules that ensures that relationships between records in linked tables are valid and that related data isn't changed or deleted inappropriately. Setting referential integrity on a link between tblCustomers and tblOrders (on the CustomerID field) would ensure, for example, that you can't enter a new order without selecting a customer. With referential integrity set, you can't delete a record from the primary table if there are matching records in the related table (unless you also choose to turn on cascading deletes), and you can't change the primary key value if there are matching records (unless you also choose to turn on cascading updates).

One-to-Many Relationships

Although Access doesn't require that linked fields have the same names (only the same data type), to make it easier to match up corresponding fields when setting up relationships, I recommend using the same name for linked primary and foreign key fields.

A one-to-many relationship (by far the most common type of relationship) is needed when a single record in one table can match several records in another table. In the Toy Workshop database, a number of one-to-many relationships are needed; they are listed below, with the "one" (or *primary*) table on the left and the "many" (or *related*) table on the right. Some of these relationships are also part of many-to-many relationships, covered below:

❑ tblCategories—tblToys

❑ tblCustomers—tblCustomerEmails

❑ tblCustomers—tblCustomerPhones

❑ tblCustomers—tblOrders

❑ tblEmployees—tblRepairs

❑ tblMailingListCompanies—tblMailingList

❑ tblMaterials—tblRepairMaterials

❑ tblMaterials—tblToyMaterials

❑ tblRepairs—tblRepairMaterials

❑ tblShippingAddresses—tblOrders

❑ tblShippingMethods—tblOrders

❑ tblToys—tblToyMaterials

❑ tblVendors—tblMaterials

❑ tblVendors—tblToys

❑ tblVendors—tblVendorEMails

❑ tblVendors—tblVendorPhones

If you get an error message "Toy Workshop can't create this relationship and enforce referential integrity" when trying to create a relationship, this indicates that data in one of the tables violates referential integrity (for example, you might have a tblOrders record without a value in the CustomerID field); fix the data, and you will be able to create the relationship.

Similarly, an error message that says, "Relationship must be on the same number of fields with the same data types" most likely indicates that the fields to be linked are of different data types; change the data type of one field so that it matches the other field (with AutoNumber matching Long Integer), and you should be able to set up the relationship.

As an example of how to set up a one-to-many relationship in the Relationships window (all the others are done similarly), let's set up the relationship between tblCustomers and tblCustomerPhones. Start by opening the Relationships window and dragging tblCustomers and tblCustomer Phones to it from the Database window (or alternately, selecting them using the Show Table dialog opened from the similarly named toolbar button). Note that the CustomerID field in tblCustomers is bold; that indicates that it is the primary key of this table. The matching CustomerID field in tblOrders is not bold, because it is a foreign key field in that table. To create the join, drag the CustomerID field in tblCustomers to the same-named field in tblOrders, as shown in Figure 1.31.

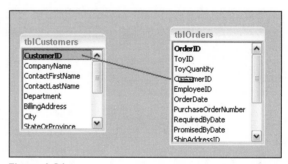

Figure 1.31

When you release the mouse, the Edit Relationships dialog opens. The Relationship Type box at the bottom of the screen displays the relationship that Access thinks is right; it is usually correct.

If the relationship type you intend to set up isn't shown in the Relationship Type box in the Edit Relationships dialog—for example, you want to set up a one-to-many relationship, and the box says Indeterminate—the most likely reason is that you have tried to link the wrong fields, or you linked the right fields, but they aren't of matching data types. Correct the problem and you should see the correct relationship type in the dialog.

In this case, the relationship type is correctly identified as one-to-many, so all you have to do is check *Enforce Referential Integrity and Cascade Update Related Fields,* and click the Create button, as shown in Figure 1.32.

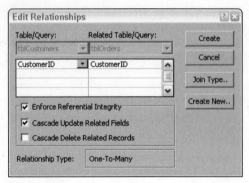

Figure 1.32

You can now see a line connecting the CustomerID field in tblCustomers to the matching field in tblOrders, as shown in Figure 1.33; note that it has a 1 on the left side (indicating that tblCustomers is the primary or "one" table), and an ∞ sign on the right side (the related or "many" table).

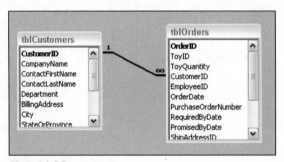

Figure 1.33

One-to-One Relationships

A one-to-one relationship (comparatively rare) is needed when a record in one table can only match a single record in another table. The linking field is the primary key field in both tables. Typically, such a relationship is created to limit access to certain data, such as confidential employee data. In the Toy Workshop sample database, there is a single one-to-one relationship, between tblEmployees and tblEmployeesConfidential. To set up this relationship, drag EmployeeID from tblEmployees to the same field in tblEmployeesConfidential; the Edit Relationships dialog will say One-to-One, as shown in Figure 1.34.

If the Edit Relationships dialog says One-to-Many instead of One-to-One, this indicates that the linking field is not the key field in both tables; change it to the key field in both, and you should be able to set up a one-to-one link.

In the Relationships window, the line representing a one-to-one relationship has a 1 at both ends, as you might expect.

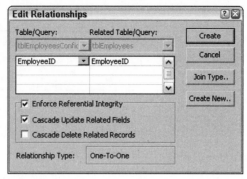

Figure 1.34

Many-to-Many Relationships

A many-to-many relationship is actually a set of two one-to-many relationships. There are two primary tables and a linking table; the linking table has two foreign key fields, one matching the primary key field of each of the primary tables. It may also (but usually doesn't) contain a few other fields that hold information related to that specific combination of records from the primary tables. In the Toy Workshop database, two many-to-many relationships are needed (the linking table is in the middle of each set):

❑ tblToys—tblToyMaterials—tblMaterials

❑ tblRepairs—tblRepairMaterials—tblMaterials

Once you have set up the two one-to-many relationships, you have a many-to-many relationship; Figure 1.35 shows the two many-to-many relationships in the Relationships window. You can see the two sets of primary tables with a linking table in between; tblMaterials serves as the primary table in two many-to-many relationships.

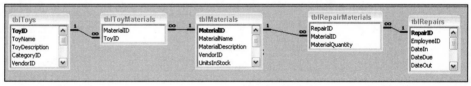

Figure 1.35

If you use a convention of naming all primary and foreign key fields with a suffix of ID, you can easily identify the fields that need to be linked to other tables in the Relationships window. However, not all key fields need to be linked to other tables—MailingListID in tblMailingList doesn't need any links because there are no tables with multiple records matching one record in tblMailingList.

Summary

Now that we have created the necessary tables for the Toy Workshop database, with appropriate relationships set up between them, we can proceed to create forms for entering and editing data, and queries for sorting and filtering.

2

Using Forms to Work with Data

In the previous chapter, we got information from the client about the business processes to be handled in the application, and set up tables to hold the application's data. The next step is to create forms for entering and editing data, and queries for filtering and sorting. You may need to create queries as form data sources or combobox row sources, so there will be some discussion of queries in this chapter, but the main focus in this chapter is on forms. Chapter 4, *Sorting and Filtering Data with Queries*, covers queries in more detail. First I'll briefly discuss the types of forms you can create with Access and their suitability for different purposes, and then we'll create forms for the Toy Workshop application, using my Design Schemes add-in to give them a consistent and attractive appearance.

Form Types

As far as database objects are concerned there is only one type of Access form, but Access forms have always had three views available (Single Form, Continuous Forms, and Datasheet)—with PivotTable and PivotChart views being added in Access 2002. The first three Form views are commonly referred to as form types, and they will be discussed in this chapter (see Chapter 5, *Using PivotTables and PivotCharts to Interact with Data*, for information on the PivotTable and PivotChart views of forms).

When you create an Access form, the Single Form view is selected by default. Often this is the most appropriate view, but the table below describes the other views and their uses.

Form View	Record Display	Comments
Single Form	Displays data one record at a time.	Can use all control types; has header and footer areas. Best when you need to display a full page of data per record. Suitable for use as either a main form or a subform. Can be nested up to 7 levels.
Continuous Forms	Displays several data records at once (usually 3 or 4).	Can use all control types except subforms; has header and footer areas. Best when you need to display less than a full page, but more than a single line of data per record, and/or you need to use command buttons or option groups. Can't be a main form with its own subforms, but can be used as a subform on a Single Form–type main form.
Datasheet	Displays records in a datasheet format (one record per row)	Can't use command buttons, listboxes, option groups, or subforms; has no header or footer areas. Best when you need only textboxes and comboboxes, and just one row of data per record. Can't be a main form with its own subforms, but can be used as a subform on a Single Form–type main form. Because of the lack of header and footer areas, datasheet forms are most suitable for use as subforms.

In addition to these three Form views, forms can also be divided into several categories depending on how they are used:

Form Type	Description	Usage
Standard	Single form, with header and footer.	Forms for reviewing, editing, and entering data.
Data entry	Single form, with footer only.	Forms for entering new data records only.
Datasheet	Datasheet form, to be used as a subform.	Datasheet display of linked data. Typically, the "many" side of the relationship is displayed in the datasheet subform, and the "one" side in the main form.

Form Type	Description	Usage
Dialog	Single form, without either header or footer.	A small form for user response or selection from an option group, combobox or listbox; the choices are used for filtering elsewhere in the database. May be bound to tblInfo to preserve the user's choices, or data may be written to global variables.
Subform	Single Form–type form designed to be used as a subform on another form. No header or footer.	Use when a Single Form–type subform is needed on another form.
Continuous	Continuous Forms–type form, designed for use either as a standalone form, or a subform on a Single Form–type form. No header or footer.	Use when you need to display one or a few lines of data per record, and may need controls other than textboxes and comboboxes.

Apart from the Form view indicated in the preceding table, each of these form types needs different settings for a number of Format and Data properties. While you could create a default form and then change its view and five or six properties, every time you create a form designed for (say) use as a datasheet subform, it would save a lot of time to be able to select your form type from a list, and have all its properties set correctly at the time it is created. This is one of the purposes of my Design Schemes add-in, along with giving you a choice of several conservative color schemes for forms (with an option for creating your own custom color scheme).

Let's start by looking at the Relationships diagram for the Toy Workshop, which is shown in Figure 2.1.

Let's analyze the tables in the database, and decide what kind of forms they need, before creating them with the Design Schemes add-in.

The diagram shows all the relationships in the database; all but one are one-to-many relationships. Some of the one-to-many relationships are suitable for display in a main form with one or more subforms (for example, a main form bound to tblCustomers with several subforms bound to tblCustomerPhones, tblCustomerEMails, and tblShippingAddresses). The primary table (tblCustomers) contains data about customers, one record per customer, while the linked tables have (at least potentially) multiple records per customer. There is a similar relationship between tblVendors (the primary table) and tblVendorPhones and tblVendorEMails (linked tables).

The relationship between tblCategories and tblToys, however, is not suitable for a main form with a subform; instead, tblCategories should be the row source of a combobox or listbox on a form where you need to select a category (the main Toys form, and possibly other forms). The relationship between tblShippingMethods and tblOrders is similar; the shipping methods are displayed for selection in a combobox or option group on the Orders form.

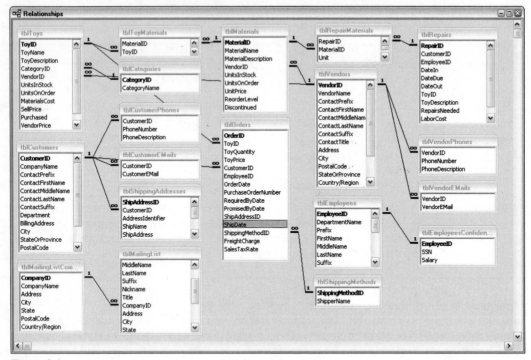

Figure 2.1

The single one-to-one relationship (tblEmployees—tblEmployeesConfidential) isn't suitable for either a main form with subform or a combobox; instead, these two tables should be displayed in separate forms, to preserve confidentiality of the SSN and salary data.

Some of the relationships between tables in the database require that data from one table be displayed in several forms: For example, tblVendors needs a form for entering and editing vendor data, but it is also the row source of a combobox on several forms. As described in the previous chapter, there are two many-to-many relationships in the database, tblToys—tblToyMaterials—tblMaterials and tblMaterials—tblRepairMaterials—tblRepairs. The linking (middle) table in each of these relationships is displayed only in a datasheet subform on one of the primary forms, for selection of a record from the other primary form (this will become clearer when the form is set up near the end of this chapter).

Some things to consider:

❑   Each foreign key needs a combobox where the value for this field can be selected from another table (in the Relationships diagram, the foreign key fields are the ones ending with ID other than the bolded primary key fields). This preserves referential integrity—you can only select values that have already been entered into the combobox's row source table.

❑   A one-to-many relationship is generally best displayed by selecting the primary form as the record source of a main form, and the linked tables as the record sources of subforms embedded on the main form.

❑   Lookup tables should be used as the row source of a combobox or listbox control, for selecting values in other tables.

❑   As a reference when creating your forms, you can print out the Relationships diagram by selecting File | Print Relationships with the diagram open. This creates an Access report in portrait mode; you can manually change the orientation to landscape so as not to cut off portions of the diagram.

The table below lists the type of form display needed for each table in the Toy Workshop database.

Table Name	Display in Form(s)	Display in Control(s)
tblCategories	Continuous Forms–type form for entering and editing data	Category selection combobox on frmToys
tblCustomerEMails	Datasheet subform for use on frmCustomers	Subform control on frmCustomers
tblCustomerPhones	Datasheet subform for use on frmCustomers	Subform control on frmCustomers
tblCustomers	Single Form–type form for entering and editing data	Customer selection combobox on frmOrders
tblEmployees	Single Form–type form for entering and editing data	Employee selection combobox on frmOrders and frmRepairs, and Supervisor selection combobox on frmEmployees
tblEmployeesConfidential	Single Form–type form for entering and editing data	
tblMailingList	Single Form–type form for entering and editing data	
tblMailingListCompanies	Single Form–type form for entering and editing data; also a form intended for use as a subform on frmMailingList	Subform control on frmMailingList
tblMaterials	Single Form–type form for entering and editing data	
tblOrders	Single Form–type form for entering and editing data	
tblRepairMaterials	Datasheet form intended for use as a subform on frmRepairs	Subform control on frmRepairs
tblRepairs	Single Form–type form for entering and editing data	
tblShippingAddresses	Continuous Forms–type form intended for use as a subform on frmCustomers and frmOrders	Shipping address selection combobox on frmOrders

Table continued on following page

Table Name	Display in Form(s)	Display in Control(s)
tblShippingMethods	Continuous Forms–type form for entering and editing data	Shipping method selection option group on frmOrders
tblToyMaterials	Datasheet form intended for use as a subform on frmToys	Subform control on frmToys
tblToys	Single Form–type form for entering and editing data	Toy selection combobox on frmOrders and frmRepairs
tblVendorEMails	Datasheet subform for use on frmVendors	Subform control on frmVendors
tblVendorPhones	Datasheet subform for use on frmVendors	Subform control on frmVendors
tblVendors	Single Form–type form for entering and editing data	Vendor selection combobox on frmMaterials and frmToys

Creating the Forms

While you could create all the forms needed for this application from scratch by selecting Design View in the Access Form Wizard and setting all the form properties manually, there is an easier way. I'll describe how to use my Design Schemes add-in's wizards and builders to eliminate a lot of the repetitive work involved in creating forms with a uniform and professional appearance.

Using the Design Schemes Add-in

First, copy the Design Schemes Add-in's library database (Design Schemes.mda) to your AddIns folder (usually C:\Documents and Settings\Administrator\Application Data\Microsoft\AddIns). Open the Toy Workshop database (or any other database), select Tools | Addins to open the Add-ins menu, and then select the Add-In Manager selection. The Add-In Manager dialog opens, as shown in Figure 2.2.

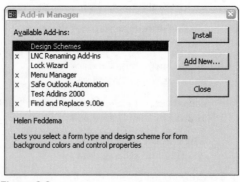

Figure 2.2

There should be a Design Schemes entry; if not (perhaps because it was placed in a nonstandard location), click the Add New button and browse for the file. Once it appears in the list of available add-ins, select it and click Install; an × appears next to the Design Schemes selection to indicate that it is installed. Close the dialog to complete the installation.

You won't see any new entries on the Add-ins menu because this add-in contains only wizards and builders, no menu add-ins. To create a form with the Design Schemes add-in, click the New button with Forms selected in the object bar, and select Custom Form Wizard from the list of selections (as shown in Figure 2.3).

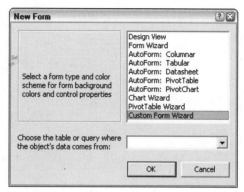

Figure 2.3

Don't select a data source on this screen; this is done on the next screen in this wizard, where you can choose the type of form to create. This screen is shown in Figure 2.4.

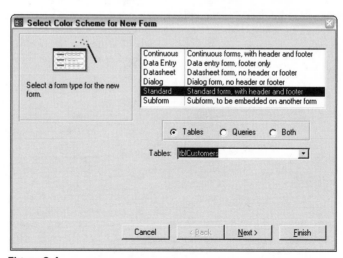

Figure 2.4

Creating a Standard Main Form

We'll start with creating a standard form to use as a main form, with subforms. The Customers form is of this type, so I selected tblCustomers in the Custom Form Wizard and accepted the default Standard Form selection, because this table needs a Single Form–type form for entering and editing data. The next screen (shown in Figure 2.5) offers a choice of four color schemes, which use standard colors that will display correctly even on low-resolution monitors.

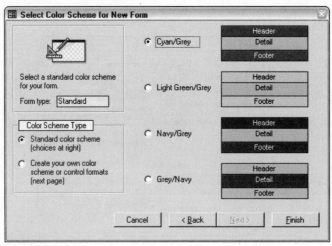

Figure 2.5

If you want to select one of the four standard color schemes, click its option button and then click the Finish button. The new form will be created, with the specified record source table or query, and opened in Design view. To create a custom color scheme, click the *Create your own color schemes or control formats* option in the Color Scheme Type option group, and then click the Next button. The next screen has a number of controls for setting every detail of color, font, and other characteristics of the form and controls on the form, as shown in Figure 2.6

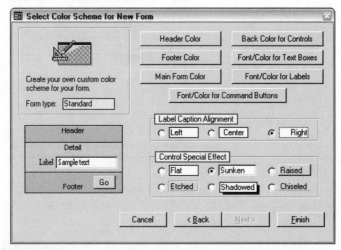

Figure 2.6

The command buttons in the upper right of the screen are used to change the color of various parts of the form and form controls. Click one of these buttons to open a standard color palette (similar to the one opened from the Build button of a color property), and select the color to use; the miniform on the lower left of the screen will reflect your choice. You can also open the color palette by clicking on a portion of the miniform.

Another standard dialog lets you select the font, weight, and color for controls on the form.

The option group in the middle of the form lets you select the alignment for labels, and the bottom option group gives you a choice of special effect for textboxes. These choices will also be displayed in the miniform.

> **Although Access lets you select the Raised special effect for labels or textboxes, I don't advise doing this. A raised textbox or label looks exactly like a command button, and users will probably try to click it and expect something to happen.**

Figure 2.7 shows the custom color scheme page of the Design Schemes Wizard, after all selections have been made.

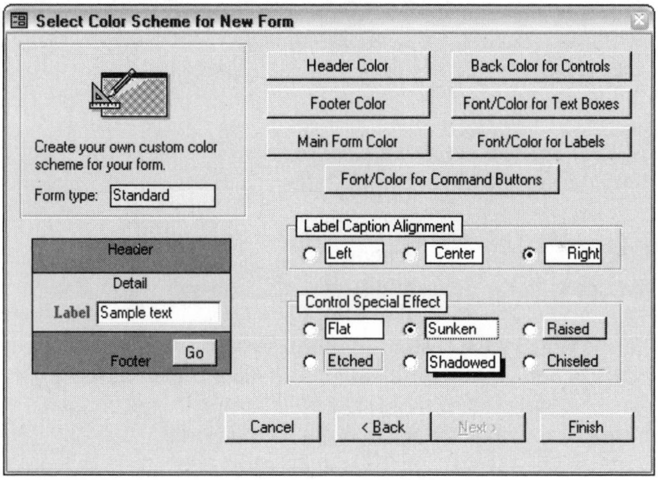

Figure 2.7

The font, weight, color, and special effect selections for textboxes and labels will be applied to all the controls on the form. Select the choices you want for the Detail section of the form; the relatively few controls in the header and footer can be changed manually if needed.

After clicking the Finish button, the new form is created, with the colors and special effects you have selected. Figure 2.8 shows a new form with a custom color scheme. The form has some code already entered into its attached module; this code will be discussed in the next section.

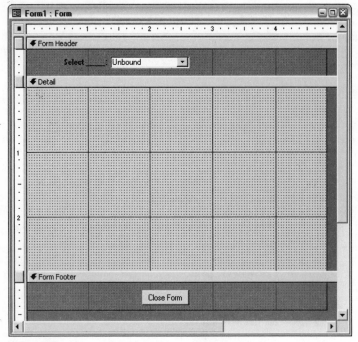

Figure 2.8

There are two field list shortcuts: Use the F8 function key to open the field list, and double-click its title bar to select all the fields in the list.

Adding Controls to a Form

Open the field list and drag all the fields to the form, as shown in Figure 2.9.

The textboxes and labels all have the custom properties you selected; the single label in the header can be changed to white for better contrast, and edited to replace the underscore with "Customer."

The new form requires several refinements (in no particular order):

❑   Make the AutoNumber CustomerID field locked, with a different color background to tell the users that it can't be edited. This is done with a builder that is part of the Design Schemes add-in. To invoke the builder, right-click the CustomerID field and select Build from its context menu; the Lock Wizard dialog appears (shown in Figure 2.10), where you can select the *Locked* option. The textbox can also be made smaller, since the ID won't be very long, and left-aligned, to make it match the other controls.

❑   Move controls around to save space on the form. Delete the Contact Last Name label, move the ContactLastName textbox up next to the ContactFirstName textbox, and edit that control's label to read Contact Name (First/Last). Similarly, delete the State/Province and Postal Code labels, move the PostalCode and StateOrProvince textboxes up and to the right of the City textbox, and edit the City label to read City/State/Zip. Because customer addresses are all in the United States, the PostalCode and StateOrProvince textboxes can be made smaller too.

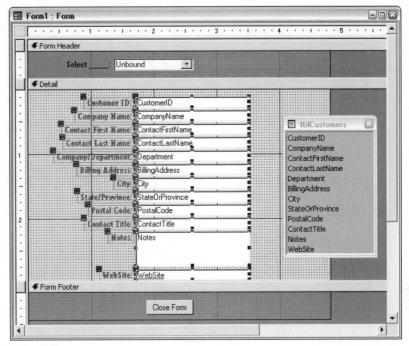

Figure 2.9

Figure 2.10

- ❑ Make the Company Name, Contact Title, Department, Notes, and Web site textboxes wider.

- ❑ Move the Contact Title textbox and label up under the name controls.

- ❑ Move the Notes and Web site controls up under the City controls

- ❑ Move the Close button to either the middle or the right side of the footer section (I prefer the right side, because sometimes there are other buttons in this section).

- ❑ Enter *Customers* into the form's Caption property.

The redesigned form is shown in Figure 2.11.

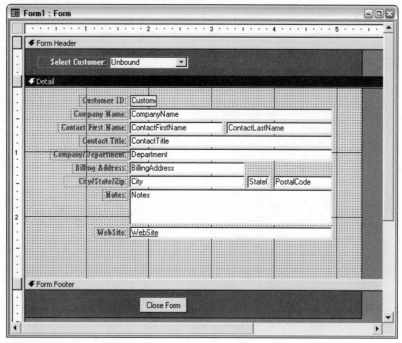

Figure 2.11

Applying a Naming Convention

It's a good idea to name database objects (tables, queries, forms, reports, macros, and modules) with a distinctive three- or four-letter tag (prefix), to identify the object type when selecting objects from drop-down lists, or working in VBA code. Controls on forms and reports should also have distinctive tags to indicate the control type, and to prevent circular reference errors resulting from controls having the same name as their bound fields. For the full process of applying the Leszynski Naming Convention (LNC) to all objects in an application created without using a naming convention, see Chapter 10, *Moving Old Data into the New Database*.

For this chapter, we have the much simpler task of using the LNC right from the start. For naming the six main database objects, the tags listed in the table below are used. (See Chapter 10 for a more extensive table with more specialized tags for subvarieties of database objects).

Object	Tag
Form	*frm*
Form (dialog)	*fdlg*
Form (menu)	*fmnu*
Form (subform)	*fsub*
Macro	*mcr*

Object	Tag
Module	*bas*
Query (any type)	*qry*
Report	*rpt*
Table	*tbl*

For this chapter, only a few form tags are needed. Standard forms will be given the tag *frm*, and sub-forms *fsub*.

Thus, the newly created form is saved as frmCustomers. This is a good time to give all the controls names with appropriate prefixes to indicate their control types, and this can be done easily using a builder that is part of the LNC Rename add-in.

First, install the LNC Rename add-in (if you don't already have it installed). This add-in is available as LNC Rename Add-in.zip (for Access 2000 and up) from www.wrox.com. After decompressing the zip file, copy the LNC Rename.mda file to the Add-ins folder (usually C:\WINDOWS\Application Data\ Microsoft\AddIns), and install it from the Add-in Manager in any database, as shown in Figure 2.12.

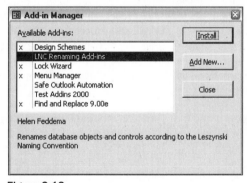

Figure 2.12

The LNC Rename add-in contains several menu add-ins, for use in renaming objects in an existing database. However, for use in a newly created database, only the builders in the LNC Rename add-in are needed. One builder (LNC Rename All Controls) renames all the controls on the currently open form; another (LNC Rename Current Control) renames the currently selected control on a form or report. To rename all the controls on frmCustomers with LNC tags, click the Detail bar (it turns black), and open its properties sheet.

> **The F4 function key is a shortcut for opening the properties sheet. Unfortunately, it is not a toggle key, so you still have to click the Close button to close the properties sheet.**

The properties sheet's title bar should say *Section: Detail*. If it doesn't, click the Detail section bar again, making sure that it is highlighted. Click the small Build button to the right of the Name property to open the Choose Builder dialog. Select the *LNC Rename All Controls* selection, and click OK to start the builder. (You may see other builders in this dialog, depending on which add-ins you have installed.)

First, you will be asking if you want to save the original control name to the control's Tag property. For a newly created form, there is no particular need to do this, so just click No in this dialog. Next, you will be presented with a series of dialogs (one for each control on the form) showing you the original control name and the proposed new control name with the appropriate LNC tag. Figure 2.13 shows one of these dialogs, for a bound textbox, which has the same name as the field to which it is bound (as is the case when you drag a control to a form from the field list).

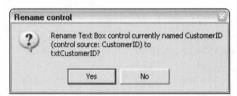

Figure 2.13

This is a good example of why you need to rename controls with tags. If you left the control with the same name as its field, you could get reference errors when using the field name or control name in code or queries. Click Yes to accept the name change, and proceed through all the controls this way. Generally, you can accept all the proposed name changes; the only exceptions are textboxes with calculated expressions, or labels with very large captions. In those cases, click No and enter an appropriate control name manually. When you have processed all the controls on the form, you will get an "All Controls Renamed!" success message.

If you later add more controls to the form, you can rename them individually by clicking the Build button next to the control's Name property in its properties sheet. In this case, select the LNC Rename Current Control builder from the Choose Builder dialog, and accept (or, rarely, manually edit) the proposed new control name. Since this builder is the default choice, generally renaming a newly created control involves only clicking the build button and pressing Enter twice.

If you add a number of new controls, you can rerun the LNC Rename All Controls builder for the form and it will rename only the controls that need renaming.

In the next section, I'll discuss using code behind forms to make forms part of a well-designed application.

Code behind Forms

VBA code is the connective tissue of an application. Without VBA code, users have to open each form or report separately from the database window, and return to the database window on closing it. An application has a main menu (perhaps one created by my Menu Manager add-in, which will be discussed in Chapter 6, *Printing Data with Reports*) with comboboxes, command buttons, and other controls powered by VBA event procedures that allow users to conveniently select which form or report to open. Similarly, VBA code on a command button or the form's Close event returns the user to the main menu when a form is closed. In addition to selecting a report to print from the main menu, an application might also include command buttons on forms to open a report filtered for the current form record, or to open another form filtered by data on the first form.

Chapter 7, *Writing VBA Code in Modules,* covers VBA code in more detail, but I will discuss event procedures for forms and controls to some extent in this chapter. VBA code on various event procedures makes it easy and intuitive to work with the data in the database, while performing various business-related tasks. When you create a new form using my Design Schemes add-in, you get a head start on writing code behind forms, with several event procedures already created for the new form. For a new Standard form, you get the event procedures listed below, with explanation under each procedure.

```
Option Compare Database
Option Explicit

Private Sub cboSelect_AfterUpdate()
'Written by Helen Feddema 10-17-2003
'Last modified 10-17-2003

On Error GoTo ErrorHandler

    Dim strSearch As String

    'For text IDs
    strSearch = "[_____ID] = " & Chr$(34) & Me![cboSelect] & Chr$(34)

    'For numeric IDs
    strSearch = "[_____ID] = " & Me![cboSelect]

    'Find the record that matches the control.
    Me.RecordsetClone.FindFirst strSearch
    Me.Bookmark = Me.RecordsetClone.Bookmark

ErrorHandlerExit:
    Exit Sub

ErrorHandler:
    MsgBox "Error No: " & Err.Number & "; Description: " & Err.Description
    Resume ErrorHandlerExit

End Sub
```

All the procedures I create have a standard error handler that pops up a message with the error number and description, and then exits the procedure. If needed, a Select Case statement under the ErrorHandler label can be set up, to process specific error numbers appropriately. I use this technique when using GetObject to create an instance of Word, Excel, or Outlook in later chapters in this book.

The comments under the procedure name will have your name and the date the form is created.

> *Occasionally, when working with add-ins, you will get the error message "Error No. 462: The remote server machine does not exist or is unavailable." This means that the Automation client has lost contact with the Automation server. When this happens, close the database and reopen it to get a fresh connection.*

The cboSelect_AfterUpdate() event procedure synchronizes the form record with the record selected from the cboSelect combobox. I use a record selector combobox on all standard forms, to make it easy to go to the correct record. I use a string variable (strSearch) to synchronize the form's RecordsetClone with the selected record. The key field (used in searching) might be a numeric field or a text field, and if it is a text field, it needs to be wrapped in quotes when creating the search string. Thus, the standard event procedure created for a Standard form by the Design Schemes add-in has two alternatives for setting the strSearch variable; for a text ID, the combobox value is wrapped in double quotes, using the Chr$(34) function, and for numeric IDs the combobox value is used alone.

Depending on the nature of the key field for the form's record source table, delete one of these alternatives—in this case, delete the text ID alternative, since CustomerID is an AutoNumber (numeric) field. Next, replace the underscore in the search string definition with the name of the key field (CustomerID). The edited strSearch line is listed below:

```
strSearch = "[CustomerID] = " & Me![cboSelect]
```

The next procedure is a standard Close button procedure (when creating an application for users who prefer to close forms by clicking on the Close button, place this code in the form's Close event procedure instead of, or in addition to, the cmdClose button's Click event procedure).

```
Private Sub cmdClose_Click()
'Written by Helen Feddema 10-17-2003
'Last modified 10-17-2003

On Error GoTo ErrorHandler

    Dim prj As Object

    Set prj = Application.CurrentProject

    If prj.AllForms("fmnuMain").IsLoaded Then
        Forms![fmnuMain].Visible = True
    Else
        DoCmd.OpenForm "fmnuMain"
    End If

ErrorHandlerExit:
    DoCmd.Close acForm, Me.Name
    Exit Sub

ErrorHandler:
    If Err.Number = 2467 Then
        Resume ErrorHandlerExit
    Else
        MsgBox "Error No: " & Err.Number & "; Description: " & Err.Description
        Resume ErrorHandlerExit
    End If
End Sub
```

This procedure uses the IsLoaded property of a form accessed through the AllForms collection, which replaces the old IsLoaded function provided with the Northwind sample database (prior to Access 2000, you had to use that function). Using this method of checking whether a form is loaded avoids the need to import the IsLoaded function into a database.

The assumption here is that the application will have a main menu, called fmnuMain, which should be opened (or reopened) when the form is closed. Some forms shouldn't return to the main menu (for example, a form opened from another form may need to return to the form that opened it); in those cases, you can replace fmnuMain with the appropriate form name, or remove the portion of the procedure that opens a form and just close the form with the DoCmd.Close line.

The form's Current procedure sets the cboSelect combobox's value to Null; this keeps it from showing the wrong data if the user navigates to another record using the navigation bar.

```
Private Sub Form_Current()
'Written by Helen Feddema 10-17-2003
'Last modified 10-17-2003

On Error GoTo ErrorHandler

    Me![cboSelect] = Null

ErrorHandlerExit:
    Exit Sub

ErrorHandler:
    MsgBox "Error No: " & Err.Number & "; Description: " & Err.Description
    Resume ErrorHandlerExit

End Sub
```

The Load event procedure has only one line of code, to size the form to fit. This ensures that the form won't open to the wrong size in case it was previously resized. There is no error handler here (only On Error Resume Next) because sometimes running the acCmdSizeToFitForm command causes an error. The On Error Resume Next statement exits the procedure without an error message in case the form can't be resized (this will happen, for example, if you are stepping through code in the module).

```
Private Sub Form_Load()
'Written by Helen Feddema 10-17-2003
'Last modified 10-17-2003

On Error Resume Next

    DoCmd.RunCommand acCmdSizeToFitForm

End Sub
```

The cboSelect combobox starts out with a row source of tblCustomers (the same as the form itself), with Column 1 as the bound field and Column 2 as the displayed field. The aim is to have the form's key field in column 1 (usually made invisible by setting the column width to zero) and one or more columns of information useful for selecting a record. The default selections are fine for the Customers form—we just need to see the company name in the drop-down list. However, it would be easier to select a company if the names were in alphabetical order, so we'll need to do a little editing of the combobox's row source.

To edit the row source, open cboSelect's properties sheet and click the Build button next to the Row Source property, then click the Yes button on the dialog asking if you want to create a query based on the table. Drag the CustomerID and CompanyName fields to the query grid, and set an Ascending sort on the CompanyName field, as shown in Figure 2.14.

You can get a preview of what will display in the combobox's drop-down list by switching to datasheet view from the query designer.

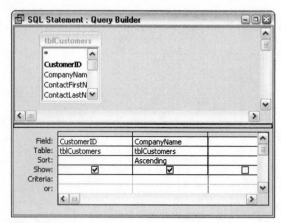

Figure 2.14

Close the query designer, and click Yes to accept the changes you have made. While in the combobox's properties sheet, you can adjust the size of the combobox itself or its drop-down list as desired (I made the combobox 2 inches wide, and set the list width to Auto). You can also set the number of rows to display in the drop-down list (I set this property to 16).

To see how the record selector combobox works, save the form, and switch to Form view. Enter a few customers (to save time, I have created a few dummy customers). Drop down the combobox, and select a customer, as shown in Figure 2.15; that customer's record is displayed in the form.

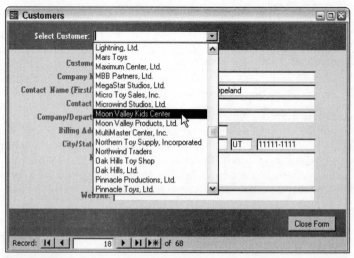

Figure 2.15

Creating and Embedding Datasheet and Single Form Subforms

As mentioned earlier in this chapter, the frmCustomers form needs several subforms. Therefore, the next step is to create these subforms based on tblCustomerPhones, tblCustomerEMails, and tblShippingAddresses. The first two tables have only a few fields, so they are most suitable for displaying in datasheet subforms; tblShippingAddresses has too many fields for datasheet display to be practical, but not enough that a Single Form–type subform is really required, so it could be either a Single Form– or Continuous Forms–type form.

To create a Datasheet form to use as a Customer Phones datasheet subform, select the Custom Form Wizard in the New Form dialog. On the first wizard screen, select the Datasheet form type and tblCustomerPhones as the record source, as shown in Figure 2.16.

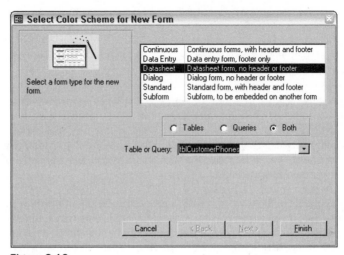

Figure 2.16

There isn't a choice of standard or custom color schemes for datasheet forms because these choices aren't relevant for datasheets, which use the color and font selections made in the Datasheet tab of the Access Options dialog.

Click the Finish button to create the new datasheet form. Drag the PhoneNumber and PhoneDescription fields to the form (CustomerID isn't needed on the form). The same text will no doubt be entered into the PhoneDescription field for different records (say, "Work" or "Home"), so to save data entry time and avoid typos, the PhoneDescription field should be changed into a combobox. To make the change, right-click the PhoneDescription textbox, select Change To from its context menu, and then Combo Box from the available choices, as shown in Figure 2.17.

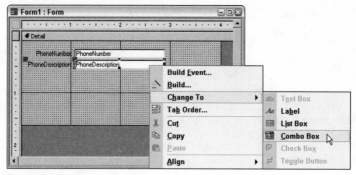

Figure 2.17

Now we can run the LNC Rename All Controls builder from the Name property of the form's Detail section, to rename the controls according to the LNC.

It's best to do any control type changing before running the builder, so you won't have to change the controls' names after changing their type.

There is no need to set a subform's caption (it won't be displayed anywhere) or to resize the controls in Design view, but you do need to remove the colons from labels, since labels are used for column headings in the datasheet. Edit the labels to remove the colons, add spaces, and make any other changes you need. I just put a space between *Phone* and *Number* in lblPhoneNumber, and changed the lblPhone Description caption to just *Description*. Save the form as fsubCustomerPhones (*fsub* is the LNC tag for forms intended for use as subforms).

The cboPhoneDescription combobox now needs a row source; it doesn't need a separate lookup table (though it could use one, if you prefer); instead, the row source consists of all the entries that have been made into this field already (alphabetized and stripped of duplicates). To create this row source, select tblCustomerPhones for the Row Source property in the combobox's properties sheet, and click the Build button next to it to open the query designer. Drag the PhoneDescription field to the query grid, and sort it Ascending. Open the query's properties sheet, and click on the upper pane of the query designer so that the properties sheet's title bar says Query Properties, and set the Unique Values property to Yes. It's also a good idea to enter Is Not Null as the criterion for the Phone Description field, to eliminate blank descriptions from the drop-down list. Once some descriptions have been entered, for future entries, you will have a choice of all the descriptions that have been entered so far.

The final touch for datasheet subforms is to adjust column sizes as needed; this is done in Datasheet view, so switch to that view to see how the columns need to be adjusted. Figure 2.18 shows the fsubCustomerPhones form in datasheet view. The column sizes are OK, so there's no need to change them (they can always be adjusted later on, if need be, after placing the subform on frmCustomers). If you do need to adjust column sizes, just stretch a column out or in using the standard double-headed resizing arrows, then save the form again.

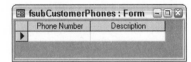

Figure 2.18

tblCustomerEMails also needs a datasheet subform. I won't go through the steps for creating this sub-form, which is even simpler than fsubCustomerPhones, since it only needs a single field (CustomerEMail). Since email addresses can be long, stretch out the txtEMail control in datasheet view to make it wider (see Figure 2.19).

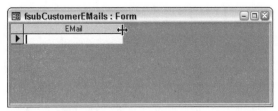

Figure 2.19

The third subform needed for frmCustomers is based on tblShippingAddresses. Since there probably won't be more than two or three shipping addresses per customer, I'll make it a Continuous Forms–type subform, choosing the Continuous form type in the Custom Form Wizard, with tblShippingAddresses as its record source. On the next screen (for consistency), select the *Create your own color scheme or control formats option;* you'll see the color scheme created for frmCustomers. Click Finish to create the subform using this color scheme.

Drag the AddressIdentifier and all the address fields to the subform, and rearrange the Ship to City, State/Province, and Postal Code fields to place them on one line, as we did for the customer address fields on frmCustomers, and make any desired changes to label captions. Figure 2.20 shows the finished subform in Design view.

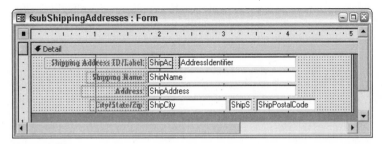

Figure 2.20

The final step is to place the subforms on frmCustomers. I like to use a tab control when a lot of data needs to be displayed on a form, because it lets you divide up the data into groups of related controls, each group displayed on a different page. You can divide up fields in a single table into groups to display on different pages, or you can embed subforms on different pages of the tab control. The interface is familiar, and the look is clean and uncluttered.

To place a tab control on frmCustomers:

1. Drag all the controls on the form way over to the right.

2. Place a tab control on the form.

3. Stretch the tab control out until it is large enough to accommodate all the moved-over controls.

To select a tab control for purposes of moving or resizing, click the top portion of the tab control, to the right of the tabs.

Click on the first page of the tab control, open the properties sheet, and enter Customer Address as its caption; enter Shipping Addresses as the caption of the next page. We'll need a third page for the customer phone numbers and emails, so right-click the tab control and select Insert page. Enter Customer Phones and Emails as the caption for the new page.

The Click event of tab controls doesn't work in Access; to respond to clicks on different tabs of a tab control, use a Select Case statement on the control's Change event instead.

After this, run the LNC Rename All Controls builder to rename all the new controls just added to the form.

When referring to tab controls, strictly speaking the term tab refers to the small protruding bit with the caption (Customer Address, and so forth), while the portion under the tab is the page. However, in ordinary usage often the page is called a tab.

Now we need to move the customer address controls to the Customer Address page of the tab control. The method you need to use here is quite unintuitive; you can't just drag the controls to the page; if you do that they will still be located on the main form and will be visible on whatever page you select. Instead, you have to select all the controls for a page, and Shift-Delete them, then click the tab of the page where you want to insert the controls (square dots will appear at the corners and sides of the selected page), then insert the controls with Ctrl-V. To check that the controls are really on that page, click the tab of another page. The controls should disappear, and they should reappear when you click the Customer Addresses page's tab again. You can now resize the frmCustomers form to eliminate the extra space on the right side. Figure 2.21 shows the form with customer address fields on the Customer Addresses page of the tab control.

Tab controls (like command buttons) have a mid-gray back color, which can't be changed. If you want a tab control to blend into the form background, you have to change the form's background to match the tab control's back color.

Save the form, and select the Shipping Addresses page of the tab control. The fsubShippingAddresses form belongs on this page, and there are two ways to place it there:

❑ Drag it to the form from the database window.

❑ Place a Subform/Subreport control on the form, and select fsubShippingAddresses as its source object.

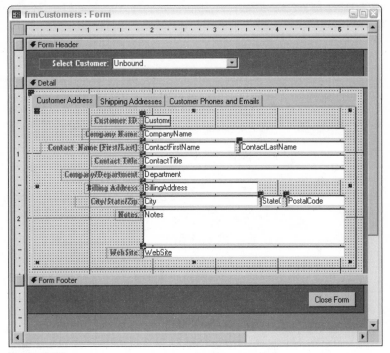

Figure 2.21

The first method is quicker, so let's do that. Resize the database window so it doesn't overlap the form, and select the ShippingAddresses page of the tab control. Drag fsubShippingAddresses to the ShippingAddresses page of the tab control (the page turns black when the subform is over it, as shown in Figure 2.22).

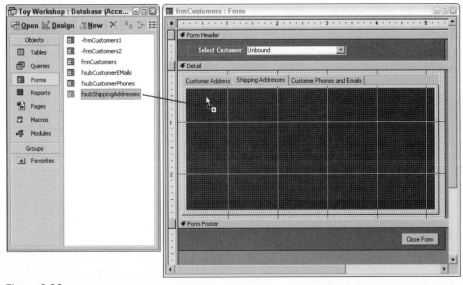

Figure 2.22

When a form is dragged to another form as a subform and there is a one-to-many relationship between the main form's table and the subform's table, the LinkMasterFields and LinkChildFields properties of the subform are automatically filled in with the linking field, as shown in Figure 2.23.

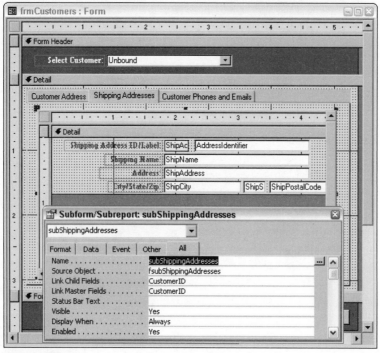

Figure 2.23

The subform doesn't need a label, because the tab caption describes it, so delete its label. I like subforms to blend in to the background, so I usually change the subform's border style to Transparent, unless I want it to have a visible border. In that case, I change its special effect to Flat.

The third page of the tab control needs two subforms: fsubCustomerPhones and fsubCustomerEMails. Drag them to this page, placing them one above the other or side by side. They do need their labels, so don't delete them; just edit the label captions as desired. Finally, run the LNC Rename All builder to rename the new subform controls and their labels.

Figures 2.24 through 2.26 show the three pages of frmCustomers, with the embedded subforms on the second and third pages.

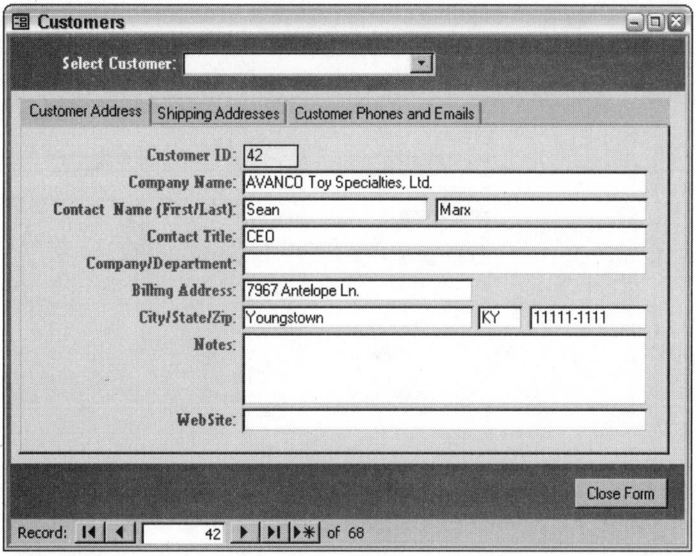

Figure 2.24

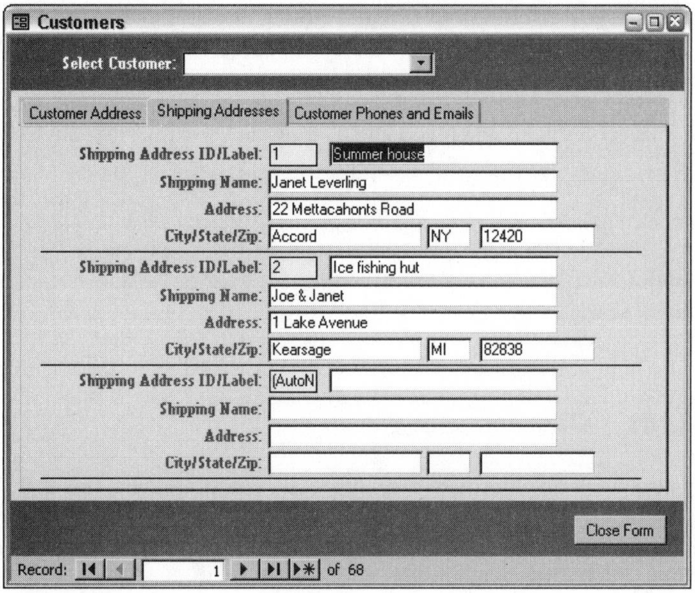

Figure 2.25

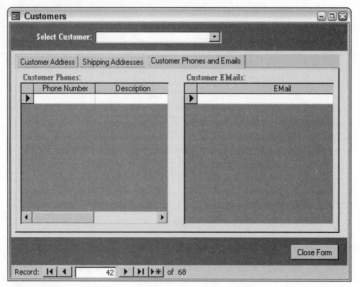

Figure 2.26

The datasheet columns need to be resized to avoid cutting off data; to do this, switch to Design view and open one of the datasheets in its own window by selecting View | Subform in New Window, switching to datasheet view in the subform, and resizing the columns. It may take some switching back and forth between the subform in its own window and the main form, to get the column sizes right. Close the subform after resizing its columns, so when you switch to Form view for the main form, you will see the new column sizes.

> *The Subform in New Window command is a little touchy, especially when the subform is very small. If this command is disabled when you try to open the subform, try clicking on the form background (outside of the subform), then click on the subform, or drag the mouse so the lasso just touches the subform. Now the command should work.*

The Vendors form is similar to frmCustomers; it needs a standard main form with two subforms. It can be created in a similar manner, with a tab control displaying data from tblVendors on one page, and Vendor phone and ID data on the other page.

The Orders form also needs a subform, to display shipping address data, but in this case the subform is not the "many" side of a one-to-many relationship, as with Customer and Vendor phones and IDs. Instead, tblShippingAddresses is the "one" side of the relationship because one shipping address could be used for multiple orders. Shipping address selection can be done with a combobox that displays the shipping addresses for the selected customer. Once the shipping address has been selected, it is displayed in a subform.

The Orders form also needs a number of comboboxes for selecting data from other tables, in addition to textboxes for entering Vendor data. To start, select the Custom Form Wizard in the New Form dialog, and select the Standard form type with tblOrders as its data source. To maintain a consistent appearance, on the next screen, select the *Create your own color scheme or control formats* option to use the color scheme created for frmCustomers.

Drag all the fields from the field list to the form. Other than OrderID, all the fields whose names end with ID are foreign key fields, and most of them need comboboxes instead of textboxes, so the next step is to convert them to comboboxes, one by one, using the Change To | Combo Box selection on their context menu, as shown in Figure 2.27 for the ToyID field.

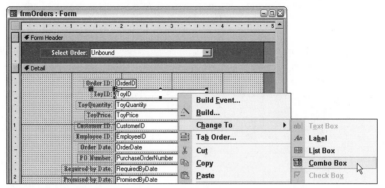

Figure 2.27

The captions of the newly converted comboboxes' attached labels should also be edited to remove ID.

The ShippingMethodID field, however, is best represented by an option group, which is not available as a Change To choice. So, remove its textbox, and place an option group on the form, and select ShippingMethodID as its field. Place five option buttons in the option group, with the default value for each one matching the ShippingMethodID for its label.

> *An option group bound to a field with an Integer value is only practical if the choices are fixed; otherwise, use a combobox or listbox for selecting a value.*

After changing the control types, you can run the LNC Rename All builder to give all the controls the appropriate tags.

The ToyID, CustomerID and EmployeeID comboboxes need similar treatment: the tblToys, tblCustomers, and tblEmployees tables need to be selected (respectively) as their row sources, and a few appropriate fields must be selected for display in each combobox's drop-down list.

As an example, I'll go through the process for cboToyID. Unlike the record selector combobox in the form's header, in this case it is a good idea to display data in the combobox after selection, to let the user know what the selection is. After selecting tblToys as the Row Source value for cboToyID, click the build button next to this property to open the query builder. In this case, we want to see the toy name and vendor name. Since tblToys only has VendorID, the vendor name can be obtained through the link to tblVendors.

To add VendorName to the query grid, add tblVendors to the query grid using the Add Table button in the query toolbar. You will see the one-to-many link between the two tables. Add VendorName to the query datasheet, and arrange the fields as shown in Figure 2.28. We need ToyID to save to the ToyID field in tblOrders, but ToyName should be displayed in the combobox after a selection is made.

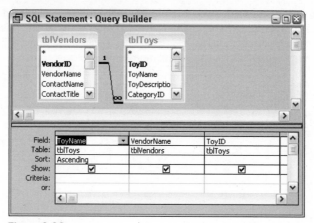

Figure 2.28

After closing the query designer, set the combobox's properties as follows (as shown in Figure 2.29), to show the three descriptive fields in the drop-down list, display ToyName in the combobox, and save ToyID to the ToyID field (to see all these properties, you need to be on the All tab of the properties sheet).

Combo Box: cboToyID

cboToyID

| Format | Data | Event | Other | All |

Name	cboToyID
Control Source	ToyID
Format	
Decimal Places	Auto
Input Mask	
Row Source Type	Table/Query
Row Source	SELECT tblToys.ToyName, tblVendors.VendorName, tblToys
Column Count	3
Column Heads	No
Column Widths	1.5";1.5";0"
Bound Column	3
List Rows	16
List Width	3"
Status Bar Text	Links to tblToys
Limit To List	Yes
Auto Expand	Yes
Default Value	

Figure 2.29

cboCustomerID needs only the CustomerName and CustomerID fields. cboEmployeeID needs a calculated field, to display employee names last name first. While this expression could be created directly in the combobox's row source, this calculated field will be used elsewhere in the database, so it will save time to create a simple select query based on tblEmployees, with two calculated name expressions: LastNameFirst and FirstNameFirst. The simplest way to do this is to select tblEmployees in the database window, click the Object Selector in the toolbar, and select Query and then Design View, as shown in Figure 2.30.

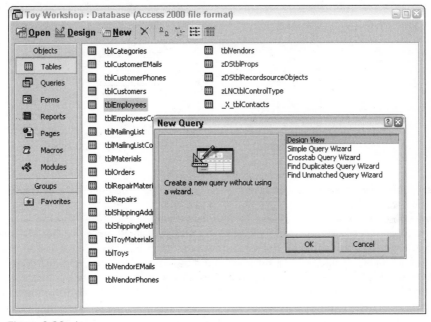

Figure 2.30

Double-click the asterisk at the top of the field list to place it on the query datasheet (the asterisk represents all the fields in the query). Then, create the two calculated fields using the expressions listed below, and save the query as qryEmployees.

```
LastNameFirst: [LastName] & ", " & [FirstName] & IIf([MiddleName]," " &
[MiddleName],"")
FirstNameFirst: [FirstName] & " " & IIf([MiddleName],[MiddleName] & " ","") &
[LastName]
```

Create a SQL statement based on qryEmployees as the row source of the cboEmployeeID combobox, and use LastNameFirst and EmployeeID for the drop-down list; the SQL statement is shown in the Query Builder in Figure 2.31.

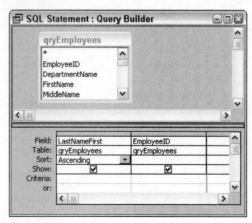

Figure 2.31

I made some of the textboxes narrower, and moved some of them side-by-side, to save space on the form.

The final touch is to provide a way to display the selected shipping address. This can be done in two ways: a subform that is refreshed after making a selection from cboShippingAddressID, or a calculated ShippingAddress field that could be displayed directly in the combobox, after selection. Because we need to display several lines of data, a subform would be better. First, cboShippingAddressID needs a special query as its row source. Because the shipping address might be either the customer's main address (in tblCustomers) or one of that customer's shipping addresses (in tblShippingAddresses), address data from these two tables needs to be combined into one data source, using a union query. More details on creating the quniCustomerAddresses union query will be given in the next chapter. For now, we'll just open the query builder from the Row Source property of the cboShippingAddressID combobox, select quniCustomerAddresses from the Show Table dialog, and add the ShipAddressID, CustomerID, and AddressIdentifier fields to the query grid.

Only the addresses for the selected customer should be available in this combobox, so the next step is to create a criterion for the CustomerID field that matches the CustomerID selected in the cboCustomerID combobox on the same form. The most accurate way to do this is to use the Expression Builder to select the combobox. Using the Expression Builder guarantees that the syntax is correct. To open the Expression Builder, right-click the Criteria row of the CustomerID field, and select Build (or click the Build button on the query toolbar). In the Expression Builder, open the Forms folder and the Loaded Forms folder under it, and select frmOrders. Select cboCustomerID in the list of controls on this form, and click the Paste button to paste it into the expression box, as shown in Figure 2.32.

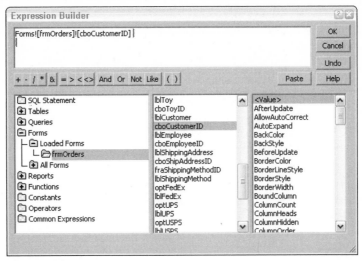

Figure 2.32

Click OK to place the expression in the Criteria row of the CustomerID field. The finished row source SQL statement is shown in Figure 2.33.

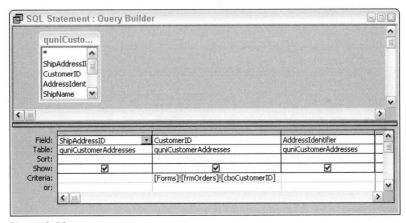

Figure 2.33

The combobox can't be filtered by CustomerID unless a customer has been selected, so cboShipAddressID should be disabled initially, and be enabled only after a customer has been selected. The code to enable cboShipAddressID needs to run off the form's Current event as well as cboCustomerID's AfterUpdate event, so that as users navigate from one record to another. cboShipAddressID will be enabled or disabled for each record, depending on whether a customer has or has not been selected. I created a private Sub procedure to do the enabling or disabling, and called it from the other event procedures as needed, to avoid having to write the same code in several procedures. The relevant procedures from frmOrders' code module are listed below.

```
Option Compare Database
Option Explicit


Private Sub EnableShippingAddress()

On Error GoTo ErrorHandler

    Dim lngCustomerID As Long

    lngCustomerID = Nz(Me![cboCustomerID])
    If lngCustomerID = 0 Then
        Me![cboShipAddressID].Enabled = False
    Else
        Me![cboShipAddressID].Enabled = True
        Me![cboShipAddressID].Requery
    End If

ErrorHandlerExit:
    Exit Sub

ErrorHandler:
    MsgBox "Error No: " & Err.Number & "; Description: " & _
        Err.Description
    Resume ErrorHandlerExit

End Sub

Private Sub cboCustomerID_AfterUpdate()

    Call EnableShippingAddress

End Sub

Private Sub Form_Current()

    Call EnableShippingAddress

End Sub
```

The cboSelect record selector combobox on frmOrders needs to display data from several other tables to allow users to select the order record they want to look at. Figure 2.34 shows the SQL statement row source for this combobox.

For purposes of debugging while working on the shipping address controls, I placed a textbox on the form to display the CustomerID from the second column of cboCustomerID. I used the Lock Wizard builder to make the textbox invisible and bright yellow (not a contradiction—you can see the yellow in Design view even when the control is invisible). Temporarily, I made the control visible so I could see it in Form view; after everything is working, it can be made invisible again. The yellow color tells me that this control should be made invisible before finalizing the application.

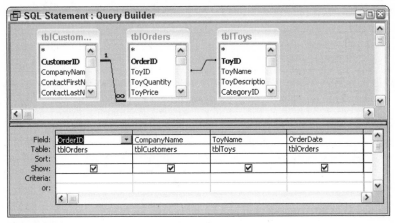

Figure 2.34

The subform that displays the selected shipping address will only display one address, so it is a Single Form–type subform created using the Subform selection in the Custom Form Wizard. The record source is the union query quniCustomerAddresses. When this subform is dragged to frmOrders, the Link ChildFields and LinkMasterFields properties aren't filled in automatically. The subform needs to be linked on both CustomerID and ShipAddressID; enter the following string in both properties to link the subform to the main form appropriately:

```
CustomerID;ShipAddressID
```

Figure 2.35 shows frmOrders, with the Selected Shipping Address subform, with several yellow controls that will be made invisible later on.

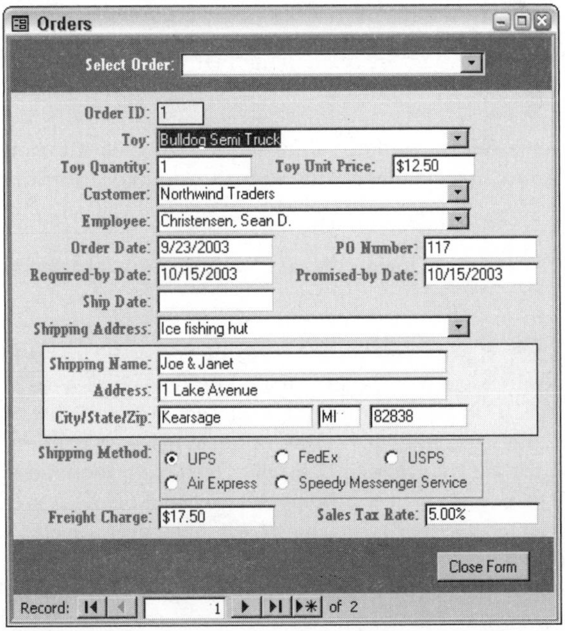

Figure 2.35

The subform's record source is a union query, so it is read-only. I gave it a light blue background (my convention for locked controls), to let users know the address can't be edited, and I also made the subform's border visible.

One more finishing touch is needed for frmOrders; when a toy is selected from cboToyID, its price needs to be picked up from tblToys and written to the ToyPrice field. Technically, this is a violation of normalization (the same data is stored in two different tables), but it is needed for business purposes because prices change, and you need to store the actual price charged when the order was made, even if that toy's price changes later on. To make this easy, I added the SellPrice field from tblToys to the combobox's row source SQL statement. The AfterUpdate event procedure of cboToyID (which follows) picks up the toy price from the fourth column of the combobox (column numbers are zero-based in code), writes it to the ToyPrice field in tblOrders, and then re-queries the txtToyPrice control.

```
Private Sub cboToyID_AfterUpdate()

On Error GoTo ErrorHandler

    Dim curToyPrice As Currency

    curToyPrice = Nz(Me![cboToyID].Column(3))
    Me![ToyPrice] = curToyPrice
    Me![txtToyPrice].Requery

ErrorHandlerExit:
    Exit Sub

ErrorHandler:
    MsgBox "Error No: " & Err.Number & "; Description: " & _
        Err.Description
    Resume ErrorHandlerExit

End Sub
```

The remaining controls on frmOrders are filled in manually; the date fields have input masks to ensure correct date entry.

tblMaterials needs a standard form with no subforms. You can create it using the Standard form type in the Custom Form Wizard, in a manner similar to frmCustomers, except without the tab control and subforms.

tblEmployees also needs a standard form, created in a similar manner, but this form has a few special features:

❑   EmployeeID is not an AutoNumber field, but a numeric ID that is filled in manually for existing employees who already have IDs, and created for new employees by adding 1 to the highest existing EmployeeID value. I made a totals query that returns the highest EmployeeID so far entered, and a subform that displays this value, to place on frmEmployees (it is set invisible). (See Chapter 4, *Sorting and Filtering Data with Queries*, for more information on totals queries.) The procedure that creates a new EmployeeID is listed below. It is called from the form's BeforeInsert event, so the new ID is created when the user starts to enter data into a new employee record.

At the same time, the code creates a new record in tblEmployeesConfidential. This is required because of the one-to-one relationship between tblEmployees and tblEmployeesConfidential. (See Chapter 7, *Writing VBA Code in Modules*, for more information on writing to tables using DAO recordsets.)

```
Private Sub NewEmployeeID()

On Error GoTo ErrorHandler

    Dim strEmployeeID As String
    Dim lngEmployeeID As Long
    Dim dbs As DAO.database
    Dim rst As DAO.Recordset

    Me![subMaxEmployeeID].Form.Requery
    lngEmployeeID = Me![subMaxEmployeeID].Form![txtNumericID] + 1
    strEmployeeID = Format(lngEmployeeID, "00000")
    Me![EmployeeID] = strEmployeeID
    Me![txtEmployeeID].Requery

    'Add a corresponding record to tblEmployeesConfidential.
    Set dbs = CurrentDb
    Set rst = dbs.OpenRecordset("tblEmployeesConfidential", dbOpenTable)
    rst.AddNew
    rst![EmployeeID] = strEmployeeID
    rst.Update
    rst.Close

ErrorHandlerExit:
    Exit Sub

ErrorHandler:
    MsgBox "Error No: " & Err.Number & "; Description: " & _
        Err.Description
    Resume ErrorHandlerExit

End Sub
```

The Department textbox should be changed to a combobox. It could have a lookup table of department names for its row source, or a SQL statement that displays all departments that have been entered. We'll use a SQL statement, done like the Description field on the phone number subforms. (The Title field could also be treated in a similar manner.)

The last special feature of this form is a combobox that selects another record in the same table. cboSupervisorID has tblEmployees as its row source, with the LastNameFirst and Employee ID fields, and also the Department field, with a criterion of Management; it is used to select the employee's supervisor.

Figure 2.36 shows the finished frmEmployees.

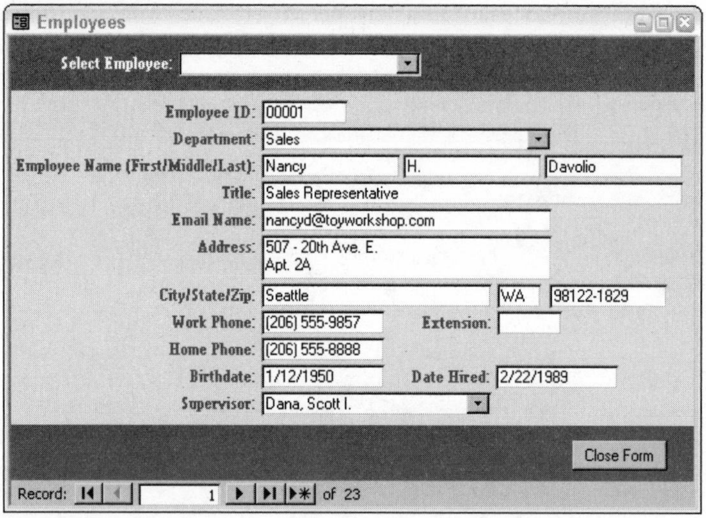

Figure 2.36

One more form with a subform needs to be created, for the tblMailingList and tblMailingListCompanies tables. There is a one-to-many relationship between these tables, but you would most likely want to view the records in tblMailingList in the main form, even though it is the "many" side of the relationship. Therefore, I made a standard form based on tblMailingList, and a subform linked on CompanyID for tblMailingListCompanies. The mailing list company is selected from a combobox, much like selecting a shipping address on frmOrders, and the address data for the selected company is displayed in a subform. I won't discuss creating this form and its subform in detail because it is virtually identical to the process of creating the shipping address selector combobox and the shipping address subform on frmOrders. The frmMailingList form is shown in Figure 2.37, on a record with a company selected.

Creating Continuous Forms

Continuous Forms–type forms are most suitable for entering and editing data when you only have a few fields to deal with and want to see several records at once. In the Toy Workshop database, tblCategories, tblShippingMethods, and tblEmployeesConfidential are good candidates for this type of form. To create a Continuous Forms–type form based on tblCategories, select the Custom Form Wizard in the New Form dialog, and select the Continuous form type with tblCategories as its data source. Since Continuous Forms–type forms do use colors and special effects, on the next screen, select the *Create your own color scheme or control formats* option to use the color scheme created for frmCustomers. Click Finish to create the form.

The new form has a standard Close button in the footer section, and a zero-height header section (Continuous Forms–type forms rarely need a record selector combobox). Drag the two fields from the field list to the form, and make a few modifications:

❑   Make the CategoryID field left-aligned and narrower (it just displays an AutoNumber ID), and use the Lock Wizard to make it locked and give it a blue background. To use the Lock Wizard, right-click the CategoryID textbox, and select Build. Accept the default Locked option in the Lock Wizard dialog, as shown earlier in Figure 2.10.

❏ Move the CategoryID textbox and label over to the left of the form, and the CategoryName textbox and label up and to the right of the CategoryID textbox.

❏ Shrink the blank space over and under the controls so there is just a small amount.

❏ (If desired) move the Close button over to the right side of the footer.

❏ Enter Toy Categories in the form's Caption property.

❏ Run the LNC Rename All Controls builder to rename all controls with the appropriate LNC tags. This is done by invoking the builder from the Build button of the Name property of the form's Detail section, as shown in Figure 2.38.

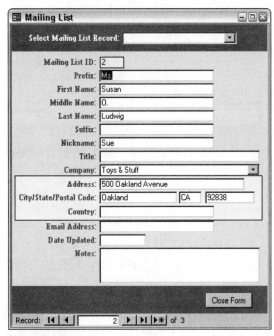

Figure 2.37

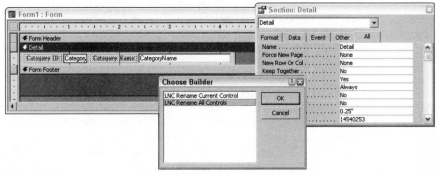

Figure 2.38

Save the new form as frmCategories, and switch to Form view. You'll see why there is no need for a record selector combobox. With only ten records, you can see all of them at once. For those rare cases where there are many records displayed on a Continuous Forms–type form, you can turn on the vertical scroll bar, or add a record selector combobox to the header, similar to the one on frmCustomers. Figure 2.39 shows the form in Form view.

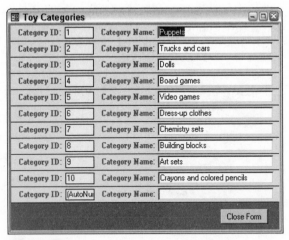

Figure 2.39

The Continuous Forms–type forms for tblShippingMethods and tblEmployeesConfidential can be created in exactly the same manner.

Creating a Form for a Many-to-Many Relationship

The last form variation needed for this application is a form used to enter data into a table that has a many-to-many relationship with another table. In the Toy Workshop database, there are two such relationships, tblToys—tblToyMaterials—tblMaterials, and tblMaterials—tblRepairMaterials—tblRepairs. I will demonstrate creating the Toys form, using an embedded datasheet subform that lets you select values from the other "many" table, tblMaterials, adding a record for each selection to the linking table, tblToyMaterials.

Start by creating a Datasheet form based on tblToyMaterials. Select the Custom Form Wizard in the New Form dialog, and select the Datasheet form type with tblCategories as its data source. Click Finish to create the new form (there are no color choices for datasheet forms).

This subform will be used to select materials, and it needs a combobox that shows you the material name, but stores the MaterialID to tblToyMaterials. Place the MaterialID field on the form, and change the textbox to a combobox. Select tblMaterials as the row source for the combobox, and select MaterialID as the bound field and MaterialName to display in the drop-down list. Select the Ascending sort for MaterialName, then drag the Unit, Quantity and Unit Cost fields to the form. Unit will appear as a combobox, because it is a lookup field. Finally, create a calculated Total Cost textbox with the following expression:

```
=[Quantity]*[UnitCost]
```

Create a standard form based on tblToys. This form has two fields (CategoryID and VendorID) that are foreign keys. They need to be converted to comboboxes so the value can be selected from (respectively) tblCategories and tblVendors. This is done in a manner similar to that used for the foreign key fields on frmOrders.

Depending on whether chkPurchased is checked or not, the Toy Materials subform is invisible or visible (materials need to be selected only for manufactured toys, not purchased toys), and controls related to either purchased or manufactured toys (but not both) are enabled or disabled appropriately. This is done with a Sub procedure called by a line of code on the checkbox's AfterUpdate event and the form's Current event. This procedure follows.

```
Private Sub EnablePurchased()

On Error GoTo ErrorHandler

    'Make subform visible only if toy is manufactured (not purchased),
    'and enable or disable other controls as needed.
    blnPurchased = Nz(Me![chkPurchased])
    If blnPurchased = True Then
        Me![subToyMaterials].Visible = False
        Me![txtVendorPrice].Enabled = True
        Me![txtVendorProductID].Enabled = True
        Me![txtMaterialsCost].Enabled = False
    Else
        Me![subToyMaterials].Visible = True
        Me![txtVendorPrice].Enabled = False
        Me![txtVendorProductID].Enabled = False
        Me![txtMaterialsCost].Enabled = True
    End If

ErrorHandlerExit:
    Exit Sub

ErrorHandler:
    MsgBox "Error No: " & Err.Number & "; Description: " & _
        Err.Description
    Resume ErrorHandlerExit

End Sub
```

Figure 2.40 shows the frmToys form on a record with a manufactured toy, with the Toy Materials subform visible.

There is an AfterUpdate event procedure on the cboMaterialID combobox on the subform that picks up the unit cost from tblMaterials and writes it to tblToyMaterials; and a calculated expression in txtTotalCost that multiplies unit cost by quantity, to get the total cost for that item. The Repairs form is done in a similar manner, except that the Select Materials subform is always visible.

The cost of materials used for manufacturing or repairing toys is calculated using totals queries, subforms, and event procedures; this technique will be discussed in detail in Chapter 4, *Sorting and Filtering Data with Queries.*

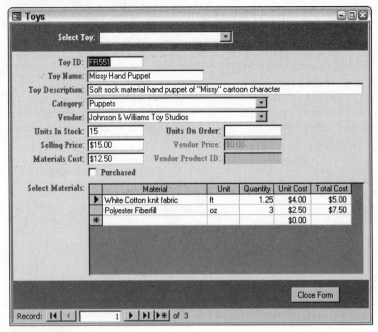

Figure 2.40

Summary

The main forms for the application are now done, though a few more specialized forms will be created in Chapter 4, in the course of discussing various types of queries used for filtering and sorting of data.

Selecting the Right Controls for Forms

In the previous chapter, in the course of creating forms for the Toy Workshop application, we also created controls to display and edit data on the forms. Most of the controls you will use (and almost all the ones automatically created when you drag fields to a form) will be of a few standard types: Textboxes, labels, comboboxes, and checkboxes are the most common. However, there are other standard control types that are useful for working with specific types of data, and some extra ActiveX controls that you can use, if you have the Developer Edition of Office (or another Microsoft application that includes these controls, such as Visual Basic). This chapter will describe the use of both standard and ActiveX controls for working with data in different ways.

Standard Controls

When you open an Access form in Design view, you have a special toolbar (called the *Toolbox*) available for placing controls on the form. If you don't see the Toolbox, you can make it appear by clicking the Toolbox button on the toolbar (this is a toggle button, so clicking it again turns the Toolbox off). I'll discuss the use of standard controls, with examples from various sample databases, and also tell you which ones aren't really useful. Figure 3.1 shows the Toolbox with the control tools labeled.

Figure 3.1

Useful Standard Controls

The controls described in the following sections are most useful on Access forms.

> When looking at Microsoft documentation and Help, sometimes you'll see Text Box, sometimes Textbox, and similarly for Listbox/List Box, Combobox/Combo Box, and Checkbox/Check Box. For the sake of consistency, I'll use the one-word variants of these control names throughout, but you may occasionally see the two-word variants in screen shots.

Label

Labels are useful for displaying text for descriptive purposes. By default, when you place a textbox on a form, it has an attached label, but you can also place standalone labels on a form, for example to label groups of controls on a form. The Information on selected book label on the frmTreeViewEBookNotes form in the EBook Companion sample database (shown in Figure 3.2) serves this purpose.

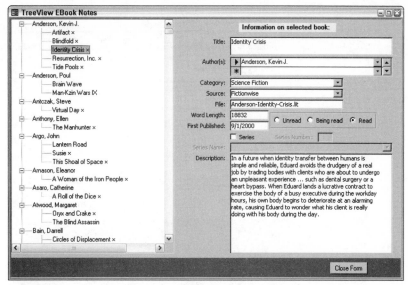

Figure 3.2

Textbox

Textboxes are most commonly used to enter and edit data in tables. However, they can also be used to display the results of calculations (calculated fields) or to display other form-related information. The txtTotalCost field on the fsubToyMaterials subform embedded on frmToys (shown in Figure 3.3) displays the result of this calculated expression:

```
=[Quantity]*[UnitCost]
```

If you want to display the form's record source on the form, you can use the expression =[RecordSource] in a textbox's control source. Several other form properties can also be displayed in textboxes in this manner, as shown in Figure 3.4.

Option Group

An option group is a frame containing two or more option buttons; only one of the option buttons can be selected at any time. (This is why they are sometimes called radio buttons, because they work like buttons on a car radio). Although you can use option buttons, checkboxes, or even toggle buttons as buttons in an option group, it's best to stick to option buttons, as they are most intuitive as a set of mutually exclusive choices. The frmOrders form in the Toy Workshop database (shown in Figure 3.5) uses an option group for selecting a shipping method.

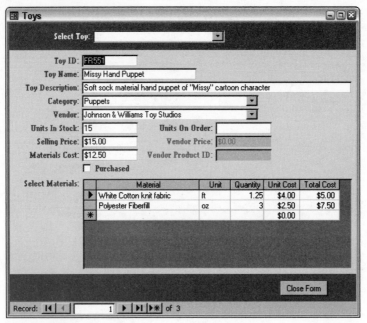

Figure 3.3

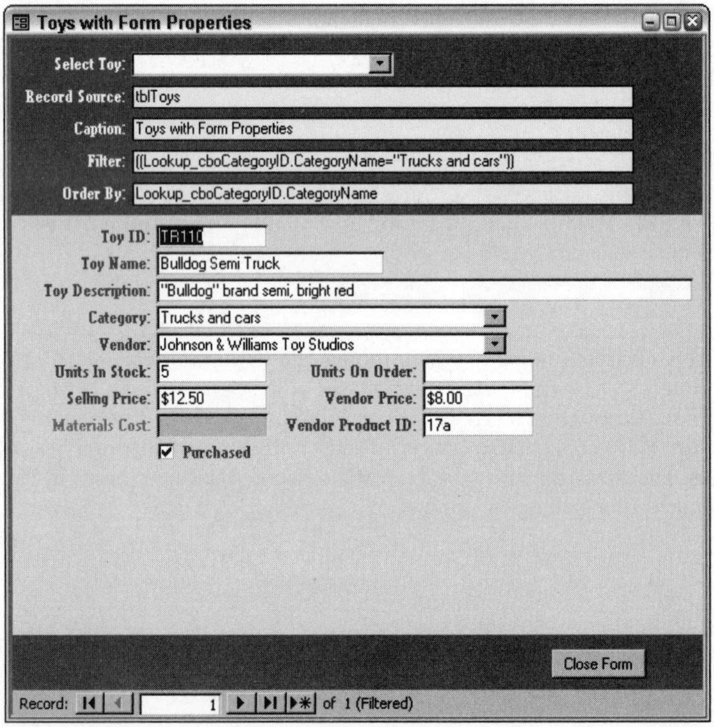

Figure 3.4

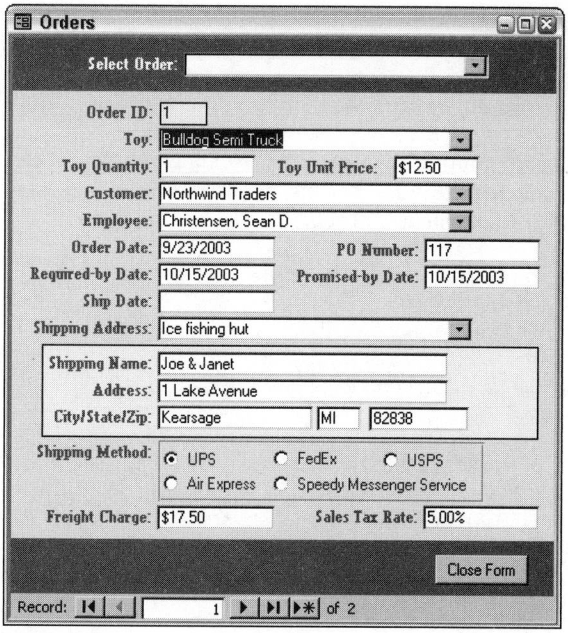

Figure 3.5

Each option button in an option group has an Integer value, so option groups are well suited for selecting a value for Long or Integer fields, such as ID fields. The ShippingMethodID field in tblOrders is such a field, so the option group (fraShippingMethodID) can be bound directly to this field. If you need to store a text string in a field, depending on the user's choice in an option group, you need to convert the Integer value to a String value, using the Switch function or a Select Case statement, such as the ones listed in the following example:

```
Private Sub fraShippingMethodID_AfterUpdate()

On Error GoTo ErrorHandler

    Dim intShipMethod As Integer
    Dim strShipMethod As String

    intShipMethod = Nz(Me![fraShippingMethodID], 1)
    strShipMethod = Switch(intShipMethod = 1, "UPS", _
        intShipMethod = 2, "FedEx", _
        intShipMethod = 3, "USPS", _
        intShipMethod = 4, "Air Express", _
        intShipMethod = 5, "Speedy Messenger Service")

    MsgBox "Selected method: " & strShipMethod

ErrorHandlerExit:
    Exit Sub

ErrorHandler:
    MsgBox "Error No: " & Err.Number & "; Description: " & _
```

```
      Err.Description
   Resume ErrorHandlerExit

End Sub
```

The Switch function is more compact than a Select Case statement, but it can only handle up to eight alternates, so if you need to handle more than eight options, or perhaps run code that depends on the chosen option, a Select Case statement is needed.

```
Private Sub fraShippingMethodID_AfterUpdate()

On Error GoTo ErrorHandler

    Dim intShipMethod As Integer
    Dim strShipMethod As String

    intShipMethod = Nz(Me![fraShippingMethodID], 1)

    Select Case intShipMethod

        Case 1
            strShipMethod = "UPS"

        Case 2
            strShipMethod = "FedEx"

        Case 3
            strShipMethod = "USPS"

        Case 4
            strShipMethod = "Air Express"

        Case 5
            strShipMethod = "Speedy Messenger Service"

    End Select

    MsgBox "Selected method: " & strShipMethod

ErrorHandlerExit:
    Exit Sub

ErrorHandler:
    MsgBox "Error No: " & Err.Number & "; Description: " & _
        Err.Description
    Resume ErrorHandlerExit

End Sub
```

Option Button

An option button is a little circle that is dark when selected and clear when not selected. Option buttons can be used as standalone controls, but they are best suited for use in option groups where only one option can be selected at a time. The interface convention is that option buttons are used for mutually exclusive choices (as part of an option group), while checkboxes are used when you need to allow multiple selections from a group of options.

Checkbox

A checkbox is a little square that is checked to indicate selection. Although you can use checkboxes inside an option group, this is not advisable; they are best used to indicate a True/False (Yes/No) choice for a single field. If you need a group of options where more than one can be selected, you can't use an option group (only one option can be selected at a time). Instead, place several standalone checkboxes on the form, and surround them with a rectangle. Using checkboxes instead of option buttons suggests to users that they can select several items from a group of choices, not just one.

Combobox

A combobox is used to make a single selection from a drop-down list of choices. The values in the list can be derived from a table, query, or SQL statement; a value list; or a field list. A very simple combobox (for example, to select a zip code) has a one-column list, and the selected item is stored in the combobox's bound field. However, comboboxes can be quite complex, with several fields showing in the drop-down list (to aid in selection), and possibly storing a value to the bound field that doesn't even appear in the drop-down list.

Table/Query Row Source

As an example of a more complex combobox, cboShipAddressID on frmOrders in the sample Toy Workshop database has a SQL statement row source that includes three fields from a union query, with a criterion on one field that filters the row source by the CustomerID of the customer selected on the form, as shown in Figure 3.6.

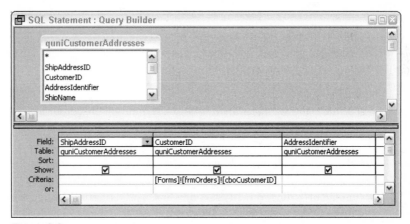

Figure 3.6

In the combobox properties sheet (shown in Figure 3.7), Table/Query is selected for the Row Source Type property.

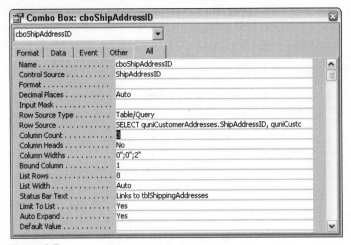

Figure 3.7

The column count is 3, for the three columns selected in the query designer. These three columns are used in different ways in the combobox. The first column (ShipAddressID) contains the value that is written to the combobox's bound field, ShipAddressID (shown in the Control Source property). The second column (CustomerID) has a criterion that limits the SQL statement results to records that have the same CustomerID as the customer selected in another combobox on the form. The third column (AddressIdentifier) contains the descriptive phrase that identifies the shipping address. Only the third column needs to show in the drop-down list, so the Column Widths are 0"; 0"; 2" to make columns 1 and 2 invisible, and column 3 visible and 2 inches wide.

Value List Row Source

As an alternative to deriving values from a table, query, or SQL statement, you can select Value List for the Row Source Type property and enter values into the Row Source property, as in the following list:

```
"UPS";"FedEx";"USPS";"Air Express";"Speedy Messenger Service"
```

For obvious reasons, value list row sources are only sensible if the list of choices is both limited and fixed; otherwise, you are better off using a lookup table as the combobox's row source.

Field List Row Source

The third type of row source available for comboboxes is a field list. This choice is useful when you need to select a field for filtering or sorting. A field list combobox is used on frmExportToWordDatasheet in the Word Data Exchange sample database for Chapter 11, *Working with Word* (and similar forms in the other export sample databases), to allow the selection of a field for filtering data. cboFilterField has Value List selected as the Row Source Type, and qryContactsAlpha as the Row Source.

> Fields displayed in a combobox with a field list row source are displayed in the order they occur in the table or query, so if you want the fields to be displayed alphabetically in the drop-down list, you have to create a special query for this purpose, with the fields arranged alphabetically. qryContactsAlpha is the alphabetized version of qryContacts. (These queries are located in the various Data Exchange sample databases.)

Simply selecting a field isn't generally useful; after selecting a field, you next need to select a value for that field, in order to do sorting or filtering. The second combobox, cboFilterValue, has a blank Row Source property; its row source is created from the AfterUpdate event of cboFilterField, and assigned to cboFilterValue. The VBA code for these two comboboxes follows:

```
Private Sub cboFilterField_AfterUpdate()

On Error GoTo ErrorHandler

    pstrFilterField = Nz(Me![cboFilterField].Value)
    If pstrFilterField = "" Then
        strTitle = "No field selected"
        strPrompt = "Please select a field for filtering"
        MsgBox strPrompt, vbCritical + vbOKOnly, strTitle
        Me![cboFilterField].SetFocus
        GoTo ErrorHandlerExit
    End If

    If pstrDataType = "C" Then
        strQuery = "qryContactsAlpha"
    ElseIf pstrDataType = "E" Then
        strQuery = "qryEBookCatalogAlpha"
    End If

    strSQL = "SELECT DISTINCT " & strQuery & ".[" & pstrFilterField & _
        "] FROM " & strQuery & " WHERE [" & pstrFilterField & "] Is Not Null;"
    Debug.Print "SQL string: " & strSQL
    With Me![cboFilterValue]
        .Value = Null
        .RowSource = strSQL
        .Requery
        .Enabled = True
        .SetFocus
        .Dropdown
    End With

    Me![txtFilterString].Value = Null

ErrorHandlerExit:
    Exit Sub

ErrorHandler:
    MsgBox "Error No: " & Err.Number & "; Description: " & _
        Err.Description
```

```
     Resume ErrorHandlerExit

End Sub

Private Sub cboFilterValue_AfterUpdate()

On Error GoTo ErrorHandler

    Dim intDataType As Integer
    Dim fld As DAO.Field
    Dim qdf As DAO.QueryDef
    Dim strTotalsQuery As String
    Dim strLinkedQuery As String
    Dim strFilter As String

    pvarFilterValue = Me![cboFilterValue].Value

    'Determine data type of selected field
    Set dbs = CurrentDb
    Set rst = dbs.OpenRecordset(pstrQuery, dbOpenDynaset)
    Set fld = rst.Fields(pstrFilterField)
    intDataType = fld.Type
    Debug.Print "Field data type: " & intDataType

    Select Case intDataType
       Case 1
          'Boolean
          strFilter = "[" & pstrFilterField & "] = " & pvarFilterValue

       Case 2, 3, 4, 6, 7
          'Various numeric
          strFilter = "[" & pstrFilterField & "] = " & pvarFilterValue

       Case 5
          'Currency
          strFilter = "[" & pstrFilterField & "] = " & CCur(pvarFilterValue)

       Case 8
          'Date
          strFilter = "[" & pstrFilterField & "] = " & Chr$(35) _
             & pvarFilterValue & Chr$(35)

       Case 10
          'Text
          strFilter = "[" & pstrFilterField & "] = " & Chr$(34) _
             & pvarFilterValue & Chr$(34)

       Case 11, 12, 15
          'OLE object, Memo, Replication ID
          strPrompt = "Can't filter by this field; please select another field"
          MsgBox strPrompt, vbCritical + vbOKOnly
          Me![cboFilterValue].SetFocus
```

```
        Me![cboFilterValue].Dropdown
        GoTo ErrorHandlerExit

    End Select

    Debug.Print "Filter string: " & strFilter

    'Apply filter to record source and make a table from it.
    Me![txtFilterString] = strFilter
    strQuery = "qmakMatchingRecords"
    strSQL = "SELECT " & pstrQuery & ".* INTO tmakMatchingRecords " _
        & "FROM " & pstrQuery & " WHERE " & strFilter & ";"
    Debug.Print "SQL Statement: " & strSQL
    Set qdf = dbs.CreateQueryDef(strQuery, strSQL)
    qdf.Execute
    Me![cboFilterField].Value = Null
    Me![cboFilterValue].Value = Null

    If pstrDataType = "C" Then
        Me![subContacts].SourceObject = "fsubContactsFiltered"
        Debug.Print "subContacts source object: " _
            & Me![subContacts].SourceObject
    ElseIf pstrDataType = "E" Then
        Me![subEBookCatalog].SourceObject = "fsubEBookCatalogFiltered"
        Debug.Print "subEBookCatalog source object: " _
            & Me![subEBookCatalog].SourceObject
    End If

ErrorHandlerExit:
    Exit Sub

ErrorHandler:
    MsgBox "Error No: " & Err.Number & "; Description: " & _
        Err.Description
    Resume ErrorHandlerExit

End Sub
```

cboFilterField's AfterUpdate event first checks that a field has been selected, and then (depending on the value of a previously set public variable) sets strQuery to one of two values. Next, a SQL string is created that displays all the values for the selected field in the query represented by strQuery. cboFilterValue is then set to Null, and its row source is set to the SQL statement. cboFilterValue is then requeried and enabled, focus is set to it, and its list is dropped down.

After a value is selected from cboFilterValue, the data type of the selected field is picked up from the field's Type property, and a Select Case statement is set up to create a filter string differently according to the field data type. For Boolean and most numeric fields, the field value is used alone. For currency fields, CCur is used to convert the field type to Currency (I have noticed that sometimes Currency fields lose their data type when picked up from code). Date field values are wrapped in the number sign character (Chr$(35)), text field values are wrapped in quotes (Chr$(34)), and several fields that can't be used for filtering get an appropriate message.

Next, the filter string is applied to the record source, and a table is created from it. Finally, depending on the value of a public variable, the appropriate source object is assigned to a subform (the table just created is the record source of the source object subform).

Add-to Combobox

The default settings for a combobox don't allow users to enter a value that isn't a selection in the list. You can set the Limit To List property to No to allow users to enter a value that isn't in the list, or you can write code on the combobox's Not In List event to automate the addition of new entries into a lookup table used as a combobox's row source (I call this an add-to combobox). I'll convert the cboCategoryID combobox on frmToys in the Toy Workshop sample database into an add-to combobox as an example. This combobox has tblCategories as its row source, and this table has only two fields: CategoryID (an AutoNumber field) and CategoryName. Since the CategoryID field's value is filled in automatically when a new record is created, the only information needed to create a new record is the category name.

To convert this combobox to an add-to combobox, check that its Limit To List property is Yes (it probably is because that is the default value), and create an event procedure stub for the Not in List property by clicking on the Build button next to this event.

> Some event procedures are displayed in the Events page of the properties sheet starting with an "On," and others are not (for example, On Not in List, After Update). In VBA code, "On" is never used as part of an event procedure name. I will not use the "On," which is unnecessary and confusing.

I make so many add-to comboboxes that I created a standard boilerplate procedure that I can just plug into a new NotInList event procedure stub, and make a few changes to customize it for the specific control, form, and table names. The Not in List event procedure with the boilerplate filler is listed below; the underscores represent the parts that need to be customized.

```
Private Sub cboCategoryID_NotInList(NewData As String, Response As Integer)
'Set Limit to List to Yes

On Error GoTo ErrorHandler

    Dim intResult As Integer
    Dim strTitle As String
    Dim intMsgDialog As Integer
    Dim strMsg1 As String
    Dim strMsg2 As String
    Dim strMsg As String
    Dim cbo As Access.ComboBox
    Dim dbs As DAO.Database
    Dim rst As DAO.Recordset
    Dim strTable As String
    Dim strEntry As String
    Dim strFieldName As String

    'The name of the lookup table
    strTable = "_____"

    'The type of item to add to the table
```

```
        strEntry = "_____"

        'The field in the lookup table in which the new entry is stored
        strFieldName = "_____"

        'The add-to combobox
        Set cbo = Me![_____]

        'Display a message box asking whether the user wants to add
        'a new entry.
        strTitle = strEntry & " not in list"
        intMsgDialog = vbYesNo + vbExclamation + vbDefaultButton1
        strMsg1 = "Do you want to add "
        strMsg2 = " as a new " & strEntry & " entry?"
        strMsg = strMsg1 + strNewData + strMsg2
        intResult = MsgBox(strMsg, intMsgDialog, strTitle)

        If intResult = vbNo Then
            'Cancel adding the new entry to the lookup table.
            intResponse = acDataErrContinue
            cbo.Undo
            GoTo ErrorHandlerExit
        ElseIf intResult = vbYes Then
            'Add a new record to the lookup table.
            Set dbs = CurrentDb
            Set rst = dbs.OpenRecordset(strTable)
            rst.AddNew
            rst(strFieldName) = strNewData
            rst.Update
            rst.Close

            'Continue without displaying default error message.
            intResponse = acDataErrAdded

        End If

ErrorHandlerExit:
    Exit Sub

ErrorHandler:
    MsgBox "Error No: " & Err.Number & "; Description: " & _
        Err.Description
    Resume ErrorHandlerExit

End Sub
```

The first step is to put the appropriate LNC variable tags in the event procedure's arguments (the tags are italicized):

```
Private Sub cboCategoryID_NotInList(strNewData As String, intResponse As Integer)
```

Next, the underscores in the boilerplate code need to be replaced with appropriate text, as follows:

❑ **The name of the lookup table:** tblCategories

❑ **The type of item to add to the table:** category

❑   **The field in the lookup table in which the new entry is stored:** CategoryName

❑   **The add-to combobox:** cboCategoryID

The edited procedure is listed below:

```
Private Sub cboCategoryID_NotInList(strNewData As String, intResponse As Integer)
'Set Limit to List to Yes.

On Error GoTo ErrorHandler

    Dim intResult As Integer
    Dim strTitle As String
    Dim intMsgDialog As Integer
    Dim strMsg1 As String
    Dim strMsg2 As String
    Dim strMsg As String
    Dim cbo As Access.ComboBox
    Dim dbs As DAO.Database
    Dim rst As DAO.Recordset
    Dim strTable As String
    Dim strEntry As String
    Dim strFieldName As String

    'The name of the lookup table
    strTable = "tblCategories"

    'The type of item to add to the table
    strEntry = "category"

    'The field in the lookup table in which the new entry is stored
    strFieldName = "CategoryName"

    'The add-to combobox
    Set cbo = Me![cboCategoryID]

    'Display a message box asking whether the user wants to add
    'a new entry.
    strTitle = strEntry & " not in list"
    intMsgDialog = vbYesNo + vbExclamation + vbDefaultButton1
    strMsg1 = "Do you want to add "
    strMsg2 = " as a new " & strEntry & " entry?"
    strMsg = strMsg1 + strNewData + strMsg2
    intResult = MsgBox(strMsg, intMsgDialog, strTitle)

    If intResult = vbNo Then
        'Cancel adding the new entry to the lookup table.
        intResponse = acDataErrContinue
        cbo.Undo
        GoTo ErrorHandlerExit
    ElseIf intResult = vbYes Then
        'Add a new record to the lookup table.
        Set dbs = CurrentDb
        Set rst = dbs.OpenRecordset(strTable)
```

```
        rst.AddNew
        rst(strFieldName) = strNewData
        rst.Update
        rst.Close

        'Continue without displaying default error message.
        intResponse = acDataErrAdded

    End If

ErrorHandlerExit:
    Exit Sub

ErrorHandler:
    MsgBox "Error No: " & Err.Number & "; Description: " & _
        Err.Description
    Resume ErrorHandlerExit

End Sub
```

When the user types a new category name into the combobox, the Not in List procedure puts up a message box asking if the user wants to add it as a new category entry; several named constants are used to handle the user's response. If the response is negative, intResponse is set to acDataErrContinue, and the value is removed from the combobox, leaving you ready to select a value from the list. If the response is positive, the a DAO recordset is created, based on the lookup table, the new value is written to the appropriate field in the table, and the record is updated. intResponse is then set to the named variable acDataErrAdded. Figure 3.8 shows the message box that appears when Construction kits is entered into cboCategoryID.

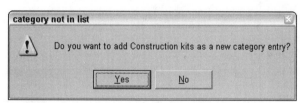

Figure 3.8

The result is that you have not just selected a category for the current record in tblToys, but added it as a category selection that will be available for selection in frmToys in future (or any other form where you can select a toy category).

Listbox

Listboxes are similar to comboboxes in many ways: they can also take a table/query, value list, or field list as a row source, and they display a list of items for the user to choose from. However, listboxes don't offer the possibility of entering data manually, and they do offer a special possibility not available for comboboxes: Listboxes have a MultiSelect property that lets users select more than one item for processing, and a handy ItemsSelected collection for working with selected items in VBA code.

I use MultiSelect listboxes for selecting multiple records from an Access table for export to Word, Outlook, or Excel. One of these listboxes is lstSelectMultiple on frmExportToWordListBox in the Word Data Exchange sample database for Chapter 11, *Working with Word*. Many of the properties of listboxes are the same as those of comboboxes; the MultiSelect property is unique, however. This property has three choices: None, Simple, and Extended, explained in the following list:

None. Only one choice can be made.

Simple. Click or press the spacebar to select or deselect items.

Extended. Multiple records can be selected, using the standard Ctrl-Click and Shift-Click keys to extend the selection (Ctrl-Click adds a single record to the previously selected items; Shift-Click extends the selection from the currently selected record through the clicked record). This is generally the best choice, since it is much easier to select large numbers of records using Shift-Click.

As with comboboxes, you can make a listbox column invisible by setting its width to zero in the Column Widths property, and you can reference data in invisible columns. Figure 3.9 shows lstSelectMultiple, with several items selected.

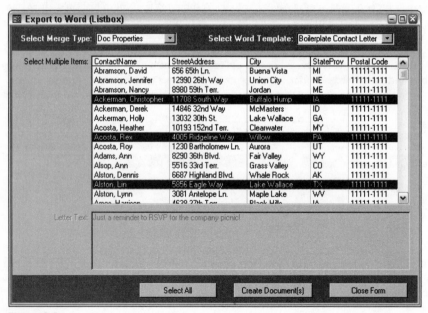

Figure 3.9

Four columns are displayed in the listbox, but if you look at the properties sheet (shown in Figure 3.10), you will see that there are actually 12 columns.

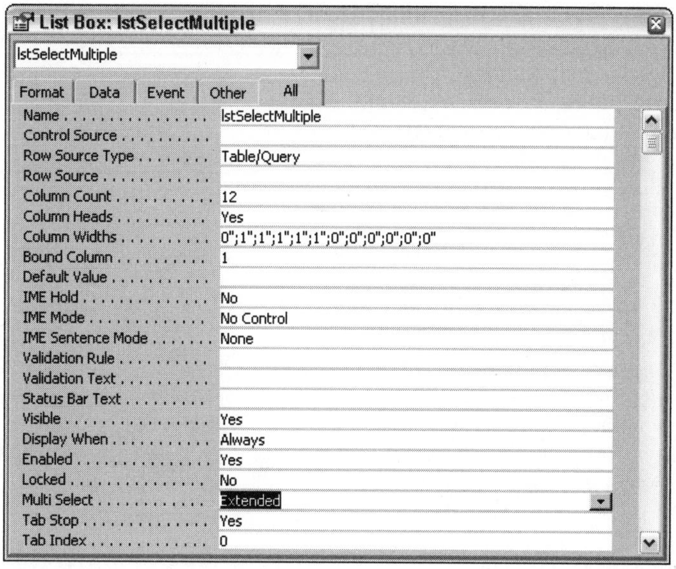

Figure 3.10

You can reference data in any of the columns in the listbox, using the following syntax:

```
strName = Nz(lst.Column(7, varItem))
```

where the *lst* variable references the listbox, the first Column argument references the column number (the first column is numbered 0), and the *varItem* variable represents the number of the selected item in the ItemsSelected collection. The Nz function is used to convert a blank value into either a zero (for numeric values) or a zero-length string (for text values), to prevent problems with storing Nulls to fields or variables that can't accept them.

The complete event procedure that creates letters for the records selected in the above listbox is listed below.

```
Private Sub cmdCreateDocuments_Click()

On Error GoTo ErrorHandler

    Dim blnSomeSkipped As Boolean
    Dim cbo As Access.ComboBox
    Dim dbs As DAO.Database
    Dim i As String
    Dim intMergeType As Integer
    Dim intSaveNameFail As String
    Dim lngContactID As Long
    Dim prps As Object
    Dim rst As DAO.Recordset
    Dim strAddress As String
    Dim strCompanyName As String
```

```
    Dim strCountry As String
    Dim strDocName As String
    Dim strDocsPath As String
    Dim strDocType As String
    Dim strEnvelopeAddress As String
    Dim strEnvelopeName As String
    Dim strFile As String
    Dim strJobTitle As String
    Dim strLetterText As String
    Dim strLongDate As String
    Dim strName As String
    Dim strNameAndJob As String
    Dim strPrompt As String
    Dim strSalutation As String
    Dim strSaveName As String
    Dim strSaveNamePath As String
    Dim strShortDate As String
    Dim strSQL As String
    Dim strTable As String
    Dim strTemplatePath As String
    Dim strTest As String
    Dim strTestFile As String
    Dim strTextFile As String
    Dim strTitle As String
    Dim strWordTemplate As String
    Dim varItem As Variant

    'Check that a letter has been selected.
    Set cbo = Me![cboSelectTemplate]
    Set lst = Me![lstSelectMultiple]
    strWordTemplate = Nz(cbo.Column(1))
    Debug.Print "Selected template: " & strWordTemplate
    If strWordTemplate = "" Then
       MsgBox "Please select a document."
       cbo.SetFocus
       cbo.Dropdown
       GoTo ErrorHandlerExit
    Else
       intMergeType = cbo.Column(3)
       Debug.Print "Merge type: " & intMergeType
    End If

    'Check that at least one contact has been selected.
    If lst.ItemsSelected.Count = 0 Then
       MsgBox "Please select at least one contact."
       lst.SetFocus
       GoTo ErrorHandlerExit
    Else
       intColumns = lst.ColumnCount
       intRows = lst.ItemsSelected.Count
    End If

    'Set global Word application variable; if Word is not running,
    'the error handler defaults to CreateObject
```

```
Set appWord = GetObject(, "Word.Application")

'Set date and folder reference variables.
strLongDate = Format(Date, "mmmm d, yyyy")
strShortDate = Format(Date, "m-d-yyyy")
strDocsPath = GetDocsDir & "Access Merge\"
strTemplatePath = TemplateDir
strWordTemplate = strTemplatePath & strWordTemplate
strLetterText = Nz(Me![LetterText])

'Check for existence of template in template folder,
'and exit if not found
strTestFile = Nz(Dir(strWordTemplate))
Debug.Print "Test file: " & strTestFile
If strTestFile = "" Then
   MsgBox strWordTemplate & " template not found; can't create document"
   GoTo ErrorHandlerExit
End If

'Open text file for writing information about skipped records
strFile = strDocsPath & "Skipped Records.txt"
Open strFile For Output As #1
Print #1, "These records were skipped when creating documents"
Print #1,

Select Case intMergeType

   Case 1
      'Bookmarks
      blnSomeSkipped = False

      For Each varItem In lst.ItemsSelected
         'Get Contact ID for reference
         lngContactID = Nz(lst.Column(0, varItem))
         Debug.Print "Contact ID: " & lngContactID

         'Check for required address information.
         strTest = Nz(lst.Column(2, varItem))
         Debug.Print "Street address: " & strTest
         If strTest = "" Then
            blnSomeSkipped = True
            Print #1,
            Print #1, "No street address for Contact " & lngContactID
            GoTo NextItem1
         End If

         strTest = Nz(lst.Column(3, varItem))
         Debug.Print "City: " & strTest
         If strTest = "" Then
            blnSomeSkipped = True
            Print #1,
            Print #1, "No city for Contact " & lngContactID
            GoTo NextItem1
         End If

         strTest = Nz(lst.Column(5, varItem))
```

```
                    Debug.Print "Postal code: " & strTest
                    If strTest = "" Then
                        blnSomeSkipped = True
                        Print #1,
                        Print #1, "No postal code for Contact " & lngContactID
                        GoTo NextItem1
                    End If

                    strName = Nz(lst.Column(7, varItem))
                    strJobTitle = Nz(lst.Column(10, varItem))
                    If strJobTitle <> "" Then
                        strNameAndJob = strName & vbCrLf & strJobTitle
                    End If
                    strAddress = Nz(lst.Column(8, varItem))
                    Debug.Print "Address: " & strAddress
                    strCountry = Nz(lst.Column(6, varItem))
                    If strCountry <> "USA" Then
                        strAddress = strAddress & vbCrLf & strCountry
                    End If
                    strCompanyName = Nz(lst.Column(9, varItem))
                    strSalutation = Nz(lst.Column(11, varItem))

                    'Open a new document based on the selected template.
                    appWord.Documents.Add strWordTemplate

                    'Write information to Word bookmarks (excluding some for One-up
                    'Label docs).
On Error Resume Next
                    With appWord.Selection
                      .GoTo What:=wdGoToBookmark, Name:="Name"
                      .TypeText Text:=strName
                     .GoTo What:=wdGoToBookmark, Name:="CompanyName"
                      If Left(cbo.Value, 12) <> "One-up Label" Then
                         .TypeText Text:=strCompanyName
                      End If
                      .GoTo What:=wdGoToBookmark, Name:="Address"
                      .TypeText Text:=strAddress
                      .GoTo What:=wdGoToBookmark, Name:="Salutation"
                      If Left(cbo.Value, 12) <> "One-up Label" Then
                         .TypeText Text:=strSalutation
                      End If
                      .GoTo What:=wdGoToBookmark, Name:="TodayDate"
                      If Left(cbo.Value, 12) <> "One-up Label" Then
                         .TypeText Text:=strLongDate
                      End If
                      .GoTo What:=wdGoToBookmark, Name:="EnvelopeName"
                      If Left(cbo.Value, 12) <> "One-up Label" Then
                         .TypeText Text:=strName
                      End If
                      .GoTo What:=wdGoToBookmark, Name:="EnvelopeCompany"
                      If Left(cbo.Value, 12) <> "One-up Label" Then
                         .TypeText Text:=strCompanyName
                      End If
                      .GoTo What:=wdGoToBookmark, Name:="EnvelopeAddress"
                      If Left(cbo.Value, 12) <> "One-up Label" Then
```

```
                    .TypeText Text:=strAddress
                End If
                .GoTo What:=wdGoToBookmark, Name:="LetterText"
                If Left(cbo.Column(1), 9) = "Freestyle" Then
                    .TypeText Text:=strLetterText
                End If
            End With

    On Error GoTo ErrorHandler
            'Check for existence of previously saved letter in documents folder,
            'and append an incremented number to save name if found
            strDocType = _
                appWord.ActiveDocument.BuiltInDocumentProperties(wdPropertySubject)
            strSaveName = strDocType & " to " & strName
            strSaveName = strSaveName & " on " & strShortDate & ".doc"
            i = 2
            intSaveNameFail = True
            Do While intSaveNameFail
                strSaveNamePath = strDocsPath & strSaveName
                Debug.Print "Proposed save name and path: " _
                    & vbCrLf & strSaveNamePath
                strTestFile = Nz(Dir(strSaveNamePath))
                Debug.Print "Test file: " & strTestFile
                If strTestFile = strSaveName Then
                    Debug.Print "Save name already used: " & strSaveName

                    'Create new save name with incremented number
                    intSaveNameFail = True
                    strSaveName = strDocType & " " & CStr(i) & " to " & strName
                    strSaveName = strSaveName & " on " & strShortDate & ".doc"
                    strSaveNamePath = strDocsPath & strSaveName
                    Debug.Print "New save name and path: " _
                        & vbCrLf & strSaveNamePath
                    i = i + 1
                Else
                    Debug.Print "Save name not used: " & strSaveName
                    intSaveNameFail = False
                End If
            Loop

            'Update fields in Word document and save it
            With appWord
                .Selection.WholeStory
                .Selection.Fields.Update
                .Selection.HomeKey Unit:=wdStory
                .ActiveDocument.SaveAs strSaveNamePath
                .Visible = True
                .ActiveWindow.WindowState = wdWindowStateNormal
                .Activate
            End With

NextItem1:
        Next varItem

        strTitle = "Merge done"
```

```
            If blnSomeSkipped = True Then
                strPrompt = "All documents created; some records skipped because " _
                    & "of missing information." & vbCrLf & "See " & strDocsPath _
                    & "Skipped Records.txt for details."
            Else
                strPrompt = "All documents created!"
            End If

            MsgBox strPrompt, vbOKOnly + vbInformation, strTitle

        Case 2
            'Doc Properties
            blnSomeSkipped = False

            For Each varItem In lst.ItemsSelected
                'Get Contact ID for reference
                lngContactID = Nz(lst.Column(0, varItem))
                Debug.Print "Contact ID: " & lngContactID

                'Check for required address information.
                strTest = Nz(lst.Column(2, varItem))
                Debug.Print "Street address: " & strTest
                If strTest = "" Then
                    blnSomeSkipped = True
                    Print #1,
                    Print #1, "No street address for Contact " & lngContactID
                    GoTo NextItem2
                End If

                strTest = Nz(lst.Column(3, varItem))
                Debug.Print "City: " & strTest
                If strTest = "" Then
                    blnSomeSkipped = True
                    Print #1,
                    Print #1, "No city for Contact " & lngContactID
                    GoTo NextItem2
                End If

                strTest = Nz(lst.Column(5, varItem))
                Debug.Print "Postal code: " & strTest
                If strTest = "" Then
                    blnSomeSkipped = True
                    Print #1,
                    Print #1, "No postal code for Contact " & lngContactID
                    GoTo NextItem2
                End If

                strName = Nz(lst.Column(7, varItem))
                strJobTitle = Nz(lst.Column(10, varItem))
                If strJobTitle <> "" Then
                    strNameAndJob = strName & vbCrLf & strJobTitle
                End If
                strAddress = Nz(lst.Column(8, varItem))
                Debug.Print "Address: " & strAddress
                strCountry = Nz(lst.Column(6, varItem))
```

```
            If strCountry <> "USA" Then
                strAddress = strAddress & vbCrLf & strCountry
            End If
            strCompanyName = Nz(lst.Column(9, varItem))
            strSalutation = Nz(lst.Column(11, varItem))

            'Open a new letter based on the selected template.
            appWord.Documents.Add strWordTemplate

            'Write information to Word custom document properties
            Set prps = appWord.ActiveDocument.CustomDocumentProperties
            prps.Item("Name").Value = strName
On Error Resume Next
            With prps
                .Item("Salutation").Value = strSalutation
                .Item("CompanyName").Value = strCompanyName
                .Item("Address").Value = strAddress
                .Item("TodayDate").Value = strLongDate
                .Item("LetterText").Value = strLetterText
            End With

On Error GoTo ErrorHandler
            'Check for existence of previously saved document in documents folder,
            'and append an incremented number to save name if found
            strDocType = _
                appWord.ActiveDocument.BuiltInDocumentProperties(wdPropertySubject)
            strSaveName = strDocType & " to " & strName
            strSaveName = strSaveName & " on " & strShortDate & ".doc"
            i = 2
            intSaveNameFail = True
            Do While intSaveNameFail
                strSaveNamePath = strDocsPath & strSaveName
                Debug.Print "Proposed save name and path: " _
                    & vbCrLf & strSaveNamePath
                strTestFile = Nz(Dir(strSaveNamePath))
                Debug.Print "Test file: " & strTestFile
                If strTestFile = strSaveName Then
                    Debug.Print "Save name already used: " & strSaveName

                    'Create new save name with incremented number
                    intSaveNameFail = True
                    strSaveName = strDocType & " " & CStr(i) & " to " & strName
                    strSaveName = strSaveName & " on " & strShortDate & ".doc"
                    strSaveNamePath = strDocsPath & strSaveName
                    Debug.Print "New save name and path: " _
                        & vbCrLf & strSaveNamePath
                    i = i + 1
                Else
                    Debug.Print "Save name not used: " & strSaveName
                    intSaveNameFail = False
                End If
            Loop

            'Update fields in Word document and save it
            With appWord
```

```
                .Selection.WholeStory
                .Selection.Fields.Update
                .Selection.HomeKey Unit:=wdStory
                .ActiveDocument.SaveAs strSaveNamePath
                .Visible = True
                .ActiveWindow.WindowState = wdWindowStateNormal
                .Activate
            End With
NextItem2:
        Next varItem

        strTitle = "Merge done"
        If blnSomeSkipped = True Then
            strPrompt = "All documents created; some records skipped because " _
                & "of missing information." & vbCrLf & "See " & strDocsPath _
                & "Skipped Records.txt for details."
        Else
            strPrompt = "All documents created!"
        End If

        MsgBox strPrompt, vbOKOnly + vbInformation, strTitle

    Case 3
        'Mail Merge
        blnSomeSkipped = False

        'Clear tblMergeList and set up recordset based on it
        strTable = "tblMailMergeList"
        strSQL = "DELETE tblMailMergeList.* FROM tblMailMergeList;"
        DoCmd.SetWarnings False
        DoCmd.RunSQL strSQL
        Set dbs = CurrentDb
        Debug.Print "Opening recordset based on " & strTable
        Set rst = dbs.OpenRecordset(strTable, dbOpenTable)

        For Each varItem In lst.ItemsSelected
            'Get Contact ID for reference
            lngContactID = Nz(lst.Column(0, varItem))
            Debug.Print "Contact ID: " & lngContactID

            'Check for required address information.
            strTest = Nz(lst.Column(2, varItem))
            Debug.Print "Street address: " & strTest
            If strTest = "" Then
                blnSomeSkipped = True
                Print #1,
                Print #1, "No street address for Contact " & lngContactID
                GoTo NextItem3
            End If

            strTest = Nz(lst.Column(3, varItem))
            Debug.Print "City: " & strTest
            If strTest = "" Then
                blnSomeSkipped = True
                Print #1,
```

```
                    Print #1, "No city for Contact " & lngContactID
                    GoTo NextItem3
                End If


                strTest = Nz(lst.Column(5, varItem))
                Debug.Print "Postal code: " & strTest
                If strTest = "" Then
                    blnSomeSkipped = True
                    Print #1,
                    Print #1, "No postal code for Contact " & lngContactID
                    GoTo NextItem3
                End If


                strName = Nz(lst.Column(7, varItem))
                strJobTitle = Nz(lst.Column(10, varItem))
                strAddress = Nz(lst.Column(8, varItem))
                Debug.Print "Address: " & strAddress
                strCountry = Nz(lst.Column(6, varItem))
                If strCountry <> "USA" Then
                    strAddress = strAddress & vbCrLf & strCountry
                End If
                strCompanyName = Nz(lst.Column(9, varItem))
                strSalutation = Nz(lst.Column(11, varItem))

                'Write data from variables to a new record in table
                With rst
                    .AddNew
                    !Name = strName
                    !JobTitle = strJobTitle
                    !CompanyName = strCompanyName
                    !Address = strAddress
                    !Salutation = strSalutation
                    !TodayDate = strLongDate
                    .Update
                End With

NextItem3:
        Next varItem
        rst.Close

        'Export merge list to a text file
        'strDBPath = Application.CurrentProject.Path & "\"
        strDocsPath = GetDocsDir & "Access Merge\"
        Debug.Print "Docs path: " & strDocsPath
        strTextFile = strDocsPath & "Mail Merge Data.txt"
        Debug.Print "Text file for merge: " & strTextFile
        DoCmd.TransferText transfertype:=acExportDelim, TableName:=strTable, _
            FileName:=strTextFile, HasFieldNames:=True

        'Open a new merge document based on the selected template.
        appWord.Documents.Add strWordTemplate
        strDocName = appWord.ActiveDocument
        Debug.Print "Initial doc name: " & strDocName

        'Check for existence of previously saved letter in documents folder,
```

```vba
        'and append an incremented number to save name if found
        strDocType = _
            appWord.ActiveDocument.BuiltInDocumentProperties(wdPropertySubject)
        strSaveName = strDocType & " on " & strShortDate & ".doc"
        i = 2
        intSaveNameFail = True
        Do While intSaveNameFail
            strSaveNamePath = strDocsPath & strSaveName
            Debug.Print "Proposed save name and path: " _
                & vbCrLf & strSaveNamePath
            strTestFile = Nz(Dir(strSaveNamePath))
            'Debug.Print "Test file: " & strTestFile
            If strTestFile = strSaveName Then
                'Debug.Print "Save name already used: " & strSaveName

                'Create new save name with incremented number
                intSaveNameFail = True
                strSaveName = strDocType & " " & CStr(i) & _
                    " on " & strShortDate & ".doc"
                strSaveNamePath = strDocsPath & strSaveName
                'Debug.Print "New save name and path: " _
                    & vbCrLf & strSaveNamePath
                i = i + 1
            Else
                'Debug.Print "Save name not used: " & strSaveName
                intSaveNameFail = False
            End If
        Loop

        'Set the merge data source to the text file just created,
        'and do the merge.
        With appWord
            .ActiveDocument.MailMerge.OpenDataSource Name:=strTextFile, _
                Format:=wdOpenFormatText
            .ActiveDocument.MailMerge.Destination = wdSendToNewDocument
            .ActiveDocument.MailMerge.Execute
            .ActiveDocument.SaveAs strSaveNamePath
            .Documents(strDocName).Close SaveChanges:=wdDoNotSaveChanges
            .Visible = True
            .ActiveWindow.WindowState = wdWindowStateNormal
            .Activate
        End With

        strTitle = "Merge done"
        If blnSomeSkipped = True Then
            strPrompt = "Merge document created; some records skipped because " _
                & "of missing information." & vbCrLf & "See " & strDocsPath _
                & "Skipped Records.txt for details."
        Else
            strPrompt = "Merge document created!"
        End If

        MsgBox strPrompt, vbOKOnly + vbInformation, strTitle

    Case 4
```

```
        'Catalog Merge
        blnSomeSkipped = False

        'Clear tblCatalogMergeList and set up recordset based on it
        strTable = "tblCatalogMergeList"
        strSQL = "DELETE tblCatalogMergeList.* FROM tblCatalogMergeList;"
        DoCmd.SetWarnings False
        DoCmd.RunSQL strSQL
        Set dbs = CurrentDb
        Debug.Print "Opening recordset based on " & strTable
        Set rst = dbs.OpenRecordset(strTable, dbOpenTable)

        For Each varItem In lst.ItemsSelected
            'Write data from listbox to a new record in table
            With rst
                .AddNew
                ![AuthorName] = Nz(lst.Column(0, varItem))
                ![BookTitle] = Nz(lst.Column(1, varItem))
                ![Category] = Nz(lst.Column(2, varItem))
                .Update
            End With

NextItem4:
        Next varItem
        rst.Close

        'Export merge list to a text file
        'strDBPath = Application.CurrentProject.Path & "\"
        strDocsPath = GetDocsDir & "Access Merge\"
        Debug.Print "Docs path: " & strDocsPath
        strTextFile = strDocsPath & "Catalog Merge Data.txt"
        Debug.Print "Text file for merge: " & strTextFile
        DoCmd.TransferText transfertype:=acExportDelim, TableName:=strTable, _
            FileName:=strTextFile, HasFieldNames:=True

        'Open a new merge document based on the selected template.
        appWord.Documents.Add strWordTemplate
        strDocName = appWord.ActiveDocument
        Debug.Print "Initial doc name: " & strDocName

        'Check for existence of previously saved letter in documents folder,
        'and append an incremented number to save name if found
        strDocType = _
            appWord.ActiveDocument.BuiltInDocumentProperties(wdPropertySubject)
        strSaveName = strDocType & " on " & strShortDate & ".doc"
        i = 2
        intSaveNameFail = True
        Do While intSaveNameFail
            strSaveNamePath = strDocsPath & strSaveName
            Debug.Print "Proposed save name and path: " _
                & vbCrLf & strSaveNamePath
            strTestFile = Nz(Dir(strSaveNamePath))
            'Debug.Print "Test file: " & strTestFile
            If strTestFile = strSaveName Then
                'Debug.Print "Save name already used: " & strSaveName
```

```vba
                    'Create new save name with incremented number
                    intSaveNameFail = True
                    strSaveName = strDocType & " " & CStr(i) & _
                        " on " & strShortDate & ".doc"
                    strSaveNamePath = strDocsPath & strSaveName
                    'Debug.Print "New save name and path: " _
                        & vbCrLf & strSaveNamePath
                    i = i + 1
                Else
                    'Debug.Print "Save name not used: " & strSaveName
                    intSaveNameFail = False
                End If
            Loop

            'Set the merge data source to the text file just created,
            'and do the merge.
            With appWord
                .ActiveDocument.MailMerge.OpenDataSource Name:=strTextFile, _
                    Format:=wdOpenFormatText
                .ActiveDocument.MailMerge.Destination = wdSendToNewDocument
                .ActiveDocument.MailMerge.Execute
                .ActiveDocument.SaveAs strSaveNamePath
                .Documents(strDocName).Close SaveChanges:=wdDoNotSaveChanges
                .Visible = True
                .ActiveWindow.WindowState = wdWindowStateNormal
                .Activate
            End With

            strTitle = "Merge done"
            If blnSomeSkipped = True Then
                strPrompt = "Merge document created; some records skipped because " _
                    & "of missing information." & vbCrLf & "See " & strDocsPath _
                    & "Skipped Records.txt for details."
            Else
                strPrompt = "Merge document created!"
            End If

            MsgBox strPrompt, vbOKOnly + vbInformation, strTitle

        Case 5
            'TypeText method
            blnSomeSkipped = False

            'Open a new document based on the selected template.
            appWord.Documents.Add strWordTemplate

            For Each varItem In lst.ItemsSelected
                'Write info from contact item to variables
                'Get Contact ID for reference
                lngContactID = Nz(lst.Column(0, varItem))
                Debug.Print "Contact ID: " & lngContactID

                'Check for required address information.
                strTest = Nz(lst.Column(2, varItem))
```

```
                Debug.Print "Street address: " & strTest
                If strTest = "" Then
                    blnSomeSkipped = True
                    Print #1,
                    Print #1, "No street address for Contact " & lngContactID
                    GoTo NextItem5
                End If

                strTest = Nz(lst.Column(3, varItem))
                Debug.Print "City: " & strTest
                If strTest = "" Then
                    blnSomeSkipped = True
                    Print #1,
                    Print #1, "No city for Contact " & lngContactID
                    GoTo NextItem5
                End If

                strTest = Nz(lst.Column(5, varItem))
                Debug.Print "Postal code: " & strTest
                If strTest = "" Then
                    blnSomeSkipped = True
                    Print #1,
                    Print #1, "No postal code for Contact " & lngContactID
                    GoTo NextItem5
                End If

                strName = Nz(lst.Column(7, varItem))
                strJobTitle = Nz(lst.Column(10, varItem))
                If strJobTitle <> "" Then
                    strName = strName & vbCrLf & strJobTitle
                End If

                strAddress = Nz(lst.Column(8, varItem))
                Debug.Print "Address: " & strAddress
                strCountry = Nz(lst.Column(6, varItem))
                If strCountry <> "USA" Then
                    strAddress = strAddress & vbCrLf & strCountry
                End If
                strCompanyName = Nz(lst.Column(9, varItem))
                strSalutation = Nz(lst.Column(11, varItem))

                'Insert data into labels.
                With appWord
                    .Selection.TypeText Text:=strName
                    .Selection.TypeParagraph
                    .Selection.TypeText Text:=strCompanyName
                    .Selection.TypeParagraph
                    .Selection.TypeText Text:=strAddress
                    .Selection.TypeParagraph
                    .Selection.MoveRight Unit:=wdCell
                End With

NextItem5:
        Next varItem
```

```
'Check for existence of previously saved document in documents folder,
'and append an incremented number to save name if found
strDocType = _
    appWord.ActiveDocument.BuiltInDocumentProperties(wdPropertySubject)
strSaveName = strDocType & " on " & strShortDate & ".doc"
i = 2
intSaveNameFail = True
Do While intSaveNameFail
    strSaveNamePath = strDocsPath & strSaveName
    Debug.Print "Proposed save name and path: " _
        & vbCrLf & strSaveNamePath
    strTestFile = Nz(Dir(strSaveNamePath))
    Debug.Print "Test file: " & strTestFile
    If strTestFile = strSaveName Then
        Debug.Print "Save name already used: " & strSaveName

        'Create new save name with incremented number
        intSaveNameFail = True
        strSaveName = strDocType & " " & CStr(i) & _
            " on " & strShortDate & ".doc"
        strSaveNamePath = strDocsPath & strSaveName
        Debug.Print "New save name and path: " _
            & vbCrLf & strSaveNamePath
        i = i + 1
    Else
        Debug.Print "Save name not used: " & strSaveName
        intSaveNameFail = False
    End If
Loop

With appWord
    .Selection.HomeKey Unit:=wdStory
    .ActiveDocument.SaveAs strSaveNamePath
    .Visible = True
    .ActiveWindow.WindowState = wdWindowStateNormal
    .Activate
End With

strTitle = "Merge done"
If blnSomeSkipped = True Then
    strPrompt = "Merge document created; some records skipped because " _
        & "of missing information." & vbCrLf & "See " & strDocsPath _
        & "Skipped Records.txt for details."
Else
    strPrompt = "Merge document created!"
End If

MsgBox strPrompt, vbOKOnly + vbInformation, strTitle

    End Select

ErrorHandlerExit:
    Close #1
    Exit Sub

ErrorHandler:
```

```
        If Err = 429 Then
            'Word is not running; open Word with CreateObject
            Set appWord = CreateObject("Word.Application")
            Resume Next
        Else
            MsgBox "Error No: " & Err.Number & "; Description: " & Err.Description
            Resume ErrorHandlerExit
        End If

    End Sub
```

If you have worked with MultiSelect listboxes on Office UserForms, you will appreciate the ItemsSelected collection available in Access VBA, which lets you process just the selected items, instead of checking for the Selected property being True for each item in the listbox, as you have to do elsewhere.

Command Button

Command buttons are used to run code; they are often placed in form header or footer sections to run procedures such as closing the form and returning to the main menu, printing a filtered report, or opening another form filtered by the record selected on the main form. The command button event procedure listed below is the standard Close button event procedure I use in most of my databases; it closes the current form and opens a main menu called fmnuMain, if there is a main menu (otherwise, it just closes the form). The procedure uses the IsLoaded property of a form in the AllForms collection to check whether the main menu is loaded or not; if it is loaded, it is made visible; otherwise, it is opened. The error handler takes care of the case where the database doesn't have a form called fmnuMain.

```
    Private Sub cmdClose_Click()

    On Error GoTo ErrorHandler

        Dim prj As Object

        Set prj = Application.CurrentProject

        If prj.AllForms("fmnuMain").IsLoaded Then
            Forms![fmnuMain].Visible = True
        Else
            DoCmd.OpenForm "fmnuMain"
        End If

    ErrorHandlerExit:
        DoCmd.Close acForm, Me.Name
        Exit Sub

    ErrorHandler:
        If Err.Number = 2467 Then
            Resume ErrorHandlerExit
        Else
            MsgBox "Error No: " & Err.Number & "; Description: " & Err.Description
            Resume ErrorHandlerExit
        End If

    End Sub
```

Image

The image control displays an image, which is selected for its Picture property using the Insert Picture dialog. You can assign an image from VBA code, as an alternative to displaying an embedded image with a bound object frame. If you need the same image (for example, a logo) for all records, an image control is perfect. If you need to display a different image for every record (say, a photo of a toy), you can save space in the database by using an image control and writing the file name to its Picture property from the form's Current event.

Compared to using a bound object frame, this method saves space in the database, but it also introduces the possibility of problems with file references—if the image file has been moved, deleted, or renamed, you will get an error when trying to assign it to the Picture property. You will probably see this problem when you navigate from record to record on frmImageControls in the sample Toy Workshop database, unless you happen to have the images referenced in the table in exactly the same location as on my computer.

frmImageControls has an image control in the form header, and a bound object frame in the Detail section, which changes its image as you navigate from record to record. It also has a combobox for selecting a picture file name; after selection, the picture is loaded to the Picture property of another image control below the combobox. This form is shown in Figure 3.11.

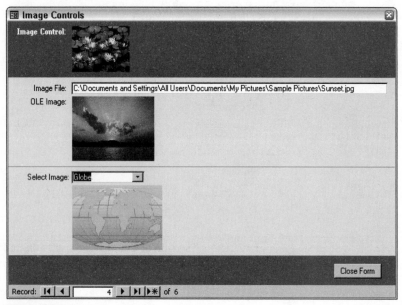

Figure 3.11

The code for loading the second image control with the selected picture follows.

```
Private Sub cboImageName_AfterUpdate()

On Error GoTo ErrorHandler

    Dim strImageFile As String

    strImageFile = Nz(Me![cboImageName].Column(1))
```

```
        If strImageFile = "" Then
            MsgBox "Please select an image"
            GoTo ErrorHandlerExit
        Else
            Me![imgSelected].Picture = strImageFile
        End If

ErrorHandlerExit:
    Exit Sub

ErrorHandler:
    MsgBox "Error No: " & Err.Number & "; Description: " & _
        Err.Description
    Resume ErrorHandlerExit

End Sub
```

Unbound Object Frame

An unbound object frame holds an OLE object—not just an image, but any type of object that supports embedding, such as an Excel worksheet or Word document. Since it is not bound, the same object is displayed on any record of a form.

Bound Object Frame

A bound object frame displays an OLE object (such as an image, an Excel worksheet, or a Word document) that has been embedded into an OLE Object field in a table. The OLE image control on frmImageControls is of this type; you can see the image change as you navigate through the records on this form. I recommend using this control just to store images; if you need to work with a Word document or an Excel worksheet, it's best to just open it in its own window, using Automation code. (See Chapters 11 through 13, which deal with Word, Outlook, and Excel data exchange, for more information on working with Office documents using Automation code.)

Subform/Subreport

The subform/subreport control is used to display data from one form (the subform) on another form (the main form). Frequently, a main form displays data from the "one" side of a one-to-many relationship, and a subform displays data from the "many" side of the relationship. The "Creating and Embedding Datasheet and Single Form Subforms" section of Chapter 2, *Using Forms to Work with Data*, has several examples of subforms used to display "many" data. Subforms can also be used to display unlinked data for reference on the form. As an example of this technique, the invisible subform subMaxEmployeeID on frmEmployees in the Toy Workshop sample database has a single textbox that contains the value of the highest EmployeeID used so far; this value is used to create an EmployeeID with the next highest number when a new employee record is created.

Line

The line control is just a line you can place on a form to separate groups of controls—frmImageControls has a line between the sections of the Detail section with a bound image frame and an image control.

Rectangle

The rectangle control is useful to indicate that a group of controls belong together, such as a group of checkbox controls.

Not-So-Useful Standard Controls

Not all of the controls on the Toolbox are useful, at least in Access 2000 or later. One should have been dropped a few versions ago, and another never was very useful to begin with.

Page Break

The page break control was once useful—in Access 1.0, this was the only way you could divide a form into pages for displaying large amounts of data. You'll still see forms with page breaks in the sample Northwind application that comes with Access (presumably carried over from version to version since Access 1.0). However, since the addition of the tab control as a standard control in Access 97, it is no longer necessary to use page breaks to convert a long form into pages; the tab control offers a much more intuitive and easy-to-use method of dividing up large amounts of data on a form.

There are some special cases in which a page break control may be useful for reports, however.

Toggle Button

The toggle button can be used either as a standalone control or as a toggle button in an option group. A toggle button has two states: raised (indicating True or Yes) and depressed (indicating False or No). The fact that I had to explain these states is part of the problem with this control: it is not, by any means, apparent to users what it means for a toggle button to be raised or depressed. Since toggle buttons look just like command buttons, most likely a user will click a toggle button and expect something to happen, assuming that it is a command button.

For a standalone control that indicates True/False or Yes/No, I recommend using a checkbox; everybody understands that a check in the checkbox means Yes (or True), and the lack of a check means No (or False). For option groups, the option button is best, since again it is intuitively obvious that the dark option button is the one that is selected. Both the checkbox and option button have analogs in paper-and-pencil procedures: checking a box on a form or darkening a circle on a multiple-choice test. The toggle button has no such analog, so I would advise not using it at all.

Special Controls

I use the term *special controls* to describe those controls that are available to all Access users, but are not part of the set of controls that have been part of Access since the earliest version. One of the special controls (the tab control) is available on the Access Toolbox, but the others are not. They must be inserted onto a form using the Insert | ActiveX Control command on the toolbar, or by clicking the More Controls tool on the Toolbox and selecting the control from a long and confusing list.

> *The list of controls that is opened from the More Controls tool on the Toolbox has (as far as I can see) an entry for every file on your computer that might represent a control for use in some application on your computer. It is not (as it should be) filtered for just those controls that will work when placed on an Access form.*

Tab Control

The tab control is a familiar interface from Options dialogs in Access and other Windows programs; clicking on a tab at the top of the control makes a page visible. The tab control allows you to divide up data from a record with many fields into groups, each of which is displayed on its own page. Additionally, you can display linked (or unlinked) data from other data sources, using subforms placed on pages of the tab control. See the "Creating and Embedding Datasheet and Single Form Subforms" section of Chapter 2, Forms, for an example of using a tab control to display data from the main form and linked subforms.

Calendar Control

The Calendar control displays a calendar for selection of a date; you can advance it by month or year. This control takes up a good deal of room on a form, so it may not be useful except when you need to select dates from a calendar (say, because appointments have to be scheduled on certain days of the week only), and you have lots of room available. The calendar control doesn't appear on the Toolbox by default, but you can add it to the Toolbox if you find it useful. To place a calendar control on a form, click the More Tools button on the Toolbox (it's the one with the hammer and wrench), and select Calendar Control 9.0 (or whatever version is available on your computer) from the list of available controls. Alternatively, you can select Insert | ActiveX Control and select the control from the Insert ActiveX Control dialog. The control can be bound to a Date/Time field, using its Control Source property. Figure 3.12 shows frmEmployeesCalendar, a version of frmEmployees that uses calendar controls to enter or edit the employee's birth date and hire date.

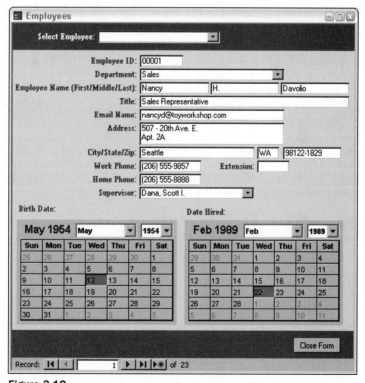

Figure 3.12

To place the calendar control (or any other special control from the list of available controls) on the Toolbox, follow the steps below:

1. Click the Toolbar Options button at the end of the Toolbox.

2. Select Add or Remove Buttons, and then Customize from the context menu.

3. Click the Commands tab.

4. Select ActiveX Controls from the Categories list.

5. Locate Calendar Control 9.0 (or another control of your choice) in the Commands list, and drag it to the desired location on the Toolbox.

6. If desired, use the Modify Selection button in the Customize dialog to display an image instead of text on the button.

For a more compact control you can use to select dates, see the section on the DateTimePicker control later in this chapter.

TreeView Control

The TreeView control has been around for a number of Office versions, and in Access 97 it had a useful wizard that helped you create the complex code needed to fill the control with data. The wizard disappeared in Access 2000, and has not reappeared since then. This control can be placed on a form by selecting Microsoft TreeView Control, v. 6.0 (or whatever version you have) from the list of controls opened from the More Controls button on the Toolbox. The frmTreeViewEBookNotes form in the EBookCompanion sample database featured in Chapter 9, *Reworking an Existing Application*, uses a treeview control to display data about ebooks. The treeview control is especially suited to displaying hierarchical data. The interface is similar to the folder tree in the Windows Explorer pane, and you can write code to run from the user's selection in the control.

The treeview control is filled with data by a function (tvwBooks_Fill) that is run from the form's Load event. The tvwBooks_Fill() function follows. The original code was generated by the Access 97 TreeView Wizard; I modified it to fit the requirements of this form, and when I need a treeview control on another form, I just copy the function again and modify it as needed.

```
Function tvwBooks_Fill()

'============================================================
'Modified from a procedure generated by the Treeview Control Wizard
'
'PURPOSE: Fill the ActiveX Treeview Control 'tvwBooks'
'ACCEPTS: Nothing
'RETURNS: Nothing
'CALLED FROM: Form Load event
'============================================================

On Error GoTo ErrorHandler

    Dim strMessage As String
    Dim dbs As DAO.Database
    Dim rst As DAO.Recordset
    Dim intVBMsg As Integer
```

```
      Dim strQuery1 As String
      Dim strQuery2 As String
      Dim nod As Object
      Dim strNode1Text As String
      Dim strNode2Text As String
      Dim strVisibleText1 As String
      Dim strVisibleText2 As String

      Set dbs = CurrentDb()
      strQuery1 = "qryEBookAuthors"
      strQuery2 = "qryEBooksByAuthor"

  With Me![tvwBooks]
     'Fill Level 1
     Set rst = dbs.OpenRecordset(strQuery1, dbOpenForwardOnly)

     'Add a node object for each record in the "qryEBookAuthors" table/query.
     'For parent nodes, the Key property is based on the the level of the tree
     'in which the node exists and the Link Master field(s) you selected when
     'linking levels in the wizard. For child nodes, the Relative property
     'is based on the level of the tree in which the Parent node exists and
     'the Link Child field(s) you selected when linking levels in the wizard.

     Do Until rst.EOF
        Debug.Print "Adding Level 1 item: " & rst![AuthorID]
        strNode1Text = StrConv("Level1 - " & rst![AuthorID], _
           vbLowerCase)
        Debug.Print "Node 1 text: " & strNode1Text
        strVisibleText1 = rst![LastNameFirst]
        Debug.Print "Level 1 visible text: " & strVisibleText1
        Set nod = .Nodes.Add(Key:=strNode1Text, _
           Text:=strVisibleText1)
        nod.Expanded = True
        rst.MoveNext
     Loop
     rst.Close

     'Fill Level 2
     Set rst = dbs.OpenRecordset(strQuery2, dbOpenForwardOnly)

     'Add a node object for each record in the "qryEBooksByAuthor"
     'table/query. For parent nodes, the Key property is based on the
     'level of the tree in which the node exists and the Link Master
     'field(s) you selected when linking levels in the wizard. For child
     'nodes, the Relative property is based on the level of the tree in
     'which the Parent node exists and the Link Child field(s) you selected
     'when linking levels in the wizard.

     Do Until rst.EOF
        Debug.Print "Adding Level 2 item: " & rst![Title]
        strNode1Text = StrConv("Level1 - " & rst![AuthorID], vbLowerCase)
        Debug.Print "Node 1 text: "; strNode1Text
        strNode2Text = StrConv("Level2 - " & rst![AuthorID] & " - " _
           & rst![Title], vbLowerCase)
        Debug.Print "Node 2 text: " & strNode2Text
```

```
            strVisibleText2 = rst![Title] & rst![BeenRead]
            Debug.Print "Visible text: " & strVisibleText2
            .Nodes.Add relative:=strNode1Text, _
                relationship:=tvwChild, _
                Key:=strNode2Text, _
                Text:=strVisibleText2
            rst.MoveNext
        Loop
        rst.Close

    End With
    dbs.Close

ErrorHandlerExit:
    Exit Function

ErrorHandler:
    Select Case Err.Number
        Case 35601
            'Element not found
            strMessage = "Possible Causes: You selected a table/query" _
                & " for a child level which does not correspond to a value" _
                & " from its parent level."
            intVBMsg = MsgBox(Error$ & strMessage, vbOKOnly + _
                vbExclamation, "Run-time Error: " & Err.Number)
        Case 35602
            'Key is not unique in collection
            strMessage = "Possible Causes: You selected a non-unique" _
                & " field to link levels."
            intVBMsg = MsgBox(Error$ & strMessage, vbOKOnly + _
                vbExclamation, "Run-time Error: " & Err.Number)
        Case Else
            intVBMsg = MsgBox(Error$ & "@@", vbOKOnly + _
                vbExclamation, "Run-time Error: " & Err.Number)
    End Select
    Resume ErrorHandlerExit

End Function
```

Each node in a treeview control needs a unique key expression and a field or expression containing text to display. In the sample treeview control, AuthorID is the unique key field for Node 1, and the author's name is displayed (last name first). Node 2 uses AuthorID concatenated with the book title as the unique expression text, and the book title plus a symbol indicating whether it has been read as the visible text. The nodes are linked to each other using the key fields, so you need to ensure that the key expressions are unique; generally this is done by including a key field from the underlying table. Figure 3.13 shows the treeview control on frmTreeViewEBookNotes in the EBookCompanion database.

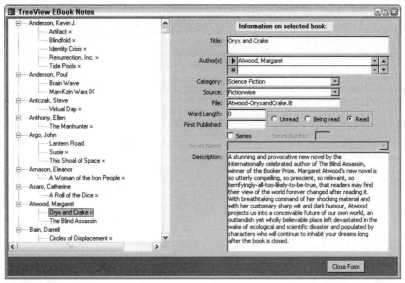

Figure 3.13

ActiveX Controls

If you have the Developer Edition of Office, or if you have other programs (such as Visual Basic) that include a set of ActiveX controls, you can also place several other controls on Access forms. The two most useful ones for Access forms are the DateTimePicker and the MonthView control, which are discussed in the next sections.

> **Caveat: If you place one of these controls on an Access form, and then send the database to someone who doesn't have these controls available (say because she has Office Pro instead of the Developer Edition), the controls won't be displayed, and generally there will be a "There is no object in this control" message. This should be taken into consideration when using these extra controls.**

DateTimePicker

The DateTimePicker control lets you select a date from a small pop-up calendar. When the calendar is closed, it takes up little space on a form. However, this control lacks the year navigation control of the regular calendar control, so it may be quite tedious to select a date with it, because you can only navigate by month. Figure 3.14 shows frmEmployeesActiveXControls, a variation of frmEmployees in the sample Toy Workshop database, with a DateTimePicker control dropped down to select the employee's birth date from its calendar.

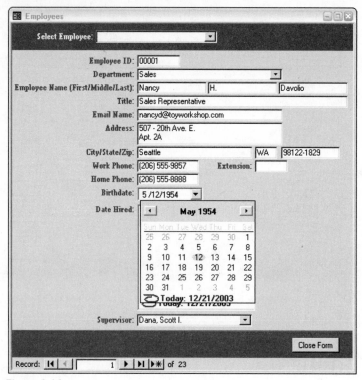

Figure 3.14

MonthView Control

The MonthView control resembles the pop-up calendar used for the DateTimePicker control, but it is always visible. It also lacks the year navigation control, so if you need a calendar that is always visible, the regular calendar control is preferable. Figure 3.15 shows a MonthView control used to select the hire date on the same form as is used for the DateTimePicker control.

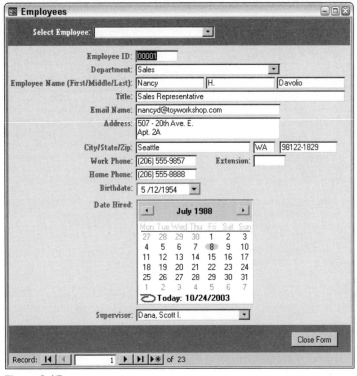

Figure 3.15

Summary

The next chapter will deal with constructing queries to filter and sort data that will be displayed on forms, using some of the controls discussed in this chapter.

Sorting and Filtering
Data with Queries

While you can base forms and reports directly on Access tables, often you'll find it more useful to prepare a select query as a record source, to avoid having to create the same calculated fields over and over again, or to work with information in linked tables. Totals queries let you extract sums, counts, and the results of other aggregate functions from data. Action queries let you update, append, and delete records, and create new tables. Union queries let you combine data from different sources into a single record source, and other SQL-specific queries let you work with tables in more specialized ways. In this chapter, I'll discuss creating all of these types of queries, using examples from various sample databases.

Select Queries

Select queries let you filter and sort data for display on forms or reports, as well as create calculated fields which can then be used as if they were table fields. A special type of select query, the totals query, lets you create sums, counts, or other mathematical functions aggregating data in fields.

Basic Select Queries

First, a digression. You don't need a select query to just sort or filter data for display on a form or report; you can do that by using the appropriate expression in the Order By or Filter property of the form or report. The expression listed below filters frmCustomers (in the sample Toy Workshop database) for customers whose title is Marketing Director:

```
ContactTitle="Marketing Director"
```

To sort frmCustomers by CompanyName, just enter CompanyName in the form's Order By property.

Although Access Help says that you can use two (or more) field names in the Order By property to sort by multiple fields, I have found that this doesn't work. Depending on the syntax used, you either get a no sort and no error message, or an Enter Parameter Value pop-up displaying the expression you entered in the Order By property.

Additionally, you can use the Sort Ascending and Sort Descending buttons on the Form toolbar in form view to sort by a field in ascending or descending order, or the Filter by Selection button to filter by the selected value.

However, if you need to filter or sort by two or more fields, you'll need to create a query. Apart from filtering and sorting, though, there is an excellent reason to create a select query for use as a record source. Typically, for each main data table in an application, you will need several standard calculated fields— for example, fields that arrange the person's name either last name first or first name first, a concatenated City/State/Zip field, or a full address field composed from several address fields. If you create these expressions in a select query, you don't have to create them separately in each form or report that needs them, and if you need to make a change in an expression, you only have to make the change once (in the query), not in all the forms and/or reports that use these expressions.

The next section describes a number of standard query field expressions that can be used to either concatenate data from several fields into useful expressions, or split up data in one field into separate fields.

Query Expressions That Split or Concatenate Name and Address Data

Sometimes you have a table (possibly imported from a flat-file database or a text file) that has a whole name in a single field (either last name first, or first name first), and you need to separate the first name, middle name (if any), and last name into individual fields. Similarly, you may have a whole address of one to three lines in a single field, or the city, state, and zip in a single field, and need to create separate fields for each address component.

At other times, you may need to do the reverse, usually when exporting to a nonrelational database, or to another Office application, such as Word. For example, you may want to put a person's complete address into a variable for export to a Word doc property, to use as an address block in a Word letter, or you may need to put a person's whole name into one field, last name first, to export to a comma-delimited text file for import into a mainframe database.

The QueryExpressions sample database has two tables of sample data. tblContactsWhole has the following fields:

❑ ContactID

❑ LastNameFirst

❑ FirstNameFirst

❑ Address

❑ CityStateZip

All the fields except ContactID contain data that you might need to split into separate fields to make it possible to sort and filter by data such as the person's last name or the city or state. This table is shown in Figure 4.1.

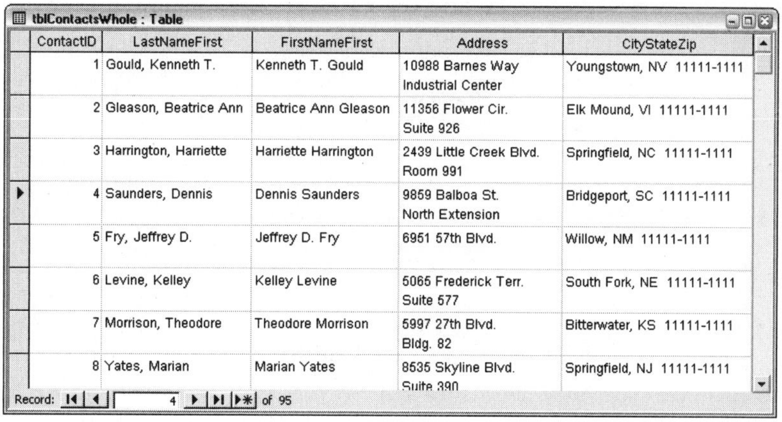

Figure 4.1

The tblContactsSeparate table illustrates the opposite scenario—a properly normalized table (like those in the Toy Workshop sample database) with name and address components stored in separate fields:

- ❑ ContactID
- ❑ FirstName
- ❑ MiddleName
- ❑ LastName
- ❑ Address1
- ❑ Address2
- ❑ Address3
- ❑ City
- ❑ StateOrProvince
- ❑ PostalCode

This table has three separate address fields, which is generally not necessary in Access since multiline address data can be stored in a single field (see the tables in the Toy Workshop sample database for examples of multiline address data). In some cases, however, it may be a good idea to store address data in several different fields, for example to separate a mailing address from a physical address—or perhaps the table was constructed by someone who didn't know that multiline addresses can be stored in one field. tblContactsSeparate is shown in Figure 4.2.

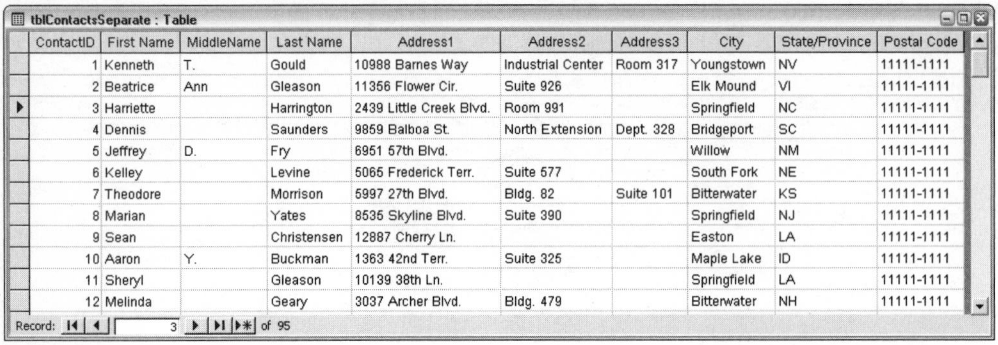

	ContactID	First Name	MiddleName	Last Name	Address1	Address2	Address3	City	State/Province	Postal Code
	1	Kenneth	T.	Gould	10988 Barnes Way	Industrial Center	Room 317	Youngstown	NV	11111-1111
	2	Beatrice	Ann	Gleason	11356 Flower Cir.	Suite 926		Elk Mound	VI	11111-1111
▶	3	Harriette		Harrington	2439 Little Creek Blvd.	Room 991		Springfield	NC	11111-1111
	4	Dennis		Saunders	9859 Balboa St.	North Extension	Dept. 328	Bridgeport	SC	11111-1111
	5	Jeffrey	D.	Fry	6951 57th Blvd.			Willow	NM	11111-1111
	6	Kelley		Levine	5065 Frederick Terr.			South Fork	NE	11111-1111
	7	Theodore		Morrison	5997 27th Blvd.	Bldg. 82	Suite 101	Bitterwater	KS	11111-1111
	8	Marian		Yates	8535 Skyline Blvd.	Suite 390		Springfield	NJ	11111-1111
	9	Sean		Christensen	12887 Cherry Ln.			Easton	LA	11111-1111
	10	Aaron	Y.	Buckman	1363 42nd Terr.	Suite 325		Maple Lake	ID	11111-1111
	11	Sheryl		Gleason	10139 38th Ln.			Springfield	LA	11111-1111
	12	Melinda		Geary	3037 Archer Blvd.	Bldg. 479		Bitterwater	NH	11111-1111

Record: ◄◄ ◄ [3] ► ►◄ ►* of 95

Figure 4.2

The Query Expressions sample database contains two empty target tables: tblTargetSeparate and tblTargetWhole, and four select queries with expressions that split or concatenate data from the raw data tables.

> *The target tables are cleared by a function run from the AutoExec macro every time the database is opened—one of the few remaining uses for macros in Access.*

Two append queries demonstrate appending split or concatenated data from the raw data tables to the target tables. To use the expressions in these queries in a real-life application, you will need to create queries based on the tables in your database and copy in the query expressions you need to use to concatenate or split data names in the queries. Edit the field names in the expressions as needed to match your tables, and (for append queries), select the appropriate target table for appending.

qrySplitAddressComponents and qrySplitNameComponents are select queries that split the address and name components into separate fields; these queries can be used as is or converted into make-table or append queries as needed. qryConcatenateAddressComponents and qryConcatenateNameComponents do the opposite: they concatenate data in separate fields into one field, for export to flat-file databases or other applications.

In the select queries qrySplitAddressComponents and qrySplitNameComponents, there are intermediate fields (the ones ending with a "Plus" and the CityStateZip field), which are used to break out a portion of a name or address that in turn needs to be further broken down. These expression names are used in turn in other query column expressions. This technique works fine in a select query, but sometimes fails in an append query (more so in older versions of Access), so in the append query, I took the entire "Plus" expression and pasted it into the other expressions that referenced it. Examine the select queries to get an idea of how the field breakdown works.

The name in a whole name field might be arranged either last name first or first name first, so I made different expressions to extract name components from each type of field; the sample append query uses the last name first version.

Here are the query column expressions used in the select queries:

qryConcatenateAddressComponents

```
CityStateZip: IIf([City],[City] & ", ","") & [StateOrProvince] & "  " &
[PostalCode]

Address: IIf(Nz([Address2])<>"",[Address1] & Chr(13) & Chr(10) &
[Address2],[Address1]) & IIf(Nz([Address3])<>"",Chr(13) & Chr(10) & [Address3])

WholeAddress: [Address] & Chr(13) & Chr(10) & [CityStateZip]
```

qryConcatenateNameComponents

```
LastNameFirst: [LastName] & IIf([FirstName],", " & [FirstName],"") &
IIf([MiddleName]," " & [MiddleName])

FirstNameFirst: IIf([MiddleName],[FirstName] & " " & [MiddleName],[FirstName]) &
IIf([LastName]," " & [LastName])
```

qrySplitAddressComponents

```
City:
IIf(InStr([CityStateZip],Chr$(44))>0,Mid([CityStateZip],1,InStr([CityStateZip],Chr$
(44))-1),[CityStateZip])

StatePlus: Mid([CityStateZip],InStr([CityStateZip],Chr$(44))+2)

State:
IIf(InStr([StatePlus],Chr$(32))>0,Mid([StatePlus],1,InStr([StatePlus],Chr$(32))-
1),[StatePlus])

Zip:
IIf(InStr([StatePlus],Chr$(32))>0,Mid([StatePlus],InStr([StatePlus],Chr$(32))+1),""
)

Address1: IIf(InStr([Address],Chr(13)),Left([Address],InStr([Address],Chr(13))-
1),[Address])

Address2:
IIf(InStr([AddressPlus],Chr(13)),Left([AddressPlus],InStr([AddressPlus],Chr(13))-
1),[AddressPlus])

Address3:
IIf(InStr([AddressPlus],Chr(10)),Mid([AddressPlus],InStr([AddressPlus],Chr(10))+1))

AddressPlus:
IIf(InStr([Address],Chr(10)),Mid([Address],InStr([Address],Chr(10))+1))
```

qrySplitNameComponents

```
FirstNameL:
IIf(InStr([FirstNamePlusL],Chr$(32))>0,Mid([FirstNamePlusL],1,InStr([FirstNamePlusL
],Chr$(32))-1),[FirstNamePlusL])

FirstNamePlusL: Mid([LastNameFirst],InStr([LastNameFirst],Chr$(44))+2)

MiddleNameL:
IIf(InStr([FirstNamePlusL],Chr$(32))>0,Mid([FirstNamePlusL],InStr([FirstNamePlusL],
Chr$(32))+1),"")

LastNameL:
IIf(InStr([LastNameFirst],Chr$(32))>0,Mid([LastNameFirst],1,InStr([LastNameFirst],C
hr$(32))-2),[LastNameFirst])

FirstNameF:
IIf(InStr([FirstNameFirst],Chr$(32))>0,Mid([FirstNameFirst],1,InStr([FirstNameFirst
],Chr$(32))-1),[FirstNameFirst])

MiddleNamePlusF:
IIf(InStr([FirstNameFirst],Chr$(32))>0,Mid([FirstNameFirst],InStr([FirstNameFirst],
Chr$(32))+1),"")

MiddleNameF:
IIf(InStr([MiddleNamePlusF],Chr$(32))>0,Mid([MiddleNamePlusF],1,InStr([MiddleNamePl
usF],Chr$(32))-1),"")

LastNameF:
IIf(InStr([MiddleNamePlusF],Chr$(32))>0,Mid([MiddleNamePlusF],InStr([MiddleNamePlus
F],Chr$(32))+1),[MiddleNamePlusF])
```

After you run qappConcatenateNameAndAddressComponents, tblTargetWhole's fields are filled with data concatenated from separate fields in the original table (tblContactsSeparate), as shown in Figure 4.3.

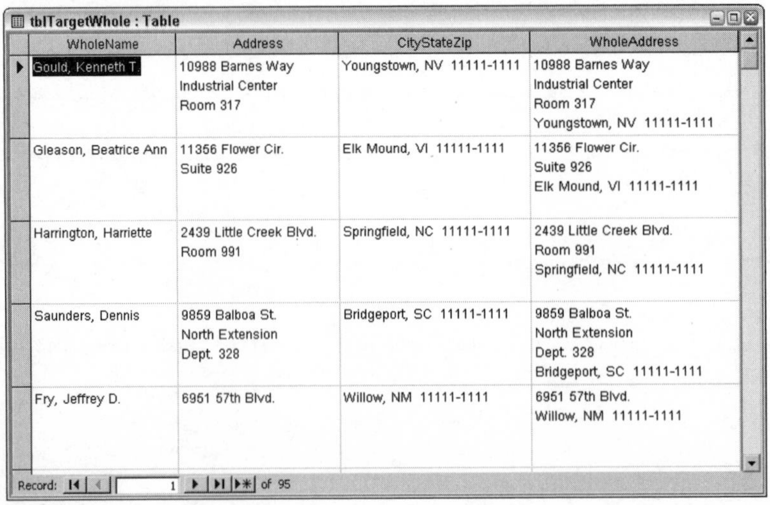
tblTargetWhole : Table

WholeName	Address	CityStateZip	WholeAddress
Gould, Kenneth T.	10988 Barnes Way Industrial Center Room 317	Youngstown, NV 11111-1111	10988 Barnes Way Industrial Center Room 317 Youngstown, NV 11111-1111
Gleason, Beatrice Ann	11356 Flower Cir. Suite 926	Elk Mound, VI 11111-1111	11356 Flower Cir. Suite 926 Elk Mound, VI 11111-1111
Harrington, Harriette	2439 Little Creek Blvd. Room 991	Springfield, NC 11111-1111	2439 Little Creek Blvd. Room 991 Springfield, NC 11111-1111
Saunders, Dennis	9859 Balboa St. North Extension Dept. 328	Bridgeport, SC 11111-1111	9859 Balboa St. North Extension Dept. 328 Bridgeport, SC 11111-1111
Fry, Jeffrey D.	6951 57th Blvd.	Willow, NM 11111-1111	6951 57th Blvd. Willow, NM 11111-1111

Record: 1 of 95

Figure 4.3

Running qappSplitNameAndAddressComponents does the reverse: it splits data that was in single fields in tblContactsWhole into separate fields in the target table, tblTargetSeparate. This table is shown in Figure 4.4.

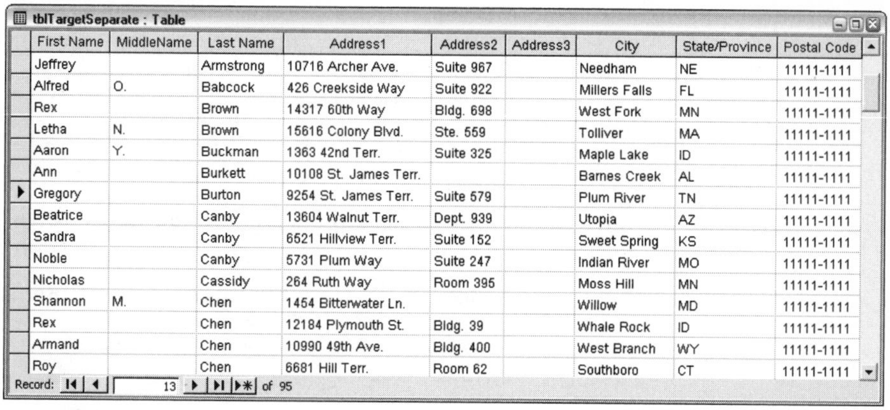
tblTargetSeparate : Table

First Name	MiddleName	Last Name	Address1	Address2	Address3	City	State/Province	Postal Code
Jeffrey		Armstrong	10716 Archer Ave.	Suite 967		Needham	NE	11111-1111
Alfred	O.	Babcock	426 Creekside Way	Suite 922		Millers Falls	FL	11111-1111
Rex		Brown	14317 60th Way	Bldg. 698		West Fork	MN	11111-1111
Letha	N.	Brown	15616 Colony Blvd.	Ste. 559		Tolliver	MA	11111-1111
Aaron	Y.	Buckman	1363 42nd Terr.	Suite 326		Maple Lake	ID	11111-1111
Ann		Burkett	10108 St. James Terr.			Barnes Creek	AL	11111-1111
Gregory		Burton	9254 St. James Terr.	Suite 579		Plum River	TN	11111-1111
Beatrice		Canby	13604 Walnut Terr.	Dept. 939		Utopia	AZ	11111-1111
Sandra		Canby	6521 Hillview Terr.	Suite 152		Sweet Spring	KS	11111-1111
Noble		Canby	5731 Plum Way	Suite 247		Indian River	MO	11111-1111
Nicholas		Cassidy	264 Ruth Way	Room 395		Moss Hill	MN	11111-1111
Shannon	M.	Chen	1454 Bitterwater Ln.			Willow	MD	11111-1111
Rex		Chen	12184 Plymouth St.	Bldg. 39		Whale Rock	ID	11111-1111
Armand		Chen	10990 49th Ave.	Bldg. 400		West Branch	WY	11111-1111
Roy		Chen	6681 Hill Terr.	Room 62		Southboro	CT	11111-1111

Record: 13 of 95

Figure 4.4

The expressions used to split or concatenate data depend on commas and spaces to parse out name and address components. If the fields in your source table don't have commas after city names, or have a comma but no space after a last name in a LastNameFirst name field, you'll need to modify the query expressions to work with the data in the source table. If (worst case) the source table data uses commas and spaces inconsistently in names and addresses, some fields will need to be cleaned up manually after appending.

You can adapt the query expressions for use in VBA code; in that case you can replace `Chr(13) & Chr(10)` with the newer (and more compact) VB named constant `vbCrLf`. Both of these represent a carriage return plus linefeed (CR + LF), with terminology harkening back to the old days of manual typewriters.

Totals Queries

Totals queries are not a separate query type—they have the same icon as regular select queries in the database window. They are simply select queries with the Total line in the query grid turned on by clicking the Totals button on the toolbar (it's the one with the big sigma). The Total line offers a choice of a set of predefined calculations using aggregate functions. The most familiar (and widely used) are Sum, Count, and Avg, but you can also use a number of other more advanced aggregate functions, as listed in the table below.

Aggregate Function	Usage	Use with Field Data Types
Sum	Totals the numeric values in a field	Number, Date/Time, Currency, AutoNumber
Avg	Averages the numeric values in a field	Number, Date/Time, Currency, AutoNumber

Table continued on following page

Aggregate Function	Usage	Use with Field Data Types
Min	Returns the lowest value in a field	Number, Date/Time, Currency, AutoNumber
Max	Returns the highest value in a field	Number, Date/Time, Currency, AutoNumber
Count	Counts the number of values in a field, excluding Nulls	Text, Memo, Number, Date/Time, Currency, AutoNumber, Yes/No, OLE Object
StDev	Returns the standard deviation of the values in a field	Number, Date/Time, Currency, AutoNumber
Var	Returns the variance of the values in a field	Number, Date/Time, Currency, AutoNumber

> Access Help says you can do a sum on a Date/Time field. Well, you can, but it's hard to see what use there is for the return value. To test this, I made a totals query with a sum on the Birthdate field in tblEmployees, and got a value of 19856. I would avoid using the sum function on Date/Time fields.

If you want to count customers in tblCustomers, all you need is the CustomerID field, with Count selected in the Total row of that field. Since CustomerID is a key field, and thus can't be blank, the count will be the same as the number of records in the table. If you do a count on the ContactTitle field, the result will be the number of records that have a value in the ContactTitle field. See Figures 4.5 and 4.6 for this query in design and Datasheet view.

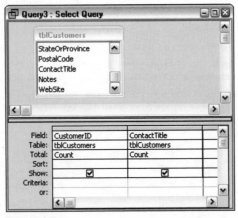

Figure 4.5

Query3 : Select Query
CountOfCustomerID
CountOfContactTitle
69
57
Record: 1 of 1

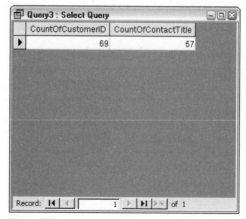

Figure 4.6

A totals query can give you different counts or totals depending on which fields are selected in the query grid. When creating a totals query, it's important to trim down the field list to remove any unnecessary fields, so the selected aggregate function will return the correct value. For example, if you base a totals query on tblOrders, and place ToyID and an ExtendedPrice calculated field on the query grid, with the Sum function selected for ExtendedPrice, you will get a sum of ExtendedPrice for each toy—that is, the total price of toys (ToyPrice * ToyQuantity) for all the orders for that toy. This query is shown in Datasheet view in Figure 4.7.

Query1 : Select Query
ToyID
ExtendedPrice
CO101
$75.00
FR551
$150.00
FR552
$150.00
TR110
$62.50
Record: 1

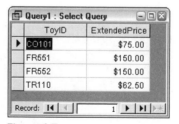

Figure 4.7

If you then remove ToyID from the query grid and replace it with CustomerID, you will get different sums, adding up the extended toy price by customer, as shown in Figure 4.8 (I added tblCustomers to the query too, so I could show the customer name and not just the CustomerID).

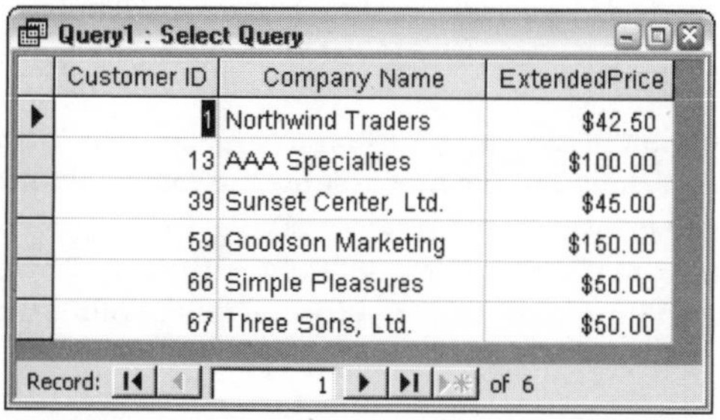

Query1 : Select Query
Customer ID
Company Name
ExtendedPrice
1
Northwind Traders
$42.50
13
AAA Specialties
$100.00
39
Sunset Center, Ltd.
$45.00
59
Goodson Marketing
$150.00
66
Simple Pleasures
$50.00
67
Three Sons, Ltd.
$50.00
Record: 1 of 6

Figure 4.8

If you find that a totals query isn't returning the correct values, remove any extraneous fields from the query grid, so you get the totals you intended.

tblToys contains several currency fields that you might want to add up, using the Sum function. You can also create a sum on a calculated field, for example a TotalCost field that multiples the UnitsInStock field by the SellPrice field, as shown in Figure 4.9 (Design view) and Figure 4.10 (Datasheet view).

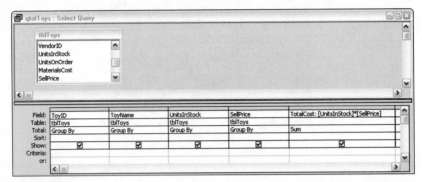

Figure 4.9

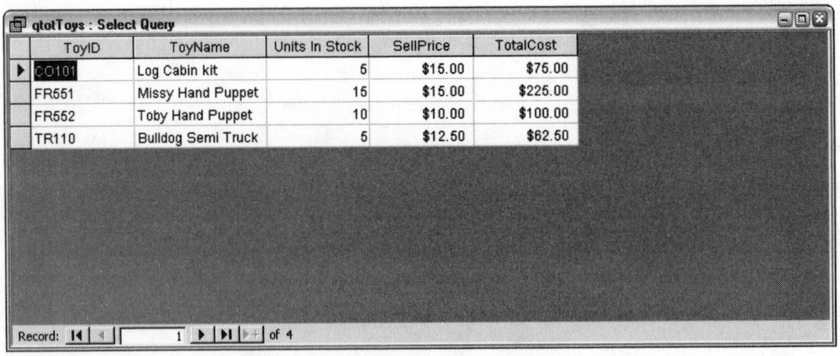

Figure 4.10

You can use the *qtot* tag to identify all totals queries, or use separate tags corresponding to the different functions, such as *qsum*, *qmin*, or *qmax*.

> When you select an aggregate function for a field, the aggregate field name in Datasheet view will be *SumOfFieldName*, *CountOfFieldName*, and so forth. If you want a less cumbersome name, you can alias the field name with another name, such as *CustomerCount*.

If you want to count the number of customers who have a specific job title, you can use a criterion on the JobTitle field plus a Count function to count just the customers with the title Marketing Director. However, you can't do this in one field—if you do, you'll get a "Data type mismatch in criteria expression" error message. Instead, drag the ContactTitle field to the query grid twice. Place the criterion on one of the columns, and select the Count function for the other column, as shown in Figure 4.11.

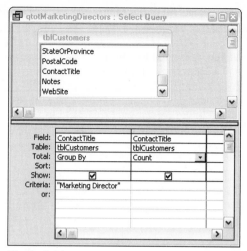

Figure 4.11

Figure 4.12 shows the same query in Datasheet view.

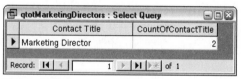

Figure 4.12

The Min and Max functions are useful for determining the lowest and highest values in a field. I use the Max function in a totals query that determines the highest value used so far in the EmployeeID field, which is not an AutoNumber field, but a text numeric field whose value is filled in by VBA code that adds 1 to the highest value. This query is shown in Design view in Figure 4.13.

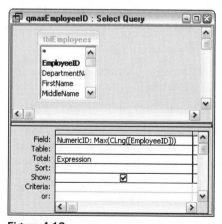

Figure 4.13

You won't see the Max function on the Total row of this query; Access sometimes converts a calculated expression that has an aggregate function selected on the Total row into a more complex expression that includes the selection function. When I created this query, the field was `NumericID: CLng ([EmployeeID]).` with the Max aggregate function; it was converted by Access into `NumericID: Max(CLng([EmployeeID]))` with Expression selected in the Total row.

Apart from the aggregate functions (Sum, Count, and so forth), you also have a choice of Group By (the default selection) and Expression in the Total row of each field in a totals query. The default selection, Group By, should be selected for the fields referenced in the aggregate function, and Expression is what you get if you use another function in a field together with an aggregate function. You can create the expression yourself, or Access may create it for you.

To prevent problems with Nulls in totals queries, use the Nz function to convert numeric values to zeroes.

Crosstab Queries

Crosstab queries are used to create cross-tabulated totals, counts, or other aggregate functions—that is, when you want a total for all the records matching each value in a field. A totals query can give you a total for all the sales made by all salespersons, but if you want to see separate sales totals for each salesperson, you need a crosstab query.

If you have Access 2002 or higher, I recommend using a PivotTable instead of a crosstab query, because they are easier to use, more attractive, and more flexible than crosstab queries. See Chapter 5, Using PivotTables and PivotCharts to Interact with Data, for more information on PivotTables.

Access provides a handy Crosstab Query Wizard that you can use to create a crosstab query. However, before you run the wizard, it's advisable to do some advance work by preparing a query that includes all the data you need. A crosstab query needs a minimum of three fields: one for the row headings, one for the column headings, and one for the data that is used for the aggregate function. Unless your data is in a flat-file table imported from a text file or a mainframe database, you'll probably need to construct a data source query based on a several tables, giving you a selection of fields useful for row and column headings, and other fields with data that can be counted, summed, or otherwise analyzed for the data area. It is often useful to create calculated fields to preprocess the data or alias fields to create appropriate column or row headings. This all-inclusive query can then be used as the data source of any number of crosstab queries, which saves considerable effort compared to creating each crosstab query from a combination of tables.

I made a query based on most of the data tables in the sample Toy Workshop database, for use as a data source for crosstab queries. This query (shown in Figure 4.14) has a number of aliased fields and a calculated TotalPrice field.

To ensure that your crosstab query's field names are what you want them to be, set the Caption property of aliased fields in the field properties sheet, as shown in Figure 4.15 for the aliased CompanyName field. Otherwise, the field may display with the original table field name, not the alias you created in the query column.

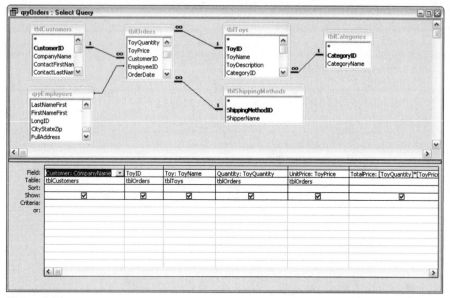

Figure 4.14

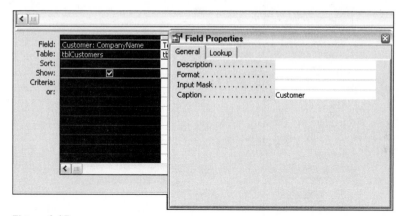

Figure 4.15

If you use a concatenated name field (last name first) or a company name for row or column headings in a crosstab query, you will see underscores replacing the final periods in names like Toy Specialities, Ltd. or Davolio, Nancy H. If you don't like the way this looks, you can use an expression like the following in the data source query to remove the trailing periods from the customer names, and a similar expression for the salesperson name:

```
Customer: IIf(Right([CompanyName],1)=".",Left([CompanyName],Len([CompanyName])-
1),[CompanyName])
```

Once the data source query has been created, you can use the Crosstab Query Wizard to create the crosstab query—or just create a new query, drag qryOrders to its top pane, switch the query type to

Crosstab Query in the Query Type selector, and select the fields for the crosstab query manually. To use the wizard, follow these steps:

1. Click the New button in the datasheet window, select Crosstab Query Wizard in the New Query dialog, and click OK.

2. On the first screen of the wizard, select qryOrders as the data source, as shown in Figure 4.16. Click Next to go to the next screen of the wizard.

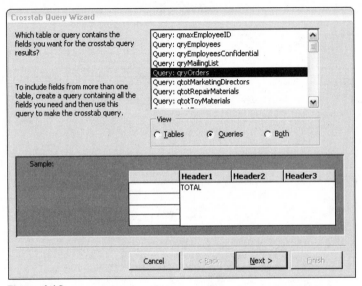

Figure 4.16

3. On the next screen, select the field or fields for use as row headings; I selected ToyCategory, as shown in Figure 4.17. Click Next to go to the next screen.

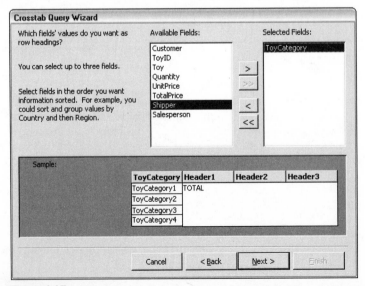

Figure 4.17

4. On the next screen, select a field for use as column headings, and click Next. I selected Salesperson, as shown in Figure 4.18.

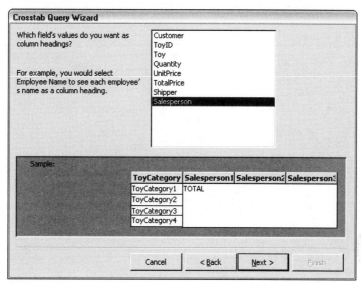

Figure 4.18

5. On the next screen, select the field with the values to be calculated and the function to use for the calculations, then click Next. I selected the TotalPrice calculated field and the Sum function, as shown in Figure 4.19.

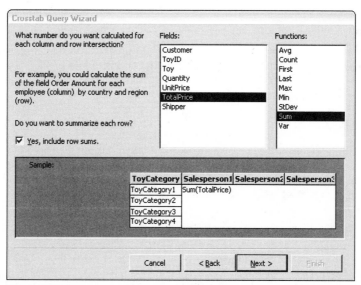

Figure 4.19

6. On the final screen, give the crosstab query a name; I use the tag qxtb for crosstab queries. I named the query qxtbToyCategoriesBySalesperson, to indicate how it tabulates the data.

Figure 4.20 shows the new crosstab query in Design view, and Figure 4.21 shows the same query in Datasheet view.

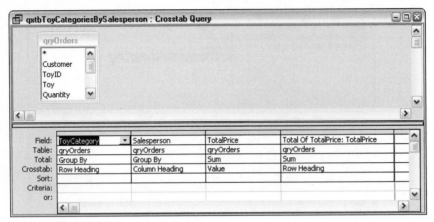

Figure 4.20

Category Name	Buckman, Aaron U	Cross, Donna Q	Davolio, Nancy H	Fields, Harriette J	Johnson, Edgar H	Thompson, Molly S	Yates, Marian
Construction kits					$30.00		$45.00
Puppets	$150.00			$100.00		$50.00	
Trucks and cars		$12.50	$50.00				

Figure 4.21

You can use the same data source query to create many different crosstab queries, selecting different fields for row and column headings, or using different functions to analyze the data.

Action Queries

Action queries can filter and sort like select queries, but they do more than select queries. They actually change data in tables, by adding new records (append query), changing data in existing records (update query), or deleting records from a table (delete query). You can even create a new table from data in another table, or several other tables, using a make-table query.

Append Queries

Append queries are used to append (add) data from one table or query to another table. As an example of a typical use of an append query, let's say that I obtained a list of companies in Excel worksheet format, and I wanted to add them to the tblMailingListCompanies table in the Toy Workshop sample database. After creating a linked table to let me work with the Excel data (see Chapter 1, *Creating an Application*, for information on creating linked tables). The linked table that displays the Excel worksheet data is called txlsMailingList.

The tag txls indicates a table linked to an Excel worksheet.

The target table (the table to which data is appended) is tblMailingListCompanies. To create an append query to append data from txlsMailingList to tblMailingList Companies, start by selecting the source table (txlsMailingList) in the database window, and selecting Query from the New Object selector, as shown in Figure 4.22.

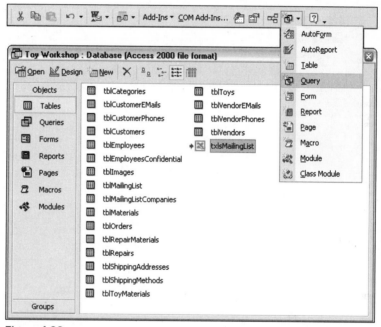

Figure 4.22

Select Design View in the New Query dialog. Since you can only append data from the source table to fields that exist in the target table, for a handy reference, open tblMailingListCompanies in Design view, and size its window and the query designer window so you can see them both. We'll need only the fields in txlsMailingList that match fields in tblMailingListCompanies; Figure 4.23 shows the selected fields.

At this point, the new query is still a select query; to change it to an append query, drop down the Query Type selector and select Append Query, as shown in Figure 4.24.

The Append dialog opens; select tblMailingListCompanies from the Table Name drop-down list, as shown in Figure 4.25.

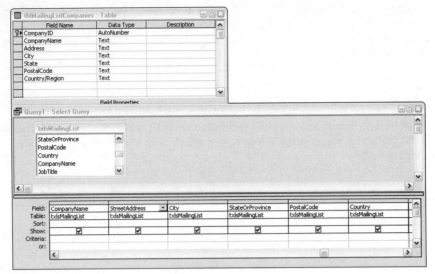

Figure 4.23

Figure 4.24

Figure 4.25

After selecting the target table, Access tries to match up the source and target fields. Generally, it misses a few, because the fields have different names in the source and target tables. In this case, CompanyName, City, and PostalCode were matched, and the other fields weren't. To manually match a field, select it from the drop-down list in the Append To row under the field, as shown in Figure 4.26.

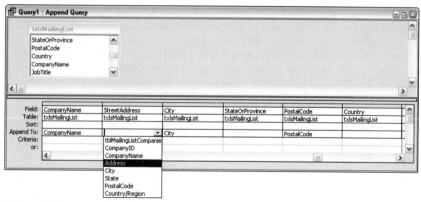

Figure 4.26

Save the query with the tag *qapp* to indicate that it is an append query. Figure 4.27 shows the query with all the fields matched up.

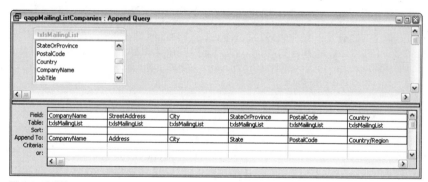

Figure 4.27

To run the append query, first close tblMailingListCompanies, then click the Run button on the toolbar (it's the one with the big red exclamation point). You'll get a confirmation message telling you how many records will be appended. After you click the Yes button, if you don't get any further messages; all the records were appended to the target table. If there are problems with appending, you will get an error message informing you of the error, and you can inspect the source table and either delete or manually correct the problem records.

Update Queries

An update query modifies data in one or more fields of a table. You can use an update query to replace a field value with another hard-coded value (say, replace all 914 area codes with 845, or replace a contact phone number or email address with a new one) or update a numeric field with the results of a calculation (add 10 percent to all prices) or replace a value in a field with a value from a field in another table. I'll give examples of several types of update queries.

Unless you are storing areas codes in a separate field, to change an area code you need to replace just the first three characters of a phone number (if you don't surround the area code with parentheses) or the second through fourth characters (if you do surround the area code with parentheses). An update expression for the first case can be done using the Left function, and one for the second case can be done with the Mid function. To create an update query, select the table to be updated in the database window, select Query from the New Object selector, then select Design View in the New Query dialog. I'll select tblEmployees, which has two phone number fields that need area code updating.

After selecting Query from the New Object selector, it becomes the default object (for the time being), so to create another query, you can just click the New Object button (it will display the Query icon, as shown in Figure 4.28.)

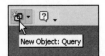

Figure 4.28

Drag the field(s) to be updated to the query designer grid. An update query might update all records in a table, but more typically you just need to update certain records. In the example, the query only needs to update phone numbers that have the 914 area code. To select just these records, both the WorkPhone and HomePhone field need a criterion that looks for 914 in positions 2 through 4. The following expression on the WorkPhone field will select the appropriate records for that field, assuming that the phone numbers are formatted with dashes:

```
Mid([WorkPhone],2,3)="914"
```

Save the query as qupdEmployeePhones (*qupd* is the LNC tag for an update query). It's still a select query—this allows switching to Datasheet view to check whether the query is selecting the right records. To check whether an update query's filter criteria are working correctly, switch to Datasheet view. Sometimes it's helpful to make a calculated field using the expression you intend to use for an update expression, to see if it works before you try to use it as an update expression. I made a calculated field using the expression `AreaCode: Mid([WorkPhone],2,3)` and switched to Datasheet view to see what I got (the results are shown in Figure 4.29).

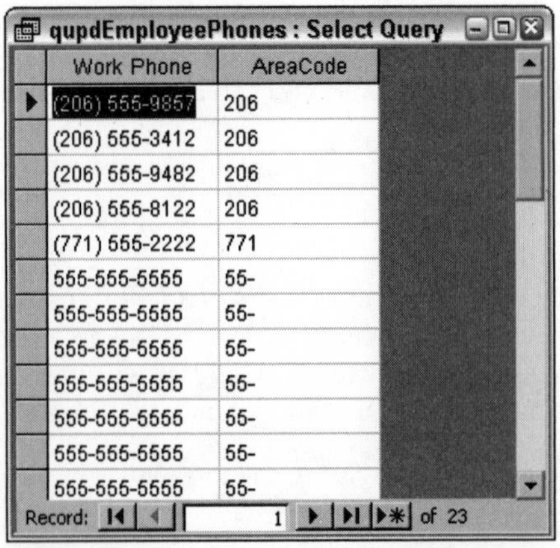

Work Phone	AreaCode
(206) 555-9857	206
(206) 555-3412	206
(206) 555-9482	206
(206) 555-8122	206
(771) 555-2222	771
555-555-5555	55-
555-555-5555	55-
555-555-5555	55-
555-555-5555	55-
555-555-5555	55-
555-555-5555	55-
555-555-5555	55-

qupdEmployeePhones : Select Query

Record: 1 of 23

Figure 4.29

The results reveal a very common problem: Some of the phone numbers have parentheses, and some don't, so the area code isn't extracted correctly for all records. If you put an input mask on a phone number field to ensure consistent data entry, this won't happen in the future, but applying an input mask won't correct existing data. Before updating the area codes, it's a good idea to make the phone number formatting consistent. This can be done with another set of filter criteria and update expressions.

In this case, the phone number format that uses dashes is correct, so we need to change the phone numbers that use parentheses. If you place the Like "(*" criterion on the WorkPhone field, the query will select just the records that need to be changed. Figure 4.30 shows the select query that filters for just the work phone numbers with parentheses, and Figure 4.31 shows the Datasheet view of the same query.

Figure 4.30

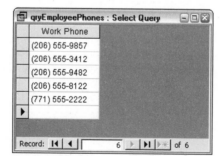

Figure 4.31

Now we need to create an update expression to convert the work phone numbers from the parentheses format to the dashed format. It's helpful to create another test expression before changing back to an update query. The following expression does the conversion correctly for the WorkPhone field:

```
NewWorkPhone: Mid([WorkPhone],2,3) & "-" & Mid([WorkPhone],7)
```

Figure 4.32 shows the query in Design view with the test expression based on the WorkPhone field, and Figure 4.33 shows the same query in Datasheet view.

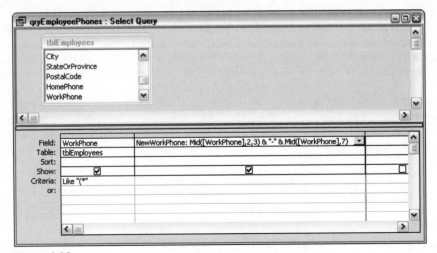

Figure 4.32

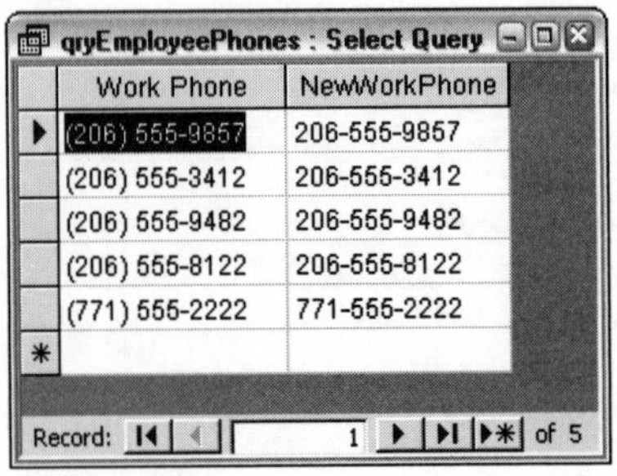

Figure 4.33

The query can now be converted to an update query, by selecting Update Query from the Query Type selector. Place the test expression above in the Update To row of the WorkPhone field (minus the label), with the `Like "(*"` criteria in the Criteria row (see Figure 4.34).

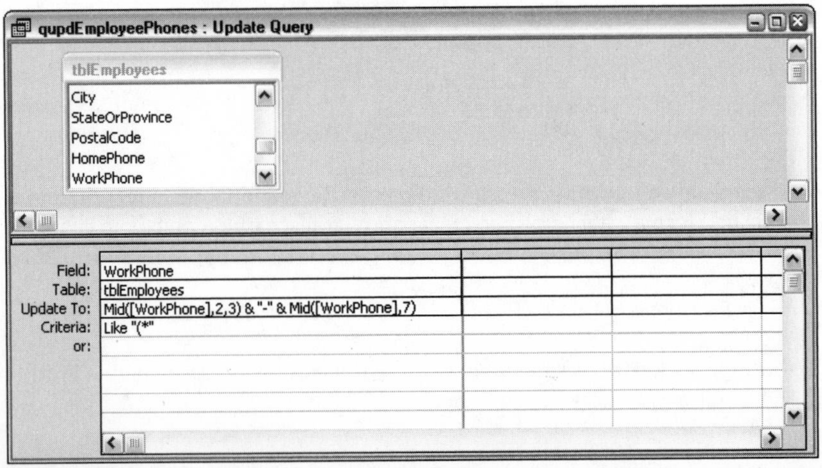

142   Figure 4.34

Run the update query by clicking the Run button on the Query Design toolbar, then modify the update query to update the HomePhone field, with a similar expression, and run it. (You can't just place filter criteria on both fields and update both phone number fields in one pass, because then the updating will be done on all the records that have either a home or work phone that needs reformatting. This could result in some phone numbers being reformatted incorrectly, if the original numbers are formatted differently.) Figure 4.35 shows tblEmployees with all the phone numbers formatted with dashes.

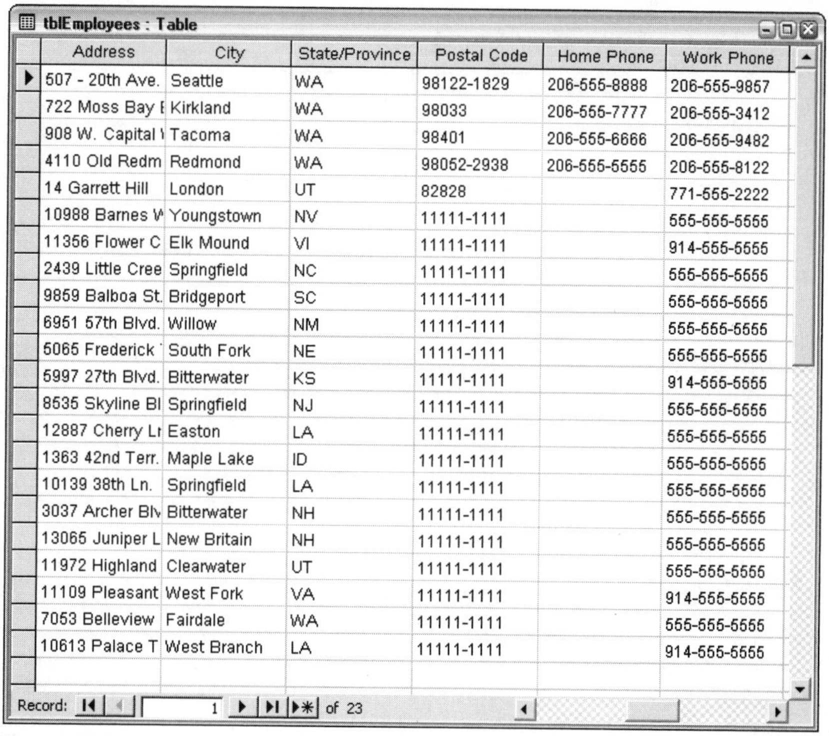

Address	City	State/Province	Postal Code	Home Phone	Work Phone
507 - 20th Ave.	Seattle	WA	98122-1829	206-555-8888	206-555-9857
722 Moss Bay F	Kirkland	WA	98033	206-555-7777	206-555-3412
908 W. Capital \	Tacoma	WA	98401	206-555-6666	206-555-9482
4110 Old Redm	Redmond	WA	98052-2938	206-555-5555	206-555-8122
14 Garrett Hill	London	UT	82828		771-555-2222
10988 Barnes W	Youngstown	NV	11111-1111		555-555-5555
11356 Flower C	Elk Mound	VI	11111-1111		914-555-5555
2439 Little Cree	Springfield	NC	11111-1111		555-555-5555
9859 Balboa St.	Bridgeport	SC	11111-1111		555-555-5555
6951 57th Blvd.	Willow	NM	11111-1111		555-555-5555
5065 Frederick `	South Fork	NE	11111-1111		555-555-5555
5997 27th Blvd.	Bitterwater	KS	11111-1111		914-555-5555
8535 Skyline Bl	Springfield	NJ	11111-1111		555-555-5555
12887 Cherry Lr	Easton	LA	11111-1111		555-555-5555
1363 42nd Terr.	Maple Lake	ID	11111-1111		555-555-5555
10139 38th Ln.	Springfield	LA	11111-1111		555-555-5555
3037 Archer Blv	Bitterwater	NH	11111-1111		555-555-5555
13065 Juniper L	New Britain	NH	11111-1111		555-555-5555
11972 Highland	Clearwater	UT	11111-1111		555-555-5555
11109 Pleasant	West Fork	VA	11111-1111		914-555-5555
7053 Belleview	Fairdale	WA	11111-1111		555-555-5555
10613 Palace T	West Branch	LA	11111-1111		914-555-5555

Record: 1 of 23

Figure 4.35

Now that all the phone numbers are formatted the same way, we're ready to do the area code updating for the WorkPhone field, using `Like "914*"` to select the records that need updating, and `"845" & Mid([WorkPhone],4)` as the update expression, as shown in Figure 4.36.

After running the modified update query, then modifying the query to update the HomePhone field similarly and running it again, all the phone numbers that had area code 914 now have area code 845, as shown in Figure 4.37.

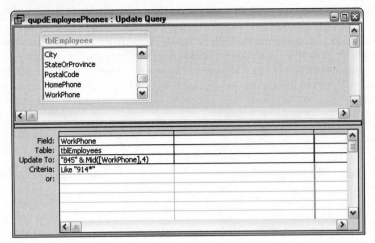

Figure 4.36

Address	City	State/Province	Postal Code	Home Phone	Work Phone
507 - 20th Ave.	Seattle	WA	98122-1829	206-555-8888	206-555-9857
722 Moss Bay E	Kirkland	WA	98033	206-555-7777	206-555-3412
908 W. Capital V	Tacoma	WA	98401	206-555-6666	206-555-9482
4110 Old Redm	Redmond	WA	98052-2938	206-555-5555	206-555-8122
14 Garrett Hill	London	UT	82828		771-555-2222
10988 Barnes W	Youngstown	NV	11111-1111		555-555-5555
11356 Flower C	Elk Mound	VI	11111-1111		845-555-5555
2439 Little Cree	Springfield	NC	11111-1111		555-555-5555
9859 Balboa St.	Bridgeport	SC	11111-1111		555-555-5555
6951 57th Blvd.	Willow	NM	11111-1111		555-555-5555
5065 Frederick	South Fork	NE	11111-1111		555-555-5555
5997 27th Blvd.	Bitterwater	KS	11111-1111		845-555-5555
8535 Skyline Bl	Springfield	NJ	11111-1111		555-555-5555
12887 Cherry Li	Easton	LA	11111-1111		555-555-5555
1363 42nd Terr.	Maple Lake	ID	11111-1111		555-555-5555
10139 38th Ln.	Springfield	LA	11111-1111		555-555-5555
3037 Archer Blv	Bitterwater	NH	11111-1111		555-555-5555
13065 Juniper L	New Britain	NH	11111-1111		555-555-5555
11972 Highland	Clearwater	UT	11111-1111		555-555-5555
11109 Pleasant	West Fork	VA	11111-1111		845-555-5555
7053 Belleview	Fairdale	WA	11111-1111		555-555-5555
10613 Palace T	West Branch	LA	11111-1111		845-555-5555

Record: 1 of 23

Figure 4.37

Make-Table Queries

When you need a table, and not a query, as a data source, a make-table query can be useful. You may need a table to use for exporting to another application, or to provide an updatable form record source in place of a nonupdatable query. As an example, I'll use a make-table query to create a table that can be imported into a flat-file mainframe database that has the entire employee name in a single field, using expressions from qryConcatenateNameComponents and qryConcatenateAddressComponents in the Query Expressions sample database.

Start by creating a query based on tblContactsSeparate, with ContactID from the table, and copy into the query grid the LastNameFirst concatenated field from qryConcatenateNameComponents. Since the target table needs to have the street address information in one field, and city, state, and zip in another field, copy the Address and CityStateZip concatenated fields from qryConcatenateAddressComponents into the new query's grid. (Just copy the expressions from the other queries, as opposed to adding the queries to the new query's pane.)

Convert the query into a make-table query by selecting Make-Table Query from the Query Type selector, and enter a name for the target table in the Make Table dialog. I use the tag *tmak* for tables created by make-table queries, so I can match them up with the queries that create them. Save the query with the tag *qmak* and the same base name (the query qmakContactsConcatenated creates the table tmakContactsConcatenated). Run the query by clicking the Run button on the toolbar; the table is created, after you click Yes on a confirmation message. tmakContactsConcatenated is shown in Datasheet view in Figure 4.38.

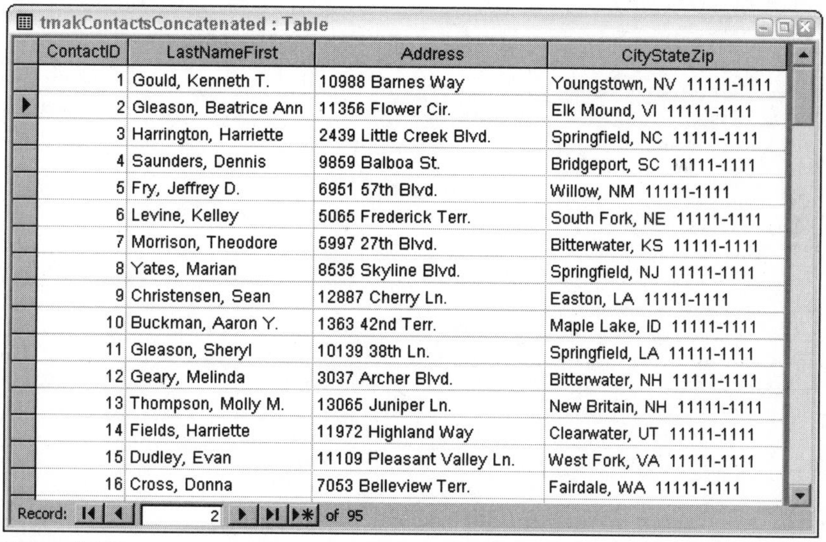

ContactID	LastNameFirst	Address	CityStateZip
1	Gould, Kenneth T.	10988 Barnes Way	Youngstown, NV 11111-1111
2	Gleason, Beatrice Ann	11356 Flower Cir.	Elk Mound, VI 11111-1111
3	Harrington, Harriette	2439 Little Creek Blvd.	Springfield, NC 11111-1111
4	Saunders, Dennis	9859 Balboa St.	Bridgeport, SC 11111-1111
5	Fry, Jeffrey D.	6951 57th Blvd.	Willow, NM 11111-1111
6	Levine, Kelley	5065 Frederick Terr.	South Fork, NE 11111-1111
7	Morrison, Theodore	5997 27th Blvd.	Bitterwater, KS 11111-1111
8	Yates, Marian	8535 Skyline Blvd.	Springfield, NJ 11111-1111
9	Christensen, Sean	12887 Cherry Ln.	Easton, LA 11111-1111
10	Buckman, Aaron Y.	1363 42nd Terr.	Maple Lake, ID 11111-1111
11	Gleason, Sheryl	10139 38th Ln.	Springfield, LA 11111-1111
12	Geary, Melinda	3037 Archer Blvd.	Bitterwater, NH 11111-1111
13	Thompson, Molly M.	13065 Juniper Ln.	New Britain, NH 11111-1111
14	Fields, Harriette	11972 Highland Way	Clearwater, UT 11111-1111
15	Dudley, Evan	11109 Pleasant Valley Ln.	West Fork, VA 11111-1111
16	Cross, Donna	7053 Belleview Terr.	Fairdale, WA 11111-1111

Record: 2 of 95

Figure 4.38

Delete Queries

A delete query deletes all the records in a table that match criteria you've specified. If you don't specify any criteria, all records will be deleted from the table. If you need to delete all records from a table in VBA code, there is little point in creating a query for that purpose, since it only takes a one-line SQL statement to delete all records from a table. The following SQL statement deletes all records from the table referenced by the strTable variable; it can be run using the RunSQL statement:

```
"DELETE * FROM " & strTable
```

The procedure that follows (from frmImportFromExcel in the sample Excel Data Exchange database for Chapter 13, *Working with Excel*) clears all records from tblCustomers, before filling it with new data imported from Excel.

```
Private Sub cmdImportDatafromWorksheet_Click()

On Error GoTo ErrorHandler

    strWorkbook = GetDocsDir & "Customers.xls"
    strTable = "tblCustomers"

    'Clear old data from table
    strSQL = "DELETE * FROM " & strTable
    DoCmd.SetWarnings False
    DoCmd.RunSQL strSQL

    'Import data from workbook into table, using the TransferSpreadsheet method
    DoCmd.TransferSpreadsheet transfertype:=acImport, _
        spreadsheettype:=acSpreadsheetTypeExcel9, _
        tablename:=strTable, _
        FileName:=strWorkbook, _
        hasfieldnames:=True

    Me![subCustomers].SourceObject = "fsubCustomers"

ErrorHandlerExit:
    Exit Sub

ErrorHandler:
    MsgBox "Error No: " & Err.Number & "; Description: " & Err.Description
    Resume ErrorHandlerExit

End Sub
```

If you need to clear just certain records from a table of imported data, a delete query is useful. After importing customer data from Excel, if you only need data for customers in the United States, you can run a delete query to delete all other records. To start, create a select query based on tblCustomers, and drag the asterisk at the top of the field list to the query grid, then drag the Country field to the grid. Uncheck the Country field's Show checkbox because this field is only used for filtering. Enter the expression Not Like "USA" as the criteria for the Country field, and convert the query to a delete query by selecting Delete Query in the Query Type selector. Save the query with the *qdel* tag. If desired, switch to

Datasheet view to check that only customers outside the United States are selected. Figure 4.39 shows the delete query.

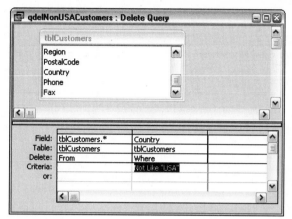

Figure 4.39

Running this query will delete all the records in tblCustomers except those in the United States—at least if data entry of country names is consistent.

SQL-specific Queries

SQL-specific queries are specialized queries that can only be created in SQL view. The most commonly used SQL-specific queries are union queries, but the others may occasionally be useful. Pass-through queries, which send SQL statements to ODBC (Open DataBase Connectivity) databases, are much less useful than in past years, because Automation code has replaced the older ODBC data exchange technology. Data-definition queries are used to create, delete, and alter tables. The last type of SQL-specific query is the Subquery, which is a SQL SELECT statement inside another query. In the following sections, I'll discuss the most useful of the SQL-specific queries.

Union Queries

Union queries combine data from two or more tables (or other queries) into a single non-updatable query. In the Toy Workshop sample database, the main customer address is in tblCustomers, and the shipping addresses are in tblShippingAddresses. For the frmOrders form, I needed a row source for the cboShipAddressID combobox, including both the main address and any shipping addresses for that customer, so I created a union query to combine address data from these two tables.

To start making a union query, make a select query based on one of the tables, and create any concatenated fields you need in Design view (you won't have this opportunity once you convert the query to a union query). In this case, I made a select query based on tblCustomers, with CustomerID, address fields, and a calculated ShipName field, as shown in Figure 4.40.

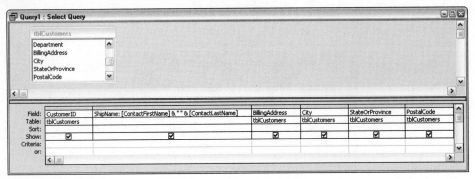

Figure 4.40

Next, switch to SQL view. The initial SQL statement of the query is:

```
SELECT tblCustomers.CustomerID, [ContactFirstName] & " " & [ContactLastName] AS
ShipName, tblCustomers.BillingAddress, tblCustomers.City,
tblCustomers.StateOrProvince, tblCustomers.PostalCode
FROM tblCustomers;
```

Although it isn't necessary, I like to remove the table names (and dividing period) before the field names, since they aren't necessary, and make the SQL statements more cumbersome. The trimmed SQL statement is:

```
SELECT CustomerID, [ContactFirstName] & " " & [ContactLastName] AS ShipName,
BillingAddress, City, StateOrProvince, PostalCode
FROM tblCustomers;
```

> There is no Search and Replace in query SQL view, so if you need to do significant editing in a query SQL statement, copy and paste it to a Notepad text document or a Word document, make any necessary changes there, and then copy and paste it back into the query.

The syntax for a concatenated or aliased field is in the opposite order from that used in Design view: the expression comes first, then the AS keyword, then the field name ([ContactFirstName] & " " & [ContactLastName] AS ShipName).

Next, create another select query based on the second table (in this case, tblShippingAddresses), including all the fields except ShipDepartment, and switch to SQL view. After trimming out the table names, the second SQL statement is as follows:

```
SELECT ShipAddressID, CustomerID, AddressIdentifier, ShipName, ShipAddress,
ShipCity, ShipStateOrProvince, ShipPostalCode
FROM tblShippingAddresses;
```

To convert the query into a union query, in the first query's SQL statement, remove the final semicolon, and type in UNION followed by a space, on a new line under the SQL statement. Switch to the second query, copy its SQL statement, return to the first query, and paste the text in after UNION. The resulting SQL statement is listed below:

```
SELECT CustomerID, [ContactFirstName] & " " & [ContactLastName] AS ShipName,
BillingAddress, City, StateOrProvince, PostalCode
FROM tblCustomers
UNION SELECT ShipAddressID, CustomerID, AddressIdentifier, ShipName, ShipAddress,
ShipCity, ShipStateOrProvince, ShipPostalCode
FROM tblShippingAddresses;
```

There is still some work to do. The component queries in a union query must have the same number of columns (fields), and the matching fields must be of matching data types (however, they don't have to have the same names). There is no ShipAddressID field in tblCustomers, so I created a dummy field with a value of 0 for this purpose. Similarly, I made a dummy field for AddressIdentifier, with a value of "Billing Address." I also aliased BillingAddress as Address, to make a more generic field name in the union query (the field names of the union query are the ones in the first component query). The final SQL statement is as follows:

```
SELECT 0 AS ShipAddressID, CustomerID, "Billing Address" AS AddressIdentifier,
[ContactFirstName] & " " & [ContactLastName] AS ShipName, BillingAddress AS
Address, City, StateOrProvince, PostalCode
FROM tblCustomers
UNION SELECT ShipAddressID, CustomerID, AddressIdentifier, ShipName, ShipAddress,
ShipCity, ShipStateOrProvince, ShipPostalCode
FROM tblShippingAddresses;
```

Now the query can be saved with the tag *quni;* a portion of the union query in Datasheet view is shown in Figure 4.41.

ShipAddressID	CustomerID	AddressIdentifier	ShipName	Address	City	StateOrProvince	PostalCode
0	62	Billing Address	Henry Maas	13374 Flower Terr.	Bay City	WV	11111-1111
0	63	Billing Address	Perry Bellows	2079 49th Blvd.	Pearblossom	MY	11111-1111
0	64	Billing Address	Anthony Nakamoto	15593 Center Ln.	Greenwood	NJ	11111-1111
0	65	Billing Address	Christopher Carrier	16889 Eagle Cir.	Springfield	MD	11111-1111
0	66	Billing Address	Suzanne Bishop	8924 First St.	Two Flags	ND	11111-1111
0	67	Billing Address	Rex Acosta	4005 Ridgeline Way	Willow	PA	11111-1111
0	68	Billing Address	Carl Richardson	3230 Ivy St.	Woodside	MA	11111-1111
0	69	Billing Address	Suanne Jones	Route 209 and Sampsonvi	Accord	NY	12424
1	1	Summer house	Janet Leverling	22 Mettacahonts Road	Accord	NY	12420
2	1	Ice fishing hut	Joe & Janet	1 Lake Avenue	Kearsage	MI	82838

Record: 68 of 71

Figure 4.41

Data-definition Queries

Data-definition queries are SQL-specific queries that use Dynamic Data Language (DDL) statements to create, delete, and alter tables, or to create indexes. Most of these actions can be performed more easily using make-table, delete, and update queries, which have the significant advantage of having a Design view you can use to create or modify query structure. However, if you need to make, delete, or modify tables from SQL statements run from VBA code, data-definition queries can occasionally be useful.

CREATE TABLE

The CREATE TABLE statement creates a new table, with fields and (optionally) an index. The SQL statement in the Sub procedure listed below creates a new table called tblMerchants with several fields and a primary key, which is shown in Design view in Figure 4.42.

```
Sub DDLCreateTable()

    strSQL = "CREATE TABLE tblMerchants (MerchantName TEXT CONSTRAINT MNIndex" _
        & " PRIMARY KEY, ContactName TEXT, Phone TEXT)"
    DoCmd.RunSQL strSQL

End Sub
```

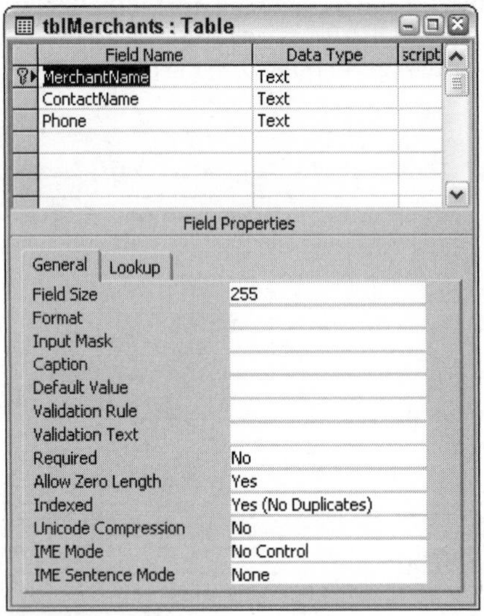

Figure 4.42

In addition to the **CREATE TABLE** *DDL statement, you can create tables programmatically by three other methods:*

* The CopyObject method of the DoCmd object, in VBA code

* A make-table query

* The Add method of the TableDefs collection in the DAO object model, in VBA code

ALTER TABLE

The ALTER TABLE statement can rename a table, or add, delete, move, or rename a field in a table. The SQL statement in the Sub procedure listed below adds a Yes/No field to the tblMerchants table just created.

```
Sub DDLAlterTable()

    strSQL = "ALTER TABLE tblMerchants ADD COLUMN Special YESNO;"
    DoCmd.RunSQL strSQL

End Sub
```

DROP

The DROP statement deletes a table or an index. The SQL statement in the Sub procedure that follows deletes tblMerchants.

```
Sub DDLDropTable()

    strSQL = "DROP TABLE tblMerchants;"
    DoCmd.RunSQL strSQL

End Sub
```

*In addition to the **DROP** DDL statement, you can delete tables programmatically by two other methods:*

* The DeleteObject method of the DoCmd object, with the acTable object type argument, in VBA code

* The Delete method of the TableDefs collection in the DAO object model, in VBA code

CREATE INDEX

The CREATE INDEX DDL statement creates an index for a table, with several variants. The Sub procedure that follows first creates a table called tblMerchants, with no index, and then creates an index that allows duplicates on the ContactName field.

```
Sub DDLCreateIndex()

    strSQL = "CREATE TABLE tblMerchants (MerchantName TEXT," _
        & " ContactName TEXT, Special YESNO, CreditLimit CURRENCY," _
        & " Phone TEXT)"
    DoCmd.RunSQL strSQL
    strSQL = "CREATE INDEX CNIndex ON tblMerchants (ContactName);"
    DoCmd.RunSQL strSQL

End Sub
```

If you don't see a table created from code in the database window immediately after running the DDL code, click another object in the Objects Bar, and then click on Tables again to refresh the display.

Subqueries

Subqueries aren't a separate query type, but just a query within another query. They may provide a more efficient structure, replacing multiple nested queries, but you can't create a subquery in Design view, and subqueries don't always perform better than nested queries (one query based on the results of another query). If you want to try replacing a nested query with a subquery, here are the steps in outline:

1. Open the base query (the one that will become the subquery) in the SQL window, highlight the SQL statement, and copy it to the clipboard with Ctrl-C.

2. Open the main query in the SQL window, and paste the subquery's SQL statement into it, usually in a WHERE clause.

3. Replace references to the base query in the main query's original SELECT statement.

4. To test the query, try to run it. If you get syntax errors, return to SQL view, and make any necessary corrections until the query runs.

As always, the devil is in the details, in this case exactly where in the main query the subquery's SQL should be inserted. As an example, let's consider a typical scenario where a nested query could be used—a totals query used as the data source for a select query. qminOldestPromisedOrder uses the Min function to get the oldest date in the PromisedByDate field of tblOrders. It returns a single record. However, what you really want here is the OrderID of that record. You can't place OrderID in the totals query itself, because then you will just get the date of every order, so you have to create another query with qminOldestPromisedOrder and tblOrders linked on the PromisedByDate field to get the OrderID and any other information you might want to see. This nested query is shown in Figure 4.43.

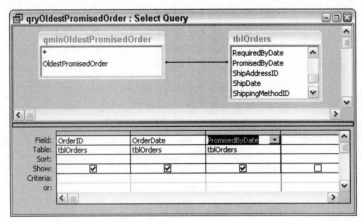

Figure 4.43

The SQL statement for the totals query is:

```
SELECT Min(tblOrders.PromisedByDate) AS OldestPromisedOrder
FROM tblOrders;
```

The nested query's SQL statement is listed below:

```
SELECT tblOrders.OrderID, tblOrders.OrderDate, tblOrders.PromisedByDate
FROM qminOldestPromisedOrder INNER JOIN tblOrders ON
qminOldestPromisedOrder.OldestPromisedOrder = tblOrders.PromisedByDate;
```

To convert these two SQL statements into a single SQL statement with a subquery, start a new query and paste the nested query's SQL into it, then replace the original FROM clause with FROM tblOrders. Next, create a WHERE statement with the PromisedByDate field from tblOrders, the In operator, and a SELECT statement based on the original totals query's SQL, replacing all references to the totals query with tblOrders. The finished SQL statement is:

```
SELECT tblOrders.OrderID, tblOrders.OrderDate, tblOrders.PromisedByDate
FROM tblOrders
WHERE tblOrders.PromisedByDate In (SELECT Min(tblOrders.PromisedByDate) AS
OldestPromisedOrder
FROM tblOrders);
```

The query with subquery is shown in Design view in Figure 4.44, and in Datasheet view in Figure 4.45. Unlike other SQL-specific queries, you can open a query with a subquery in Design view, but any editing of the subquery SQL statement has to be done manually.

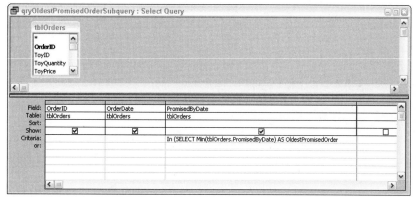

Figure 4.44

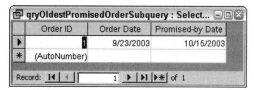

Figure 4.45

Summary

In this chapter, I discussed creating select queries for sorting, filtering, and preprocessing data, totals queries for doing calculations on data, crosstab queries for cross-tabulating data, and SQL-specific queries for specialized tasks. The next chapter will deal with using PivotTables and PivotCharts, a step up from crosstab queries, to chart and analyze your data in a dynamic, interactive format.

Using PivotTables
and PivotCharts to
Interact with Data

PivotTables and PivotCharts are views (usually of a form) that let you interactively select fields for sorting, grouping, and analyzing data in Access tables. A limited version of PivotTables was available in Access 2000, but Access 2002 (Office XP) greatly enhanced PivotTables and introduced PivotCharts. I assume that you have Office XP or higher in this chapter.

If you have Office 2000, see Chapter 4, Sorting and Filtering Data with Queries, for information on crosstab queries, an older (nondynamic) method of analyzing Access data.

When creating a totals query or a crosstab query to analyze your data, you select the fields and the aggregate functions or calculated expressions for use in the query. These choices are static (only the data changes). To analyze sales by day, week, month, and year, you have to create four separate queries. To swap row and column headings, you have to create two queries. PivotTables and PivotCharts give you much greater flexibility. With an appropriate data source query, you can swap rows and columns, sort and group by various fields and expressions, and even filter the PivotTable or PivotChart on the fly—without modifying its design.

In this chapter, I use the term PivotObject to refer to either a PivotTable or PivotChart.

Unlike other Access objects (such as forms and reports), where a great deal of programming effort may be required to prepare a form or report that is easy for the end user to use, PivotTables are easy and intuitive to use and don't require any programming to set up (except perhaps if you are going to put one on the Web, which is beyond the scope of this book). Therefore, you won't see any code in this chapter—just information on how to create a suitable data source query, and how to create and modify PivotObjects in PivotTable or PivotChart view.

Creating a Data Source Query

Although you can switch to PivotTable or PivotChart view from a form, table, or query, in most cases this won't produce good results. A useful PivotObject is generally based on a query combining data from several tables, giving you a selection of fields useful for row and column headings, and other fields with data that can be counted, summed, or otherwise analyzed for the data area. Rarely, a single table might contain all the data needed for a PivotObject—generally, that would be a flat-file table imported from a mainframe database, or perhaps a table created from data in other tables using a make-table query.

When creating a query to use as a data source for PivotObjects, include all the data you might want to analyze. In the case of date and time data in particular, it is often useful to write some column expressions to preprocess the data to create appropriate column or row headings. Typically, you will need to include several linked tables in the query, far more than you would use for a form or report—possibly all the data tables in the database. As an example (possibly carried to a ridiculous extreme), I made a query called qryNorthwindEverything that includes all the tables in the Northwind sample database—or actually, copies of these tables renamed with appropriate LNC tags, in the sample PivotTables and PivotCharts database. This query is shown in design view in Figure 5.1.

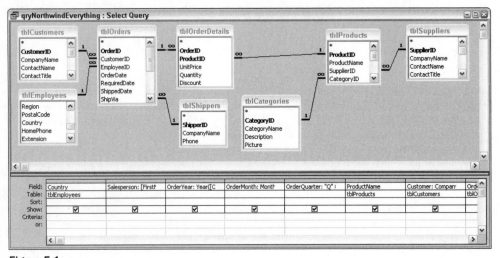

Figure 5.1

The calculated expressions for this query are explained below.

Concatenate the salesperson's first and last name:

    Salesperson: [FirstName] & " " & [LastName]

Extract the year from the order date:

    OrderYear: Year([OrderDate])

Extract the month number from the order date, and get the month name from it:

```
OrderMonth: MonthName(Month([OrderDate]))
```

Create an expression with the letter "Q," the quarter number, and the year from the order date:

```
OrderQuarter: "Q" & DatePart("q",[OrderDate]) & ", " & Year([OrderDate])
```

Customer name (CompanyName in tblCustomers):

```
Customer: CompanyName
```

Price, calculated as UnitPrice * Quantity * Discount (if any):

```
Price: CCur(tblOrderDetails.[UnitPrice]*tblOrderDetails.Quantity*IIf([Discount]>0,
[Discount],1))
```

Supplier name (CompanyName in tblSuppliers):

```
Supplier: CompanyName
```

Shipper name (CompanyName in tblShippers):

```
Shipper: CompanyName
```

With a query like this, you can make PivotObjects that analyze just about anything you want in the Northwind database.

PivotTables

For the very limited type of PivotTable that can be created in Access 2000, see the Sales Analysis form in the original Northwind database that comes with Office 2000. To edit an Access 2000 PivotTable, you have to open Excel in a full window; on this form, click the Edit Pivot Table button.

There are several ways to create a PivotTable in Access 2002 or higher. You can switch to PivotTable view from a form, query, or report (I don't recommend this except for a query that you have prepared for use with PivotObjects); create a new form, and select AutoForm: PivotTable (see Figure 5.2); or select PivotTable Wizard from the same list of selections. Selecting AutoForm: PivotTable opens a form with the selected query or table as its data source, in PivotTable view, ready to place fields in its drop zones.

A drop zone (also called drop area) is one of four labeled areas in a PivotObject where you can drop a field from the field list.

If you choose PivotTable Wizard on the New Form dialog instead, after an unnecessarily complex and confusing opening screen you will be asked for the fields you want to include in the PivotTable, and then the blank PivotTable will open. Because (if you follow my recommendations) you will have already prepared a query with suitable fields, this step isn't necessary. I recommend just selecting AutoForm: PivotTable instead, and using drag and drop to move fields to the PivotTable's drop zones as needed.

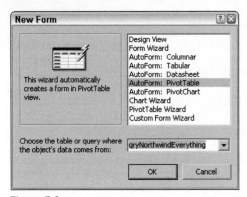

Figure 5.2

You will only use three to five fields at any time on a PivotTable, but there is an advantage to having more fields available in the field list. It gives you the flexibility to modify the PivotTable to display different data—and flexibility is what PivotTables are about!

I use the tag fpvt for PivotTable forms.

A PivotTable requires at least three fields: One for the row headings, one for the column headings, and one for the data in the center of the table. But (unlike crosstab queries) you aren't stuck with your initial choices; with a PivotTable, you can change your selections interactively at any time.

The new PivotTable with qryNorthwindEverything as its data source is shown in Figure 5.3. It has labeled drop zones where you can drop row fields (the left edge), filter fields (the top), column fields (under the top), and detail or totals fields (data fields) (center). The PivotTable field List displays all the fields in the query, so you can drag them to the PivotTable.

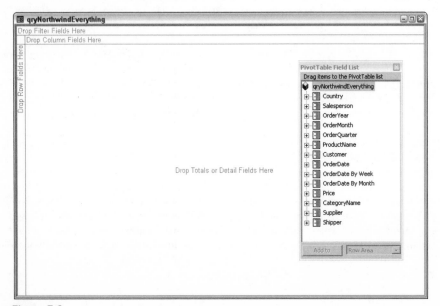

Figure 5.3

You can see the advantage of preprocessing data for a PivotObject in the field list—you have a choice of Year, Month, or Quarter for date columns, and Customer, Supplier, and Shipper are separate, easily identifiable selections (remember, the field is actually CompanyName in all three tables). With a picture in your mind of how you want to see the data, all you need to do is drag the field(s) of your choice to each area. To see food categories on the left, drag the CategoryName field to the Rows drop area. To see results for salespersons by category, drag the Salesperson field to the Columns drop area. To filter by country, drag the Country field to the Filter drop area. Finally, to show price data in the data area of the PivotTable, drag the Price field to the Totals/Details drop area. The initial PivotTable created by these actions is shown in Figure 5.4.

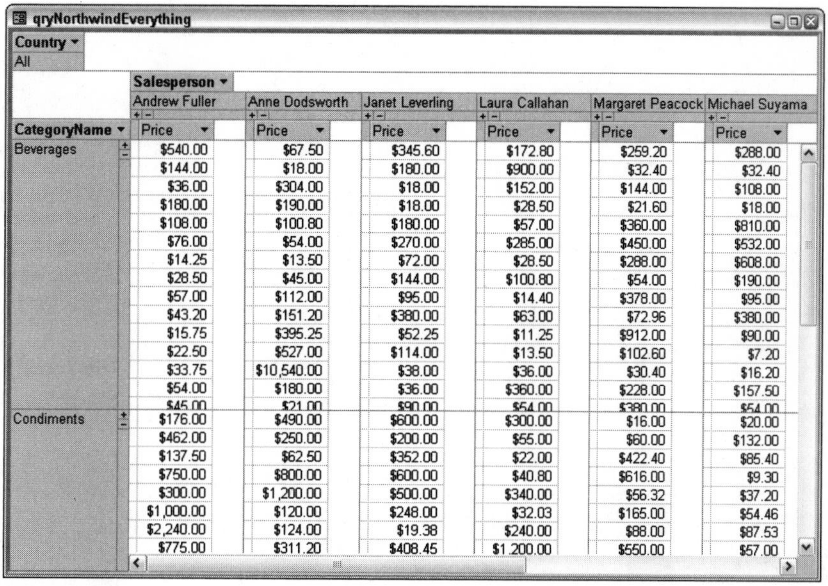

Figure 5.4

Just as it is, with no more tinkering, this PivotTable is very useful—and very flexible. Unlike the limited Access 2000 PivotTables, you don't need to open Excel to modify a PivotTable; you can adjust it right in Access PivotTable view. Note that the field selected for the rows, columns, and filters has a drop-down arrow next to it; clicking on this arrow lets you select values for filtering the data. For example, drop down the Country selections, and check only UK to see just UK data, as shown in Figure 5.5.

> **To deselect all the values before selecting one, uncheck the All box.**

After selecting UK, only results for salespersons based in the UK are displayed in the PivotTable. Similarly, you can filter for specific categories or salespersons. If you just want to see results for Steven Buchanan and Michael Suyama for the Beverages and Dairy Products food categories, select Steven Buchanan and Michael Suyama in the Salesperson drop-down list, and Beverages and Dairy Products in the CategoryName list. The filtered PivotTable is shown in Figure 5.6.

Figure 5.5

qryNorthwindEverything			
Country ▾			
UK			

		Salesperson ▾		
		Michael Suyama	Steven Buchanan	Grand Total
		+ −	+ −	+ −
CategoryName ▾		Price ▾	Price ▾	No Totals
Beverages	+ −	$288.00	$216.00	
		$32.40	$720.00	
		$108.00	$142.50	
		$18.00	$4.75	
		$810.00	$99.75	
		$532.00	$8.10	
		$608.00	$1.80	
		$190.00	$10.13	
		$95.00	$6.75	
		$380.00	$157.50	
		$90.00	$5.60	
		$7.20	$54.00	
		$16.20	$2,108.00	
		$157.50	$864.00	
		$54.00	$72.00	
Dairy Products	+ −	$201.60	$168.00	
		$63.00	$42.00	
		$63.00	$210.00	
		$210.00	$210.00	
		$26.25	$35.00	
		$456.00	$103.13	
		$400.00	$87.50	
		$300.00	$1.88	
		$60.00	$20.00	
		$140.00	$46.88	
		$3.00	$6.00	
		$100.00	$35.00	
		$437.50	$660.00	
		$11.25	$220.00	
		$48.00	$2,750.00	
Grand Total	+ −			

Figure 5.6

This basic PivotTable displays the prices for all the orders for Beverages and Dairy Products placed by Steven Buchanan and Michael Suyama. It is very useful as is, but when I look at it I can see some ways it could be improved—and because it is a PivotTable, it is just a matter of a few mouse clicks to customize it just as I prefer.

For example, I think it would be useful to have the order date alongside the price. All I have to do is drag the OrderDate field from the Field List to the data area, placing it to the left of Price. Now I have more filter options, with drop-down arrows next to OrderDate and Price.

> If the Field List disappears (as it does every once in a while, all on its own), make it visible again by clicking the Field List button on the PivotTable toolbar or by right-clicking the PivotTable and selecting Field List from the context menu.

I wanted to show orders only for 1995; to do this I dragged the OrderYear field to the data area (one of the date expressions created in the data source query) to the left of Order Date, so that I could filter by year. Figure 5.7 shows the PivotTable, filtered for 1995 orders.

qryNorthwindEverything							
Country ▾ UK							
	Salesperson ▾						
	Michael Suyama			Steven Buchanan			Grand Total
CategoryName ▾	OrderYear ▾	OrderDate ▾	Price ▾	OrderYear ▾	OrderDate ▾	Price ▾	No Totals
Beverages	1995	03-Jan-95	$32.40	1995	17-Apr-95	$216.00	
	1995	25-Aug-95	$108.00	1995	22-Nov-95	$142.50	
	1995	25-Aug-95	$190.00	1995	28-Sep-95	$10.13	
	1995	14-Nov-95	$95.00	1995	04-Jan-95	$2,108.00	
	1995	17-Mar-95	$7.20	1995	17-Apr-95	$72.00	
	1995	03-Jul-95	$16.20	1995	03-Oct-95	$36.00	
	1995	14-Nov-95	$157.50	1995	13-Apr-95	$62.00	
	1995	28-Dec-95	$420.00	1995	17-Jul-95	$540.00	
	1995	23-Jan-95	$57.60	1995	21-Jul-95	$180.00	
	1995	25-Sep-95	$94.50				
	1995	19-May-95	$27.90				
	1995	24-Feb-95	$72.00				
	1995	13-Nov-95	$94.50				
Dairy Products	1995	28-Apr-95	$63.00	1995	27-Jun-95	$103.13	
	1995	06-Jun-95	$63.00	1995	17-Jul-95	$87.50	
	1995	19-Sep-95	$210.00	1995	06-Dec-95	$1.88	
	1995	10-Mar-95	$456.00	1995	22-Aug-95	$35.00	
	1995	23-Jan-95	$60.00	1995	21-Jul-95	$660.00	
	1995	23-Feb-95	$140.00	1995	04-Jan-95	$476.00	
	1995	17-Mar-95	$3.00	1995	07-Jun-95	$360.00	
	1995	20-Dec-95	$100.00	1995	10-Jan-95	$103.20	
	1995	06-Jun-95	$4.00	1995	04-Jan-95	$291.90	
	1995	16-Jun-95	$37.50	1995	21-Jul-95	$1,044.00	
	1995	23-Feb-95	$880.00	1995	22-Aug-95	$417.60	
	1995	20-Apr-95	$528.00	1995	28-Sep-95	$522.00	
	1995	13-Nov-95	$346.50				
	1995	14-Nov-95	$1,925.00				
	1995	28-Dec-95	$385.00				
Grand Total							

Figure 5.7

After selecting 1995 as the filter value for OrderYear, there is no need to see the OrderYear column, so I used the standard datasheet column resizing arrow in the column heading to shrink the OrderYear column to nothing, and I also widened the Price column somewhat, to display all of the larger numbers.

> You won't see the familiar Undo button when working on PivotObjects; if you make a mistake, you have to fix it manually.

Say that I don't want to see each order separately, but just the total for each salesperson, and I also want to see Grand Totals (note that the initial PivotTable has GrandTotal areas, but no totals are displayed in these areas). To create Price totals, I select the Price column by left-clicking its header, click the Sum button on the PivotTable toolbar, and select Sum from the list of aggregate functions (they are similar to the choices in a totals query). (Alternately, I could just drag the Price field to the Grand Total column to create a sum—but if I want a choice of aggregate functions, the toolbar button provides more selections.) Now the PivotTable displays the sum of orders for each salesperson, each food category group, and the grand total in the lower-right corner. To see daily order totals, click the tiny plus (+) sign under the Grand Total column; Figure 5.8 shows a portion of the PivotTable with column and daily totals.

qryNorthwindEverything							
Country ▾							
UK							
	Salesperson ▾						
	Michael Suyama		Steven Buchanan		Grand Total		
	+ −		+ −		+ −		
CategoryName ▾	OrderDate ▾	Price ▾	OrderDate ▾	Price ▾	OrderDate ▾	Price ▾	
Dairy Products	28-Apr-95	$63.00	27-Jun-95	$103.13	28-Apr-95	$63.00	
	06-Jun-95	$63.00	17-Jul-95	$87.50	06-Jun-95	$63.00	
	19-Sep-95	$210.00	06-Dec-95	$1.88	19-Sep-95	$210.00	
	10-Mar-95	$456.00	22-Aug-95	$35.00	10-Mar-95	$456.00	
	23-Jan-95	$60.00	21-Jul-95	$660.00	23-Jan-95	$60.00	
	23-Feb-95	$140.00	04-Jan-95	$476.00	23-Feb-95	$140.00	
	17-Mar-95	$3.00	07-Jun-95	$360.00	17-Mar-95	$3.00	
	20-Dec-95	$100.00	10-Jan-95	$103.20	27-Jun-95	$103.13	
	06-Jun-95	$4.00	04-Jan-95	$291.90	17-Jul-95	$87.50	
	16-Jun-95	$37.50	21-Jul-95	$1,044.00	06-Dec-95	$1.88	
	23-Feb-95	$880.00	22-Aug-95	$417.60	20-Dec-95	$100.00	
	20-Apr-95	$528.00	28-Sep-95	$522.00	06-Jun-95	$4.00	
	13-Nov-95	$346.50			16-Jun-95	$37.50	
	14-Nov-95	$1,925.00			22-Aug-95	$35.00	
	28-Dec-95	$385.00			23-Feb-95	$880.00	
	Sum of Price	$12,422.06	Sum of Price	$9,638.58	Sum of Price	$22,060.64	
Grand Total					03-Jan-95	$32.40	
					17-Apr-95	$216.00	
					25-Aug-95	$108.00	
					25-Aug-95	$190.00	
					14-Nov-95	$95.00	
					22-Nov-95	$142.50	
					17-Mar-95	$7.20	
					03-Jul-95	$16.20	
					28-Sep-95	$10.13	
					14-Nov-95	$157.50	
					28-Dec-95	$420.00	
					23-Jan-95	$57.60	
					04-Jan-95	$2,108.00	
					17-Apr-95	$72.00	
					25-Sep-95	$94.50	
	Sum of Price	$18,032.36	Sum of Price	$15,088.55	Sum of Price	$33,120.91	

Figure 5.8

To see just the totals, without details, I clicked on the tiny minus (−) signs for each salesperson, each food category (you can make different selections for each column and row, if desired), and the grand total.

> **To remove a total, right-click the total, then select Remove from its context menu.**

If the plain grayscale PivotTable isn't fancy enough for you, select fonts and colors that please you by clicking the element you want to change and selecting a font, size, and text color from the Formatting (PivotTable/PivotChart) toolbar. The formatting you select will be applied to all the elements of that type. For example, I selected the total under Michael Suyama's column, and made it 11 pt, bold, and red;

the result was that all the column totals had this formatting. I made the salesperson and category names 11 pt, bold, and bright blue on a white background, and the grand totals 12 pt and bold underlined. The resulting formatted PivotTable is shown in Figure 5.9.

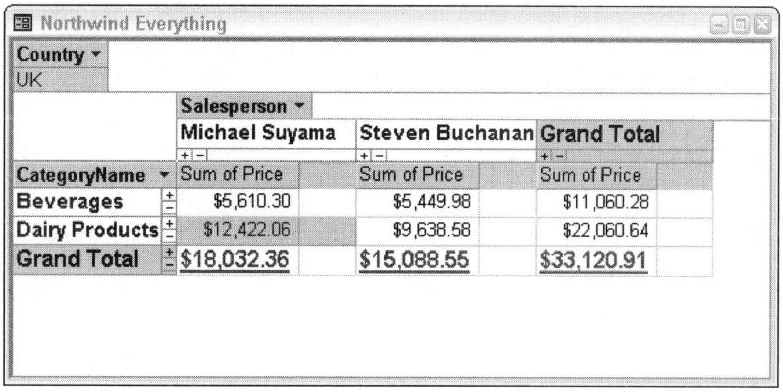

Figure 5.9

How about swapping rows and columns? With a PivotTable, this is delightfully simple. All you have to do is drag the Salesperson field to the row drop area (drop it when you see the blue vertical bar, as shown in Figure 5.10) and then drag the CategoryName field to the column drop area.

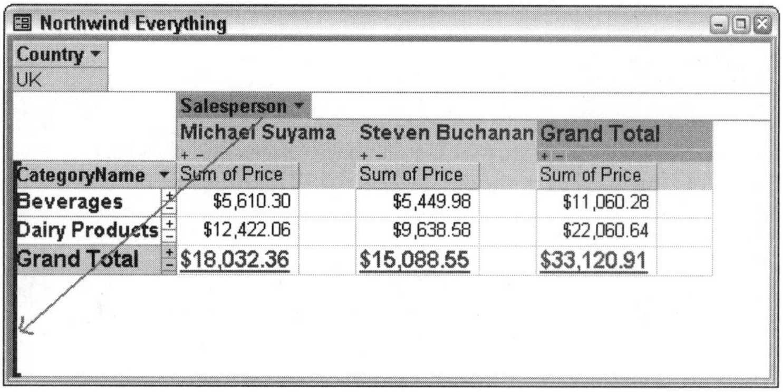

Figure 5.10

After swapping, initially the details are shown; you can return to the summary display by clicking the tiny minus (-) sign in the row headings again. Curiously, after swapping rows and columns, the column headings revert to the default gray background, so I had to reapply the white background. Figure 5.11 shows the swapped PivotTable, with details displayed.

When you add Totals to a column, each column has its own total, as well as the grand total, displayed in the lower-right corner. There is also a Grand Total column at the right of the PivotTable, with a subtotal for each salesperson (as shown in Figure 5.11). If you don't want to see this column, you can click the Subtotal button on the PivotTable toolbar to hide it. This button is a toggle button, so clicking it again makes the Grand Total column reappear.

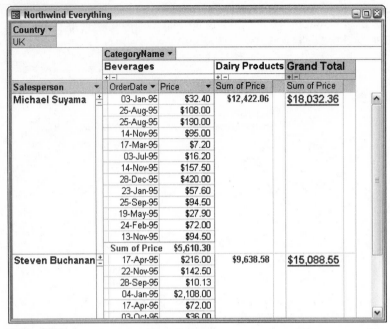

Figure 5.11

The PivotTable Toolbar

PivotTables have their own toolbar, with several buttons you can use to modify PivotTable elements. Some of them will be familiar to you from other toolbars (query and datasheet); others are unique to PivotTables. The PivotTable toolbar is shown in Figure 5.12, and its buttons are explained in the table that follows the figure.

Figure 5.12

Note that some toolbar buttons are only enabled if the appropriate PivotTable element is selected; for example, you can only sort if a column is selected, and you can only use expand or collapse if there are two (or more) row fields or column fields.

Toolbar Button	Function	Comments
![icon]	Switch to another view	Rarely, if ever needed for PivotTables
![icon]	Save	Saves the form

Toolbar Button	Function	Comments
	Search	Opens the Search pane
	Print	Prints the PivotTable
	Preview	Previews the PivotTable
	Copy	Copies the selected object
	Sort Ascending	Row or Column selected
	Sort Descending	Row or Column selected
	AutoFilter	Switches between the selected filter and showing all
	Show Top/Bottom Items	Shows the top or bottom n records; Row or Column selected
	AutoCalc	Creates a standard aggregate function; Row or Column selected
	Subtotal—toggles Grand Total column (with row subtotals) on or off	Row or Column must have at least two detail items; there must be a Totals field already
	Calculated Totals and Fields	Lets you create calculated expressions and totals
	Show As	Lets you show a total as a percentage of a selected total
	Collapse	Hides lower level—select the higher of two row or column levels
	Expand	Displays lower level—select the higher of two row or column levels
	Hide Details	Hides all the details; click the – sign on a row or column to just hide details for that row or column
	Show Details	Shows all the details; click the – sign on a row or column to just show details for that row or column
	Refresh	Refreshes data; useful when a PivotTable is based on a remote data source

Table continued on following page

Toolbar Button	Function	Comments
	Export to Excel	Exports the PivotTable to Excel
	Field List	Displays the field list
	Properties	Lets you set many properties of various Pivot-Table elements; different properties can be set depending on which element is selected
	Database Window	Shows the database window
	New Object selector	Lets you create a new object
	Access Help	Opens Access Help

The PivotTable Properties Sheet

To fine-tune your PivotTable, open the properties sheet for any element and make changes (the PivotTable properties sheet has different pages and options depending on the element selected when it is opened). For example, to put a space between *Category* and *Name* for the *CategoryName* field, select the CategoryName field and open the properties sheet. Click the Captions tab and place the space between *Category* and *Name* in the Caption field, as shown in Figure 5.13.

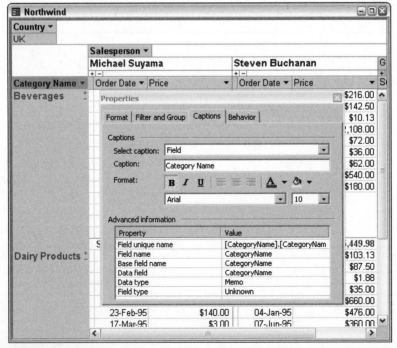

Figure 5.13

You can use this page of the properties sheet to modify font and color properties as well, though it is generally easier to use the toolbar buttons for that purpose. The Format page of the properties sheet lets you make adjustments to the format of the selected element, as well as sort by Ascending or Descending (again, most of these properties can also be adjusted from the toolbar). The Filter and Group page lets you set up more elaborate filtering and grouping, and the Behavior page lets you set options related to the drop zone indicators and expand indicators (for example, if you are preparing a PivotTable for a presentation, you may wish to turn off these features).

> **I have found that when I change the Caption property of a row or column, or the filter field name in a PivotTable, often the change doesn't stick—it reverts to the original name either immediately after changing it or after closing and reopening the PivotTable. For this reason, for PivotObjects alone, I recommend not giving controls the usual LNC tags.**

PivotCharts

Like PivotTables, PivotCharts are easier to work with if you first prepare a data source query. The same qryNorthwindEverything query that was used for PivotTables in the previous section is also useful for creating PivotCharts. A PivotChart has drop zones for category fields and series fields (similar to the row and column fields for PivotTables), and filter and data fields (similar to the filter and detail/total fields for PivotTables); however, some PivotChart types (such as the pie chart) only require a series field (no category field) and a data field.

I use the tag fpvc for PivotChart forms.

To create a PivotChart, create a new form and select AutoForm: PivotChart from the New Form dialog; select qryNorthwindEverything as its data source. The new, blank PivotChart is shown in Figure 5.14.

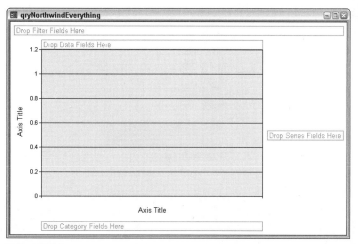

Figure 5.14

To start with a simple column graph (the default chart type), I dragged Country to the filter area, and filtered for USA, dragged CategoryName to the Categories drop area, OrderQuarter to the Series drop area, and Price to the data area. Note that Price appears on the chart as Sum of Price. If I dragged OrderDate to this area, it would appear as Count of OrderDate. Access places numeric fields as Sum, and other fields as Count, when they are placed in the Data area. The initial chart is shown in Figure 5.15.

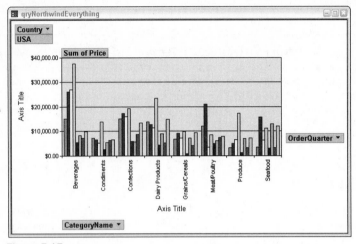

Figure 5.15

There are many more formatting options for PivotCharts than for PivotTables, and you can use them to prepare impressive charts, selecting an appropriate chart type for the data you are displaying. The column colors in the starter chart indicate the quarter for which the price is being summed, but without a legend the users won't know which is which. Therefore, the first step is to add a legend to the chart, by clicking the Show Legend button on the PivotChart toolbar. To restrict the data to just 1995, I dropped down the OrderQuarter selector and checked only the 1995 quarters, as shown in Figure 5.16.

Figure 5.16

Next step is to replace the Axis Title placeholders with real titles for the X- and Y-axes; this is done by right-clicking the placeholder and opening the properties sheet from its context menu; here, the caption is edited on the Format page. I entered Food Categories as the X (bottom) axis title, and formatted it for 11 pt and bold. Similarly, I changed the Y- (left) axis title to Total Sales, 11 pt bold. The enhanced, but still rather plain chart is shown in Figure 5.17.

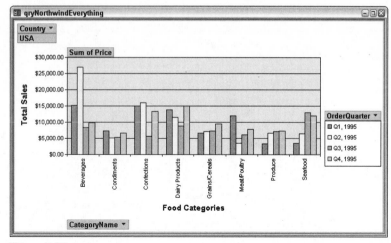

Figure 5.17

There are many choices for chart and graph types; to see them, click the Chart Type button on the PivotChart toolbar. Figure 5.18 shows the choices for column graphs; click the other chart types to see their selections.

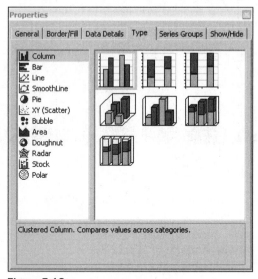

Figure 5.18

I selected the 3D, angled view, and in the same properties sheet I modified some of the visual effects of the graph on the 3D view page and the Fill page; the best way to learn about these selections is to experiment with them. I rotated the graph to display the columns better, and selected the Calm Water background for the chart. The modified chart is shown in Figure 5.19.

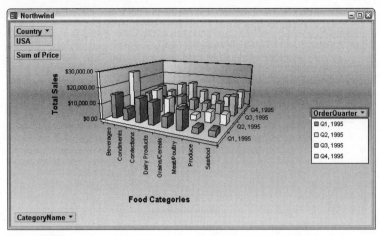

Figure 5.19

With the 3D graph, there are labels for the four quarters, so the legend could be removed, though I like to keep it, for clarity. You can swap rows and columns very easily with a PivotChart—just click the By Row/By Column toolbar button..

For some data, a line graph may be more suitable. Figure 5.20 shows a SmoothLine graph showing 1995 sales by month (using a count, not a sum) for all the UK salespersons.

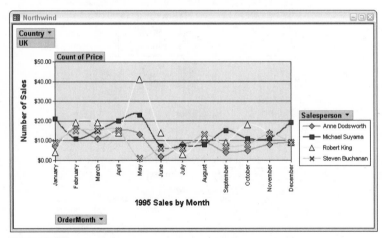

Figure 5.20

A pie chart is appropriate when you only want to look at data for a category, such as displaying sales by food categories. I created a PivotChart with Price for the data field and CategoryName for the Categories field, and added a title to the chart by opening its properties sheet and clicking the Add Title button on the General page. Then, I selected the placeholder Chart Workspace Title and edited the title in the Caption property of the Format page of its properties sheet. I also hid the field buttons and drop zones for a cleaner look by unchecking the Field Buttons/Drop Zones checkbox on the Show/Hide page of the chart's properties sheet. Figure 5.21 shows the modified 3D pie chart.

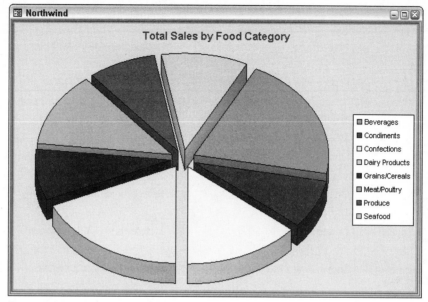

Figure 5.21

The PivotChart Toolbar

Like PivotTables, PivotCharts have their own toolbar, with several buttons you can use to modify PivotChart elements; some of them will be familiar to you from other toolbars. The PivotChart toolbar is shown in Figure 5.22, and its buttons are explained in the table following the figure.

Figure 5.22

> Some toolbar buttons are only enabled if the appropriate PivotChart element is selected. For example, you can only collapse or expand levels if there are two or more fields in the Categories (or Series) area.

Toolbar Button	Function	Comments
	Switch to another view	Rarely, if ever needed for PivotCharts
	Save	Saves the form

Table continued on following page

Toolbar Button	Function	Comments
	Search	Opens the Search pane
	Print	Prints the PivotChart
	Preview	Previews the PivotChart
	Undo	When it is enabled (rarely), undoes the last action
	Chart Type	Select the chart type
	Delete	Delete the selected element
	Show Legend	Makes the legend visible
	By Row/By Column	Swaps rows and columns
	Sort Ascending	Row or Column selected
	Sort Descending	Row or Column selected
	AutoFilter	Switches between the selected filter and showing all
	Show Top/Bottom Items	Category or Series selected
	AutoCalc	Data total selected
	Collapse	Hides lower level—select the higher of two category or series levels
	Expand	Displays lower level—select the higher of two category or series levels
	Drill into	Drills down into the data
	Drill out	Drills up out of the data
	Refresh	Useful when a PivotChart is based on a remote data source
	Multiple Plots	Lets you create a multi-chart—each value in the multi-chart field has its own chart

Toolbar Button	Function	Comments
	Multiple Plots Unified Field	Uses the same scale for all multi-charts
	Field List	Displays the field list
	Properties	Lets you set many properties of various PivotChart elements; different properties can be set depending on which element is selected
	Database Window	Shows the database window
	New Object selector	Lets you create a new object
	Access Help	Opens Access Help

Embedded PivotCharts

PivotCharts can also be embedded in standard forms, so that each record will have its own chart based on data in that record. To create an embedded PivotChart, first create the main form (I made a simple form based on the Northwind tblEmployees table), then create a PivotChart form as usual, and drag the PivotChart form to the main form where you want to embed it.

Next, to filter the PivotChart subform for just the current record, set the subform's LinkChildFields and LinkMasterFields properties to the appropriate linking field (EmployeeID, in this case). Figure 5.23 shows the Employees with Chart form, with a line graph showing 1995 sales by food category for 1995.

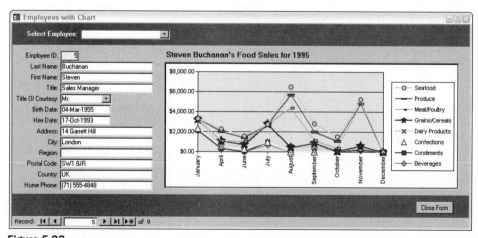

Figure 5.23

Summary

PivotTables and PivotCharts are especially useful when you are designing an application for users who like to tinker with their data and examine it from different perspectives. Instead of preparing static forms and reports to let the user look at the same data in different ways, you can just create an all-inclusive query with appropriate calculated fields, create one PivotTable and one PivotChart based on the query, and let the user tinker with it as needed, to view the data in all sorts of different ways.

In the next chapter, I'll describe how to create reports to display and print your data.

Printing Data with Reports

After you have created tables, forms, and queries for a database and entered some data, you need to create reports for printing the data. Although you can create reports at any time after creating the tables, it's a good idea to wait to create reports until you have a fair amount of representative data entered into the database's tables, in case you need to modify table structure or relationships as you enter data. In an ideal world, you would be able to set up all the tables and fields perfectly right at the start, but in the real world it is more than likely that as you create forms and then enter data you will find that a few fields have to be changed to different data types, that some fields aren't needed, or that a few new fields have to be created. This means you will have to make some changes to the forms—and if you have already created a number of reports, you'll also have to change the reports to match the table changes.

Report Design Principles

Although Access lets you save a form as a report (in Access 2000—this less-than-useful feature was dropped in Access 2002) or even print a form (see the "Filtered by Form Report" section later in this chapter for more details on why this is not a good idea), neither of these choices will result in a well-formatted report. Forms use interactive controls such as comboboxes, command buttons and option groups—none of which make sense on reports. Additionally, most forms have header and footer sections that generally contain interactive controls, and any or all form sections may have colored backgrounds, which print poorly and waste toner or ink. See Figure 6.1 for an example of a form in print preview.

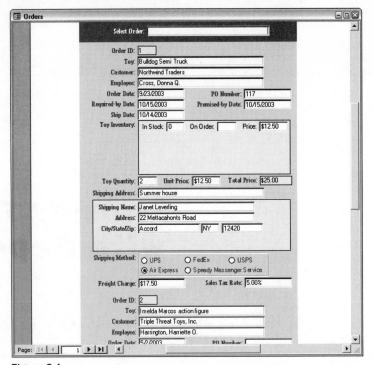

Figure 6.1

Forms (at least Single Form–type forms) generally display data one record at a time. A well-designed report, on the other hand, usually displays data from multiple records on one page, often grouped by one or more fields; some reports summarize data and only display overall and possibly group totals or counts. A report header should generally contain the report title, and possibly information such as the date the report was printed. A report footer may contain grand totals. Report page headers and footers should contain information such as the group header (in case report groups are more than one page long) and page number. And for grouped reports, the group header should contain the group header name, and the group footer might contain group subtotals.

The Report Wizard

Access has a Report Wizard, but generally you'll have to do as much work on a report created by this wizard as you would when creating a report from scratch (or in some cases, more work). This is primarily because of problems with arranging controls on the report design grid. The Report Wizard has two AutoReport selections. If I select the AutoReport: Columnar selection in the New Report dialog with qryOrders as the record source, I'll get the report shown in Figure 6.2.

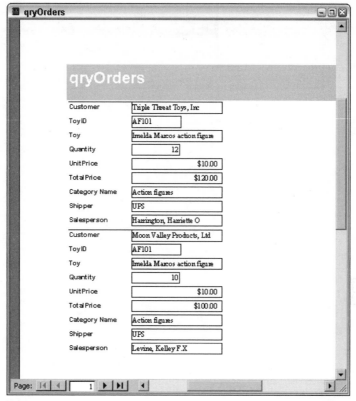

Figure 6.2

To view a report in the sample Toy Workshop (Reports Finish) database, select it by figure number from the Reports selector combobox on the main menu.

This report simply lists all the fields in qryOrders, from top to bottom, with a line between records. This is generally not a very useful format, unless you just need a basic printout of all the data for proofreading—but even for that purpose, you'll have to do some reformatting to prevent the truncation of data in some fields. If you select tblOrders instead of qryOrders, and the AutoReport: Tabular selection, you get the report shown in Figure 6.3.

This report squashes all the selected fields into a letter landscape page, resulting in both labels and data being truncated. If you only have a few fields, this Wizard selection produces an acceptable report, but if you have lots of fields, you will have to do a lot of resizing to get an acceptable report.

For a plainer (but still ugly and virtually useless) report, there's the AutoReport selection from the New Object selector. This creates a plain text report that arranges all the controls on the report, from top to bottom, with no header or footer, as shown in Figure 6.4.

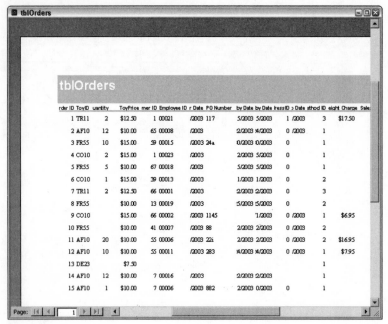

Figure 6.3

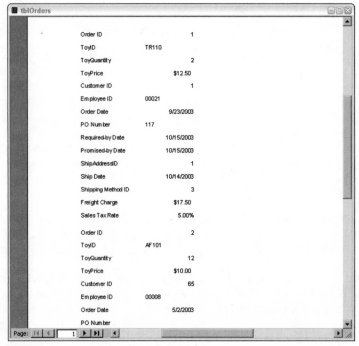

Figure 6.4

You can create a grouped report—a report where data is arranged hierarchically, sorted and grouped by several fields—with the Report Wizard. However, there is no explicit Grouped Report selection. Instead, to create a grouped report you select Report Wizard from the New Report dialog and make choices in pages of the Wizard. If you select tblOrders as the record source, select all the fields in the table, select three fields for sorting and grouping, and leave all other selections at the default, you'll get the report shown in Figure 6.5.

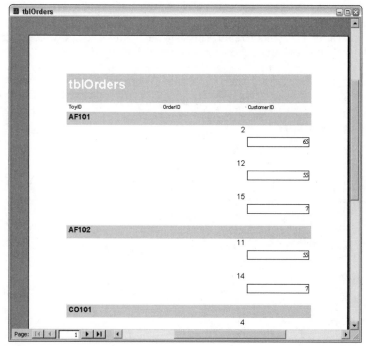

Figure 6.5

Actually, what you see is only a small portion of the report. Totally ignoring the reality of paper sizes, and despite the fact that the report is formatted for letter-sized paper with portrait orientation, the Report Wizard creates a 22-inch wide report, of which only the first three fields are visible. This report is useless (and ugly to boot).

With a wizard like this, you're better off doing it yourself! Instead of selecting the Report Wizard from the New Report dialog, just select Design view, choose a table or query record source, and place the controls on the report grid as you wish. Or, to save time and ensure a consistent appearance for all the reports in an application, you may want to create a set of report templates, and use them as the basis for the reports you create.

Using Report Templates

Instead of using the Report Wizard, I recommend creating a set of report templates that can be customized for each application you create. You'll need at least a portrait and landscape template in letter size (or whatever paper size you use most frequently) and possibly another set of portrait and landscape templates in a larger size. My generic report templates include grouped and tabular reports with two groups, each with both a group header and footer. For plainer reports that don't need grouping, just delete any groups that aren't needed. I also have a subreport template with no groups.

Each group section in a report needs its own font style and size for descriptive text and group fields, to differentiate the groups, and this means that you need to place controls with appropriately formatted dummy text in each section of the template. It is rare to need more than two or three group levels in a report (though Access allows up to ten). My generic report templates have two groups, each with a header and a footer, supplied with preformatted textboxes with sample text. I use the Arial font throughout, mostly 9 pt, with italics and bold for emphasis in group header and footer sections, and larger sizes only in the report header. The generic report template for a letter-sized portrait tabular report (rtmpTabularReportLetterPortrait) is shown in Design view in Figure 6.6.

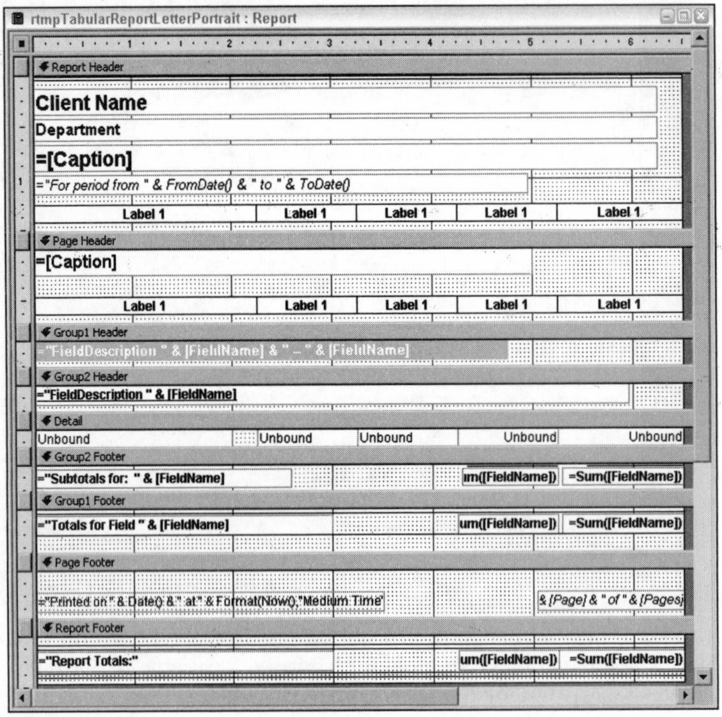

Figure 6.6

To use these report templates for an application, copy them into the application database and edit them as needed to replace the dummy text in the title and subtitle labels ("Client Name" and "Department") with whatever standard text is appropriate for the application. In the sample database, I replaced Client Name with Toy Workshop, and deleted the Department label, moving the Caption label up.

The txtCaptionRH textbox has the control source =[Caption], which prints the report's caption. This ensures that the report's caption in print preview will match the caption printed on the report itself and also the report name displayed in the report selector combobox on the standard main menu (this feature is discussed in the "Creating a Main Menu with the Menu Manager Add-In" section later in this chapter).

The txtDateRange textbox displays a date range; this control source expression picks up a From Date and To Date from textboxes on my standard main menu (see the "Creating a Main Menu with the Menu Manager" section later in this chapter for more details on this menu feature). This textbox is only needed for reports you want to filter by a date range, so it can be deleted from any report that doesn't need this feature.

The tabular report template has two sets of column heading labels, one in the report header section, and one in the page header section; the page header section is set to not print on the first page of the report. The page header section also displays the report caption, in a smaller type size than in the report header.

The Group 1 header text has a textbox with dummy text for a descriptive word or phrase, the group field, and another field (optional). It is formatted with a light gray background and white text. The Group 2 group header text is black text on a white background, underlined. The Detail section has textboxes in Arial 9, without labels (in this template, the labels are located over the columns, in the header sections). The Group 1 and Group 2 footer sections have textboxes with "Subtotals for" (or "Totals for") text and the group field, and sums under several of the fields, which can be eliminated if they aren't needed.

The page footer has calculated fields that display the date and time the report was printed, and the page number, in Page *x* of *y* format.

Tabular Reports

A tabular report is laid out like a datasheet, with data displayed in rows and columns, with or without grouping. Columns are identified by labels in the page header or a group header. To create a tabular report, follow these steps:

1. Make a copy of one of the tabular report templates (probably rtmpTabularReportLetterLandscape).

2. Select an appropriate record source, such as qryOrdersFull for the sample tabular report.

3. Enter the report's caption in its Caption property.

4. Edit the captions of the lblTitle and lblSubtitle labels in the report header as needed (unless you have already standardized them in the application's templates).

5. If grouping on one or more fields is needed, select the group(s) in the Sorting and Grouping dialog. I selected ToyCategory and Customer, with header and footer turned on for both fields.

6. To sort on another field that doesn't need grouping, select it on another row in the Sorting and Grouping dialog, but don't turn on the header or footer

7. Place the fields you want on the report in the detail section, resize them as needed, and give the labels in the report header and page header sections appropriate captions.

8. Run the LNC Rename All Controls builder from the Name property of the Detail section to give all the controls the appropriate LNC tags.

9. Save the report with the *rpt* tag.

Figure 6.7 shows the new report in Design view, and Figure 6.8 shows it in Datasheet view.

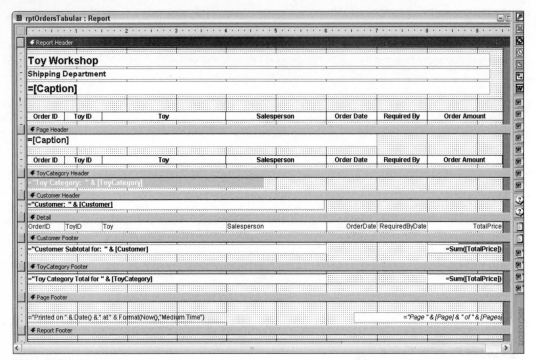

Figure 6.7

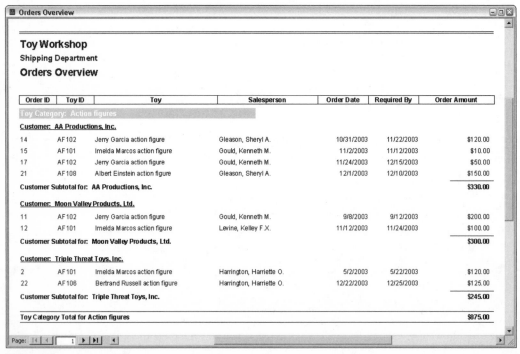

Figure 6.8

Grouped Reports

Grouped reports display data hierarchically, sometimes indenting data from lower groups (indentation is practical only for reports with a small number of fields). The lowest level may contain data from individual records or summarized data. You can create a grouped report using the Report Wizard, but the results are not likely to be acceptable (see the "Report Wizard" section earlier in this chapter for an example). Therefore, I prefer to create grouped reports directly from Design view, using a copy of the appropriate report template.

As an example of a simple grouped report, I started by making a copy of the letter portrait grouped report template, and selected qryOrders as its record source. I selected ToyCategory and Salesperson as sorting and grouping levels with both headers and footers, and Customer and ToyID for further sorting, without headers and footers, as shown in Figure 6.9.

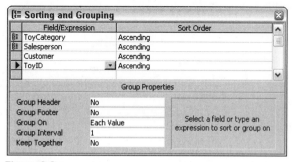

Figure 6.9

I edited the dummy text and field names in the group header and footer textboxes, replacing "Client Name" with "Toy Workshop" in txtTitle and placing "Shipping" before "Department" in txtSubtitle. I also removed txtDateRange, because it isn't needed for this report. In the Detail section, I placed a textbox to display the customer name, with Hide Duplicates and CanGrow both set to Yes (to prevent printing the customer name more than once in a group and to let long customer names wrap to the next row). I created a calculated field to concatenate information about the toy purchased, with the control source listed below:

```
=[Quantity] & " of Toy ID " & [ToyID] & " (" & [Toy] & ") @ " &
Format([UnitPrice],"Currency")
```

and I placed the TotalPrice field on the report, changing its label caption to "Order Price."

There are several group subtotals on this report. If you look at the textboxes that display these subtotals, you'll see that they all have the same expression for the ControlSource property:

```
=Sum([TotalPrice])
```

This expression yields different values depending on where it is placed in the report. In a group footer, it yields a subtotal for that group, and in the report footer, it yields a grand total for the entire report.

The report is shown in print preview in Figure 6.10.

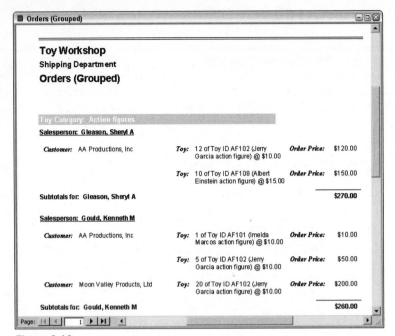

Figure 6.10

This page of the report shows two orders for one customer under Sheryl Gleason's group, and two orders for one customer and one order for another customer under Kenneth Gould's record. If you wanted a more compact report format, with customer subtotals, you could add a group header and footer for the Customer field and eliminate the calculated field, placing Quantity, ToyID, Toy, and UnitPrice textboxes directly on the form. I added more descriptive text to the group footer subtotals, to clearly differentiate the group levels, made them right-aligned, and moved them closer to the totals. I also added descriptive column labels to the Customer group header, to identify the fields. Version 2 of the report is shown in Figure 6.11.

One more change might be beneficial: Set the Force New Page property of the ToyCategory group footer to After Section so that each toy category starts on a new page. Figure 6.12 shows the third page of version 3 of the report, with a small category on its own page.

> *If you see blank report pages between pages with text when printing or previewing a report, this is probably because you accidentally moved or resized a control so that it goes beyond the available report width. Curiously, Access doesn't show guidelines for the report size in Design view, nor does it prevent you from dragging a control too far to the right, so this is a common occurrence. If you drag or resize a control beyond the available space, Access just changes the report width correspondingly—and you get the overflow printing on the next page, on an extra, unnumbered page.*

> *To fix the problem, check that no controls go beyond the available space for the report width, and set the report width back to its original value, which should be the paper width minus the left and right margins.*

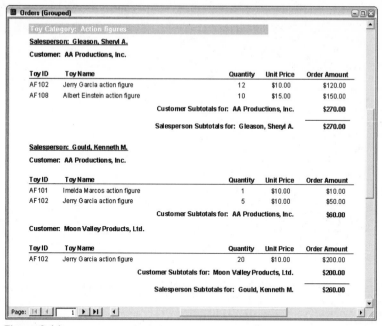

Figure 6.11

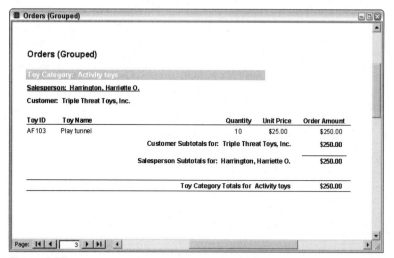

Figure 6.12

One final touch that could be added to a grouped report is running sums, and possibly page totals. Access doesn't support page totals directly. This means that if you place a textbox with a Sum or Count expression in a report's page footer section, you'll just see #Error when you preview or print the report.

However, there is a workaround for the lack of support for page totals: Create a one-line event procedure for the Print event of the Detail section, which adds the values of the TotalPrice field and places the sum in an unbound txtPageTotal textbox. This event procedure is:

```
Private Sub Detail1_Print(Cancel As Integer, PrintCount As Integer)

On Error GoTo ErrorHandler

    Me![txtPageTotal] = Nz(Me![txtPageTotal]) + Nz(Me![TotalPrice])

ErrorHandlerExit:
    Exit Sub

ErrorHandler:
    MsgBox "Error No: " & Err.Number & "; Description: " & _
        Err.Description
    Resume ErrorHandlerExit

End Sub
```

Running sums are easier: all you need to do is add a textbox bound to the field for which you want a running sum, and set its RunningSum property to either Over Group (to reset the running sum every time a new group starts) or Over All, to keep on adding to the running sum all through the report. Figure 6.13 shows version 4 of the grouped report, with a page total and both group and overall running sums.

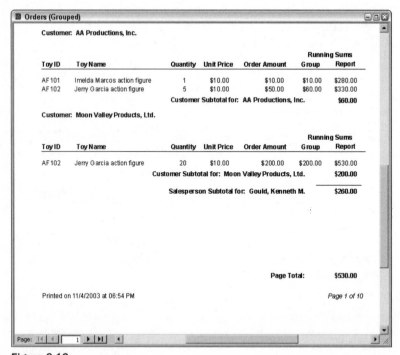

Figure 6.13

Labels Reports

There is one Report Wizard selection that is genuinely useful—the Label Wizard. To create a mailing labels report, select a table or query in the database window (I selected qryEmployees, which has several concatenated fields handy for this purpose), select Report from the New Object selector, and select Label Wizard from the New Report dialog. The first screen of the wizard lets you select a standard label format or create your own custom format. I selected Avery #5160 labels, a standard three-across U.S. label format, as shown in Figure 6.14.

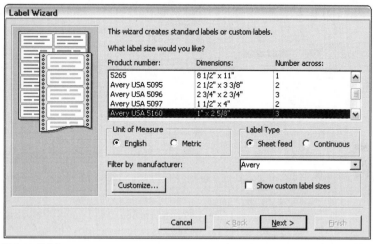

Figure 6.14

On the next screen of the wizard (shown in Figure 6.15), select a font and color. For mailing labels, generally the default Arial 8 pt font is a good choice for a three-across label format; if you select a larger size, you may not have enough room to print longer addresses on the labels.

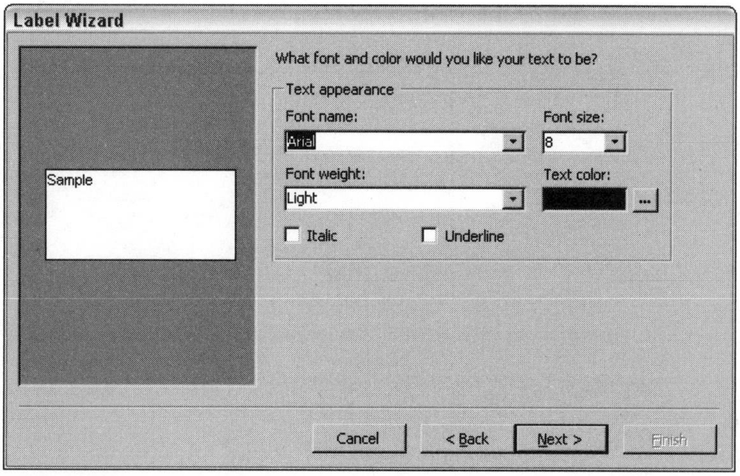

Figure 6.15

On the next screen, select fields to place on the label. Here is where the concatenated fields come in handy—all I have to do is place the FirstNameFirst field on the label, press Enter, and place the FullAddress field under it, as shown in Figure 6.16.

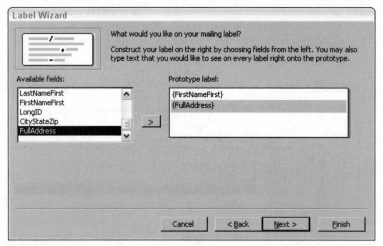

Figure 6.16

The next screen of the wizard (not shown) lets you select a field for sorting; I selected the PostalCode field for this purpose. On the last screen of the wizard, name the report, I named the report rptEmployees5160Labels. The mailing labels report is shown in Figure 6.17.

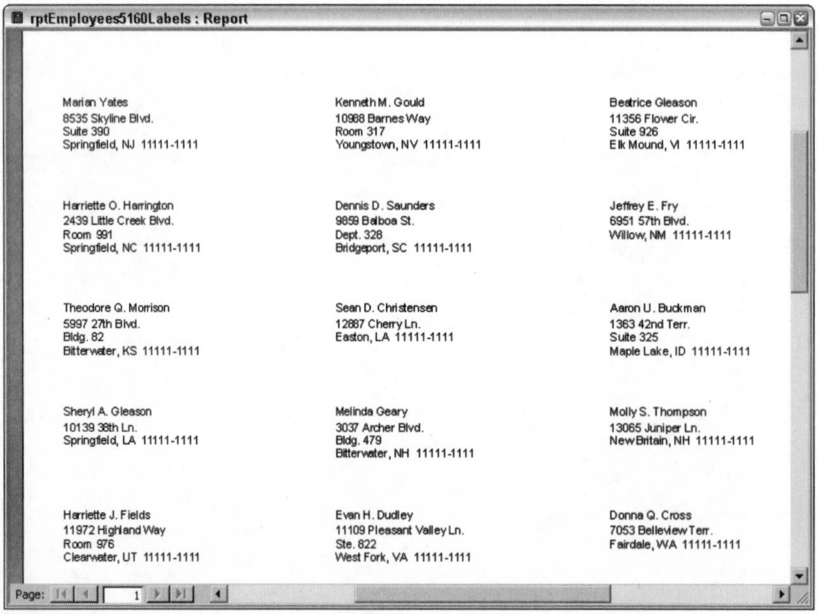

Figure 6.17

Columnar Reports

In the section on using the Report Wizard earlier in this chapter, the sample columnar report produced by the AutoReport: Columnar selection didn't look too promising. However, there is one type of report that benefits from a simple top-to-bottom format: a name and address report, say for use as an address book. Starting with the selection of Design View in the New Report dialog, I created a columnar report based on qryEmployees and placed a few fields on it:

- ❏ EmployeeID
- ❏ FirstNameFirst
- ❏ DepartmentName
- ❏ Title
- ❏ EmailName
- ❏ FullAddress

Concatenated name and address fields are especially useful on reports, because they automatically eliminate spaces and blank rows between name and address components.

I ran the LNC Rename add-in from the Name property of the report's Detail section to rename all controls, changed the captions of some labels, and saved the report as rptEmployeeAddressBook. The resulting report is shown in Figure 6.18.

Figure 6.18

189

For an address book report, it would be nice to have the records sorted by the LastNameFirst field, and to have large letters (A, B, and so forth) setting off each group of names. To do this, switch to Design view and open the Sorting and Grouping dialog. Create an expression for the first sort level as follows: Select the LastName field for the first line, set the Group Header property to Yes, select Prefix Characters for its Group On property, and 1 as the group interval. Finally, to make sure that the big letter won't print on the last line of a page, set the Keep Together property to With First Detail (see Figure 6.19).

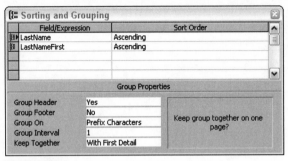

Figure 6.19

Select the LastNameFirst field for the second line, and set its Group Footer property to Yes, and the Keep Together property to Yes. Close the Sorting/Grouping dialog, and place a textbox in the LastName group header, with a control source of =Left([LastName],1). Make it several sizes larger than the main font (I made it 12 pt and bold). In the LastNameFirst footer section, place a horizontal line to divide the addresses.

Next, the report needs to be formatted for the appropriate paper size for printing pages that can be put into a Junior-size DayTimer, Filofax, or similar small notebook, which takes 3.75" × 6.75" paper. Unlike Outlook, Access doesn't have a wide selection of standard paper sizes to pick from, so you need to create a custom size for this purpose. The exact details of how to do this depend on your printer. You can access the printer's properties sheet from the Properties button on the Access Page Setup dialog. For my HP LaserJet 3200 printer, a custom size is created in the printer's properties sheet's Custom Paper Size dialog, as shown in Figure 6.20.

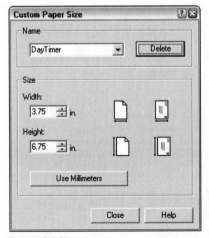

Figure 6.20

Save the custom paper size, and then select it in main printer properties sheet dialog (shown in Figure 6.21).

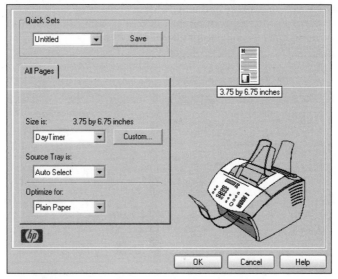

Figure 6.21

After closing the printer properties sheet, the selected size appears in the Page Setup dialog, as shown in Figure 6.22.

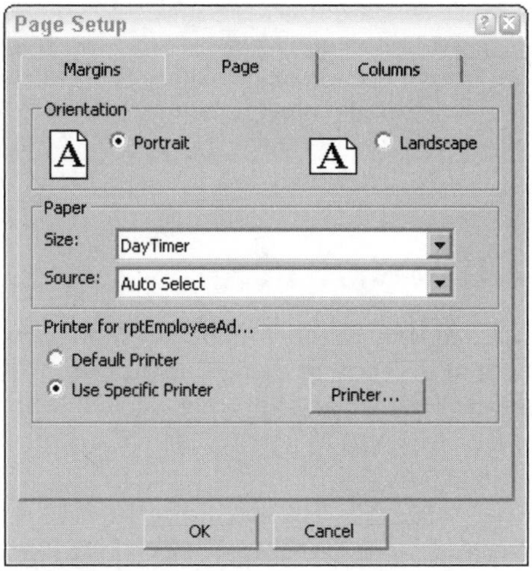

Figure 6.22

After selecting this small paper size, you won't see Access resizing the report to match the selected paper size; you have to do this yourself. I made the report's margins .5 inches all around, in the Page Setup dialog, and the report width 2.75 inches (I also made the divider line in the LastNameFirst footer 2.75

inches wide). The report doesn't need a page header or footer, so I turned them off from the View menu. Figure 6.23 shows the G and H pages of this report. You will get either two or three addresses per page, depending on how long the address is, and whether there is a new letter section. The Keep Together property settings prevent an address from being split over two pages, and also prevent the big letter from printing at the bottom of a page.

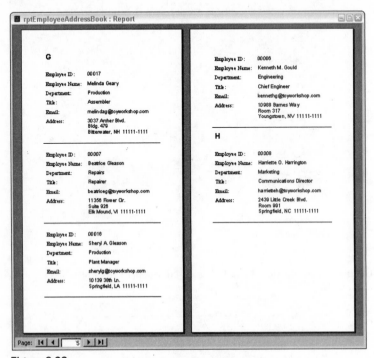

Figure 6.23

Reports with Subreports

Just as with forms, you can place reports on other reports as subreports. However, this isn't necessary nearly as often for reports as for forms because there is no problem with using nonupdatable queries as report record sources. This means that instead of placing a linked subreport on a main report, it's often easier to just add the linked table to the report's record source, and place data from the linked table in the appropriate section of a grouped report.

However, there are some circumstances in which a subreport may be useful. If you need to display the same linked information on numerous reports, you can create a subreport, format it as needed, and place the same subreport on all the reports that need it, which saves time. You can also use subreports to display unlinked data on reports, such as a PivotTable or PivotChart showing company-wide sales. Figure 6.24 shows a variant of the Orders grouped report, with a PivotTable showing toy sales by shipper in the report header, in the form of an embedded PivotTable subform.

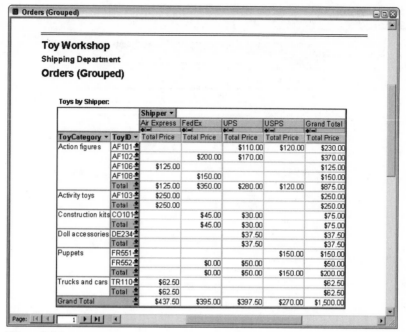

Figure 6.24

You can embed a form on a report, but not a report on a form.

For an example of a linked subreport, see the Single Order report in the next section, which uses a subreport linked on ShipAddressID and CustomerID to display the shipping address for an order.

Filtered by Form Reports

Sometimes you need to print a report with data for the current form record. You may be tempted to print the form, but this is rarely workable. Well-designed forms have controls that don't make sense on reports, such as command buttons, option groups, listboxes, and comboboxes; and they generally have colored backgrounds and control special effects that don't print well. Additionally, forms are generally designed to display one data record at a time, while reports (with the exception of some name and address reports) are usually designed to display data from multiple records on one page. If you print a form filtered for the current record, you'll get a report that looks like Figure 6.25.

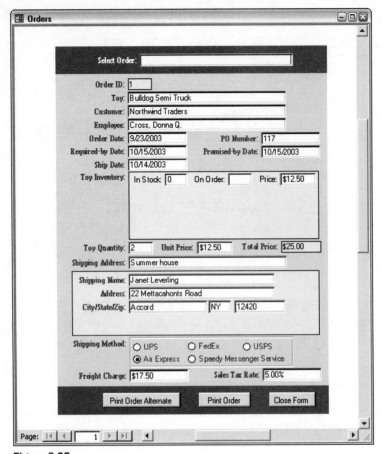

Figure 6.25

The form header and footer print, though the combobox and command button are meaningless on a report, and the subforms aren't sized properly. What you need here is a report that prints the data for a single form record in a format suitable for printing. (Printing a report for each order, as it is entered, ensures that there is a paper record of orders, in case of a power outage or other disaster.) In many cases, you can use the same report to print a single record as for printing multiple records, by just applying a filter so the report prints only the current record. However, in this case it's best to create a report with a different format, to give full details about the individual order in a compact format. The single-record report is shown in Figure 6.26. (This report is opened by clicking the Print Report command button in the footer of the fpriOrders form.)

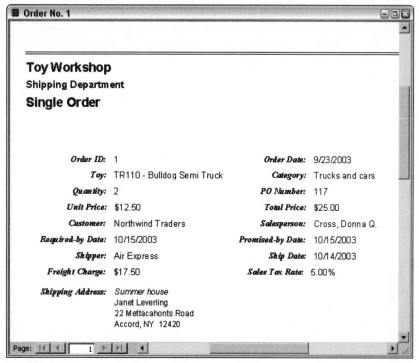

Figure 6.26

The report's caption is set to Order No. *n* by the code, and you can see this caption in the report's title bar in print preview, but curiously, the textbox with the control source =[Caption] is not displayed correctly in print preview, although it does print correctly. If this isn't acceptable, you can change the control source of txtCaptionRH to ="Order No. " & [OrderID]; this will make it display correctly in print preview, as well as on the printed report. (I did this for the sample report.)

A report designed to print just a single order generally doesn't need a page header; if it will never be longer than one page, it may not need a page footer either (though if you want to see the date and time the report was printed, the page footer is a good place for this information). Similarly, there is no need for a report footer. There is no need for report groups because you only need to sort and group records if you are printing multiple records, so all the data can be displayed in the Detail section. All of these requirements make for a report that is formatted very differently than a grouped report intended to print data from multiple records.

There are a variety of ways to filter a report by the current form record. One is to use the form's key field as a criterion in the report's record source; this is the method I use for the Single Order report shown in Figure 6.26. This method is suitable for a special report only used to print data from a single selected record. You can also create a filter string in code and use it to set a report's Filter property, as in the code segment listed below. This method is more suitable when the same report is used for printing both a single record and multiple records.

```
Private Sub cmdPrintOrderAlternate_Click()

On Error GoTo ErrorHandler

    Dim lngOrderID As Long
    Dim strCaption As String
    Dim strReport As String
    Dim rpt As Access.Report
    Dim strFilter As String

    lngOrderID = Nz(Me![OrderID])
    If lngOrderID = 0 Then
        GoTo ErrorHandlerExit
    Else
        strReport = "rptOrdersGroupedV3"
        strCaption = "Order No. " & lngOrderID
        strFilter = "[OrderID] = " & lngOrderID
    End If

    DoCmd.OpenReport reportname:=strReport, _
        View:=acViewPreview, _
        windowmode:=acHidden
    Set rpt = Reports(strReport)
    rpt.Caption = strCaption
    rpt.FilterOn = True
    rpt.Filter = strFilter
    DoCmd.OpenReport reportname:=strReport, _
        View:=acNormal

ErrorHandlerExit:
    Exit Sub

ErrorHandler:
    MsgBox "Error No: " & Err.Number & "; Description: " & _
        Err.Description
    Resume ErrorHandlerExit

End Sub
```

The Single Order report is opened by code on a command button, which follows. The code first checks whether there is an Order ID and exits the procedure if none is found (this indicates a new record, not yet filled in). Then, a variable is set to the Single Order report name, and another variable is created for the report caption, with the current order number. The report is opened in hidden mode, the caption is set, and then it is printed.

```
Private Sub cmdPrintOrder_Click()

On Error GoTo ErrorHandler

    Dim lngOrderID As Long
    Dim strCaption As String
    Dim strReport As String
    Dim rpt As Access.Report

    lngOrderID = Nz(Me![OrderID])

If lngOrderID = 0 Then
    GoTo ErrorHandlerExit
    Else
        strReport = "rptSingleOrder"
        strCaption = "Order No. " & lngOrderID
    End If

    DoCmd.OpenReport reportname:=strReport, _
        View:=acViewPreview, _
        windowmode:=acHidden
    Set rpt = Reports(strReport)
    rpt.Caption = strCaption
    DoCmd.OpenReport reportname:=strReport, _
        View:=acNormal

ErrorHandlerExit:
    Exit Sub

ErrorHandler:
    MsgBox "Error No: " & Err.Number & "; Description: " & _
        Err.Description
    Resume ErrorHandlerExit

End Sub
```

Summary Reports

Creating a summary report in Access is delightfully simple (though not very intuitive). All you have to do is create a grouped report with sums, counts, or other aggregate functions in a group footer and then set the Visible property of the Detail section of the report to No. You may need to do some reformatting, such as removing a group header or changing the formatting of a label or textbox control in the group footer as well. If the standard report was formatted for landscape printing, you may be able to change it to portrait for the summary report. Figure 6.27 shows a summary report based on the tabular Orders report.

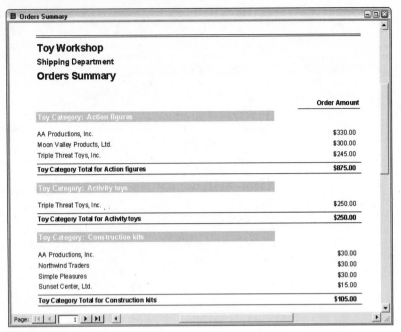

Figure 6.27

Special Formatting for Reports

You can use several techniques to apply special formatting to reports: conditional formatting done both from the interface and from VBA code, and watermarks.

Conditional Formatting of Report Controls and Sections

You can use conditional formatting with both form and report controls, but it is more useful on reports. One typical use is to emphasize records that have a Currency value over (or under) a certain number. As an example, let's use conditional formatting on a Sales Results report to make records where the sales total per salesperson is over $300 bold, and those with sales under $25 italicized. Other records are in plain text. In design view, select the txtSumTotalPriceGF textbox in the Salesperson footer, and select Format | Conditional Formatting from the menu. Set the criteria for the formatting in the Conditional Formatting dialog, as shown in Figure 6.28.

With reports you also have another option: formatting controls or making sections visible or invisible from the Format event of a report section, depending on the values of certain fields. Version 2 of the Sales Results report shown in Figure 6.29 uses an event procedure on the Salesperson group footer's Format event to make records where the sales total per salesperson is over $300 bold, and those with sales under $25 italicized. Other records are in plain text. The code uses an If . . . ElseIf . . . Else . . . End If structure to cover all the cases. This is necessary, because otherwise the formatting applied to one row will be carried over to the next record, unless that record is specifically formatted. (Version 1 of this report, using conditional formatting, looks exactly the same.)

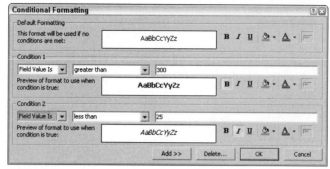

Figure 6.28

If you want to make a section visible or invisible, you have to use code, as conditional formatting is only available for controls. To make an entire report section visible or invisible, reference the section by its named constant, using the following syntax:

```
Me.Section(acDetail).Visible
```

The named constants for various report sections are listed in the table below:

Named Constant	Report Section
acDetail	Detail
acHeader	Report Header
acFooter	Report Footer
acPageHeader	Page Header
acPageFooter	Page Footer
acGroupLevel1Header	Group 1 Header
acGroupLevel1Footer	Group 1 Footer
acGroupLevel2Header	Group 2 Header
acGroupLevel2Footer	Group 2 Footer

(and so forth for further group headers and footers).

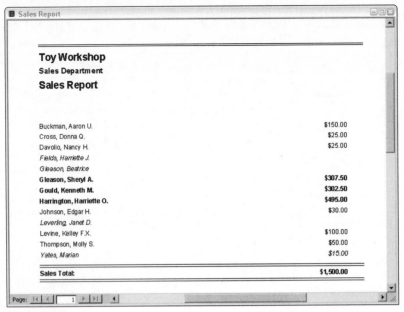

Figure 6.29

```
Private Sub SalespersonFooter_Format(Cancel As Integer, FormatCount As Integer)

On Error GoTo ErrorHandler

    Dim curSales As Currency

    curSales = Nz(Me![txtSumTotalPriceGF])
    If curSales > 300 Then
        Me![txtSalespersonGF].FontWeight = 700
        Me![txtSumTotalPriceGF].FontWeight = 700
        Me![txtSalespersonGF].FontItalic = False
        Me![txtSumTotalPriceGF].FontItalic = False
    ElseIf curSales < 25 Then
        Me![txtSalespersonGF].FontWeight = 500
        Me![txtSumTotalPriceGF].FontWeight = 500
        Me![txtSalespersonGF].FontItalic = True
        Me![txtSumTotalPriceGF].FontItalic = True
    Else
        Me![txtSalespersonGF].FontWeight = 500
        Me![txtSumTotalPriceGF].FontWeight = 500
        Me![txtSalespersonGF].FontItalic = False
        Me![txtSumTotalPriceGF].FontItalic = False
    End If

ErrorHandlerExit:
    Exit Sub

ErrorHandler:
```

```
        MsgBox "Error No: " & Err.Number & "; Description: " & _
            Err.Description
        Resume ErrorHandlerExit

    End Sub
```

Another type of special formatting uses the row count, rather than the value of a field. If you want to shade alternate rows of a financial report, for example, you can use the following code in the Detail section's Format event procedure:

```
Private Sub Detail1_Format(Cancel As Integer, FormatCount As Integer)

On Error GoTo ErrorHandler

    Const vbLightGrey = 12632256

    If Me.CurrentRecord Mod 2 = 0 Then
        Me.Section(acDetail).BackColor = vbLightGrey
    Else
        Me.Section(acDetail).BackColor = vbWhite
    End If

ErrorHandlerExit:
    Exit Sub

ErrorHandler:
    MsgBox "Error No: " & Err.Number & "; Description: " & _
        Err.Description
    Resume ErrorHandlerExit

End Sub
```

The code uses the Mod operator to determine whether the current record (row) is even or not, and makes even rows gray and odd rows white. The shaded report is shown in Figure 6.30.

When creating a report with alternate line shading, make sure that the textboxes in the Detail section have their BackStyle property set to Transparent so that the gray section back color can show through them.

Placing a Watermark on a Report

To print an image as a report background (sometimes called a *watermark*), select the image for the report's Picture property, using the MS Picture Builder to browse for it. To keep the report readable, the image should be light in tone. Some versions of Office include a Confidential.wmf or Confidential.bmp file you can use as a report watermark, but you don't have to limit yourself to that image: whatever text you want for use as a report watermark can be created using WordArt and Paint. Here is how I made a diagonal "Company Confidential" watermark for use on reports.

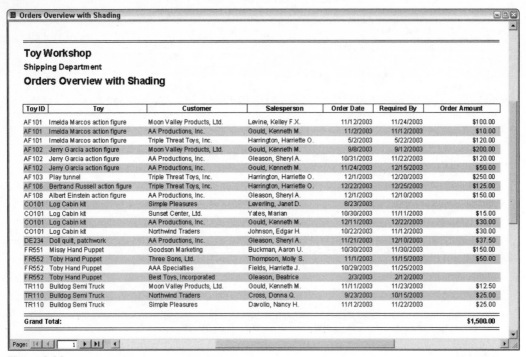

Figure 6.30

1. Open Word.

2. Select Insert | Picture | Word Art.

3. I like the second image down in the left column from the WordArt Gallery (shown in Figure 6.31) for watermarks (of course, you can select any style you prefer).

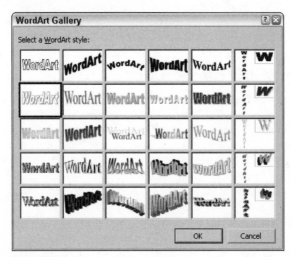

Figure 6.31

4. Enter "Company Confidential" (or other text) as the WordArt text.

5. To make the WordArt image slanted, for diagonal display on the report, select it and click the Format WordArt button on the WordArt toolbar.

6. In the Format WordArt dialog, enter 300 in the Rotation box. Figure 6.32 shows the rotated WordArt, with its properties sheet and the WordArt toolbar.

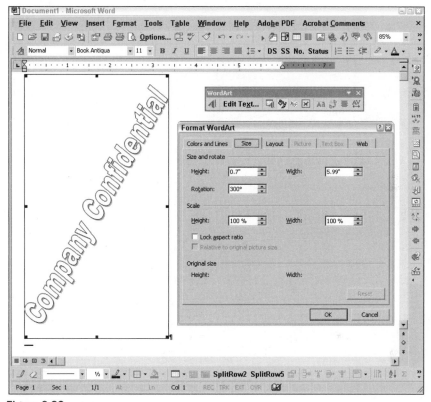

Figure 6.32

7. Press Alt-PrintScreen to capture the WordArt image on the clipboard.

8. Open Paint from the Accessories program group (or another image editing program of your choice), and paste in the image with Ctrl-V.

9. Use the Paint Select tool to outline the WordArt image, as shown in Figure 6.33.

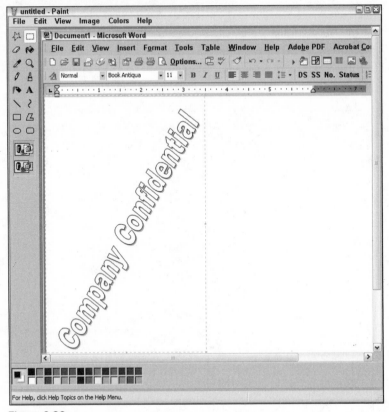

Figure 6.33

10. Save the cropped image as Company Confidential Watermark.bmp.

11. Back in Access, open a report in Design view and set the BackStyle property of all the textboxes and labels (except shaded ones) to Transparent.

12. Select the new Company Confidential Watermark.bmp image for the Picture property of a report. Figure 6.34 shows a version of the Orders grouped report with this watermark.

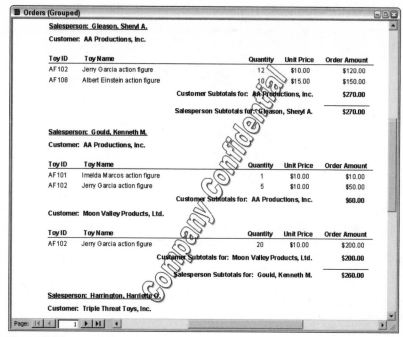

Figure 6.34

Creating a Main Menu with the Menu Manager Add-In

When all of the major forms and reports for the database have been created, you can run my Menu Manager add-in to create a main menu for the database, allowing users to select forms and reports from a combobox on the main menu.

Installation

To install the add-in, copy the Menu Manager add-in's library database (Menu Manager.mda) to your AddIns folder (usually C:\Documents and Settings\Administrator\Application Data\Microsoft\AddIns). Open the Toy Workshop database (or any other database where you want to create a main menu), select Tools | Addins to open the Add-ins menu, and select the Add-In Manager selection. The Add-In Manager dialog opens, as shown in Figure 6.35.

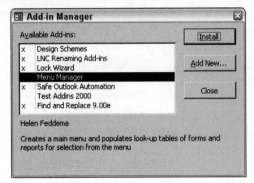

Figure 6.35

There should be a Menu Manager entry; if not (perhaps because it was placed in a nonstandard location), click the Add New button and browse for the file. Once it appears in the list of available add-ins, select it and click Install. A × appears next to the Menu Manager selection to indicate that it is installed. Close the dialog to complete the installation.

The Add-ins menu will now have three new selections: Create Main Menu, Change Menu Picture, and Refresh Lookup Tables, as shown in Figure 6.36.

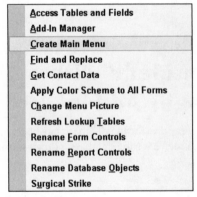

Figure 6.36

Preparation

Before running the Create Main Menu command, there are a few things you should check, to prevent errors. The Menu Manager add-in assumes that the main form in the database (the one used most frequently) has the prefix fpri, so first select the form you want to be the main form, and give it this prefix. I renamed the main Orders form as fpriOrders.

When changing a form name, if there are comboboxes or subforms on the form, check their row or record sources to see if there are references to the form name that also need to be changed. In this case, a reference to frmOrders in cboShipAddressID's row source needed to be changed to fpriOrders.

If you don't make this change, you will get the annoying "Enter Parameter Value" error message, which doesn't tell you where the incorrect or missing parameter is needed. An incorrect reference to a form name in the following places can cause this message:

*   **ORDER BY** *clause on a form or subform*

*   *Combobox or listbox row source*

*   *Query criteria*

*   *Subform data source*

The Menu Manager also needs references to the Data Access Objects (DAO), Scripting Runtime and Word object libraries, so you'll need to check that you have these references, or add them if you don't. To check your references, open a code module and select References from the Tools menu to open the References dialog. Figure 6.37 shows the References dialog for the Toy Workshop database.

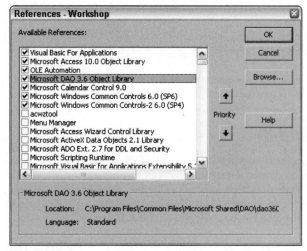

Figure 6.37

The DAO 3.6 Object Library reference is checked, but not the Scripting Runtime and Word 10.0 Object Libraries, so you'll need to scroll down the list of references and check them. Figure 6.38 shows the Scripting Runtime selection checked, and the Word object library selection being checked.

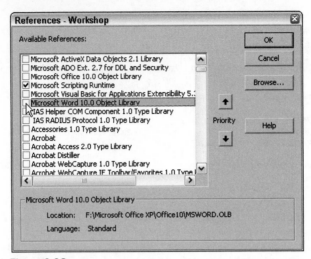

Figure 6.38

The list of available references is alphabetical—sort of. There are two exceptions: the checked references are all at the top of the list, and any references that have previously been checked are listed directly under the checked references, before the A's, to make it easier to locate and check them again.

If you see #Name instead of your primary form name next to the large button on the top left of the menu, this is a sign that you have a missing reference.

Running the Add-in

To create a main menu for an application, select the Create Main Menu selection on the Add-ins menu. After some flickering as various database objects are processed, the Menu Sidebar Picture Picker dialog opens, as shown in Figure 6.39. Here you can enter an application title, and select one of a set of standard sidebar pictures for your application. These pictures use a color palette that works well even on low-resolution monitors, and can be stretched without distortion.

After entering an application title, and selecting an image, click the Apply Picture button to create the main menu. You will get a confirmation message asking if you want to open the main menu now; on clicking Yes, the main menu will open, as shown in Figure 6.40.

After creating a main menu using the add-in, select Tools | Startup from the database window, and select fmnuMain as the Display Form/Page, as shown in Figure 6.41. From now on, when the database is opened, the main menu will automatically open.

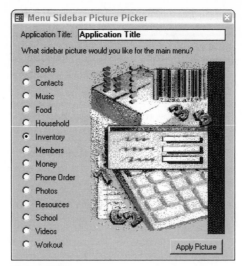

Figure 6.39

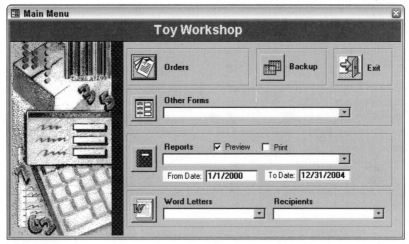

Figure 6.40

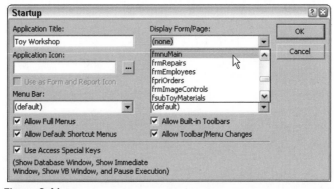

Figure 6.41

Curiously, the forms in the Display Form/Page drop-down list aren't in alphabetical order, so you may have to scroll down a few screens to find fmnuMain.

The main menu has several large command buttons with images, and comboboxes displaying lists of database objects for the user to select, as an alternative to the confusing (and difficult to maintain) array of pop-up menus created by the built-in Access Menu Wizard.

❑ The large Orders button opens the application's primary form (in this case, fpriOrders). The primary form is indicated by the "fpri" tag; its name is saved in tblInfo.

❑ The Backup button offers to create a backup copy of the database, including the date and an incrementing number. The backups are created in a folder called "Backups" under the database folder. This folder will be created if it doesn't already exist.

❑ The Exit button closes the database and exits from Access.

❑ The Other Forms button opens the form selected from its combobox, which lists all forms with a check in the Use checkbox in tlkpForms, excluding the primary form, system forms, and other inappropriate entries, based on their LNC tags. To remove a form from the drop-down list (without removing it from the database), just uncheck the Use checkbox for the form's record in tlkpForms.

❑ The Reports button and combobox work similarly, with the addition of a few extra controls useful for reports, where users can choose to open the report in print preview or just print it, and a set of date textboxes, which can be used to filter a report by a date range. To remove a report from the drop-down list (without removing it from the database), just uncheck the Use checkbox for the report's record in tlkpReports.

❑ The Word Letters and Recipients button and comboboxes let you select a Word template and a recipient for a letter. Automation code on the command button fills custom document properties in the Word letter with name and address data from Access. To test this feature with sample data, select Test Letter in the Word Letters combobox, then select a recipient from Recipients and click the Word command button. To replace these with real templates and data, see Chapter 11, *Working with Word.*

The tlkpForms and tlkpReports lookup tables contain several fields of useful information, other than what is displayed in the drop-down lists. The tlkpForms lookup table is shown in Figure 6.42.

The DisplayName field is filled with form captions. If you forgot to enter a caption for a form or report, the DisplayName field will contain "[No caption]" (see frmRepairs). After entering the form's caption in its properties sheet, you can manually edit the caption in tlkpForms to match (or run the Refresh Lookup Tables command from the Add-ins menu). A portion of the tlkpReports lookup table is shown in Figure 6.43.

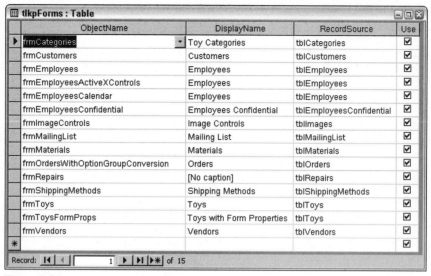

tlkpForms : Table

ObjectName	DisplayName	RecordSource	Use
frmCategories	Toy Categories	tblCategories	☑
frmCustomers	Customers	tblCustomers	☑
frmEmployees	Employees	tblEmployees	☑
frmEmployeesActiveXControls	Employees	tblEmployees	☑
frmEmployeesCalendar	Employees	tblEmployees	☑
frmEmployeesConfidential	Employees Confidential	tblEmployeesConfidential	☑
frmImageControls	Image Controls	tblImages	☑
frmMailingList	Mailing List	tblMailingList	☑
frmMaterials	Materials	tblMaterials	☑
frmOrdersWithOptionGroupConversion	Orders	tblOrders	☑
frmRepairs	[No caption]	tblRepairs	☑
frmShippingMethods	Shipping Methods	tblShippingMethods	☑
frmToys	Toys	tblToys	☑
frmToysFormProps	Toys with Form Properties	tblToys	☑
frmVendors	Vendors	tblVendors	☑
*			☑

Record: 1 of 15

Figure 6.42

tlkpReports : Table

ObjectName	DisplayName	RecordSource	Width	Use
rptEmployeeAddressBook	Employee Address Book	qryEmployees	2.75	☑
rptEmployees5160Labels	Employees #5160 Labels	qryEmployees	2.3375	☑
rptEmployees5161Labels	Employees #5161 Labels	qryEmployees	3.65	☑
rptOrdersAutoReportTabular	tblOrders	tblOrders	9	☑
rptOrdersAutoReportWizard	tblOrders	tblOrders	3.21458333333	☑
rptOrdersColumnarWizard	qryOrders	qryOrders	6.5	☑
rptOrdersGrouped	Orders (Grouped)	qryOrders	6.5	☑
rptOrdersGroupedConfidential	Orders (Grouped)	qryOrders	6.5	☑
rptOrdersGroupedV1	Orders (Grouped)	qryOrders	6.5	☑
rptOrdersGroupedV2	Orders (Grouped)	qryOrders	6.5	☑
rptOrdersGroupedV3	Orders (Grouped)	qryOrders	6.5	☑
rptOrdersGroupedV4	Orders (Grouped)	qryOrders	6.5	☑
rptOrdersGroupedWithPivotChart	Orders (Grouped)	qryOrders	6.5	☑
rptOrdersGroupedWizard	tblOrders	tblOrders	21.8333333333	☑
rptOrdersTabular	Orders Overview	qryOrdersFull	9.51041666667	☑
rptOrdersTabularShading	Orders Overview with Shading	qryOrdersFull	9.51041666667	☑
rptRelationships	Relationships for Toy Workshop		9.91666666667	☑
rptSales	Sales Report	qryOrders	6.5	☑
rptSingleOrder	Single Order	qrySelectedOrder	6.5	☑

Record: 23 of 25

Figure 6.43

The DisplayName field is what shows in the drop-down list; it is picked up from the report's caption. The RecordSource field lists the report's record source, and the Width field gives the report's width, which is used to create a LTR or LGL prefix to indicate whether reports use letter- or legal-sized paper. If you only use letter-sized paper, and don't need the prefix, you can replace the calculated expression listed below

```
Description: IIf([Width]>11.25,"LGL: " & [DisplayName],"LTR: " & [DisplayName])
```

with the DisplayName field in the cboReports combobox's row source.

The RecordSource property is used to determine whether or not a report has any records, before attempting to open it. This feature will only work with table or query record sources, so if you frequently use SQL statement record sources for reports, and you don't want to convert them to saved queries, you can comment out (or delete) the lines of code that check the record source before opening the report.

The Use field is checked when you want the form or report to appear in the drop-down list on the menu; uncheck it to hide the form or report, for example for a form that is only opened from another form. You'll probably want to uncheck any report templates (they start with the tag rtmp). I unchecked the Use checkbox for the report templates in the Toy Workshop database.

You can change the menu picture at any time by running the Change Menu Picture command from the Add-ins menu; it opens the Picture Picker dialog again. After creating new forms and reports, you can either add them to the lookup tables manually, using a drop-down list on the Object Name field in Datasheet view and entering the other information manually (OK for just a few changes), or you can run the Refresh Lookup Tables command to rerun the functions that fill the lookup tables with form and report names and other information.

The main menu is bound to a table called tblInfo, which stores selections for future use. This technique allows you to preserve your selections for a form, report, Word template, and/or date range from one application session to another. The table can also be used to store other miscellaneous information you need to use in the database (as a more stable alternative to global variables, or to preserve information indefinitely). I use extra fields in tblInfo to store information for creating faxes in Chapter 14, *Working Outside of Office*.

Summary

Now that all the main database objects (forms, queries, and reports) have been created, you can write VBA code to add more functionality. The next chapter discusses the creation of both code behind forms and code modules.

7

Writing VBA Code in Modules

There were some code samples in previous chapters, mostly event procedures for various form and control events. In this chapter, I'll explain the Visual Basic window's components and discuss the use of procedures in code behind forms (CBF) and standard modules, and present some more advanced code samples.

When you open a module (or click the New button when the Modules object is selected in the Object Bar), a new window opens: the *Visual Basic Window*. If you have worked with VBA code in Word, Excel, or another application, this window will be familiar, though there are a few differences in Access. Figure 7.1 shows the Visual Basic window; I'll describe its main components briefly.

The Project Explorer

On the upper left of the Visual Basic window, the *Project Explorer* lists the modules in the current database (and possibly modules in add-in libraries). The current database's modules are divided into three categories, in separate folders. Figure 7.2 shows the Project Explorer with the top folder closed, so you can see all three folders.

The *Microsoft Access Class Objects* folder contains code behind forms (and code behind reports). You'll see an entry for each form or report that has a code module. Figure 7.3 shows a selection of form and report modules.

If you have created UserForms for a Word template, you will recognize the *UserForm* selection on the Insert Module selector. You can create a UserForm in Access and place controls on it—but there's no point in doing this, because there's no way to run UserForms in Access, and in any case, Access has its own forms, with more functionality than UserForms (most notably, Access forms can be bound to data).

The *Modules* folder contains standard modules, and the *Class Modules* folder contains class modules.

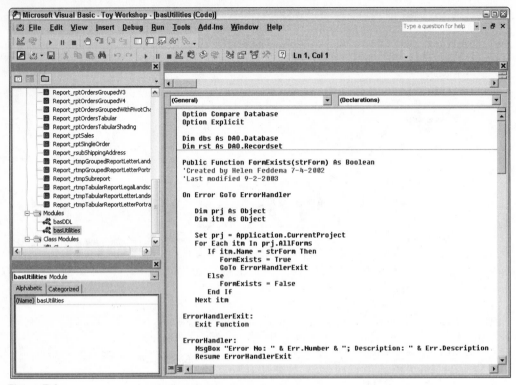

Figure 7.1

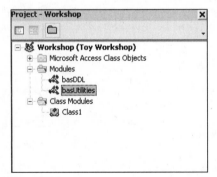

Figure 7.2

The Properties Sheet

The *Properties Sheet* in the lower left of the Visual Basic window displays the properties for the selected module—in Access, there is just one property to work with, the module name. New modules are called Module*n* (for standard modules) or Class*n* (for class modules). I suggest renaming standard modules with the LNC tag *bas*, with a meaningful base name. For class modules, on the other hand, just use a meaningful base name, since the module name is the name of the custom object that will be referenced in code.

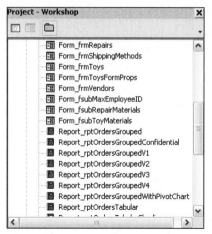

Figure 7.3

The Immediate Window

The *Immediate Window* (AKA the Debug Window) displays the results of Debug.Print statements, which you can insert in your code for debugging purposes. Debug.Print statements are especially useful for displaying the value of variables, filter strings, or SQL statements constructed in code, so you can see what's wrong if they don't work as expected. You can also test functions by typing them directly into the Immediate window, preceded by a question mark. Figure 7.4 shows several Debug.Print statements (from the AfterUpdate event of the Shipping Address selector combobox on fpriOrders) and two tests of the Mid function with a phone number.

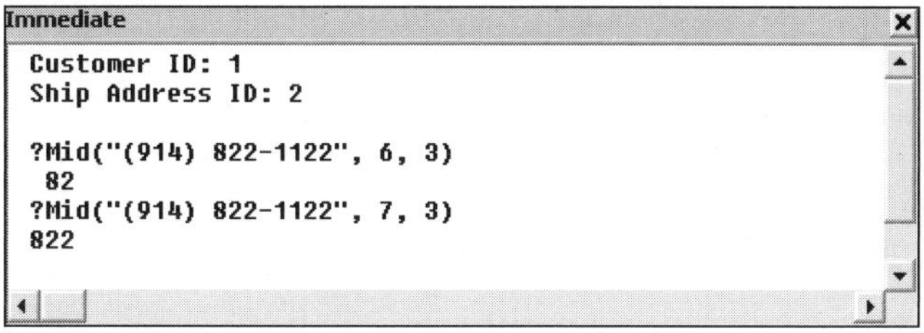

```
Customer ID: 1
Ship Address ID: 2

?Mid("(914) 822-1122", 6, 3)
 82
?Mid("(914) 822-1122", 7, 3)
822
```

Figure 7.4

The Module Pane

The *Module Pane* displays the contents of the module selected in the Project Explorer. You can see a portion of the basUtilities module's contents displayed in the Module pane in Figure 7.4. You create and edit VBA code in the module pane. You can open a module directly in the Visual Basic window, by double-clicking it in the Project Explorer. Alternately (in the case of form and report modules), you can open a form or report module by clicking the Code button on the Form Design toolbar, as shown in Figure 7.5.

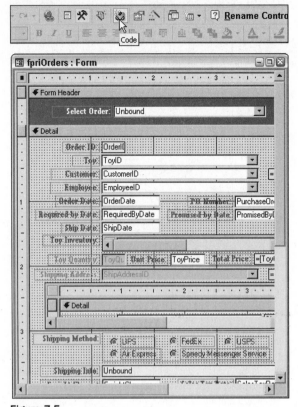

Figure 7.5

The Module pane has two unlabeled drop-down lists at the top: the *Object* selector on the left and the *Procedure* selector on the right. For code behind forms modules, the Object selector lets you select a form section or control, and the Procedure selector lets you select an event procedure for the selected object. For standard modules, the Object selector has only one choice, (General), and the Procedure selector lets you select either the Declarations section, or a procedure in the module.

Getting Help

For more details on working in the Visual Basic window, open the Visual Basic User Interface Help book from Microsoft Visual Basic Help, and select a topic. Figure 7.6 shows the Help topic for the Debug toolbar.

When using Visual Basic window Help, bear in mind that it is generic in nature, not customized for the Access Visual Basic window. For example, you'll find UserForm topics, although UserForms aren't functional in Access.

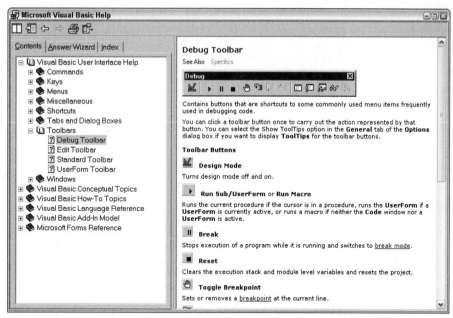

Figure 7.6

Module Types

Access has three types of modules: Code behind Forms, Standard, and Class modules. A *Code behind Forms* module contains declarations, event procedures, and possibly other procedures that relate to a specific form (or report). A *Standard* module contains declarations and procedures that can be used throughout an application. And *Class* modules are used to define custom objects you can work with in code.

Statements for Use in Modules

Modules contain declarations of variables (and sometimes constants), and Sub and function procedures that can be used anywhere in a database (for standard modules) or in a specific form or report (for Code behind Forms modules). Functions yield a return value, and Sub procedures don't—at least theoretically. The idea is that you should use a Sub when you want to do something, and a function when you need a return value to work with elsewhere in your code. However, the lines are sometimes blurred in Access. For example, if you need to run a procedure from a macro, it has to be a function because only functions are selectable for the RunCode macro action. This means that if you need to run a Sub from a macro action (say, the AutoExec macro that runs when a database is opened), you need to convert it into a function, with a throwaway return value.

Statements are used in all types of modules to process data in a systematic way, using logical structures to control data flow. The following sections describe the most useful statements.

Call

The *Call* statement is used to run a Sub procedure, with the following syntax:

```
Call NewEmployeeID
```

You can omit the word "Call" and the line of code will still run, but in the interests of clarity I recommend leaving it in so that you know that a procedure is being called.

Do While . . . Loop

The *Do While . . . Loop* logical structure runs a code segment repeatedly so long as a condition is met. The function that follows (from the basUtilities module in the Outlook Data Exchange database for Chapter 12, *Working with Outlook*) strips nonalphanumeric characters from a text string, using a Do While . . . Loop structure to process the characters in the string one by one.

```
Public Function StripChars(strText As String) As String

On Error GoTo ErrorHandler

    Dim strTestString As String
    Dim strTestChar As String
    Dim lngFound As Long
    Dim i As Integer
    Dim strStripChars As String

    strStripChars = " ()-"
    strTestString = strText

    i = 1
    Do While i <= Len(strTestString)
      'Find a strippable character
      strTestChar = Mid$(strTestString, i, 1)
      lngFound = InStr(strStripChars, strTestChar)
      If lngFound > 0 Then
        strTestString = Left(strTestString, i - 1) & Mid(strTestString, i + 1)
      Else
        i = i + 1
      End If
    Loop

    StripChars = strTestString

ErrorHandlerExit:
    Exit Function

ErrorHandler:
    MsgBox "Error No: " & Err.Number & "; Description: " & _
```

```
        Err.Description
    Resume ErrorHandlerExit

End Function
```

Do Until . . . Loop

The *Do Until . . . Loop* logical structure runs a code segment repeatedly until a condition is met. The code segment below processes all records in a recordset based on an Access table, adding text to nodes of a treeview control. The code is from the tvwBooks_Fill function from frmTreeViewBookNotes in the EBook Companion sample database for Chapter 9, *Reworking an Existing Application*.

```
Do Until rst.EOF
    Debug.Print "Adding Level 1 item: " & rst![AuthorID]
    strNode1Text = StrConv("Level1 - " & rst![AuthorID], _
        vbLowerCase)
    Debug.Print "Node 1 text: " & strNode1Text
    strVisibleText1 = rst![LastNameFirst]
    Debug.Print "Level 1 visible text: " & strVisibleText1
    Set nod = .Nodes.Add(Key:=strNode1Text, _
        Text:=strVisibleText1)
    nod.Expanded = True
    rst.MoveNext
Loop
rst.Close
```

For . . . Next

The *For . . . Next* statement repeats processing for a specified number of times. Before the For Each . . . Next statement was added to Access VBA, you had to use the For . . . Next statement to process members of collections, but now it is rarely used. One example of the use of For . . . Next comes from the cmdSelectAll command button on the frmExportToWordDatasheet form in the Word Data Exchange sample database for Chapter 11, *Working with Word*. You need to use For . . . Next in this case because the rows in a listbox aren't a collection.

```
Private Sub cmdSelectAll_Click()

On Error GoTo ErrorHandler

    'Select all rows in listbox
    Set lst = Me![lstSelectMultiple]
    intRows = lst.ListCount - 1

    For intIndex = 0 To intRows
        lst.Selected(intIndex) = True
    Next intIndex

ErrorHandlerExit:
    Exit Sub

ErrorHandler:
```

```
      MsgBox "Error No: " & Err.Number & "; Description: " & _
         Err.Description
      Resume ErrorHandlerExit

   End Sub
```

For Each . . . Next

The *For Each . . . Next* statement is a variant of the For . . . Next statement, which processes all the members of a collection without having to know how many there are. The following code segment (from the FormExists function in basUtilities) uses a For Each . . . Next statement to process the items in the AllForms collection of the current project.

```
   On Error GoTo ErrorHandler

      Dim prj As Object
      Dim itm As Object

      Set prj = Application.CurrentProject
      For Each itm In prj.AllForms
         If itm.Name = strForm Then
            FormExists = True
            GoTo ErrorHandlerExit
         Else
            FormExists = False
         End If
      Next itm

   ErrorHandlerExit:
      Exit Function

   ErrorHandler:
      MsgBox "Error No: " & Err.Number & "; Description: " & Err.Description
      Resume ErrorHandlerExit

   End Function
```

GoTo

The *GoTo* statement goes to a specific label in a procedure. The `On Error GoTo ErrorHandler` line that is used in my standard error handler goes to the ErrorHandler label when an error occurs.

If . . . Then . . . Else

An *If . . . Then . . . Else* statement lets you run one code segment if a condition is met and another code segment if the condition isn't met. Optionally, you can add one or more *ElseIf* statements to an If . . . Then . . . Else statement to run a second (or further) code segment if the first condition isn't met.

The command button event procedure listed below (from the standard main menu form created by my Menu Manager add-in, described in Chapter 6, *Printing Data with Reports*) has several nested If . . . Then . . . Else statements, one with an ElseIf clause:

```
Private Sub cmdReports_Click()

On Error GoTo ErrorHandler

    Dim strReportName As String
    Dim strRecordSource As String

    If Nz(Me![cboReports]) <> "" Then
        strReportName = Me![cboReports]
        strRecordSource = Me![cboReports].Column(2)
        If Nz(DCount("*", strRecordSource)) > 0 Then
            If Me![fraReportMode] = 1 Then
                    DoCmd.OpenReport ReportName:=strReportName, view:=acPreview
             ElseIf Me![fraReportMode] = 2 Then
                DoCmd.OpenReport ReportName:=strReportName, view:=acNormal
            End If
        Else
            MsgBox "No records for this report"
            GoTo ErrorHandlerExit
        End If
    Else
        Me![cboReports].SetFocus
        Me![cboReports].Dropdown
    End If

ErrorHandlerExit:
    Exit Sub

ErrorHandler:
    MsgBox "Error No: " & Err.Number & "; Description: " & _
        Err.Description
    Resume ErrorHandlerExit

End Sub
```

Select Case . . . End Select

The *Select Case . . . End Select* statement lets you respond to any number of different values of a field or control (or other alternatives) and (unlike the Switch function) doesn't require that the responses are all of the same data type. Typically, in a line of code before the Select Case . . . End Select statement, a variable is set to a value picked up from a control on a form (or a field), and then a case is set up for each expected value of the field or control, possibly with a Case Else to handle other possibilities.

You can set a variable for each case, call procedures from the cases, or run code of various types. The Select Case statement that follows (from the fraFilter_AfterUpdate event procedure on the Dynamic Contact Search form in the sample Toy Workshop database, described in more detail in the "Sort and Filter Forms" section later in this chapter) responds to the user's choice of a filter type in an option group. Depending on the choice, some controls on the form are enabled, others are disabled, and various other properties are set as needed.

```
Select Case intFilter

    Case 1
    'Unfiltered
    Me![cboCity].Enabled = False
    Me![cboCity].ControlSource = ""
    Me![cboCountry].Enabled = False
    Me![cboCountry].ControlSource = ""
    Me![cboCompany].Enabled = False
    Me![cboCompany].ControlSource = ""
    Me![cboLastMeetingDate].Enabled = False
    Me![cboLastMeetingDate].ControlSource = ""
    Me![cboSalary].Enabled = False
    Me![cboSalary].ControlSource = ""
    Me![cmdContacts].Caption = "Open Unfiltered Contacts Form"
    Me![txtFilter].Visible = False
    Me![subSearchResults].Form.RecordSource = "qryContacts"

    Case 2
    'Filter by City
    Me![cboCity].Enabled = True
    Me![cboCity].ControlSource = "FilterValue"
    Me![cboCity].SetFocus
    Me![cboCity].Dropdown
    Me![cboCountry].Enabled = False
    Me![cboCountry].ControlSource = ""
    Me![cboCompany].Enabled = False
    Me![cboCompany].ControlSource = ""
    Me![cboLastMeetingDate].Enabled = False
    Me![cboLastMeetingDate].ControlSource = ""
    Me![cboSalary].Enabled = False
    Me![cboSalary].ControlSource = ""
    Me![cmdContacts].Caption = "Open Filtered Contacts Form"
    Me![txtFilter].Visible = True

    Case 3
    'Filter by Country
    Me![cboCity].Enabled = False
    Me![cboCity].ControlSource = ""
    Me![cboCountry].Enabled = True
    Me![cboCountry].ControlSource = "FilterValue"
    Me![cboCountry].SetFocus
    Me![cboCountry].Dropdown
    Me![cboCompany].Enabled = False
    Me![cboCompany].ControlSource = ""
    Me![cboLastMeetingDate].Enabled = False
    Me![cboLastMeetingDate].ControlSource = ""
    Me![cboSalary].Enabled = False
    Me![cboSalary].ControlSource = ""
    Me![cmdContacts].Caption = "Open Filtered Contacts Form"
    Me![txtFilter].Visible = True

    Case 4
```

```
        'Filter by Company Name
        Me![cboCity].Enabled = False
        Me![cboCity].ControlSource = ""
        Me![cboCountry].Enabled = False
        Me![cboCountry].ControlSource = ""
        Me![cboCompany].Enabled = True
        Me![cboCompany].ControlSource = "FilterValue"
        Me![cboCompany].SetFocus
        Me![cboCompany].Dropdown
        Me![cboLastMeetingDate].Enabled = False
        Me![cboLastMeetingDate].ControlSource = ""
        Me![cboSalary].Enabled = False
        Me![cboSalary].ControlSource = ""
        Me![cmdContacts].Caption = "Open Filtered Contacts Form"
        Me![txtFilter].Visible = True

    Case 5
        'Filter by Last Meeting Date
        Me![cboCity].Enabled = False
        Me![cboCity].ControlSource = ""
        Me![cboCountry].Enabled = False
        Me![cboCountry].ControlSource = ""
        Me![cboCompany].Enabled = False
        Me![cboCompany].ControlSource = ""
        Me![cboLastMeetingDate].Enabled = True
        Me![cboLastMeetingDate].ControlSource = "FilterValue"
        Me![cboLastMeetingDate].SetFocus
        Me![cboLastMeetingDate].Dropdown
        Me![cboSalary].Enabled = False
        Me![cboSalary].ControlSource = ""
        Me![cmdContacts].Caption = "Open Filtered Contacts Form"
        Me![txtFilter].Visible = True

    Case 6
        'Filter by Salary
        Me![cboCity].Enabled = False
        Me![cboCity].ControlSource = ""
        Me![cboCountry].Enabled = False
        Me![cboCountry].ControlSource = ""
        Me![cboCompany].Enabled = False
        Me![cboCompany].ControlSource = ""
        Me![cboLastMeetingDate].Enabled = False
        Me![cboLastMeetingDate].ControlSource = ""
        Me![cboSalary].Enabled = True
        Me![cboSalary].ControlSource = "FilterValue"
        Me![cboSalary].SetFocus
        Me![cboSalary].Dropdown
        Me![cmdContacts].Caption = "Open Filtered Contacts Form"
        Me![txtFilter].Visible = True

End Select
```

With . . . End With

A *With . . . End With* statement lets you work with a variety of properties and methods of an object, without repeating its name. The code segment listed below is from the cmdImportDatafromWordTable_Click event procedure from the Word Data Exchange database for Chapter 11, *Working with Word*. It first sets an appWord variable to reference the Word instance, and then uses a With . . . End With statement to work with the Word Selection object.

```
Set doc = appWord.Documents.Add(strDocName)
appWord.Visible = True
doc.Activate
With appWord.Selection
   .GoTo What:=wdGoToTable, Which:=wdGoToFirst, Count:=1, Name:=""
   lngStartRows = .Information(wdMaximumNumberOfRows)
   Debug.Print "Total table rows: " & lngStartRows
   .MoveDown Unit:=wdLine, Count:=1
   .MoveRight Unit:=wdCell
   .MoveLeft Unit:=wdCell
End With
```

Standard Module Code Samples

Almost all applications need some standard code that can be used throughout the application. My Menu Manager add-in includes a basUtilities module with some standard procedures, and you can add your own as needed (each of the sample databases has different extra procedures in basUtilities, depending on its needs). Some of these standard module procedures are described in the following sections.

Using Data in tblInfo

I use fields in tblInfo (the table to which the main menu is bound) to store miscellaneous information I need to use in a database. To retrieve information from this table or store a new value in a field, I use functions like the following so that I can set the value of a variable with the GetDocsDir function in VBA code, retrieving the value from tblInfo. The GetDocsDir function (from basWordAutomation in the Word Data Exchange sample database) picks up the value of the DocsPath field from tblInfo, falling back on the default path C:\My Documents if the field is empty. Finally, the subfolder Access Merge\ is appended to the documents path to get the folder for creating merge documents.

```
Public Function GetDocsDir() As String

On Error GoTo ErrorHandler

   Set dbs = CurrentDb
   Set rst = dbs.OpenRecordset("tblInfo", dbOpenDynaset)

   With rst
      .MoveFirst
      strDocsDir = Nz(![DocsPath])
      If strDocsDir = "" Then
         GetDocsDir = "C:\My Documents\"
      Else
```

```
            GetDocsDir = ![DocsPath]
        End If
    End With

    GetDocsDir = GetDocsDir & "Access Merge\"

ErrorHandlerExit:
    Exit Function

ErrorHandler:
    MsgBox "Error No: " & Err.Number & "; Description: " & _
        Err.Description
    Resume ErrorHandlerExit

End Function
```

The syntax for using this function in a procedure is:

```
strDocsDir = GetDocsDir
```

To save a value to tblInfo from code (this would be required if the value can't be picked up from a control on a form bound to tblInfo), a procedure like the following will do the job (also from basWordAutomation in the Word Data Exchange sample database).

```
Public Sub SaveDocsDir(strDocsDir)

On Error GoTo ErrorHandler

    Set dbs = CurrentDb
    Set rst = dbs.OpenRecordset("tblInfo", dbOpenDynaset)

    With rst
        .MoveFirst
        .Edit
        ![DocsPath] = strDocsDir
        .Update
        .Close
    End With

ErrorHandlerExit:
    Exit Sub

ErrorHandler:
    MsgBox "Error No: " & Err.Number & "; Description: " & _
        Err.Description
    Resume ErrorHandlerExit

End Sub
```

The Sub procedure can be called with a line like one of the following (depending on whether you need to hard-code the path or pick it up from a control on a form):

```
Call SaveDocsDir("C:\My Documents")

Call SaveDocsDir(Nz(Me![txtDocsDir].Value))
```

Date Range Code on Main Menu

The standard main menu created by my Menu Manager add-in has two textboxes that can be used to create a date range for filtering reports. The basUtilities standard module (also created by Menu Manager) has two functions that retrieve the dates from these textboxes, each with a fallback date in case the textbox is blank.

```
Public Function ToDate() As Date

On Error GoTo ErrorHandler

    'Pick up To date from Info table
    Set dbs = CurrentDb
    Set rst = dbs.OpenRecordset("tblInfo", dbOpenTable)
    With rst
       .MoveFirst
       ToDate = Nz(![ToDate], "12/31/2004")
       .Close
    End With

ErrorHandlerExit:
    Exit Function

ErrorHandler:
    MsgBox "Error No: " & Err.Number & "; Description: " & _
       Err.Description
    Resume ErrorHandlerExit

End Function

Public Function FromDate() As Date

On Error GoTo ErrorHandler

    'Pick up from date from Info table
    Set dbs = CurrentDb
    Set rst = dbs.OpenRecordset("tblInfo", dbOpenTable)
    With rst
       .MoveFirst
       FromDate = Nz(![FromDate], "1/1/2003")
       .Close
    End With

ErrorHandlerExit:
    Exit Function

ErrorHandler:
    MsgBox "Error No: " & Err.Number & "; Description: " & _
       Err.Description
    Resume ErrorHandlerExit

End Function
```

Instead of a hard-coded fallback date, you could use the DateAdd function to create fallback From and To dates. The following expressions yield dates from one year before the present to the present date:

```
FromDate = Nz(![ToDate], DateAdd("yyyy", -1, Date))

ToDate = Nz(![FromDate], Date)
```

If dates have been entered into the textboxes, the FromDate and ToDate functions are set to the specified dates; otherwise, default dates of 1/1/2003 and 12/31/2004 are used. A textbox in the standard report template header displays the FromDate and ToDate values, and they are used as a criterion for filtering the report's record source. Figure 7.7 shows the main menu, with dates, and a filtered report, and Figure 7.8 shows the report's record source, with a criteria expression using FromDate and ToDate.

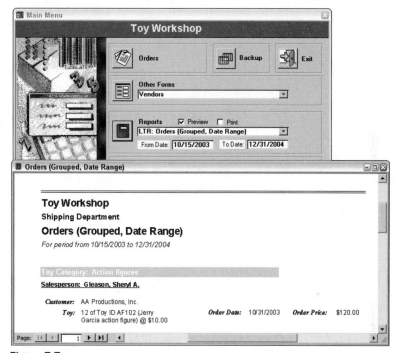

Figure 7.7

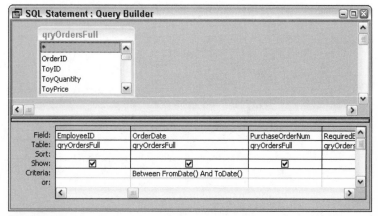

Figure 7.8

Code Behind Forms Code Samples

I have discussed creating event procedures for forms and form controls in preceding chapters; here, I'll give some examples of standard event procedures and some event procedures for special purposes.

The AfterUpdate event procedure listed below puts different text into a locked textbox control on the fpriOrders form in the sample Toy Workshop database, depending on which option the user selects in the `Shipping Method` option group:

```
Private Sub fraShippingMethodID_AfterUpdate()

On Error GoTo ErrorHandler

    Dim intShip As Integer
    Dim strShipInfo As String

    intShip = Nz(Me![fraShippingMethodID].Value)

    Select Case intShip

        Case 1
            'UPS
            strShipInfo = "UPS pickup at 3 PM"

        Case 2
            'FedEx
            strShipInfo = "Put in FedEx box on corner of 4th and Main St."

        Case 3
            'USPS
            strShipInfo = "U.S. Mail pickups at 10 AM and 4 PM"

        Case 4
            'Air Express
            strShipInfo = "Call Air Express for pickup at 555-111-2222"

        Case 5
            'Speedy Messenger Service
            strShipInfo = "Call Extension 45 for Speedy pickup"

        Case Else
            'No selection made
            strShipInfo = "No shipping selection made"

    End Select

    Me![txtShippingInfo].Value = strShipInfo

ErrorHandlerExit:
    Exit Sub

ErrorHandler:
```

```
      MsgBox "Error No: " & Err.Number & "; Description: " & _
          Err.Description
      Resume ErrorHandlerExit

End Sub
```

For the Select Case statement to work on a new record, you have two alternatives: (1) Don't assign a default value to the Shipping Method option group, so the user will always need to select a value, or (2) assign the default text for the default method to the txtShippingInfo textbox from the form's BeforeInsert event.

Figure 7.9 shows the fpriOrders form in the sample Toy Workshop (Modules Finish) database after selecting UPS as the shipping method.

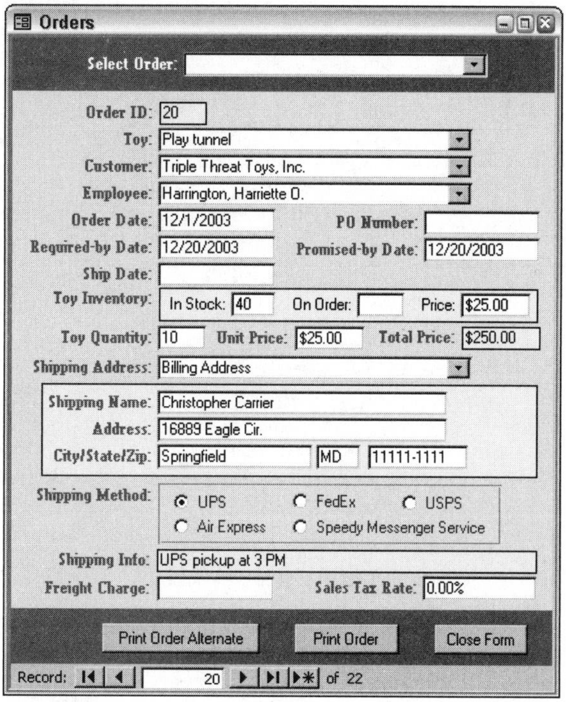

Figure 7.9

Setting the value of the txtShippingInfo textbox from the option group's AfterUpdate event is fine if you only need to see the message when an option is selected for a new order, or changed for an existing order. However, if you always want to see the appropriate message when navigating from record to record, it's best to move the code from the event procedure to a Sub procedure that can be called from the option group's AfterUpdate event procedure and the form's Current event procedure, using the syntax

```
Call ShippingMethod
```

The option group event procedure is now:

```
Private Sub fraShippingMethodID_AfterUpdate()

    Call ShippingInfo

End Sub
```

This procedure doesn't need an error handler, because the ShippingInfo Sub has its own error handler. The new Sub procedure contains exactly the same code as the original fraShippingMethodID_AfterUpdate event procedure.

There is one final modification that might be needed in some cases, such as when you need to respond to identical option groups on several different forms. While you could create the same Sub procedure in each form's module, it is more efficient to place the Sub procedure in a standard module and make it public instead of private. In this case, you need to make a change in the procedure, replacing the Me keyword that references the form (this keyword will only work in a code behind forms module) with an Access form argument that is set with the Me keyword when the procedure is called. The public Sub procedure is listed below:

```
Public Sub ShippingInfo(frm As Access.Form)

On Error GoTo ErrorHandler

    Dim intShip As Integer
    Dim strShipInfo As String

    intShip = Nz(frm![fraShippingMethodID].Value)

    Select Case intShip

        Case 1
            'UPS
            strShipInfo = "UPS pickup at 3 PM"

        Case 2
            'FedEx
            strShipInfo = "Put in FedEx box on corner of 4th and Main St."

        Case 3
            'USPS
            strShipInfo = "U.S. Mail pickups at 10 AM and 4 PM"

        Case 4
            'Air Express
            strShipInfo = "Call Air Express for pickup at 555-111-2222"

        Case 5
            'Speedy Messenger Service
            strShipInfo = "Call Extension 45 for Speedy pickup"

        Case Else
            'No selection made
```

```
            strShipInfo = "No shipping selection made"

    End Select

    frm![txtShippingInfo].Value = strShipInfo

ErrorHandlerExit:
    Exit Sub

ErrorHandler:
    MsgBox "Error No: " & Err.Number & "; Description: " & _
        Err.Description
    Resume ErrorHandlerExit

End Sub
```

and this is the modified option group event procedure:

```
Private Sub fraShippingMethodID_AfterUpdate()

    Call ShippingInfo(Me)

End Sub
```

The same Call line is needed in the Form_Current event procedure, so that you will see the correct message when navigating from record to record on the form.

New Thing Form

When adding a new record to a table, it may not be a good idea to let users add records on the same form used to edit existing records. It is far too easy to create a record missing crucial data because Access saves a record when (for example) you move the focus to a subform, and it's not easy to put error trapping on all the possible events where a save may occur.

Instead, it is sometimes advisable to use a special *New Thing* form to accept the data, and only create a new table record if there is valid data in all fields that must be filled in for a valid record. For example, to add records to tblEmployees, you can use frmNewEmployee, and keep frmEmployees for editing existing records in that table. A New Thing form can be implemented in several ways, ranging from the most complex to the simplest:

❑   Create a Class module and all the required code to create a custom object corresponding to the table, and check the properties of the object; if the properties corresponding to required fields have valid values, copy them to a new record in the table. In my opinion, this is overkill just to save a new record in a more secure manner.

❑   Bind the New Thing form to a temp table that has the same fields as the regular table, with the exception of an AutoNumber field (if there is one). After the new record has been validated, append the record from the temp table to the regular table. This method can be useful, especially if you want to be able to work with the data on the New Thing form before appending it to the main table (for example, to print a report with the new record's data).

❑   On an unbound form, check the values of required fields directly from the values in controls on the form, and add a new record to the table only if all required fields have valid values. This is relatively easy to implement; I'll give details for this method below.

To create a New Thing form for adding new employees to tblEmployees in the sample Toy Workshop database (Modules Start), first make a copy of frmEmployees and name it frmNewEmployee. You will need to make several changes to both frmEmployees and frmNewEmployee, as listed below.

frmEmployees Changes

❑   Set the form's AllowAdditions property to No.

❑   Delete the subMaxEmployeeID subform.

❑   Remove the Form_BeforeInsert and NewEmployeeID procedures from the form's code module.

❑   Add a New Employee button to the footer of frmEmployees to open frmNew Employee.

frmNewEmployee Changes

❑   Delete the form's record source (this makes it an unbound form).

❑   Set the form's Data Entry property to Yes.

❑   Remove the record selector combobox from the form header (it's not needed for creating a new form), and shrink the header to nothing.

❑   Delete the control source of each bound control on the form (but leave the row sources of comboboxes).

❑   Set the form's caption to "New Employee."

❑   Rename the original Close Form button to Cancel and Close, and add another button with the caption "Save and Close." The Cancel and Close button just closes the form, without creating a new Employee record (the code returns to frmEmployees rather than to the main menu). The Save and Close button does the checking of required fields and either informs the user about missing information in a field or appends a new record to tblEmployees. The cmdClose and cmdSave Click event procedures are listed below.

```
Private Sub cmdClose_Click()

On Error GoTo ErrorHandler


    Set prj = Application.CurrentProject

    If prj.AllForms("frmEmployees").IsLoaded Then
        Forms![frmEmployees].Visible = True
    Else
        DoCmd.OpenForm "frmEmployees"
    End If

ErrorHandlerExit:
    DoCmd.Close acForm, Me.Name
```

```
        Exit Sub

ErrorHandler:
    If Err.Number = 2467 Then
        Resume ErrorHandlerExit
    Else
        MsgBox "Error No: " & Err.Number & "; Description: " & Err.Description
        Resume ErrorHandlerExit
    End If

End Sub

Private Sub cmdSave_Click()

On Error GoTo ErrorHandler

    Dim dbs As DAO.Database
    Dim rst As DAO.Recordset
    Dim strPrompt As String
    Dim strTitle As String

    'Check values of variables and exit if required data is missing
    strTitle = "Missing data"
    If Nz(Me![txtFirstName].Value) = "" Then
        strPrompt = "First name missing; can't add new employee record"
        MsgBox strPrompt, vbOKOnly, strTitle
        GoTo ErrorHandlerExit
    ElseIf Nz(Me![txtLastName].Value) = "" Then
        strPrompt = "Last name missing; can't add new employee record"
        MsgBox strPrompt, vbOKOnly, strTitle
        GoTo ErrorHandlerExit
    ElseIf Nz(Me![txtTitle].Value) = "" Then
        strPrompt = "Title missing; can't add new employee record"
        MsgBox strPrompt, vbOKOnly, strTitle
        GoTo ErrorHandlerExit
    ElseIf Nz(Me![txtDateHired].Value, #1/1/1980#) = #1/1/1980# Then
        strPrompt = "Date hired missing; can't add new employee record"
        MsgBox strPrompt, vbOKOnly, strTitle
        GoTo ErrorHandlerExit
    End If

    'All required fields have data; add new records to tblEmployees
    'and tblEmployeesConfidential
    Set dbs = CurrentDb
    Set rst = dbs.OpenRecordset("tblEmployees")
    rst.AddNew
    rst![EmployeeID] = mstrEmployeeID
    rst![DepartmentName] = Nz(Me![cboDepartmentName].Value)
    rst![FirstName] = Me![txtFirstName].Value
    rst![MiddleName] = Nz(Me![txtMiddleName].Value)
    rst![LastName] = Me![txtLastName].Value
    rst![Title] = Me![txtTitle].Value
    rst![EmailName] = Nz(Me![txtEmailName].Value)
    rst![Extension] = (Me![txtExtension].Value)
```

```
    rst![Address] = Nz(Me![txtAddress].Value)
    rst![City] = Nz(Me![txtCity].Value)
    rst![StateOrProvince] = Nz(Me![txtStateOrProvince].Value)
    rst![PostalCode] = Nz(Me![txtPostalCode].Value)
    rst![HomePhone] = Nz(Me![txtHomePhone].Value)
    rst![WorkPhone] = Nz(Me![txtWorkPhone].Value)
    rst![Birthdate] = Nz(Me![txtBirthdate].Value)
    rst![DateHired] = Me![txtDateHired].Value
    rst![SupervisorID] = Nz(Me![cboSupervisorID].Value)
    rst.Update
    rst.Close

    Set prj = Application.CurrentProject

    If prj.AllForms("frmEmployees").IsLoaded Then
        Forms![frmEmployees].Visible = True
        Forms![frmEmployees].Requery
    Else
        DoCmd.OpenForm "frmEmployees"
    End If

    DoCmd.Close acForm, Me.Name

ErrorHandlerExit:
    Exit Sub

ErrorHandler:
    If Err.Number = 2467 Then
        Resume ErrorHandlerExit
    Else
        MsgBox "Error No: " & Err.Number & "; Description: " & Err.Description
        Resume ErrorHandlerExit
    End If

End Sub
```

❑ Add a module-level mstrEmployeeID variable to the Declarations section of the code behind forms module.

❑ Remove the section that adds a new record to tblEmployeesConfidential from the NewEmployeeID procedure, and modify the remaining code to write the new Employee ID to the textbox on the form. The modified procedure is below.

```
Private Sub NewEmployeeID()

On Error GoTo ErrorHandler

    Dim lngEmployeeID As Long

    Me![subMaxEmployeeID].Form.Requery
    lngEmployeeID = Me![subMaxEmployeeID].Form![txtNumericID] + 1
    mstrEmployeeID = Format(lngEmployeeID, "00000")
    Me![txtEmployeeID] = mstrEmployeeID

ErrorHandlerExit:
```

```
      Exit Sub

ErrorHandler:
    MsgBox "Error No: " & Err.Number & "; Description: " & _
       Err.Description
    Resume ErrorHandlerExit

End Sub
```

❑   Remove the Current event procedure, since there is no record selector combo box to clear.

❑   Move the Call NewEmployeeID line from the BeforeInsert event to the Load event of the form (BeforeInsert won't work on an unbound form).

The finished frmEmployees and frmNewEmployee forms can be seen in the Modules Finish version of the sample Toy Workshop database. frmNewEmployee is shown in Figure 7.10.

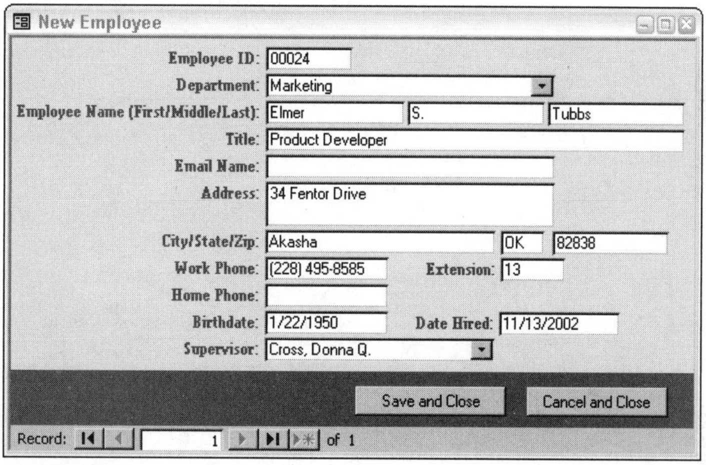

Figure 7.10

Sort and Filter Forms

If you have data that you need to view sorted and/or filtered by different fields, you can use code on the AfterUpdate event of a set of comboboxes to create a filter string, which can then be used to filter the data source of a subform showing the filter results, or to filter a form popped up from a command button. The Dynamic Search form shown in Figure 7.11 is based on a table of 500 contacts, with comboboxes allowing you to filter the data for a value in any of five fields.

Initially, the form opens unfiltered, and all the contacts are displayed in the datasheet subform. You can sort by any column by selecting the column and clicking the Sort Ascending or Sort Descending toolbar button—no need to write code for that. Figure 7.12 shows the datasheet sorted by the Company Name field.

To filter the contacts by a value, select one of the field options, and then select a value in the corresponding combobox. Figure 7.13 shows the results of filtering by Last Meeting Date = 5/9/2002.

235

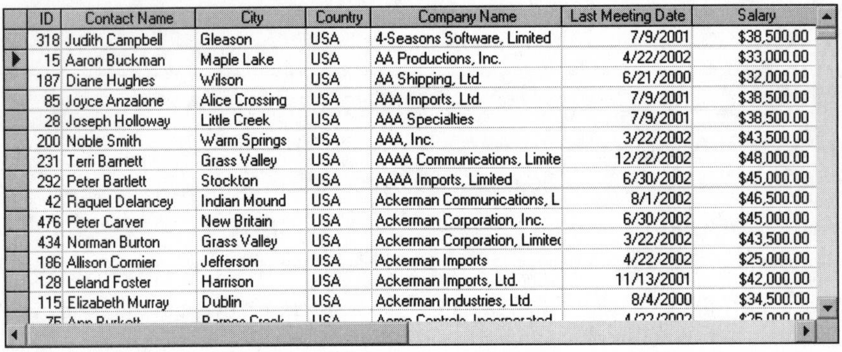

ID	Contact Name	City	Country	Company Name	Last Meeting Date	Salary
318	Judith Campbell	Gleason	USA	4-Seasons Software, Limited	7/9/2001	$38,500.00
15	Aaron Buckman	Maple Lake	USA	AA Productions, Inc.	4/22/2002	$33,000.00
187	Diane Hughes	Wilson	USA	AA Shipping, Ltd.	6/21/2000	$32,000.00
85	Joyce Anzalone	Alice Crossing	USA	AAA Imports, Ltd.	7/9/2001	$38,500.00
28	Joseph Holloway	Little Creek	USA	AAA Specialties	7/9/2001	$38,500.00
200	Noble Smith	Warm Springs	USA	AAA, Inc.	3/22/2002	$43,500.00
231	Terri Barnett	Grass Valley	USA	AAAA Communications, Limite	12/22/2002	$48,000.00
292	Peter Bartlett	Stockton	USA	AAAA Imports, Limited	6/30/2002	$45,000.00
42	Raquel Delancey	Indian Mound	USA	Ackerman Communications, L	8/1/2002	$46,500.00
476	Peter Carver	New Britain	USA	Ackerman Corporation, Inc.	6/30/2002	$45,000.00
434	Norman Burton	Grass Valley	USA	Ackerman Corporation, Limited	3/22/2002	$43,500.00
186	Allison Cormier	Jefferson	USA	Ackerman Imports	4/22/2002	$25,000.00
128	Leland Foster	Harrison	USA	Ackerman Imports, Ltd.	11/13/2001	$42,000.00
115	Elizabeth Murray	Dublin	USA	Ackerman Industries, Ltd.	8/4/2000	$34,500.00
75	Ann Burkett	Barnes Creek	USA	Acme Controls, Incorporated	4/22/2002	$25,000.00

Figure 7.11

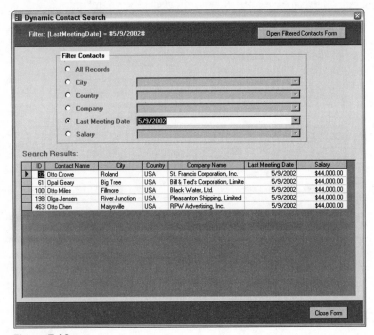

Figure 7.12

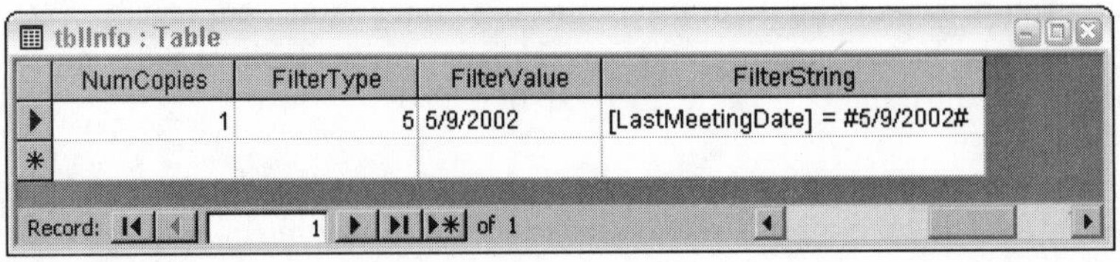

	NumCopies	FilterType	FilterValue	FilterString
▶	1	5	5/9/2002	[LastMeetingDate] = #5/9/2002#
*				

Record: ◀◀ ◀ 1 ▶ ▶◀ ▶* of 1

Figure 7.13

The Dynamic Search form is bound to tblInfo, so that filter-related information can be saved in this table. Figure 7.14 shows the latest filter selection saved to the FilterType, FilterValue, and FilterString fields in tblInfo.

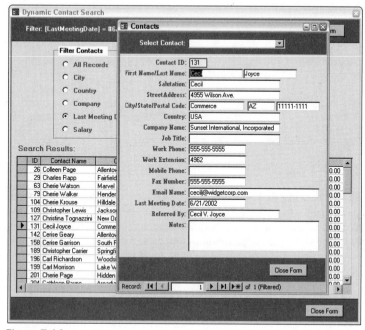

Figure 7.14

AfterUpdate events on the five field comboboxes create a filter string and save it to the FilterString field in tblInfo. The AfterUpdate event procedure for the Company combobox follows. Because CompanyName is a text field, the value picked up from the combobox is wrapped in single quotes, using Chr$(39). (Numeric values don't need the quotes, and dates are wrapped in number signs.) The filter string is then used to create a query called qryFilteredContacts, using the CreateAndTestQuery function, and the newly created query is assigned to the datasheet subform's RecordSource property.

```
Private Sub cboCompany_AfterUpdate()

On Error GoTo ErrorHandler

    Dim strCompany As String

    strCompany = Nz(Me![cboCompany])
    If strCompany = "" Then
        GoTo ErrorHandlerExit
    End If

    strFilter = "[CompanyName] = " & Chr$(39) & strCompany & Chr$(39)
    Me![FilterString] = strFilter
    DoCmd.RunCommand acCmdSaveRecord
    strRecordSource = "qryContacts"
```

237

```
      strQuery = "qryFilteredContacts"
      strSQL = "SELECT * FROM " & strRecordSource & " WHERE " _
          & strFilter & ";"
      Debug.Print "SQL Statement: " & strSQL
      Debug.Print CreateAndTestQuery(strQuery, strSQL) _
          & " records found"
      Me![subSearchResults].Form.RecordSource = strQuery

ErrorHandlerExit:
    Exit Sub

ErrorHandler:
    MsgBox "Error No: " & Err.Number & "; Description: " & _
        Err.Description
    Resume ErrorHandlerExit

End Sub
```

The option group's AfterUpdate event procedure enables the appropriate combobox, depending on the option chosen, and disables the others, and makes the txtFilter textbox visible or invisible, depending on whether a filter field is selected or not. Appropriate text is also written to the caption of the cmdContacts command button. If the Unfiltered option is selected, qryContacts is assigned to the datasheet subform's record source. If a filter field is selected, that assignment is made from the AfterUpdate event procedure of that field's combobox.

```
Private Sub fraFilter_AfterUpdate()

On Error GoTo ErrorHandler

    Dim intFilter As Integer

    intFilter = Me![fraFilter].Value
    Me![FilterValue] = Null

    Select Case intFilter

        Case 1
        'Unfiltered
        Me![cboCity].Enabled = False
        Me![cboCity].ControlSource = ""
        Me![cboCountry].Enabled = False
        Me![cboCountry].ControlSource = ""
        Me![cboCompany].Enabled = False
        Me![cboCompany].ControlSource = ""
        Me![cboLastMeetingDate].Enabled = False
        Me![cboLastMeetingDate].ControlSource = ""
        Me![cboSalary].Enabled = False
        Me![cboSalary].ControlSource = ""
        Me![cmdContacts].Caption = "Open Unfiltered Contacts Form"
        Me![txtFilter].Visible = False
        Me![subSearchResults].Form.RecordSource = "qryContacts"

        Case 2
        'Filter by City
        Me![cboCity].Enabled = True
```

```
Me![cboCity].ControlSource = "FilterValue"
Me![cboCity].SetFocus
Me![cboCity].Dropdown
Me![cboCountry].Enabled = False
Me![cboCountry].ControlSource = ""
Me![cboCompany].Enabled = False
Me![cboCompany].ControlSource = ""
Me![cboLastMeetingDate].Enabled = False
Me![cboLastMeetingDate].ControlSource = ""
Me![cboSalary].Enabled = False
Me![cboSalary].ControlSource = ""
Me![cmdContacts].Caption = "Open Filtered Contacts Form"
Me![txtFilter].Visible = True

Case 3
'Filter by Country
Me![cboCity].Enabled = False
Me![cboCity].ControlSource = ""
Me![cboCountry].Enabled = True
Me![cboCountry].ControlSource = "FilterValue"
Me![cboCountry].SetFocus
Me![cboCountry].Dropdown
Me![cboCompany].Enabled = False
Me![cboCompany].ControlSource = ""
Me![cboLastMeetingDate].Enabled = False
Me![cboLastMeetingDate].ControlSource = ""
Me![cboSalary].Enabled = False
Me![cboSalary].ControlSource = ""
Me![cmdContacts].Caption = "Open Filtered Contacts Form"
Me![txtFilter].Visible = True

Case 4
'Filter by Company Name
Me![cboCity].Enabled = False
Me![cboCity].ControlSource = ""
Me![cboCountry].Enabled = False
Me![cboCountry].ControlSource = ""
Me![cboCompany].Enabled = True
Me![cboCompany].ControlSource = "FilterValue"
Me![cboCompany].SetFocus
Me![cboCompany].Dropdown
Me![cboLastMeetingDate].Enabled = False
Me![cboLastMeetingDate].ControlSource = ""
Me![cboSalary].Enabled = False
Me![cboSalary].ControlSource = ""
Me![cmdContacts].Caption = "Open Filtered Contacts Form"
Me![txtFilter].Visible = True

Case 5
'Filter by Last Meeting Date
Me![cboCity].Enabled = False
Me![cboCity].ControlSource = ""
Me![cboCountry].Enabled = False
Me![cboCountry].ControlSource = ""
Me![cboCompany].Enabled = False
Me![cboCompany].ControlSource = ""
```

```
        Me![cboLastMeetingDate].Enabled = True
        Me![cboLastMeetingDate].ControlSource = "FilterValue"
        Me![cboLastMeetingDate].SetFocus
        Me![cboLastMeetingDate].Dropdown
        Me![cboSalary].Enabled = False
        Me![cboSalary].ControlSource = ""
        Me![cmdContacts].Caption = "Open Filtered Contacts Form"
        Me![txtFilter].Visible = True

        Case 6
        'Filter by Salary
        Me![cboCity].Enabled = False
        Me![cboCity].ControlSource = ""
        Me![cboCountry].Enabled = False
        Me![cboCountry].ControlSource = ""
        Me![cboCompany].Enabled = False
        Me![cboCompany].ControlSource = ""
        Me![cboLastMeetingDate].Enabled = False
        Me![cboLastMeetingDate].ControlSource = ""
        Me![cboSalary].Enabled = True
        Me![cboSalary].ControlSource = "FilterValue"
        Me![cboSalary].SetFocus
        Me![cboSalary].Dropdown
        Me![cmdContacts].Caption = "Open Filtered Contacts Form"
        Me![txtFilter].Visible = True

    End Select

    DoCmd.RunCommand acCmdSaveRecord
    If intFilter > 1 Then
        strFilter = " WHERE [ContactID] = 0"
        strRecordSource = "qryContacts"
        strQuery = "qryFilteredContacts"
        strSQL = "SELECT * FROM " & strRecordSource & strFilter & ";"
        Debug.Print "SQL Statement: " & strSQL
        Debug.Print CreateAndTestQuery(strQuery, strSQL) & "records found"
        Me![subSearchResults].Form.RecordSource = strQuery
    End If

ErrorHandlerExit:
    Exit Sub

ErrorHandler:
    MsgBox "Error No: " & Err.Number & "; Description: " & _
        Err.Description
    Resume ErrorHandlerExit

End Sub
```

The Contacts command button's Click event procedure is listed below. If the Unfiltered option is selected in the option group, the strFilter variable is set to a zero-length string; otherwise the saved filter string is picked up from the FilterString field. The Contacts form is then opened, either unfiltered or filtered by the selected filter string, and the search form is closed.

```
Private Sub cmdContacts_Click()

On Error GoTo ErrorHandler

    Dim strFormName As String

    strFormName = "frmContacts"
    If Me![fraFilter].Value = 1 Then
        strFilter = ""
    Else
        'Pick up saved filter string
        strFilter = Me![FilterString]
    End If

    DoCmd.OpenForm FormName:=strFormName, _
        view:=acNormal, _
        windowmode:=acWindowNormal, _
        wherecondition:=strFilter
    Me.Visible = False

ErrorHandlerExit:
    Exit Sub

ErrorHandler:
    MsgBox "Error No: " & Err.Number & "; Description: " & _
        Err.Description
    Resume ErrorHandlerExit

End Sub
```

DblClick Event from Datasheet Subform

If you need to run an event procedure from a datasheet subform, you don't have the usual options of a command button or option group. For datasheet subforms, I like to use the DblClick event on a textbox. The datasheet subform (fsubSearchResults) on the Dynamic Search form has a DblClick event procedure on both txtContactID and txtContactName. The txtContactName DblClick event procedure is listed below. First the code checks that a contact has been selected, and then the FilterContact Sub procedure is called, with the selected ContactID value as its argument.

```
Private Sub txtContactName_DblClick(Cancel As Integer)

On Error GoTo ErrorHandler

    lngContactID = Nz(Me![ContactID])
    If lngContactID <> 0 Then
        Call FilterContact(lngContactID)
```

```
        End If

ErrorHandlerExit:
    Exit Sub

ErrorHandler:
    MsgBox "Error No: " & Err.Number & "; Description: " & _
        Err.Description
Resume ErrorHandlerExit

End Sub
```

The FilterContact procedure is listed below. The code is simpler than the filter field combobox code on the main form; it just creates a filter string based on ContactID, then opens frmContacts with the filter string for its wherecondition argument.

```
Private Sub FilterContact(lngID As Long)

On Error GoTo ErrorHandler


    Dim strFilter As String

    strFilter = "[ContactID] = " & lngID
    DoCmd.OpenForm FormName:="frmContacts", _
        view:=acNormal, _
        wherecondition:=strFilter

ErrorHandlerExit:
    Exit Sub

ErrorHandler:
    MsgBox "Error No: " & Err.Number & "; Description: " & _
        Err.Description
    Resume ErrorHandlerExit

End Sub
```

Figure 7.15 shows frmContacts opened for just the selected contact.

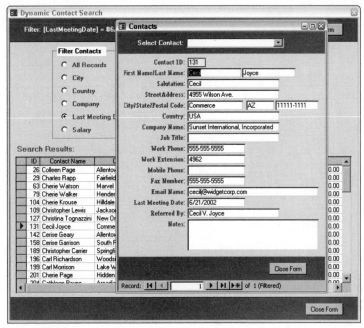

Figure 7.15

Summary

Using Sub and function procedures in Code Behind Forms and standard modules, you can write code to tie your forms, queries, and reports together into a smoothly functioning application. The next chapter will deal with the changes you need to make during an application's life cycle, while working with a client.

Part II: Modifying, Updating, and Maintaining Access Applications

Managing the
Application Life Cycle

When you complete an application and deliver it to your client, that may not be the end of the road. As an application is put into use, it will need to be tweaked, and as it is used over the years, the client will want to add new features. Additionally, every few years, you (and the client) need to make a decision about whether to upgrade the application to a new version of Office. (For recent Office versions, the decision to upgrade an Access application is a separate decision from the decision to upgrade to the new Office version in general.)

In my experience, if you deliver an application to a client and never hear from him (or her) again, that is a sign that the application is not being used. If it is used, some changes will always be needed.

Modifying an Application

When the client starts using an application, quite often—in fact, typically—some modifications will be needed. Some of the changes may be simply things that weren't foreseen when the application was planned, but that become evident when it is used (for example, the need to keep some information confidential). Others may be new features that are needed because of new business requirements (for example, the client is now selling to customers outside of the United States, so country data must be stored in the database, or the client wants to generate Word letters to customers, so a Prefix field is needed for customer names). And finally, a new version of Access may offer features that could enhance the application.

It's a good idea to include a few hours of development time for unforeseen modifications when planning an application, because otherwise the client may balk at paying for them. However, it's also advisable to be reasonable about making minor changes without charge, especially if you really should have foreseen the need for them. When a client has a brand-new requirement that wasn't included in the original requirements of the application, this is new work, and of course should be paid for as such. (For more information on dealing with clients on issues related to changes, see the "Client Relations" section later in this chapter.)

Some requirements are so commonly needed that it is worthwhile to anticipate them. While it isn't a problem to have a few unused fields in a table and form, adding fields later on (and modifying queries, forms, and reports accordingly) can be quite time-consuming. One of these requirements is the division of names into separate fields. Even if the client doesn't request it, it's highly advisable to break down names into at least three fields (FirstName, MiddleName, and LastName for European-derived names; other types of names may need different fields) and often two more fields as well (Prefix and Suffix).

A single field holding an entire name (usually first name first) won't allow you to easily sort by last name or print a report with names arranged last name first. If you have separate fields for the different components of a name, you can rearrange them as needed or just use certain components, such as first names for name badges for a party or last names for locker or helmet labels.

If the application creates Word letters (or might at some point include such a component), then you need five name fields. The prefix (Mr., Dr., Father, and so on) is needed so that letters can be addressed properly, and a separate field for suffix is needed so that the suffix (if any) can be placed in the correct order when printing names last name first. If users have to enter the suffix (Jr., III, Ph.D.) in the LastName field, reports with names arranged last name first will print with very odd formatting, such as:

```
Yates Ph.D., Dr. Marian
Saunders Jr., Mr. Dennis
```

With suffix information in its own field, you can place the suffix after the middle name when printing names last name first, using a concatenated query expression such as:

```
LastNameFirst: [LastName] & IIf([Prefix],", " & [Prefix],"") & IIf([FirstName]," "
& [FirstName],"") & IIf([MiddleName]," " & [MiddleName]) & IIf([Suffix],", " &
[Suffix],"")
```

to print these names correctly:

```
Yates, Dr. Marian, Ph.D.
Saunders, Mr. Dennis, Jr.
```

Upgrading to a New Office Version

Some Office upgrades have included major changes to Access; others have made only a few insignificant changes (though of course, a change that is highly significant to one person may be insignificant to another). From my point of view, the upgrade from Office 97 to Office 2000 was significant, and Access gained several highly useful new features with Office XP. Office 2003, however, hardly changed Access at all, though Outlook had major enhancements that could be significant if an application works with Outlook components. The table below lists the more significant changes to Access in Office 2000, Office XP, and Office 2003.

Office Version	Changes from Previous Version
2000	Objects Bar replaces tabbed database window
	Database object groups
	New object shortcuts
	Name AutoCorrect (this is more a problem than a welcome new feature!)
	Print Relationships Diagram
	ADO object library
	Grouping of form and report controls
	Conditional formatting of form controls
	Snapshot format for distributing reports
	Data Access Pages
	Personalized menus (an Office-wide feature)
	Compact on close
	Convert to Access 97 format
	Projects for working with SQL Server
	Exchange/Outlook Wizard for importing or linking Outlook data (has serious limitations)
XP (2002)	Printer object
	FileDialog object (this is an Office-wide feature)
	Enhancements to Data Access Pages
	Enhancements to PivotTables
	PivotCharts
	Multiple Undo/Redo
	Ask a Question box
2003	Object dependencies
	Form and report error checking
	Propagating field properties
	Smart tags
	Database backup
	XML support
	Multifield sorting in controls
	Enhanced fonts and Help in SQL view

Upgrading an Application to a New Database Format

Many of the new features in any Access version are primarily of interest to people who work in Access databases in Design view (both end users and developers), rather than people who enter and edit data in Access databases. If you (and your client) are considering whether to upgrade an application to the next version of Access, three questions need to be asked:

❑   Does the new version have a feature that will significantly enhance the application with new functionality?

❑   Does the new version have a feature that will make the application easier to use or more efficient?

❑   Will all the people working on the database at the client's site be upgraded to the new Office version?

If the answer to all these questions is "No," then it's not very likely that the client will want to upgrade to the new version of Office, at least not for Access-related reasons. You (as the developer) may want the Print Relationships Diagram in Access 2000, or the FileDialog object in Access XP, or object dependencies in Access 2003—but these features don't mean a thing to the client who is looking at the overall functionality of the application for running a business or other enterprise, or the clerks who enter and modify data in the application.

On the other hand, if the client wants to display application data in attractive charts and is thrilled by the interactive features of PivotCharts, then an upgrade to Office XP is definitely called for, and if XML support is a welcome enhancement to the application, that calls for an upgrade to Office 2003.

As a developer, you should always upgrade to a new version of Access, so that you can use new features that make it easier to work with database objects in Design view, and also so you can create databases in the new format for clients who have also upgraded to the latest version of Office. However, in Office XP and Office 2003, you can still work with databases in Access 2000 format (with full read/write access) for clients who haven't upgraded yet.

There are two ways to safely work with different Access database formats on one computer:

❑   Set up separate boot partitions for different Office versions (this is best when you need to be absolutely sure that every aspect of an application will work in a specific version of Access).

❑   Leave the database in Access 2000 format, and work with it in Access 2002 or 2003.

Setting Up Separate Boot Partitions for Different Office Versions

Even though you can work with Access 2000 databases in Access 2002 or 2003 (see the next section for details), this is not the exactly the same as working in Access 2000. When working in Office 2000, if your application includes Automation code to work with Word, Outlook, or Excel, you are working with Word 2000, Outlook 2000, or Excel 2000. If you use ActiveX controls in the application (such as the Calendar control or the DateTimePicker control), they are the versions of those controls that come with Office 2000. Because of these considerations, in order to make absolutely sure that your application will work in Office 2000, you need to test it in Office 2000, ideally with the same operating system the client is using.

I recommend installing each version of Office in a separate boot partition, using an application such as System Commander (see the V-Comm Web site, www.v-com.com/, for information on this product), or Boot Magic (included with PartitionMagic (see the PowerQuest Web site, www.powerquest.com/, for information on these products). System Commander and Boot Magic let you set up multiple boot partitions, with different operating systems if desired, and to have different versions of Office running in each partition. On different computers, I currently have the OS/Office combinations listed in the table below:

Operating System	Office Version
Windows XP	Office XP
Windows 2000	Office 2003
Windows ME	Office 2000
Windows XP	Office 2003
Windows 2000	Office XP

As new versions of Windows and Office come out I add new partitions, and as the last client using an older version upgrades, I reformat the older OS/Office partitions and install a newer OS/Office combination. I keep all the operating systems on Drive C and all data on Drive D. I install applications (the ones that give me a choice) on Drive E. This means that when I wipe a boot partition to install a new OS, I don't lose any data, and I can work with the same documents in all partitions. I still have to install applications in each partition, but I install them to the same folder on the E drive (except for those that work differently with different operating systems, such as Norton SystemWorks), which can save a considerable amount of hard drive real estate.

Working with Access 2000 Databases in Higher Versions of Access

Office XP added a new Access format (the Access 2002 database format), but unlike earlier upgrades users aren't required to use the new format when creating new databases, nor are users required to upgrade Access 2000 databases to the new format to have full read/write functionality, unless they want to take advantage of new features such as PivotCharts or the Printer object. The Access 2002 format is also available for use in Access 2003, where it is labeled the Access 2002 - 2003 format. You can work with Access 2000 format databases in both Access 2002 and 2003, as long as you don't use any features not available in Access 2000 and take some care with references.

If you want to create a new database in Access 2000 format while running Access 2002 or 2003, you have to first select Access 2000 as the database format on the Advanced page of the Options dialog, as shown in Figure 8.1.

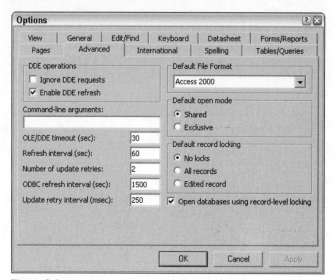

Figure 8.1

Apart from the obvious limitations of working with an older database format (you can't use PivotCharts or enhanced PivotTables, or the Printer object), there are a few problems that can occur when an Access 2000 database is opened alternately in Access 2000 and a higher version of Access. This will be the case if your client is working in Access 2000, and you are working in Access 2002 (or 2003), or if the client's workstations have different versions of Office installed. There is generally no problem with references when opening an Access 2000 database in a higher version of Access; references to the Office 2000 versions of Access, Office, and other Office components such as Word or Outlook will be upgraded from the v. 9.0 object libraries to the v. 10.0 or v. 11.0 object libraries.

However, downgrading doesn't always work automatically. When an Access 2000 database is opened in Access 2002, then in Access 2000 again, the Access object library reference (and the Office object library reference, if you have one) will be downgraded from a higher version to v. 9.0 without problems, and the DAO 3.6 reference works for both Office versions, so it is OK, but references to other Office object libraries are generally not downgraded. That means that the database now has missing references to Word, Excel, or Outlook 10.0 or 11.0, and they will cause errors when the code is run.

The Test References sample database is an Access 2000 format database with references to the Outlook and Word object libraries. If you open it in Access 2000, its references are initially to the Office 2000 (v. 9.0) versions of various object libraries, as shown in Figure 8.2.

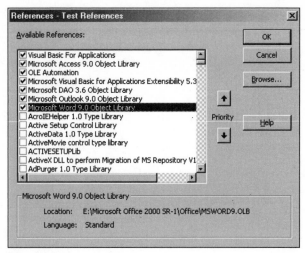

Figure 8.2

The database has two macros (mcrTestOutlookAutomationCode and mcrTestWordAutomationCode) that run functions that set up a reference to the Outlook and Word object libraries, respectively, and display information picked up from Word or Outlook in a message box. The two functions for testing references are:

```
Option Compare Database
Option Explicit

Public Function TemplateDir() As String

On Error GoTo ErrorHandler

    Dim appWord As Word.Application

    Set appWord = CreateObject("Word.Application")
    TemplateDir = _
        appWord.Options.DefaultFilePath(wdUserTemplatesPath) _
        & "\"
    MsgBox "Word template folder: " & TemplateDir

ErrorHandlerExit:
    Exit Function

ErrorHandler:
    MsgBox "Error No: " & Err.Number & "; Description: " _
        & Err.Description
```

```
       Resume ErrorHandlerExit

End Function

Public Function CurrentOutlookFolder()

On Error GoTo ErrorHandler

    Dim appOutlook As Outlook.Application
    Dim exp As Outlook.Explorer
    Dim fld As Outlook.MAPIFolder

    Set appOutlook = CreateObject("Outlook.Application")
    Set exp = appOutlook.ActiveExplorer
    Set fld = exp.CurrentFolder
    CurrentOutlookFolder = fld.Name
    MsgBox "Current Outlook folder: " & _
        CurrentOutlookFolder

ErrorHandlerExit:
    Exit Function

ErrorHandler:
    If Err.Number = 91 Then
        MsgBox "Please run Outlook and try again"
    Else
        MsgBox "Error No: " & Err.Number & _
            "; Description: " & Err.Description
        Resume ErrorHandlerExit
    End If

End Function
```

When the references are set correctly, you will get the message boxes shown in Figures 8.3 and 8.4 when running these macros.

Figure 8.3

Figure 8.4

When the sample database is opened in Access 2002 (Office XP), its references are automatically upgraded to the Office XP (v. 10.0) versions, as shown in Figure 8.5.

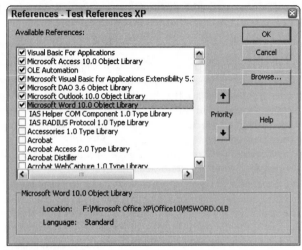

Figure 8.5

To open the References dialog, select References from the Tools menu in the Visual Basic window.

Now for the real challenge: Close the sample Test References database, then reopen it in Access 2000 once more, and open the References dialog. Now you will see the Outlook and Word references labeled "MISSING," as shown in Figure 8.6.

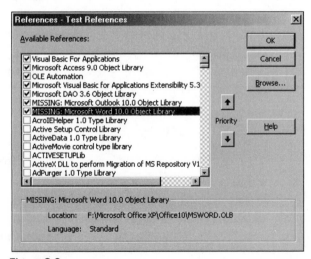

Figure 8.6

If you try to run the macros, you will get a compile error, "Can't find project or library," with the line that declares the appWord or appOutlook variable highlighted.

You could uncheck the references marked "MISSING" and reselect the v. 9.0 object libraries while the database is open in Access 2000. However, that would only be a temporary fix. If the database is opened in Access 2002 or 2003 and then again in Access 2000, the problem will recur.

Fortunately, there is a way to avoid this problem. You can avoid errors with missing references in Access 2000 databases that will be used in Access 2000 and higher versions by setting references to the Office 2000 (v. 9.0) object libraries from a database that has been opened in a higher version of Access. If you have different Office versions installed in different boot partitions, and you have installed both Office versions to locations accessible in all partitions, this is a straightforward process, because both sets of object libraries can be found on your computer (in different folders). Even if you don't have a multiboot setup for different Office versions, you can still use this technique, by placing the Office 2000 versions of the Outlook, Word, and possibly other object library files in a folder on your computer (you may have to copy them from another computer or temporarily install Office 2000 to obtain these library files).

The table below lists the object library names and standard locations for the main Office components for Office 97 through Office 2003 (the file paths may be different on your computer, depending on your Windows version and the folder where you installed Office).

Application Version	Object Library Name in References Dialog	File Name and Path
Office 2000		
Access 2000	Microsoft Access 9.0 Object Library	C:\Program Files\Microsoft Office\Office\msacc9.olb
Excel 2000	Microsoft Excel 9.0 Object Library	C:\Program Files\Microsoft Office\Office\excel9.olb
Outlook 2000	Microsoft Outlook 9.0 Object Library	C:\Program Files\Microsoft Office\Office\msoutl9.olb
Word 2000	Microsoft Word 9.0 Object Library	C:\Program Files\Microsoft Office\Office\msword9.olb
DAO 3.51	Microsoft DAO 3.51 Object Library	C:\Program Files\Common Files\Microsoft Shared\DAO\dao350.dll
ADO 2.1	Microsoft ActiveX Data Objects 2.1 Library	C:\Program Files\Common Files\system\ado\msado21.tlb
Office 2000	Microsoft Office 9.0 Object Library	C:\Program Files\Microsoft Office\Office\mso9.dll

Application Version	Object Library Name in References Dialog	File Name and Path
Office XP		
Access 2002	Microsoft Access 10.0 Object Library	C:\Program Files\Microsoft Office\Office10\msacc.olb
Excel 2002	Microsoft Excel 10.0 Object Library	C:\Program Files\Microsoft Office\Office10\excel.exe
Outlook 2002	Microsoft Outlook 10.0 Object Library	C:\Program Files\Microsoft Office\Office10\msoutl.olb
Word 2002	Microsoft Word 10.0 Object Library	C:\Program Files\Microsoft Office\Office10\msword.olb
DAO 3.6	Microsoft DAO 3.6 Object Library	C:\Program Files\Common Files\Microsoft Shared\DAO\dao360.dll
ADO 2.5	Microsoft ActiveX Data Objects 2.5 Library	C:\Program Files\Common Files\system\ado\msado25.tlb
Office XP	Microsoft Office 10.0 Object Library	C:\Program Files\Common Files\Microsoft Shared\Office10\mso.dll
Office 2003		
Access 2003	Microsoft Access 11.0 Object Library	C:\Program Files\Microsoft Office\Office11\msacc.olb
Excel 2003	Microsoft Excel 11.0 Object Library	C:\Program Files\Microsoft Office\Office11\excel.exe
Outlook 2003	Microsoft Outlook 11.0 Object Library	C:\Program Files\Microsoft Office\Office11\msoutl.olb
Word 2003	Microsoft Word 11.0 Object Library	C:\Program Files\Microsoft Office\Office11\msword.olb
DAO 3.6	Microsoft DAO 3.6 Object Library	C:\Program Files\Common Files\Microsoft Shared\DAO\dao360.dll
ADO 2.5	Microsoft ActiveX Data Objects 2.5 Library	C:\Program Files\Common Files\system\ado\msado25.tlb
Office 2003	Microsoft Office 11.0 Object Library	C:\Program Files\Common Files\Microsoft Shared\Office11\mso.dll

The DAO and ADO object libraries are not tightly associated with specific Office versions, so you may have DAO 3.51 in Office 97 or Office 2000, or DAO 3.6 in Office 2000 or higher.

Start by copying the Office 2000 object libraries from the location listed in the table to an Office 2000 Object Libraries folder in a location that is accessible to all Office versions (mine is under the main Documents folder on Drive D). Open the Test References database in Access 2002 or 2003 (the process is exactly the same for Office XP and Office 2003). Initially, the References dialog shows v. 11.0 references, as shown in Figure 8.7.

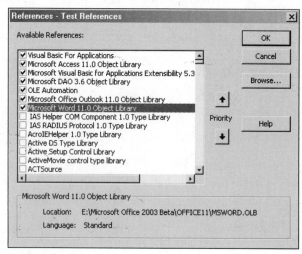

Figure 8.7

There's no need to set references to Access 9.0 or Office 9.0 in Access 2002 or 2003, because these references will be downgraded automatically when the database is opened in Access 2000. However, Word and Outlook references aren't downgraded, so uncheck them, then click the Browse button and browse to the folder where the Office 2000 object libraries are located, as shown in Figure 8.8.

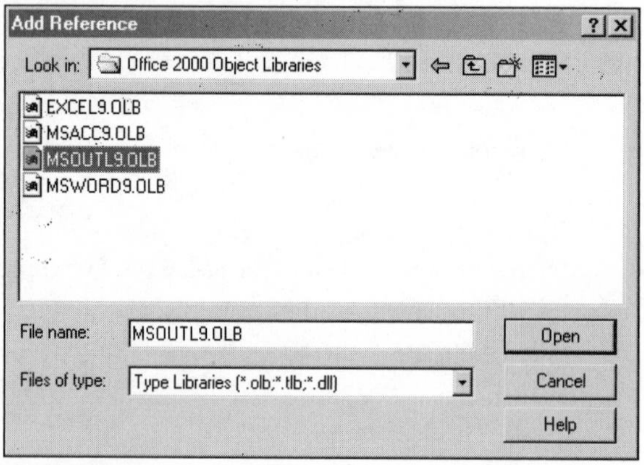

Figure 8.8

Select the Outlook object library and click Open, then click the Browse button again and repeat the process to select the Word object library. The new v. 9.0 references now appear at the bottom of the References dialog, as shown in Figure 8.9.

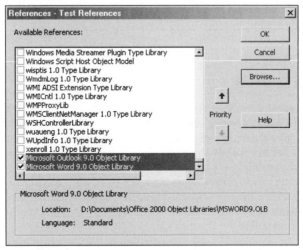

Figure 8.9

The next time the References dialog is opened, you'll see the v. 11.0 Access object library reference near the top of the dialog, and the v. 9.0 references will be at the bottom of the list of checked references, as shown in Figure 8.10.

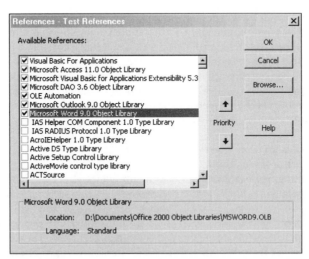

Figure 8.10

Now this Access 2000 database can be opened in Access 2000, Access 2002 or Access 2003, and the Office 2000 versions of the Word and Outlook objects libraries will be correctly referenced.

Working with Clients

Although this isn't a touchy-feely book about interpersonal relations (I'm a techie, not a psychologist), over the years I have figured out a few principles for promoting good relationships with clients. In this section, I'll discuss these principles in more detail and give examples of implementing client-requested modifications to an application.

Client Relations

When working on an application for a client, it's important to consider the long term—ideally, you want to keep a good client for many years to come, so it's worthwhile to make a few changes or add a new feature the client isn't sure about, free of charge, as a gesture of goodwill. Needless to say, there is a balance here. Doing work for free makes sense as an investment of your time in exchange for goodwill when dealing with a reasonable client who will probably be paying you for work for many years to come and recommending you to other potential clients. But if you make changes or add features to an application free of charge for a client who just wants the maximum work done for the minimum charge and who will take advantage of your consideration to ask for more and more changes free of charge, this can become a very bad situation.

I don't know if I can tell you how to accurately classify clients, other than just by proceeding cautiously and observing how a client reacts to common situations such as an application needing some tweaking after delivery. As always, the best predictor for future behavior is past behavior—a client who complains vociferously about having to pay for new features he requested after the application was created according to his original specifications, and pays late, is probably going to continue to behave in the same way in the future.

After working with a client for a while, you will generally have a good idea whether you and the client tend to think alike about possible database features and changes. If you find that a particular client generally approves of changes you think are needed, you can feel comfortable with just going ahead and making any changes that seem to be called for without prior approval. Other clients may see things differently from you, so when doing work for them and because you can't predict what they would like based on your own preferences, if you realize that another change might be needed, while working on something else, it's best to check in advance before making any changes that haven't been specifically requested by the client.

One situation that comes up from time to time is a client request that you know is not appropriate—either it just won't work or it will lead to serious problems elsewhere in the application or it just isn't the best way to do something. For example, the client might want to have three phone number fields in the Customers table, to store work, home, and fax numbers.

You can just tell the client, "that won't work," or something similar, and provide a technical explanation of why this violates the first normal form, but that is rarely a good idea. The client will feel insulted, and probably won't understand the explanation in any case. In these cases, when feasible, I generally say something like, "I can do that, but there are a few other alternatives you might also want to consider," and perhaps do a demo of the alternatives (in this case, having the phone numbers in a separate linked table).

Ask the client to consider the case of entering a customer's cell phone number. Hopefully, the limitations of having three fixed fields in tblCustomers will now become apparent (there is no Cell Phone field!), and the client will see the benefits of putting phone numbers into a separate table—without the need for an insulting lecture from you. At this point, several things can happen: (1) The client goes along with the more reasonable alternative; (2) the client provides a good reason for having a non-normalized table (say, meeting very specific government requirements based on outdated database technology); (3) the client will insist on having the three separate phone fields, without any good reason. (1) and (2) you can work with; but (3) will clue you in that this is an unreasonable client who will probably be difficult to work with in the future.

Making Client-Requested Changes

After the client has spent some time working in the application, he or she will probably request some new features. Sometimes the requests spring from changes to business procedures, and sometimes the client realizes that existing procedures can be made more efficient after working with the application in its new format.

Application-Specific Changes

Usually, after you complete an application's tables and create some forms for data entry, the client gets a copy of the database and starts entering data (for the case where you need to write code or create queries to import old data, see Chapter 10, *Moving Old Data into a New Database*). Generally, after working with the application, the client will request some changes. For example, in the Toy Workshop database, after entering a few orders, the client asked for a display of the available inventory for a toy.

To display the available inventory, I created a subform (fsubToyInventory) with tblToys as its record source, linked on ToyID. I could have just placed the UnitsInStock field on the form—that would have satisfied the letter of the client's request—but looking at the field list, I saw a few other fields that would also be useful, UnitsOnOrder and SellPrice. In cases like this, I generally go ahead and make whatever changes seem reasonable—the only exception being cases where a client is absolutely insistent on pre-approving any changes. I dragged ToyID, UnitsInStock, UnitsOnOrder, and SellPrice to the subform, and made ToyID invisible, using the Lock Wizard, as shown in Figure 8.11.

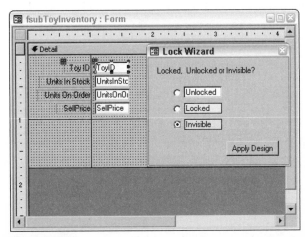

Figure 8.11

The reason for making ToyID invisible, instead of just omitting it, is that in case of problems (such as the subform not displaying the appropriate data) I can temporarily make it visible for debugging purposes. The yellow color reminds me that this field should be made invisible before finalizing the form.

I placed the subform on fpriOrders in the sample Toy Workshop database, under the cboToyID combobox (after moving down the other controls) and rearranged the controls on the subform and the subform itself to save space. I locked the subform and made its back color light blue as a visual indicator that it was locked. fpriOrders with the new Toy Inventory subform is shown in Figure 8.12.

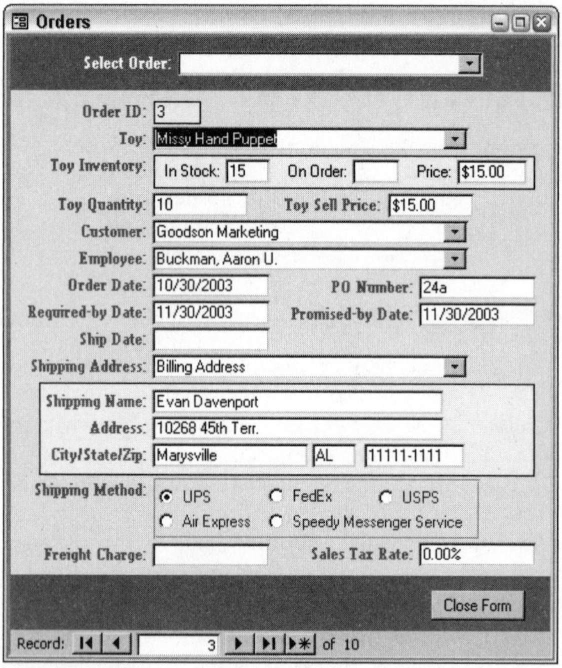

Figure 8.12

The new subform will correctly display toy inventory when navigating from record to record, but it doesn't refresh automatically when a new toy is selected from cboToyID; to do that, the combobox's AfterUpdate event procedure needs a line that requeries the subform. I added this line to the existing event procedure, which also copies the toy's price from tblToys to the ToyPrice field on fpriOrders. The ToyPrice field can be edited as needed to adjust the selling price for an order.

```
Private Sub cboToyID_AfterUpdate()

On Error GoTo ErrorHandler

    Dim curToyPrice As Currency

    curToyPrice = Nz(Me![cboToyID].Column(3))
    Me![ToyPrice] = curToyPrice
    Me![txtToyPrice].Requery
```

```
    Me![subToyInventory].Requery

ErrorHandlerExit:
   Exit Sub

ErrorHandler:
   MsgBox "Error No: " & Err.Number & "; Description: " & _
      Err.Description
   Resume ErrorHandlerExit

End Sub
```

Now that we can see the available inventory, some more coding is called for to prevent placing an order for more toys than are available. This code could be run from the BeforeUpdate event of the txtToyQuantity text box, or perhaps on the form's BeforeUpdate event. I would write this code without conferencing with the client because it is simple to do and obviously needed. If the client wants serious error trapping, I could make a special form for creating a new order, either bound to a temporary table or storing its values in variables, and only transfer the data to a new record in tblOrders after checking that all fields have correct data (I wouldn't go ahead with this without checking with the client because it is a more time-consuming project). (See Chapter 7, *Writing VBA Code in Modules*, for more information on creating a separate form for entering new records.) Another possibility would be triggering toy orders to vendors if there isn't enough inventory to fill an order—again, I would check whether the client wants this feature before doing it.

For now, a simple BeforeUpdate event procedure for txtToyQuantity will do.

```
   Private Sub txtToyQuantity_BeforeUpdate(Cancel As Integer)

   On Error GoTo ErrorHandler

      Dim lngAvailable As Long
      Dim lngNeeded As Long
      Dim strPrompt As String
      Dim strTitle As String

      lngAvailable = Nz(Me![subToyInventory]![UnitsInStock])
      lngNeeded = Nz(Me![txtToyQuantity].Value)
      If lngAvailable < lngNeeded Then
         strTitle = "Not enough inventory"
         strPrompt = lngNeeded & " needed; only " & lngAvailable & " available"
         MsgBox strPrompt, vbOKOnly, strTitle
         Me![txtToyQuantity].Undo
         Cancel = True
      End If

   ErrorHandlerExit:
      Exit Sub

   ErrorHandler:
      MsgBox "Error No: " & Err.Number & "; Description: " & _
         Err.Description
      Resume ErrorHandlerExit

   End Sub
```

I also added a locked text box to display the total price for the toy order (ToyQuantity * ToyPrice), with a control source of `=[ToyQuantity]*[ToyPrice]`.

> **If you get an error message for a calculated field, it may be missing an equal sign.**
> **All calculated control source expressions must start with an equal sign.**

If there is enough inventory to provide the desired quantity of a toy, then an AfterUpdate event procedure is also needed to deduct the amount just ordered from inventory. I moved the declarations from the BeforeUpdate event procedure to the Declarations section of the Code Behind Forms module because they will also be used in the AfterUpdate event procedure. The txtToyQuantity AfterUpdate event procedure is:

```
Private Sub txtToyQuantity_AfterUpdate()

On Error GoTo ErrorHandler

    Dim strToyID As String
    Dim dbs As DAO.Database
    Dim rst As DAO.Recordset
    Dim strSearch As String

    'Check that a toy has been selected and an amount entered.
    strToyID = Nz(Me![ToyID])
    lngNeeded = Nz(Me![txtToyQuantity].Value)
    If lngNeeded = 0 Then
        GoTo ErrorHandlerExit
    ElseIf strToyID = "" Then
        GoTo ErrorHandlerExit
    Else
        strSearch = "[ToyID] = " & Chr$(39) & strToyID & Chr$(39)
        Debug.Print "Search string: " & strSearch
    End If

    Set dbs = CurrentDb
    Set rst = dbs.OpenRecordset("tblToys", dbOpenDynaset)
    rst.FindFirst strSearch
    If rst.NoMatch = True Then
        strTitle = "Toy not found"
        strPrompt = "Can't find Toy ID " & strToyID & " in tblToys"
        MsgBox strPrompt, vbOKOnly, strTitle
        GoTo ErrorHandlerExit
    Else
        'Found the toy; ask for confirmation of reducing inventory.
        strTitle = "Use inventory"
        strPrompt = "Take " & lngNeeded & " of Toy ID " & strToyID _
            & " from inventory for this order?"
        intReturn = MsgBox(strPrompt, vbOKCancel, strTitle)
```

```
            If intReturn = vbCancel Then
                Me![txtToyQuantity].Value = Null
                GoTo ErrorHandlerExit
            ElseIf intReturn = vbOK Then
                rst.Edit
    rst![UnitsInStock] = rst![UnitsInStock] - lngNeeded
                rst.Update
                rst.Close
                Me![subToyInventory].Requery
            End If
        End If

ErrorHandlerExit:
    Exit Sub

ErrorHandler:
    MsgBox "Error No: " & Err.Number & "; Description: " & _
        Err.Description
    Resume ErrorHandlerExit

End Sub
```

This procedure first checks that a toy has been selected and a nonzero amount entered, and exits the procedure if either test fails. If the tests are passed, a search string is created for searching for the selected toy in tblToys, using the Chr$(39) function to wrap the Toy ID with single quotes. A Debug.Print statement is used to display the search string in the Immediate window, which lets you inspect it, in case it isn't working right.

Next, a DAO recordset is set up based on tblToys, and the strSearch variable is used with the FindFirst method to attempt to locate the selected toy in tblToys. If it isn't found, an informative message is popped up, and the procedure is exited. If the record is found, an informative message is popped up to confirm removing the specified amount from inventory. If the user clicks Cancel, the amount is cleared from txtToyQuantity, and the procedure is exited. If the user clicks OK, the tblToys record is edited to subtract the amount needed from the amount in the UnitsInStock field, and to store the resulting amount back in UnitsInStock. The record is updated, the recordset closed, and the subToyInventory subform is requeried to reflect the change in the table.

At this point, the client reviews the modified form and suggests that the confirmation is premature before the other order information has been entered (a good point!), so I move the toy inventory and quantity controls down lower on the form. Some more checking is needed to ensure that a customer, employee, and the three dates have been filled in. I could modify the txtToyQuantity BeforeUpdate event procedure, but it's less cumbersome to just make txtToyQuantity disabled initially, and enable it only after all the relevant fields have been filled in. This is done by calling a procedure called CheckData (listed below) from various control AfterUpdate procedures. The modified fpriOrders is shown in Figure 8.13, with the confirmation message for removing items from inventory.

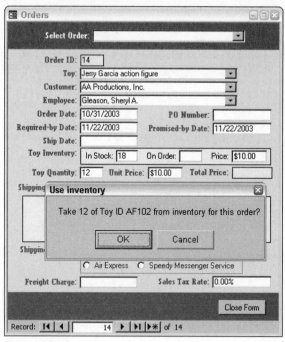

Figure 8.13

The entire Code Behind Forms module for fpriOrdersfollows. There is no error trapping for the calls to Sub procedures, because they have their own error trapping.

```
Option Compare Database
Option Explicit

Dim lngAvailable As Long
Dim lngNeeded As Long
Dim strPrompt As String
Dim strTitle As String
Dim intReturn As Integer


Private Sub EnableShippingAddress()

On Error GoTo ErrorHandler

   Dim lngCustomerID As Long

   lngCustomerID = Nz(Me![cboCustomerID])
   If lngCustomerID = 0 Then
      Me![cboShipAddressID].Enabled = False
   Else
      Me![cboShipAddressID].Enabled = True
      Me![cboShipAddressID].Requery
   End If
```

```
    ErrorHandlerExit:
       Exit Sub

    ErrorHandler:
       MsgBox "Error No: " & Err.Number & "; Description: " & _
          Err.Description
       Resume ErrorHandlerExit

End Sub

Private Sub cboCustomerID_AfterUpdate()

    Call EnableShippingAddress
    Call EnableQuantity

End Sub

Private Sub cboEmployeeID_AfterUpdate()

    Call EnableQuantity

End Sub

Private Sub cboSelect_AfterUpdate()

On Error GoTo ErrorHandler

    Dim strSearch As String

    strSearch = "[OrderID] = " & Me![cboSelect]

    'Find the record that matches the control
    Me.RecordsetClone.FindFirst strSearch
    Me.Bookmark = Me.RecordsetClone.Bookmark

ErrorHandlerExit:
   Exit Sub

ErrorHandler:
   MsgBox "Error No: " & Err.Number & "; Description: " & _
      Err.Description
   Resume ErrorHandlerExit

End Sub

Private Sub cboShipAddressID_AfterUpdate()

On Error GoTo ErrorHandlerExit

    On Error Resume Next
    DoCmd.RunCommand acCmdSaveRecord
    Debug.Print "Customer ID: " & Me![CustomerID]
    Debug.Print "Ship Address ID: " & Me![ShipAddressID]
```

```
    Me![subSelectedShippingAddress].Requery

ErrorHandlerExit:
    Exit Sub

ErrorHandler:
    MsgBox "Error No: " & Err.Number & "; Description: " & _
        Err.Description
    Resume ErrorHandlerExit

End Sub

Private Sub cboToyID_AfterUpdate()

On Error GoTo ErrorHandler

    Dim curToyPrice As Currency

    curToyPrice = Nz(Me![cboToyID].Column(3))
    Me![ToyPrice] = curToyPrice
    Me![txtToyPrice].Requery
    Me![subToyInventory].Requery
    Call EnableQuantity

ErrorHandlerExit:
    Exit Sub

ErrorHandler:
    MsgBox "Error No: " & Err.Number & "; Description: " & _
        Err.Description
    Resume ErrorHandlerExit

End Sub

Private Sub cmdClose_Click()

On Error GoTo ErrorHandler

    Dim prj As Object

    Set prj = Application.CurrentProject

    If prj.AllForms("fmnuMain").IsLoaded Then
        Forms![fmnuMain].Visible = True
    Else
        DoCmd.OpenForm "fmnuMain"
    End If

ErrorHandlerExit:
    DoCmd.Close acForm, Me.Name
    Exit Sub

ErrorHandler:
    If Err.Number = 2467 Then
```

```
            Resume ErrorHandlerExit
        Else
            MsgBox "Error No: " & Err.Number & "; Description: " & Err.Description
            Resume ErrorHandlerExit
        End If

End Sub

Private Sub Form_BeforeInsert(Cancel As Integer)

On Error GoTo ErrorHandler

    Me![txtToyQuantity].Enabled = False

ErrorHandlerExit:
    Exit Sub

ErrorHandler:
    MsgBox "Error No: " & Err.Number & "; Description: " & _
        Err.Description
    Resume ErrorHandlerExit

End Sub

Private Sub Form_Current()

On Error GoTo ErrorHandlerExit

    Me![cboSelect].Value = Null
    Call EnableShippingAddress
    Call EnableQuantity

ErrorHandlerExit:
    Exit Sub

ErrorHandler:
    MsgBox "Error No: " & Err.Number & "; Description: " & _
        Err.Description
    Resume ErrorHandlerExit

End Sub

Private Sub Form_Load()

On Error Resume Next

    DoCmd.RunCommand acCmdSizeToFitForm

End Sub

Private Sub txtOrderDate_AfterUpdate()

    Call EnableQuantity
```

```
End Sub

Private Sub txtPromisedByDate_BeforeUpdate(Cancel As Integer)

    Call EnableQuantity

End Sub

Private Sub txtRequiredByDate_BeforeUpdate(Cancel As Integer)

    Call EnableQuantity

End Sub

Private Sub txtToyQuantity_AfterUpdate()

On Error GoTo ErrorHandler

    Dim strToyID As String
    Dim dbs As DAO.Database
    Dim rst As DAO.Recordset
    Dim strSearch As String

    strToyID = Nz(Me![ToyID])
    lngNeeded = Nz(Me![txtToyQuantity].Value)
    Set dbs = CurrentDb
    Set rst = dbs.OpenRecordset("tblToys", dbOpenDynaset)
    strSearch = "[ToyID] = " & Chr$(39) & strToyID & Chr$(39)
    rst.FindFirst strSearch
    If rst.NoMatch = True Then
        strTitle = "Toy not found"
        strPrompt = "Can't find Toy ID " & strToyID & " in tblToys"
        MsgBox strPrompt, vbOKOnly, strTitle
        GoTo ErrorHandlerExit
    Else
        'Found the toy; ask for confirmation of reducing inventory
        strTitle = "Use inventory"
        strPrompt = "Take " & lngNeeded & " of Toy ID " & strToyID _
            & " from inventory for this order?"
        intReturn = MsgBox(strPrompt, vbOKCancel, strTitle)
        If intReturn = vbCancel Then
            Me![txtToyQuantity].Value = Null
            GoTo ErrorHandlerExit
        ElseIf intReturn = vbOK Then
            rst.Edit
            rst![UnitsInStock] = rst![UnitsInStock] - lngNeeded
            rst.Update
            rst.Close
            Me![subToyInventory].Requery
        End If
    End If

ErrorHandlerExit:
```

```
      Exit Sub

ErrorHandler:
    MsgBox "Error No: " & Err.Number & "; Description: " & _
        Err.Description
    Resume ErrorHandlerExit

End Sub

Private Sub txtToyQuantity_BeforeUpdate(Cancel As Integer)

On Error Resume Next

    Dim strToyID As String
    Dim dbs As DAO.Database
    Dim rst As DAO.Recordset
    Dim strSearch As String

    'Check that an amount has been entered
    strToyID = Nz(Me![ToyID])
    lngNeeded = Nz(Me![txtToyQuantity].Value)
    lngAvailable = Nz(Me![subToyInventory]![UnitsInStock])
    If lngNeeded = 0 Then
        GoTo ErrorHandlerExit
    Else
        strSearch = "[ToyID] = " & Chr$(39) & strToyID & Chr$(39)
        Debug.Print "Search string: " & strSearch
    End If

    If lngAvailable < lngNeeded Then
        strTitle = "Not enough inventory"
        strPrompt = lngNeeded & " needed; only " & lngAvailable & " available"
        MsgBox strPrompt, vbOKOnly, strTitle
        Me![txtToyQuantity].Undo
        Cancel = True
    End If

ErrorHandlerExit:
    Exit Sub

ErrorHandler:
    MsgBox "Error No: " & Err.Number & "; Description: " & _
        Err.Description
    Resume ErrorHandlerExit

End Sub

Sub CheckData()

On Error GoTo ErrorHandler

    strTitle = "Missing data"
    If Nz(Me![cboToyID].Value) = "" Then
```

```
          strPrompt = "Please select a toy"
          MsgBox strPrompt, vbOKOnly, strTitle
          Me![cboToyID].SetFocus
          GoTo ErrorHandlerExit
      End If

      If Nz(Me![cboCustomerID].Value) = 0 Then
          strPrompt = "Please select a customer"
          MsgBox strPrompt, vbOKOnly, strTitle
          Me![cboCustomerID].SetFocus
          GoTo ErrorHandlerExit
      End If

      If Nz(Me![cboEmployeeID].Value) = "" Then
          strPrompt = "Please select an employee"
          MsgBox strPrompt, vbOKOnly, strTitle
          Me![cboEmployeeID].SetFocus
          GoTo ErrorHandlerExit
      End If

      If Nz(Me![txtOrderDate].Value) = "" Then
          strPrompt = "Please enter an order date"
          MsgBox strPrompt, vbOKOnly, strTitle
          Me![txtOrderDate].SetFocus
          GoTo ErrorHandlerExit
      End If

      If Nz(Me![txtRequiredByDate].Value) = "" Then
          strPrompt = "Please enter a required-by date"
          MsgBox strPrompt, vbOKOnly, strTitle
          Me![txtRequiredByDate].SetFocus
          GoTo ErrorHandlerExit
      End If

      If Nz(Me![txtPromisedByDate].Value) = "" Then
          strPrompt = "Please enter a required-by date"
          MsgBox strPrompt, vbOKOnly, strTitle
          Me![txtPromisedByDate].SetFocus
          GoTo ErrorHandlerExit
      End If

      If Nz(Me![txtToyQuantity].Value) = 0 Then
          strPrompt = "Please enter an amount to order"
          MsgBox strPrompt, vbOKOnly, strTitle
          Me![txtToyQuantity].SetFocus
          GoTo ErrorHandlerExit
      End If

ErrorHandlerExit:
   Exit Sub

ErrorHandler:
```

```
         MsgBox "Error No: " & Err.Number & "; Description: " & _
            Err.Description
         Resume ErrorHandlerExit

   End Sub

   Sub EnableQuantity()

   On Error GoTo ErrorHandler

         If Nz(Me![cboToyID].Value) = "" Then
            Me![txtToyQuantity].Enabled = False
            GoTo ErrorHandlerExit
         End If

         If Nz(Me![cboCustomerID].Value) = 0 Then
            Me![txtToyQuantity].Enabled = False
            GoTo ErrorHandlerExit
         End If

         If Nz(Me![cboEmployeeID].Value) = "" Then
            Me![txtToyQuantity].Enabled = False
            GoTo ErrorHandlerExit
         End If

         If Nz(Me![txtOrderDate].Value) = "" Then
            Me![txtToyQuantity].Enabled = False
            GoTo ErrorHandlerExit
         End If

         If Nz(Me![txtRequiredByDate].Value) = "" Then
            Me![txtToyQuantity].Enabled = False
            GoTo ErrorHandlerExit
         End If

         If Nz(Me![txtPromisedByDate].Value) = "" Then
            Me![txtToyQuantity].Enabled = False
            GoTo ErrorHandlerExit
         End If

         Me![txtToyQuantity].Enabled = True

   ErrorHandlerExit:
      Exit Sub

   ErrorHandler:
      MsgBox "Error No: " & Err.Number & "; Description: " & _
         Err.Description
      Resume ErrorHandlerExit

   End Sub
```

Standard Changes

Certain application features are quite likely to be needed at some point in an application, even though the client may not have originally requested them, or may even have specifically stated that they would not be needed. Some of these features are so commonly needed (database backup, generating Word letters, filtering reports by a date range) that I have built them into my standard main menu, which is created for an application by running the Menu Manager add-in. (See Chapter 6, *Printing Data with Reports*, for more details on using this add-in.) This eliminates the need to discuss why a certain feature is a good idea (and why the client should pay for its development)—it's just there, and the client can use it or not, as he or she prefers. Splitting a name into separate fields is one of these often-needed changes, and another is the need to generate Word letters to customers.

Adding More Name Fields

At the initial Q&A session for setting up the Toy Workshop application, the client said that there was no need to store prefixes and suffixes for names in most of the tables in the application that store name information. The tblCustomers, tblEmployees, and tblVendors tables don't have Prefix and Suffix fields. However, tblMailingList does have these fields, because it was anticipated that Word letters might be sent to the mailing list at some point. Now the Toy Workshop client has hired a new employee whose name includes a suffix ("Jr."), and he wants to send Word letters to vendors and possibly customers as well as to people on his mailing list.

This means that the tblEmployees, tblVendors, and tblCustomers tables need a Prefix and Suffix field so that the "Jr." can be stored in the proper field and letters can be addressed using the appropriate prefix (Mr., Ms., Dr., and so on). Currently there is just a ContactName field in tblVendors, so the information in that field needs to be extracted and put into separate fields, which can be done with query expressions modified from the queries in the Query Expressions sample database for Chapter 4, *Sorting and Filtering Data with Queries*.

There are several stages to making these changes. First, the new fields need to be added to the tables. Next, controls bound to the new fields need to be placed on various forms. And finally, queries and reports that display name data need to be modified to include the Prefix and Suffix fields, where relevant. The first step is to open each table with name fields in Design view and add the new fields. Figure 8.14 shows tblCustomers with the new ContactPrefix and ContactSuffix fields.

> *If you try to modify the structure of a table while an object bound to that table is open, you will get the error message "You can't open the table 'tblInfo' for modification" (with the name of the table you are trying to modify). Close any objects bound to the table, and try again. If you still get the same error message, closing the database and reopening using Shift-Enter to bypass startup code should do the trick.*

Similar fields are also added to tblEmployees and tblVendors (leaving the original ContactName field in tblVendors, because it contains the whole name that needs to be split up among the new fields). After adding the new fields to the tables, forms bound to the tables need new Prefix and Suffix controls. Figure 8.15 shows the main Employees form, with the new Prefix and Suffix fields, for the employee with the Jr. suffix.

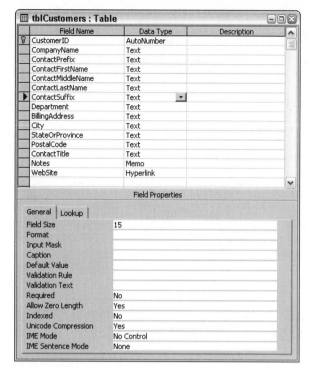

Figure 8.14

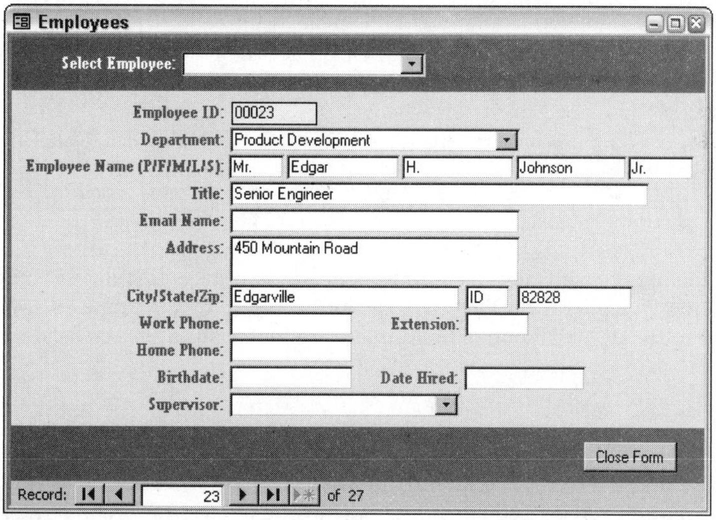

Figure 8.15

The Customer Address tab on frmCustomers also needs two more controls, for the ContactPrefix and ContactSuffix fields. Before modifying the final form, frmVendors, an update query is needed to fill the separate fields with first name and last name information from the ContactName field. I started by importing qrySplitNameComponents from the Query Expressions sample database for Chapter 4, *Sorting and Filtering Data with Queries*. Next, create a new query based on tblVendors, and create expressions for the new ContactFirstName and ContactLastName fields. For ContactFirstName, the FirstNameF expression from qrySplitNameComponents is fine, if we simply substitute ContactName for FirstNameFirst, as shown in Figure 8.16.

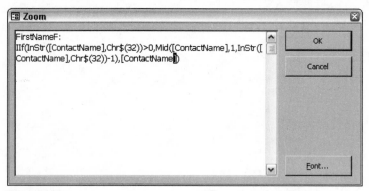

Figure 8.16

For the remaining name fields, I could use the full set of fields in qrySplitNameComponents, pasting the MiddleNamePlusF expression into the expressions for the MiddleNameF and LastNameF fields as needed. However, eyeballing tblVendors shows that in fact there are no middle names in the ContactName field for any records, so instead I'll create a simpler LastName expression, on the assumption that the last name starts after the space in the ContactName field. The expressions for extracting the first name and last name from the ContactName field are:

```
FirstName: IIf(InStr([ContactName],Chr$(32))>0,Mid([ContactName],1,
InStr([ContactName],Chr$(32))-1),[ContactName])
LastName: IIf(InStr([ContactName],Chr$(32))>0,Mid([ContactName],
InStr([ContactName],Chr$(32))+1),[ContactName])
```

After checking the query results in Datasheet view, to see that the correct name components are being extracted (as shown in Figure 8.17), the query can be converted to an update query, by moving the field expressions to the Update To column of the ContactFirstName and ContactLastName fields.

The update query is shown in Design view in Figure 8.18.

After running the query, the tblVendors table now has data in the ContactFirstName and ContactLastName fields; the other fields will have to be filled in manually, when and if the information is available. The redundant ContactName field can now be removed from tblVendors. frmVendors now needs controls to display the data from the separate name fields, and its txtContactName control can be removed. The modified frmVendors form is shown in Figure 8.19.

Figure 8.17

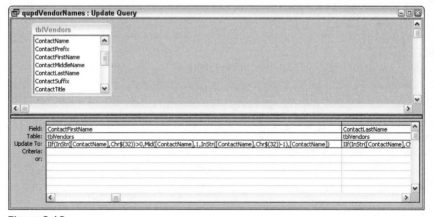

Figure 8.18

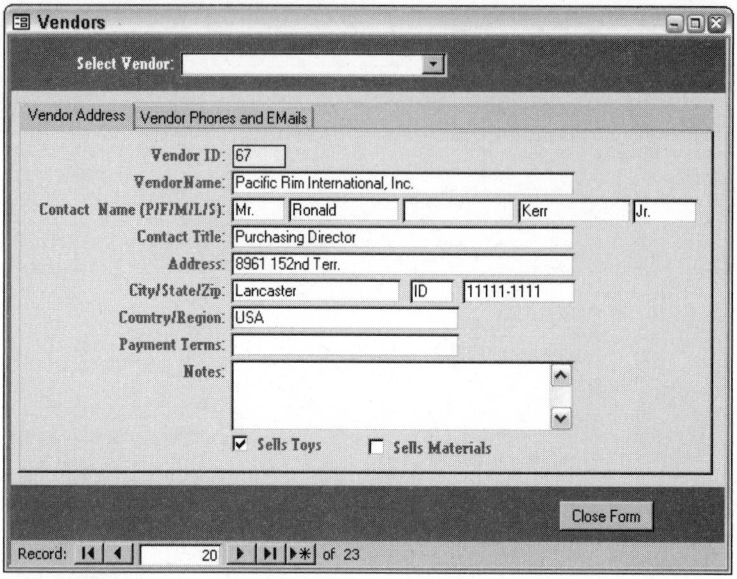

Figure 8.19

Customizing the Main Menu's Word Letters Component

The client may not have originally planned on sending Word letters to clients, but as the application is used and more features are added to it, quite often there will be a need to generate Word letters. My standard main menu has a Word Letters section that can be customized to send a letter to a recipient selected from a table in the database.

The main menu of the Toy Workshop database already contains the controls and code needed to generate a letter to a single recipient, using a Word template selected from a combobox and a table of sample data. To customize this component to work with your application's data, you need to make several changes:

1. Add the required doc properties to the client's Word template(s).

2. Add the templates to tlkpLetters.

3. Replace the sample zstblSampleData table in cboLetter's RowSource property with a reference to the database table that contains the letter recipient data.

4. Modify the cmdLetters Click event procedure (if necessary), depending on what fields need to be printed on the Word letter.

The original cmdLetters Click event procedure is:

```
Private Sub cmdLetters_Click()

On Error GoTo ErrorHandler

    Dim strLetter As String
```

```
      Dim strRecipient As String
      Dim strTestFile As String
      Dim ctl As Access.Control
      Dim docs As Word.Documents
      Dim prps As Object
      Dim strDocsPath As String
      Dim strTemplatePath As String

      'Check that a letter has been selected
      strLetter = Nz(Me![cboLetters])
      Set ctl = Me![cboLetters]
      If strLetter = "" Then
         ctl.SetFocus
         ctl.Dropdown
         GoTo ErrorHandlerExit
      End If

      'Check that a recipient has been selected.
      strRecipient = Nz(Me![cboRecipients])
      Set ctl = Me![cboRecipients]
      If strRecipient = "" Then
         ctl.SetFocus
         ctl.Dropdown
         GoTo ErrorHandlerExit
      End If

      Set appWord = GetObject(, "Word.Application")
      strDocsPath = DocsDir
      strTemplatePath = TemplateDir
      strLetter = strTemplatePath & strLetter

      'Check for existence of template in template folder,
      'and exit if not found
      strTestFile = Nz(Dir(strLetter))
      Debug.Print "Test file: " & strTestFile
      If strTestFile = "" Then
         MsgBox strLetter & " template not found; can't create letter"
         GoTo ErrorHandlerExit
      End If

      Set docs = appWord.Documents
      docs.Add strLetter
      Set ctl = Me![cboRecipients]

On Error Resume Next
      Set prps = appWord.ActiveDocument.CustomDocumentProperties
      prps.Item("Name").Value = Nz(ctl.Column(6))
      prps.Item("Street").Value = Nz(ctl.Column(1))
      prps.Item("City").Value = Nz(ctl.Column(2))
      prps.Item("State").Value = Nz(ctl.Column(3))
      prps.Item("Zip").Value = Nz(ctl.Column(4))
      prps.Item("Country").Value = Nz(ctl.Column(5))

On Error GoTo ErrorHandlerExit
      'Update fields and make letter visible
```

279

```
    With appWord
        .Visible = True
        .Selection.WholeStory
        .Selection.Fields.Update
        .Visible = True
        .Activate
    End With

ErrorHandlerExit:
    Exit Sub

ErrorHandler:
    If Err = 429 Then
        'Word is not running; open Word with CreateObject
        Set appWord = CreateObject("Word.Application")
        Resume Next
    Else
        MsgBox "Error No: " & Err.Number & "; Description: " & Err.Description
        Resume ErrorHandlerExit
    End If

End Sub
```

The cboLetters combobox has a lookup table, tlkpLetters, as its row source. When a template is selected from this combobox, the code looks for the template in the folder designated as the Word UserTemplates folder (see Chapter 11, *Working with Word*, for more details on the TemplateDir function that is used to find this folder). If the template is found, a new letter is created from it, and a set of doc properties is filled with name and address data from the selected recipient from cboRecipients.

There are two ways you can customize Word templates to work with this code: add the appropriate doc properties to existing templates, or make copies of the sample template (Test Letter.dot) and modify their text as needed. If the templates aren't very complicated, it's easier to make copies of Test Letter.dot and add the appropriate logo, text, headers, and footers, but if the templates are complex, you'll probably want to add the necessary doc properties to them.

To quickly (and accurately) copy doc properties from one Word template to another, you can use the procedure that follows, run from a standard module. It is in basUtilities in the Toy Workshop sample database. Modify the template path, original document name, and target document name as required, and run the procedure from the module window with the F5 hot key.

```
Sub CopyDocProps()

On Error GoTo ErrorHandler

    Dim appWord As Word.Application
    Dim strTemplatePath As String
    Dim strOriginalDoc As String
    Dim strTargetDoc As String
    Dim prp As Object
```

```
        Dim prpsOriginal As Object
        Dim prpsTarget As Object
        Dim docOriginal As Word.Document
        Dim docTarget As Word.Document

        Set appWord = GetObject(, "Word.Application")
        strTemplatePath = _
            appWord.Options.DefaultFilePath(wdUserTemplatesPath) _
            & "\Access Merge\"
        Debug.Print "Templates folder: " & strTemplatePath
        strOriginalDoc = strTemplatePath & "Test Letter.dot"
        strTargetDoc = strTemplatePath & "TW Contact Letter.dot"
        Set docOriginal = appWord.Documents.Open(strOriginalDoc)
        Set docTarget = appWord.Documents.Open(strTargetDoc)
        Set prpsOriginal = docOriginal.CustomDocumentProperties
        Set prpsTarget = docTarget.CustomDocumentProperties

    On Error Resume Next
        For Each prp In prpsOriginal
            Debug.Print "Adding " & prp.Name & " to " & strTargetDoc
            prpsTarget.Add Name:=prp.Name, LinkToContent:=False, _
                Value:=prp.Value, Type:=msoPropertyTypeString
        Next prp

        appWord.Visible = True

ErrorHandlerExit:
    Exit Sub

ErrorHandler:
    If Err = 429 Then
        'Word is not running; open Word with CreateObject
        Set appWord = CreateObject("Word.Application")
        Resume Next
    Else
        MsgBox "Error No: " & Err.Number & "; Description: " & Err.Description
        Resume ErrorHandlerExit
    End If

End Sub
```

The CopyDocProps procedure uses some properties of the DocProperty object in the Office object model, because these properties allow you to specify the type of doc property you are creating, and (more importantly) these properties are read/write, which is not the case with doc properties in the Word object model. Because of this, you need to set a reference to the Office object library in a database that uses this code.

While running the procedure, you'll see the doc property names in the Immediate window, and afterward, you can see the new doc properties on the Custom page of the properties sheet in the target document, as shown in Figure 8.20.

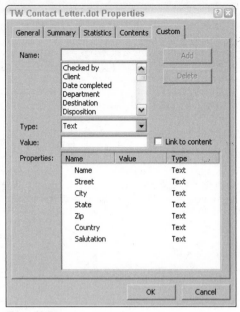

Figure 8.20

The next step is to make field codes visible on the template (which should be open after running the CopyDocProps procedure), delete the FormText, MailMerge, or other codes, and insert DocProperty codes where you want the data from the name and address doc properties to appear in the document. Figure 8.21 shows the FormText fields in the original TW Contact Letter template being replaced by DocProperty codes.

> *Inserting DocProperty fields is a multistep process, and it is different in Word 2000 and Word 2002 (or higher). For a complete explanation of how to insert a DocProperty field in a document, see my white paper "Adding Custom Doc Properties to a Word Template," which can be downloaded from the Downloads page on my Web site (www.helenfeddema.com).*

After inserting DocProperty fields where needed, the next step is to add the template to the tlkpLetters lookup table so that it will be available for the cboLetters combobox on the main menu. Next, the SQL statement in the cboRecipients RowSource property needs to have zstblSampleData replaced by the table you want to use for selecting letter recipients (I'll use the tblVendors table), and you can modify calculated expressions as needed. I also added the FirstName field to the query, to use for the Salutation doc property. The SQL statement is shown in Figure 8.22.

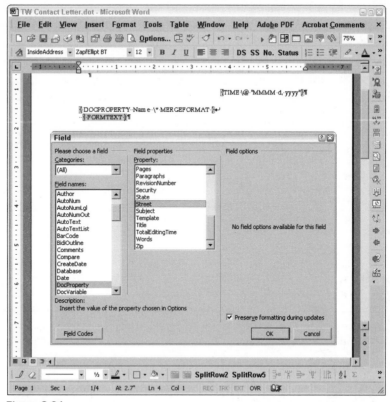

Figure 8.21

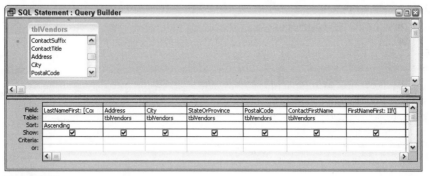

Figure 8.22

If the SQL statement has a different number of columns after your modifications, modify the Columns and ColumnWidths properties of the combobox accordingly (all columns except the first should have a width of zero) because they don't need to show in the drop-down list).

Finally, the Click event procedure of the cmdLetters command button needs tweaking, to match up the SQL statement fields with the doc properties. The table below shows how the fields match the doc properties (you need to know the zero-based column position to reference the field in VBA code):

Row Source Field	Doc Property	Column Position
LastNameFirst	[not used]	0
Address	Street	1
City	City	2
StateOrProvince	State	3
PostalCode	Zip	4
ContactFirstName	Salutation	5
FirstNameFirst	Name	6

The modified procedure is:

```
Private Sub cmdLetters_Click()

On Error GoTo ErrorHandler

    Dim strLetter As String
    Dim strRecipient As String
    Dim strTestFile As String
    Dim cbo As Access.ComboBox
    Dim docs As Word.Documents
    Dim prps As Object
    Dim strDocsPath As String
    Dim strTemplatePath As String

    'Check that a letter has been selected
    strLetter = Nz(Me![cboLetters])
    Set cbo = Me![cboLetters]
    If strLetter = "" Then
        cbo.SetFocus
        cbo.Dropdown
        GoTo ErrorHandlerExit
    End If

    'Check that a recipient has been selected.
    strRecipient = Nz(Me![cboRecipients])
    Set cbo = Me![cboRecipients]
    If strRecipient = "" Then
        cbo.SetFocus
        cbo.Dropdown
```

```
          GoTo ErrorHandlerExit
      End If

      Set appWord = GetObject(, "Word.Application")
      strDocsPath = DocsDir
      'Reference a subfolder under the Templates folder (optional)
      strTemplatePath = TemplateDir & "Access Merge\"
      strLetter = strTemplatePath & strLetter

      'Check for existence of template in template folder,
      'and exit if not found
      strTestFile = Nz(Dir(strLetter))
      Debug.Print "Test file: " & strTestFile
      If strTestFile = "" Then
          MsgBox strLetter & " template not found; can't create letter"
          GoTo ErrorHandlerExit
      End If

      Set docs = appWord.Documents
      docs.Add strLetter
      Set cbo = Me![cboRecipients]

  On Error Resume Next
      Set prps = appWord.ActiveDocument.CustomDocumentProperties
      prps.Item("Name").Value = Nz(cbo.Column(6))
      prps.Item("Street").Value = Nz(cbo.Column(1))
      prps.Item("City").Value = Nz(cbo.Column(2))
      prps.Item("State").Value = Nz(cbo.Column(3))
      prps.Item("Zip").Value = Nz(cbo.Column(4))
      prps.Item("Salutation").Value = Nz(cbo.Column(5))

  On Error GoTo ErrorHandlerExit
      'Update fields and make letter visible
      With appWord
          .Visible = True
          .Selection.WholeStory
          .Selection.Fields.Update
          .Visible = True
          .Activate
      End With

  ErrorHandlerExit:
      Exit Sub

  ErrorHandler:
      If Err = 429 Then
          'Word is not running; open Word with CreateObject.
          Set appWord = CreateObject("Word.Application")
          Resume Next
      Else
          MsgBox "Error No: " & Err.Number & "; Description: " & Err.Description
          Resume ErrorHandlerExit
      End If

  End Sub
```

With these changes in place, after selecting the TW Contact Letter template and a recipient, a letter similar to the one in Figure 8.23 is generated.

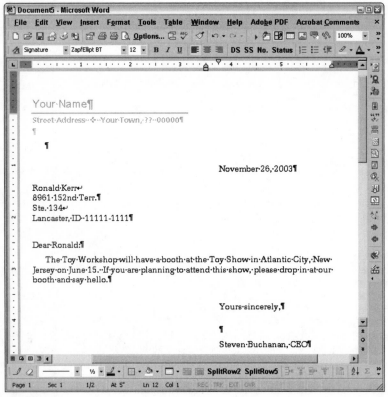

Figure 8.23

You might want to have more choices when creating documents, such as sending letters to everyone or to multiple (but not all) recipients. Or you might want to create a catalog merge, to put data from different records into rows of a Word table. If you have huge numbers of recipients, too many to produce a separate Word letter for each one in a single session, you need to do a mail merge. All these alternate methods of creating Word documents filled with Access data are discussed in detail in Chapter 11, *Working with Word*.

Summary

With a little common sense (and patience), you should be able to work harmoniously with clients through many years of application and Office upgrades—or at least, the ones you would want to keep as long-term clients—making changes to their applications that will enhance their usefulness, so the clients will return to you to make further changes in the future.

Reworking an Existing Application

When you are given the task of reworking an application developed by another person (perhaps a client with only basic end-user Access skills), you have to make a decision on whether to rework the database or scrap it and start over from the beginning. If the database does work (mostly), you can rework it—apply a naming convention, normalize tables and relationships, create an attractive main menu, and standardize the appearance of forms and reports. If it is basically nonfunctional, you will need to create a new database, and then move data from the old, nonworking database into the new one (this task is covered in Chapter 10, *Moving Old Data into a New Database*). In this chapter, I will concentrate on fixing and enhancing a database that is basically functional, but needs work to become an efficient and attractive application.

I'll explain why a naming convention is essential for making your database self-documenting, and walk you through using the LNC Rename add-in I created to make it easier to apply a naming convention. I will also explain (using a real-life example) how to normalize a database's tables, and rework its forms and reports as needed.

Applying a Naming Convention

Access lets you give database objects (tables, queries, and so forth) any name you want, up to 64 characters in length, with spaces and most punctuation marks. Unfortunately, Access does not automatically apply an appropriate prefix to objects as you create them (a feature that has long been requested by developers!). Considering that the original Leszynski-Reddick Naming Convention (the predecessor to the Leszynski Naming Convention) was developed for Access 1.0 in 1993, auto-prefixing of database objects is long overdue. However, Microsoft hasn't yet built this essential feature into Access, so it is up to the user (or developer) to manually apply a naming convention to database objects and variables.

While freestyle Access object and control naming is certainly an improvement over older database programs (such as dBASE), which had strict limits on object and field name length and format, this flexibility has a downside. In the interface, you can see what type of object you are dealing with, because Access places different types of objects on separate pages in the database window. For queries (as shown in Figure 9.1), you can tell the query type by its icon, where a union query has the linked circles icon, and a crosstab query has the datasheet icon, instead of the standard select query linked datasheets icon.

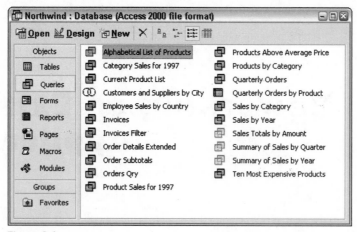

Figure 9.1

However, when you are working in VBA code—referencing database objects and creating and using variables—the lack of a built-in identifier causes serious problems. There is no way to tell whether the word "Sales" refers to a table, query, form, report, or variable (and if a variable, what data type). Additionally, when you are working with forms and reports, especially those created by the Access Form Wizard or Report Wizard, typically all bound controls have the same name as their fields (see Figure 9.2), and so do controls that you manually drag to a form or report in Design view. Unfortunately, this causes reference confusion and, in some cases, circular reference errors.

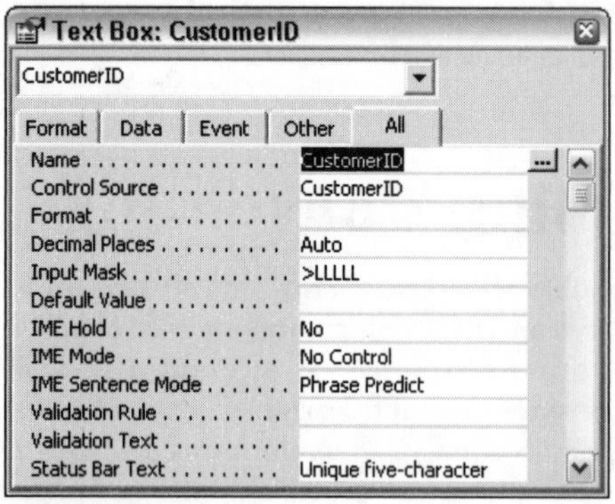

Figure 9.2

> If you see #Error in a control in form view, this is most likely the result of a circular reference error, caused by a control having the same name as the field to which it is bound. The circular reference occurs when an expression in a control's Control Source property references the field to which the control is bound, while the control itself has the same name. See Figure 9.3 for an example of an expression that will cause #Error to appear in a control. The fix is simple: Give the control a prefix so that it has a different name than the field.

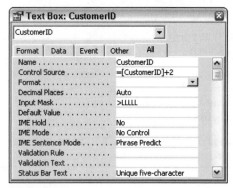

Figure 9.3

When creating a database from scratch, you can (and should) give all newly created objects, controls, and variables names that indicate (respectively) the object, control, or data type. The Leszynski-Reddick Naming Convention (1993) was the first widely accepted naming convention for Access, and is based on the Hungarian notation for naming objects developed by Charles Simonyi. There are now two variants of the original convention: the Leszynski Naming Convention (which I use) and the Reddick VBA Naming convention. The important thing is not which naming convention you use, but that you use one If your database will be viewed by other developers, it is advisable to use one of the two widely accepted conventions (Leszynski or Reddick).

The latest version of the LNC may be downloaded from www.kwery.com and the latest version of the RVBA convention from www.xoc.net.

The Leszynski Naming Convention

The Leszynski Naming Convention uses prefixes to indicate the object type, control type, or variable data type, and (optionally) the field data type. Use of distinctive prefixes makes your database self-documenting; when you see `frmSales` in code, you will know that it is a form, and when you see `curSales` you will know that it is a Currency variable. When selecting a query from a drop-down list, you will know that a query starting with *qmak* is a make-table query, while one starting with *quni* is a union query. This information will allow you to avoid errors such as using the SetFocus method (a control method) with a field, or trying to open a table.

Hungarian notation (named after Charles Simonyi's native country) breaks down object names into the following elements:

```
[prefix(es)][tag]BaseName[Suffix/Qualifier]
```

These elements are described in the following table.

Component	Description	Example
Prefix(es)	A lowercase letter that adds extra information to the tag.	*p* for Public variable
Tag	A three-letter sequence indicating the object type.	*tbl* for table
BaseName	A word or two describing the object. If several words are used, each starts with a capital letter, and there are no spaces between them.	*OutlookContacts*—contacts imported from Outlook
Suffix (RVBA), Qualifier (LNC)	A word giving more specific information about an object.	*ByDate*—the data is sorted by date

I use LNC notation for database objects, controls on forms and reports, and variables. I don't use field prefixes (although some developers do), because giving prefixes only to controls prevents confusion—if a name (such as StreetAddress) has no prefix, I know that it is a field name. Also, using field prefixes would interfere with the operation of my LNC Rename add-in (to be described later in this chapter).

The basic LNC object prefixes are described in the following table.

Object	Tag
Incomplete objects, backup objects, or objects that are under development	_ or– (In Access 2000 and 2002, dashes sort to the beginning of the database object list; in Access 2003, underscores sort to the beginning)
Hidden system objects	*zh*
Displayed system objects	*zs*
Programmatically created temporary objects	*zt*
Backup copies of objects, for later copying or reuse	*zz*

The basic LNC variable prefixes are described in the following table.

Variable type	Tag
Local variable	[no prefix]
Local static variable	*s*
Module-level variable	*m*
Public variable in a form or report module	*p*
Public variable declared in the Declarations section of a standard module	*g*

The basic LNC database object tags are described in the following table.

Object	Tag
Class module	*cls*
Form	*frm*
Form (dialog)	*fdlg*
Form (menu)	*fmnu*
Form (message)	*fmsg*
Form (subform)	*fsub*
Macro	*mcr*
Module	*bas*
Query (any type)	*qry*
Query (append)	*qapp*
Query (crosstab)	*qxtb*
Query (data definition)	*qddl*
Query (delete)	*qdel*
Query (form filter)	*qflt*
Query (lookup)	*qlkp*
Query (make-table)	*qmak*
Query (select)	*qry* (or *qsel*)
Query (SQL pass-through)	*qspt*

Table continued on following page

Object	Tag
Query (union)	*quni*
Query (update)	*qupd*
Report	*rpt*
Report (subreport)	*rsub*
Table	*tbl*
Table (attached dBASE)	*tdbf*
Table (attached Excel)	*txls*
Table (attached FoxPro)	*tfox*
Table (attached Lotus)	*twks*
Table (attached ODBC)	*todb*
Table (attached Paradox)	*tpdx*
Table (attached SQL Server)	*tsql*
Table (attached text)	*ttxt*
Table (lookup)	*tlkp*

The following table lists the LNC table field tags (I don't use these personally, but I am including them for completeness).

Object	Tag
Autonumber (random nonsequential)	*idn*
Autonumber (replication ID)	*idr*
Autonumber (sequential)	*ids*
Binary	*bin*
Byte	*byt*
Currency	*cur*
Date/Time	*dtm*
Double	*dbl*
Hyperlink	*hlk*
Integer	*int*
Long	*lng*
Memo	*mem*

Object	Tag
OLE	*ole*
Single	*sng*
Text (character)	*chr*
Yes/No (Boolean)	*bln*

The following table lists the LNC tags for VBA variables.

Object	Tag
Combobox	*cbo*
CommandBar	*cbr*
Control (generic; useful when cycling through controls on a form or report)	*ctl*
Currency	*cur*
Database	*dbs*
Double	*dbl*
Form	*frm*
Integer	*int*
Label	*lbl*
List box	*lst*
Long	*lng*
QueryDef	*qdf*
Report	*rpt*
Single	*sng*
Snapshot	*snp*
String	*str*
Table	*tbl*
Textbox	*txt*
Type (user-defined)	*typ*
Variant	*var*

The LNC tags for form and report controls are listed in the following table.

Object	Tag
Bound object frame	*Frb*
Chart (graph)	*Cht*
Check box	*Chk*
Combobox	*Cbo*
Command button	*Cmd*
Custom control	*Ocx*
Frame	*Fra*
Hyperlink	*Hlk*
Image	*Img*
Label	*Lbl*
Line	*Lin*
Listbox	*Lst*
Option button	*Opt*
Option group	*Grp*
Page (on a tab control)	*Pge*
Page break	*Brk*
Rectangle (shape)	*Shp*
Subform/report	*Sub*
Tab control	*tab*
Textbox	*txt*
Toggle button	*tgl*
Unbound object frame	*fru*

The following table lists some typical LNC names of database objects, controls, and variables.

Object/variable name	LNC naming elements	Description
tblEmployees	tag + base name	A table of employee data
qupdSales	tag + base name	A query that updates sales data
fsubDayMax	tag + base name + qualifier	A subform that shows the maximum day
intLines	tag + base name	An Integer variable to hold a value representing the number of lines

Object/variable name	LNC naming elements	Description
curSales	tag + base name	A Currency variable holding a Sales value
pstrForm	prefix + tag + base name	A public String variable holding a form name
zztblContacts	prefix + tag + base name	A backup Contacts table, for copying and filling with imported data

In addition to the standard LNC tags, you can create your own custom tags as needed. I use the *tmak* tag for tables created from make-table queries, with the same base name, so when I see a table called tmakNewContacts, I know that it was created by a query called qmakNewContacts. This lets me know that if I want to modify the table, I need to modify the query that generates it, because changes to the table will be lost the next time the query is run. I also use *qtot* as a prefix for totals queries—although totals queries are just a type of select queries, when you are selecting a query to use as the source object for a totals subform, it is useful to know which queries are totals queries.

Applying the LNC to a Database

When you are reworking an application created by someone else, with no naming convention, applying a naming convention manually is a daunting (and time-consuming) task—and also one that a client probably doesn't want to pay for! You not only have to rename each object, and each form or report control, but also have to correct all the references to the renamed objects and controls in other database objects and code. To make this task less burdensome, I created the LNC Rename add-in, an Access add-in that automates the process of renaming database objects and form and report controls, and also corrects references to them in code.

This add-in piggybacks on another add-in, Rick Fisher's very useful Find And Replace, for some of its functionality (FAR does the search and replace work in code). The latest version of Find And Replace may be downloaded from Rick Fisher's Web site, www.RickWorld.com.

If you don't already have LNC Rename installed, you will need to install it. This add-in is available as LNC Rename Add-in.zip (for Access 2000 and up) from www.wrox.com. The .zip file for this add-in includes a 30-day trial version of FAR. To install FAR, extract the Repl9.exe file and follow the instruction in its Readme file. After installing FAR, and copying the LNC Rename.mda file to the Add-ins folder (usually C:\WINDOWS\Application Data\Microsoft\AddIns), you can install LNC Rename from the Add-in Manager in any database, as shown in Figure 9.4.

The sample Northwind database that comes with Access has no consistent naming convention, so it is a good example for running the LNC Rename add-in. For trying out the LNC Rename add-in, make a copy of the Northwind database (located in the Samples subfolder under the main Office folder); alternately, you can use the sample database in the LNC Rename Add-in.zip file.

After installing the LNC Rename add-in, you will now have three new selections on the Add-ins menu: Rename Form Controls, Rename Report Controls, and Rename Database Objects, as shown in Figure 9.5.

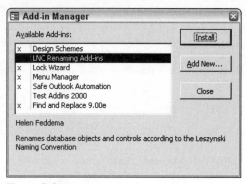

Figure 9.4

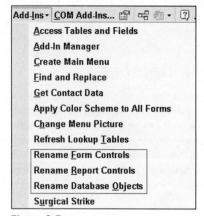

Figure 9.5

LNC Menu Add-Ins

The first step in renaming objects is to rename the main database objects. In the copy of Northwind.mdb, drop down the Add-Ins menu and select Rename Database Objects. The Choose Database Object dialog opens, as shown in Figure 9.6.

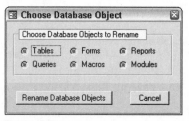

Figure 9.6

I recommend doing the renaming in the following order: tables, queries, forms, reports, and (optionally) macros and modules (you may not feel the need to rename macros and modules, because they are rarely referenced by other database objects). After selecting a database object type from the option group, click the Rename Database Objects button to open another dialog, listing each object of the selected type in the database with its current name and suggested new name. Figure 9.7 shows this dialog for tables.

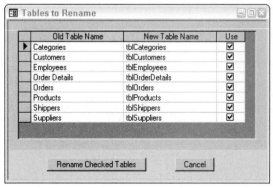

Figure 9.7

You can edit the suggested new names as desired, and (if you don't wish to rename all the objects), uncheck the Use checkbox for selected objects. Clicking the Rename Checked Tables button starts the process of renaming the tables and all references to them. In a database with no naming convention (such as Northwind), the same name is typically used for several different types of database objects, such as tables and forms, so you will need to verify all the proposed name changes. The first confirmation dialog that appears when renaming Northwind tables is shown in Figure 9.8.

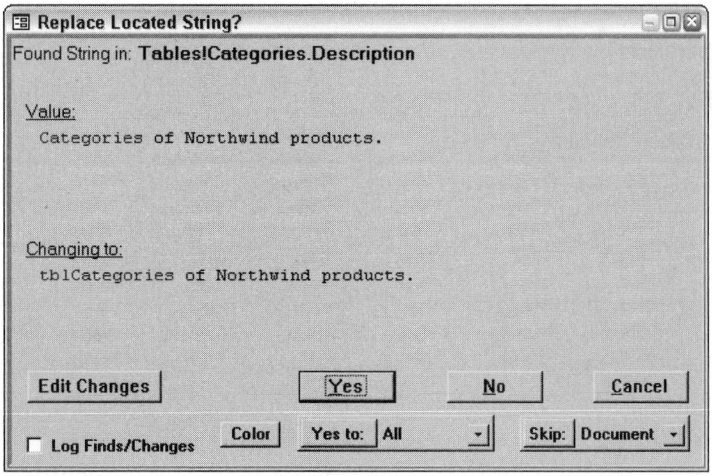

Figure 9.8

You wouldn't want to change the word "Categories" in the table description to "tblCategories," so click No on this dialog (and any other dialogs that would make an inappropriate change). Figure 9.9 shows an appropriate reference change, in the row source of a lookup field.

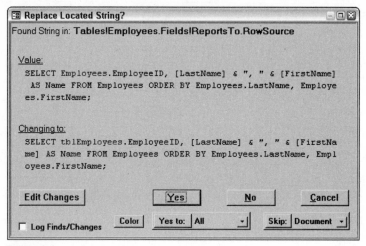

Figure 9.9

Some object renaming hints:

❑ SELECT clauses reference tables or queries.

❑ The IsLoaded function references forms.

❑ Forms! references reference forms.

❑ Reports! references reference reports.

❑ Text in Description fields and label captions generally doesn't need renaming.

❑ Source objects are forms or reports.

❑ Record sources and row sources are tables or queries.

When renaming forms, I like to use the tag fsub for subforms, and similarly rsub for subreports.

When renaming queries, the query type may not be apparent from its name. If you select the Queries tab of the database window first, and size it so you can see all the queries, it will be a handy reference when renaming queries because you can tell the query type from its icon. See Figure 9.10 for an illustration of this technique.

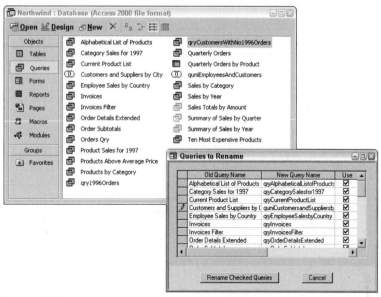

Figure 9.10

After renaming all the database objects, the next step is to rename controls on forms and reports. Some developers don't bother with renaming report controls, because they are rarely referenced elsewhere in the database, but personally I like to give them correct names too—and you should at least rename any report controls that *are* referenced in code, for example in a Format event procedure.

To rename form controls, select the Rename Form Controls selection on the Add-ins menu; the Forms to Rename dialog opens (as shown in Figure 9.11), listing all the forms in the database. If you don't want to rename controls on all the forms, just uncheck the ones you want to skip, and then click the Rename Controls on Checked Forms button to start renaming controls on the selected forms.

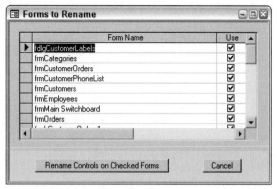

Figure 9.11

The process of renaming controls starts with a question about whether you want to save the original control name to the control's Tag property. Saving original names to the Tag property is a good idea if you are reworking a complex application that has references to controls in VBA code or elsewhere. In case you find a mystery reference in code, you can search for the original control name in the Tag property using Find and Replace.

Next, you will get a series of dialogs, each displaying the current control name and the proposed new name, using the appropriate LNC control tag, and removing spaces and most punctuation marks (see Figure 9.12). Most of the proposed names can be accepted as is, but occasionally you will come across a control that can't be renamed automatically, such as controls with calculated expression control sources, or labels with long captions.

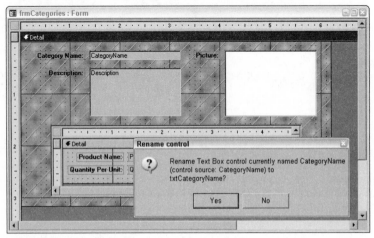

Figure 9.12

After each selected form's controls have been processed, you will get a confirmation message asking if you want to save and close that form; if you have any questions about renaming objects on a form, click No to leave the form open in Design view, so you can review the name changes before closing it; if all the changes are fine, click Yes on this dialog. You will get a confirmation message when all the forms have been processed.

Renaming of report controls is similar, so I will not discuss that process.

LNC Rename Property Wizards

In addition to the three menu add-ins discussed previously, LNC Rename also includes some Property Wizards that let you rename an individual control or all controls on the currently open form or report. To rename an individual control (perhaps one newly added to a form), select the control in Design view, open its properties sheet, and click the Build button beside the Name property (it's the tiny button with three dots), as shown in Figure 9.13.

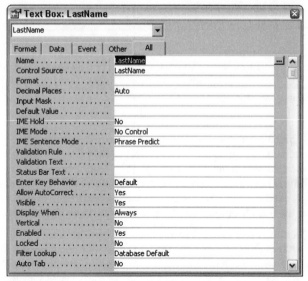

Figure 9.13

The Choose Builder dialog opens, as shown in Figure 9.14, where you can see two LNC Rename Property Wizards (and perhaps others you may have installed).

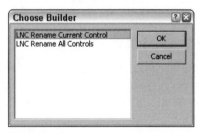

Figure 9.14

Select the LNC Rename Current Control builder to rename the current control. You will get a dialog like the one shown in Figure 9.15, where you can select Yes to accept the proposed name or No to edit it.

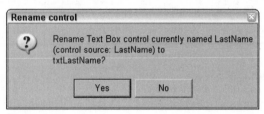

Figure 9.15

The process of renaming a single control sounds more complex than it is—in most cases, all you need to do is click the Build button and press Enter twice, to rename a control with the standard tag.

To rename all the controls on a form that is open in Design view, select the Detail section, open its properties sheet, click the Build button next to the Name property to open the Choose Builder dialog, and this time select the LNC Rename All Controls selection. Dialogs for all the controls on the form will open in turn, letting you rename all the controls on the form.

> **Access 2000 added an AutoCorrect feature that many developers hoped would make it easier to rename database objects, but unfortunately this feature has several serious flaws, which make it practically unworkable. Basically, AutoCorrect fixes some (but not all) references to renamed objects, and none of the references in VBA code, which makes it pretty much worthless because you will have to use a utility such as FAR to correct the missed references. It's easier to just use FAR directly.**
>
> **Additionally, AutoCorrect has a very annoying feature of "correcting" references that should not be corrected. For example, if you are working on the design of a form called frmOrders, and you make a backup copy of the form, called -frmOrders1, you will find that references to frmOrders (say, in a query criterion) may be changed to -frmOrders1, resulting in errors.**
>
> **I recommend turning off AutoCorrect in the General tab of the Access Options dialog and using LNC Rename and/or FAR to rename database objects as needed.**

Creating a Main Menu

If the database you are reworking has no main menu—or an ugly or cumbersome one, such as a menu created by the Access Menu Builder—you can use another of my add-ins, Menu Manager, to create a new main menu. Use of this add-in is covered in Chapter 6, *Printing Data with Reports,* so it will not be discussed here.

Normalizing Tables and Relationships

My EBook Companion database started life as a quick-and-dirty database to store information about downloaded ebooks, for my personal use. I guess this is a case of the shoemaker's children going barefoot, because this database was definitely not normalized! The original tblEBooks table has two sets of Author fields (first, middle, and last names for author and coauthor) and the Title field is the key field, as shown in Figure 9.16.

As I added more and more ebooks to the database, I found that this non-normalized structure wouldn't work, and not just for theoretical considerations—some books I needed to add to the database had more than two authors, and there were different books with the same name. The database needed to be normalized to avoid these problems. Working through the process of normalizing this database should give you a good idea of what is involved in normalizing a client database that you have to rework.

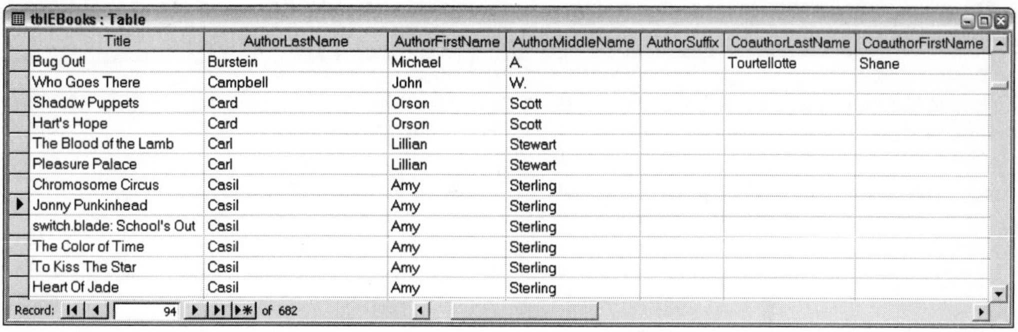

tblEBooks : Table							
Title	AuthorLastName	AuthorFirstName	AuthorMiddleName	AuthorSuffix	CoauthorLastName	CoauthorFirstName	
Bug Out!	Burstein	Michael	A.		Tourtellotte	Shane	
Who Goes There	Campbell	John	W.				
Shadow Puppets	Card	Orson	Scott				
Hart's Hope	Card	Orson	Scott				
The Blood of the Lamb	Carl	Lillian	Stewart				
Pleasure Palace	Carl	Lillian	Stewart				
Chromosome Circus	Casil	Amy	Sterling				
Jonny Punkinhead	Casil	Amy	Sterling				
switch.blade: School's Out	Casil	Amy	Sterling				
The Color of Time	Casil	Amy	Sterling				
To Kiss The Star	Casil	Amy	Sterling				
Heart Of Jade	Casil	Amy	Sterling				

Record: |◄| ◄ | 94 ► |►I|►*| of 682   ◄

Figure 9.16

For tblEBooks, ISBN would be the obvious choice as a unique ID for books. But the ISBN isn't generally available at the time ebooks are downloaded, so I just added a BookID AutoNumber field to tblEBooks, to give each book a unique ID—that was easy!

The next step was more complicated—authors (as many as are needed for each book) had to be moved into a separate table, linked on BookID, and author data needed its own separate table, with one record for each author, to avoid the duplicate author data in the original tblEBooks. A book can have multiple authors and an author can write many books, so the tblEBooks table and tblAuthors table should be linked many-to-many through the linking table, tblEBookAuthors.

> *The Original EBook Companion database has the old, non-normalized tables; the EBook Companion database has the normalized tables and modified forms and reports, after all the changes discussed in the following sections have been made.*

To start, I moved the author data from the old, non-normalized tblEBooks table into new, normalized tables using several queries. First, I made qryAuthors, containing the AuthorFirstName, AuthorMiddleName, and AuthorLastName fields from tblEBooks, and I set the query's Unique Values property to Yes to eliminate duplicates. I made a similar query (qryCoauthors) using the CoauthorFirstName, CoauthorMiddleName, and CoauthorLastName fields, with the addition of a criterion of Is Not Null on the CoauthorLastName field, so the query's results contained only records that had coauthor data.

Next, I constructed a union query (quniAuthors) to join the author and coauthor data into a single recordset, using the following SQL statement:

```
SELECT qryAuthors.AuthorLastName AS LastName, qryAuthors.AuthorFirstName AS
FirstName, qryAuthors.AuthorMiddleName AS MiddleName
FROM qryAuthors
UNION SELECT qryCoauthors.CoauthorLastName AS LastName,
qryCoauthors.CoauthorFirstName AS FirstName, qryCoauthors.CoauthorMiddleName AS
MiddleName
FROM qryCoauthors;
```

So that I could tinker with the author names without affecting the data in tblEBooks (not absolutely necessary, but a good idea), I made a make-table query (qmakAuthors), sorted by last name, first name, and middle name (this query is shown in Design view in Figure 9.17). The table made by this query is called tmakAuthors.

I use the tmak prefix to match up a table with the make-table that created it, so I know at a glance which tables in the database window were created by make-table queries.

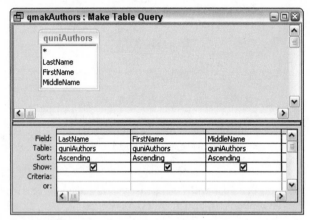

Figure 9.17

I did a little clean-up on the resulting table (fixed a few typos in author names, removed some duplicates that snuck in despite setting Unique Values to True, moved a "Jr." into a Suffix field I added to the table), and then I made a new, empty table (tblAuthors) to hold the cleaned-up author data, and an append query (qappAuthors) to move the data from tmakAuthors into tblAuthors. The qappAuthors query is shown in Figure 9.18.

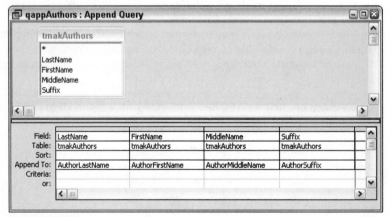

Figure 9.18

The new tblAuthors table has an AuthorID AutoNumber field. A portion of tblEBookAuthors is shown in Figure 9.19.

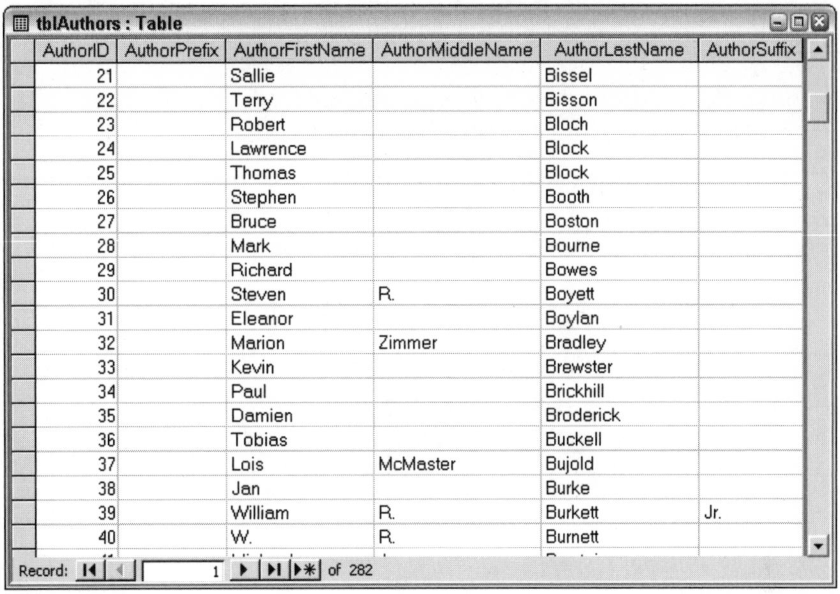

	AuthorID	AuthorPrefix	AuthorFirstName	AuthorMiddleName	AuthorLastName	AuthorSuffix
	21		Sallie		Bissel	
	22		Terry		Bisson	
	23		Robert		Bloch	
	24		Lawrence		Block	
	25		Thomas		Block	
	26		Stephen		Booth	
	27		Bruce		Boston	
	28		Mark		Bourne	
	29		Richard		Bowes	
	30		Steven	R.	Boyett	
	31		Eleanor		Boylan	
	32		Marion	Zimmer	Bradley	
	33		Kevin		Brewster	
	34		Paul		Brickhill	
	35		Damien		Broderick	
	36		Tobias		Buckell	
	37		Lois	McMaster	Bujold	
	38		Jan		Burke	
	39		William	R.	Burkett	Jr.
	40		W.	R.	Burnett	

Record: 1 of 282

Figure 9.19

The final step in normalizing the tables is to create the linking table, tblEBookAuthors. This table sets up the many-to-many relationship between tblEbooks and tblAuthors. In Access, a many-to-many relationship is actually two one-to-many relationships, with the linking table being on the "many" side of both relationships. A many-to-many relationship is needed here because there are (potentially) many records in tblEBookAuthors for one ebook, or one author, because an author can write many books, and a book can have more than one author.

tblEBookAuthors needs only two fields, AuthorID and BookID; these fields are the key fields of tblAuthors and tblEBooks, respectively, and the foreign keys in the one-to-many relationships between tblAuthors and tblEBookAuthors, and tblEBooks and tblEBookAuthors. Figure 9.20 shows the one-to-many relationship being set up between tblAuthors and tblEBookAuthors; the other relationship is done in a similar manner.

The two finished relationships are shown in the Relationships window in Figure 9.21.

The final step of the normalizing process is the most complex: filling tblEBookAuthors with data linking authors to their books. This requires matching up the new BookID field in tblEBooks with the appropriate AuthorID in tblAuthors, using the old author data fields to find the author in tblAuthors. To facilitate this matching, I made two queries that combine the author first, middle. and last name components into a single AuthorName field. qryEBooksWithAuthorNames is shown in Design view in Figure 9.22, and in Datasheet view in Figure 9.23.

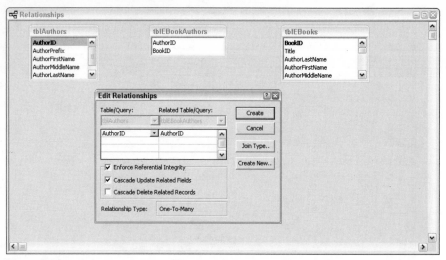

Figure 9.20

Figure 9.21

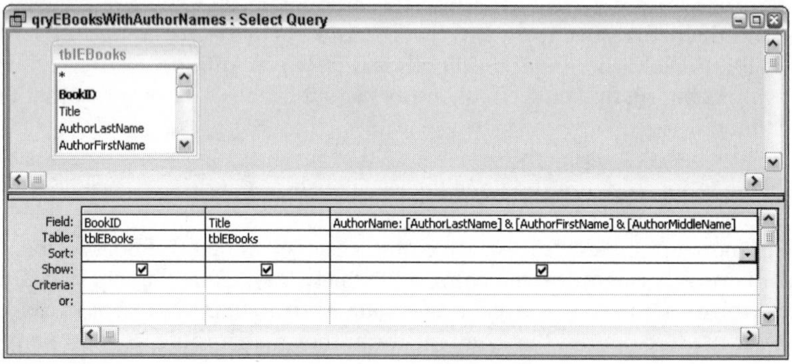

Figure 9.22

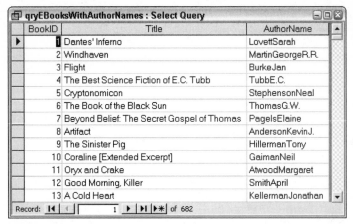

Figure 9.23

Next, I made a query (qryAuthorNames) based on tblAuthors, containing the AuthorID field and a similar AuthorName concatenated field. I then joined the two queries on the AuthorName field in qryEBooksAndAuthors, linking the tables with a LEFT JOIN, so that there would be one record for each record in tblEBooks. This query is shown in Design view in Figure 9.24.

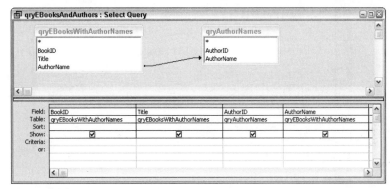

Figure 9.24

After checking the query in Datasheet view (as shown in Figure 9.25), I made a similar query for the coauthor names (qryEBooksAndCoauthors) and a union query to combine their data. This is necessary, because otherwise there would be only one record in tblEBookAuthors for each book, and the coauthor data would be lost.

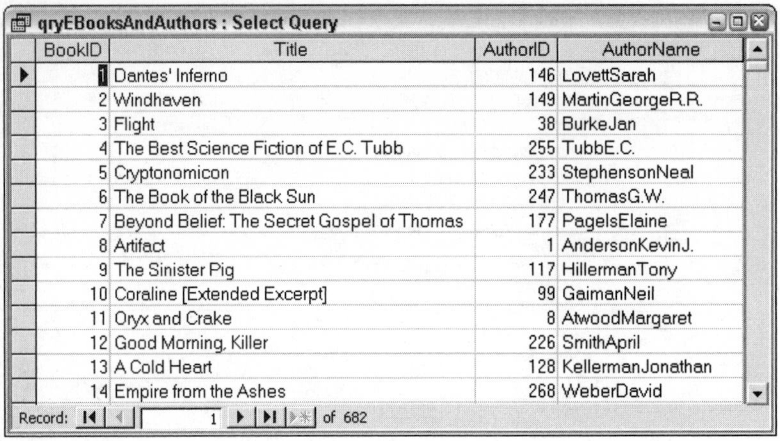

qryEBooksAndAuthors : Select Query

BookID	Title	AuthorID	AuthorName
1	Dantes' Inferno	146	LovettSarah
2	Windhaven	149	MartinGeorgeR.R.
3	Flight	38	BurkeJan
4	The Best Science Fiction of E.C. Tubb	255	TubbE.C.
5	Cryptonomicon	233	StephensonNeal
6	The Book of the Black Sun	247	ThomasG.W.
7	Beyond Belief: The Secret Gospel of Thomas	177	PagelsElaine
8	Artifact	1	AndersonKevinJ.
9	The Sinister Pig	117	HillermanTony
10	Coraline [Extended Excerpt]	99	GaimanNeil
11	Oryx and Crake	8	AtwoodMargaret
12	Good Morning, Killer	226	SmithApril
13	A Cold Heart	128	KellermanJonathan
14	Empire from the Ashes	268	WeberDavid

Record: 1 of 682

Figure 9.25

The union query that combines author and coauthor book data is shown in Figure 9.26.

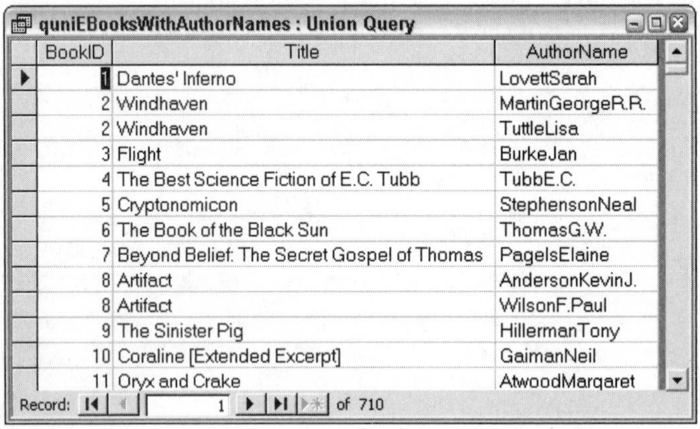

quniEBooksWithAuthorNames : Union Query

BookID	Title	AuthorName
1	Dantes' Inferno	LovettSarah
2	Windhaven	MartinGeorgeR.R.
2	Windhaven	TuttleLisa
3	Flight	BurkeJan
4	The Best Science Fiction of E.C. Tubb	TubbE.C.
5	Cryptonomicon	StephensonNeal
6	The Book of the Black Sun	ThomasG.W.
7	Beyond Belief: The Secret Gospel of Thomas	PagelsElaine
8	Artifact	AndersonKevinJ.
8	Artifact	WilsonF.Paul
9	The Sinister Pig	HillermanTony
10	Coraline [Extended Excerpt]	GaimanNeil
11	Oryx and Crake	AtwoodMargaret

Record: 1 of 710

Figure 9.26

I made an append query based on the union query, linked to tblAuthors on the AuthorName field, renamed it with the qapp prefix, and ran the qappEBooksAndAuthors query to fill tblEBookAuthors. This query is shown in Design view in Figure 9.27.

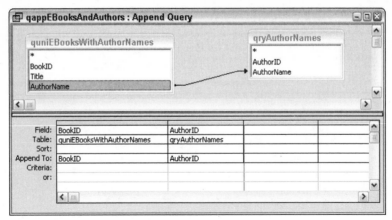

Figure 9.27

A portion of tblEBookAuthors is shown in Figure 9.28.

tblEBookAuthors : Table

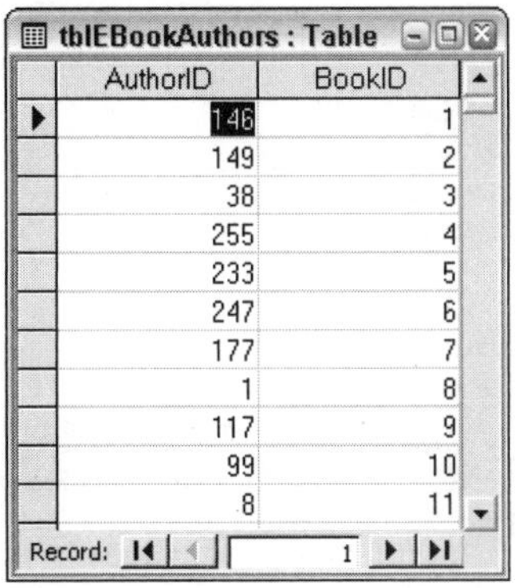

AuthorID	BookID
146	1
149	2
38	3
255	4
233	5
247	6
177	7
1	8
117	9
99	10
8	11

Record: 1

Figure 9.28

Reworking Forms to Enter and Display Many-to-Many Linked Data

Because of the changes to tables, some changes to the database's forms are also required. Displaying (and entering) data into tables linked many-to-many requires some rather unintuitive techniques. The EBook Companion database has two forms used to enter and display data, fpriEBookNotes, a standard form with a combobox record selector for selecting books by author or title, and frmTreeViewEBookNotes, which uses a TreeView control for book selection. Both of these forms need reworking as a consequence of the normalization of the tables in the database, and a new form for working with author data is also needed.

Reworking the fpriEBookNotes Form

The original data entry form, fpriEBookNotes, has two sets of fields for the author and coauthor name, as shown in Figure 9.29.

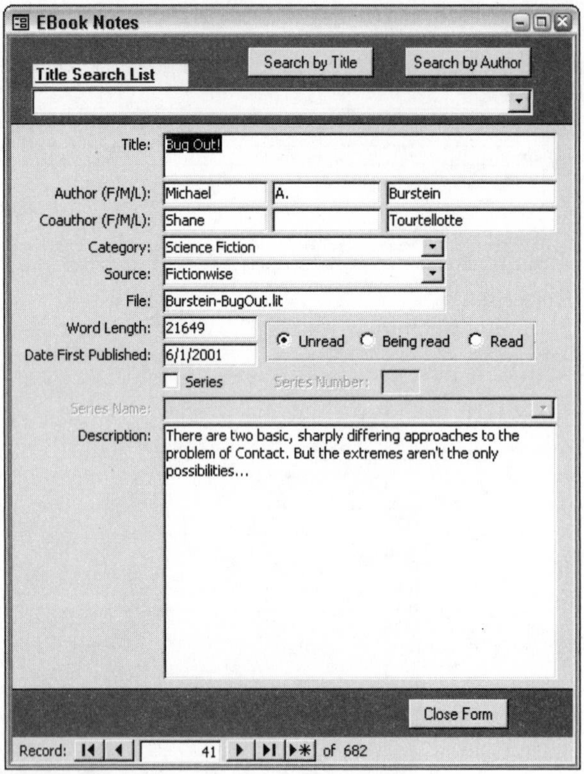

Figure 9.29

Now that the tables have been normalized so that author information is stored in its own table, a different interface is needed to allow users to select authors for an ebook. I have found that the best way to work with many-to-many relationships on a form is a subform with the linking table (in this case, tblEBookAuthors) as its record source. The subform has a single control: a combobox that displays the information to be selected (in this case, a query based on tblAuthors). Figure 9.30 shows the fsubEBookAuthors subform in Design view. The subform's LinkChildFields and LinkMasterFields properties are set to BookID, so it always displays the correct author information for the current book record.

The author information is most conveniently displayed in last name first format, so I made a query (qryEBookAuthors) containing only the AuthorID field and a calculated expression for a LastNameFirst field (I made a query, rather than just creating the expression in the subform's record source so that it would be available for use elsewhere in the database).

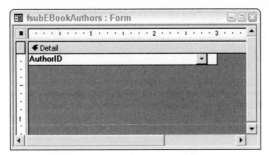

Figure 9.30

The LastNameFirst calculated expression is:

```
LastNameFirst: Trim(IIf([AuthorFirstName],[AuthorLastName]
& IIf([AuthorPrefix],[AuthorPrefix] & " ","") & IIf([AuthorFirstName],
", " & [AuthorFirstName],"") & IIf([AuthorMiddleName]," "
& [AuthorMiddleName]),[AuthorLastName])) & IIf([AuthorSuffix],
" " & [AuthorSuffix],"")
```

The expression uses the Iif and Trim functions to concatenate the various components of an author's name, without creating extra spaces if some components are missing. qryEBookAuthors is the row source of the cboAuthor combobox on fsubEBookAuthors. The significant properties of this combobox are shown in Figure 9.31.

Combo Box: cboAuthor

cboAuthor

| Format | Data | Event | Other | All |

Name	cboAuthor
Control Source	AuthorID
Format	
Decimal Places	Auto
Input Mask	
Row Source Type	Table/Query
Row Source	qryEBookAuthors
Column Count	2
Column Heads	No
Column Widths	0";3"
Bound Column	1
List Rows	16
List Width	Auto
Status Bar Text	
Limit To List	Yes

Figure 9.31

The combobox's control source is the AuthorID field in tblEBookAuthors (the linking table in the many-to-many relationship). Because the subform is linked to the main form on the BookID field, BookID is automatically filled with the correct value when a new subform record is created. These two fields are the only fields in tblEBookAuthors, so that means that no code is needed to enter data into the linking table. Just select an author from the drop-down list (as shown in Figure 9.32), and both fields in the linking table are filled in with the BookID and AuthorID values.

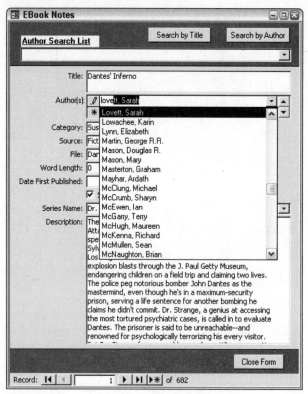

Figure 9.32

The combobox's row source (as mentioned above) is qryEBookAuthors, with the author's name displayed last name first. The column count is 2, the column widths are 0" and 3", and the bound column is 1, which means that the first column (the AuthorID column) is invisible in the drop-down list, but its value is written to the AuthorID field in the subform's record source, tblEBookAuthors. Sixteen rows of author names are displayed, and the Limit to List property is set to Yes so that only authors in tblAuthors can be selected.

The fsubEBookAuthors subform looks like a datasheet, but it is actually a Continuous Forms–type form, with its single control (cboAuthor) taking up the entire area of the subform. The reason for making this form Continuous Forms rather than Datasheet is that a datasheet subform would have a visible column heading, instead of just showing the author name selector combobox. The subform technique lets you add as many authors to a book as needed—just move to a new row on the subform, and select another author.

The fpriEBookNotes form header has two record selector comboboxes and two command buttons that let you switch the comboboxes (only one is visible at any time). Because of the normalization of the database's tables, I had to modify the code on the AfterUpdate event procedures of the comboboxes, and also their row sources. cboTitleSearchList originally had qryEBooksByTitle (based on the non-normalized tblEBooks) as a row source, and cboAuthorSearchList also had a row source query that needs to be replaced.

The event procedures for both record selectors need changes; instead of using the old (possibly nonunique) search fields, I revised them to use the new unique AutoNumber field, BookID. I made two queries (qryEBookAuthorSearch and qryEBookTitleSearch) based on qryEBooksAndAuthors, containing only three fields: LastNameFirst, Title, and BookID. Whether you are searching by author or by title, the target is a specific book, so only BookID is needed for synchronizing. The only difference between these queries is the order of the LastNameFirst and Title fields. The qryEBookAuthorSearch query is shown in Design view in Figure 9.33.

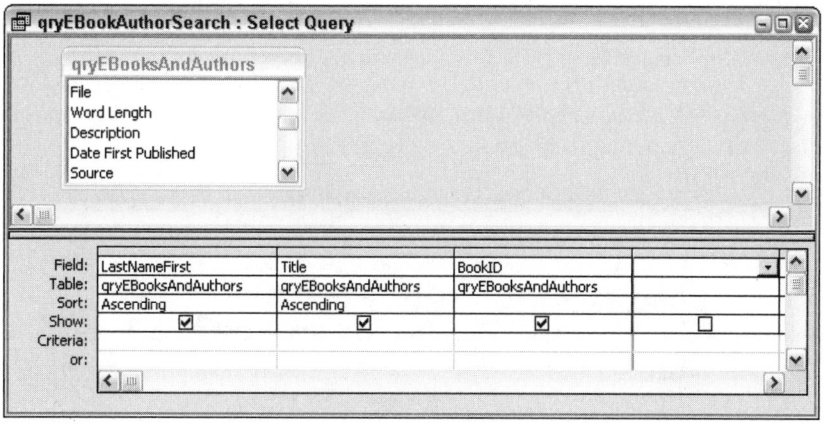

Figure 9.33

Several of the comboboxes' properties need to be modified to correctly reference the new row source query's columns:

❑ Column Count is set to 3

❑ The Bound Column is set to 2 (the BookID field)

❑ ColumnWidths are set to 3";1.5";0" (or 1.5";3";0"), so the BookID field won't be displayed in the drop-down list

The original cboAuthorSearchList event procedure is:

```
Private Sub cboAuthorSearchList_AfterUpdate()

On Error GoTo ErrorHandler

    strSearch = "[Title] = " & Chr$(34) & _
        Me![cboAuthorSearchList].Column(1) & Chr$(34)

    'Find the record that matches the control.
    Me.Requery
    Me.RecordsetClone.FindFirst strSearch
    Me.Bookmark = Me.RecordsetClone.Bookmark

ErrorHandlerExit:
```

```
    Exit Sub

ErrorHandler:
    MsgBox "Error No: " & Err.Number & "; Description: " & Err.Description
    Resume ErrorHandlerExit

End Sub
```

The only difference in the new event procedures is the search string:

```
    strSearch = "[BookID] = " & Me![cboAuthorSearchList].Column(2)
```

Column numbers in VBA code are zero-based, so Column(2) is actually the third column of the row source.

Figure 9.34 shows a book being selected from the cboTitleSearchList combobox.

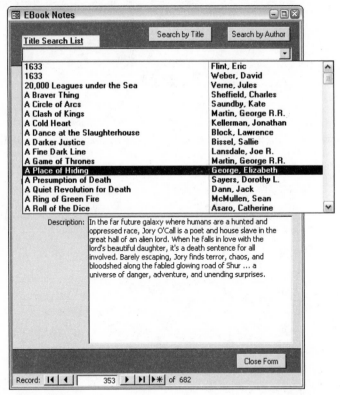

Figure 9.34

Reworking the frmTreeViewEBookNotes Form

frmTreeViewEBookNotes has a TreeView control, which is filled with data from code (this is necessary because the old Access 97 TreeView Wizard was dropped in Access 2000, and has not yet reappeared in successive versions of Access). Additionally, it has a subform that displays data for the book selected in the TreeView control.

The function that fills the TreeView control required modification to work with the new, normalized tables. The original code is listed below (stripped of Debug.Print statements):

```
Function tvwBooks_Fill()
'Modified from a procedure generated by the Treeview Control Wizard
'Called from Form_Load event

On Error GoTo ErrorHandler

    Dim strMessage As String
    Dim dbs As DAO.Database
    Dim rst As DAO.Recordset
    Dim intVBMsg As Integer
    Dim strQuery1 As String
    Dim strQuery2 As String
    Dim nod As Object
    Dim strNode1Text As String
    Dim strNode2Text As String
    Dim strVisibleText As String

    Set dbs = CurrentDb()
    strQuery1 = "qryEBookAuthors"
    strQuery2 = "qryEBooksByAuthor"

With Me![tvwBooks]
    'Fill Level 1
    Set rst = dbs.OpenRecordset(strQuery1, dbOpenForwardOnly)

    Do Until rst.EOF
       strNode1Text = StrConv("Level1" & rst![LastNameFirst], _
          vbLowerCase)
       Set nod = .Nodes.Add(, , strNode1Text, rst![LastNameFirst])
       nod.Expanded = True
       rst.MoveNext
    Loop
    rst.Close

    'Fill Level 2
    Set rst = dbs.OpenRecordset(strQuery2, dbOpenForwardOnly)

    Do Until rst.EOF
       strNode1Text = StrConv("Level1" & rst![LastNameFirst], vbLowerCase)
       strNode2Text = StrConv("Level2" & rst![Title], vbLowerCase)
       strVisibleText = rst![Title] & rst![BeenRead]
       .Nodes.Add strNode1Text, tvwChild, strNode2Text, strVisibleText
```

315

```
            rst.MoveNext
        Loop
        rst.Close

    End With
    dbs.Close

ErrorHandlerExit:
    Exit Function

ErrorHandler:
    Select Case Err.Number
        Case 35601
            'Element not found
            strMessage = "Possible Causes: You selected a table/query" _
                & " for a child level that does not correspond to a value" _
                & " from its parent level."
            intVBMsg = MsgBox(Error$ & strMessage, vbOKOnly + _
                vbExclamation, "Run-time Error: " & Err.Number)
        Case 35602
            'Key is not unique in collection
            strMessage = "Possible Causes: You selected a nonunique" _
                & " field to link levels."
            intVBMsg = MsgBox(Error$ & strMessage, vbOKOnly + _
                vbExclamation, "Run-time Error: " & Err.Number)
        Case Else
            intVBMsg = MsgBox(Error$ & "@@", vbOKOnly + _
                vbExclamation, "Run-time Error: " & Err.Number)
    End Select
    Resume ErrorHandlerExit

End Function
```

The original versions of the two queries used in this code (qryEBookAuthors and qryEBooksByAuthor) both pick up author names (concatenated into the LastNameFirst expression from the original, non-normalized tblEBooks. The LastNameFirst field is used as the Node 1 key expression, and the Title field is the key expression for Node 2. Since neither of these values is (necessarily) unique, this could cause problems when filling the TreeView control, when either an author name or a book title is not unique. See the TreeView Control section of Chapter 3, *Selecting the Right Controls for Forms*, for a more detailed explanation of TreeView controls.

After normalizing the EBookCompanion tables, and modifying the queries as needed, I rewrote the tvwBooks_Fill function to use AuthorID as the Node 1 key, with LastNameFirst as the visible text for that node. For the Node 2 key expression, I used AuthorID concatenated with Title, to ensure uniqueness of books by different authors with the same title, and Title plus a BeenRead symbol for the Node 2 visible text (BeenRead uses a division sign to indicate that the book is being read, and a small multiplication sign to indicate that it has been read). The modified function is:

```
Function tvwBooks_Fill()
'Modified from a procedure generated by the Treeview Control Wizard
'Called from Form_Load event

On Error GoTo ErrorHandler

    Dim strMessage As String
```

```
      Dim dbs As DAO.Database
      Dim rst As DAO.Recordset
      Dim intVBMsg As Integer
      Dim strQuery1 As String
      Dim strQuery2 As String
      Dim nod As Object
      Dim strNode1Text As String
      Dim strNode2Text As String
      Dim strVisibleText1 As String
      Dim strVisibleText2 As String

      Set dbs = CurrentDb()
      strQuery1 = "qryEBookAuthors"
      strQuery2 = "qryEBooksByAuthor"

   With Me![tvwBooks]
      'Fill Level 1
      Set rst = dbs.OpenRecordset(strQuery1, dbOpenForwardOnly)

      Do Until rst.EOF
         strNode1Text = StrConv("Level1 - " & rst![AuthorID], _
            vbLowerCase)
         strVisibleText1 = rst![LastNameFirst]
         Set nod = .Nodes.Add(Key:=strNode1Text, _
            Text:=strVisibleText1)
         nod.Expanded = True
         rst.MoveNext
      Loop
      rst.Close

      'Fill Level 2
      Set rst = dbs.OpenRecordset(strQuery2, dbOpenForwardOnly)

      Do Until rst.EOF
         strNode1Text = StrConv("Level1 - " & rst![AuthorID], vbLowerCase)
         strNode2Text = StrConv("Level2 - " & rst![AuthorID] & " - " _
            & rst![Title], vbLowerCase)
         strVisibleText2 = rst![Title] & rst![BeenRead]
         .Nodes.Add relative:=strNode1Text, _
            relationship:=tvwChild, _
            Key:=strNode2Text, _
            Text:=strVisibleText2
         rst.MoveNext
      Loop
      rst.Close

   End With
   dbs.Close

ErrorHandlerExit:
   Exit Function

ErrorHandler:
   Select Case Err.Number
      Case 35601
         'Element not found
```

```
                    strMessage = "Possible Causes: You selected a table/query" _
                        & " for a child level that does not correspond to a value" _
                        & " from its parent level."
                    intVBMsg = MsgBox(Error$ & strMessage, vbOKOnly + _
                        vbExclamation, "Run-time Error: " & Err.Number)
                Case 35602
                    'Key is not unique in collection.
                    strMessage = "Possible Causes: You selected a nonunique" _
                        & " field to link levels."
                    intVBMsg = MsgBox(Error$ & strMessage, vbOKOnly + _
                        vbExclamation, "Run-time Error: " & Err.Number)
                Case Else
                    intVBMsg = MsgBox(Error$ & "@@", vbOKOnly + _
                        vbExclamation, "Run-time Error: " & Err.Number)
            End Select
            Resume ErrorHandlerExit

    End Function
```

There is another function related to the TreeView control: the Node_Click event procedure, which synchronizes the Books subform with the node (book title) clicked in the TreeView control. The original tvwBooks_NodeClick event procedure is:

```
    Private Sub tvwBooks_NodeClick(ByVal Node As Object)

    On Error GoTo ErrorHandler

        Dim frm As Access.Form
        Dim strNodeText As String

        Set frm = Me![subBookInformation].Form

        If Left(Node.Key, 6) = "level2" Then
            If Right(Node.Text, 1) = Chr$(215) Or _
                Right(Node.Text, 1) = Chr$(247) Then
                strNodeText = Left(Node.Text, Len(Node.Text) - 1)
            Else
                strNodeText = Node.Text
            End If

            Debug.Print "Node text: " & strNodeText
            Me![txtSelectedBook].Value = strNodeText
            frm.Requery
            frm![txtSeriesNumber].Enabled = frm![chkSeries].Value
            frm![cboSeriesName].Enabled = frm![chkSeries].Value
            frm.Visible = True
        Else
            frm.Visible = False
        End If

    ErrorHandlerExit:
        Exit Sub

    ErrorHandler:
```

```
    MsgBox "Error No: " & Err.Number & "; Description: " & Err.Description
    Resume ErrorHandlerExit

End Sub
```

I added a strTitlePlus variable to contain the Node 2 key expression (Author ID plus Title), and wrote this variable to the txtSelectedBook textbox on the main form (this textbox's value is used to synchronize the subform with the selected book). The modified procedure is:

```
Private Sub tvwBooks_NodeClick(ByVal Node As Object)

On Error GoTo ErrorHandler

    Dim frm As Access.Form
    Dim strNodeText As String
    Dim strTitlePlus As String

    Set frm = Me![subBookInformation].Form

    If Left(Node.Key, 6) = "level2" Then
        If Right(Node.Text, 1) = Chr$(215) Or _
            Right(Node.Text, 1) = Chr$(247) Then
            strNodeText = Left(Node.Text, Len(Node.Text) - 1)
        Else
            strNodeText = Node.Text
        End If

        strTitlePlus = Mid(Node.Key, 10)
        Me![txtSelectedBook].Value = strTitlePlus
        frm.Requery
        frm![txtSeriesNumber].Enabled = frm![chkSeries].Value
        frm![cboSeriesName].Enabled = frm![chkSeries].Value
        frm.Visible = True
    Else
        frm.Visible = False
    End If

ErrorHandlerExit:
    Exit Sub

ErrorHandler:
    MsgBox "Error No: " & Err.Number & "; Description: " & Err.Description
    Resume ErrorHandlerExit

End Sub
```

The subform on frmTreeViewEBookNotes (fsubBooks) is very similar to the main fpriEBookNotes form, without the header or footer, so the only modification needed was to replace the original txtAuthors textbox with a copy of the new subEBookAuthors subform from the main fpriEBookNotes form. (There is no problem with using the same subform on two main forms in this database because only one of them would be open at any given time.) I also added an invisible BookID control to the subform for debugging purposes. The modified frmTreeViewEBookNotes form is shown in Figure 9.35.

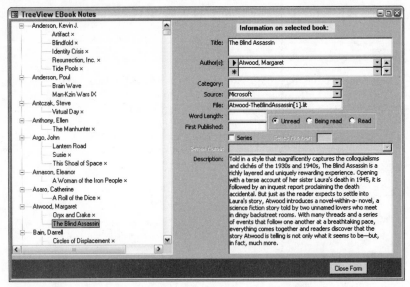

Figure 9.35

Creating the New frmAuthors Form

The original EBook Companion database didn't need an Authors form because author names were entered directly into the non-normalized tblEBooks. Now that there is a separate tblAuthors, a form is needed for entering and editing author data. I made a simple form (frmAuthors) bound to tblAuthors for this purpose. This form is shown in Figure 9.36.

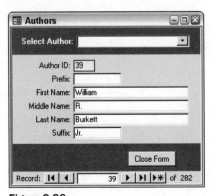

Figure 9.36

The final touch is to turn the cboAuthor combobox into an add-to combobox, by adding a NotInList event procedure that opens a New Author form. This event procedure allows entry of author data on the fly, in case the author of a newly entered book is not already in the tblAuthors table. The event procedure is:

```
        Private Sub cboAuthor_NotInList(strNewData As String, intResponse As Integer)

    On Error GoTo ErrorHandler

        Dim strTitle As String
        Dim intMsgDialog As Integer
        Dim strMsg As String
        Dim ctl As Control
        Dim strEntry As String
        Dim strFormName As String
        Dim intReturn As Integer

        strFormName = "fdlgNewAuthor"
        strEntry = "author"
        Set ctl = Me![cboAuthor]

        'Display a message box asking if the user wants to add
        'a new entry.
        strTitle = strEntry & " not in list"
        intMsgDialog = vbYesNo + vbExclamation + vbDefaultButton1
        strMsg = "Do you want to add a new " & strEntry & " entry?"
        intReturn = MsgBox(strMsg, intMsgDialog, strTitle)

        If intReturn = vbNo Then
           intResponse = acDataErrContinue
           ctl.Undo
           GoTo ErrorHandlerExit
        ElseIf intReturn = vbYes Then
           'Open form for adding new record
           ctl.Undo
           intResponse = acDataErrContinue
           DoCmd.OpenForm strFormName
        End If

    ErrorHandlerExit:
        Exit Sub

    ErrorHandler:
        MsgBox "Error No: " & Err.Number & "; Description: " & _
            Err.Description
        Resume ErrorHandlerExit

    End Sub
```

For full details on creating an add-to combobox, see the "Add-to Combobox" section of Chapter 3, *Selecting the Right Controls for Forms*.

Reworking Reports to Enter and Display Many-to-Many Linked Data

After normalizing the database's tables, and reworking the forms, the reports also need some work. The original reports were based on a query (qryEBooks) that included the author name fields in the old, non-normalized tblEBooks. I replaced this query with a new query, qryEBooksAndAuthors, that links the three tables in the many-to-many relationship, so that I would have the AuthorID available for linking purposes. This query is shown in Design view in Figure 9.37.

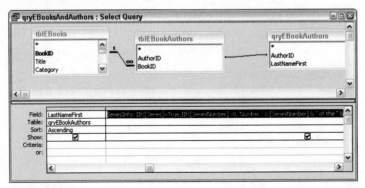

Figure 9.37

> While a query combining several linked tables is rarely useful as a record source (because it is not editable), such queries are very useful as report record sources because reports display data, but don't permit editing.

qryEBooksAndAuthors has several calculated fields, which manipulate data from several fields in tblEBooks to display it in a more attractive format on the reports. The SeriesInfo field first checks whether the book is part of a series (indicated by a True value in the Series field), and if it is, it next checks whether a number has been entered into the SeriesNumber field. If a number has been entered, the text "Number " is concatenated with the series number, the linking text " of the " and the series name (with the word "The" added only if the series name itself does not start with "The").

```
SeriesInfo: IIf([Series]=True,IIf([SeriesNumber]>0,"Number " & [SeriesNumber]
& " of the " & IIf(Left([SeriesName],4)="The",Mid([SeriesName],5),[SeriesName])
& " series","The " & IIf(Left([SeriesName],4)="The",Mid([SeriesName],5),
[SeriesName]) & " series"))
```

The expression yields series information for books such as the following:

❑ Number 9 of the Man-Kzin Wars series *(series number entered)*

❑ The Company series *(no series number entered)*

The ReadStat field translates the numeric ReadStatus value into a text phrase that is used as a group value for sorting some of the reports:

```
ReadStat: Switch([ReadStatus]=2,"Books Being Read",[ReadStatus]=1,
"Unread Books",[ReadStatus]=3,"Read Books")
```

The UniqueAuthorName field (used in reports for accurate grouping of author names) simply concatenates the author name (last name first) and the Author ID, with a dash in between:

```
UniqueAuthorName: [LastNameFirst] & " - " & [tblEBookAuthors].[AuthorID]
```

In the reports themselves, I removed the txtAuthors control and replaced it with a subreport to display authors data as needed. In the case of a single-author book (the standard case), this subform is invisible; if there are two or more authors, the subreport becomes visible and the coauthor(s) are displayed.

The subreport (rsubCoauthors) has as its record source a select query that shows all the authors for a given book except the author for the current record. To determine which books have multiple authors, I made a totals query (qryMultipleAuthorEBooks) based on qryEBooksAndAuthors, with a count on the AuthorID field, and a criterion selecting only records with a value greater than one in this field. This query is shown in Design view in Figure 9.38.

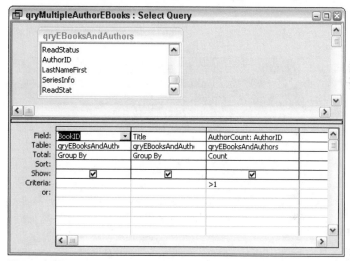

Figure 9.38

This query doesn't (and can't) contain the author name, because then it couldn't count the authors. Thus I needed to link it to the main report query, qryEBooksAndAuthors, in order to get the coauthor names to display on the subreport. qryEBookCoauthors, with the two linked queries, is shown in Design view in Figure 9.39.

The same query is shown in Datasheet view in Figure 9.40.

The subreport needs to display just the coauthor names. That means that for each report record, if the book has multiple authors, the subreport should display only the author(s) that don't match the main author name for that record. (The main author name is just the one that comes first in alphabetical order.) Thus, for BookID 2 (Windhaven), on the record that shows it as a book by author George R. R. Martin, Lisa Tuttle should be displayed as the coauthor, and on the record that shows it as a book by Lisa Tuttle, George R. R. Martin should display as the coauthor.

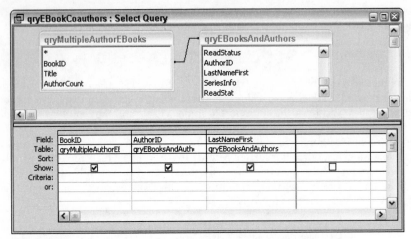

Figure 9.39

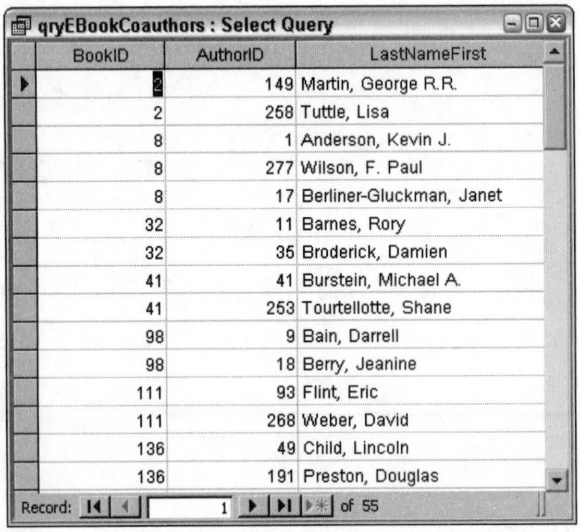

Figure 9.40

To accomplish this, I created yet another query (qryCoauthors), linking qryEBookCoauthors with qryEBooksAndAuthors on BookID, to limit the query results to just books with multiple authors. I put a criterion of:

```
<>[qryEBooksAndAuthors].[AuthorID]
```

on the AuthorID field from qryEBookCoauthors, which means that the matching records in the two source queries will have the same BookID, but different AuthorIDs. I aliased the LastNameFirst field in qryEBooksAndAuthors as MainAuthor and the same field in qryEBookCoauthors as Coauthor, and the AuthorID fields in the two tables as MainAuthorID and CoauthorID. This query (qryCoauthors) is shown in Design view in Figure 9.41 and in Datasheet view in Figure 9.42.

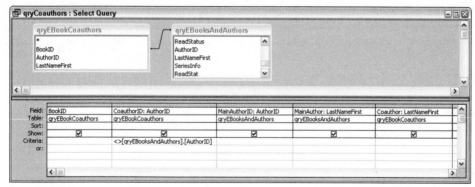

Figure 9.41

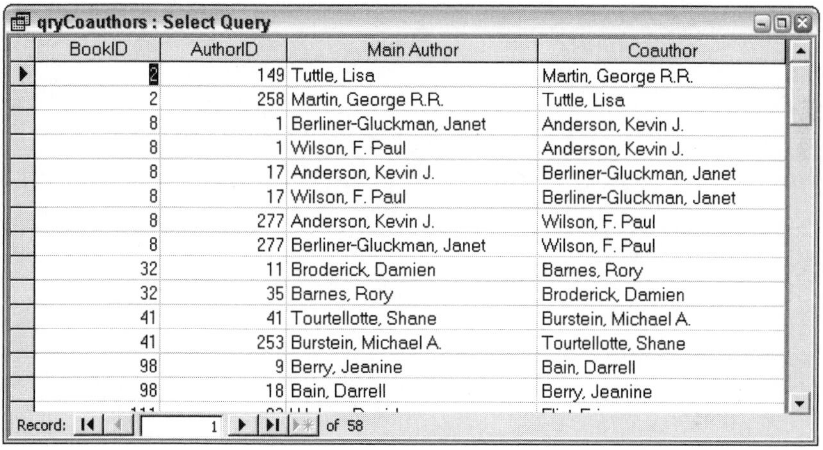

Figure 9.42

Note that for a book with three authors (such as BookID 8, Artifact), there are six records, representing all the possible combinations of three authors (two pairs for each author, listing one of the authors with each of the other two coauthors). For the more common two-author book, there are two records, one with the first author as the main author and the other author as the coauthor, and one with the reverse.

With qryCoauthors as the record source, displaying only the Coauthor field, the subreport rsubCoathors is linked to the main report by BookID to Book and AuthorID to MainAuthorID, and it displays the coauthors for the book, for multiple-authors books only. Because there may be multiple records when only coauthor names are displayed, the txtCoauthor textbox's HideDuplicates property is set to Yes.

In the original reports, the Authors textbox (displaying the author names from the original, non-normalized table) was in the LastNameFirst group header, but in the new version of the report, the subCoauthors subreport is placed in the Detail section, because an author might write some books alone and others with a coauthor. There is code on the Format event of the report's Detail section that makes the subreport visible only if the book has multiple authors (using the previously created qryMultipleAuthorEBooks), and also makes the series information visible only for series books, depending on the value of the Series field. This event procedure is:

```
Private Sub Detail1_Format(Cancel As Integer, FormatCount As Integer)

On Error GoTo ErrorHandler

    Dim lngBookID As Long

    lngBookID = Me![BookID]
    If Me![Series] = True Then
        Me![txtSeries].Visible = True
    Else
        Me![txtSeries].Visible = False
    End If

    If Nz(DCount("*", "qryMultipleAuthorEBooks", "BookID = " _
        & lngBookID)) > 0 Then
        Me![subCoauthors].Visible = True
    Else
        Me![subCoauthors].Visible = False
    End If

ErrorHandlerExit:
    Exit Sub

ErrorHandler:
    MsgBox "Error No: " & Err.Number & "; Description: " & _
        Err.Description
    Resume ErrorHandlerExit

End Sub
```

The rptEBooksByAuthor report is shown in Design view in Figure 9.43 and in Print Preview in Figure 9.44.

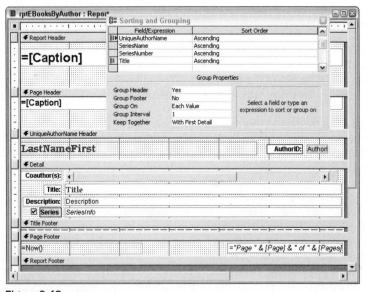

Figure 9.43

The report controls with a yellow background (txtAuthorID and txtSeries) are invisible—I use the convention of a bright yellow background for controls on forms and reports that are intended to be invisible on the finished form or report, but may be set visible temporarily for debugging purposes. The yellow color reminds me to set these controls to invisible before finishing the application.

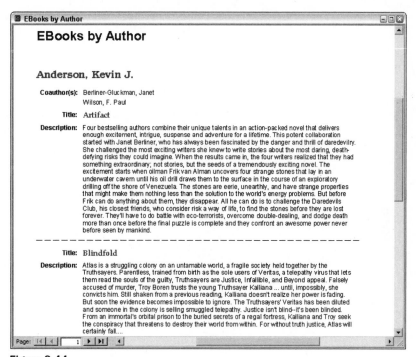

Figure 9.44

Two authors can have the same name (for example, Elizabeth George the mystery writer and Elizabeth George the Christian writer), so I use the UniqueAuthorName concatenated field (created in qryEBooksAndAuthors) for the first group in the Sorting and Grouping dialog, to guarantee that each author will have a distinct group in the report, but I only display the author name on the report. I didn't need to treat book names similarly—although two books can have the same name (for example, Partner in Crime by J.A. Jance and Partner in Crime by Rajnar Vajra), a book title would be unique for a specific author.

There are several other reports in this database. They differ from rptEBooksByAuthor only in sorting, filtering, and arrangement of the book data, so I will not discuss them specifically here.

After normalizing the database, applying a naming convention, and modifying the existing queries, forms, and reports as needed, you are now ready to proceed with further changes, on a sound foundation of normalized tables, and forms and reports that display the data in the tables.

Summary

In this chapter, I discussed the importance of applying a naming convention to your databases, and showed you how to normalize a database. The next chapter, *Moving Old Data into a New Database*, will use similar techniques with append and update queries when you need to move data from an old, non-normalized database into a brand-new database.

10

Moving Old Data into a New Database

There are two situations where you need to move old data into a new database: (1) When you are reworking an application that was developed in a non-normalized fashion, and you make a fresh start by creating a brand-new database with properly normalized tables, and then need to import data into the new tables from the old, non-normalized tables, and (2) when you develop a new Access application, and need to import data into it from another application such as dBASE or Excel, possibly after that data has been exported to an intermediate format such as comma-delimited text files.

In both cases, you can use a variety of techniques, involving both queries and VBA code, to extract the data you need from the old tables or text files and place it into the appropriate normalized tables.

Getting at the Old Data

Whether your old data is in the form of Access tables in another database or external files of some sort, the first step is to link to these tables (or import, if you prefer) to bring the data into your application, where you can work with it. For the Toy Workshop sample database, the client has sent me an Excel worksheet containing customer data entered before the Access database was created. I need to either link to this worksheet or import data from it into a new Access table so that I can work with the data. Since I only need to pull the Excel data into my new tables once, I will import the data in order to have full read-write access to all the fields in the table.

To import the worksheet, select Tables in the object bar, and click the New button in the datasheet window. Select Import Table in the New Table dialog, as shown in Figure 10.1.

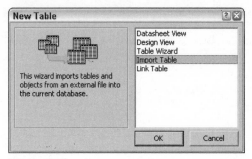

Figure 10.1

Select the appropriate file format (in this case, Microsoft Excel (*.xls)) in the Files of type selector in the Import dialog, browse to the folder where the file is located, select it and click the Import button, as shown in Figure 10.2.

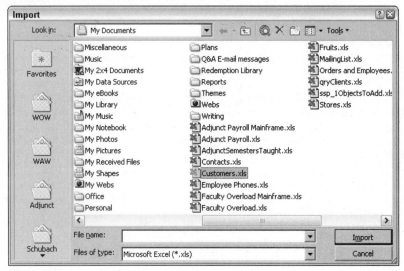

Figure 10.2

The Import Spreadsheet Wizard opens; generally, you can accept the defaults throughout the wizard, checking *First Row Contains Column Headings* on the first page, as shown in Figure 10.3.

You can check the *No primary key* option on the next to last page of the wizard because Access will create its own primary key when new records are added to tblCustomers. On the last page of the wizard, give the table the name tblRawCustomers (the word "Raw" in front of the base name of a table is my convention for marking raw data for import into normalized tables), and click Finish. Figures 10.4 and 10.5 show tblRawCustomers in Datasheet view. The first figure shows the name and part of the main address data; the second shows some of the phone numbers and email addresses.

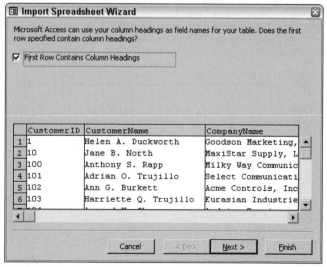

Figure 10.3

	CustomerID	CustomerName	CompanyName	JobTitle	MainAddressStreet
▶	55	Joseph H. Holloway	AAA Specialties	President	14635 Flower Ln.
	113	Florence E. Hall	Plutonic Center, Inc.	Advertising Director	13068 44th Terr.
	45	Molly U. Thompson	QLR Productions	Communications Director	13065 Juniper Ln.
	402	Penny F. Bellows	Margay Insurance, Ltd.	Director of Marketing	16205 19th Way
	138	Richard X. Carver	Foothill Marketing	MIS Manager	8992 51st Cir.
	200	Amber Q. Herman	Pueblo Management, Limited		3647 69th Blvd.
	203	Perry P. Bellows	Richland Marketing, Incorporated	MIS Manager	2079 49th Blvd.
	122	Lawrence K. Piper	Turnkey Associates, Ltd.	Sales Manager	1940 John Wayne Cir.
	237	Melvin E. Ferris	Black Oak Insurance, Ltd.	Purchasing Director	4976 51st St.
	453	Amanda O. Thompson	Homewood Manufacturing, Incorporated	Regional Sales Director	859 South St.
	367	Rex S. Galbraith	Quantum Systems		14843 21st Blvd.
	312	Rex C. Fuller	Almagamated Center, Inc.	Controller	717 24th Terr.

tblRawCustomers : Table

Record: ◀ ◀ 1 ▶ ▶l ▶✱ of 500

Figure 10.4

tblRawCustomers : Table

Phone1	Phone2	CallbackPhone	CarPhone	CellPhone	Pager	Email1	Email2
(614) 700-3475						josephh@toywkshop.com	
(925) 118-8839					(977) 848-5566	florenceh@toywkshop.com	fhall@frm.com
(120) 749-4563	(121) 987-6829					mollyt@toywkshop.com	mthompson@ibm.com
(555) 692-6722				(417) 630-6043		pennyb@toywkshop.com	pbellows@xrx.com
(514) 605-1191						richardc@toywkshop.com	rcarver@yto.com
(502) 830-6937	(812) 113-7189			(893) 636-1215		amberh@toywkshop.com	aherman@geq.com
(736) 113-1146			(121) 755-9277	(502) 830-6937		perryb@toywkshop.com	pbellows@qju.com
(714) 824-1077	(835) 121-1317			(104) 868-7499		lawrencep@toywkshop.com	lpiper@uof.com
(100) 352-6717					(716) 129-8363	melvinf@toywkshop.com	mferris@wmf.com
(437) 752-7529				(396) 547-9819		amandat@toywkshop.com	athompson@wud.com
(706) 111-1039				(513) 435-1278		rexg@toywkshop.com	rgalbraith@sbf.com
(106) 454-9142		(509) 856-1294				rexf@toywkshop.com	rfuller@uya.com

Record: ◀ ◀ 1 ▶ ▶l ▶✱ of 500

Figure 10.5

In addition to the main address, there are also two sets of fields for shipping addresses. Data from tblRawCustomers needs to be appended to several linked tables. Figure 10.6 shows a portion of the Relationships diagram showing how the normalized tables are linked.

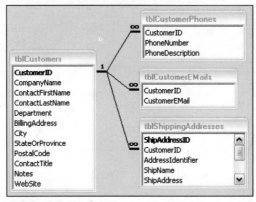

Figure 10.6

A simple append query (with some calculated fields to do splitting and concatenating as needed) will suffice to add the new customer records to tblCustomers, but to add new records to the linked tables, VBA code is needed. I'll discuss both of these methods in the next sections.

Using Queries with Calculated Fields to Append Data from a Non-Normalized Table to a Normalized Table

The query that appends records from tblRawCustomers to tblCustomers needs several calculated fields, to match the structure of the normalized tblCustomers:

❑ FirstName, MiddleName, and LastName fields that extract their data from the CustomerName field

❑ A StreetAddress field that concatenates data from the MainStreetAddress and MainAddressStreet2 fields

I'll modify some of the boilerplate calculated fields from queries in the Query Expressions database to do these tasks. (See Chapter 4, *Sorting and Filtering Data with Queries,* for more information on the Query Expressions database and the calculated fields in its queries.)

To start, select tblRawCustomers in the database window and select Query in the New Object selector on the toolbar, as shown in Figure 10.7.

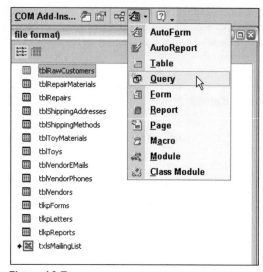

Figure 10.7

Select Design View in the New Query dialog, and select Append Query in the Query Type selector on the Query Design toolbar. Select tblCustomers in the Append dialog, as shown in Figure 10.8.

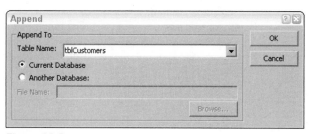

Figure 10.8

Save the new append query as qappRawCustomers. Not all of the fields in tblRawCustomers are needed in this query—just the ones that correspond to fields in tblCustomers, with the exception of Customer ID. If the matching fields in the source table and target table have the same names (for example, CompanyName), Access will automatically select the target field in the Append To row for the tblRawCustomers field. If the field has a different name, you have to select it manually from the list of available fields in tblCustomers.

If the target table for an append query has an AutoNumber field, don't append to that field unless the following conditions are met: (1) The fields in the source and target tables are of matching data types (you can use one of the conversion functions in a calculated field if necessary to convert the data type), and (2) the target table is empty. If you try to append to an AutoNumber field when the target table has data, you'll probably get a key violation error. If you omit the AutoNumber field, Access will create the new AutoNumber automatically.

The source table (tblRawCustomers) has a CustomerName field that includes a middle initial. The target table only has two name fields: ContactFirstName and ContactLastName. We can either throw away the middle initial from the source table or add a ContactMiddleName field to the target table. I chose to add a MiddleName field to the target table.

The table below shows the status of each field in tblRawCustomers (the source table of the append query), and its matching field (if any) in tblCustomers (the target table).

tblRawCustomers Field	tblCustomers Field(s)	Comments
CustomerID	CustomerID	Leave out of query—this is an Auto-Number field, whose value will be created automatically.
CustomerName	FirstName	The CustomerName field in tblRawCustomers is the source of three fields in tblCustomers, using calculated expressions.
	MiddleName	
	LastName	
CompanyName	CompanyName	
JobTitle	ContactTitle	
MainAddressStreet	BillingAddress	The two street address fields in tblRawCustomers are concatenated into the BillingAddress field in tblCustomers.
MainAddressStreet2		
MainAddressCity	City	
MainAddressState	StateOrProvince	
MainAddressPostalCode	PostalCode	
ShippingAddressStreet		Data in these fields will be appended to tblShippingAddresses.
ShippingAddressStreet2		
ShippingAddressCity		
ShippingAddressState		
ShippingAddressPostalCode		
ShippingAddressCountry		
Shipping2AddressStreet		
Shipping2AddressStreet2		

tblRawCustomers Field	tblCustomers Field(s)	Comments
Shipping2AddressCity		
Shipping2AddressState		
Shipping2AddressPostalCode		
Shipping2AddressCountry		
Shipping2AddressCountry		
Fax		Data in these fields will be appended to tblCustomerPhones.
Phone1		
Phone2		
CallbackPhone		
CarPhone		
CellPhone		
Pager		
Email1		Data in these fields will be appended to tblCustomerEMails.
Email2		
Email3		

To use the boilerplate query expressions for splitting and concatenating name and address data, start by importing the qrySplitNameComponents and qryConcatenateAddressComponents queries from the Query Expressions database into the current database. The qrySplitNameComponents append query contains expressions for splitting name fields into their components. There are two versions of the expressions for splitting names in this query—one set of fields to split a last name first name field (indicated by an "L" suffix), and another set of fields to split a first name first name field (indicated by an "F" suffix). The CustomerName field in tblRawCustomers has a first name first CustomerName field, so the FirstNameF, MiddleNamePlusF, MiddleNameF, and LastNameF fields are the ones to use. Copy these fields from qrySplitNameComponents to qappRawCustomers.

Each of these copied fields needs to be edited to replace the original field names with the appropriate field names from the source table. You can edit directly in the Zoom window (opened from the field by pressing Shift-F2). I recommend changing the font to a larger size by clicking the Font button and selecting 10 pt (or larger). Figure 10.9 shows the FirstNameF field with the original FirstNameFirst field being replaced by CustomerName.

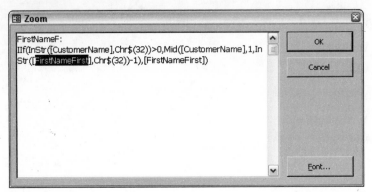

Figure 10.9

Replace FirstNameFirst with CustomerName in the FirstNameF and MiddleNamePlusF fields. The MiddleNameF and LastNameF fields both reference the intermediate field MiddleNamePlusF. This technique works fine in a select query (and it makes the calculated expressions far more comprehensible), but for an append query you need to replace the calculated field MiddleNamePlusF with the actual calculated expression (because each field in an append query must have a target field). This modification is difficult to do in the Zoom window, so I prefer to open a blank Word or Notepad document, paste the query expression into it, and use Search and Replace to replace [MiddleNamePlusF] (don't forget the brackets!) with the expression for the MiddleNamePlusF calculated field, as shown in Figure 10.10. After replacing all the occurrences of MiddleNamePlusF, paste the modified expression back into the query.

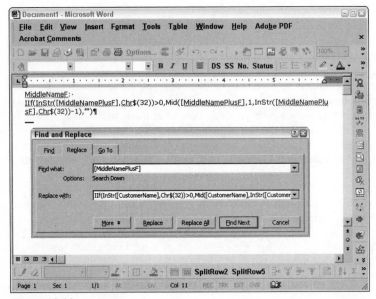

Figure 10.10

After doing this, the MiddleNamePlusF field can be deleted from the append query. The modified append query calculated name fields are listed below:

```
FirstNameF:
IIf(InStr([CustomerName],Chr$(32))>0,Mid([CustomerName],1,InStr([CustomerName],
Chr$(32))-1),[CustomerName])
MiddleNameF: IIf(InStr(IIf(InStr([CustomerName],Chr$(32))>0,Mid([CustomerName],
InStr([CustomerName],Chr$(32))+1),""),Chr$(32))>0,Mid(IIf(InStr([CustomerName],
Chr$(32))>0,Mid([CustomerName],InStr([CustomerName],Chr$(32))+1),""),1,
InStr(IIf(InStr([CustomerName],Chr$(32))>0,Mid([CustomerName],
InStr([CustomerName],Chr$(32))+1),""),Chr$(32))-1),"")
LastNameF: IIf(InStr(IIf(InStr([CustomerName],Chr$(32))>0,Mid([CustomerName],
InStr([CustomerName],Chr$(32))+1),""),Chr$(32))>0,Mid(IIf(InStr([CustomerName],
Chr$(32))>0,Mid([CustomerName],InStr([CustomerName],Chr$(32))+1),""),
InStr(IIf(InStr([CustomerName],Chr$(32))>0,Mid([CustomerName],
InStr([CustomerName],Chr$(32))+1),""),Chr$(32))+1),IIf(InStr([CustomerName],
Chr$(32))>0,Mid([CustomerName],InStr([CustomerName],Chr$(32))+1),""))
```

The next task is to concatenate the data from the two main street address fields into the Address field in the target table. Start by copying the Address field from qryConcatenateAddressComponents into qappRawCustomers. This field concatenates data from three separate street address fields, and there are only two address fields in the source table, so the final `& IIf(Nz([Address3])<>"",Chr(13) & Chr(10) & [Address3])` portion of the expression can be deleted. The Address1 field needs to be replaced with MainAddressStreet, and the Address2 field with MainAddressStreet2. The modified expression is:

```
Address: IIf(Nz([MainAddressStreet2])<>"",[MainAddressStreet] & Chr(13)
& Chr(10) & [MainAddressStreet2],[MainAddressStreet])
```

> **Chr(13) & Chr(10) puts a CR + LF (carriage return plus linefeed) into a query expression. In VBA code, you can use the vbCrLf named constant instead.**

The append query is now finished. It is shown in Design view in Figure 10.11.

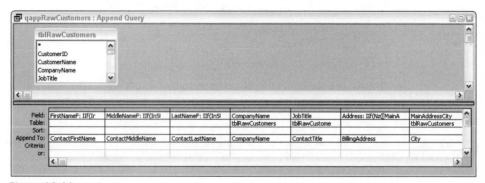

Figure 10.11

Now you can run the append query. Often, there will be a problem with appending some of the records. When I ran qappRawCustomers, I got the error message shown in Figure 10.12.

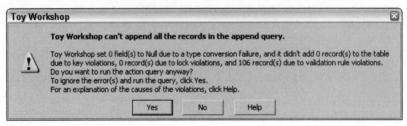

Figure 10.12

The error message shows that 106 records have validation rule problems. However, an examination of tblCustomers reveals that none of its fields have validation rules (it's not at all uncommon for append query error messages to be misleading). If you run the query, the 106 problem records will be discarded, and there is no easy way to append those 106 records later, after fixing the problem.

> *When I get an error running an append query, I cancel the update and make a copy of the target table with a dash prefix and the suffix "BeforeAppend" (in this case, the copy is -tblCustomersBeforeAppend). The copy preserves the data in the target table before appending, for use after resolving the issue that caused the problem while appending. After fixing the problem, I'll delete tblCustomers and copy tblCustomersBeforeAppend to tblCustomers, before running the append query.*

After running the append query, skipping the records that can't be appended, tblCustomers now has most of the records from tblRawCustomers—excluding the 106 problem records. To identify the 106 problem records, I use one of the selections in the New Query dialog. Create a new query, selecting the Find Unmatched Query Wizard in the New Query dialog, as shown in Figure 10.13.

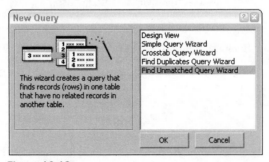

Figure 10.13

Select tblRawCustomers on the first screen of the wizard, and tblCustomers on the second screen. They can't be linked by CustomerID, so I'll use CompanyName, as shown in Figure 10.14.

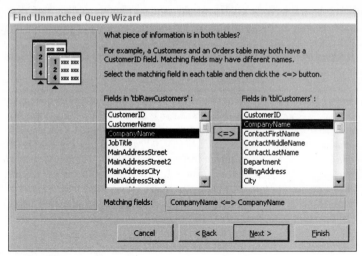

Figure 10.14

This won't link the two tables with perfect precision, but it's close enough to diagnose the problem. On the next screen of the wizard, select the first few fields (CustomerID, CustomerName, JobTitle, and CompanyName) for the query, and save it as qryUnmatchedCustomers. Figure 10.15 shows this query and some of the appended records in tblCustomers in Datasheet view.

qryUnmatchedCustomers : Select Query			tblCustomers : Table			
CompanyName	**JobTitle**			**Postal Code**	**Contact Title**	**Note:**
Goodson Marketing, Limited			+	13055-1098	Media Director	
Milky Way Communications, Limited			+	40469-5639	Director of Sales	
Pinnacle, Ltd.			+	76680-8108	Regional Manager	
Hillside Communications, Incorporated			+	71695-4840	Personnel Manager	
BME Industries			+	10081-1238	Communications Director	
Allied Industries, Ltd.			+	48523-1180	Regional Manager	
High-End Communications, Incorporated			+	57557-1020	Plant Manager	
Sunset International, Incorporated			+	38501-1009	Office Manager	
Margay, Ltd.			+	10245-1071	Regional Sales Director	
Secura Publishing, Inc.			+	36242-4222	Vice President	
Three Sons Management, Limited			+	13218-1174	Advertising Director	
Eastern Shipping, Ltd.			+	71319-3438	Advertising Director	
Dolphin Alternatives, Ltd.			+	11329-6470	Personnel Manager	
Stellar, Limited			+	73357-9734	Regional Sales Director	
Value Trend Advertising, Incorporated			+	83130-5211	Regional Sales Director	
Pueblo Management, Limited			+	43348-1267	Transportation Manager	
MLS International			+	46279-4491	Transportation Manager	
AA Shipping, Ltd.			+	84463-7695	Chief Engineer	
Venus International, Limited			+	42642-1069	MIS Manager	
New Value Advertising, Inc.			+	44996-6697	Public Relations Director	
Bright Flower Shipping, Ltd.			+	12201-5633	Purchasing Director	
Whooping Crane Management			+	10461-9538	Sales Manager	
White Peak Products, Ltd.			+	12017-5923	Director of Marketing	
Campbell Supply, Inc.			+	93334-3598	Plant Manager	
Lakeview International, Inc.			+	94656-1279	Communications Director	
Record: 1 of 94			Record: 371 of 463			

Figure 10.15

One thing stands out: all the records in qryUnmatchedCustomers have no data in the JobTitle field, while the appended records in tblCustomers all have data in the corresponding ContactTitle field, so it looks like this field is the one that caused the problem. Looking at the ContactTitle field in tblCustomers in Design view, the problem is clear: its AllowZeroLength property is set to No, so the records with no job title could not be appended.

From time to time, I like to make copies of database objects I am working on, in case a modification doesn't work out and I need to return to a previous version. To make a copy of an object quickly, I use a macro in the AutoKeys macro group (one of the few uses left for Access macros). This macro (hot key Ctrl-D) makes a copy of a database object with a dash (Access 2000 and 2002) or underscore (Access 2003) in front of its name (so that all the copies sort to the top of the database window, for easy clean-up). The macro has a SendKeys statement with the following keystrokes: **%fa{home}+^{right 2}-{end}**. *To use this macro, after adding it to your AutoKeys macro group, select a database object, and press Ctrl-D. The Save As dialog pops up, prefilled with the object name preceded by a dash. You can accept that name, or (if you want to save multiple backup copies), add a digit at the end of the name. Figure 10.16 shows the Save As dialog when making a second backup copy of tblCustomers.*

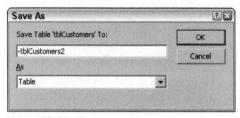

Figure 10.16

Now tblCustomers (with the missing records) can be deleted, and the backup copy made before doing the append (-tblCustomersBeforeAppend) can be copied to tblCustomers. Open tblCustomers in Design view, change AllowZeroLength to Yes for the ContactTitle field, check that any other field that could legitimately be blank also has this property set to Yes, and save the table. Generally speaking, only a few fields in a table—if any—should have the AllowZeroLength property set to Yes. If a record isn't valid unless it has a value in a field (say, a Social Security number for an employee), set the AllowZeroLength property to Yes; otherwise, it should be No. Try running qappRawCustomers again—this time all the records are appended.

Deleting the original tblCustomers and recreating it from the backup table deleted the links between tblCustomers and its linked tables, so open the Relationships diagram and redo the links. tblCustomer needs to be linked one-to-many to tblCustomerPhones, tblCustomerEMails, tblShippingAddresses, and tblOrders.

Using VBA Code to Move Data from a Non-Normalized Table to Linked Normalized Tables

The next task in moving data from tblRawCustomers involves the three sets of fields that don't belong in tblCustomers, but need to be appended to the three linked tables (tblCustomerPhones, tblCustomerEMails, and tblShippingAddresses). When the records were appended from tblRawCustomers to tblCustomers, new CustomerIDs were created for the records, and the CustomerID is needed to link these new records to their matching new records in the linked tables. This means that the new CustomerID needs to be written back to the CustomerID field in tblRawCustomers. tblRawCustomers has 500 records, while the original tblCustomers had 69 records, and now has 569 records. So the last 500 records of tblCustomers are the ones whose CustomerIDs (numbering 70 to 569) need to be written to the corresponding records in tblRawCustomers.

To do the updating, first create a select query based on tblCustomers, with the criterion >69 and an ascending sort on its CustomerID field, and save it as qryNewCustomers. Figure 10.17 shows this query in Design view.

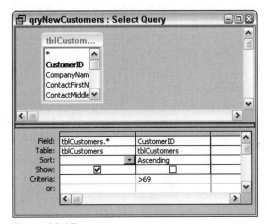

Figure 10.17

Next (just to make absolutely sure that the records are sorted by CustomerID), make a select query based on tblRawCustomers, sorted ascending by CustomerID, and save it as qryRawCustomers. Now there are two queries, each with 500 records, sorted by CustomerID, with matching records, as shown in Figure 10.18.

341

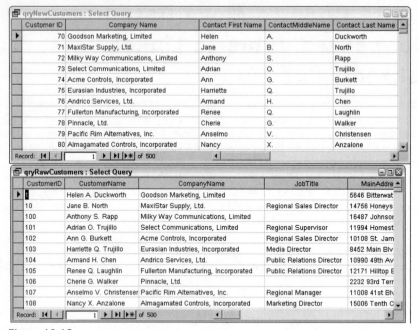

Figure 10.18

To write the new CustomerID values to tblRawCustomers, I set up two DAO recordsets and iterated through them record by record, writing the value from the recordset based on qryNewCustomers to the recordset based on qryRawCustomers. The code goes to the first record of rstOld, and then loops through rstNew, using the CStr function to convert the numeric CustomerID in rstNew to a string that is saved to the record in rstOld. The modified record in rstOld is updated, and the code moves to the next record in both recordsets. This procedure is:

```
Public Sub NewCustomerIDs()

On Error GoTo ErrorHandler

    Dim rstOld As DAO.Recordset
    Dim rstNew As DAO.Recordset

    Set dbs = CurrentDb
    Set rstOld = dbs.OpenRecordset("qryRawCustomers")
    Set rstNew = dbs.OpenRecordset("qryNewCustomers")
    rstOld.MoveFirst
    Do While Not rstNew.EOF
        rstOld.Edit
        rstOld![CustomerID] = CStr(rstNew![CustomerID])
        rstOld.Update
        rstOld.MoveNext
        rstNew.MoveNext
    Loop

ErrorHandlerExit:
```

```
      Exit Sub

ErrorHandler:
   MsgBox "Error No: " & Err.Number & "; Description: " & _
      Err.Description
   Resume ErrorHandlerExit

End Sub
```

You can run a Sub procedure by calling it from code in another procedure or by pressing the F5 hot key with the cursor inside the procedure. Subs can't be run from macros, but If you need to run code from a macro, you can just convert the Sub procedure to a function with no return value, and call it from a RunCode action in a macro.

Now the matching records in tblRawCustomers and tblCustomers have the same CustomerID, as shown in Figure 10.19.

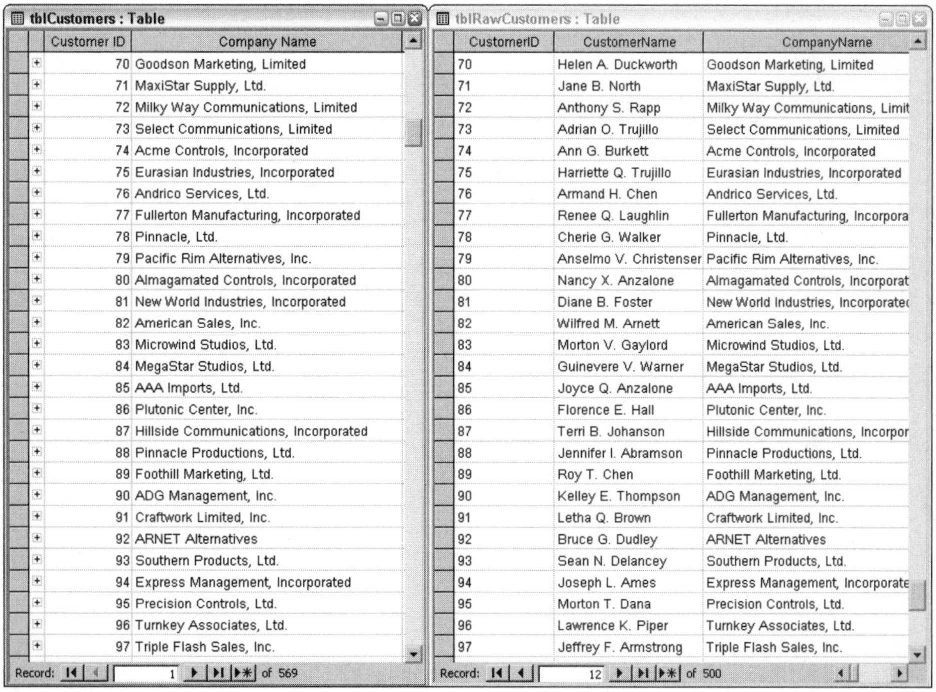

tblCustomers : Table			tblRawCustomers : Table		
Customer ID	Company Name		CustomerID	CustomerName	CompanyName
70	Goodson Marketing, Limited		70	Helen A. Duckworth	Goodson Marketing, Limited
71	MaxiStar Supply, Ltd.		71	Jane B. North	MaxiStar Supply, Ltd.
72	Milky Way Communications, Limited		72	Anthony S. Rapp	Milky Way Communications, Limit
73	Select Communications, Limited		73	Adrian O. Trujillo	Select Communications, Limited
74	Acme Controls, Incorporated		74	Ann G. Burkett	Acme Controls, Incorporated
75	Eurasian Industries, Incorporated		75	Harriette Q. Trujillo	Eurasian Industries, Incorporated
76	Andrico Services, Ltd.		76	Armand H. Chen	Andrico Services, Ltd.
77	Fullerton Manufacturing, Incorporated		77	Renee Q. Laughlin	Fullerton Manufacturing, Incorpora
78	Pinnacle, Ltd.		78	Cherie G. Walker	Pinnacle, Ltd.
79	Pacific Rim Alternatives, Inc.		79	Anselmo V. Christensen	Pacific Rim Alternatives, Inc.
80	Almagamated Controls, Incorporated		80	Nancy X. Anzalone	Almagamated Controls, Incorporat
81	New World Industries, Incorporated		81	Diane B. Foster	New World Industries, Incorporated
82	American Sales, Inc.		82	Wilfred M. Arnett	American Sales, Inc.
83	Microwind Studios, Ltd.		83	Morton V. Gaylord	Microwind Studios, Ltd.
84	MegaStar Studios, Ltd.		84	Guinevere V. Warner	MegaStar Studios, Ltd.
85	AAA Imports, Ltd.		85	Joyce Q. Anzalone	AAA Imports, Ltd.
86	Plutonic Center, Inc.		86	Florence E. Hall	Plutonic Center, Inc.
87	Hillside Communications, Incorporated		87	Terri B. Johanson	Hillside Communications, Incorpor
88	Pinnacle Productions, Ltd.		88	Jennifer I. Abramson	Pinnacle Productions, Ltd.
89	Foothill Marketing, Ltd.		89	Roy T. Chen	Foothill Marketing, Ltd.
90	ADG Management, Inc.		90	Kelley E. Thompson	ADG Management, Inc.
91	Craftwork Limited, Inc.		91	Letha Q. Brown	Craftwork Limited, Inc.
92	ARNET Alternatives		92	Bruce G. Dudley	ARNET Alternatives
93	Southern Products, Ltd.		93	Sean N. Delancey	Southern Products, Ltd.
94	Express Management, Incorporated		94	Joseph L. Ames	Express Management, Incorporate
95	Precision Controls, Ltd.		95	Morton T. Dana	Precision Controls, Ltd.
96	Turnkey Associates, Ltd.		96	Lawrence K. Piper	Turnkey Associates, Ltd.
97	Triple Flash Sales, Inc.		97	Jeffrey F. Armstrong	Triple Flash Sales, Inc.

Record: 1 of 569   Record: 12 of 500

Figure 10.19

Since CustomerID is a text field in tblRawCustomers (and thus is sorted alphabetically), the first group of new fields (numbered 70 to 99) is at the end of the table.

The next step is to write procedures for adding records to the linked tables, using the new, correct CustomerIDs as the foreign keys. But first, I'll create concatenated fields in qryRawCustomers, to combine the two street address fields into one for the first and second shipping addresses. These fields are similar to the ones for the main address fields, but with the appropriate field names replaced. The two concatenated fields follow, and they are shown in Datasheet view in Figure 10.20.

```
ShippingAddress1: IIf(Nz([ShippingAddressStreet2])<>"",[ShippingAddressStreet]
& Chr(13) & Chr(10) & [ShippingAddressStreet2],[ShippingAddressStreet])
ShippingAddress2: IIf(Nz([Shipping2AddressStreet2])<>"",[Shipping2AddressStreet]
& Chr(13) & Chr(10) & [Shipping2AddressStreet2],[Shipping2AddressStreet])
```

Email2	Email3	ShippingAddress1	ShippingAddress2
		11671 47th Ln. Room 100	5333 Flower Ave.
		1732 Shasta Way	
rpiper@era.com		7336 Division Ln. Dept. 769	4186 36th Ave. Room 225
		235 56th Blvd. Bldg. 420	717 24th Terr. Suite 581
		8535 Skyline Blvd. Suite 390	

Figure 10.20

The procedure that creates new records in tblCustomerPhones is listed below. The procedure sets up recordsets based on qryRawCustomers and tblCustomerPhones, and loops through the records in qryRawCustomers. The code checks each phone number field, and if it has a phone number, then the code creates a new record in tblCustomerPhones, writing the CustomerID, phone number, and phone description to the new record.

```
Public Sub NewCustomerPhones()

On Error GoTo ErrorHandler

    Dim rstCustomers As DAO.Recordset
    Dim rstPhones As DAO.Recordset
    Dim lngCustomerID As Long

    Set dbs = CurrentDb
    Set rstCustomers = dbs.OpenRecordset("qryRawCustomers")
    Set rstPhones = dbs.OpenRecordset("tblCustomerPhones")
    Do While Not rstCustomers.EOF
        'Pick up CustomerID from tblRawCustomers
        lngCustomerID = CLng(rstCustomers![CustomerID])
        'For each phone number field with a value, add a record
        'to tblCustomerPhones for this CustomerID.
        If Nz(rstCustomers![Fax]) <> "" Then
            rstPhones.AddNew
            rstPhones![CustomerID] = lngCustomerID
            rstPhones![PhoneDescription] = "Fax"
            rstPhones![PhoneNumber] = rstCustomers![Fax]
            rstPhones.Update
        End If
```

```
            If Nz(rstCustomers![Phone1]) <> "" Then
                rstPhones.AddNew
                rstPhones![CustomerID] = lngCustomerID
                rstPhones![PhoneDescription] = "Phone 1"
                rstPhones![PhoneNumber] = rstCustomers![Phone1]
                rstPhones.Update
            End If
            If Nz(rstCustomers![Phone2]) <> "" Then
                rstPhones.AddNew
                rstPhones![CustomerID] = lngCustomerID
                rstPhones![PhoneDescription] = "Phone 2"
                rstPhones![PhoneNumber] = rstCustomers![Phone2]
                rstPhones.Update
            End If
            If Nz(rstCustomers![CallbackPhone]) <> "" Then
                Debug.Print "Callback number: " & rstCustomers![CallbackPhone]
                rstPhones.AddNew
                rstPhones![CustomerID] = lngCustomerID
                rstPhones![PhoneDescription] = "Callback Phone"
                rstPhones![PhoneNumber] = rstCustomers![CallbackPhone]
                rstPhones.Update
            End If
            If Nz(rstCustomers![CarPhone]) <> "" Then
                rstPhones.AddNew
                rstPhones![CustomerID] = lngCustomerID
                rstPhones![PhoneDescription] = "Car Phone"
                rstPhones![PhoneNumber] = rstCustomers![CarPhone]
                rstPhones.Update
            End If
            If Nz(rstCustomers![CellPhone]) <> "" Then
                rstPhones.AddNew
                rstPhones![CustomerID] = lngCustomerID
                rstPhones![PhoneDescription] = "Cell Phone"
                rstPhones![PhoneNumber] = rstCustomers![CellPhone]
                rstPhones.Update
            End If
            If Nz(rstCustomers![Pager]) <> "" Then
                rstPhones.AddNew
                rstPhones![CustomerID] = lngCustomerID
                rstPhones![PhoneDescription] = "Pager"
                rstPhones![PhoneNumber] = rstCustomers![Pager]
                rstPhones.Update
            End If
            rstCustomers.MoveNext
        Loop

ErrorHandlerExit:
        Exit Sub

ErrorHandler:
        MsgBox "Error No: " & Err.Number & "; Description: " & _
            Err.Description
        Resume ErrorHandlerExit

End Sub
```

Access sometimes copies links when you make a copy of a table, which can lead to problems in code or queries. If you see an error message like the one in Figure 10.21 when running this procedure (or any procedure), you need to put the offending table (usually a table that was copied from another table) into the Relationships diagram and delete any links to it.

Figure 10.21

Figure 10.22 shows tblCustomerPhones with some of the phone numbers added by the NewCustomerPhones procedure.

CustomerID	PhoneNumber	PhoneDescription
70	(934) 471-6509	Fax
70	(100) 752-3843	Phone 1
70	(112) 102-9619	Phone 2
70	(911) 622-6352	Car Phone
71	(510) 125-4057	Fax
71	(523) 615-6767	Phone 1
71	(120) 100-6841	Cell Phone
72	(440) 100-6429	Fax
72	(118) 505-9973	Phone 1
72	(562) 121-7046	Phone 2
72	(108) 122-1155	Callback Phone
73	(703) 854-8079	Fax
73	(543) 481-1049	Phone 1
74	(564) 102-6616	Fax
74	(491) 493-5747	Phone 1
74	(975) 120-5759	Cell Phone
74	(913) 106-4782	Pager
75	(577) 132-3489	Fax
75	(697) 790-1052	Phone 1

Record: 1 of 1645

Figure 10.22

The next procedure adds email addresses to tblCustomerEMails in a similar manner:

```
Public Sub NewCustomerEMails()

On Error GoTo ErrorHandler

    Dim rstCustomers As DAO.Recordset
    Dim rstEMails As DAO.Recordset
    Dim lngCustomerID As Long

    Set dbs = CurrentDb
    Set rstCustomers = dbs.OpenRecordset("qryRawCustomers")
    Set rstEMails = dbs.OpenRecordset("tblCustomerEmails")
    Do While Not rstCustomers.EOF
        'Pick up CustomerID from tblRawCustomers
        lngCustomerID = CLng(rstCustomers![CustomerID])
        'For each email field with a value, add a record
        'to tblCustomerEMails for this CustomerID
        If Nz(rstCustomers![EMail1]) <> "" Then
            rstEMails.AddNew
            rstEMails![CustomerID] = lngCustomerID
            rstEMails![CustomerEMail] = rstCustomers![EMail1]
            rstEMails.Update
        End If
        If Nz(rstCustomers![EMail2]) <> "" Then
            rstEMails.AddNew
            rstEMails![CustomerID] = lngCustomerID
            rstEMails![CustomerEMail] = rstCustomers![EMail2]
            rstEMails.Update
        End If
        If Nz(rstCustomers![EMail3]) <> "" Then
            rstEMails.AddNew
            rstEMails![CustomerID] = lngCustomerID
            rstEMails![CustomerEMail] = rstCustomers![EMail3]
            rstEMails.Update
        End If
        rstCustomers.MoveNext
    Loop

ErrorHandlerExit:
    Exit Sub

ErrorHandler:
    MsgBox "Error No: " & Err.Number & "; Description: " & _
        Err.Description
    Resume ErrorHandlerExit

End Sub
```

Figure 10.23 shows some of the email addresses added to tblCustomerEMails by the NewCustomerEMails procedure.

Figure 10.23

The final procedure creates new shipping address records in tblShippingAddresses; it is:

```
Public Sub NewCustomerShippingAddresses()

On Error GoTo ErrorHandler

    Dim rstCustomers As DAO.Recordset
    Dim rstShippingAddresses As DAO.Recordset
    Dim lngCustomerID As Long

    Set dbs = CurrentDb
    Set rstCustomers = dbs.OpenRecordset("qryRawCustomers")
    Set rstShippingAddresses = dbs.OpenRecordset("tblShippingAddresses")
    Do While Not rstCustomers.EOF
        'Pick up CustomerID from tblRawCustomers
        lngCustomerID = CLng(rstCustomers![CustomerID])
        'For each set of shipping address fields with values, add a record
        'to tblShippingAddresses for this CustomerID.
        If Nz(rstCustomers![ShippingAddress1]) <> "" And _
            Nz(rstCustomers![ShippingAddressCity]) <> "" And _
            Nz(rstCustomers![ShippingAddressState]) <> "" And _
            Nz(rstCustomers![ShippingAddressPostalCode]) <> "" Then
            rstShippingAddresses.AddNew
            rstShippingAddresses![CustomerID] = lngCustomerID
            rstShippingAddresses![AddressIdentifier] = "Shipping Address 1"
            rstShippingAddresses![ShipName] = rstCustomers![CustomerName]
            rstShippingAddresses![ShipAddress] = _
                rstCustomers![ShippingAddress1]
```

```
            rstShippingAddresses![ShipCity] = _
                rstCustomers![ShippingAddressCity]
            rstShippingAddresses![ShipStateOrProvince] = _
                rstCustomers![ShippingAddressState]
            rstShippingAddresses![ShipPostalCode] = _
                rstCustomers![ShippingAddressPostalCode]
            rstShippingAddresses.Update
        End If
        If Nz(rstCustomers![ShippingAddress2]) <> "" And _
           Nz(rstCustomers![Shipping2AddressCity]) <> "" And _
           Nz(rstCustomers![Shipping2AddressState]) <> "" And _
           Nz(rstCustomers![Shipping2AddressPostalCode]) <> "" Then
            rstShippingAddresses.AddNew
            rstShippingAddresses![CustomerID] = lngCustomerID
            rstShippingAddresses![AddressIdentifier] = "Shipping Address 2"
            rstShippingAddresses![ShipName] = _
                rstCustomers![CustomerName]
            rstShippingAddresses![ShipAddress] = _
                rstCustomers![ShippingAddress2]
            rstShippingAddresses![ShipCity] = _
                rstCustomers![Shipping2AddressCity]
            rstShippingAddresses![ShipStateOrProvince] = _
                rstCustomers![Shipping2AddressState]
            rstShippingAddresses![ShipPostalCode] = _
                rstCustomers![Shipping2AddressPostalCode]
            rstShippingAddresses.Update
        End If
        rstCustomers.MoveNext
    Loop

ErrorHandlerExit:
    Exit Sub

ErrorHandler:
    MsgBox "Error No: " & Err.Number & "; Description: " & _
        Err.Description
    Resume ErrorHandlerExit

End Sub
```

There was an error (shown in Figure 10.24) when running the NewCustomerShippingAddresses procedure.

Figure 10.24

I examined the data in tblRawCustomers and saw that one record did not have a value in this field. There should be a value in this field, but if there isn't, the best way to work around the problem is just to skip saving that record to tblShippingAddresses. I modified the If . . . Then clause that checks each shipping address to only process an address if there is data in the address, city, state, and postal code fields.

If you have a problem while running a procedure to add records to a linked table, you can just delete the records that the procedure added to the linked table before it stopped with the error, and run the procedure again after fixing any problems.

After making this change, the procedure completed without errors. The modified procedure is:

```
Public Sub NewCustomerShippingAddresses()

On Error GoTo ErrorHandler

    Dim rstCustomers As DAO.Recordset
    Dim rstShippingAddresses As DAO.Recordset
    Dim lngCustomerID As Long

    Set dbs = CurrentDb
    Set rstCustomers = dbs.OpenRecordset("qryRawCustomers")
    Set rstShippingAddresses = dbs.OpenRecordset("tblShippingAddresses")
    Do While Not rstCustomers.EOF
        'Pick up CustomerID from tblRawCustomers
        lngCustomerID = CLng(rstCustomers![CustomerID])
        'For each set of shipping address fields with values, add a record
        'to tblShippingAddresses for this CustomerID.
        If Nz(rstCustomers![ShippingAddress1]) <> "" And _
           Nz(rstCustomers![ShippingAddressCity]) <> "" And _
           Nz(rstCustomers![ShippingAddressState]) <> "" And _
           Nz(rstCustomers![ShippingAddressPostalCode]) <> "" Then
           rstShippingAddresses.AddNew
           rstShippingAddresses![CustomerID] = lngCustomerID
           rstShippingAddresses![AddressIdentifier] = "Shipping Address 1"
           rstShippingAddresses![ShipName] = rstCustomers![CustomerName]
           rstShippingAddresses![ShipAddress] = rstCustomers![ShippingAddress1]
           rstShippingAddresses![ShipCity] = rstCustomers![ShippingAddressCity]
           rstShippingAddresses![ShipStateOrProvince] =
rstCustomers![ShippingAddressState]
           rstShippingAddresses![ShipPostalCode] =
rstCustomers![ShippingAddressPostalCode]
           rstShippingAddresses.Update
        End If
        If Nz(rstCustomers![ShippingAddress2]) <> "" And _
           Nz(rstCustomers![Shipping2AddressCity]) <> "" And _
           Nz(rstCustomers![Shipping2AddressState]) <> "" And _
           Nz(rstCustomers![Shipping2AddressPostalCode]) <> "" Then
           rstShippingAddresses.AddNew
           rstShippingAddresses![CustomerID] = lngCustomerID
           rstShippingAddresses![AddressIdentifier] = "Shipping Address 2"
           rstShippingAddresses![ShipName] = rstCustomers![CustomerName]
           rstShippingAddresses![ShipAddress] = rstCustomers![ShippingAddress2]
           rstShippingAddresses![ShipCity] = rstCustomers![Shipping2AddressCity]
```

```
            rstShippingAddresses![ShipStateOrProvince] =
rstCustomers![Shipping2AddressState]
            rstShippingAddresses![ShipPostalCode] =
rstCustomers![Shipping2AddressPostalCode]
            rstShippingAddresses.Update
         End If
         rstCustomers.MoveNext
      Loop

ErrorHandlerExit:
   Exit Sub

ErrorHandler:
   MsgBox "Error No: " & Err.Number & "; Description: " & _
      Err.Description
   Resume ErrorHandlerExit

End Sub
```

Figure 10.25 shows tblShippingAddresses with some of the new shipping addresses appended by the NewCustomerShippingAddresses procedure.

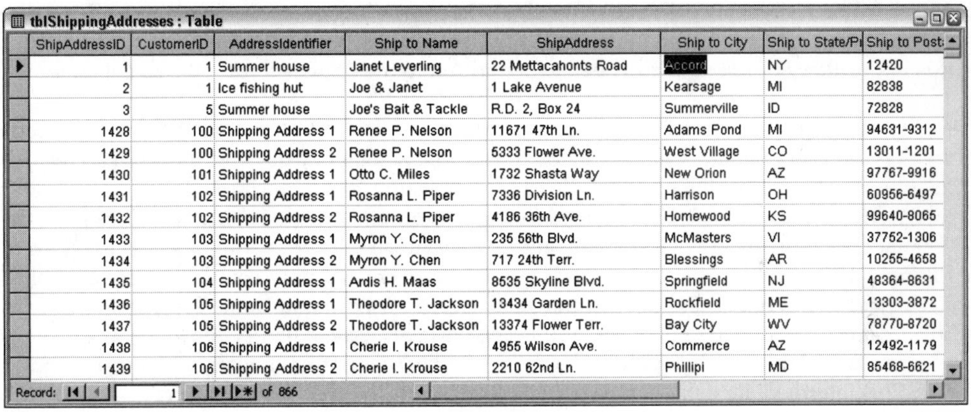
tblShippingAddresses : Table

ShipAddressID	CustomerID	AddressIdentifier	Ship to Name	ShipAddress	Ship to City	Ship to State/Pı	Ship to Post:
1	1	Summer house	Janet Leverling	22 Mettacahonts Road	Accord	NY	12420
2	1	Ice fishing hut	Joe & Janet	1 Lake Avenue	Kearsage	MI	82838
3	5	Summer house	Joe's Bait & Tackle	R.D. 2, Box 24	Summerville	ID	72828
1428	100	Shipping Address 1	Renee P. Nelson	11671 47th Ln.	Adams Pond	MI	94631-9312
1429	100	Shipping Address 2	Renee P. Nelson	5333 Flower Ave.	West Village	CO	13011-1201
1430	101	Shipping Address 1	Otto C. Miles	1732 Shasta Way	New Orion	AZ	97767-9916
1431	102	Shipping Address 1	Rosanna L. Piper	7336 Division Ln.	Harrison	OH	60956-6497
1432	102	Shipping Address 2	Rosanna L. Piper	4186 36th Ave.	Homewood	KS	99640-8065
1433	103	Shipping Address 1	Myron Y. Chen	235 56th Blvd.	McMasters	VI	37752-1306
1434	103	Shipping Address 2	Myron Y. Chen	717 24th Terr.	Blessings	AR	10255-4658
1435	104	Shipping Address 1	Ardis H. Maas	8535 Skyline Blvd.	Springfield	NJ	48364-8631
1436	105	Shipping Address 1	Theodore T. Jackson	13434 Garden Ln.	Rockfield	ME	13303-3872
1437	105	Shipping Address 2	Theodore T. Jackson	13374 Flower Terr.	Bay City	WV	78770-8720
1438	106	Shipping Address 1	Cherie I. Krouse	4955 Wilson Ave.	Commerce	AZ	12492-1179
1439	106	Shipping Address 2	Cherie I. Krouse	2210 62nd Ln.	Phillipi	MD	85468-6621

Record: 1 of 866

Figure 10.25

Denormalizing Data

Sometimes you may need to do the opposite of the last section's tasks—export data from linked, normalized tables to a non-normalized table—generally because such a table structure is required for compatibility with a flat-file mainframe database, or to meet government requirements (which are often based on outdated database technology). The task of extracting data from separate linked (normalized) tables, and appending it to a single flat-file table, is sometimes called *denormalizing* because you are reversing the usual process of separating data into linked, normalized tables. As an example of such a table, I made a structure-only copy of tblRawCustomers, by copying the table to the clipboard, then pasting it with the Structure Only option selected in the Paste Table As dialog, as shown in Figure 10.26.

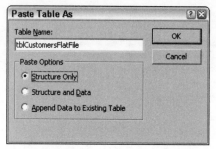

Figure 10.26

The target table (tblCustomersFlatFile) has three sets of fields of the same type (phones, emails, and shipping addresses). To fill these fields with data from tblCustomers (the "one" table in the relationships), and the three linked "many" tables, three procedures are needed to pick up data from tblCustomers and the three "many" tables. The first procedure uses a query to fill the target table (tblCustomersFlatFiles) with records, one record per CustomerID, and also to fill the separate phone fields with data from the linked tblCustomerPhones. The two other procedures work with the two linked tables, updating the records in tblCustomersFlatFiles with email and shipping address data from the linked tables. I use a query to work with the shipping address data, because calculated fields are needed to split the street address into two fields. The appending or updating has to be done in code, because the query and the linked tables have multiple records per CustomerID, so data from different records in the query or linked tables need to be written to the same record in the target table.

The query (qryCustomersAndPhones) includes two tables, tblCustomers and tblCustomerPhones. To ensure that the query includes all the Customer records, whether or not they have linked records in tblCustomerPhones, select the middle (LEFT JOIN) selection in the Join Type dialog for the join between the table. This query needs a few calculated fields: CustomerName (to concatenate data from the separate Contact Name fields in tblCustomers) and a set of Address1 and Address2 fields to separate data in the Billing Address field in tblCustomers. These fields are created based on the boilerplate fields in two queries from the Query Expressions sample database: qryConcatenateNameComponents and qrySplitAddressComponents, as in the "Using Queries with Calculated Fields to Append Data from a Non-Normalized Table to a Normalized Table" section earlier in this chapter, with one exception: the AddressPlus intermediate fields can be used to simplify the query field expressions, since this is a select query, not an append query. The query expressions for the concatenated name field and the split billing address fields are:

```
FirstNameFirst: IIf([ContactMiddleName],[ContactFirstName] & " " &
[ContactMiddleName],[ContactFirstName]) & IIf([ContactLastName]," " &
[ContactLastName],[ContactLastName])
AddressPlus:
IIf(InStr([BillingAddress],Chr(10)),Mid([BillingAddress],InStr([BillingAddress],
Chr(10))+1))
Address1:
IIf(InStr([BillingAddress],Chr(13)),Left([BillingAddress],InStr([BillingAddress],
Chr(13))-1),[BillingAddress])
Address2: IIf(InStr([AddressPlus],Chr(13)),Left([AddressPlus],
InStr([AddressPlus],Chr(13))-1),[AddressPlus])
```

The first query (qryCustomersAndPhones) is shown in Design view in Figure 10.27.

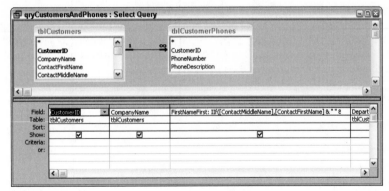

Figure 10.27

Figure 10.28 shows the same query in Datasheet view, with just the CustomerID, CompanyName, PhoneNumber, and PhoneDescription fields showing. The number of records per CustomerID is equal to the number of phones for that customer in the linked tblCustomerPhones table.

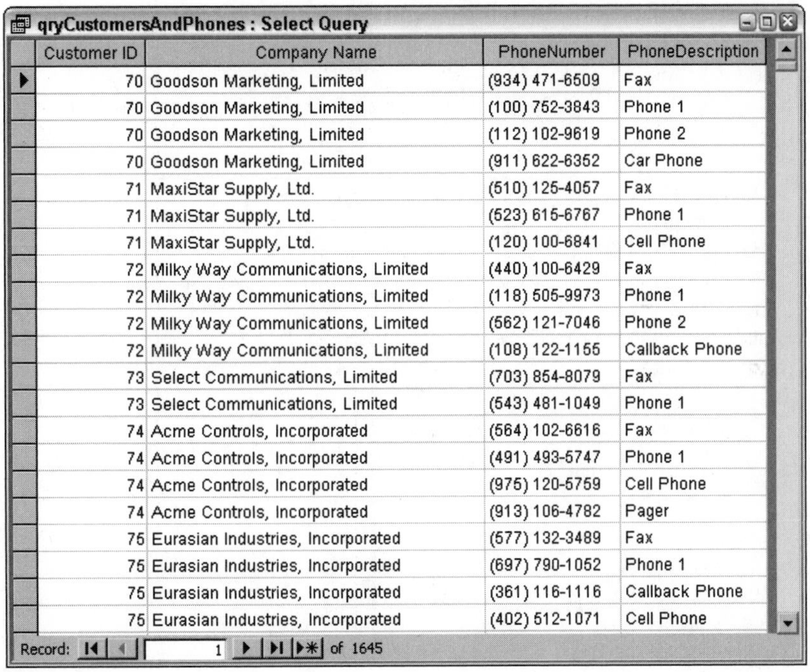

Customer ID	Company Name	PhoneNumber	PhoneDescription
70	Goodson Marketing, Limited	(934) 471-6509	Fax
70	Goodson Marketing, Limited	(100) 752-3843	Phone 1
70	Goodson Marketing, Limited	(112) 102-9619	Phone 2
70	Goodson Marketing, Limited	(911) 622-6352	Car Phone
71	MaxiStar Supply, Ltd.	(510) 125-4057	Fax
71	MaxiStar Supply, Ltd.	(523) 615-6767	Phone 1
71	MaxiStar Supply, Ltd.	(120) 100-6841	Cell Phone
72	Milky Way Communications, Limited	(440) 100-6429	Fax
72	Milky Way Communications, Limited	(118) 505-9973	Phone 1
72	Milky Way Communications, Limited	(562) 121-7046	Phone 2
72	Milky Way Communications, Limited	(108) 122-1155	Callback Phone
73	Select Communications, Limited	(703) 854-8079	Fax
73	Select Communications, Limited	(543) 481-1049	Phone 1
74	Acme Controls, Incorporated	(564) 102-6616	Fax
74	Acme Controls, Incorporated	(491) 493-5747	Phone 1
74	Acme Controls, Incorporated	(975) 120-5759	Cell Phone
74	Acme Controls, Incorporated	(913) 106-4782	Pager
75	Eurasian Industries, Incorporated	(577) 132-3489	Fax
75	Eurasian Industries, Incorporated	(697) 790-1052	Phone 1
75	Eurasian Industries, Incorporated	(361) 116-1116	Callback Phone
75	Eurasian Industries, Incorporated	(402) 512-1071	Cell Phone

Record: 1 of 1645

Figure 10.28

The procedure that creates new records in tblCustomersFlatFile uses two recordsets, one based on qryCustomersAndPhones (the source data) and one based on tblCustomersFlatFile (the target table). The code loops through rstCustomers, starting out by checking whether the CustomerID value is the same as in the previous record (the lngOldCustomerID variable is set to 0 before processing the first record). If the CustomerID is different, a new record is added to the flat file table, and its name and address fields are filled in from tblCustomers. Then, for all records (whether the CustomerID is the same or different), the value of the PhoneDescription field is checked, and the phone number is saved to the appropriate field in tblCustomersFlatFile. After updating the record, the code moves to the last record and edits it again in case there are more records for the same CustomerID.

```vb
Public Sub AppendCustomersAndPhones()

On Error GoTo ErrorHandler

    Dim rstCustomers As DAO.Recordset
    Dim rstFlatFile As DAO.Recordset
    Dim lngCustomerID As Long
    Dim lngOldCustomerID As Long
    Dim strPhoneDesc As String

    lngOldCustomerID = 0
    Set dbs = CurrentDb
    Set rstCustomers = dbs.OpenRecordset("qryCustomersAndPhones")
    Set rstFlatFile = dbs.OpenRecordset("tblCustomersFlatFile")
    Do While Not rstCustomers.EOF
        lngCustomerID = rstCustomers![CustomerID]
        Debug.Print "Customer ID: " & lngCustomerID
        Debug.Print "Old Customer ID: " & lngOldCustomerID
        'Check whether this record has a new CustomerID.
        If lngCustomerID <> lngOldCustomerID Then
            'New record has different CustomerID;
            'add a new record to target table and fill the name and
            'address fields
            rstFlatFile.AddNew
            rstFlatFile![CustomerID] = lngCustomerID
            rstFlatFile![CompanyName] = rstCustomers![CompanyName]
            rstFlatFile![CustomerName] = rstCustomers![FirstNameFirst]
            rstFlatFile![JobTitle] = rstCustomers![ContactTitle]
            rstFlatFile![MainAddressStreet] = rstCustomers![Address1]
            rstFlatFile![MainAddressStreet2] = rstCustomers![Address2]
            rstFlatFile![MainAddressCity] = rstCustomers![City]
            rstFlatFile![MainAddressState] = rstCustomers![StateOrProvince]
            rstFlatFile![MainAddressPostalCode] = rstCustomers![PostalCode]
        End If

        'Determine type of phone number from its description, and store
        'it in the appropriate field.
        'Phone numbers need to be updated for all records in the source query.
        strPhoneDesc = Nz(rstCustomers![PhoneDescription])
        Debug.Print "Phone description: " & strPhoneDesc
        Select Case strPhoneDesc

            Case "Phone 1"
                rstFlatFile![Phone1] = rstCustomers![PhoneNumber]

            Case "Phone 2"
                rstFlatFile![Phone2] = rstCustomers![PhoneNumber]

            Case "Fax"
```

```
                    rstFlatFile![Fax] = rstCustomers![PhoneNumber]

            Case "Callback Phone"
               rstFlatFile![CallbackPhone] = rstCustomers![PhoneNumber]

            Case "Car Phone"
               rstFlatFile![CarPhone] = rstCustomers![PhoneNumber]

            Case "Cell Phone"
               rstFlatFile![CellPhone] = rstCustomers![PhoneNumber]

            Case "Pager"
               rstFlatFile![Pager] = rstCustomers![PhoneNumber]

            Case Else
               'Other phones can't be stored in the target table, so
               'they won't be processed.
         End Select

         lngOldCustomerID = lngCustomerID
         rstFlatFile.Update
         rstFlatFile.MoveLast
         rstFlatFile.Edit
         rstCustomers.MoveNext
      Loop

ErrorHandlerExit:
   Exit Sub

ErrorHandler:
   MsgBox "Error No: " & Err.Number & "; Description: " & _
      Err.Description
   Resume ErrorHandlerExit

End Sub
```

After running this procedure, there are 569 records in tblCustomersFlatFile (the same number of records as tblCustomers), with their phone number fields filled in.

The next procedure updates the records in tblCustomersFlatFile with email addresses. It cycles through a recordset based on tblCustomerEMails, and for each record it searches for the matching CustomerID record in tblCustomersFlatFile. An intCount variable is set to 1 every time a new CustomerID occurs in tblCustomerEMails, and incremented by 1 with each successive record that has the same CustomerID. This variable is used to create a field name ("Email" & CStr(intCount)), and the email address from the current record in tblCustomerEMails is written to the EMail1, EMail2, or EMail3 field in tblCustomersFlatFile, depending on whether it is the first, second, or third email address for that customer in tblCustomerEMails (if there are more than three email addresses, the extra ones are not written to the flat-file table). The UpdateEMails procedure is listed below:

```
Public Sub UpdateEMails()

On Error GoTo ErrorHandler

   Dim rstEMails As DAO.Recordset
```

355

```
        Dim rstFlatFile As DAO.Recordset
        Dim strCustomerID As String
        Dim strOldCustomerID As String
        Dim strEMail As String
        Dim strSearch As String
        Dim intCount As Integer
        Dim strFieldName As String

        strOldCustomerID = ""
        Set dbs = CurrentDb
        Set rstEMails = dbs.OpenRecordset("tblCustomerEMails", dbOpenDynaset)
        Set rstFlatFile = dbs.OpenRecordset("tblCustomersFlatFile", dbOpenDynaset)
        Do While Not rstEMails.EOF
            strCustomerID = rstEMails![CustomerID]
            strSearch = "[CustomerID] = " & Chr$(39) & strCustomerID _
                & Chr$(39)
            Debug.Print "Search string: " & strSearch
            Debug.Print "Customer ID: " & strCustomerID
            Debug.Print "Old Customer ID: " & strOldCustomerID
            'Check whether this record has a new CustomerID
            If strCustomerID <> strOldCustomerID Then
                'New record has different CustomerID;
                'Set email count back to one
                intCount = 1
            Else
                'Increment email count by one
                intCount = intCount + 1
            End If

            'Store the email address in the appropriate field of the
            'flat-file table (Email1, Email2, or EMail3; if there are
            'more than three emails, only the first three will be stored).
            If intCount < 4 Then
                rstFlatFile.FindFirst strSearch
                strEMail = Nz(rstEMails![CustomerEMail])
                Debug.Print "Email address: " & strEMail
                rstFlatFile.Edit
                strFieldName = "Email" & CStr(intCount)
                Debug.Print "Field name: " & strFieldName
                rstFlatFile(strFieldName) = strEMail
                rstFlatFile.Update
                rstFlatFile.FindFirst strSearch
                rstFlatFile.Edit
            End If

            strOldCustomerID = strCustomerID
            rstEMails.MoveNext
        Loop

ErrorHandlerExit:
        Exit Sub

ErrorHandler:
        MsgBox "Error No: " & Err.Number & "; Description: " & _
```

```
        Err.Description
    Resume ErrorHandlerExit

End Sub
```

The procedure for adding shipping addresses to tblCustomersFlatFile is similar, except that it uses a select query based on tblShippingAddresses, with calculated fields to separate out the street address field into two fields (similar to the fields in qryCustomerNamesAndPhones). This procedure is:

```
Public Sub UpdateShippingAddresses()

On Error GoTo ErrorHandler

    Dim rstShipping As DAO.Recordset
    Dim rstFlatFile As DAO.Recordset
    Dim strCustomerID As String
    Dim strOldCustomerID As String
    Dim strSearch As String
    Dim intCount As Integer

    strOldCustomerID = ""
    Set dbs = CurrentDb
    Set rstShipping = dbs.OpenRecordset("qryShippingAddresses", dbOpenDynaset)
    Set rstFlatFile = dbs.OpenRecordset("tblCustomersFlatFile", dbOpenDynaset)
    Do While Not rstShipping.EOF
        strCustomerID = rstShipping![CustomerID]
        strSearch = "[CustomerID] = " & Chr$(39) & strCustomerID _
            & Chr$(39)
        Debug.Print "Search string: " & strSearch
        Debug.Print "Customer ID: " & strCustomerID
        Debug.Print "Old Customer ID: " & strOldCustomerID
        'Check whether this record has a new CustomerID.
        If strCustomerID <> strOldCustomerID Then
            'New record has different CustomerID;
            'Set email count back to one
            intCount = 1
        Else
            'Increment address count by one
            intCount = intCount + 1
        End If

        'Store the shipping address info in the appropriate set of
        'fields in the flat-file table; if there are more than three
        'shipping addresses, only the first two will be stored.
        rstFlatFile.FindFirst strSearch
        rstFlatFile.Edit
        If intCount = 1 Then
            rstFlatFile![ShippingAddressStreet] = _
                Nz(rstShipping![ShippingAddress1])
            rstFlatFile![ShippingAddressStreet2] = _
                Nz(rstShipping![ShippingAddress2])
            rstFlatFile![ShippingAddressCity] = _
                Nz(rstShipping![ShipCity])
```

```
            rstFlatFile![ShippingAddressState] = _
                Nz(rstShipping![ShipStateOrProvince])
            rstFlatFile![ShippingAddressPostalCode] = _
                Nz(rstShipping![ShipPostalCode])
            rstFlatFile![ShippingAddressCountry] = "USA"
        ElseIf intCount = 2 Then
            rstFlatFile![Shipping2AddressStreet] = _
                Nz(rstShipping![ShippingAddress1])
            rstFlatFile![Shipping2AddressStreet2] = _
                Nz(rstShipping![ShippingAddress2])
            rstFlatFile![Shipping2AddressCity] = _
                Nz(rstShipping![ShipCity])
            rstFlatFile![Shipping2AddressState] = _
                Nz(rstShipping![ShipStateOrProvince])
            rstFlatFile![Shipping2AddressPostalCode] = _
                Nz(rstShipping![ShipPostalCode])
            rstFlatFile![Shipping2AddressCountry] = "USA"
        End If
        rstFlatFile.Update
        rstFlatFile.FindFirst strSearch
        rstFlatFile.Edit

        strOldCustomerID = strCustomerID
        rstShipping.MoveNext
    Loop

ErrorHandlerExit:
    Exit Sub

ErrorHandler:
    MsgBox "Error No: " & Err.Number & "; Description: " & _
        Err.Description
    Resume ErrorHandlerExit

End Sub
```

If you need to run the code that fills tblCustomersFlatFile with denormalized data on a regular basis (say, for a monthly export to a mainframe database), you can convert the Sub procedures to functions, so that they can be run from a macro with RunCode actions. You'll also need to make a structure-only copy of tblCustomersFlatFile with the zz prefix (indicating a table for copying), so you can make a fresh copy of tblCustomersFlatFile by copying from zstblCustomersFlatFile. The macro's actions are:

```
DeleteObject, Table, tblCustomersFlatFile
CopyObject, tblCustomersFlatFile, Table, zztblCustomersFlatFile
RunCode, AppendCustomersAndPhones
RunCode, UpdateEMails
RunCode, UpdateShippingAddresses
```

The mcrCreateFlatFileTable macro can be run every time you want to create the flat-file table with fresh data.

Summary

Using the techniques in this chapter, you should be able to use append and update queries, and VBA code, to move data from old, non-normalized tables into a database with properly normalized tables.

Part III: Working with Other Office Components (and More)

11

Working with Word

You can create great reports with Access (see Chapter 6, *Printing Data with Reports*), but there are times when it is convenient (or necessary) to create Word documents to print your Access data. You may already have created Word templates, and want to print letters created from these templates using data stored in Access tables. You may need to do a mass mailing, but with more control over data selection than the Word Mail Merge Wizard allows. Or you may need to put Access data into a Word document so that it can be distributed to anyone who has the standard edition of Office, which includes Word, but not Access.

> For other ways of distributing documents filled with Access data to persons who don't have Access, see the section on emailing reports in .snp or .pdf formats in Chapter 12, Working with Outlook.

You may also need to import data from Word. You won't see a Word selection in the *Files of type* selection list in the Access Import dialog, but it is possible to import data from Word documents into an Access table, at least if the data is in one or more Word tables. You can write VBA code to do the import, using the Word object model.

This chapter will explain how to use the Word object model to export Access data to Word documents and to import data in Word tables into Access. The following table lists the sample files referenced in this chapter and indicates where they should be placed.

Document Name	Document Type	Place in Folder
Avery 5160 Labels.dot	Word template	\Templates\Access Merge
Avery 5160 Merge Labels.dot	Word template	\Templates\Access Merge
Avery 5161 Labels.dot	Word template	\Templates\Access Merge
Avery 5161 Merge Labels.dot	Word Labels template	\Templates\Access Merge

Table continued on following page

Document Name	Document Type	Place in Folder
Avery 5162 Merge Labels.dot	Word Labels template	\Templates\Access Merge
Boilerplate Contact Letter BM.dot	Word template	\Templates\Access Merge
Boilerplate Contact Letter DP.dot	Word template	\Templates\Access Merge
Catalog.dot	Word Catalog Merge template	\Templates\Access Merge
Contact Merge Letter.dot	Word Mail Merge template	\Templates\Access Merge
Freestyle Contact Letter BM.dot	Word template	\Templates\Access Merge
Freestyle Contact Letter DP.dot	Word template	\Templates\Access Merge
Northwind Invoice.dot	Word template	\Templates\Access Merge
One-up Label BM.dot	Word template	\Templates\Access Merge
One-up Label DP.dot	Word template	\Templates\Access Merge
Employee Phones.doc	Word document	\My Documents\Access Merge
Logons and Passwords.doc	Word document	\My Documents\Access Merge
Word Data Exchange.mdb	Access 2000 database	Wherever you want

Writing Automation Code

To work with Office documents (such as Word documents) in VBA code, you need to write Automation code. Automation (previously called OLE—Object Linking and Embedding—or OLE Automation) lets you work with the object models of Office applications (and some non-Office applications). The object models represent the objects, properties, methods, and events of that program in a form that can be used in code. When working with Word, this means that you can work with documents, styles, ranges, bookmarks, and just about any other components you can manipulate in the Word interface.

The first step in writing Automation code is to set a reference to the appropriate object model, in this case Word. Open an Access module, drop down the Tools menu in the Visual Basic window, and select References. The References dialog opens, with the currently selected references checked. By default, a brand-new Access 2000 or higher database has only the references shown in Figure 11.1.

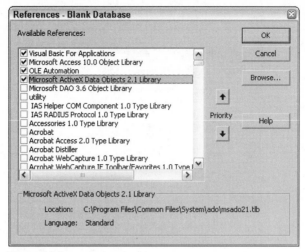

Figure 11.1

Some Handy Toolbar Buttons

To save time when working with modules and references, I suggest placing a Visual Basic Editor button on the main Access toolbar and a References button on the Visual Basic window toolbar. To place a Visual Basic Editor button on the main Access toolbar, follow these steps:

1. With the database window visible, right-click the grey background of the Database toolbar and select Customize from the context menu, as shown in Figure 11.2.

Figure 11.2

2. In the Customize dialog, select Tools in the Categories well, and locate the Visual Basic Editor command in the Commands well, as shown in Figure 11.3.

3. Using the mouse, drag the Visual Basic Editor command to the Database toolbar, and close the Customize dialog. The command will become a toolbar button, as shown in Figure 11.4.

To add a References button to the Visual Basic window Standard toolbar, use the new Visual Basic Editor button to open that window, open the Customize dialog from the Standard toolbar, and drag the References command from the Tools category to that toolbar. You may also want to drag the Compile Project command from the Debug category to this toolbar; both buttons are shown in Figure 11.5.

Figure 11.3

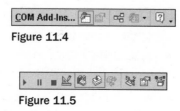

Figure 11.4

Figure 11.5

The Word Object Model

There are several handy built-in tools you can use when working with the Word object model in Access databases. They are described in the next sections.

Viewing the Word Object Model Diagram

To view the Word object model, open the Visual Basic window from a Word document, and type object model into the Answer box on the toolbar, then select Microsoft Word Objects to open the corresponding Help topic. The first page of the Word object model diagram from this Help topic opens, as shown in Figure 11.6.

Some Help topics have their own subsidiary windows. Clicking the red triangle next to the Document object, for example, opens another Help window, shown in Figure 11.7.

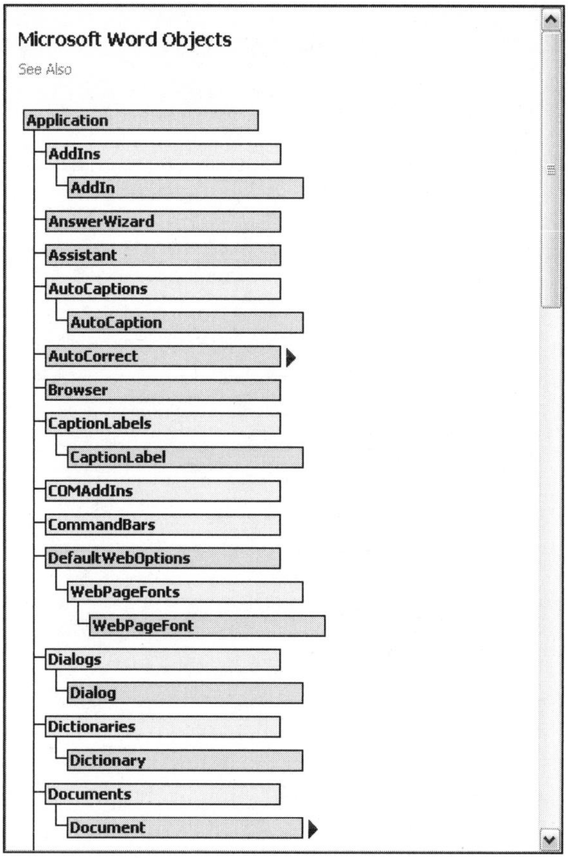

Microsoft Word Objects
See Also

- Application
  - AddIns
    - AddIn
  - AnswerWizard
  - Assistant
  - AutoCaptions
    - AutoCaption
  - AutoCorrect ▶
  - Browser
  - CaptionLabels
    - CaptionLabel
  - COMAddIns
  - CommandBars
  - DefaultWebOptions
    - WebPageFonts
      - WebPageFont
  - Dialogs
    - Dialog
  - Dictionaries
    - Dictionary
  - Documents
    - Document ▶

Figure 11.6

The Word object model is very extensive, and you can explore all of it by paging through the diagram in Help, and clicking on the red triangles to see more detail. However, when writing Automation code to work with Word, most likely you will be working with just a few components of this large and complex object model, primarily the Application object, the Documents, Templates, Tables, Bookmarks, and Styles collections, and perhaps the FileDialog and FileSearch objects.

Along with the diagrams in Help, there is another way to view the Word object model, which is generally more helpful when you are writing VBA code: Use the Object Browser, which is opened from the Visual Basic window of any Office component, using the F2 function key. This dialog lets you select objects and their properties, methods, and events, and open Help topics as needed. To view Word objects, select Word in the unlabeled Libraries selector at the upper left of the window. The Classes list contains objects, collections, and enumerations (abbreviated *enums*)—collections of named constants that can be used as argument values. When you make a selection in the Classes list, all the attributes of the selection object, collection, or enum are displayed in the Members list.

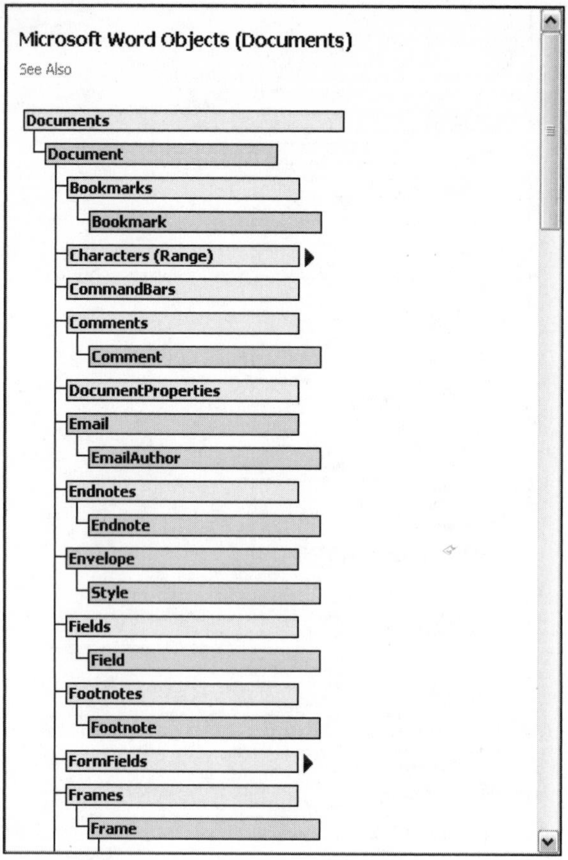

Figure 11.7

Figure 11.8 shows the properties and methods of the Bookmarks collection.

On selecting a property, method, or event of an entry in the Classes list, you will see its syntax displayed in the Object Browser's status bar. Figure 11.9 shows the syntax for the SetWidth method of the Column object. The method's argument names (*ColumnWidth* and *RulerStyle*) are in italics, and for each argument, either its data type (Single) is given, or the enum used to select appropriate values (WdRulerStyle). For enum settings, you can click the enum name to open it and see the available selections.

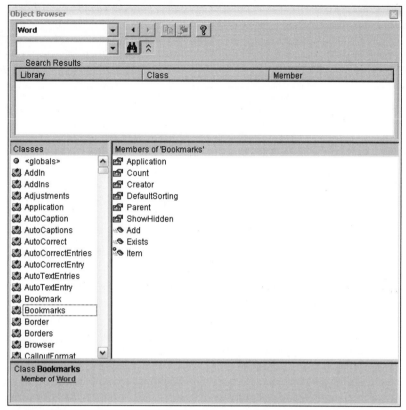

Figure 11.8

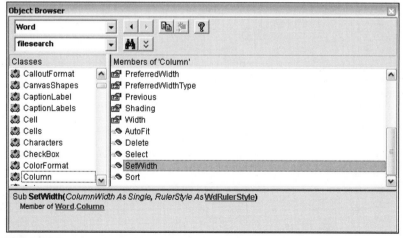

Figure 11.9

A Note on Enums

Enums (short for enumerations) are collections of named constants, used to set values of properties and method arguments of methods, or to check the return values of functions. If you have a reference set to the appropriate object model, you can use named constants that are members of an enum when writing code.

Using these named arguments for property values and arguments makes your code much more readable. For example, when writing Word Automation code:

```
gappWord.Selection.MoveDown unit:=wdLine, Count:=1, Extend:=wdExtend
```

is a lot more comprehensible than:

```
gappWord.Selection.MoveDown 5, 1, 1
```

However, there are circumstances where you need to use the numeric values for setting property and argument values:

❑ When writing VBS code (such as the code behind Outlook forms). VBS code does not support most named constants, so you must use the numeric values instead.

❑ When writing VBA code using late binding. In this type of code, variables are not declared as specific data types, and there may not be a reference set to the appropriate object model, so named constants won't be recognized.

When you need to know the numeric (or other) values behind named constants, you can open an enum in the Object Browser, select the named constant whose value you need to know, and see its numeric value in the status bar, as shown in Figure 11.10.

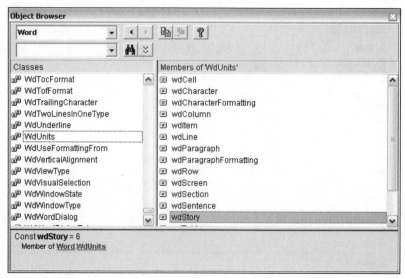

Figure 11.10

You can also search for an individual member of an enum (such as wdLine) in the Object Browser's Search box to find out its value.

The Basic Automation Commands

To initiate an Automation session, you need to create an Automation object representing the Office component, in this case, Word. This is done by setting an object variable to the top-level Application object in the Word object model, using either the CreateObject or GetObject function. CreateObject creates a new instance of Word, while GetObject uses an existing instance of Word. To avoid creating extra Word instances, I like to use the GetObject function initially, with a fallback to CreateObject in a procedure's error handler, so that an existing instance of Word will be used, if there is one, and a new instance will only be created if it is needed.

While you can use the GetObject function to create an instance of (say) a Word document, I find it more useful to create a Word application object that can then be used for all Automation work with Word, since most Automation code needs to work with properties and methods of the Application object itself, as well as properties and methods of lower-level objects such as the Document object. The syntax for setting a reference to an existing instance of Word, using the GetObject function, is:

```
Set gappWord = GetObject(, "Word.Application")
```

If this line of code fails (because Word is not running), error 429 occurs, and the following error handler then runs a line of code using the CreateObject function to create a new instance of Word, and resumes running the code after the GetObject line.

ErrorHandler:

```
If Err.Number = 429 Then
    'Word is not running; open Word with CreateObject
    Set gappWord = CreateObject("Word.Application")
    Resume Next
Else
    MsgBox "Error No: " & Err.Number & "; Description: "
    Resume ErrorHandlerExit
End If
```

Using the gappWord variable, you can access any of the objects in the Word object model, to create documents and work with them as needed. The code samples in the "Exporting Access Data to Word Documents" and "Importing Data from Word Tables into Access" sections in this chapter (and the Word Data Exchange sample database) all use the gappWord variable as the starting point for working with various components of the Word object model.

To ensure that there is an instance of Word to work with, I run a function called OpenWord from the Word Data Exchange's AutoExec macro, which uses GetObject to set the value of the global gappWord variable, if Word is running, and uses Shell to run Word in hidden mode otherwise (I use Shell instead of

CreateObject here for pragmatic reasons—it works in Office 2000, XP, and 2003, while I have had some problems with CreateObject in 2003). The OpenWord function is listed below:

```
Public Function OpenWord()

On Error GoTo ErrorHandler

    Set gappWord = GetObject(, "Word.Application")

ErrorHandlerExit:
    Exit Function

ErrorHandler:
    If Err = 429 Then
        'Word is not running; open Word with Shell
        Shell "WinWord.exe", vbHide
        Resume Next
    Else
        MsgBox "Error No: " & Err.Number & "; Description: " & Err.Description
        Resume ErrorHandlerExit
    End If

End Function
```

A Word VBA Shortcut

Word lets you record macros, so if you want to write VBA code to perform a certain action in Word, you can record a macro as follows: Turn the Word macro recorder on by double-clicking the REC button on the Word status bar, go through the steps you want to perform, and stop the recorder by clicking the Stop Recording button on the small Macro Recorder toolbar. The resulting saved macro (by default called Macro*n*) contains the VBA code to do the steps you recorded. This code is likely to be verbose and in need of trimming (for example, you rarely need to assign a value to every single argument of a method), but it is very helpful as a preliminary step to writing Automation code.

The macro listed below was recorded from the following actions: Search for the first text formatted with the Comment style, and apply the Heading 4 style to that text (the replacement text came from a previous search and replace action):

```
Sub Macro7()
'
' Macro7 Macro
' Macro recorded 9/4/2003 by Helen Feddema
'
    Selection.Find.ClearFormatting
    Selection.Find.Style = ActiveDocument.Styles("Comment")
    Selection.Find.ParagraphFormat.Borders.Shadow = False
    With Selection.Find
        .Text = ""
        .Replacement.Text = "^p^mPrivate Function"
        .Forward = True
        .Wrap = wdFindContinue
        .Format = True
```

```
            .MatchCase = False
            .MatchWholeWord = False
            .MatchWildcards = False
            .MatchSoundsLike = False
            .MatchAllWordForms = False
        End With
        Selection.Find.Execute
        Selection.Style = ActiveDocument.Styles("Heading 4")
    End Sub
```

Trimmed of unnecessary argument settings and formatted with a With . . . End With structure for clarity, the code becomes:

```
    With Selection.Find
        .ClearFormatting
        .Style = ActiveDocument.Styles("Comment")
        .Text = ""
        .Execute
    End With

    Selection.Style = ActiveDocument.Styles("Heading 4")
```

Exporting Access Data to Word Documents

Word offers several document types that are useful for creating merge documents. In addition to standard templates, you can create templates based on mail merge documents, catalog merge documents, and label documents to use in mail merge from Access. Documents made from these different types of templates can be filled with data from Access in a variety of ways, as described in the following sections.

Merge Types

There are several ways you can export data from Access tables to Word documents, each with its advantages and disadvantages, described in the following sections.

Mail Merge

A mail merge involves a link between an Access table or query (or some other data source), and a Word mail merge document. The Word document has to be set up with a link to a specific data source.

Advantage:

❑   Mail merge can handle very large numbers of records, more than you could generate as separate Word documents.

Disadvantages:

- ❏ A Word mail merge document must be prepared, with its data source set up and merge fields placed as needed.

- ❏ If you move or rename the data source, the Word mail merge document won't work properly (however, this problem can be avoided—at least for mail merges run from Access—by creating and assigning the data source in code).

- ❏ Mail merges can be very slow, and memory-intensive.

- ❏ It is difficult to customize a single merge record, because it is part of a huge merge document.

Document Properties

This method (my personal favorite) involves writing data to custom document properties (abbreviated *doc properties*) in a Word document. A separate Word document is created for each Access record.

Advantages:

- ❏ Each record has its own Word document, which makes it easy to customize one or a few of the documents.

- ❏ Since the data is stored in doc properties, the same piece of data (such as an address) can be displayed in multiple DocProperty fields on the same document. This is handy when doing a letter and envelope together.

Disadvantages:

- ❏ The Word document must be prepared with the required doc properties.

- ❏ Users may not realize that the merge data comes from doc properties and may type over information in a DocProperty field, only to see it revert to the stored data when the document is printed and the fields are refreshed. Depending on whether security or freedom to modify the documents is more important, this may be an advantage or disadvantage.

Bookmarks

Data is written to bookmarks in a Word document. A separate Word document is created for each Access record.

Advantage:

- ❏ The data written to bookmarks is just text in the document and can be overwritten (for purposes of customizing one or more documents) without any problems. As with the Doc Properties method, this can be either an advantage or a disadvantage.

Disadvantages:

- ❏ The Word document must be prepared with the required bookmarks.

- ❏ Each bookmark has its own name, so if you need to write data to multiple locations in a document (say the name and address for a letter and its envelope), you need to write the same data to two (or more) bookmarks.

TypeText Method

You can write Access data directly to a Word document, using the TypeText method of the Word Selection object. This method is generally used for simple tabular data, such as mailing labels. You can either create a single document with all the data (labels) or a separate document for each record (letters).

Advantage:

❑   The method is very simple and requires no preparation of Word documents or templates—you can even write data using TypeText to a newly created, blank Word document.

Disadvantage:

❑   It is difficult to use this method to create documents with any significant formatting because there is no way to target the data to a specific location.

Merge Examples

The sample database, Word Data Exchange.mdb, illustrates exporting Access data to Word using all of the techniques just described. It contains several tables of data that you might want to export to Word documents—a table of contacts (tblContacts), and several linked tables of information about ebooks (tblAuthors, tblEBooks, and tblEBookAuthors).

Main Menu

The main menu of this database was created using my Menu Manager add-in (see Chapter 6, *Printing Data with Reports,* for a discussion of this add-in), with some modifications. My standard main menu includes controls for selecting a Word letter and recipient, for a convenient way of sending a standard letter to a single recipient. For the Word Data Exchange database, I added a txtLetterText textbox, to allow entry of a few sentences of text for a freestyle letter (as opposed to a saved template with boiler-plate text), and a Docs Path textbox, to allow editing the Documents path (this path is picked up from tblInfo in various procedures in the database).

The main menu is bound to the information table, tblInfo, which contains miscellaneous information to be used throughout the database. I added three more fields to this table, MergeType, LetterText, and DocsPath, to use for doing mail merges of various types. The MergeType field holds an integer repre-senting the type of letter to be created (1 for Boilerplate or 2 for Freestyle). A Boilerplate letter has stan-dard text in the template; a Freestyle letter picks up the text entered into the txtLetterText control on the menu (this control is bound to the LetterText field in tblInfo). The DocsPath field stores the user's Documents path, for use in saving documents.

Several standard Word templates are included in the sample files; they are listed in tlkpTemplates. The doc properties versions of the Boilerplate and Freestyle contact letters, and a One-up Label, are used for the main menu. To test creating a boilerplate letter, select Boilerplate Contact Letter from the Word Letter combobox, and a recipient from the Recipient combobox, as shown in Figure 11.11, and click the large Word button.

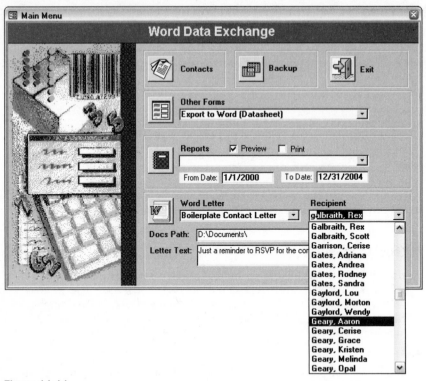

Figure 11.11

The cmdLetters button's Click event procedure follows. The code starts by declaring variables to use in creating the letter. Although you can write data from Access fields directly to Word doc properties, I prefer to assign most values to variables, using the Nz function to prevent Nulls from being assigned to the variables (and thus to the doc properties), since Nulls can cause problems.

> The prps variable (representing the Word custom doc properties) must be declared as *Object*, because if it is declared as Word.CustomProperties—the "correct" data type—it doesn't work. You get no error message, but no data is written to the doc properties.

Two If . . . Then structures check that a letter and a recipient have been selected, and exit the procedure if one or the other is missing. Next, a gappWord variable is set, to allow working with Word, using the GetObject function with a fallback to CreateObject in the error handler, as described in the "Basic Automation Commands" section earlier in this chapter.

Next, variables are assigned the values of the Access Merge subfolder under the user's Documents path (which is picked up from tblInfo, via the GetDocsDir function) and the User Templates folder, picked up from the Word Options dialog via the TemplateDir function. The code looks for the selected template in the Templates\Access Merge folder, and if it is not found, puts up an informative message and exits the procedure. If there is no Access Merge subfolder under the Documents folder or the Templates folder, this subfolder is created in the GetDocsDir or TemplateDir function, using the FileSystemObject's CreateFolder method.

The FileSystemObject is part of the Microsoft Scripting Runtime library, so databases using this object need to have a reference set to this library.

Finally, a new document is created based on the selected template, and a section of code assigns values to name and address variables from fields in qryContacts for the selected recipient, picked up from columns of cboRecipients.

When picking up data from a column of a combobox, note that column numbering is zero-based, so to reference the third column, you need to use the syntax **cboRecipients.Column(2)**.

Because this procedure is used to create both boilerplate and freestyle letters, an If . . . Then structure determines whether text from txtLetterText should be written to the LetterText doc property. Next, a section of code creates a save name for the document, based on text in the template's Subject property, the recipient's name, and the current date, and checks whether a document with this name exists in the Documents\Access Merge folder. If it does, then an incrementing number is added to the name, so you won't overwrite an existing document. If you don't need to preserve multiple copies of letters, you can comment out or delete the code that creates the incrementing number for the save name, and just overwrite earlier versions of letters, if they exist.

The final section of code updates fields for the new document, saves it with the save name just created, and makes it visible.

```
Private Sub cmdLetters_Click()

On Error GoTo ErrorHandler

    Dim strLetter As String
    Dim strRecipient As String
    Dim strTestFile As String
    Dim cbo As Access.ComboBox
    Dim docs As Word.Documents
    Dim strLongDate As String
    Dim strShortDate As String
    Dim strDocType As String
    Dim strName As String
    Dim strSaveName As String
    Dim i As Integer
    Dim intSaveNameFail As Integer
    Dim strSaveNamePath As String
    Dim strJobTitle As String
    Dim strNameAndJob As String

    'Must declare as Object because it doesn't work if declared as
    'CustomProperties
    Dim prps As Object
    'Dim prps As Word.CustomProperties
    Dim strDocsPath As String
    Dim strTemplatePath As String

    'Check that a letter has been selected.
```

```
   strLetter = Nz(Me![cboLetters])
   Set cbo = Me![cboLetters]
   If strLetter = "" Then
      cbo.SetFocus
      cbo.Dropdown
      GoTo ErrorHandlerExit
   End If

   'Check that a recipient has been selected.
   strRecipient = Nz(Me![cboRecipients])
   Set cbo = Me![cboRecipients]
   If strRecipient = "" Then
      cbo.SetFocus
      cbo.Dropdown
      GoTo ErrorHandlerExit
   End If

   Set gappWord = GetObject(, "Word.Application")
   If CheckDocsDir = False Then
      GoTo ErrorHandlerExit
   End If
   strDocsPath = GetDocsDir
   strTemplatePath = TemplateDir
   strLetter = strTemplatePath & strLetter
   strLongDate = Format(Date, "mmmm d, yyyy")
   strShortDate = Format(Date, "m-d-yyyy")

   'Check for existence of template in template folder,
   'and exit if not found
   strTestFile = Nz(Dir(strLetter))
   Debug.Print "Test file: " & strTestFile
   If strTestFile = "" Then
      MsgBox strLetter & " template not found; can't create letter"
      GoTo ErrorHandlerExit
   End If

   Set docs = gappWord.Documents
   docs.Add strLetter
   Set cbo = Me![cboRecipients]

On Error Resume Next
   'Assign values to many doc properties, so the same code can
   'be used with different templates.
   strName = Nz(cbo.Column(7))
   strJobTitle = Nz(cbo.Column(10))
   If strJobTitle <> "" Then
      strNameAndJob = strName & vbCrLf & strJobTitle
   Else
      strNameAndJob = strName
   End If

   Set prps = gappWord.ActiveDocument.CustomDocumentProperties
   prps.Item("TodayDate").Value = strLongDate
   prps.Item("Name").Value = strNameAndJob
```

```
      prps.Item("Address").Value = Nz(cbo.Column(8))
      prps.Item("Street").Value = Nz(cbo.Column(2))
      prps.Item("City").Value = Nz(cbo.Column(3))
      prps.Item("State").Value = Nz(cbo.Column(4))
      prps.Item("Zip").Value = Nz(cbo.Column(5))
      prps.Item("Country").Value = Nz(cbo.Column(6))
      prps.Item("CompanyName").Value = Nz(cbo.Column(9))
      Debug.Print "Salutation: " & Nz(cbo.Column(11))
      prps.Item("Salutation").Value = Nz(cbo.Column(11))
      If InStr(strLetter, "Freestyle") > 0 Then
          prps.Item("LetterText").Value = Nz(Me![txtLetterText])
      End If

On Error GoTo ErrorHandlerExit
      'Check for existence of previously saved letter in documents folder,
      'and append an incremented number to save name if found
      strDocType = _
          gappWord.ActiveDocument.BuiltInDocumentProperties(wdPropertySubject)
      strSaveName = strDocType & " to " & strName
      strSaveName = strSaveName & " on " & strShortDate & ".doc"
      i = 2
      intSaveNameFail = True
      Do While intSaveNameFail
          strSaveNamePath = strDocsPath & strSaveName
          Debug.Print "Proposed save name and path: " _
              & vbCrLf & strSaveNamePath
          strTestFile = Nz(Dir(strSaveNamePath))
          Debug.Print "Test file: " & strTestFile
          If strTestFile = strSaveName Then
              Debug.Print "Save name already used: " & strSaveName

              'Create new save name with incremented number
              intSaveNameFail = True
              strSaveName = strDocType & " " & CStr(i) & " to " & _
                  strName
              strSaveName = strSaveName & " on " & strShortDate & ".doc"
              strSaveNamePath = strDocsPath & strSaveName
              Debug.Print "New save name and path: " _
                  & vbCrLf & strSaveNamePath
              i = i + 1
          Else
              Debug.Print "Save name not used: " & strSaveName
              intSaveNameFail = False
          End If
      Loop

      'Update fields in Word document and save it
      With gappWord
          .Selection.WholeStory
          .Selection.Fields.Update
          .Selection.HomeKey Unit:=wdStory
          .ActiveDocument.SaveAs strSaveName
          .Visible = True
          .ActiveWindow.WindowState = wdWindowStateNormal
```

```
        .Activate
    End With

ErrorHandlerExit:
    Exit Sub

ErrorHandler:
    If Err = 429 Then
        'Word is not running; open Word with CreateObject.
        Set gappWord = CreateObject("Word.Application")
        Resume Next
    Else
        MsgBox "Error No: " & Err.Number & "; Description: " & Err.Description
        Resume ErrorHandlerExit
    End If

End Sub
```

A letter created by this code is shown in Figure 11.12.

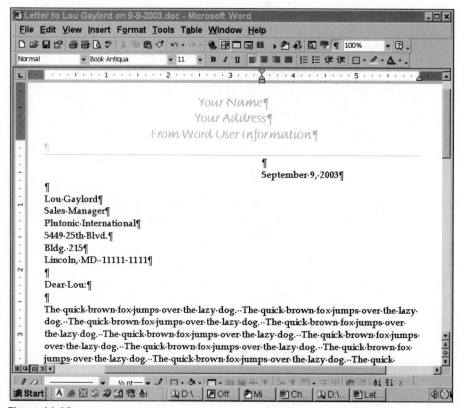

Figure 11.12

If you choose the Freestyle letter, any text you type into the txtLetterText textbox will be printed on the letter; this option is handy for quick notes. The third option, One-up Label, creates a single label for the selected recipient. This is a type of label that prints on a form that is the same size as a U.S. #10 envelope; it is handy when you need to print a single label, and don't want to waste a whole sheet of labels.

Other Forms

There are several other forms in the database that do different types of mail merges, going beyond the simple letter to one recipient selection available on the main menu.

MultiSelect Listbox Form

Often you will need to do a mail merge to multiple recipients—but not necessarily all the records in a table or query. Access offers a special type of control that is very handy for this purpose—the *MultiSelect listbox*. To create a MultiSelect listbox, place a listbox on a form, open its properties sheet, select the Other tab, and set its Multiselect property to either Simple or Extended. The *Simple* setting only supports selection with the mouse or spacebar; the *Extended* selection (generally the best selection) lets you select multiple items with Ctrl-click and Shift-click, the same as making a selection in an Explorer pane.

frmExportToWordListBox has two comboboxes, for selecting a merge type (with more choices than on the main menu) and a Word template, and a MultiSelect listbox that is dynamically assigned a row source depending on your selection in the cboSelectTemplate combobox. The code for cboSelectMergeType's AfterUpdate event follows (stripped of its standard error handler); it simply clears the row source of the other combobox and the listbox and requeries the other combobox.

```
Private Sub cboSelectMergeType_AfterUpdate()

    Me![cboSelectTemplate].Value = Null
    Me![cboSelectTemplate].Requery
    Me![lstSelectMultiple].RowSource = ""

End Sub
```

The cboSelectTemplate combobox's AfterUpdate event procedure follows (also stripped of its error handler). This code picks up the template name and data source from cboSelectTemplate, enables (or disables) txtLetterText, depending on whether the template contains the word "Freestyle," assigns the appropriate row source to the listbox, and sets its column properties to 3 equal-sized columns for a Catalog merge and 12 columns of different sizes for other merge documents.

```
Private Sub cboSelectTemplate_AfterUpdate()

    Dim strDataSource As String
    Dim strTemplate As String

    Set lst = Me![lstSelectMultiple]
    strTemplate = Me![cboSelectTemplate].Column(1)
    strDataSource = Me![cboSelectTemplate].Column(2)
    lst.RowSource = strDataSource
    If InStr(strTemplate, "Freestyle") > 0 Then
        Me![txtLetterText].Enabled = True
    Else
        Me![txtLetterText].Enabled = False
```

```
        End If

    If InStr(strTemplate, "Catalog") > 0 Then
        lst.ColumnWidths = ""
        lst.ColumnCount = 3
    Else
        lst.ColumnWidths = -
            "0 in;1.25 in;1.25 in;1 in;.6 in;.6 in;0 in;0 in;0 in;0 in;0 in;0 in"
        lst.ColumnCount = 12
    End If

End Sub
```

Figure 11.13 shows the listbox form, with the Bookmarks merge type, Freestyle contact letter, and all recipients selected (using the Select All button). Clicking the Create Document(s) button generates a set of separate documents to all 500 recipients (don't do this unless you have lots of memory and disk space!).

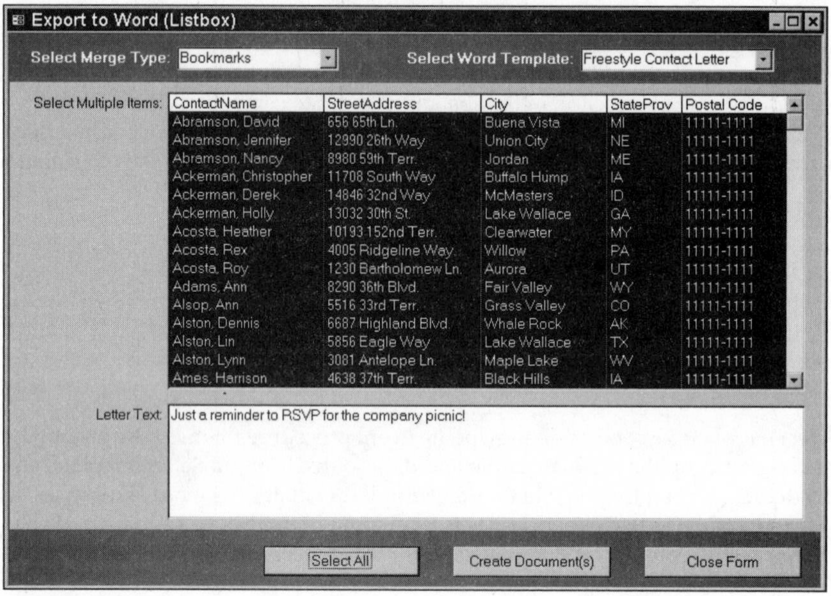

Figure 11.13

There is a textbox on the main menu that displays the Documents path (default: C:\My Documents or C:\Documents and Settings*LogonName*\My Documents, depending on your operating system); this information is stored in tblInfo. Before running merge code, check that the correct path is displayed, and edit it if needed. (See Figure 11.11 earlier for a view of the Docs Path textbox.)

The cmdCreateDocuments_Click event procedure follows, with interspersed explanatory text.

```
Private Sub cmdCreateDocuments_Click()

On Error GoTo ErrorHandler

    Dim blnSomeSkipped As Boolean
    Dim cbo As Access.ComboBox
    Dim dbs As DAO.Database
    Dim i As String
    Dim intMergeType As Integer
    Dim intSaveNameFail As String
    Dim lngContactID As Long
    Dim prps As Object
    Dim rst As DAO.Recordset
    Dim strAddress As String
    Dim strCompanyName As String
    Dim strCountry As String
    Dim strDocName As String
    Dim strDocsPath As String
    Dim strDocType As String
    Dim strEnvelopeAddress As String
    Dim strEnvelopeName As String
    Dim strFile As String
    Dim strJobTitle As String
    Dim strLetterText As String
    Dim strLongDate As String
    Dim strName As String
    Dim strNameAndJob As String
    Dim strPrompt As String
    Dim strSalutation As String
    Dim strSaveName As String
    Dim strSaveNamePath As String
    Dim strShortDate As String
    Dim strSQL As String
    Dim strTable As String
    Dim strTemplatePath As String
    Dim strTest As String
    Dim strTestFile As String
    Dim strTextFile As String
    Dim strTitle As String
    Dim strWordTemplate As String
    Dim varItem As Variant
```

This starts like the single letter, checking that a letter and at least one recipient have been selected.

```
    Set cbo = Me![cboSelectTemplate]
    Set lst = Me![lstSelectMultiple]
    strWordTemplate = Nz(cbo.Column(1))
    Debug.Print "Selected template: " & strWordTemplate
```

```
    If strWordTemplate = "" Then
        MsgBox "Please select a document"
        cbo.SetFocus
        cbo.Dropdown
        GoTo ErrorHandlerExit
    Else
        intMergeType = cbo.Column(3)
        Debug.Print "Merge type: " & intMergeType
    End If

    'Check that at least one contact has been selected.
    If lst.ItemsSelected.Count = 0 Then
        MsgBox "Please select at least one contact"
        lst.SetFocus
        GoTo ErrorHandlerExit
    Else
        intColumns = lst.ColumnCount
        intRows = lst.ItemsSelected.Count
    End If
```

Set up Word application variable and other variables to reference the Access Merge subfolder under the Documents and Templates folders and the current date in different formats.

```
    'Set Word application variable; if Word is not running,
    'the error handler defaults to CreateObject
    Set gappWord = GetObject(, "Word.Application")

    'Set date and folder reference variables.
    strLongDate = Format(Date, "mmmm d, yyyy")
    strShortDate = Format(Date, "m-d-yyyy")
    If CheckDocsDir = False Then
        GoTo ErrorHandlerExit
    End If
    strDocsPath = GetDocsDir
    strTemplatePath = TemplateDir
    strWordTemplate = strTemplatePath & strWordTemplate
    strLetterText = Nz(Me![LetterText])
```

Check for the existence of template in template folder, and exit if not found.

```
    strTestFile = Nz(Dir(strWordTemplate))
    Debug.Print "Test file: " & strTestFile
    If strTestFile = "" Then
        MsgBox strWordTemplate & " template not found; can't create document"
        GoTo ErrorHandlerExit
    End If
```

Open a text file that will be filled with information about any records skipped because they were missing required name or address data.

```
    strFile = strDocsPath & "Skipped Records.txt"
    Open strFile For Output As #1
    Print #1, "These records were skipped when creating documents."
    Print #1,
```

Set up a Select Case statement that processes each merge type separately, based on the merge type selected in cboMergeType.

```
Select Case intMergeType

    Case 1
        'Bookmarks
        blnSomeSkipped = False
```

Work with the ItemsSelected collection of the listbox, which represents the items that the user has selected. The value for each field is picked up from the appropriate column of a row in the listbox, iterating through all the selected rows.

```
For Each varItem In lst.ItemsSelected
    'Get Contact ID for reference
    lngContactID = Nz(lst.Column(0, varItem))
    Debug.Print "Contact ID: " & lngContactID
```

Check for required information in various fields and skip to the next record (and write the Contact ID to the text file) in case anything is missing.

```
        'Check for required address information.
        strTest = Nz(lst.Column(2, varItem))
        Debug.Print "Street address: " & strTest
        If strTest = "" Then
            blnSomeSkipped = True
            Print #1,
            Print #1, "No street address for Contact " & lngContactID
            GoTo NextItem1
        End If

        strTest = Nz(lst.Column(3, varItem))
        Debug.Print "City: " & strTest
        If strTest = "" Then
            blnSomeSkipped = True
            Print #1,
            Print #1, "No city for Contact " & lngContactID
            GoTo NextItem1
        End If

        strTest = Nz(lst.Column(5, varItem))
        Debug.Print "Postal code: " & strTest
        If strTest = "" Then
            blnSomeSkipped = True
            Print #1,
            Print #1, "No postal code for Contact " & lngContactID
            GoTo NextItem1
        End If

        strName = Nz(lst.Column(7, varItem))
        strJobTitle = Nz(lst.Column(10, varItem))
        If strJobTitle <> "" Then
            strNameAndJob = strName & vbCrLf & strJobTitle
```

```
            Else
                strNameAndJob = strName
            End If
            strAddress = Nz(lst.Column(8, varItem))
            Debug.Print "Address: " & strAddress
            strCountry = Nz(lst.Column(6, varItem))
            If strCountry <> "USA" Then
                strAddress = strAddress & vbCrLf & strCountry
            End If
            strCompanyName = Nz(lst.Column(9, varItem))
            strSalutation = Nz(lst.Column(11, varItem))

            'Open a new document based on the selected template.
            gappWord.Documents.Add strWordTemplate
```

The following writes information to bookmarks in the Word document. All bookmarks that exist in any of the templates are included, with an On Error Resume Next statement to prevent errors from missing bookmarks, and If . . . Then statements for special cases (the bookmark exists, but should only be filled for certain documents).

```
On Error Resume Next
            With gappWord.Selection
                .GoTo What:=wdGoToBookmark, Name:="Name"
                .TypeText Text:=strName
                .GoTo What:=wdGoToBookmark, Name:="CompanyName"
                If Left(cbo.Value, 12) <> "One-up Label" Then
                    .TypeText Text:=strCompanyName
                End If
                .GoTo What:=wdGoToBookmark, Name:="Address"
                .TypeText Text:=strAddress
                .GoTo What:=wdGoToBookmark, Name:="Salutation"
                If Left(cbo.Value, 12) <> "One-up Label" Then
                    .TypeText Text:=strSalutation
                End If
                .GoTo What:=wdGoToBookmark, Name:="TodayDate"
                If Left(cbo.Value, 12) <> "One-up Label" Then
                    .TypeText Text:=strLongDate
                End If
                .GoTo What:=wdGoToBookmark, Name:="EnvelopeName"
                If Left(cbo.Value, 12) <> "One-up Label" Then
                    .TypeText Text:=strName
                End If
                .GoTo What:=wdGoToBookmark, Name:="EnvelopeCompany"
                If Left(cbo.Value, 12) <> "One-up Label" Then
                    .TypeText Text:=strCompanyName
                End If
                .GoTo What:=wdGoToBookmark, Name:="EnvelopeAddress"
                If Left(cbo.Value, 12) <> "One-up Label" Then
                    .TypeText Text:=strAddress
                End If
                .GoTo What:=wdGoToBookmark, Name:="LetterText"
                If Left(cbo.Column(1), 9) = "Freestyle" Then
                    .TypeText Text:=strLetterText
                End If
            End With
```

A save name is created (the same as for the single document).

```
On Error GoTo ErrorHandler
        'Check for existence of previously saved letter in documents folder,
        'and append an incremented number to save name if found
        strDocType = _
            gappWord.ActiveDocument.BuiltInDocumentProperties(wdPropertySubject)
        strSaveName = strDocType & " to " & strName
        strSaveName = strSaveName & " on " & strShortDate & ".doc"
        i = 2
        intSaveNameFail = True
        Do While intSaveNameFail
            strSaveNamePath = strDocsPath & strSaveName
            Debug.Print "Proposed save name and path: " _
                & vbCrLf & strSaveNamePath
            strTestFile = Nz(Dir(strSaveNamePath))
            Debug.Print "Test file: " & strTestFile
            If strTestFile = strSaveName Then
                Debug.Print "Save name already used: " & strSaveName

                'Create new save name with incremented number
                intSaveNameFail = True
                strSaveName = strDocType & " " & CStr(i) & " to " & strName
                strSaveName = strSaveName & " on " & strShortDate & ".doc"
                strSaveNamePath = strDocsPath & strSaveName
                Debug.Print "New save name and path: " _
                    & vbCrLf & strSaveNamePath
                i = i + 1
            Else
                Debug.Print "Save name not used: " & strSaveName
                intSaveNameFail = False
            End If
        Loop
```

Word fields are updated and the document is saved.

```
        'Update fields in Word document and save it
        With gappWord
            .Selection.WholeStory
            .Selection.Fields.Update
            .Selection.HomeKey Unit:=wdStory
            .ActiveDocument.SaveAs strSaveNamePath
            .Visible = True
            .ActiveWindow.WindowState = wdWindowStateNormal
            .Activate
        End With

NextItem1:
```

Proceed to the next item in the ItemsSelected collection.

```
        Next varItem
```

Generate a "Merge done" message, with info about text file if some records have been skipped.

```
            strTitle = "Merge done"
            If blnSomeSkipped = True Then
               strPrompt = "All documents created; some records skipped because " _
                  & "of missing information." & vbCrLf & "See " & strDocsPath _
                  & "Skipped Records.txt for details."
            Else
               strPrompt = "All documents created!"
            End If

            MsgBox strPrompt, vbOKOnly + vbInformation, strTitle

         Case 2
```

The first portion of code is the same as for the Bookmarks case.

```
            'Doc Properties
            blnSomeSkipped = False

            For Each varItem In lst.ItemsSelected
               'Get Contact ID for reference
               lngContactID = Nz(lst.Column(0, varItem))
               Debug.Print "Contact ID: " & lngContactID

               'Check for required address information
               strTest = Nz(lst.Column(2, varItem))
               Debug.Print "Street address: " & strTest
               If strTest = "" Then
                  blnSomeSkipped = True
                  Print #1,
                  Print #1, "No street address for Contact " & lngContactID
                  GoTo NextItem2
               End If

               strTest = Nz(lst.Column(3, varItem))
               Debug.Print "City: " & strTest
               If strTest = "" Then
                  blnSomeSkipped = True
                  Print #1,
                  Print #1, "No city for Contact " & lngContactID
                  GoTo NextItem2
               End If

               strTest = Nz(lst.Column(5, varItem))
               Debug.Print "Postal code: " & strTest
               If strTest = "" Then
                  blnSomeSkipped = True
                  Print #1,
                  Print #1, "No postal code for Contact " & lngContactID
                  GoTo NextItem2
               End If

               strName = Nz(lst.Column(7, varItem))
```

```
        strJobTitle = Nz(lst.Column(10, varItem))
        If strJobTitle <> "" Then
            strNameAndJob = strName & vbCrLf & strJobTitle
        Else
            strNameAndJob = strName
        End If
        strAddress = Nz(lst.Column(8, varItem))
        Debug.Print "Address: " & strAddress
        strCountry = Nz(lst.Column(6, varItem))
        If strCountry <> "USA" Then
            strAddress = strAddress & vbCrLf & strCountry
        End If
        strCompanyName = Nz(lst.Column(9, varItem))
        strSalutation = Nz(lst.Column(11, varItem))

        'Open a new letter based on the selected template.
        gappWord.Documents.Add strWordTemplate
```

Instead of using bookmarks, the information is written to Word doc properties, with an On Error Resume Next statement because not all doc properties exist in all the templates.

```
        'Write information to Word custom document properties
        Set prps = gappWord.ActiveDocument.CustomDocumentProperties
        prps.Item("Name").Value = strName
On Error Resume Next
        With prps
            .Item("Salutation").Value = strSalutation
            .Item("CompanyName").Value = strCompanyName
            .Item("Address").Value = strAddress
            .Item("TodayDate").Value = strLongDate
            .Item("LetterText").Value = strLetterText
        End With
```

The document is saved and updated similarly to the Bookmarks case.

```
On Error GoTo ErrorHandler
        'Check for existence of previously saved document in documents folder,
        'and append an incremented number to save name if found
        strDocType = _
            gappWord.ActiveDocument.BuiltInDocumentProperties(wdPropertySubject)
        strSaveName = strDocType & " to " & strName
        strSaveName = strSaveName & " on " & strShortDate & ".doc"
        i = 2
        intSaveNameFail = True
        Do While intSaveNameFail
            strSaveNamePath = strDocsPath & strSaveName
            Debug.Print "Proposed save name and path: " _
                & vbCrLf & strSaveNamePath
            strTestFile = Nz(Dir(strSaveNamePath))
            Debug.Print "Test file: " & strTestFile
            If strTestFile = strSaveName Then
                Debug.Print "Save name already used: " & strSaveName

                'Create new save name with incremented number
```

```
                    intSaveNameFail = True
                    strSaveName = strDocType & " " & CStr(i) & " to " & strName
                    strSaveName = strSaveName & " on " & strShortDate & ".doc"
                    strSaveNamePath = strDocsPath & strSaveName
                    Debug.Print "New save name and path: " _
                        & vbCrLf & strSaveNamePath
                    i = i + 1
                Else
                    Debug.Print "Save name not used: " & strSaveName
                    intSaveNameFail = False
                End If
            Loop

            'Update fields in Word document and save it
            With gappWord
                .Selection.WholeStory
                .Selection.Fields.Update
                .Selection.HomeKey Unit:=wdStory
                .ActiveDocument.SaveAs strSaveNamePath
                .Visible = True
                .ActiveWindow.WindowState = wdWindowStateNormal
                .Activate
            End With
NextItem2:
        Next varItem

        strTitle = "Merge done"
        If blnSomeSkipped = True Then
            strPrompt = "All documents created; some records skipped because " _
                & "of missing information." & vbCrLf & "See " & strDocsPath _
                & "Skipped Records.txt for details."
        Else
            strPrompt = "All documents created!"
        End If

        MsgBox strPrompt, vbOKOnly + vbInformation, strTitle

    Case 3
        'Mail Merge
        blnSomeSkipped = False
```

A table that holds the specific records to merge is cleared of old data, and a recordset based on it is opened.

```
            'Clear tblMergeList and set up recordset based on it
            strTable = "tblMailMergeList"
            strSQL = "DELETE tblMailMergeList.* FROM tblMailMergeList;"
            DoCmd.SetWarnings False
            DoCmd.RunSQL strSQL
            Set dbs = CurrentDb
            Debug.Print "Opening recordset based on " & strTable
            Set rst = dbs.OpenRecordset(strTable, dbOpenTable)
```

Records are checked for missing information, as in the Bookmarks case.

```
For Each varItem In lst.ItemsSelected
    'Get Contact ID for reference
    lngContactID = Nz(lst.Column(0, varItem))
    Debug.Print "Contact ID: " & lngContactID

    'Check for required address information.
    strTest = Nz(lst.Column(2, varItem))
    Debug.Print "Street address: " & strTest
    If strTest = "" Then
        blnSomeSkipped = True
        Print #1,
        Print #1, "No street address for Contact " & lngContactID
        GoTo NextItem3
    End If

    strTest = Nz(lst.Column(3, varItem))
    Debug.Print "City: " & strTest
    If strTest = "" Then
        blnSomeSkipped = True
        Print #1,
        Print #1, "No city for Contact " & lngContactID
        GoTo NextItem3
    End If

    strTest = Nz(lst.Column(5, varItem))
    Debug.Print "Postal code: " & strTest
    If strTest = "" Then
        blnSomeSkipped = True
        Print #1,
        Print #1, "No postal code for Contact " & lngContactID
        GoTo NextItem3
    End If

    strName = Nz(lst.Column(7, varItem))
    strJobTitle = Nz(lst.Column(10, varItem))
    strAddress = Nz(lst.Column(8, varItem))
    Debug.Print "Address: " & strAddress
    strCountry = Nz(lst.Column(6, varItem))
    If strCountry <> "USA" Then
        strAddress = strAddress & vbCrLf & strCountry
    End If
    strCompanyName = Nz(lst.Column(9, varItem))
    strSalutation = Nz(lst.Column(11, varItem))
```

The data from the current record is written to a new record in the tblMailMergeList table.

```
'Write data from variables to a new record in table
With rst
    .AddNew
    !Name = strName
    !JobTitle = strJobTitle
    !CompanyName = strCompanyName
```

```
            !Address = strAddress
            !Salutation = strSalutation
            !TodayDate = strLongDate
            .Update
         End With

   NextItem3:
```

Proceed to the next selected item.

```
         Next varItem
         rst.Close
```

The data in the filled tblMailMergeList table is exported to a text file. This file will be the data source of the Word mail merge document.

```
         'Export merge list to a text file
         If CheckDocsDir = False Then
            GoTo ErrorHandlerExit
         End If
         strDocsPath = GetDocsDir
         Debug.Print "Docs path: " & strDocsPath
         strTextFile = strDocsPath & "Mail Merge Data.txt"
         Debug.Print "Text file for merge: " & strTextFile
         DoCmd.TransferText transfertype:=acExportDelim, TableName:=strTable, _
            FileName:=strTextFile, HasFieldNames:=True
```

A new document is created from the selected mail merge template.

```
         'Open a new merge document based on the selected template.
         gappWord.Documents.Add strWordTemplate
         strDocName = gappWord.ActiveDocument
         Debug.Print "Initial doc name: " & strDocName
```

A save name is created, based on the name in the template's Subject property plus the date.

```
         'Check for existence of previously saved letter in documents folder,
         'and append an incremented number to save name if found
         strDocType = _
            gappWord.ActiveDocument.BuiltInDocumentProperties(wdPropertySubject)
         strSaveName = strDocType & " on " & strShortDate & ".doc"
         i = 2
         intSaveNameFail = True
         Do While intSaveNameFail
            strSaveNamePath = strDocsPath & strSaveName
            Debug.Print "Proposed save name and path: " _
               & vbCrLf & strSaveNamePath
            strTestFile = Nz(Dir(strSaveNamePath))
            'Debug.Print "Test file: " & strTestFile
            If strTestFile = strSaveName Then
               'Debug.Print "Save name already used: " & strSaveName

               'Create new save name with incremented number
```

```
                intSaveNameFail = True
                strSaveName = strDocType & " " & CStr(i) & _
                    " on " & strShortDate & ".doc"
                strSaveNamePath = strDocsPath & strSaveName
                'Debug.Print "New save name and path: " _
                    & vbCrLf & strSaveNamePath
                i = i + 1
            Else
                'Debug.Print "Save name not used: " & strSaveName
                intSaveNameFail = False
            End If
    Loop
```

The previously created text file is assigned as the merge document's data source, the merge is performed, and the resulting document is saved and opened.

```
With gappWord
    .ActiveDocument.MailMerge.OpenDataSource Name:=strTextFile, _
        Format:=wdOpenFormatText
    .ActiveDocument.MailMerge.Destination = wdSendToNewDocument
    .ActiveDocument.MailMerge.Execute
    .ActiveDocument.SaveAs strSaveNamePath
    .Documents(strDocName).Close SaveChanges:=wdDoNotSaveChanges
    .Visible = True
    .ActiveWindow.WindowState = wdWindowStateNormal
    .Activate
End With
```

A "Merge done" message pops up, with information on the text file if any records have been skipped.

```
    strTitle = "Merge done"
    If blnSomeSkipped = True Then
        strPrompt = "Merge document created; some records skipped because " _
            & "of missing information." & vbCrLf & "See " & strDocsPath _
            & "Skipped Records.txt for details."
    Else
        strPrompt = "Merge document created!"
    End If

    MsgBox strPrompt, vbOKOnly + vbInformation, strTitle

Case 4
    'Catalog Merge
    blnSomeSkipped = False
```

The Catalog merge is very similar to mail merge; the only difference is in the appearance of the final document. A catalog merge document is a tabular document, with one record per row, rather than one record per page as in a mail merge document.

```
    'Clear tblCatalogMergeList and set up recordset based on it
    strTable = "tblCatalogMergeList"
    strSQL = "DELETE tblCatalogMergeList.* FROM tblCatalogMergeList;"
    DoCmd.SetWarnings False
```

```
            DoCmd.RunSQL strSQL
            Set dbs = CurrentDb
            Debug.Print "Opening recordset based on " & strTable
            Set rst = dbs.OpenRecordset(strTable, dbOpenTable)

            For Each varItem In lst.ItemsSelected
                'Write data from listbox to a new record in table
                With rst
                    .AddNew
                    ![AuthorName] = Nz(lst.Column(0, varItem))
                    ![BookTitle] = Nz(lst.Column(1, varItem))
                    ![Category] = Nz(lst.Column(2, varItem))
                    .Update
                End With

NextItem4:
            Next varItem
            rst.Close

            'Export merge list to a text file
            'strDBPath = Application.CurrentProject.Path & "\"
            If CheckDocsDir = False Then
                GoTo ErrorHandlerExit
            End If
            strDocsPath = GetDocsDir
            Debug.Print "Docs path: " & strDocsPath
            strTextFile = strDocsPath & "Catalog Merge Data.txt"
            Debug.Print "Text file for merge: " & strTextFile
            DoCmd.TransferText transfertype:=acExportDelim, TableName:=strTable, _
                FileName:=strTextFile, HasFieldNames:=True

            'Open a new merge document based on the selected template.
            gappWord.Documents.Add strWordTemplate
            strDocName = gappWord.ActiveDocument
            Debug.Print "Initial doc name: " & strDocName

            'Check for existence of previously saved letter in documents folder,
            'and append an incremented number to save name if found
            strDocType = _
                gappWord.ActiveDocument.BuiltInDocumentProperties(wdPropertySubject)
            strSaveName = strDocType & " on " & strShortDate & ".doc"
            i = 2
            intSaveNameFail = True
            Do While intSaveNameFail
                strSaveNamePath = strDocsPath & strSaveName
                Debug.Print "Proposed save name and path: " _
                    & vbCrLf & strSaveNamePath
                strTestFile = Nz(Dir(strSaveNamePath))
                'Debug.Print "Test file: " & strTestFile
                If strTestFile = strSaveName Then
                    'Debug.Print "Save name already used: " & strSaveName

                    'Create new save name with incremented number
                    intSaveNameFail = True
```

```
            strSaveName = strDocType & " " & CStr(i) & _
               " on " & strShortDate & ".doc"
            strSaveNamePath = strDocsPath & strSaveName
            'Debug.Print "New save name and path: " _
               & vbCrLf & strSaveNamePath
            i = i + 1
         Else
            'Debug.Print "Save name not used: " & strSaveName
            intSaveNameFail = False
         End If
      Loop

      'Set the merge data source to the text file just created,
      'and do the merge.
      With gappWord
         .ActiveDocument.MailMerge.OpenDataSource Name:=strTextFile, _
            Format:=wdOpenFormatText
         .ActiveDocument.MailMerge.Destination = wdSendToNewDocument
         .ActiveDocument.MailMerge.Execute
         .ActiveDocument.SaveAs strSaveNamePath
         .Documents(strDocName).Close SaveChanges:=wdDoNotSaveChanges
         .Visible = True
         .ActiveWindow.WindowState = wdWindowStateNormal
         .Activate
      End With

      strTitle = "Merge done"
      If blnSomeSkipped = True Then
         strPrompt = "Merge document created; some records skipped because " _
            & "of missing information." & vbCrLf & "See " & strDocsPath _
            & "Skipped Records.txt for details."
      Else
         strPrompt = "Merge document created!"
      End If

      MsgBox strPrompt, vbOKOnly + vbInformation, strTitle

   Case 5
      'TypeText method
      blnSomeSkipped = False
```

The TypeText merge is similar to the Bookmarks and Doc Properties merges in the initial sections of code.

```
      'Open a new document based on the selected template.
      gappWord.Documents.Add strWordTemplate

      For Each varItem In lst.ItemsSelected
         'Write info from contact item to variables
         'Get Contact ID for reference
         lngContactID = Nz(lst.Column(0, varItem))
         Debug.Print "Contact ID: " & lngContactID

         'Check for required address information
         strTest = Nz(lst.Column(2, varItem))
```

```
Debug.Print "Street address: " & strTest
If strTest = "" Then
   blnSomeSkipped = True
   Print #1,
   Print #1, "No street address for Contact " & lngContactID
   GoTo NextItem5
End If

strTest = Nz(lst.Column(3, varItem))
Debug.Print "City: " & strTest
If strTest = "" Then
   blnSomeSkipped = True
   Print #1,
   Print #1, "No city for Contact " & lngContactID
   GoTo NextItem5
End If

strTest = Nz(lst.Column(5, varItem))
Debug.Print "Postal code: " & strTest
If strTest = "" Then
   blnSomeSkipped = True
   Print #1,
   Print #1, "No postal code for Contact " & lngContactID
   GoTo NextItem5
End If

strName = Nz(lst.Column(7, varItem))
strJobTitle = Nz(lst.Column(10, varItem))
If strJobTitle <> "" Then
   strName = strName & vbCrLf & strJobTitle
End If

strAddress = Nz(lst.Column(8, varItem))
Debug.Print "Address: " & strAddress
strCountry = Nz(lst.Column(6, varItem))
If strCountry <> "USA" Then
   strAddress = strAddress & vbCrLf & strCountry
End If
strCompanyName = Nz(lst.Column(9, varItem))
strSalutation = Nz(lst.Column(11, varItem))
```

Insert data directly into a cell in the table of the selected labels document.

```
'Insert data into labels
With gappWord
   .Selection.TypeText Text:=strName
   .Selection.TypeParagraph
   .Selection.TypeText Text:=strCompanyName
   .Selection.TypeParagraph
   .Selection.TypeText Text:=strAddress
   .Selection.TypeParagraph
   .Selection.MoveRight Unit:=wdCell
```

```
            End With

NextItem5:
        Next varItem

        'Check for existence of previously saved document in documents folder,
        'and append an incremented number to save name if found
        strDocType = _
            gappWord.ActiveDocument.BuiltInDocumentProperties(wdPropertySubject)
        strSaveName = strDocType & " on " & strShortDate & ".doc"
        i = 2
        intSaveNameFail = True
        Do While intSaveNameFail
            strSaveNamePath = strDocsPath & strSaveName
            Debug.Print "Proposed save name and path: " _
                & vbCrLf & strSaveNamePath
            strTestFile = Nz(Dir(strSaveNamePath))
            Debug.Print "Test file: " & strTestFile
            If strTestFile = strSaveName Then
                Debug.Print "Save name already used: " & strSaveName

                'Create new save name with incremented number
                intSaveNameFail = True
                strSaveName = strDocType & " " & CStr(i) & _
                    " on " & strShortDate & ".doc"
                strSaveNamePath = strDocsPath & strSaveName
                Debug.Print "New save name and path: " _
                    & vbCrLf & strSaveNamePath
                i = i + 1
            Else
                Debug.Print "Save name not used: " & strSaveName
                intSaveNameFail = False
            End If
        Loop

        With gappWord
            .Selection.HomeKey Unit:=wdStory
            .ActiveDocument.SaveAs strSaveNamePath
            .Visible = True
            .ActiveWindow.WindowState = wdWindowStateNormal
            .Activate
        End With

        strTitle = "Merge done"
        If blnSomeSkipped = True Then
            strPrompt = "Merge document created; some records skipped because " _
                & "of missing information." & vbCrLf & "See " & strDocsPath _
                & "Skipped Records.txt for details."
        Else
            strPrompt = "Merge document created!"
        End If

        MsgBox strPrompt, vbOKOnly + vbInformation, strTitle
```

```
      End Select

ErrorHandlerExit:
    Close #1
    Exit Sub

ErrorHandler:
    If Err = 429 Then
        'Word is not running; open Word with CreateObject.
        Set gappWord = CreateObject("Word.Application")
        Resume Next
    Else
        MsgBox "Error No: " & Err.Number & "; Description: " & Err.Description
        Resume ErrorHandlerExit
    End If

End Sub
```

Figure 11.14 shows the Ebook Catalog merge document selected, and books by David Weber selected in the listbox (for this selection, the listbox is filled with book data instead of contact data).

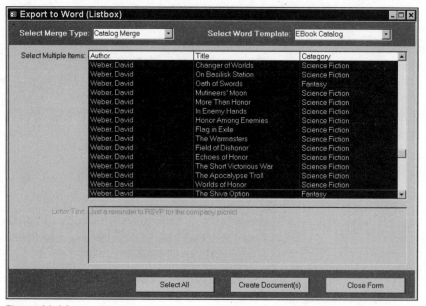

Figure 11.14

The resulting Catalog Merge document is shown in Figure 11.15.

The Catalog Merge type is rather flaky, compared to regular mail merge. In Word 2000, there is a bug that places each record on its own page. In Word 2002 and 2003, that bug is gone, but catalog merges are very prone to crashing Word (though, after recovering from the crash, the catalog merge document is usually there).

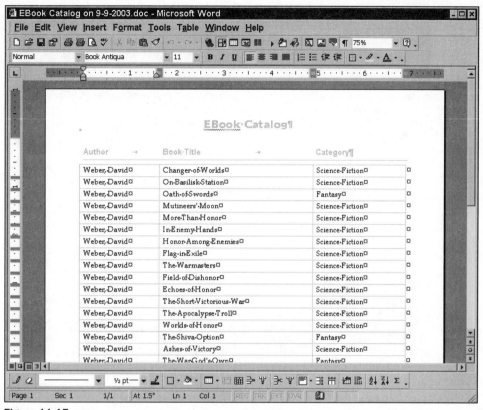

Figure 11.15

Datasheet Form

After working with the listbox form for selecting multiple recipients, you may realize that it has some limitations. It is easy to select all recipients for a letter or document, or just a few recipients chosen on an ad hoc basis, but it isn't easy to select large numbers of recipients based on the value of a field—for example, sending a letter to all the recipients in the state of Ohio, or printing an ebook catalog for books in the Alternate History category. There is no way to do this kind of selection in a listbox, so I made another form, with a datasheet subform, to make it possible to select recipients using a filter based on a field value. frmExportToWordDatasheet is shown in its initial state in Figure 11.16.

Occasionally, when working with Automation code, you will get the error message "Error No. 462: The remote server machine does not exist or is unavailable." This means that the Automation client has lost contact with the Automation server. When this happens, close the database and reopen it to get a fresh connection.

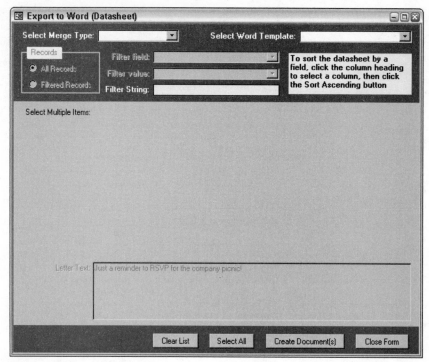

Figure 11.16

The header of this form has comboboxes for selecting the merge type and template. After you make your selections, a datasheet subform becomes visible, listing either contact or book data (depending on the selected template). Additionally, several other controls for sorting and filtering data are enabled. The Records option group lets you select to merge all or filtered records (by default, All is selected). If you leave All selected, all the records from the underlying query are displayed in the datasheet subform. If you select the Filtered Records option, the Filter field combobox is enabled, so you can select a field for filtering. On selecting a field, its values are displayed in the Filter Value combobox. When you select a filter value, the filtered records are displayed in the datasheet.

You can also sort the data in the datasheet by clicking the column heading and then clicking the Sort Ascending (or Sort Descending) button on the database toolbar. Sorting the data makes it easy to see (for example) whether there are any contacts in a specific state.

When the datasheet displays all data, it is locked (to prevent alteration of the data). When it is filtered, the datasheet is bound to a temporary table created in code, and in that case the datasheet is editable, so you can (if desired) delete records you don't want to merge, without modifying the underlying data in the tables. Figure 11.17 shows the datasheet form with the TypeText merge selected, the Avery 5161 Labels document, and a filter for the state of Alaska.

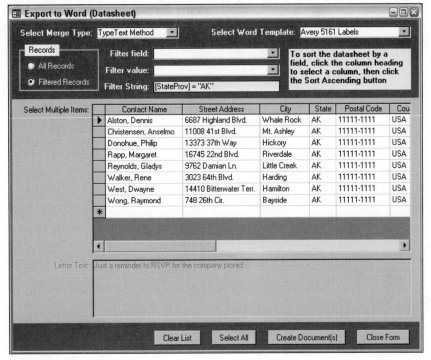

Figure 11.17

The resulting labels document is shown in Figure 11.18.

The code on the cboSelectTemplate combobox (stripped of its standard error handler) follows. After setting variables with values picked up from the combobox, and a public variable (pstrDataDype) that is set from the selection in the other combobox, the code makes either the subContacts or the subEBookCatalog datasheet visible, and the other one invisible. If the subContacts datasheet is visible, it is locked so that data in it can't be modified.

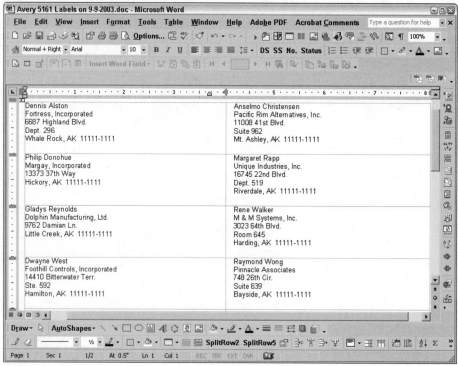

Figure 11.18

Next, the filter comboboxes are cleared, and the cboFilterField combobox is assigned the appropriate query as its data source, depending on the selected template. Finally, txtLetterText is enabled only if a freestyle template has been selected.

```
Private Sub cboSelectTemplate_AfterUpdate()

On Error GoTo ErrorHandler

    Dim strDataSource As String
    Dim strTemplate As String

    strTemplate = Me![cboSelectTemplate].Column(1)
    strDataSource = Me![cboSelectTemplate].Column(2)
    pstrDataType = Me![cboSelectTemplate].Column(4)
    Debug.Print "Data type: " & pstrDataType
    pstrQuery = strDataSource
    If pstrDataType = "C" Then
        Me![subContacts].Visible = True
        Me![subContacts].Locked = True
        Me![subEBookCatalog].Visible = False
    ElseIf pstrDataType = "E" Then
        Me![subContacts].Visible = False
        Me![subEBookCatalog].Visible = True
```

```
        End If

      Me![cboFilterField].Value = Null
      Me![cboFilterValue].Value = Null
      Me![cboFilterField].RowSource = pstrQuery & "Alpha"
      Me![fraRecords].Enabled = True

      If InStr(strTemplate, "Freestyle") > 0 Then
          Me![txtLetterText].Enabled = True
      Else
          Me![txtLetterText].Enabled = False
      End If

ErrorHandlerExit:
    Exit Sub

ErrorHandler:
    MsgBox "Error No: " & Err.Number & "; Description: " & _
        Err.Description
    Resume ErrorHandlerExit
End Sub
```

The AfterUpdate event procedures for the two filter fields follow with explanatory text.

```
Private Sub cboFilterField_AfterUpdate()

On Error GoTo ErrorHandler
```

Set a public variable representing the filter field if one has been selected; otherwise exit the procedure with an error message.

```
      pstrFilterField = Nz(Me![cboFilterField].Value)
      If pstrFilterField = "" Then
          strTitle = "No field selected"
          strPrompt = "Please select a field for filtering"
          MsgBox strPrompt, vbCritical + vbOKOnly, strTitle
          Me![cboFilterField].SetFocus
          GoTo ErrorHandlerExit
      End If
```

Set the strQuery variable to the appropriate query (contacts or books data).

```
      If pstrDataType = "C" Then
          strQuery = "qryContactsAlpha"
      ElseIf pstrDataType = "E" Then
          strQuery = "qryEBookCatalogAlpha"
      End If
```

Create a SQL statement for the non-null values of the selected field, and assign it as the row source of cboFilterValue, for selecting values. Finally, delete the old make-table query and its table, if they exist.

```
        strSQL = "SELECT DISTINCT " & strQuery & ".[" & pstrFilterField & _
            "] FROM " & strQuery & " WHERE [" & pstrFilterField & "] Is Not Null;"
        Debug.Print "SQL string: " & strSQL
        With Me![cboFilterValue]
            .Value = Null
            .RowSource = strSQL
            .Requery
            .Enabled = True
            .SetFocus
            .Dropdown
        End With

        Me![txtFilterString].Value = Null
        CallClearTables

ErrorHandlerExit:
    Exit Sub

ErrorHandler:
    MsgBox "Error No: " & Err.Number & "; Description: " & _
        Err.Description
    Resume ErrorHandlerExit

End Sub

Private Sub cboFilterValue_AfterUpdate()

On Error GoTo ErrorHandler

    Dim intDataType As Integer
    Dim fld As DAO.Field
    Dim qdf As DAO.QueryDef
    Dim strTotalsQuery As String
    Dim strLinkedQuery As String
    Dim strFilter As String
```

Set a public variant variable to the selected value (I use the Variant data type because the value could be of different data types depending on the field).

```
        pvarFilterValue = Me![cboFilterValue].Value

        'Determine data type of selected field
        Set dbs = CurrentDb
        Set rst = dbs.OpenRecordset(pstrQuery, dbOpenDynaset)
        Set fld = rst.Fields(pstrFilterField)
        intDataType = fld.Type
        Debug.Print "Field data type: " & intDataType
```

Create an appropriate filter string according to the data type of the selected field value.

```
        Select Case intDataType
            Case 1
                'Boolean
```

```
            strFilter = "[" & pstrFilterField & "] = " & pvarFilterValue

        Case 2, 3, 4, 6, 7
            'Various numeric
            strFilter = "[" & pstrFilterField & "] = " & pvarFilterValue

        Case 5
            'Currency
            strFilter = "[" & pstrFilterField & "] = " & CCur(pvarFilterValue)

        Case 8
            'Date
            strFilter = "[" & pstrFilterField & "] = " & Chr$(35) _
                & pvarFilterValue & Chr$(35)

        Case 10
            'Text
            strFilter = "[" & pstrFilterField & "] = " & Chr$(34) _
                & pvarFilterValue & Chr$(34)

        Case 11, 12, 15
            'OLE object, Memo, Replication ID
            strPrompt = "Can't filter by this field; please select another field"
            MsgBox strPrompt, vbCritical + vbOKOnly
            Me![cboFilterValue].SetFocus
            Me![cboFilterValue].Dropdown
            GoTo ErrorHandlerExit

    End Select

    Debug.Print "Filter string: " & strFilter
```

Apply the filter to the record source and make a table from it.

```
    Me![txtFilterString] = strFilter
    strQuery = "qmakMatchingRecords"
    strSQL = "SELECT " & pstrQuery & ".* INTO tmakMatchingRecords " _
        & "FROM " & pstrQuery & " WHERE " & strFilter & ";"
    Debug.Print "SQL Statement: " & strSQL
    Set qdf = dbs.CreateQueryDef(strQuery, strSQL)
    qdf.Execute
    Me![cboFilterField].Value = Null
    Me![cboFilterValue].Value = Null
```

Depending on the data type, assign the filtered subform as a source object to the appropriate datasheet subform.

```
    If pstrDataType = "C" Then
        Me![subContacts].SourceObject = "fsubContactsFiltered"
        Debug.Print "subContacts source object: " _
            & Me![subContacts].SourceObject
    ElseIf pstrDataType = "E" Then
        Me![subEBookCatalog].SourceObject = "fsubEBookCatalogFiltered"
        Debug.Print "subEBookCatalog source object: " _
```

```
                & Me![subEBookCatalog].SourceObject
        End If

ErrorHandlerExit:
    Exit Sub

ErrorHandler:
    MsgBox "Error No: " & Err.Number & "; Description: " & _
        Err.Description
    Resume ErrorHandlerExit

End Sub
```

The cmdCreateDocuments code is very similar to the code on the listbox form. The only difference is that instead of picking up selected data from rows and columns in the listbox, the code picks up values from a recordset: qryContacts or qryEBookCatalog if all records are to be merged, or tmakMatchingRecords (a table created by a make-table query) for filtered data. A portion of the code showing the recordset creation and the beginning of the Bookmarks case follows.

```
    'Determine whether it is a Contacts or EBook merge, and whether all
    'records or filtered records are to be merged.
    If Me![fraRecords].Value = 1 Then
        'All records
        If pstrDataType = "C" Then
            strDataSource = "qryContacts"
        ElseIf pstrDataType = "E" Then
            strDataSource = "qryEBookCatalog"
        End If
    ElseIf Me![fraRecords].Value = 2 Then
        'Filtered records
        strDataSource = "tmakMatchingRecords"
    End If

    Set dbs = CurrentDb
    Set rstData = dbs.OpenRecordset(strDataSource, dbOpenDynaset)

    Select Case intMergeType

        Case 1
            'Bookmarks
            blnSomeSkipped = False

            With rstData
                Do While Not .EOF
                    'Get Contact ID for reference
                    lngContactID = Nz(![ContactID])
                    Debug.Print "Contact ID: " & lngContactID

                    'Check for required address information
                    strTest = Nz(![StreetAddress])
                    Debug.Print "Street address: " & strTest
                    If strTest = "" Then
                        blnSomeSkipped = True
```

```
                    Print #1,
                    Print #1, "No street address for Contact " & lngContactID
                    GoTo NextItem1
               End If
```

Invoice Creation Dialog

The last example of exporting Access data to Word illustrates exporting data from linked tables. The target is an invoice document (similar to the Northwind invoice report in the sample Northwind database that comes with Access). The invoice needs information from a customer record in the main body of the invoice, and a list of as many items as needed (the invoice details). The data for the invoice comes from several Northwind tables (given appropriate LNC tags). The form (shown in Figure 11.19) is very simple: a small dialog that lets you select the order from a combobox that displays the order number, company name, and the date when its list is dropped down (this information is displayed in the locked blue textboxes).

I use a convention of giving locked controls a light blue background to tell users that they can't modify data in these controls.

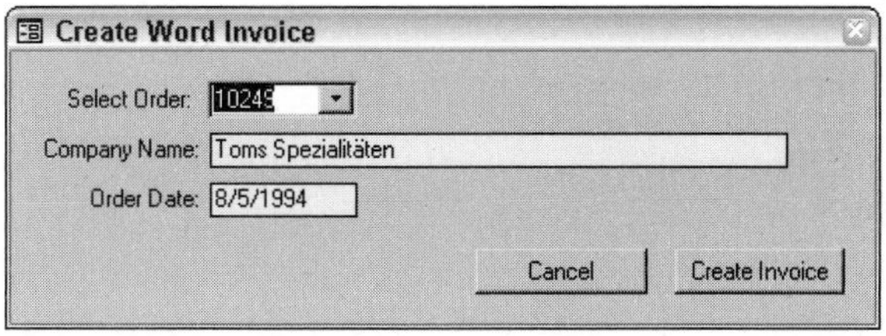

Create Word Invoice

Select Order: 10249

Company Name: Toms Spezialitäten

Order Date: 8/5/1994

Cancel   Create Invoice

Figure 11.19

The Create Invoice button's Click event procedure follows with explanatory text.

```
Private Sub cmdCreateInvoice_Click()

On Error GoTo ErrorHandler

    Dim dbs As DAO.Database
    Dim docs As Word.Documents
    Dim prps As Object
    Dim rst As DAO.Recordset
    Dim blnSaveNameFail As Boolean
    Dim lngOrderID As Long
    Dim strShipName As String
    Dim strShipAddress As String
    Dim strShipCityStateZip As String
    Dim strShipCountry As String
    Dim strCustomerID As String
    Dim strCompanyName As String
    Dim strBillToAddress As String
    Dim strBillToCityStateZip As String
    Dim strBillToCountry As String
    Dim strSalesperson As String
```

```
Dim dteTodayDate As Date
Dim dteOrderDate As Date
Dim dteRequiredDate As Date
Dim dteShippedDate As Date
Dim strShipper As String
Dim curSubtotal As Currency
Dim curFreight As Currency
Dim curTotal As Currency
Dim lngProductID As Long
Dim strProductName As String
Dim dblQuantity As Double
Dim strUnitPrice As String
Dim strDiscount As String
Dim strExtendedPrice As String
Dim strDoc As String
Dim strDocsPath As String
Dim strSaveName As String
Dim strSaveNamePath As String
Dim strShortDate As String
Dim strTemplatePath As String
Dim strTest As String
Dim strTestFile As String
Dim strWordTemplate As String
Dim strMessageTitle As String
Dim strMessage As String
Dim intReturn As Integer
Dim intCount As Integer
```

Run make-table queries to create tables to use for export. I use make-table queries instead of select queries, because the queries have a criterion limiting the Order ID to the one selected on the form, and such parameter queries can't be used in a recordset. Instead, the code runs make-table queries to create tables, which will be used in the recordsets later in the procedure.

```
DoCmd.SetWarnings False
DoCmd.OpenQuery "qmakInvoice"
DoCmd.OpenQuery "qmakInvoiceDetails"
```

Check that there is at least one detail item before creating invoice.

```
intCount = DCount("*", "tmakInvoiceDetails")
Debug.Print "Number of Detail items: " & intCount

If intCount < 1 Then
   MsgBox "No detail items for invoice; canceling"
   GoTo ErrorHandlerExit
End If
```

Create a recordset based on the table of invoice data, and assign variables to be used to set doc properties for this invoice from the table.

```
Set dbs = CurrentDb
Set rst = dbs.OpenRecordset("tmakInvoice", dbOpenDynaset)
With rst
```

The Nz function is used to convert any Nulls to zeros or zero-length strings, to prevent problems with exporting to Word doc properties.

```
        lngOrderID = Nz(![OrderID])
        Debug.Print "Order ID: " & lngOrderID
        strShipName = Nz(![ShipName])
        strShipAddress = Nz(![ShipAddress])
        strShipCityStateZip = Nz(![ShipCityStateZip])
        strShipCountry = Nz(![ShipCountry])
        strCompanyName = Nz(![CompanyName])
        strCustomerID = Nz(![CustomerID])
        strCompanyName = Nz(![CompanyName])
        strBillToAddress = Nz(![BillToAddress])
        strBillToCityStateZip = Nz(![BillToCityStateZip])
        strBillToCountry = Nz(![BillToCountry])
        strSalesperson = Nz(![Salesperson])
        dteOrderDate = Nz(![OrderDate])
        dteRequiredDate = Nz(![RequiredDate])
        dteShippedDate = Nz(![ShippedDate])
        strShipper = Nz(![Shipper])
        curSubtotal = Nz(![Subtotal])
        curFreight = Nz(![Freight])
        curTotal = Nz(![Total])
    End With
    rst.Close

    Set gappWord = GetObject(, "Word.Application")
    If CheckDocsDir = False Then
        GoTo ErrorHandlerExit
    End If
    strDocsPath = GetDocsDir
    strTemplatePath = TemplateDir
    strWordTemplate = strTemplatePath & "Northwind Invoice.dot"
```

Check for the existence of the selected template in the template folder, and exit if it is not found.

```
    strTestFile = Nz(Dir(strWordTemplate))
    Debug.Print "Test file: " & strTestFile
    If strTestFile = "" Then
        MsgBox strWordTemplate & " template not found; can't create invoice"
        GoTo ErrorHandlerExit
    End If
```

This date string is used in creating the invoice's save name; I use a date format with dashes to prevent problems when creating a save name for the document later on.

```
    strShortDate = Format(Date, "m-d-yyyy")
```

This date variable is used to print the current day's date on the invoice (unlike a Word date code, it remains stable when the invoice is reopened later).

```
    dteTodayDate = Date

    Set docs = gappWord.Documents
    docs.Add strWordTemplate
```

Write information to Word custom document properties from previously created variables. There is no need for an `On Error Resume Next` statement before this block of code in this procedure, because it writes data to only one template, which has all the required doc properties.

```
Set prps = gappWord.ActiveDocument.CustomDocumentProperties
With prps
    .Item("TodayDate").Value = dteTodayDate
    .Item("OrderID").Value = lngOrderID
    .Item("ShipName").Value = strShipName
    .Item("ShipAddress").Value = strShipAddress
    .Item("ShipCityStateZip").Value = strShipCityStateZip
    .Item("ShipCountry").Value = strShipCountry
    .Item("CompanyName").Value = strCompanyName
    .Item("CustomerID").Value = strCustomerID
    .Item("CompanyName").Value = strCompanyName
    .Item("BillToAddress").Value = strBillToAddress
    .Item("BillToCityStateZip").Value = strBillToCityStateZip
    .Item("BillToCountry").Value = strBillToCountry
    .Item("Salesperson").Value = strSalesperson
    .Item("OrderDate").Value = dteOrderDate
    .Item("RequiredDate").Value = dteRequiredDate
    .Item("ShippedDate").Value = dteShippedDate
    .Item("Shipper").Value = strShipper
    .Item("Subtotal").Value = curSubtotal
    .Item("Freight").Value = curFreight
    .Item("Total").Value = curTotal
End With
```

Highlight the entire Word document and update fields so that the data written to the custom doc props is displayed in the DocProperty fields.

```
With gappWord
    .Selection.WholeStory
    .Selection.Fields.Update
    .Selection.HomeKey Unit:=wdStory
    .Visible = True
    .Activate
End With
```

Go to the table in the invoice document, and fill it with Details data from the recordset of linked Details data.

```
With gappWord.Selection
    .GoTo What:=wdGoToTable, Which:=wdGoToFirst, Count:=3, Name:=""
    .MoveDown Unit:=wdLine, Count:=1
End With
```

Set up a recordset of linked Details data to put into the table on the Word invoice.

```
Set rst = dbs.OpenRecordset("tmakInvoiceDetails", dbOpenDynaset)
```

Save Details information to variables, using the Format function to apply the appropriate formatting to Currency and Percent fields, because they don't keep their Access formatting when assigned to Word numeric doc properties.

```
        With rst
            .MoveFirst
            Do While Not .EOF
                lngProductID = Nz(![ProductID])
                Debug.Print "Product ID: " & lngProductID
                strProductName = Nz(![ProductName])
                Debug.Print "Product Name: " & strProductName
                dblQuantity = Nz(![Quantity])
                Debug.Print "Quantity: " & dblQuantity
                strUnitPrice = Format(Nz(![UnitPrice]), "$##.00")
                Debug.Print "Unit price: " & strUnitPrice
                strDiscount = Format(Nz(![Discount]), "0%")
                Debug.Print "Discount: " & strDiscount
                strExtendedPrice = Format(Nz(![ExtendedPrice]), "$#,###.00")
                Debug.Print "Extended price: " & strExtendedPrice
Move through the table, writing values from the variables to cells in the Word table.
                With gappWord.Selection
                    .TypeText Text:=CStr(lngProductID)
                    .MoveRight Unit:=wdCell
                    .TypeText Text:=strProductName
                    .MoveRight Unit:=wdCell
                    .TypeText Text:=CStr(dblQuantity)
                    .MoveRight Unit:=wdCell
                    .TypeText Text:=strUnitPrice
                    .MoveRight Unit:=wdCell
                    .TypeText Text:=strDiscount
                    .MoveRight Unit:=wdCell
                    .TypeText Text:=strExtendedPrice
                    .MoveRight Unit:=wdCell
                End With
            .MoveNext
            Loop
            .Close
        End With
        dbs.Close
```

Delete the last, empty row of the table.

```
        Selection.SelectRow
        Selection.Rows.Delete
```

Check for the existence of a previously saved letter in documents folder, and append an incremented number to the save name if found.

```
        strSaveName = "Invoice to " & strCompanyName & " for Order " _
            & lngOrderID & " on " & strShortDate & ".doc"

        intCount = 2
        blnSaveNameFail = True
        Do While blnSaveNameFail
            strSaveNamePath = strDocsPath & strSaveName
            Debug.Print "Proposed save name and path: " _
                & vbCrLf & strSaveNamePath
            strTestFile = Nz(Dir(strSaveNamePath))
```

```
        If strTestFile = strSaveName Then

            'Create new save name with incremented number
            blnSaveNameFail = True
          strSaveName = "Invoice " & CStr(intCount) & " to " & strCompanyName _
          & " for Order " & lngOrderID & " on " & strShortDate & ".doc"

            strSaveNamePath = strDocsPath & strSaveName
            intCount = intCount + 1
        Else
            blnSaveNameFail = False
        End If
    Loop
```

Save the document with the save name just created.

```
        gappWord.ActiveDocument.SaveAs strSaveNamePath

ErrorHandlerExit:
    'Close any open recordset or database, in case code stops because
    'of an error
    On Error Resume Next
    rst.Close
    dbs.Close
    Exit Sub

ErrorHandler:
    If Err = 429 Then
        'Word is not running; open Word with CreateObject.
        Set gappWord = CreateObject("Word.Application")
        Resume Next
    Else
        MsgBox "Error No: " & Err.Number & "; Description: " & Err.Description
        Resume ErrorHandlerExit
    End If

End Sub
```

An invoice document created from this code is shown in Figure 11.20.

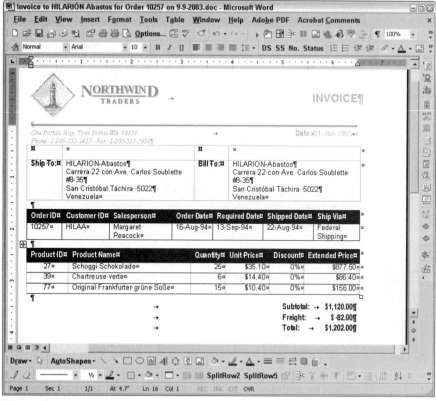

Figure 11.20

Importing Data from Word Tables into Access

Although you'll be more likely to want to export Access data into Word documents than the reverse, sometimes you need to import data from Word into Access tables. If the Word data is in tables, this can be done with VBA code that works through the cells of the table(s) and saves the data in the cells to fields in an Access table. frmImportFromWord has a tab control with two pages. The Single Table tab displays data imported from a single Word table (a phone list), and the Multiple Tables tab displays data imported from a Word document containing multiple tables with headings and filling two linked Access tables. If there is data in tblEmployeePhones, it is displayed in the subform on the Single Table tab, as shown in Figure 11.21.

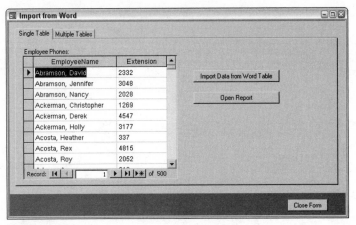

Figure 11.21

Clicking the Import Data from Word Table button clears the old data, and then imports new data from a Word document containing a list of employees and their extensions. This event procedure follows, with explanatory text.

```
Private Sub cmdImportDatafromWordTable_Click()

On Error GoTo ErrorHandler

    Dim rst As DAO.Recordset
```

Clear the Access table of old data.

```
    DoCmd.SetWarnings False
    strSQL = "DELETE * FROM tblEmployeePhones"
    DoCmd.RunSQL strSQL
    Me![subEmployeePhones].SourceObject = ""
```

Set a reference to the Word application object, and set variables for document name and path.

```
    Set gappWord = GetObject(, Word.Application)
    If CheckDocsDir = False Then
        GoTo ErrorHandlerExit
    End If
    strDocsPath = GetDocsDir
    strDocName = "Employee Phones.doc"
    strDocName = strDocsPath & strDocName
    Debug.Print "Document name: " & strDocName
    Set dbs = CurrentDb
```

Create a recordset for the Access table to be filled with data from the Word table.

```
    Set rst = dbs.OpenRecordset("tblEmployeePhones", dbOpenDynaset)

    'Set a reference to the Word document.
```

414

```
        Set doc = gappWord.Documents.Add(strDocName)
        gappWord.Visible = True
        doc.Activate
        With gappWord.Selection
```

Go the first table in the document.

```
        .GoTo What:=wdGoToTable, Which:=wdGoToFirst, Count:=1, Name:=""
```

Set a variable with the total number of table rows.

```
        lngStartRows = gappWord.Selection.Information(wdMaximumNumberOfRows)
        Debug.Print "Total table rows: " & lngStartRows
```

Move to and select the first cell in the table.

```
        .MoveDown Unit:=wdLine, Count:=1
        .MoveRight Unit:=wdCell
        .MoveLeft Unit:=wdCell
    End With
    lngRows = 0
```

Iterate through the table, until reaching the last row, and write information from the Word table cells to the Access table, using the recordset.

```
    Do While lngRows < lngStartRows
        'Write info to Access table
        With rst
            .AddNew
            lngRows = gappWord.Selection.Information(wdStartOfRangeRowNumber)
            Debug.Print "Current row: " & lngRows
            Debug.Print "Employee name: " & gappWord.Selection.Text
            ![EmployeeName] = gappWord.Selection.Text
            gappWord.Selection.MoveRight Unit:=wdCell
            ![Extension] = gappWord.Selection.Text
            gappWord.Selection.MoveRight Unit:=wdCell
            .Update
        End With
    Loop

    Me![subEmployeePhones].SourceObject = "Table.tblEmployeePhones"

ErrorHandlerExit:
    rst.Close
    Exit Sub

ErrorHandler:
    If Err = 429 Then
        'Word is not running; open Word with CreateObject.
        Set gappWord = CreateObject("Word.Application")
        Resume Next
    Else
        MsgBox "Error No: " & Err.Number & "; Description: " & Err.Description
```

```
            Resume ErrorHandlerExit
        End If

    End Sub
```

The other tab on frmExportToWord displays Logon information, if tblLogons and the linked table tblLogonValues have data. Clicking the Import Data from Word Tables button runs a Click event procedure that sets up two recordsets, based on the two Access tables, and fills them from data in the Word document; this procedure follows with explanatory text.

```
    Private Sub cmdImportDatafromWordTables_Click()

    On Error GoTo ErrorHandler

        Dim strSiteName As String
        Dim strIDName As String
        Dim strIDValue As String
        Dim rstOne As DAO.Recordset
        Dim rstMany As DAO.Recordset
        Dim lngID As Long
        Dim strSQL As String
```

Clear the Access tables of old data.

```
        DoCmd.SetWarnings False
        strSQL = "DELETE * FROM tblLogonValues"
        DoCmd.RunSQL strSQL
        strSQL = "DELETE * FROM tblLogons"
        DoCmd.RunSQL strSQL
```

Remove the subform's source object.

```
        Me![subLogons].SourceObject = ""
```

Set a reference to the Word application object and folder reference variables.

```
        Set gappWord = GetObject(, Word.Application)
        If CheckDocsDir = False Then
            GoTo ErrorHandlerExit
        End If
        strDocsPath = GetDocsDir
        strDocName = "Logons and Passwords.doc"
        strDocName = strDocsPath & strDocName
        Debug.Print "Document name: " & strDocName
        Set dbs = CurrentDb
```

Create recordsets for the two linked Access tables to be filled from the Word tables.

```
        Set rstOne = dbs.OpenRecordset("tblLogons", dbOpenDynaset)
        Set rstMany = dbs.OpenRecordset("tblLogonValues", dbOpenDynaset)
```

Set a reference to the Word documents.

```
        Set doc = gappWord.Documents.Add(strDocName)
        gappWord.Visible = True
        doc.Activate
        gappWord.Selection.HomeKey Unit:=wdStory

    NextItem:
```

Search for the next Heading 3 style, and pick up the site name from the text formatted with this style.

```
        gappWord.Selection.Find.ClearFormatting
        gappWord.Selection.Find.Style = ActiveDocument.Styles("Heading 3")
        With gappWord.Selection.Find
            .Text = ""
            .Replacement.Text = ""
            .Forward = True
            .Wrap = wdFindStop
            .Format = True
        End With
        gappWord.Selection.Find.Execute

        If gappWord.Selection.Find.Found = False Then
            GoTo ErrorHandlerExit
        End If
```

Save the site name to the Access table.

```
        gappWord.Selection.MoveLeft Unit:=wdCharacter, Count:=1, Extend:=wdExtend
        strSiteName = gappWord.Selection
        Debug.Print "Site name: " & strSiteName
        rstOne.AddNew
        rstOne!SiteName = strSiteName
        lngID = rstOne!id
        Debug.Print "ID: " & lngID
        rstOne.Update
```

Go to next table in the Word document.

```
        gappWord.Selection.MoveRight Unit:=wdCharacter, Count:=1
        gappWord.Selection.GoTo What:=wdGoToTable, Which:=wdGoToNext, _
            Count:=1, Name:=""
        lngStartRows = gappWord.Selection.Information(wdMaximumNumberOfRows)
```

Select the current cell.

```
        gappWord.Selection.MoveRight Unit:=wdCell
        gappWord.Selection.MoveLeft Unit:=wdCell

    AddValues:
        If gappWord.Selection.Type = wdSelectionIP Then GoTo NextItem
        gappWord.Selection.MoveLeft Unit:=wdCharacter, Count:=1, Extend:=wdExtend
```

Save the ID name and value to variables.

```
strIDName = gappWord.Selection
Debug.Print "ID name: " & strIDName
gappWord.Selection.MoveRight Unit:=wdCell
strIDValue = gappWord.Selection
Debug.Print "ID value: " & strIDValue
```

Write the ID name and value to the "many" table.

```
With rstMany
    Debug.Print "Processing ID " & lngID
    .AddNew
    ![id] = lngID
    ![ItemName] = strIDName
    ![ItemValue] = strIDValue
    .Update
End With
```

Check whether the selection is still in the table, and go to the next heading if it is not.

```
gappWord.Selection.MoveRight Unit:=wdCell
lngRows = gappWord.Selection.Information(wdMaximumNumberOfRows)
Debug.Print "Start rows: " & lngStartRows & vbCrLf & "Rows: " & lngRows
If lngRows = lngStartRows Then
    If gappWord.Selection.Information(wdWithInTable) = True Then
        GoTo AddValues
    Else
        GoTo NextItem
    End If
End If
```

Assign tblLogons as the source object of the datasheet subform.

```
    Me![subLogons].SourceObject = "Table.tblLogons"

ErrorHandlerExit:
    rstOne.Close
    rstMany.Close
    Exit Sub

ErrorHandler:
    If Err = 429 Then
        'Word is not running; open Word with CreateObject.
        Set gappWord = CreateObject("Word.Application")
        Resume Next
    Else
        MsgBox "Error No: " & Err.Number & "; Description: " & Err.Description
        Resume ErrorHandlerExit
    End If

End Sub
```

Figure 11.22 shows the Multiple Tables tab, with data from tblLogons and the linked tblLogonValues tables displayed in a subform.

You can assign a table as the source object of a subform control, which lets you use the subdatasheet feature of linked tables on a form.

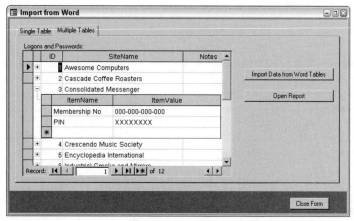

Figure 11.22

The Open Report button on both tabs opens an Access report based on the tables filled with imported data; the Employee Phones report is shown in Figure 11.23.

Employee Name	Extension
Abramson, David	2332
Abramson, Jennifer	3048
Abramson, Nancy	2028
Ackerman, Christopher	1269
Ackerman, Derek	4547
Ackerman, Holly	3177
Acosta, Heather	337
Acosta, Rex	4815
Acosta, Roy	2052
Adams, Ann	218
Alsop, Ann	2355
Alston, Dennis	1744
Alston, Lin	1714
Alston, Lynn	3852
Ames, Harrison	4913
Ames, Joseph	3972

Figure 11.23

Automation Problems and How to Avoid Them

When working with Access 2000 databases in higher versions of Access, you may encounter some problems. The next section will help you avoid these problems or deal with them if they occur.

References

You can work with an Access 2000 database (without converting it) in Access 2002 and Access 2003. This is a very handy feature, especially when users with different Office versions work with the same database. However, there are a few gotchas, especially when you work with other Office components. When you set a reference to the object model of another Office component, such as Word, you will see a specific Office version in the References dialog. For example, when you set a reference to Word from an Access 2000 database while working in Office 2000, you set a reference to Word 9.0. When you set a reference to Word from an Access 2000 database while working in Office XP, however, you set a reference to Word 10.

The Word 10 (XP) reference will work fine for Automation code so long as you are operating in Office XP, but if you open the same database in Office 2000, on opening the database you will get a mysterious error referencing the Format function (or some other perfectly legitimate function), and if you open the References dialog, you will see a reference to the Word 10.0 object library (as shown in Figure 11.24), marked "MISSING."

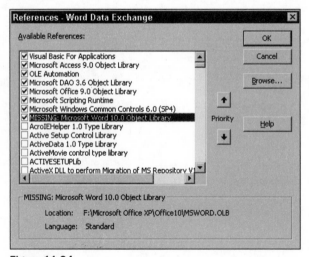

Figure 11.24

Note that the references to Access and Office (which were set to v. 10.0 when the database was opened in Office XP) were automatically downgraded to v. 9.0. In my experience, the Word and Outlook references aren't downgraded automatically, while the Access, Office, and Excel references are usually downgraded automatically. To temporarily fix this problem, you can uncheck the missing v. 10.0 reference, and check the v. 9.0 reference. This will fix the problem so long as you don't open the database in Access 2002 again. For a permanent fix (necessary when the database is shared among users with different Office versions), use the following steps:

1. Copy the Office 9.0 type libraries (or at least the Word and Outlook ones) to a separate folder, in a location that is accessible when you are working in higher Office versions.

2. Open the Access 2000 database in Access 2002 (Office XP), uncheck the Word 10.0 and/or Outlook 10.0 references if they are checked, and set references to the Word 9.0 and/or Outlook 9.0 object libraries.

After this, the references will remain set to the v. 9.0 object libraries regardless of which version of Office is in use, and there won't be any reference errors.

The process is the same for Access 2003; for that Office version, the references are v. 11.0.

Getting the Documents Directory from Word

In my Automation code, I retrieve the User Templates folder from the Word Options dialog using the following line of code:

```
TemplateDir = pgappWord.Options.DefaultFilePath(wdUserTemplatesPath)
```

This line of code reliably retrieves the folder specified in the File Locations path of the user's Word Options dialog (shown in Figure 11.25).

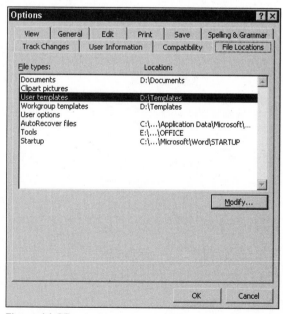

Figure 11.25

There is another named constant that should retrieve the location of the Documents folder from the same dialog:

```
DocsDir = pgappWord.Options.DefaultFilePath(wdDocumentsPath)
```

In my experience, this line of code, when used in a VBA procedure, more often than not returns the current folder, not the Document folder. Because of this problem, I generally store the Documents path in a field in tblInfo, a little table containing miscellaneous information that I use in most of my databases. The first of the following two functions checks whether the path entered into the DocsPath textbox on the main menu is valid, and if so, the second function retrieves the path from tblInfo, defaulting to C:\My Documents if the field is blank. It also checks whether there is an Access Merge subfolder under the Documents folder, and creates one if needed.

```
Public Function CheckDocsDir() As Boolean

On Error GoTo ErrorHandler

    Set dbs = CurrentDb
    Set rst = dbs.OpenRecordset("tblInfo", dbOpenDynaset)

    With rst
        .MoveFirst
        strFolderPath = Nz(![DocsPath])
        If strFolderPath = "" Then
            strFolderPath = "C:\My Documents\"
        End If
    End With

    'Test the validity of the folder path
    Debug.Print "Folder path: " & strFolderPath

    If strFolderPath = "" Then
        strTitle = "No path entered"
        strPrompt = "Please enter a Docs folder path on the main menu"
        MsgBox strPrompt, vbOKOnly + vbCritical, strTitle
        CheckDocsDir = False
        GoTo ErrorHandlerExit
    Else
        Set fso = CreateObject("Scripting.FileSystemObject")
        If fso.FolderExists(strFolderPath) = False Then
            strTitle = "Folder path invalid"
            strPrompt = "Please enter a valid Docs folder path on the main menu"
            MsgBox strPrompt, vbOKOnly + vbCritical, strTitle
            GoTo ErrorHandlerExit
            CheckDocsDir = False
        End If
    End If

    CheckDocsDir = True

ErrorHandlerExit:
    Exit Function

ErrorHandler:
```

```
        MsgBox "Error No: " & Err.Number & "; Description: " & _
            Err.Description
        Resume ErrorHandlerExit

End Function

Public Function GetDocsDir() As String

On Error GoTo ErrorHandler

    Dim strFolderPath As String

    Set dbs = CurrentDb
    Set rst = dbs.OpenRecordset("tblInfo", dbOpenDynaset)

    With rst
        .MoveFirst
        strFolderPath = Nz(![DocsPath])
        If strFolderPath = "" Then
            strFolderPath = "C:\My Documents\"
        End If
    End With

    'Test the validity of the folder path
    Debug.Print "Folder path: " & strFolderPath

    If strFolderPath = "" Then
        strTitle = "No path entered"
        strPrompt = "Please enter a Docs folder path on the main menu"
        MsgBox strPrompt, vbOKOnly + vbCritical, strTitle
        GoTo ErrorHandlerExit
    Else
        Set fso = CreateObject("Scripting.FileSystemObject")
        If fso.FolderExists(strFolderPath) = False Then
            strTitle = "Folder path invalid"
            strPrompt = "Please enter a valid Docs folder path on the main menu"
            MsgBox strPrompt, vbOKOnly + vbCritical, strTitle
            GoTo ErrorHandlerExit
        End If
    End If

    strDocsDir = strFolderPath & "Access Merge\"
    Debug.Print "Access Merge subfolder: " & strDocsDir

    'Test for existence of Access Merge subfolder, and create
    'it if it is not found
    Set fso = CreateObject("Scripting.FileSystemObject")
    If Not fso.FolderExists(strDocsDir) Then
        'Access Merge subfolder does not exist; create it
        fso.CreateFolder strDocsDir
    End If

    GetDocsDir = strDocsDir

ErrorHandlerExit:
```

```
    Exit Function

ErrorHandler:
    MsgBox "Error No: " & Err.Number & "; Description: " & _
        Err.Description
    Resume ErrorHandlerExit

End Function
```

The CheckDocsDir and GetDocsDir functions are used whenever the code in the Word Data Exchange sample database needs to save a document, using the following code segment:

```
If CheckDocsDir = False Then
    GoTo ErrorHandlerExit
End If
strDocsPath = GetDocsDir
```

If you want to test whether the Word wdDocumentsPath named constant correctly retrieves the Documents path on your computer, run the DocsDir function in the Immediate window by typing:

```
?DocsDir
```

and then typing:

```
?GetDocsDir
```

and see what they return. On my computer, the DocsDir function generally returns D:\Documents\ Writing\Wiley\Chapters (the current path), while the GetDocsDir function returns D:\Documents\Access Merge, which is correct on my computer.

Summary

Using the Word object model to create Word documents filled with Access data gives you the freedom to create highly formatted Word documents, and also lets you distribute these documents to people who don't have Access, letting you use both Office components for their strongest features—Access for data management and Word for document production.

12

Working with Outlook

Since Office 97, Outlook has been the Office component that handles email, tasks, contacts, appointments, and a few extras—the rarely used journal and yellow notes. Unless you're using a non-Office product for these purposes, you probably use Outlook to handle your email and calendar (appointments), and perhaps tasks as well. However, if you use Access to store contact information, you need a way to get information from an Access table of contacts into Outlook so that you can send email messages to your contacts. If you enter contact data in Outlook (for example, storing an email address from an incoming message as a contact), you also need a way to get contact information from Outlook into an Access table.

Apart from dealing with contacts, there are also circumstances when you need to move Outlook data into Access tables and export data from Access tables to various sorts of Outlook items. This chapter will deal with writing Automation code for exporting Access data to Outlook and importing Outlook data into Access. The sample database for this chapter is Outlook Data Exchange.mdb, an Access 2000 database that can also be used in higher versions of Access. There is also a supplementary Outlook Data Exchange with Redemption.mdb database, illustrating use of Dmitry Streblechenko's Redemption Library to avoid the annoying Object Model Guardian pop-up when working with mail messages and contacts in VBA code.

Writing Automation Code

To work with Outlook folders and items in VBA code, you need to write Automation code. See Chapter 11, *Working with Word,* for an explanation of Automation. Any Access database that works with Outlook needs a reference to the Outlook object model, which is set in the References dialog, opened from the Tools menu in the Visual Basic window, as shown in Figure 12.1.

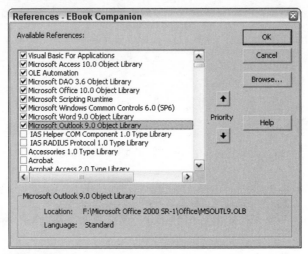

Figure 12.1

As explained in Chapter 11, the Outlook reference will be upgraded when a database is opened in a higher version of Office, but will not be downgraded when the database is opened in a lower version. This can be a problem with an Access 2000 database that is opened in both Access 2000 and Access 2002 or 2003. To prevent problems, set a reference to the Outlook 9.0 (2000) object model while the database is open in Access 2002 or 2003. See the References section in Chapter 11, for more details on this technique.

To save time when working with references and VBA code in general, see the "Some Handy Toolbar Buttons" section in Chapter 11, which shows you how to put buttons on your toolbar to quickly open the Visual Basic window and the References dialog.

The Outlook Object Model

The Outlook object model is a collection of objects that lets you work with Outlook components in VBA code. There are two ways you can get information about the Outlook object model: through the object model diagram in Help and through the Object Browser.

Viewing the Outlook Object Model Diagram

Curiously, it is much more difficult to view the Outlook object model than the Word object model—you won't find it by searching on "object model" in Help, as with Word. To locate the diagram in Office 2000, follow these steps:

1. Open Help from the main Outlook window, and click on the Contents page.

2. Select the Advanced Customization book.

3. Select the Microsoft Outlook Visual Basic Reference book.

4. Select the Microsoft Outlook Objects topic.

For Office XP, follow these steps:

1. Open Help from the main Outlook window, and click on the Contents page.
2. Select the Forms and Programming Information book.
3. Select the Outlook VBA Language Reference book.
4. Select the Microsoft Outlook Visual Basic Reference book.
5. Select the Microsoft Outlook Object Model topic.

For Office 2003, follow these steps:

1. Open Help from the main Outlook window, and click the Table of Contents link.
2. Select the Microsoft Outlook Visual Basic Reference book.
3. Select the Microsoft Outlook Object Model topic.

The object model diagram is shown in Figure 12.2.

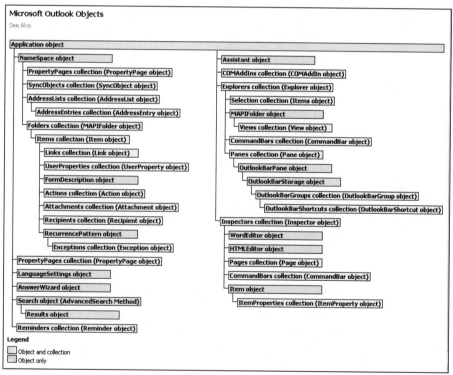

Figure 12.2

You won't see familiar Outlook items such as contacts, tasks, or appointments in the object model, and you will see strange objects such as the NameSpace object and the Explorers and Inspectors collections.

However, you can work with Outlook items in VBA code—you just need to know how to get at them, by working down the branches of the object model, as described in the next section.

In addition to the object model diagram in Help, you can also use the Object Browser (opened by F2 in the Visual Basic window). Select Outlook in the unlabeled Libraries selector, and then select the Outlook component you want to examine in the Classes list. Its properties, methods, and events are displayed in the Members list, as shown for the AppointmentItem object in Figure 12.3.

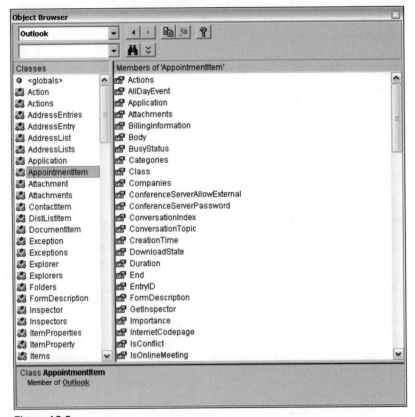

Figure 12.3

More than other Office components, the names of Outlook fields (properties) are often significantly different from the field names that appear in the Outlook interface, for example in the Field Chooser. Additionally, there are some highly useful properties that don't appear in the Field Chooser at all; you can only work with them in Visual Basic for Applications (VBA) or Visual Basic Script (VBS) code. To avoid confusion, in this chapter, I will use the term *field* for properties of objects (and other Outlook components) as they appear in the interface, and *property* when working in VBA code.

> Since Office 2000, Outlook uses two dialects of Visual Basic: VBS for code behind forms, and VBA for application-wide programming.

The Outlook Field Chooser is shown in Figure 12.4.

Figure 12.4

If you examine the fields shown on the first page of the Frequently-used fields section of the Field Chooser and try to locate their corresponding properties in the Object Browser, you may not find them—at least not under the same names. There are two problems: (1) Different names for fields and their corresponding properties, and (2) some selections in the Field Chooser don't represent properties at all, but collections (Attachment represents the Attachments collection, and Contacts represents the Links collection). The table below shows how the fields shown in Figure 12.4 match up to property names.

Field Name	Property or Collection Name
Assistant's Phone	AssistantTelephoneNumber
Attachment	Attachments (collection)
Business Address	BusinessAddress
Business Fax	BusinessFaxNumber
Business Home Page	BusinessHomePage
Business Phone	BusinessTelephoneNumber
Business Phone 2	Business2TelephoneNumber
Callback	CallbackTelephoneNumber
Car Phone	CarTelephoneNumber
Categories	Categories (an enumerated property)
Company	CompanyName
Company Main Phone	CompanyMainTelephoneNumber
Contacts	Links (collection)

For a full listing of Outlook ContactItem fields and their corresponding properties, see my white paper on Outlook Fields and Properties, which can be downloaded from the Downloads page of my Web site, www.helenfeddema.com.

The Basic Automation Commands

To initiate an Automation session for working with Outlook, you need to create an Automation object representing the Outlook Application object, which is at the top of the Outlook object model. This can be done with either the CreateObject or GetObject function. CreateObject creates a new instance of Outlook, while GetObject uses an existing instance of Outlook. To avoid creating extra Outlook instances, I like to use the GetObject function initially, with a fallback to CreateObject in a procedure's error handler, so that an existing instance of Outlook will be used, if there is one, and a new instance will be created if it is needed.

While you can use the GetObject function to create an instance of (say) an Outlook folder, I find it more useful to create a Outlook application object that can then be used for all Automation work with Outlook, since most Automation code needs to work with properties and methods of the Application object itself, and the NameSpace object on the next level down, as well as with the properties and methods of lower-level objects such as the MAPIFolder and ContactItem objects. The syntax for setting a reference to an existing instance of Outlook, using the GetObject function, is:

```
Set gappOutlook = GetObject(, "Outlook.Application")
```

If this line of code fails (because Outlook is not running), error 429 occurs, and the following error handler then runs a line of code using the CreateObject function to create a new instance of Outlook and resumes running the code after the GetObject line.

```
If Err.Number = 429 Then
    'Outlook is not running; open Outlook with CreateObject.
    Set gappOutlook = CreateObject("Outlook.Application")
    Resume Next
Else
    MsgBox "Error No: " & Err.Number & "; Description: "
    Resume ErrorHandlerExit
End If
```

Using the gappOutlook variable, you can access any of the objects in the Outlook object model to work with folders and items of various types. The code samples in the "Exporting Data from Access to Outlook Items" and "Importing Data from Outlook Items to Access" sections in this chapter (and the Outlook Data Exchange sample database) all use the gappOutlook variable as the starting point for working with various components of the Outlook object model.

Unlike Word, Outlook has no macro recorder, so unfortunately, you can't record a macro to get a shortcut to the syntax needed for various Outlook actions.

NameSpaces and Other Oddly Named Objects

If you are unfamiliar with the Outlook object model, you will probably be puzzled at the names of its major objects, which don't correspond to what you see in the interface. The strangest ones are the

NameSpace object, which represents the data stored in Outlook folders; the Inspector object, representing the window in which an Outlook item (such as a contact or mail message) is displayed; and the Explorer object, representing a pane in which the contents of a folder are displayed, such as the Tasks folder (when you open Outlook in the interface, you are looking at an Explorer).

These three high-level objects, in addition to the Application object itself, are used to get at the other Outlook components you need to work with, such as folders and items. To work with a folder, for example, you must first set a reference to the Outlook Application object, then the NameSpace object, and then you can retrieve one of the default local folders using the GetDefaultFolder method, or a custom folder by referencing it as a member of the top-level Folders collection, or some folder underneath that folder (note that the singular of Folders in VBA code is not Folder, as you would expect, but MAPIFolder).

Syntax for Referencing Outlook Objects

The following code segments show how to set a reference to various types of Outlook folders and items, in different situations, as described in comments in the following code. The appOutlook variable would only be needed if you haven't declared a global gappOutlook variable in the Declarations section of a standard module, which is the technique I use in the sample databases for this chapter.

```
Dim appOutlook As Outlook.Application
Dim nms As Outlook.NameSpace
Dim flds As Outlook.Folders
Dim fld As Outlook.MAPIFolder
Dim exp As Outlook.Explorer
Dim ins As Outlook.Inspector
```

Declare this variable as Object so it can be used for any type of item. This is useful when iterating through a folder that may contain several different sorts of items (such as a contacts folder containing both contact items and distribution lists).

```
Dim itm As Object
```

Declare these variables as specific item types.

```
Dim msg As Outlook.MailItem
Dim con As Outlook.ContactItem

Set nms = gappOutlook.GetNamespace("MAPI")
Set flds = nms.Folders("Personal Folders").Folders
```

Set a reference to the default local Contacts folder.

```
Set fld = nms.GetDefaultFolder(olFolderContacts)
```

Set a reference to a folder called Custom Contacts under the top-level Personal Folders folder's Folders collection (via the previously set flds variable).

```
Set fld = flds("Custom Contacts")
```

Set a reference to a custom public folder.

```
Set flds = nms.Folders("Public Folders").Folders
Set fld = flds("All Public Folders").Folders("Custom Folder")
```

Set a reference to the currently open folder, via the active Explorer.

```
Set exp = gappOutlook.ActiveExplorer
Set fld = exp.CurrentFolder
```

Test whether the current folder is a Contacts folder.

```
If fld.DefaultItemType <> olContactItem Then
    MsgBox "This folder is not a Contacts folder; canceling"
    GoTo ErrorHandlerExit
End If
```

Set a reference to the currently open item, via the active Inspector.

```
Set ins = gappOutlook.ActiveInspector
Set itm = ins.CurrentItem
```

Test whether the open item is a mail message and set a mail message variable to it if so; this allows you to use IntelliSense to select specific MailItem properties.

```
If itm.Class = olMail Then
    Set msg = itm
End If
```

Set a reference to the contact whose name is "Helen Feddema."

```
Set fld = nms.GetDefaultFolder(olFolderContacts)
Set con = fld.Items("Helen Feddema")
```

Set a reference to a built-in Outlook item property.

```
strFullName = con.FullName
```

Set a reference to a custom Outlook item property.

```
blnCustomer = con.UserProperties("Customer")
```

Referencing Outlook Items in the Interface and in Code

Microsoft has chosen to use the word "Note" to reference different item types (a mail message's message class and a Note in the interface), and to give items confusingly different names in code than they have in the user interface (a Journal item has a message class of Activity). Here is a table that will help you find the correct syntax for referencing an object in different situations.

Interface Name	Object Model Name	Message Class
Contact	ContactItem	IPM.Contact
Task	TaskItem	IPM.Task
Mail Message	MailItem	IPM.Note
Appointment	AppointmentItem	IPM.Appointment
Journal Entry	JournalItem	IPM.Activity
Note	NoteItem	IPM.StickyNote

Additionally, there are named constants (listed in the table below) that reference the standard Outlook items, which can be used as arguments for various methods in VBA code.

Interface Name	OlItemType Enum	OlObjectClass Enum
Contact	olContactItem	olContact
Task	olTaskItem	olTask
Mail Message	olMailItem	olMail
Appointment	olAppointmentItem	olAppointment
Journal Entry	olJournalItem	olJournal
Note	olNoteItem	olNote

Constants from the OlItemType enum are used in determining what type of item you are dealing with. Those in the OlObjectClassEnum (a much larger group) are used in determining what type of object you are dealing with. For example, if you wanted to determine whether an item in a folder is a mail message, you would check whether its Class property is olMail. To determine whether a folder is a Contacts folder, you would check whether the value of its Class property is olContact. The OlItemType constants are used to create new items of specific types, using the Application object's CreateItem method.

The Outlook-Exchange Wizard

Access has a way to import from Outlook items or set up linked tables. If you select File | Get External Data | Import, and select the Outlook() or Exchange() selection in the Files of type selector, then select a profile, the Import Exchange/Outlook Wizard opens, as shown in Figure 12.5.

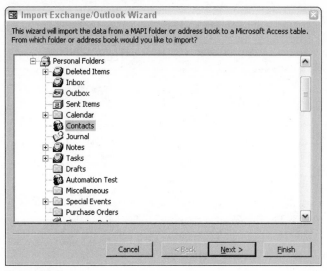

Figure 12.5

However, if you proceed through the steps of this Wizard, you will end up with a table that may not be very useful. Here is what you will get for the main Outlook item types:

❑ **Contacts.** A limited selection of standard fields is imported; it may be sufficient for many purposes.

❑ **Tasks.** You get the correct number of records, but Subject, Start Date, Due Date, and in fact all fields for which a table field is created, are blank. This is no use at all.

❑ **Appointments.** The table has Subject and Notes, but omits Start Time and End Time. This is not much use.

❑ **Mail messages.** The table has Subject, To, and Body. It omits attachments, except for noting that the message has one. This may be useful, if you don't care about attachments.

See the tables in the Outlook Data Exchange database with the otbl tag for examples of what you get when you use this Wizard. Because of its inadequacies, you will do better to write VBA code to import data from Outlook, as described in the "Importing Data from Outlook Items to Access" section of this chapter.

Exporting Data from Access to Outlook Items

The Outlook Data Exchange sample database has three forms that illustrate exporting data from Access tables to Outlook items, for the most commonly used items: Appointments, Contacts, Mail Messages, and Tasks. Additionally, the main menu has a set of controls for quickly creating a mail message to a recipient, and a Docs Path textbox, to allow editing the Documents path (the path is picked up from tblInfo in various procedures in the database). The first of the following two functions checks whether the path entered into the DocsPath textbox on the main menu is valid, and if so, the second function retrieves the path from tblInfo, defaulting to C:\My Documents if the field is blank. It also checks whether there is an Access Merge subfolder under the Documents folder, and creates one if needed.

```
Public Function CheckDocsDir() As Boolean

On Error GoTo ErrorHandler

    Set dbs = CurrentDb
    Set rst = dbs.OpenRecordset("tblInfo", dbOpenDynaset)

    With rst
       .MoveFirst
       strFolderPath = Nz(![DocsPath])
       If strFolderPath = "" Then
          strFolderPath = "C:\My Documents\"
       End If
    End With

    'Test the validity of the folder path
    Debug.Print "Folder path: " & strFolderPath

    If strFolderPath = "" Then
       strTitle = "No path entered"
       strPrompt = "Please enter a Docs folder path on the main menu"
       MsgBox strPrompt, vbOKOnly + vbCritical, strTitle
       CheckDocsDir = False
       GoTo ErrorHandlerExit
    Else
       Set fso = CreateObject("Scripting.FileSystemObject")
       If fso.FolderExists(strFolderPath) = False Then
          strTitle = "Folder path invalid"
          strPrompt = "Please enter a valid Docs folder path on the main menu"
          MsgBox strPrompt, vbOKOnly + vbCritical, strTitle
          GoTo ErrorHandlerExit
          CheckDocsDir = False
       End If
    End If

    CheckDocsDir = True

ErrorHandlerExit:
    Exit Function

ErrorHandler:
    MsgBox "Error No: " & Err.Number & "; Description: " & _
       Err.Description
    Resume ErrorHandlerExit

End Function

Public Function GetDocsDir() As String
```

```
On Error GoTo ErrorHandler

    Dim strFolderPath As String

    Set dbs = CurrentDb
    Set rst = dbs.OpenRecordset("tblInfo", dbOpenDynaset)

    With rst
        .MoveFirst
        strFolderPath = Nz(![DocsPath])
        If strFolderPath = "" Then
            strFolderPath = "C:\My Documents\"
        End If
    End With

    'Test the validity of the folder path
    Debug.Print "Folder path: " & strFolderPath

    If strFolderPath = "" Then
        strTitle = "No path entered"
        strPrompt = "Please enter a Docs folder path on the main menu"
        MsgBox strPrompt, vbOKOnly + vbCritical, strTitle
        GoTo ErrorHandlerExit
    Else
        Set fso = CreateObject("Scripting.FileSystemObject")
        If fso.FolderExists(strFolderPath) = False Then
            strTitle = "Folder path invalid"
            strPrompt = "Please enter a valid Docs folder path on the main menu"
            MsgBox strPrompt, vbOKOnly + vbCritical, strTitle
            GoTo ErrorHandlerExit
        End If
    End If

    strDocsDir = strFolderPath & "Access Merge\"
    Debug.Print "Access Merge subfolder: " & strDocsDir

    'Test for existence of Access Merge subfolder, and create
    'it if it is not found
    Set fso = CreateObject("Scripting.FileSystemObject")
    If Not fso.FolderExists(strDocsDir) Then
        'Access Merge subfolder does not exist; create it
        fso.CreateFolder strDocsDir
    End If

    GetDocsDir = strDocsDir

ErrorHandlerExit:
    Exit Function

ErrorHandler:
    MsgBox "Error No: " & Err.Number & "; Description: " & _
        Err.Description
    Resume ErrorHandlerExit

End Function
```

The CheckDocsDir and GetDocsDir functions are used whenever the code in the Outlook Data Exchange sample database needs to save a document (in this database, the documents are the saved reports to be attached to mail messages), using the following code segment:

```
If CheckDocsDir = False Then
    GoTo ErrorHandlerExit
End If
strDocsPath = GetDocsDir
```

Creating a Mail Message from the Main Menu

The main menu of the Outlook Data Exchange database has a section where you can type the subject and message text of an email message, select a recipient from tblContacts (a table of contact data with an EMailName field), and send a message to the recipient by clicking the large EMail command button. The main menu is shown in Figure 12.6, with a recipient selected.

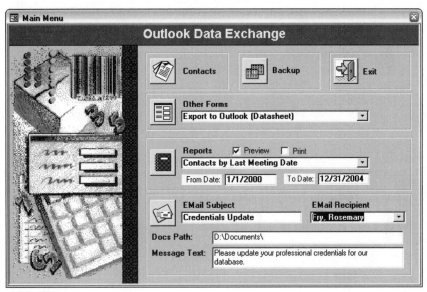

Figure 12.6

The AfterUpdate event procedure for the large EMail command button is listed below, with explanatory text.

```
Private Sub cmdEMail_Click()

On Error GoTo ErrorHandler

    Dim strEMailRecipient As String
    Dim dteLastMeeting As Date
    Dim strSubject As String
    Dim strMessage As String
    Dim strBody As String
```

This variable represents an Outlook folder—note that the object name is not Folder, but MAPIFolder.

```
Dim fld As Outlook.MAPIFolder
Dim msg As Outlook.MailItem
```

Check the Access table record for required email information. The information is picked up from columns of the selected record in the combobox, using the zero-based Column (*n*) syntax.

```
strEMailRecipient = Nz(Me![cboRecipients].Column(1))
If strEMailRecipient = "" Then
   GoTo ErrorHandlerExit
Else
```

A Debug.Print statement is useful for debugging.

```
    Debug.Print "EMail recipient: " & strEMailRecipient
End If
dteLastMeeting = CDate(Me![cboRecipients].Column(2))
```

The Nz function is used to set the strSubject variable to "Reminder" in case nothing has been entered into the MessageSubject field.

```
strSubject = Nz(Me![MessageSubject], "Reminder")
```

The Nz function is initially used to set the strMessage variable to a zero-length string ("") if nothing has been entered into the MessageSubject field (to prevent errors with Nulls).

```
strMessage = Nz(Me![MessageText])
If strMessage <> "" Then
   strBody = strMessage
Else
```

If nothing was entered, a message including the last meeting date is created.

```
    strBody = "Your last meeting was on " & dteLastMeeting _
    & "; please call to arrange a meeting by the end of the year."
End If
```

A new mail message is created, working down from the Outlook Application object, to the NameSpace object, then to the Outbox folder, and the Add method of its Items collection.

```
Set gappOutlook = GetObject(, Outlook.Application)
Set nms = gappOutlook.GetNamespace("MAPI")
Set fld = nms.GetDefaultFolder(olFolderOutbox)

Set msg = fld.Items.Add
```

Various properties of the new mail message are set, and it is sent.

```
With msg
    .To = strEMailRecipient
    .Subject = strSubject
    .Body = strBody
    .Send
End With

ErrorHandlerExit:
    Exit Sub

ErrorHandler:
```

This error handler runs the CreateObject function to create an Outlook instance, in case Outlook is not running.

```
If Err = 429 Then
    'Outlook is not running; open Outlook with CreateObject.
    Set gappOutlook = CreateObject("Outlook.Application")
    Resume Next
Else
    MsgBox "Error No: " & Err.Number & "; Description: " & Err.Description
    Resume ErrorHandlerExit
End If

End Sub
```

When you click the EMail button, you will probably see the message shown in Figure 12.7. This is part of the obnoxious Object Model Guardian that appears when you access Outlook mail messages and contacts.

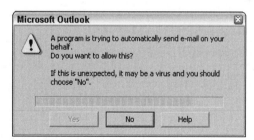

Figure 12.7

To create the message, click the Yes button in this dialog. For a way of avoiding the Object Model Guardian dialog, see the section, "Using the Redemption Library to Avoid the Object Model Guardian," later in this chapter.

A mail message created by this procedure is shown in Figure 12.8.

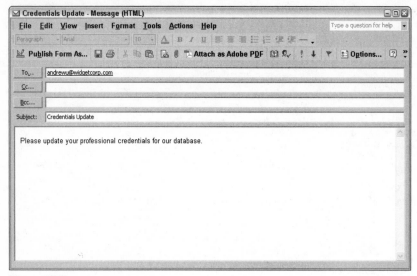

Figure 12.8

MultiSelect Listbox Form

For creating various types of Outlook items, with data from multiple records in an Access table, I created frmExportToOutlookListBox, which uses a MultiSelect listbox as a way of selecting multiple records from a table, with a combobox in the header for selecting an Outlook item type. The cboSelectOutlookItem combobox has as its row source the table tlkpOutlookItemTypes, which follows.

ItemTypeID	ItemType	ItemConstant	DataSource
0	Mail message	olMailItem	qryContactsEMail
1	Appointment	olAppointmentItem	qryAppointments
2	Contact	olContactItem	qryContacts
3	Task	olTaskItem	qryTasks

Information from different columns in the selected row of the table is used in the code on the combobox's AfterUpdate event and the Create Items command button in the form footer. Figure 12.9 shows the listbox dialog, with Contact selected as the Outlook item type.

Figure 12.9

For the Contact selection, qryContacts is assigned as the row source of lstSelectMultiple; this query displays data from tblContacts. The code for cboSelectOutlookItem's AfterUpdate event procedure follows, with commentary.

```
Private Sub cboSelectOutlookItem_AfterUpdate()

On Error GoTo ErrorHandler
```

Set a variable for the listbox.

```
    Set lst = Me![lstSelectMultiple]
```

Set variables representing the data in different columns of the listbox.

```
    lngItemId = Me![cboSelectOutlookItem].Column(0)
    strItemType = Me![cboSelectOutlookItem].Column(1)
    strItemConstant = Me![cboSelectOutlookItem].Column(2)
    strDataSource = Me![cboSelectOutlookItem].Column(3)
```

Assign the appropriate data source as the listbox's row source.

```
    lst.RowSource = strDataSource
```

For mail messages only, enable the txtMessageText textbox.

```
    If lngItemId = 0 Then
        'Mail message selected
        Me![txtMessageText].Enabled = True
    Else
        Me![txtMessageText].Enabled = False
    End If
```

Set up a Select Case statement to set the appropriate number of columns, and column sizes, for each data source.

```
    Select Case strDataSource

        Case "qryContacts"
            lst.ColumnCount = 13
            lst.ColumnWidths = _
                "0 in;1.25 in;1.25 in;1 in;.6 in;.6 in;0 in;0 in;0 in;0 in;0 in;0 in;0 in"

        Case "qryAppointments"
            lst.ColumnCount = 8
            lst.ColumnWidths = _
                "0 in;1.25 in;1.25 in;1.5 in;1.5 in;0 in;1.25 in;1.25 in"

        Case "qryTasks"
            lst.ColumnCount = 7
            lst.ColumnWidths = _
                "0 in;1.5 in;0 in;1.25 in;1 in;1 in;.75 in"

        Case "qryContactsEMail"
            lst.ColumnCount = 5
            lst.ColumnWidths = _
                "0 in;1.25 in;1.25 in;1.75 in;1.25 in"

    End Select

ErrorHandlerExit:
    Exit Sub

ErrorHandler:
    MsgBox "Error No: " & Err.Number & "; Description: " & _
        Err.Description
    Resume ErrorHandlerExit

End Sub
```

As a quick way of selecting all the records, the Select All button in the form footer iterates through all the rows in the listbox, setting the Selected property of each row to True. This procedure is:

```
Private Sub cmdSelectAll_Click()

On Error GoTo ErrorHandler
```

Set a variable to the listbox.

```
    Set lst = Me![lstSelectMultiple]
```

Count the number of rows in the listbox, and save this number to a variable.

```
    intRows = lst.ListCount - 1
```

Select all the rows in the listbox.

```
    For intIndex = 0 To intRows
        lst.Selected(intIndex) = True
    Next intIndex

ErrorHandlerExit:
    Exit Sub

ErrorHandler:
    MsgBox "Error No: " & Err.Number & "; Description: " & _
        Err.Description
    Resume ErrorHandlerExit

End Sub
```

The main procedure on the listbox form is the Click event procedure of cmdCreateItems, which follows, with explanatory text.

```
Private Sub cmdCreateItems_Click()

On Error GoTo ErrorHandler
```

Declare variables for values from the Access tables, Outlook objects, and listbox rows and columns.

```
    Dim strContactName As String
    Dim strTaskName As String
    Dim dteStartDate As Date
    Dim dteDueDate As Date
    Dim strStatus As String
    Dim lngStatus As Long
    Dim strSalutation As String
    Dim strPostalCode As String
    Dim strStateProv As String
    Dim strCity As String
    Dim strStreetAddress As String
    Dim nms As Outlook.NameSpace
    Dim fldCalendar As Outlook.MAPIFolder
    Dim fldContacts As Outlook.MAPIFolder
    Dim fldTasks As Outlook.MAPIFolder
    Dim appt As Outlook.AppointmentItem
    Dim msg As Outlook.MailItem
    Dim con As Outlook.ContactItem
    Dim tsk As Outlook.TaskItem
    Dim lnks As Outlook.Links
    Dim itm As Object
    Dim blnSomeSkipped As Boolean
    Dim cbo As Access.ComboBox
    Dim dbs As DAO.Database
    Dim dteLastMeeting As Date
    Dim i As String
    Dim lngAppointmentID As Long
    Dim lngContactID As Long
    Dim strBody As String
    Dim strCompanyName As String
```

```
Dim strCountry As String
Dim strDocName As String
Dim strDocsPath As String
Dim strDocType As String
Dim strEMailRecipient As String
Dim strFullName As String
Dim strFile As String
Dim strJobTitle As String
Dim strLongDate As String
Dim strMessage As String
Dim strName As String
Dim strNameAndJob As String
Dim strPrompt As String
Dim strShortDate As String
Dim strSubject As String
Dim strTest As String
Dim strTestFile As String
Dim strTextFile As String
Dim strTitle As String
Dim varItem As Variant
```

Check that an Outlook item type has been selected, and exit if it has not.

```
Set cbo = Me![cboSelectOutlookItem]
Set lst = Me![lstSelectMultiple]
lngItemId = Nz(cbo.Column(0))
strItemType = Nz(cbo.Column(1))
Debug.Print "Selected Outlook item type: " & strItemType
If strItemType = "" Then
    MsgBox "Please select an Outlook item type."
    cbo.SetFocus
    cbo.Dropdown
    GoTo ErrorHandlerExit
End If
```

Check that at least one record has been selected in the listbox, and exit if it has not.

```
If lst.ItemsSelected.Count = 0 Then
    MsgBox "Please select at least one record."
    lst.SetFocus
    GoTo ErrorHandlerExit
Else
    intColumns = lst.ColumnCount
    intRows = lst.ItemsSelected.Count
End If
```

Set a global Outlook application variable; if Outlook is not running, the error handler defaults to CreateObject.

```
Set gappOutlook = GetObject(, "Outlook.Application")
```

Open a text file for writing information about skipped records.

```
strFile = strDocsPath & "Skipped Records.txt"
Open strFile For Output As #1
Print #1, "These records were skipped when creating Outlook items"
Print #1,
```

Set up a Select Case statement to deal with each Outlook item type.

```
Select Case strItemType

    Case "Mail message"
```

Set blnSomeSkipped to False to start with—it will be set to True if any records have to be skipped because of missing data.

```
blnSomeSkipped = False
```

Set up a For Each . . . Next loop to deal with each selected item in the listbox, using the handy Access ItemsSelected collection.

```
For Each varItem In lst.ItemsSelected
```

Get the Contact ID for use later in the code.

```
lngContactID = Nz(lst.Column(0, varItem))
Debug.Print "Contact ID: " & lngContactID
```

Check for required email information, and set blnSomeSkipped to True if anything is missing.

```
strTest = Nz(lst.Column(3, varItem))
Debug.Print "Email address: " & strTest
If strTest = "" Then
   blnSomeSkipped = True
```

Print a line about the missing information to the Skipped Records text file.

```
Print #1,
Print #1, "No email address for Contact " & lngContactID
GoTo NextItemMail
End If
```

As with the main menu, either pick up the message text from the MessageText field in tblInfo or create a message about the last meeting date.

```
strEMailRecipient = Nz(lst.Column(3, varItem))
dteLastMeeting = Nz(lst.Column(4, varItem))
strMessage = Nz(Me![MessageText])
If strMessage <> "" Then
   strBody = strMessage
Else
```

```
                  strBody = "Your last meeting was on " & dteLastMeeting _
                     & "; please call to arrange a meeting by the end of the year."
               End If
```

Create the new mail message, using the CreateItem method of the Application object, and set the values of several of its fields. The new item will be created in the default folder for mail messages (the Outbox).

```
            Set gappOutlook = GetObject(, Outlook.Application)
            Set msg = gappOutlook.CreateItem(olMailItem)
            With msg
               .To = strEMailRecipient
               .Subject = "Meeting reminder"
               .Body = strBody
               .Send
            End With
```

Go the next record.

```
   NextItemMail:
            Next varItem
```

When all the selected records have been processed, put up an informative message box.

```
            strTitle = "Done"
            If blnSomeSkipped = True Then
               strPrompt = "All mail messages created; some records skipped because " _
                  & "of missing information." & vbCrLf & "See " & strDocsPath _
                  & "Skipped Records.txt for details."
            Else
               strPrompt = "All mail messages created!"
            End If

            MsgBox strPrompt, vbOKOnly + vbInformation, strTitle

         Case "Appointment"
```

Much of the code is similar to the mail message code; only segments that differ will be explained in detail.

```
            blnSomeSkipped = False

            For Each varItem In lst.ItemsSelected
               'Get Appointment ID for reference
               lngAppointmentID = Nz(lst.Column(0, varItem))
               Debug.Print "Appointment ID: " & lngAppointmentID

               'Check for required appointment information.
               strTest = Nz(lst.Column(1, varItem))
```

```
      Debug.Print "Topic: " & strTest
      If strTest = "" Then
         blnSomeSkipped = True
         Print #1,
         Print #1, "No topic for Appointment " & lngAppointmentID
         GoTo NextItemAppt
      Else
         strSubject = lst.Column(1, varItem)
      End If

      strTest = Nz(lst.Column(3, varItem))
      Debug.Print "Start time: " & strTest
      If strTest = "" Then
         blnSomeSkipped = True
         Print #1,
         Print #1, "No start time for Appointment " & lngAppointmentID
         GoTo NextItemAppt
      End If

      'Create new appointment in default Calendar folder
      Set gappOutlook = GetObject(, Outlook.Application)
      Set nms = gappOutlook.GetNamespace("MAPI")
      Set appt = gappOutlook.CreateItem(olAppointmentItem)
      With appt
         .Subject = strSubject
         dteStartDate = Nz(lst.Column(3, varItem))
         .Start = dteStartDate
         If IsDate(lst.Column(4, varItem)) = True Then
            dteEndDate = lst.Column(4, varItem)
            .End = dteEndDate
         End If
         .Location = Nz(lst.Column(2, varItem))
         .Categories = Nz(lst.Column(7, varItem))
```

Appointments can have one or more contacts, which are stored in the Links collection of the AppointmentItem object. To add a contact to an appointment, first the contact is located in a Contacts folder (here the default local Contacts folder is searched), and then the ContactItem is added to the Links collection.

```
         If Nz(lst.Column(5, varItem)) > 0 Then
            'There is a contact for this appointment; attempt to
            'locate this contact in the default Contacts folder.
            Set nms = gappOutlook.GetNamespace("MAPI")
            Set fldContacts = nms.GetDefaultFolder(olFolderContacts)
On Error Resume Next
            lngContactID = Nz(lst.Column(5, varItem))
            'Find the contact, using the CustomerID field
            Set con = fldContacts.Items.Find("[CustomerID] = " & lngContactID)
            If con Is Nothing Then
               strPrompt = "Can't find Contact ID " & lngContactID _
                  & " in your default local Contacts folder"
               Debug.Print strPrompt
```

```
                      Else
                          Set lnks = .Links
                          lnks.Add con
                      End If
On Error GoTo ErrorHandler
                  End If
                  .Close(olSave)
              End With
NextItemAppt:
          Next varItem

          strTitle = "Done"
          If blnSomeSkipped = True Then
              strPrompt = "All appointments created; some records skipped because " _
                  & "of missing information." & vbCrLf & "See " & strDocsPath _
                  & "Skipped Records.txt for details."
          Else
              strPrompt = "All appointments created!"
          End If

          MsgBox strPrompt, vbOKOnly + vbInformation, strTitle

      Case "Contact"
          blnSomeSkipped = False

          For Each varItem In lst.ItemsSelected
              'Get Contact ID for reference
              lngContactID = Nz(lst.Column(0, varItem))
              Debug.Print "Contact ID: " & lngContactID

              'Check for required name information
              strTest = Nz(lst.Column(1, varItem))
              Debug.Print "Contact name: " & strTest
              If strTest = "" Then
                  blnSomeSkipped = True
                  Print #1,
                  Print #1, "No name for Contact " & lngContactID
                  GoTo NextItemContact
              End If

              strFullName = Nz(lst.Column(7, varItem))
              strJobTitle = Nz(lst.Column(10, varItem))
              strStreetAddress = Nz(lst.Column(2, varItem))
              strCity = Nz(lst.Column(3, varItem))
              strStateProv = Nz(lst.Column(4, varItem))
              strPostalCode = Nz(lst.Column(5, varItem))
              strCountry = Nz(lst.Column(6, varItem))
              strCompanyName = Nz(lst.Column(9, varItem))
              strSalutation = Nz(lst.Column(11, varItem))
              strEMailRecipient = Nz(lst.Column(12, varItem))
```

```
                    'Create new contact item in default local Contacts folder
                    Set gappOutlook = GetObject(, Outlook.Application)
                    Set con = gappOutlook.CreateItem(olContactItem)
                    With con
                        .CustomerID = lngContactID
                        .FullName = strFullName
                        .JobTitle = strJobTitle
                        .BusinessAddressStreet = strStreetAddress
                        .BusinessAddressCity = strCity
                        .BusinessAddressState = strStateProv
                        .BusinessAddressPostalCode = strPostalCode
                        .BusinessAddressCountry = strCountry
                        .CompanyName = strCompanyName
                        .NickName = strSalutation
                        .Email1Address = strEMailRecipient
                        .Close(olSave)
                    End With

NextItemContact:
            Next varItem

            strTitle = "Done"
            If blnSomeSkipped = True Then
                strPrompt = "All contacts created; some records skipped because " _
                    & "of missing information." & vbCrLf & "See " & strDocsPath _
                    & "Skipped Records.txt for details."
            Else
                strPrompt = "All contacts created!"
            End If

            MsgBox strPrompt, vbOKOnly + vbInformation, strTitle

        Case "Task"
            blnSomeSkipped = False


            For Each varItem In lst.ItemsSelected
                'Check for required task information
                strTest = Nz(lst.Column(1, varItem))
                Debug.Print "Task: " & strTest
                If strTest = "" Then
                    blnSomeSkipped = True
                    Print #1,
                    Print #1, "No task name"
                    GoTo NextItemTask
                End If

                strTaskName = Nz(lst.Column(1, varItem))
                lngContactID = Nz(lst.Column(2, varItem))
                dteStartDate = Nz(lst.Column(4, varItem))
                dteDueDate = Nz(lst.Column(5, varItem))
```

```
            strStatus = Nz(lst.Column(6, varItem))
            lngStatus = Switch(strStatus = "Not started", 0, _
            strStatus = "In progress", 1, _
            strStatus = "Completed", 2, "", 0)

            'Create new task item in default local Tasks folder
            Set gappOutlook = GetObject(, Outlook.Application)
            Set tsk = gappOutlook.CreateItem(olTaskItem)
            With tsk
                .Subject = strTaskName
                .StartDate = dteStartDate
                .DueDate = dteDueDate
                .Status = lngStatus
```

Tasks can have one or more contacts, which are stored in the Links collection of the TaskItem object. To add a contact to a task, first the contact is located in a Contacts folder (here the default local Contacts folder is searched), and then the ContactItem is added to the Links collection.

```
            If lngContactID > 0 Then
                'There is a contact for this appointment; attempt to
                'locate this contact in the default Contacts folder.
                Set nms = gappOutlook.GetNamespace("MAPI")
                Set fldContacts = nms.GetDefaultFolder(olFolderContacts)
                'Find contact, using the Subject field
                Set con = fldContacts.Items.Find("[Subject] = " & strSubject)
                If con Is Nothing Then
                    strPrompt = "Can't find Contact ID " & lngContactID _
                        & " in your default local Contacts folder"
                    Debug.Print strPrompt
                Else
                    Set lnks = .Links
                    lnks.Add con
                End If
            .Close(olSave)
        End With

NextItemTask:
        Next varItem

        strTitle = "Done"
        If blnSomeSkipped = True Then
            strPrompt = "All tasks created; some records skipped because " _
                & "of missing information." & vbCrLf & "See " & strDocsPath _
                & "Skipped Records.txt for details."
        Else
            strPrompt = "All tasks created!"
        End If

        MsgBox strPrompt, vbOKOnly + vbInformation, strTitle

    End Select
```

```
ErrorHandlerExit:
    Close #1
    Exit Sub

ErrorHandler:
    If Err = 429 Then
        'Outlook is not running; open Outlook with CreateObject
        Set gappOutlook = CreateObject("Outlook.Application")
        Resume Next
    Else
        MsgBox "Error No: " & Err.Number & "; Description: " & Err.Description
        Resume ErrorHandlerExit
    End If

End Sub
```

Figure 12.10 shows an appointment (with a contact) created from one of the records in tblAppointments.

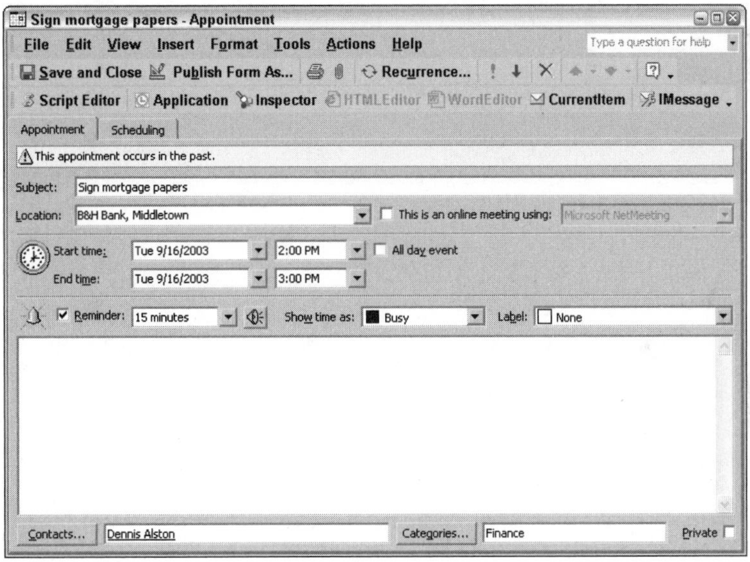

Figure 12.10

Datasheet Form

While the listbox form lets you select multiple Access records for creating Outlook items, you may realize that it has some limitations. It is easy to select all the records in a table, or just a few records selected on an ad hoc basis, but it isn't easy to select large numbers of filtered records—say, creating contact items for all contacts in the state of Idaho. There is no way to do this kind of selection in a listbox, so I made another form, with a datasheet subform, to make it possible to select records using a filter. frmExportToOutlookDatasheet is shown in its initial state in Figure 12.11.

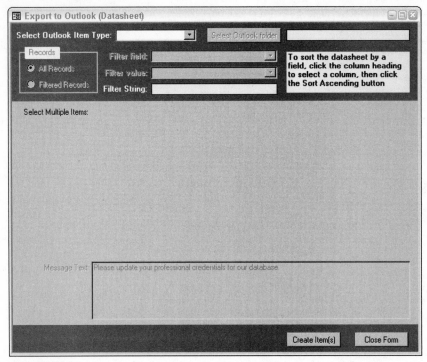

Figure 12.11

As with the listbox form, selecting an Outlook item type from cboSelectOutlookItem selects the appropriate data source, in this case by making one subform visible and the others invisible (each record source has its own subform). cboSelectOutlookItem's AfterUpdate event procedure follows.

```
Private Sub cboSelectOutlookItem_AfterUpdate()


On Error GoTo ErrorHandler

   Me![txtFilterString].Value = Null
   Me![txtSelectedFolder].Value = Null
   plngItemId = Me![cboSelectOutlookItem].Column(0)
   pstrItemType = Me![cboSelectOutlookItem].Column(1)
   pstrItemConstant = Me![cboSelectOutlookItem].Column(2)
   pstrDataSource = Me![cboSelectOutlookItem].Column(3)
   pstrQuery = Nz(Me![cboSelectOutlookItem].Column(3)) & "Alpha"

   If plngItemId <> 0 Then
      Me![cmdSelectOutlookFolder].Enabled = True
   Else
      Me![cmdSelectOutlookFolder].Enabled = False
   End If
```

```
    If plngItemId = 0 Then
        'Mail message selected
        Me![txtMessageText].Enabled = True
    Else
        Me![txtMessageText].Enabled = False
    End If

    Select Case pstrDataSource

        Case "qryContacts"
            Me![subContacts].Visible = True
            Me![subContacts].Locked = True
            Me![subAppointments].Visible = False
            Me![subTasks].Visible = False
            Me![subEMail].Visible = False

        Case "qryAppointments"
            Me![subContacts].Visible = False
            Me![subAppointments].Visible = True
            Me![subAppointments].Locked = True
            Me![subTasks].Visible = False
            Me![subEMail].Visible = False

        Case "qryTasks"
            Me![subContacts].Visible = False
            Me![subAppointments].Visible = False
            Me![subTasks].Visible = True
            Me![subTasks].Locked = True
            Me![subEMail].Visible = False

        Case "qryContactsEMail"
            Me![subContacts].Visible = False
            Me![subAppointments].Visible = False
            Me![subTasks].Visible = False
            Me![subEMail].Visible = True
            Me![subEMail].Locked = True

    End Select

    Me![cboFilterField].Value = Null
    Me![cboFilterValue].Value = Null
    Me![cboFilterField].RowSource = pstrDataSource & "Alpha"
    Me![fraRecords].Enabled = True

ErrorHandlerExit:
    Exit Sub

ErrorHandler:
    MsgBox "Error No: " & Err.Number & "; Description: " & _
        Err.Description
    Resume ErrorHandlerExit

End Sub
```

This procedure also enables the fraRecords option group, where you can select All Records or Filtered Records, and clears the two comboboxes used to select a filter.

Initially, on selecting an Outlook item type, all records are displayed. If you want to filter the records, click Filtered Records in the Records option group. The AfterUpdate procedure of this option group enables the Filter field combobox and sets its row source to the appropriate query. This procedure follows, with commentary for the first Case statement (the others are similar).

```
Private Sub fraRecords_AfterUpdate()

On Error GoTo ErrorHandler

    Dim intRecords As Integer
```

Call a procedure that clears the source objects of all the subforms and the values of the filter controls.

```
    Call ClearList
```

Set a variable representing the choice in fraRecords.

```
    intRecords = Nz(Me![fraRecords].Value, 1)
```

Set up a Select Case statement for the selected data source (the public variable pstrDataSource was set by the selection in cboSelectOutlookItemType).

```
    Select Case pstrDataSource

    Case "qryContacts"
```

Make the subContacts subform visible, and the other subforms invisible.

```
        Me![subContacts].Visible = True
        Me![subContacts].Locked = True
        Me![subAppointments].Visible = False
        Me![subTasks].Visible = False
        Me![subEMail].Visible = False
        If intRecords = 1 Then
```

If All Records was selected in the Records option group, make fsubContactsAll the source object of subContacts, and disable the filter controls.

```
            Me![subContacts].SourceObject = "fsubContactsAll"
            Me![cboFilterField].Enabled = False
            Me![cboFilterField].Value = ""
            Me![cboFilterValue].Enabled = False
        ElseIf intRecords = 2 Then
```

If Filtered Records was selected in the Records option group, clear the source object of subContacts (it will be set later, after making filter selections), and enable cboFilterField.

```
            Me![subContacts].SourceObject = ""
            Me![cboFilterField].Enabled = True
            Me![cboFilterField].Value = ""
            Me![cboFilterValue].Enabled = False
        End If

    Case "qryAppointments"
        Me![subContacts].Visible = False
        Me![subAppointments].Visible = True
        Me![subAppointments].Locked = True
        Me![subTasks].Visible = False
        Me![subEMail].Visible = False
        If intRecords = 1 Then
            Me![subAppointments].SourceObject = "fsubAppointmentsAll"
            Me![cboFilterField].Enabled = False
            Me![cboFilterField].Value = ""
            Me![cboFilterValue].Enabled = False
        ElseIf intRecords = 2 Then
            Me![subAppointments].SourceObject = ""
            Me![cboFilterField].Enabled = True
            Me![cboFilterField].Value = ""
            Me![cboFilterValue].Enabled = False
        End If

    Case "qryTasks"
        Me![subContacts].Visible = False
        Me![subAppointments].Visible = False
        Me![subTasks].Visible = True
        Me![subTasks].Locked = True
        Me![subEMail].Visible = False
        If intRecords = 1 Then
            Me![subTasks].SourceObject = "fsubTasksAll"
            Me![cboFilterField].Enabled = False
            Me![cboFilterField].Value = ""
            Me![cboFilterValue].Enabled = False
        ElseIf intRecords = 2 Then
            Me![subTasks].SourceObject = ""
            Me![cboFilterField].Enabled = True
            Me![cboFilterField].Value = ""
            Me![cboFilterValue].Enabled = False
        End If

    Case "qryContactsEMail"
        Me![subContacts].Visible = False
        Me![subAppointments].Visible = False
        Me![subTasks].Visible = False
        Me![subEMail].Visible = True
        Me![subEMail].Locked = True
```

```
            If intRecords = 1 Then
                Me![subEMail].SourceObject = "fsubEmailAll"
                Me![cboFilterField].Enabled = False
                Me![cboFilterField].Value = ""
                Me![cboFilterValue].Enabled = False
            ElseIf intRecords = 2 Then
                Me![subEMail].SourceObject = ""
                Me![cboFilterField].Enabled = True
                Me![cboFilterField].Value = ""
                Me![cboFilterValue].Enabled = False
            End If

    End Select

ErrorHandlerExit:
    Exit Sub

ErrorHandler:
    MsgBox "Error No: " & Err.Number & "; Description: " & _
        Err.Description
    Resume ErrorHandlerExit

End Sub
```

Using public variables set from the user's initial selection in cboSelectOutlookItemType lets me clear this combobox, but preserve the selected values for use in code running from other controls. I could also save the selection to tblInfo, but in this case, public variables work fine. Saving to tblInfo would be required if I need to preserve the values from one database session to another, or if I want to easily check their values for debugging purposes.

On selecting a field for filtering from cboFilterField, the public variable pstrFilterField is set, and a SQL statement is constructed, using the public variables pstrQuery and pstrFilterField. The SQL statement is assigned as the row source of cboFilterValue, that combobox is requeried, and its list is dropped down. Finally, the make-table query and the table it makes are deleted (if they exist). This procedure follows.

```
Private Sub cboFilterField_AfterUpdate()

On Error GoTo ErrorHandler

    pstrFilterField = Nz(Me![cboFilterField].Value)
    If pstrFilterField = "" Then
        strTitle = "No field selected"
        strPrompt = "Please select a field for filtering"
        MsgBox strPrompt, vbCritical + vbOKOnly, strTitle
        Me![cboFilterField].SetFocus
        GoTo ErrorHandlerExit
    End If

    strSQL = "SELECT DISTINCT " & pstrQuery & ".[" & pstrFilterField & _
        "] FROM " & pstrQuery & " WHERE [" & pstrFilterField & "] Is Not Null;"
    Debug.Print "SQL string: " & strSQL
    With Me![cboFilterValue]
        .Value = Null
```

```
            .RowSource = strSQL
            .Requery
            .Enabled = True
            .SetFocus
            .Dropdown
        End With

        Me![txtFilterString].Value = Null
        Call ClearTables

ErrorHandlerExit:
    Exit Sub

ErrorHandler:
    MsgBox "Error No: " & Err.Number & "; Description: " & _
        Err.Description
    Resume ErrorHandlerExit

End Sub
```

The AfterUpdate procedure of cboFilterValue is more complex; it follows, with commentary.

```
    Private Sub cboFilterValue_AfterUpdate()

    On Error GoTo ErrorHandler

        Dim intDataType As Integer
        Dim fld As DAO.Field
        Dim qdf As DAO.QueryDef
        Dim strTotalsQuery As String
        Dim strLinkedQuery As String
        Dim strFilter As String
```

Set a public variable to the selected filter value.

```
        pvarFilterValue = Me![cboFilterValue].Value
        Debug.Print "Selected value: " & pvarFilterValue
```

Determine the data type of the selected field.

```
        Set dbs = CurrentDb
        Set rst = dbs.OpenRecordset(pstrQuery, dbOpenDynaset)
        Set fld = rst.Fields(pstrFilterField)
        intDataType = fld.Type
        Debug.Print "Field data type: " & intDataType
```

Set up a Select Case statement to create an appropriate filter string for different data types.

```
        Select Case intDataType
            Case 1
                'Boolean
                strFilter = "[" & pstrFilterField & "] = " & pvarFilterValue
```

```
        Case 2, 3, 4, 6, 7
            'Various numeric
            strFilter = "[" & pstrFilterField & "] = " & pvarFilterValue

        Case 5
            'Currency
```

Use CCur to make sure the value is passed as a Currency value.

```
            strFilter = "[" & pstrFilterField & "] = " & CCur(pvarFilterValue)

        Case 8
            'Date
```

Wrap the value in # characters.

```
            strFilter = "[" & pstrFilterField & "] = " & Chr$(35) _
                & pvarFilterValue & Chr$(35)

        Case 10
            'Text
```

Wrap the value in double quotes.

```
            strFilter = "[" & pstrFilterField & "] = " & Chr$(34) _
                & pvarFilterValue & Chr$(34)

        Case 11, 12, 15
            'OLE object, Memo, Replication ID
```

Inform the user that you can't filter by this type of field.

```
            strPrompt = "Can't filter by this field; please select another field"
            MsgBox strPrompt, vbCritical + vbOKOnly
            Me![cboFilterValue].SetFocus
            Me![cboFilterValue].Dropdown
            GoTo ErrorHandlerExit

    End Select
```

Display the filter string just created in the Immediate window for purposes of debugging.

```
    Debug.Print "Filter string: " & strFilter
```

Write the filter string to a locked textbox on the form.

```
    Me![txtFilterString] = strFilter
```

Apply the filter to the selected record source and make a table from it, using a SQL statement to create the make-table query. Making a table rather than just using the query as the subform's source object allows deletion of records on the subform, without affecting the underlying data.

```
    strQuery = "qmakMatchingRecords"
    strSQL = "SELECT " & pstrQuery & ".* INTO tmakMatchingRecords " _
        & "FROM " & pstrQuery & " WHERE " & strFilter & ";"
    Debug.Print "SQL Statement: " & strSQL
    Set qdf = dbs.CreateQueryDef(strQuery, strSQL)
    qdf.Execute
    Me![cboFilterField].Value = Null
    Me![cboFilterValue].Value = Null
```

Display the selected data source name to the Immediate window for purposes of debugging.

```
    Debug.Print "Data source: " & pstrDataSource
```

Set up a Select Case statement to select the appropriate filtered subform as the selected subform's source object. The filtered subforms have the table made by the make-table query earlier (tmakMatchingRecords) as their record source.

```
    Select Case pstrDataSource

        Case "qryContacts"
            Me![subContacts].SourceObject = "fsubContactsFiltered"
            Debug.Print "subContacts source object: " _
                & Me![subContacts].SourceObject

        Case "qryAppointments"
            Me![subAppointments].SourceObject = "fsubAppointmentsFiltered"
            Debug.Print "subAppointments source object: " _
                & Me![subAppointments].SourceObject

        Case "qryTasks"
            Me![subTasks].SourceObject = "fsubTasksFiltered"
            Debug.Print "subTasks source object: " _
                & Me![subTasks].SourceObject

        Case "qryContactsEMail"
            Me![subEMail].SourceObject = "fsubEMailFiltered"
            Debug.Print "subEMail source object: " _
                & Me![subEMail].SourceObject

    End Select

ErrorHandlerExit:
    Exit Sub

ErrorHandler:
    MsgBox "Error No: " & Err.Number & "; Description: " & _
        Err.Description
    Resume ErrorHandlerExit

End Sub
```

Figure 12.12 shows contacts filtered by state.

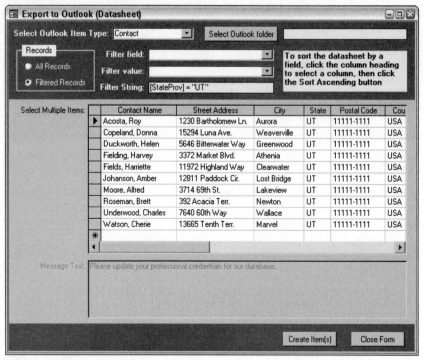

Figure 12.12

The listbox form automatically created items in the default local Contacts, Tasks, Calendar, or Outbox folder. The datasheet form lets you select a folder for creating items. To select an Outlook folder (this option is available for Appointments, Contacts, and Tasks), click the Select Outlook folder command button in the form header. The Click event procedure on this form (listed below) pops up the Outlook Select Folder dialog (shown in Figure 12.13), where you can select a folder. Unfortunately, there is no way to filter this dialog so that it offers all the Outlook folders on your system, whether they are the right type or not. You can't create contacts in a Tasks folder or vice versa, so the code checks the folder type by examining its DefaultItemType property to see whether it matches the item type selected in the cboSelectOutlookItemType combobox. (The exception is mail messages, which are always created in the Outbox—or the Drafts folder, if you are using the Redemption Library; the Select Outlook folder command button is disabled if you select Mail message as the Outlook item type.)

```
Private Sub cmdSelectOutlookFolder_Click()

On Error GoTo ErrorHandler

    Dim nms As Outlook.NameSpace

    Set gappOutlook = GetObject(, Outlook.Application)
    Set nms = gappOutlook.GetNamespace("MAPI")

SelectFolder:
```

Set a public variable to the selected folder. This is the actual folder object itself, not the folder name.

```
    Set pfld = nms.PickFolder
    If pfld Is Nothing Then
        GoTo ErrorHandlerExit
    End If
```

Test whether folder is the right type for the selected Outlook item type.

```
    Debug.Print "Default item type: " & pfld.DefaultItemType
    If pfld.DefaultItemType <> plngItemId Then
        MsgBox "Please select a " & pstrItemType & " folder"
        GoTo SelectFolder
    End If
```

Display the name of the selected folder in a textbox on the form.

```
    pstrFolderName = pfld.Name
    Me![txtSelectedFolder].Value = pstrFolderName

ErrorHandlerExit:
    Exit Sub

ErrorHandler:
    If Err = 429 Then
        'Outlook is not running; open Outlook with CreateObject.
        Set gappOutlook = CreateObject("Outlook.Application")
        Resume Next
    Else
        MsgBox "Error No: " & Err.Number & "; Description: " & Err.Description
        Resume ErrorHandlerExit
    End If

End Sub
```

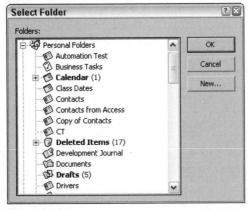

Figure 12.13

Figure 12.14 shows the Contacts from Access folder, with the Utah contacts exported from Access.

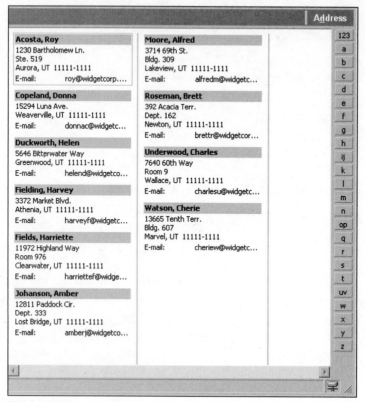

Figure 12.14

The Create Items command button does the work of creating the items, in the selected folder. Its procedure is similar to that of the button on the listbox form, except that instead of picking up data from columns of a listbox, it uses a DAO recordset to pick up data from fields of a query or table. The cmdCreateItems Click event procedure follows, with commentary.

```
Private Sub cmdCreateItems_Click()

On Error GoTo ErrorHandler
```

Declare variables for values from the Access tables, Outlook objects, and DAO objects for working with recordsets.

```
Dim blnSomeSkipped As Boolean
Dim dteDueDate As Date
Dim dteEndDate As Date
Dim dteEndTime As Date
Dim dteLastMeeting As Date
Dim dteStartDate As Date
Dim dteStartTime As Date
```

```
Dim fldContacts As Outlook.MAPIFolder
Dim intRecords As Integer
Dim lngAppointmentID As Long
Dim lngContactID As Long
Dim lngStatus As Long
Dim lnks As Outlook.Links
Dim rstData As DAO.Recordset
Dim strBody As String
Dim strCity As String
Dim strCompanyName As String
Dim strContactName As String
Dim strCountry As String
Dim strEMailRecipient As String
Dim strFile As String
Dim strFullName As String
Dim strJobTitle As String
Dim strMessage As String
Dim strMessageText As String
Dim strPostalCode As String
Dim strSalutation As String
Dim strStateProv As String
Dim strStatus As String
Dim strStreetAddress As String
Dim strSubject As String
Dim strTaskName As String
Dim strTest As String
Dim strTestFile As String
```

Check that an Outlook item type has been selected, and exit if it has not.

```
Debug.Print "Selected item type: " & pstrItemType
If pstrItemType = "" Then
    Me![cboSelectOutlookItem].SetFocus
    Me![cboSelectOutlookItem].Dropdown
    MsgBox "Please select an Outlook item type", vbCritical
    GoTo ErrorHandlerExit
End If

intRecords = Me![fraRecords].Value
strMessageText = Nz(Me![MessageText])
```

Set a global Outlook application variable; if Outlook is not running, the error handler defaults to CreateObject.

```
Set gappOutlook = GetObject(, "Outlook.Application")
Set nms = appOutlook.GetNamespace("MAPI")
```

Open a text file for writing information about skipped records.

```
strFile = strDocsPath & "Skipped Records.txt"
Open strFile For Output As #1
Print #1, "These records were skipped when creating documents"
Print #1,
```

Determine what type of Outlook item is to be used, what Outlook folder is to be used, and whether all records or filtered records are to be merged.

```
Debug.Print "Data source: " & pstrDataSource

If Me![fraRecords].Value = 2 Then
```

Filtered records—change data source to the filtered table.

```
    pstrDataSource = "tmakMatchingRecords"
Else
```

For the All Records selection, keep the selection made in cboSelectOutlookItem.

```
End If
```

Set up a Select Case statement to set the global pfld variable appropriately for each item type, in case a specific folder is not selected.

```
Select Case plngItemId

    Case 0
        Set pfld = nms.GetDefaultFolder(olFolderOutbox)
        pstrFolderName = "Outbox"

    Case 1
        pstrFolderName = "Calendar"
        Set pfld = nms.GetDefaultFolder(olFolderCalendar)

    Case 2
        pstrFolderName = "Contacts"
        Set pfld = nms.GetDefaultFolder(olFolderContacts)

    Case 3
        pstrFolderName = "Tasks"
        Set pfld = nms.GetDefaultFolder(olFolderTasks)

End Select

Debug.Print "Selected folder: " & pstrFolderName
```

Set up a DAO recordset based on the selected data source.

```
Set dbs = CurrentDb
Set rstData = dbs.OpenRecordset(pstrDataSource, dbOpenDynaset)
```

Set up a Select Case statement to deal with each Outlook item type.

```
Select Case pstrItemType

    Case "Appointment"
```

Set blnSomeSkipped to False to start with—it will be set to True if any records have to be skipped because of missing data.

```
blnSomeSkipped = False
```

Set up a For Each . . . Next loop to deal with each item in the datasheet.

```
With rstData
    Do While Not .EOF
```

Get the Appointment ID use later in the code.

```
lngAppointmentID = Nz(![AppointmentID])
Debug.Print "Appointment ID: " & lngAppointmentID
```

Check for required appointment information, and set blnSomeSkipped to True if anything is missing.

```
strTest = Nz(![Topic])
Debug.Print "Topic: " & strTest
If strTest = "" Then
    blnSomeSkipped = True
    Print #1,
    Print #1, "No topic for Appointment " & lngAppointmentID
    GoTo NextItemAppt
Else
    strSubject = Nz(![Topic])
End If

strTest = Nz(![StartTime])
Debug.Print "Start time: " & strTest
If strTest = "" Then
    blnSomeSkipped = True
```

Print a line about the missing information to the Skipped Records text file.

```
    Print #1,
    Print #1, "No start time for Appointment " & lngAppointmentID
    GoTo NextItemAppt
End If
```

Create a new appointment in the selected folder.

```
Set appt = pfld.Items.Add
appt.Subject = strSubject
```

Write StartTime and EndTime properties only if there is a valid date in the corresponding Access table fields.

```
If IsDate(![StartTime]) = True Then
    dteStartTime = CDate(![StartTime])
    Debug.Print dteStartTime
    appt.Start = dteStartTime
```

```
                                 End If
                                 If IsDate(![EndTime]) = True Then
                                     dteEndTime = CDate(![EndTime])
                                     Debug.Print dteEndTime
                                     appt.Start = dteEndTime
                                 End If
                                 appt.Location = Nz(![Location])
                                 appt.Categories = Nz(![Category])

                                 lngContactID = Nz(![ContactID])
                                 strContactName = Nz(![ContactName])
                                 Debug.Print "Contact name: " & strContactName
```

Appointments can have one or more contacts, which are stored in the Links collection of the AppointmentItem object. To add a contact to an appointment, first the contact is located in a Contacts folder (here the default local Contacts folder is searched), and then the ContactItem is added to the Links collection.

```
                      If lngContactID > 0 Then
                          Set fldContacts = nms.GetDefaultFolder(olFolderContacts)
On Error Resume Next
                          Set con = fldContacts.Items.Find("[CustomerID] = " _
                              & lngContactID)
                          If con Is Nothing Then
                              strPrompt = "Can't find Contact ID " & lngContactID _
                                  & " in your default local Contacts folder"
                              Debug.Print strPrompt
                          Else
                              Set lnks = appt.Links
                              lnks.Add con
                          End If
On Error GoTo ErrorHandler
                      End If
                      appt.Close (olSave)
```

Go the next record.

```
NextItemAppt:
                  .MoveNext
              Loop
              .Close
          End With
```

When all the selected records have been processed, put up an informative message box.

```
                  strTitle = "Done"
                  If blnSomeSkipped = True Then
                      strPrompt = "All appointments created; some records skipped " _
                          & "because of missing information." & vbCrLf & _
                              "See " & strDocsPath & "Skipped Records.txt for details."
                  Else
                      strPrompt = "All appointments created in " & pstrFolderName _
                          & " folder"
```

```
            End If

            MsgBox strPrompt, vbOKOnly + vbInformation, strTitle
```

Other cases are handled similarly.

```
    Case "Contact"
        blnSomeSkipped = False

        With rstData
            Do While Not .EOF
                'Get Contact ID for reference
                lngContactID = Nz(![ContactID])
                Debug.Print "Contact ID: " & lngContactID

                'Check for required name information
                strTest = Nz(![ContactName])
                Debug.Print "Contact name: " & strTest
                If strTest = "" Then
                    blnSomeSkipped = True
                    Print #1,
                    Print #1, "No name for Contact " & lngContactID
                    GoTo NextItemContact
                End If

                strFullName = Nz(![FirstNameFirst])
                strJobTitle = Nz(![JobTitle])
                strStreetAddress = Nz(![StreetAddress])
                strCity = Nz(![City])
                strStateProv = Nz(![StateProv])
                strPostalCode = Nz(![PostalCode])
                strCountry = Nz(![Country])
                strCompanyName = Nz(![CompanyName])
                strSalutation = Nz(![Salutation])
                strEMailRecipient = Nz(![EmailName])

                'Create new contact item in selected folder
                Set con = pfld.Items.Add
                With con
                    .CustomerID = lngContactID
                    .FullName = strFullName
                    .JobTitle = strJobTitle
                    .BusinessAddressStreet = strStreetAddress
                    .BusinessAddressCity = strCity
                    .BusinessAddressState = strStateProv
                    .BusinessAddressPostalCode = strPostalCode
                    .BusinessAddressCountry = strCountry
                    .CompanyName = strCompanyName
                    .NickName = strSalutation
                    .Email1Address = strEMailRecipient
                    .Close (olSave)
                End With

NextItemContact:
```

```
               .MoveNext
         Loop
         .Close
      End With

      strTitle = "Done"
      If blnSomeSkipped = True Then
         strPrompt = "All contacts created; some records skipped because " _
            & "of missing information." & vbCrLf & "See " & strDocsPath _
            & "Skipped Records.txt for details."
      Else
         strPrompt = "All contacts created in " & pstrFolderName & " folder"
      End If

      MsgBox strPrompt, vbOKOnly + vbInformation, strTitle

   Case "Mail message"
      blnSomeSkipped = False

      With rstData
         Do While Not .EOF
            'Get Contact ID for reference
            lngContactID = Nz(![ContactID])
            Debug.Print "Contact ID: " & lngContactID

            'Check for required email information
            strTest = Nz(![EmailName])
            Debug.Print "Email address: " & strTest
            If strTest = "" Then
               blnSomeSkipped = True
               Print #1,
               Print #1, "No email address for Contact " & lngContactID
               GoTo NextItemMail
            End If

            strEMailRecipient = Nz(![EmailName])
            dteLastMeeting = Nz(![LastMeetingDate])
            strMessage = Nz(Me![MessageText])
            If strMessage <> "" Then
               strBody = strMessage
            Else
               strBody = "Your last meeting was on " & dteLastMeeting _
                  & "; please call to arrange a meeting by the end of the year."
            End If

            'Create new mail message
            Set msg = pfld.Items.Add
            With msg
               .To = strEMailRecipient
               .Subject = "Reminder"
               .Body = strBody
               .Send
            End With
```

```
NextItemMail:
            .MoveNext
        Loop
        .Close
    End With

    strTitle = "Done"
    If blnSomeSkipped = True Then
        strPrompt = "All mail messages created; some records skipped " _
            & " because of missing information." & vbCrLf & "See " _
                & strDocsPath _
            & "Skipped Records.txt for details."
    Else
        strPrompt = "All mail messages created in " & pstrFolderName
    End If

    MsgBox strPrompt, vbOKOnly + vbInformation, strTitle

Case "Task"
    blnSomeSkipped = False

    With rstData
        Do While Not .EOF
            'Check for required task information
            strTest = Nz(![TaskName])
            Debug.Print "Task: " & strTest
            If strTest = "" Then
                blnSomeSkipped = True
                Print #1,
                Print #1, "No task name"
                GoTo NextItemTask
            End If

            strTaskName = Nz(![TaskName])
            lngContactID = Nz(![ContactID])
            dteStartDate = Nz(![StartDate])
            dteDueDate = Nz(![DueDate])
            strStatus = Nz(![Status])
```

Convert the Status text from the Access table into a Long value for writing to the Outlook record.

```
            lngStatus = Switch(strStatus = "Not started", 0, _
                strStatus = "In progress", 1, _
                strStatus = "Completed", 2, "", 0)

            'Create new task item in selected Tasks folder
            Set tsk = pfld.Items.Add
            tsk.Subject = strTaskName
            tsk.StartDate = dteStartDate
            tsk.DueDate = dteDueDate
            tsk.Status = lngStatus
```

Tasks can have one or more contacts, which are stored in the Links collection of the TaskItem object. To add a contact to a task, first the contact is located in a Contacts folder (here the default local Contacts folder is searched) and then the ContactItem is added to the Links collection.

```
            lngContactID = Nz(![ContactID])
            strContactName = Nz(![ContactName])
            Debug.Print "Contact name: " & strContactName

            'Add contact to item, using the Links collection
            If lngContactID > 0 Then
                'There is a contact for this appointment; attempt to
                'locate this contact in the default Contacts folder.
                Set fldContacts = nms.GetDefaultFolder(olFolderContacts)
On Error Resume Next
                Set con = fldContacts.Items.Find("[CustomerID] = " _
                    & lngContactID)
                If con Is Nothing Then
                    strPrompt = "Can't find Contact ID " & lngContactID _
                        & " in your default local Contacts folder"
                    Debug.Print strPrompt
                Else
                    Set lnks = tsk.Links
                    lnks.Add con
                End If
            End If
            tsk.Close (olSave)

NextItemTask:
            .MoveNext
        Loop
        .Close
    End With

    strTitle = "Done"
    If blnSomeSkipped = True Then
        strPrompt = "All tasks created; some records skipped because " _
            & "of missing information." & vbCrLf & "See " & strDocsPath _
            & "Skipped Records.txt for details."
    Else
        strPrompt = "All tasks created in " & pstrFolderName & " folder"
    End If

    MsgBox strPrompt, vbOKOnly + vbInformation, strTitle

End Select

ErrorHandlerExit:
    Close #1
    Exit Sub

ErrorHandler:
    If Err = 429 Then
        'Outlook is not running; open Outlook with CreateObject.
        Set appOutlook = CreateObject("Outlook.Application")
```

```
        Resume Next
    Else
        MsgBox "Error No: " & Err.Number & "; Description: " & Err.Description
        Resume ErrorHandlerExit
    End If

End Sub
```

Email a Report Form

The final form illustrating exporting Access data to Outlook shows you how to output an Access report to one of a variety of formats and then email the exported report. The EMail Access Report form is shown in Figure 12.15.

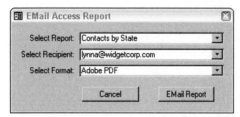

Figure 12.15

It is a simple form, with three comboboxes for selecting the report, recipient, and format, and a command button to save the report to the selected format and email it to the recipient. The cboSelectReport combobox has tlkpReports as its row source, a lookup table that lists report names and their record sources. cboSelectRecipient uses qryContacts as its row source with contact names and email addresses. cboSelectFormat has tlkpFormats as its row source, listing the available formats and their extensions (for use in code.

The available formats have their advantages and disadvantages, which are listed in the following table.

Format Type	Advantages	Disadvantages
Access Snapshot	Excellent appearance; not editable.	Users who don't have Access have to install the Snapshot Viewer to view it.
Adobe PDF	Excellent appearance; not editable. Almost everybody has the Adobe Viewer, or can easily download and install it.	You have to purchase Adobe Acrobat to generate these files (or use a third-party utility that doesn't work as well, and is probably illegal).
Comma-Delimited Text File	Widely supported format; excellent for importing into other databases.	Doesn't look like the report.
Excel Worksheet	Many users have Excel; a good choice if the data needs to be manipulated.	Doesn't look like the report.

Table continued on following page

Format Type	Advantages	Disadvantages
Plain Text	The lowest common denominator format; anyone who has even Notepad can view this format.	Doesn't look like the report.
Rich Text	Looks somewhat like the report, though there are some appearance problems.	Need Word to view it.

The code on the cmdEMailReport command button's Click event calls one of a group of Sub procedures, depending on the chosen format. This procedure is listed below, with commentary.

```
Private Sub cmdEMailReport_Click()

On Error GoTo ErrorHandler

    Dim strFormatType As String
```

Pick up format type from combobox.

```
    strFormatType = Me![cboSelectFormat].Column(0)
    Debug.Print "Selected format: " & strFormatType
```

Set up Select Case statement to process each format type separately by calling a Sub procedure.

```
    Select Case strFormatType

        Case "Access Snapshot"
            Call SendReportSNP(Me)

        Case "Adobe PDF"
            Call SendReportPDF(Me)

        Case "Rich Text"
            Call SendReportRTF(Me)

        Case "Comma-Delimited Text File"
            Call SendReportCSV(Me)

        Case "Plain Text"
            Call SendReportTXT(Me)

        Case "Excel Worksheet"
            Call SendReportWKS(Me)

    End Select

ErrorHandlerExit:
    Exit Sub

ErrorHandler:
```

```
      MsgBox "Error No: " & Err.Number & "; Description: " & _
         Err.Description
      Resume ErrorHandlerExit

   End Sub
```

The procedures for the different formats (located in the basOutlookAutomation module) follow, with commentary (full commentary only for the first procedure).

```
   Sub SendReportSNP(frm As Access.Form)

   On Error GoTo ErrorHandler
```

Set variables for the report name, data source, display name, email address, Contact ID, output file name, and extension, file path, and concatenated file name and path.

```
      strReport = Nz(frm![cboSelectReport].Column(0))
      strDataSource = Nz(frm![cboSelectReport].Column(2))
      strDisplayName = Nz(frm![cboSelectReport].Column(1))
      strEMailRecipient = Nz(frm![cboSelectRecipient].Column(0))
      lngContactID = frm![cboSelectRecipient].Column(2)
      strFileName = Mid(Nz(frm![cboSelectReport].Column(0)), 4)
      strExtension = Nz(frm![cboSelectFormat].Column(1))
      strFilePath = GetDocsDir()
      strFileAndPath = strFilePath & strFileName & strExtension
      Debug.Print "File name and path: " & strFileAndPath
```

Initialize the progress bar (using an arbitrary division of four units).

```
      varReturn = SysCmd(acSysCmdInitMeter, _
         "Creating output file ...", 4)
```

Update the progress bar.

```
      varReturn = SysCmd(acSysCmdUpdateMeter, 1)
```

Use the FileSystemObject to test whether there is an old file, and delete it if there is one.

```
      Set fso = CreateObject("Scripting.FileSystemObject")
      If fso.FileExists(strFileAndPath) = True Then
         fso.DeleteFile strFileAndPath
      End If

      'Update the progress bar
      varReturn = SysCmd(acSysCmdUpdateMeter, 2)
```

Create the new snapshot file in the Documents\Access Merge folder, using the OutputTo method.

```
      DoCmd.OutputTo objecttype:=acOutputReport, _
         objectname:=strReport, _
         outputformat:=acFormatSNP, _
         outputfile:=strFileAndPath, _
```

473

```
        autostart:=False

    'Update the progress bar
    varReturn = SysCmd(acSysCmdUpdateMeter, 3)
```

Test for the existence of the specified report file, using the FileSystemObject, with a loop to prevent premature cancellation.

```
TryAgain:
    Set fso = CreateObject("Scripting.FileSystemObject")
    If fso.FileExists(strFileAndPath) = False Then
        GoTo TryAgain
    End If

    'Update the progress bar
    varReturn = SysCmd(acSysCmdUpdateMeter, 4)
```

Create the new mail message and attach the snapshot file to it.

```
    Set appOutlook = GetObject(, Outlook.Application)
    Set itm = appOutlook.CreateItem(olMailItem)
    With itm
        .To = strEMailRecipient
        .Subject = strDisplayName & " report"
        .Body = "This file was exported from " & strReport _
            & " on " & Format(Date, "m/d/yyyy") & "." & vbCrLf & vbCrLf _
            & "You need the Access Snapshot Viewer to view this file." _
            & vbCrLf & vbCrLf
        .Attachments.Add strFileAndPath
        .Display
    End With

ErrorHandlerExit:
    'Remove the progress bar
    varReturn = SysCmd(acSysCmdRemoveMeter)
    Exit Sub

ErrorHandler:
    If Err = 429 Then
        'Outlook is not running; open Outlook with CreateObject.
        Set appOutlook = CreateObject("Outlook.Application")
        Resume Next
    Else
        MsgBox "Error No: " & Err.Number & "; Description: " & Err.Description
        Resume ErrorHandlerExit
    End If

End Sub

Sub
SendReportRTF(frm As Access.Form)

On Error GoTo ErrorHandler
```

```
strReport = Nz(frm![cboSelectReport].Column(0))
strDataSource = Nz(frm![cboSelectReport].Column(2))
strDisplayName = Nz(frm![cboSelectReport].Column(1))
strEMailRecipient = Nz(frm![cboSelectRecipient].Column(0))
lngContactID = frm![cboSelectRecipient].Column(2)
strFileName = Mid(Nz(frm![cboSelectReport].Column(0)), 4)
strExtension = Nz(frm![cboSelectFormat].Column(1))
strFilePath = GetDocsDir()
strFileAndPath = strFilePath & strFileName & strExtension
Debug.Print "File name and path: " & strFileAndPath


'Initialize the progress bar (using an arbitrary division of four units).
varReturn = SysCmd(acSysCmdInitMeter, _
    "Creating output file ...", 4)


'Update the progress bar.
varReturn = SysCmd(acSysCmdUpdateMeter, 1)


'Delete old file, if there is one
Set fso = CreateObject("Scripting.FileSystemObject")
If fso.FileExists(strFileAndPath) = True Then
    fso.DeleteFile strFileAndPath
End If


'Update the progress bar.
varReturn = SysCmd(acSysCmdUpdateMeter, 2)


'Create new rich text file in Documents\Access Merge folder
DoCmd.OutputTo objecttype:=acOutputReport, _
    objectname:=strReport, _
    outputformat:=acFormatRTF, _
    outputfile:=strFileAndPath, _
    autostart:=False


'Test for existence of specified report file, with loop
'to prevent premature cancellation
TryAgain:
    Set fso = CreateObject("Scripting.FileSystemObject")
    If fso.FileExists(strFileAndPath) = False Then
        GoTo TryAgain
    End If


'Update the progress bar.
varReturn = SysCmd(acSysCmdUpdateMeter, 3)


'Create new mail message and attach rich text file to it
Set appOutlook = GetObject(, Outlook.Application)
Set itm = appOutlook.CreateItem(olMailItem)
With itm
    .To = strEMailRecipient
    .Subject = strDisplayName & " report"
    .Body = "This file was exported from " & strReport _
        & " on " & Format(Date, "m/d/yyyy") & "." & vbCrLf & vbCrLf _
        & "You need Word to view this file." _
        & vbCrLf & vbCrLf
```

```
            .Attachments.Add strFileAndPath
            .Display
        End With

        'Update the progress bar.
        varReturn = SysCmd(acSysCmdUpdateMeter, 4)

ErrorHandlerExit:
        'Remove the progress bar.
        varReturn = SysCmd(acSysCmdRemoveMeter)
        Exit Sub

ErrorHandler:
        If Err = 429 Then
            'Outlook is not running; open Outlook with CreateObject.
            Set appOutlook = CreateObject("Outlook.Application")
            Resume Next
        Else
            MsgBox "Error No: " & Err.Number & "; Description: " & Err.Description
            Resume ErrorHandlerExit
        End If

End Sub

Sub SendReportTXT(frm As Access.Form)

On Error GoTo ErrorHandler

        strReport = Nz(frm![cboSelectReport].Column(0))
        strDataSource = Nz(frm![cboSelectReport].Column(2))
        strDisplayName = Nz(frm![cboSelectReport].Column(1))
        strEMailRecipient = Nz(frm![cboSelectRecipient].Column(0))
        lngContactID = frm![cboSelectRecipient].Column(2)
        strFileName = Mid(Nz(frm![cboSelectReport].Column(0)), 4)
        strExtension = Nz(frm![cboSelectFormat].Column(1))
        strFilePath = GetDocsDir()
        strFileAndPath = strFilePath & strFileName & strExtension
        Debug.Print "File name and path: " & strFileAndPath

        'Initialize the progress bar (using an arbitrary division of four units).
        varReturn = SysCmd(acSysCmdInitMeter, _
            "Creating output file ...", 4)

        'Update the progress bar.
        varReturn = SysCmd(acSysCmdUpdateMeter, 1)

        'Delete old file, if there is one
        Set fso = CreateObject("Scripting.FileSystemObject")
        If fso.FileExists(strFileAndPath) = True Then
            fso.DeleteFile strFileAndPath
        End If

        'Update the progress bar.
        varReturn = SysCmd(acSysCmdUpdateMeter, 2)
```

```
    'Create new rich text file in Documents\Access Merge folder
    DoCmd.OutputTo objecttype:=acOutputReport, _
        objectname:=strReport, _
        outputformat:=acFormatTXT, _
        outputfile:=strFileAndPath, _
        autostart:=False


    'Test for existence of specified report file, with loop
    'to prevent premature cancellation
TryAgain:
    Set fso = CreateObject("Scripting.FileSystemObject")
    If fso.FileExists(strFileAndPath) = False Then
        GoTo TryAgain
    End If

    'Update the progress bar.
    varReturn = SysCmd(acSysCmdUpdateMeter, 3)

    'Create new mail message and attach text file to it
    Set appOutlook = GetObject(, Outlook.Application)
    Set itm = appOutlook.CreateItem(olMailItem)
    With itm
        .To = strEMailRecipient
        .Subject = strDisplayName & " report"
        .Body = "This file was exported from " & strReport _
            & " on " & Format(Date, "m/d/yyyy") & "." & vbCrLf & vbCrLf
        .Attachments.Add strFileAndPath
        .Display
    End With

    'Update the progress bar.
    varReturn = SysCmd(acSysCmdUpdateMeter, 4)

ErrorHandlerExit:
    'Remove the progress bar
    varReturn = SysCmd(acSysCmdRemoveMeter)
    Exit Sub

ErrorHandler:
    If Err = 429 Then
        'Outlook is not running; open Outlook with CreateObject.
        Set appOutlook = CreateObject("Outlook.Application")
        Resume Next
    Else
        MsgBox "Error No: " & Err.Number & "; Description: " & Err.Description
        Resume ErrorHandlerExit
    End If

End Sub

Sub SendReportWKS(frm As Access.Form)

On Error GoTo ErrorHandler
```

```
    strReport = Nz(frm![cboSelectReport].Column(0))
    strDataSource = Nz(frm![cboSelectReport].Column(2))
    strDisplayName = Nz(frm![cboSelectReport].Column(1))
    strEMailRecipient = Nz(frm![cboSelectRecipient].Column(0))
    lngContactID = frm![cboSelectRecipient].Column(2)
    strFileName = Mid(Nz(frm![cboSelectReport].Column(0)), 4)
    strExtension = Nz(frm![cboSelectFormat].Column(1))
    strFilePath = GetDocsDir()
    strFileAndPath = strFilePath & strFileName & strExtension
    Debug.Print "File name and path: " & strFileAndPath

    'Initialize the progress bar (using an arbitrary division of four units).
    varReturn = SysCmd(acSysCmdInitMeter, _
        "Creating output file ...", 4)

    'Update the progress bar.
    varReturn = SysCmd(acSysCmdUpdateMeter, 1)

    'Delete old file, if there is one
    Set fso = CreateObject("Scripting.FileSystemObject")
    If fso.FileExists(strFileAndPath) = True Then
        fso.DeleteFile strFileAndPath
    End If

    'Update the progress bar.
    varReturn = SysCmd(acSysCmdUpdateMeter, 2)

    'Create new worksheet file in Documents\Access Merge folder
    DoCmd.OutputTo objecttype:=acOutputReport, _
        objectname:=strReport, _
        outputformat:=acFormatXLS, _
        outputfile:=strFileAndPath, _
        autostart:=False

    'Test for existence of specified report file, with loop
    'to prevent premature cancellation
TryAgain:
    Set fso = CreateObject("Scripting.FileSystemObject")
    If fso.FileExists(strFileAndPath) = False Then
        GoTo TryAgain
    End If

    'Update the progress bar.
    varReturn = SysCmd(acSysCmdUpdateMeter, 3)

    'Create new mail message and attach worksheet file to it
    Set appOutlook = GetObject(, Outlook.Application)
    Set itm = appOutlook.CreateItem(olMailItem)
    With itm
        .To = strEMailRecipient
        .Subject = strDisplayName & " report"
        .Body = "This file was exported from " & strReport _
            & " on " & Format(Date, "m/d/yyyy") & "." & vbCrLf & vbCrLf _
            & "You need Excel to view this file." _
            & vbCrLf & vbCrLf
```

```
        .Attachments.Add strFileAndPath
        .Display
    End With

    'Update the progress bar.
    varReturn = SysCmd(acSysCmdUpdateMeter, 4)

ErrorHandlerExit:
    'Remove the progress bar
    varReturn = SysCmd(acSysCmdRemoveMeter)
    Exit Sub

ErrorHandler:
    If Err = 429 Then
        'Outlook is not running; open Outlook with CreateObject.
        Set appOutlook = CreateObject("Outlook.Application")
        Resume Next
    Else
        MsgBox "Error No: " & Err.Number & "; Description: " & Err.Description
        Resume ErrorHandlerExit
    End If

End Sub

Sub SendReportCSV(frm As Access.Form)

On Error GoTo ErrorHandler

    strReport = Nz(frm![cboSelectReport].Column(0))
    strDataSource = Nz(frm![cboSelectReport].Column(2))
    strSpec = Mid(strDataSource, 4) & " Export Specification"
    strDisplayName = Nz(frm![cboSelectReport].Column(1))
    strEMailRecipient = Nz(frm![cboSelectRecipient].Column(0))
    lngContactID = frm![cboSelectRecipient].Column(2)
    strFileName = Mid(Nz(frm![cboSelectReport].Column(0)), 4)
    strExtension = Nz(frm![cboSelectFormat].Column(1))
    strFilePath = GetDocsDir()
    strFileAndPath = strFilePath & strFileName & strExtension
    Debug.Print "File name and path: " & strFileAndPath

    'Initialize the progress bar (using an arbitrary division of 5 units).
    varReturn = SysCmd(acSysCmdInitMeter, _
        "Creating output file ...", 5)

    'Update the progress bar.
    varReturn = SysCmd(acSysCmdUpdateMeter, 1)

    'Delete old file, if there is one
    Set fso = CreateObject("Scripting.FileSystemObject")
    If fso.FileExists(strFileAndPath) = True Then
        fso.DeleteFile strFileAndPath
    End If

    'Update the progress bar.
    varReturn = SysCmd(acSysCmdUpdateMeter, 2)
```

Create a new comma-delimited text file in the Documents\Access Merge folder, using the TransferText method.

```
    DoCmd.TransferText transfertype:=acExportDelim, _
       specificationname:=strSpec, _
       TableName:=strDataSource, _
       FileName:=strFileAndPath, _
       HasFieldNames:=True

    'Update the progress bar.
    varReturn = SysCmd(acSysCmdUpdateMeter, 3)

    'Test for existence of specified report file, with loop
    'to prevent premature cancellation
TryAgain:
    Set fso = CreateObject("Scripting.FileSystemObject")
    If fso.FileExists(strFileAndPath) = False Then
       GoTo TryAgain
    End If

    'Update the progress bar.
    varReturn = SysCmd(acSysCmdUpdateMeter, 4)

    'Create new mail message and attach comma-delimited text file to it
    Set appOutlook = GetObject(, Outlook.Application)
    Set itm = appOutlook.CreateItem(olMailItem)
    With itm
       .To = strEMailRecipient
       .Subject = strDisplayName & " report"
       .Body = "This file was exported from " & strDataSource & _
          " on " & Format(Date, "m/d/yyyy") & "." & vbCrLf & vbCrLf
       .Attachments.Add strFileAndPath
       .Display
    End With

    'Update the progress bar.
    varReturn = SysCmd(acSysCmdUpdateMeter, 5)

ErrorHandlerExit:
    'Remove the progress bar.
    varReturn = SysCmd(acSysCmdRemoveMeter)
    Exit Sub

ErrorHandler:
    If Err = 429 Then
       'Outlook is not running; open Outlook with CreateObject.
       Set appOutlook = CreateObject("Outlook.Application")
       Resume Next
    Else
       MsgBox "Error No: " & Err.Number & "; Description: " & Err.Description
       Resume ErrorHandlerExit
    End If

End Sub

Sub SendReportPDF(frm As Access.Form)
```

This code assumes that you have installed Adobe Acrobat and have assigned the PDF printer to a copy of each report, with "PDF" appended to its name.

```
On Error GoTo ErrorHandler

    strReport = Nz(frm![cboSelectReport].Column(0)) & "PDF"
    strDataSource = Nz(frm![cboSelectReport].Column(2))
    strDisplayName = Nz(frm![cboSelectReport].Column(1))
    strEMailRecipient = Nz(frm![cboSelectRecipient].Column(0))
    lngContactID = frm![cboSelectRecipient].Column(2)
    strFileName = Nz(frm![cboSelectReport].Column(1))
    strExtension = Nz(frm![cboSelectFormat].Column(1))
    strFilePath = GetDocsDir()
    strFileAndPath = strFilePath & strFileName & strExtension
    Debug.Print "File name and path: " & strFileAndPath

    'Initialize the progress bar (using an arbitrary division of 3 units)
    varReturn = SysCmd(acSysCmdInitMeter, _
        "Creating output file ...", 4)

    'Update the progress bar.
    varReturn = SysCmd(acSysCmdUpdateMeter, 1)
```

Create the PDF file by printing the report to the PDF printer, previously selected for this report.

```
    DoCmd.OpenReport strReport, acViewNormal

    varReturn = SysCmd(acSysCmdUpdateMeter, 2)

    'Test for existence of specified report file, with loop
    'to prevent premature cancellation
TryAgain:
    Set fso = CreateObject("Scripting.FileSystemObject")
    If fso.FileExists(strFileAndPath) = False Then
        GoTo TryAgain
    End If

    'Update the progress bar.
    varReturn = SysCmd(acSysCmdUpdateMeter, 3)

    'Create new mail message and attach PDF file to it
    Set appOutlook = GetObject(, Outlook.Application)
    Set itm = appOutlook.CreateItem(olMailItem)
    With itm
        .To = strEMailRecipient
        .Subject = strDisplayName & " report"
        .Body = "This file was exported from " & strReport & _
            " on " & Format(Date, "m/d/yyyy") & "." _
            & vbCrLf & vbCrLf _
            & "You need the Adobe Acrobat Viewer to open this file." _
            & vbCrLf & vbCrLf
        .Attachments.Add strFileAndPath
        .Display
    End With
```

```
        'Update the progress bar.
        varReturn = SysCmd(acSysCmdUpdateMeter, 4)

ErrorHandlerExit:
    'Remove the progress bar
    varReturn = SysCmd(acSysCmdRemoveMeter)
    Exit Sub

ErrorHandler:
    If Err = 429 Then
        'Outlook is not running; open Outlook with CreateObject.
        Set appOutlook = CreateObject("Outlook.Application")
        Resume Next
    Else
        MsgBox "Error No: " & Err.Number & "; Description: " & Err.Description
        Resume ErrorHandlerExit
    End If

End Sub
```

Figure 12.16 shows the EBooks by Category report exported to Adobe PDF format.

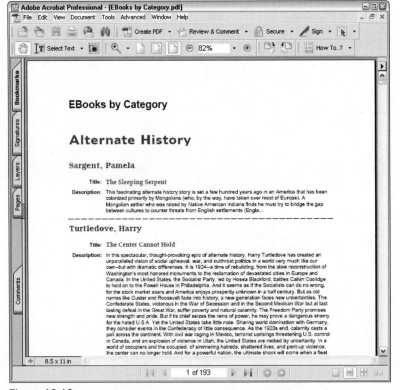

Figure 12.16

Importing Data from Outlook Items to Access

In addition to exporting Access data to Outlook items, you can also import data from Outlook items into Access tables. For the most common case of importing Outlook contacts to Access, I have written an add-in to do the importing (the Outlook Automation add-in, available from the Code Samples page of my Web site, www.helenfeddema.com). My add-in is complex, because it handles custom properties as well as built-in properties, but for importing data from standard items in the default local folder, much simpler VBA code will do. The Import from Outlook form has a Tab control with two pages, one for importing data from a single currently open Outlook item, and the other for importing from multiple selected Outlook items. This form is shown in its initial state in Figure 12.17.

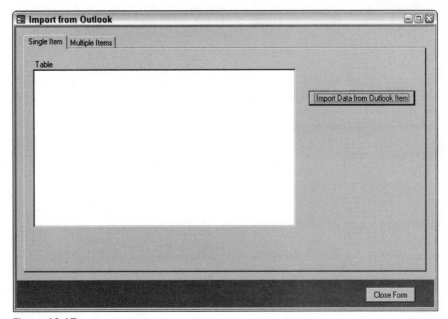

Figure 12.17

To import data from the current Outlook item, I use the Inspector object, an oddly named object in the Outlook object model that represents whatever item (if any) is currently open. The cmdImportDatafromOutlookItem_Click event procedure follows, with commentary.

```
Private Sub cmdImportDatafromOutlookItem_Click()

On Error GoTo ErrorHandler

    Set appOutlook = GetObject(, Outlook.Application)
```

Set an Inspector variable to the ActiveInspector property of the Outlook Application object, which represents the currently open item. If no item is open, a case in the error handler exits the procedure.

```
Set ins = appOutlook.ActiveInspector
```

Set a variable representing the item type of the Inspector, picked up from its Class property.

```
lngItemType = Nz(ins.CurrentItem.Class)
Debug.Print "Item type: " & lngItemType
```

Exit if no usable item has been selected (a second check in case there is a strange item open with no class).

```
If lngItemType = 0 Then
    strPrompt = "No Outlook item open; exiting"
    MsgBox strPrompt, vbOKOnly, "No item open"
    GoTo ErrorHandlerExit
End If

Set dbs = CurrentDb
Set subTable = Me![subTableSingle]
```

Set up a Select Case statement to process each item type correctly.

```
Select Case lngItemType

    Case olAppointment
        strTable = "tblAppointmentsFromOutlook"
```

Clear old data from the table, using a SQL statement delete query.

```
        strSQL = "DELETE * FROM " & strTable
        DoCmd.SetWarnings False
        DoCmd.RunSQL strSQL
```

Set up a recordset based on the appropriate table for import.

```
        Set rst = dbs.OpenRecordset(strTable, dbOpenDynaset)
        With rst
            Set appt = ins.CurrentItem
```

Add a record to the table, and copy values from the Outlook item to its fields.

```
            .AddNew
            ![Subject] = appt.Subject
            ![Location] = appt.Location
            ![StartTime] = appt.Start
            ![EndTime] = appt.End
            ![Category] = appt.Categories
            .Update
            appt.Close (olSave)
        End With
```

Assign the appropriate source object to the subTable subform.

```
                subTable.SourceObject = "fsubAppointmentsFromOutlook"

    Case olContact
        strTable = "tblContactsFromOutlook"

        'Clear old data from table
        strSQL = "DELETE * FROM " & strTable
        DoCmd.SetWarnings False
        DoCmd.RunSQL strSQL

        'Set up recordset based on table
        Set rst = dbs.OpenRecordset(strTable, dbOpenDynaset)
        With rst
            Set con = ins.CurrentItem
            .AddNew
            ![FirstName] = con.FirstName
            ![LastName] = con.LastName
            ![Salutation] = con.NickName
            ![StreetAddress] = con.BusinessAddressStreet
            ![City] = con.BusinessAddressCity
            ![StateOrProvince] = con.BusinessAddressState
            ![PostalCode] = con.BusinessAddressPostalCode
            ![Country] = con.BusinessAddressCountry
            ![CompanyName] = con.CompanyName
            ![JobTitle] = con.JobTitle
            ![WorkPhone] = con.BusinessTelephoneNumber
            ![MobilePhone] = con.MobileTelephoneNumber
            ![FaxNumber] = con.BusinessFaxNumber
            ![EmailName] = con.Email1Address
            .Update
            con.Close (olSave)
        End With

        subTable.SourceObject = "fsubContactsFromOutlook"

    Case olMail
        strTable = "tblMailMessagesFromOutlook"

        'Clear old data from table
        strSQL = "DELETE * FROM " & strTable
        DoCmd.SetWarnings False
        DoCmd.RunSQL strSQL

        'Set up recordset based on table
        Set rst = dbs.OpenRecordset(strTable, dbOpenDynaset)
        With rst
            Set msg = ins.CurrentItem
            Set msgReply = msg.Reply
            .AddNew
            ![Subject] = msg.Subject
            ![From] = msgReply.To
            ![To] = msg.To
            ![Sent] = msg.SentOn
```

```
            ![Message] = msg.Body
            .Update
            msg.Close (olSave)
            msgReply.Close (olDiscard)
        End With

        subTable.SourceObject = "fsubMailMessagesFromOutlook"

    Case olTask
        strTable = "tblTasksFromOutlook"

        'Clear old data from table
        strSQL = "DELETE * FROM " & strTable
        DoCmd.SetWarnings False
        DoCmd.RunSQL strSQL

        'Set up recordset based on table
        Set rst = dbs.OpenRecordset(strTable, dbOpenDynaset)
        With rst
            Set tsk = ins.CurrentItem
            .AddNew
            ![Subject] = tsk.Subject
            ![StartDate] = tsk.StartDate
            ![DueDate] = tsk.DueDate
            ![PercentComplete] = tsk.PercentComplete
```

Set up a Select Case statement to convert Outlook numeric status values to text for storage in the Access table.

```
            lngStatus = tsk.Status

            Select Case lngStatus
                Case olTaskComplete
                    strStatus = "Complete"

                Case olTaskDeferred
                    strStatus = "Deferred"

                Case olTaskInProgress
                    strStatus = "In progress"

                Case olTaskNotStarted
                    strStatus = "Not started"

                Case olTaskWaiting
                    strStatus = "Waiting"

            End Select
            ![Status] = strStatus
            .Update
            tsk.Close (olSave)
        End With

        subTable.SourceObject = "fsubTasksFromOutlook"
```

```
        Case Else
            MsgBox "Item type not supported for import; exiting"
            subTable.SourceObject = ""

    End Select

ErrorHandlerExit:
    Exit Sub

ErrorHandler:
    If Err = 429 Then
        'Outlook is not running; open Outlook with CreateObject.
        Set appOutlook = CreateObject("Outlook.Application")
        Resume Next
    ElseIf Err = 91 Then
        strPrompt = "No Outlook item open; exiting"
        MsgBox strPrompt, vbOKOnly, "No item open"
        GoTo ErrorHandlerExit
    Else
        MsgBox "Error No: " & Err.Number & "; Description: " & Err.Description
        Resume ErrorHandlerExit
    End If

End Sub
```

Figure 12.18 shows the form with data written to tblAppointmentsFromOutlook for an appointment item.

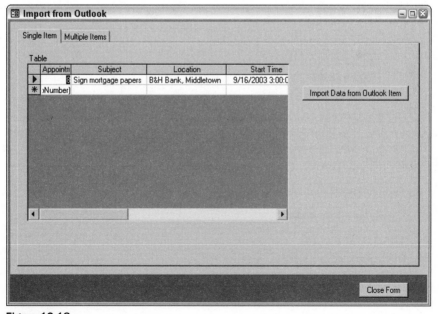

Figure 12.18

The other tab of the Import from Outlook form imports multiple items from Outlook, using the Outlook Selection object (introduced in Office 2000). This object represents the items selected in the current folder, allowing you to use an Outlook folder much like a MultiSelect listbox, selecting items for import into Outlook. Figure 12.19 shows an Outlook tasks folder with several tasks selected for import.

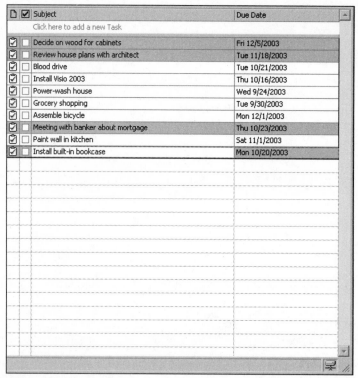

☐ ☑	Subject	Due Date
	Click here to add a new Task	
☑ ☐	Decide on wood for cabinets	Fri 12/5/2003
☑ ☐	Review house plans with architect	Tue 11/18/2003
☑ ☐	Blood drive	Tue 10/21/2003
☑ ☐	Install Visio 2003	Thu 10/16/2003
☑ ☐	Power-wash house	Wed 9/24/2003
☑ ☐	Grocery shopping	Tue 9/30/2003
☑ ☐	Assemble bicycle	Mon 12/1/2003
☑ ☐	Meeting with banker about mortgage	Thu 10/23/2003
☑ ☐	Paint wall in kitchen	Sat 11/1/2003
☑ ☐	Install built-in bookcase	Mon 10/20/2003

Figure 12.19

Clicking the cmdImportDataFromOutlook button on the Multiple Items page of the Import from Outlook form runs a procedure that is similar to the one on the Single Items page, except that it iterates through the Selection object (representing the items selected in the currently open folder) to process all the selected items. The procedure follows, with commentary on the Selection-related features.

```
Private Sub cmdImportDatafromOutlookItems_Click()

On Error GoTo ErrorHandler

    Set appOutlook = GetObject(, Outlook.Application)
    Set nms = appOutlook.GetNamespace("MAPI")
```

Set up an Explorer variable to represent the current window displaying a folder in Outlook, and a MAPIFolder variable to represent the folder displayed in the Explorer.

```
    Set exp = appOutlook.ActiveExplorer
    Set fld = exp.CurrentFolder
    Debug.Print "Folder default item type: " & fld.DefaultItemType
```

Store the folder item type to a variable for use later in the code.

```
lngItemType = fld.DefaultItemType
Debug.Print "Folder item type: " & fld.DefaultItemType
```

Set up a Selection variable.

```
Set sel = exp.Selection
```

Count the number of selected items, and exit if none is selected.

```
lngSelectionCount = sel.Count
Debug.Print "Number of selected contacts: " & lngSelectionCount

'Exit if no contact has been selected.
If lngSelectionCount = 0 Then
   MsgBox "No items selected; exiting"
   GoTo ErrorHandlerExit
End If
```

Set up a DAO recordset based on the appropriate table for import.

```
Set dbs = CurrentDb
Set subTable = Me![subTableMultiple]
```

Set up a Select Case statement to process items correctly for the folder type selected.

```
Select Case lngItemType

   Case olAppointmentItem
      strTable = "tblAppointmentsFromOutlook"

      'Clear old data from table
      strSQL = "DELETE * FROM " & strTable
      DoCmd.SetWarnings False
      DoCmd.RunSQL strSQL

      'Set up recordset based on table
      Set rst = dbs.OpenRecordset(strTable, dbOpenDynaset)
      With rst
         For Each itm In sel
            If itm.Class = olAppointment Then
               Set appt = itm
               .AddNew
               ![Subject] = appt.Subject
               ![Location] = appt.Location
               ![StartTime] = appt.Start
               ![EndTime] = appt.End
               ![Category] = appt.Categories
               .Update
               appt.Close (olSave)
            End If
         Next itm
      End With
```

```
            subTable.SourceObject = "fsubAppointmentsFromOutlook"

    Case olContactItem
        strTable = "tblContactsFromOutlook"

        'Clear old data from table
        strSQL = "DELETE * FROM " & strTable
        DoCmd.SetWarnings False
        DoCmd.RunSQL strSQL

        'Set up recordset based on table
        Set rst = dbs.OpenRecordset(strTable, dbOpenDynaset)
        With rst
```

Note that although the Selection object is a collection of items, it does not have an Items collection—you just iterate through it directly.

```
        For Each itm In sel
            If itm.Class = olContact Then
                Set con = itm
                .AddNew
                ![FirstName] = con.FirstName
                ![LastName] = con.LastName
                ![Salutation] = con.NickName
                ![StreetAddress] = con.BusinessAddressStreet
                ![City] = con.BusinessAddressCity
                ![StateOrProvince] = con.BusinessAddressState
                ![PostalCode] = con.BusinessAddressPostalCode
                ![Country] = con.BusinessAddressCountry
                ![CompanyName] = con.CompanyName
                ![JobTitle] = con.JobTitle
                ![WorkPhone] = con.BusinessTelephoneNumber
                ![MobilePhone] = con.MobileTelephoneNumber
                ![FaxNumber] = con.BusinessFaxNumber
                ![EmailName] = con.Email1Address
                .Update
                con.Close (olSave)
            End If
        Next itm
    End With

    subTable.SourceObject = "fsubContactsFromOutlook"

Case olMailItem
    strTable = "tblMailMessagesFromOutlook"

    'Clear old data from table
    strSQL = "DELETE * FROM " & strTable
    DoCmd.SetWarnings False
    DoCmd.RunSQL strSQL

    'Set up recordset based on table
```

```
                    Set rst = dbs.OpenRecordset(strTable, dbOpenDynaset)
                    With rst
                        For Each itm In sel
                            If itm.Class = olMail Then
                                Set msg = itm
                                Set msgReply = msg.Reply
                                .AddNew
                                ![Subject] = msg.Subject
                                ![From] = msgReply.To
                                ![To] = msg.To
                                ![Sent] = msg.SentOn
                                ![Message] = msg.Body
                                .Update
                                msg.Close (olSave)
                                msgReply.Close (olDiscard)
                            End If
                        Next itm
                    End With

                    subTable.SourceObject = "fsubMailMessagesFromOutlook"

                Case olTaskItem
                    strTable = "tblTasksFromOutlook"

                    'Clear old data from table
                    strSQL = "DELETE * FROM " & strTable
                    DoCmd.SetWarnings False
                    DoCmd.RunSQL strSQL

                    'Set up recordset based on table
                    Set rst = dbs.OpenRecordset(strTable, dbOpenDynaset)
                    With rst
                        For Each itm In sel
                            If itm.Class = olTask Then
                                Set tsk = itm
                                .AddNew
                                ![Subject] = tsk.Subject
                                ![StartDate] = tsk.StartDate
                                ![DueDate] = tsk.DueDate
                                ![PercentComplete] = tsk.PercentComplete
```

Set up a Select Case statement to convert Outlook numeric status values to text for the Access table.

```
                        lngStatus = tsk.Status

                        Select Case lngStatus
                            Case olTaskComplete
                                strStatus = "Complete"

                            Case olTaskDeferred
                                strStatus = "Deferred"

                            Case olTaskInProgress
                                strStatus = "In progress"
```

```
                        Case olTaskNotStarted
                            strStatus = "Not started"

                        Case olTaskWaiting
                            strStatus = "Waiting"

                    End Select
                    ![Status] = strStatus
                    .Update
                    tsk.Close (olSave)
                End If
            Next itm
        End With

        subTable.SourceObject = "fsubTasksFromOutlook"

    Case Else
        MsgBox "Folder type not supported for import; exiting"
        subTable.SourceObject = ""

    End Select

ErrorHandlerExit:
    Exit Sub

ErrorHandler:
    If Err = 429 Then
        'Outlook is not running; open Outlook with CreateObject.
        Set appOutlook = CreateObject("Outlook.Application")
        Resume Next
    Else
        MsgBox "Error No: " & Err.Number & "; Description: " & Err.Description
        Resume ErrorHandlerExit
    End If

End Sub
```

Using the Redemption Library to Avoid the Object Model Guardian

As a response to Outlook's vulnerability to various email viruses, Microsoft added some security features to Outlook 2000 (optional for that version, built in to later versions) that unfortunately made life much more difficult for Office users, especially those who write VBA code to work with Outlook objects. If you have Office XP or 2003, Outlook 2000 with the Outlook security patch, or Office 2000 with Service Pack 2, you will see the pop-up shown in Figure 12.20 whenever your Access code works with Outlook objects, if the code works with mail messages, address books, and contacts.

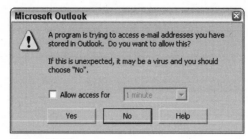

Figure 12.20

This pop-up is the Object Model Guardian. While Microsoft's intention with this irritating "feature" was to protect Outlook objects from modification by hackers, in real life the Object Model Guardian mostly appears as an annoying interruption in the smooth running of Office VBA code. Instead of your code running automatically, somebody has to hover over the computer, responding to pop-ups, giving access for a few minutes at a time (10 minutes is the top choice, which may not be enough for lengthy merges). Running a long merge over lunch is out of the question, because if no one responds to the dialog, the merge stops dead.

Since the introduction of the Outlook 2000 security patch, the only way to avoid this annoying pop-up has been to avoid upgrading to Office XP or 2003, stay in Outlook 2000, and not install the security patch that implements this feature. However, this is no longer the case—Dmitry Streblechenko developed the Redemption Library for Outlook, which lets your VBA code run unaffected by the security patch, and also adds a number of extra features that are very useful for working with Outlook objects in code.

The Redemption Libary for Outlook can be downloaded from www.dimastr.com. Two versions are available: a free version for noncommercial use and a distributable version with extra features for $199.99. The distributable version is required for commercial use of the Redemption Library.

To use the Redemption library in your code, you need to download and install it and set a reference to the SafeOutlook Library in the References dialog. I recommend placing the Redemption.dll file in the AddIns folder (typically C:\Documents and Settings\Administrator\Application Data\Microsoft\ AddIns for a standalone Office installation in Windows 2000, or C:\Windows\Application Data\ Microsoft\Addins for Windows ME). Placing this file in the Addins folder will make it easy to install as an add-in in Access.

To set the reference, open any Access 2000 or higher database, open a module, and select References from the Tools menu. If you placed Redemption.dll in the Addins folder, scroll down until you can see the SafeOutlook Library selection, and check it, as shown in Figure 12.21.

If you have downloaded and installed the Redemption library, you can test working with Outlook without the annoying Object Model Guardian pop-ups, using the Outlook Data Exchange with Redemption database, which has a reference set to the SafeOutlook library and some necessary modifications to code on some of the procedures that work with mail messages and contacts.

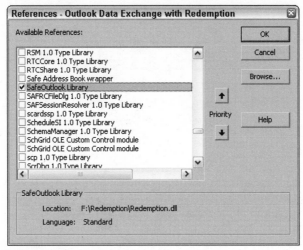

Figure 12.21

First, you need to declare two sets of contact and mail message variables, both as Object.

```
'Must declare Redemption objects and corresponding Outlook objects as Object
Private ocon As Object
Private con As Object
Private omsg As Object
Private msg As Object
```

Then, whenever your code works with a contact or mail message, replace the original line setting the ContactItem (con) or MailItem (msg) variable with a set of lines like the following:

```
'Set the standard and Safe ContactItem variables
Set ocon = ins.CurrentItem
Set con = New Redemption.SafeContactItem
con.Item = ocon
```

From this point on, you can use the con (or msg) variable as usual, and you will not see the annoying Object Model Guardian when the code runs.

Summary

Using the Outlook object model, you can create Outlook contacts, tasks, mail messages, and appointments from data in Access tables, or import Outlook data into Access tables, which lets you use Outlook for its superior mail handling and calendar features, but maintain your contacts data in an Access table.

13

Working with Excel

Excel is the Office component that is used to analyze data, particularly numeric data. In early versions of Office, you had to use Excel to produce attractive charts or pivot tables, but Access has had a charting component since v. 1.0 (MS Graph) and PivotTables since Access 2000, and PivotCharts were introduced in Access 2002 (Office XP). Because of these enhancements to Access, you no longer need to export data to Excel in order to produce elegant, interactive PivotTables and (if you have Office XP or higher) PivotCharts (see Chapter 5, *Using PivotTables and PivotCharts to Interact with Data*, for information on PivotTables and PivotCharts). However, there are still circumstances in which you will need to export Access data to an Excel worksheet or chart, primarily when you need to give the data to someone who doesn't have Access and needs to work interactively with your data.

If you just need to send somebody a read-only image of attractively formatted Access data, you can prepare a report (possibly including a PivotTable or PivotChart image), export it to either the Access Snapshot or Adobe PDF format, and email it as an attachment, as described in the "Email a Report Form" section of Chapter 12, Working with Outlook.

This chapter explains how to export Access data to Excel worksheets, using the OutputTo and TransferSpreadsheet methods and Automation code, and how to import data from Excel worksheets into Access tables. The following table lists the sample files referenced in this chapter, and where they should be placed.

Document Name	Document Type	Place in Folder
Excel Data Exchange.mdb	Access 2000 database	Anywhere you want
Categories.xls	Excel worksheet	\My Documents\Access Merge
Customers.xls	Excel worksheet	\My Documents\Access Merge

The main menu of the Excel Data Exchange database was created with my Menu Manager add-in (see Chapter 6, *Printing Data with Reports,* for more information on this add-in.) In addition to the standard main menu sections, the main menu also has a Docs Path textbox to allow editing the Documents path (the path is picked up from tblInfo in various procedures in the database) The main menu is shown in Figure 13.1.

Figure 13.1

The first of the following two functions checks whether the path entered into the DocsPath textbox on the main menu is valid, and if so, the second function retrieves the path from tblInfo, defaulting to C:\My Documents if the field is blank. It also checks whether there is an Access Merge subfolder under the Documents folder, and creates one if needed.

```
    Public Function CheckDocsDir() As Boolean

  On Error GoTo ErrorHandler

    Set dbs = CurrentDb
    Set rst = dbs.OpenRecordset("tblInfo", dbOpenDynaset)

    With rst
       .MoveFirst
       strFolderPath = Nz(![DocsPath])
       If strFolderPath = "" Then
          strFolderPath = "C:\My Documents\"
       End If
    End With

    'Test the validity of the folder path
    Debug.Print "Folder path: " & strFolderPath

    If strFolderPath = "" Then
       strTitle = "No path entered"
       strPrompt = "Please enter a Docs folder path on the main menu"
```

```
            MsgBox strPrompt, vbOKOnly + vbCritical, strTitle
            CheckDocsDir = False
            GoTo ErrorHandlerExit
        Else
            Set fso = CreateObject("Scripting.FileSystemObject")
            If fso.FolderExists(strFolderPath) = False Then
                strTitle = "Folder path invalid"
                strPrompt = "Please enter a valid Docs folder path on the main menu"
                MsgBox strPrompt, vbOKOnly + vbCritical, strTitle
                GoTo ErrorHandlerExit
                CheckDocsDir = False
            End If
        End If

    CheckDocsDir = True

ErrorHandlerExit:
    Exit Function

ErrorHandler:
    MsgBox "Error No: " & Err.Number & "; Description: " & _
        Err.Description
    Resume ErrorHandlerExit

End Function

Public Function GetDocsDir() As String

On Error GoTo ErrorHandler

    Dim strFolderPath As String

    Set dbs = CurrentDb
    Set rst = dbs.OpenRecordset("tblInfo", dbOpenDynaset)

    With rst
        .MoveFirst
        strFolderPath = Nz(![DocsPath])
        If strFolderPath = "" Then
            strFolderPath = "C:\My Documents\"
        End If
    End With

    'Test the validity of the folder path
    Debug.Print "Folder path: " & strFolderPath

    If strFolderPath = "" Then
        strTitle = "No path entered"
        strPrompt = "Please enter a Docs folder path on the main menu"
        MsgBox strPrompt, vbOKOnly + vbCritical, strTitle
        GoTo ErrorHandlerExit
    Else
        Set fso = CreateObject("Scripting.FileSystemObject")
        If fso.FolderExists(strFolderPath) = False Then
            strTitle = "Folder path invalid"
```

```
              strPrompt = "Please enter a valid Docs folder path on the main menu"
              MsgBox strPrompt, vbOKOnly + vbCritical, strTitle
              GoTo ErrorHandlerExit
        End If
    End If

    strDocsDir = strFolderPath & "Access Merge\"
    Debug.Print "Access Merge subfolder: " & strDocsDir

    'Test for existence of Access Merge subfolder, and create
    'it if it is not found
    Set fso = CreateObject("Scripting.FileSystemObject")
    If Not fso.FolderExists(strDocsDir) Then
        'Access Merge subfolder does not exist; create it
        fso.CreateFolder strDocsDir
    End If

    GetDocsDir = strDocsDir

ErrorHandlerExit:
    Exit Function

ErrorHandler:
    MsgBox "Error No: " & Err.Number & "; Description: " & _
        Err.Description
    Resume ErrorHandlerExit

End Function
```

Writing Automation Code

If you are going to work with Excel worksheets in code—as opposed to simply exporting data from a table or query to a worksheet—you need to set a reference to the Excel object model in your database, so that you can work with Excel objects using Automation code. (See Chapter 11, *Working with Word*, or an explanation of using Automation code to communicate with another Office application.) To set a reference to the Excel object model, open the database's Visual Basic window, drop down the Tools menu, and select References. Locate the Microsoft Excel Object Library and check it, as shown in Figure 13.2. The version will vary according to the version of Office you are running: 9.0 for Office 2000, 10.0 for Office XP, and 11.0 for Office 2003.

Unlike Word and Outlook, Excel references are generally upgraded and downgraded appropriately if an Access 2000 database is opened alternately in Access 2000 and higher versions, so you can set the reference to the version you are currently using. The version number should change as needed, depending on the version of Office you are using.

The "Some Handy Toolbar Buttons" section in Chapter 11 describes how to put buttons on your toolbar to quickly open the Visual Basic window and the References dialog, which can save time when working with references and VBA code in general.

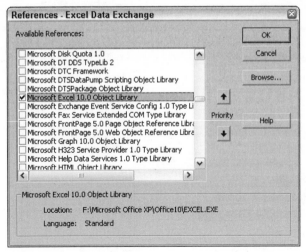

Figure 13.2

The Excel Object Model

The Excel object model is a collection of objects that let you work with Excel components in VBA code. You can get information about the Excel object model through the object model diagram in Help or the Object Browser in the Visual Basic window.

Viewing the Excel Object Model

As with Word, it is easy to find a diagram of the Excel object model in Help. First, open the Visual Basic window from an Excel worksheet. Type "object model" into the Answer box on the toolbar, and then select Microsoft Excel Objects (or Microsoft Excel Object Model, for Excel 2003) to open the corresponding Help topic. A portion of the Excel object model diagram in this Help topic is shown in Figure 13.3.

Directly under the top-level Application object, you can see Workbooks and Worksheets and Charts, representing the familiar Excel worksheets and charts you work with in the interface. In addition to these objects, when you work with Excel using Automation code you will also need to work with the Range object, which represents a set of cells designated by row and column references. You can see the Range object in the secondary diagram opened by clicking on the red triangle next to the Worksheets collection, as shown in Figure 13.4.

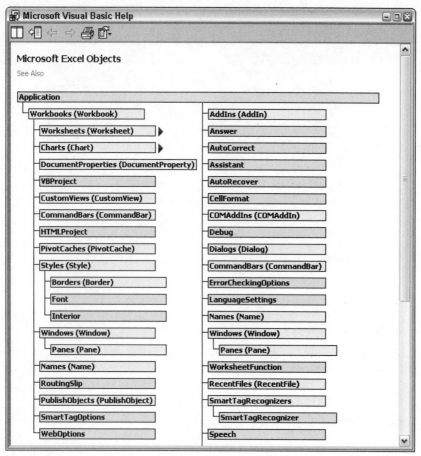

Figure 13.3

Along with the diagrams in Help, there is another way to view the Excel object model, which may be more helpful when you are writing VBA code: This is the Object Browser, which is opened from the Visual Basic window of any Office component, using the F2 function key. This dialog lets you select objects and their properties, methods, and events, and open Help topics as needed. To view Excel objects, select Excel in the unlabeled Libraries selector at the upper left of the window. The Classes list contains objects, collections, and enumerations (abbreviated *enums*)—collections of named constants that can be used as argument values. When you make a selection in the Classes list, all the attributes of the selected object, collection, or enum are displayed in the Members list.

```
Microsoft Visual Basic Help                                    [_][□][X]

Microsoft Excel Objects (Worksheet)
See Also

┌──────────────────────────────────────────────────────────────────┐
│ Worksheets (Worksheet)                                             │
└──────────────────────────────────────────────────────────────────┘
  ┌─ Names (Name)                    ┌─ Comments (Comment)
  ┌─ Range                           ┌─ CustomProperties
      ┌─ Areas                           └─ CustomProperty
      ┌─ Borders (Border)            ┌─ HPageBreaks (HPageBreak)
      ┌─ Errors                      ┌─ VPageBreaks (VPageBreak)
          └─ Error                   ┌─ Hyperlinks (Hyperlink)
      ┌─ Font                        ┌─ Scenarios (Scenario)
      ┌─ Interior                    ┌─ OLEObjects (OLEObject)
      ┌─ Characters                  ┌─ Outline
          └─ Font                    ┌─ PageSetup
      ┌─ Name                            └─ Graphic
      ┌─ Style                       ┌─ QueryTables (QueryTable)
          ┌─ Borders (Border)            └─ Parameters (Parameter)
          ┌─ Font                    ┌─ PivotTables (PivotTable)
          └─ Interior                    ┌─ CalculatedFields
      ┌─ FormatConditions (FormatCondition)  ┌─ CalculatedMembers
      ┌─ Hyperlinks (Hyperlink)                  └─ CalculatedMember
      ┌─ Validation                  ┌─ CubeFields
      ┌─ Comment                         └─ CubeField
      └─ Phonetics (Phonetic)                └─ TreeviewControl
```

Figure 13.4

Figure 13.5 shows the properties and methods of the Worksheets collection.

On selecting a property, method, or event of an entry in the Classes list, you will see its syntax displayed in the Object Browser's status bar. Figure 13.6 shows the syntax for the PrintOut method of the Worksheets collection. The method's argument names (From, To, and so forth) are italicized and bracketed. Unlike Word, the data type of the arguments is not given, although the enum used to select appropriate values is listed, where relevant. For enum settings, you can click the enum name to open it and see the available selections. (See Chapter 11, *Working with Word*, for more information on using enums.)

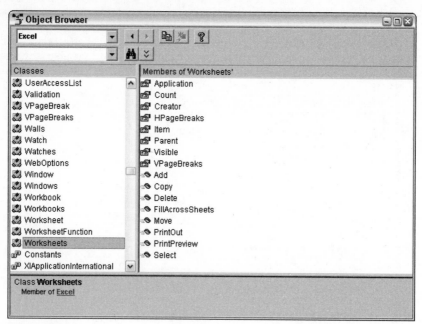

Figure 13.5

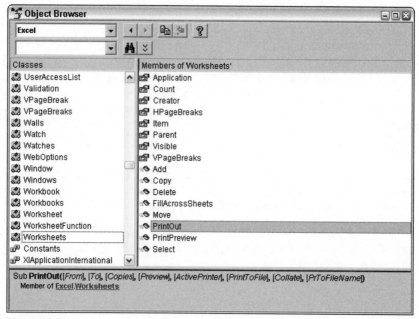

Figure 13.6

The Basic Automation Commands

To initiate an Automation session, the first step is to create an Automation object representing the Office component, in this case, Excel. This is generally done by setting an object variable to the top-level Application object in the Excel object model, using either the CreateObject or GetObject function. CreateObject creates a new instance of Excel, while GetObject uses an existing instance of Excel. To avoid creating extra Excel instances, I like to use the GetObject function initially, with a fallback to CreateObject in a procedure's error handler, so that an existing instance of Excel will be used, if there is one, and a new instance will only be created if it is needed.

With Excel (unlike Word and Outlook), it can be useful to just set a reference to a Workbook or Worksheet object, but you will often need to use methods or properties of the Excel Application object, so in that case it is best to create a Excel application object that can then be used for all Automation work with Excel. The syntax for setting a reference to an existing instance of Excel, using the GetObject function, follows:

```
Set gappExcel = GetObject(, "Excel.Application")
```

If this line of code fails (because Excel is not running), error 429 occurs, and the following error handler then runs a line of code using the CreateObject function to create a new instance of Excel and resumes running the code after the GetObject line.

```
ErrorHandler:
If Err.Number = 429 Then
    'Excel is not running; open Excel with CreateObject
    Set gappExcel = CreateObject("Excel.Application")
    Resume Next
Else
    MsgBox "Error No: " & Err.Number & "; Description: "
    Resume ErrorHandlerExit
End If
```

Using the gappExcel variable, you can access any of the objects in the Excel object model, to create workbooks, worksheets, and charts, and work with them as needed. Some of the code samples in the "Exporting Data from Access to Excel" and "Importing Data from Excel" sections in this chapter (and the Excel Data Exchange sample database) use the gappExcel variable as the starting point for working with various components of the Excel object model, using Automation code.

Workbooks, Worksheets, and Ranges

Although people generally refer to .xls files as worksheets, technically they are workbooks, each containing one or more worksheets. This means that when you need to work with worksheets, you have to first set a reference to the relevant workbook, then work down to the specific worksheet you need to work with. The sample code segment that follows creates a new workbook, sets a reference to the first worksheet in the new workbook, and makes it visible.

```
Set wkb = gappExcel.Workbooks.Add
Set wks = wkb.Worksheets(1)
wks.Activate
gappExcel.Application.Visible = True
```

This code is useful for creating a brand-new worksheet for accepting data from Access. If you need to work with a named worksheet, use the following syntax, which sets a reference to a workbook, then to a specific worksheet, and prints a value from one of the worksheet's cells to the Immediate window.

```
    If CheckDocsDir = False Then
        GoTo ErrorHandlerExit
    End If
strWorkbook = GetDocsDir & "Categories.xls"
Set wkb = GetObject(strWorkbook)
Set wks = wkb.Sheets("Northwind Food Categories")
Debug.Print wks.Range("B3").Value
```

Unlike Word and Outlook, where you are usually creating separate objects (Word documents and Outlook items) from records in an Access table, when exporting Access data to Excel you are creating a worksheet with rows in the worksheet corresponding to records in an Access table or query. Because of this, it generally isn't necessary to screen data for missing values in fields. If you are creating Outlook mail messages, you need to check that the Access record has an email address, and if you are creating Word letters, you need to check that the Access record has a complete mailing address—but it won't cause problems if a cell in an Excel worksheet is missing an email address value or a street address. Because of this, when exporting data to Excel or importing data from Excel I generally prefer to export or import the entire table, query, or datasheet, and do whatever filtering or data type conversion is needed in the target application. However, there are times when you need to work with Excel worksheets using Automation code, primarily when you want to format a worksheet (data exported to worksheets).

A Shortcut: Using the Excel Macro Recorder

As with Word (but unlike Outlook), Excel has a macro recorder that you can use to capture the VBA syntax corresponding to various actions in the Excel interface. To use this handy feature, turn on the macro recorder by selecting Tools | Macro | Record New Macro, and click OK (there is no REC button on the Excel status bar). Go through the steps you want to perform, and stop the recorder by clicking the Stop Recording button on the small Macro Recorder toolbar. The resulting saved macro (by default called Macro*n*) contains the VBA code to do the steps you recorded. This code is likely to be verbose, and in need of trimming (for example, you rarely need to assign a value to every single argument of a method), but it is very helpful as a preliminary step to writing Automation code.

The following macro was recorded from these actions: Select Column I in a worksheet and sort by it.

```
Columns("I:I").Select
Range("A1:K92").Sort Key1:=Range("I1"), Order1:=xlAscending, Header:= _
    xlGuess, OrderCustom:=1, MatchCase:=False, Orientation:=xlTopToBottom, _
    DataOption1:=xlSortNormal
```

To modify this code for use in Automation code, all you need to do is insert an Excel Application variable in front of each line.

```
gappExcel.Columns("I:I").Select
gappExcel.Range("A1:K92").Sort Key1:=Range("I1"), Order1:=xlAscending, Header:= _
    xlGuess, OrderCustom:=1, MatchCase:=False, Orientation:=xlTopToBottom, _
    DataOption1:=xlSortNormal
```

Exporting Data from Access to Excel

There are several techniques you can use to export data from Access tables or queries to Excel. Some of them (the OutputTo and TransferSpreadsheet methods) export all the data from an Access table or query to an Excel worksheet. You can also use Automation code to create a worksheet, and then format it. The following sections show how to export data from Access to Excel, using a variety of methods.

MultiSelect Listbox Form

To allow selection of records from an Access data source, I created a form with a MultiSelect listbox to use for selecting records on an ad hoc basis. The form header has two comboboxes, for selecting a data source and export type. The Select Data Source combobox has as its row source the table tlkpDataSources, with a DataType field describing the type of data, and a DataSource field, with the name of a query. The Select Export Type combobox has tlkpExportTypes as its row source, with an AutoNumber ExportID field, and ExportType and FileType fields. The combobox displays a concatenated expression combining ExportType and FileType, and the ExportID numeric value is used in a Select Case statement for calling the appropriate Sub procedure to do the export.

When you select a data source from cboSelectDataSource, an AfterUpdate event procedure assigns the appropriate record source to the MultiSelect listbox on the form and formats its columns appropriately. The data source value is saved to a public variable (pstrDataSource), so it can be used in other code, even if the combobox has been cleared.

```
Private Sub cboSelectDataSource_AfterUpdate()

On Error GoTo ErrorHandler

    Set lst = Me![lstSelectMultiple]
    pstrDataSource = Me![cboSelectDataSource].Column(1)
    lst.RowSource = pstrDataSource

    Select Case pstrDataSource

        Case "qryContacts"
            lst.ColumnCount = 13
            lst.ColumnWidths = _
                "0 in;1.25 in;1.25 in;1 in;.6 in;.6 in;0 in;0 in;0 in;0 in;0 in;0 in;0 in"

        Case "qryEBooksAndAuthors"
            lst.ColumnCount = 7
            lst.ColumnWidths = _
                "0 in;1.5 in;1.5 in;1.5 in;1.5 in;1.25 in;1.25 in"

        Case "qryEmployeePhones"
            lst.ColumnCount = 4
            lst.ColumnWidths = "1.5 in;1 in;1.5 in;1.5 in"

    End Select

ErrorHandlerExit:
```

```
      Exit Sub

ErrorHandler:
   MsgBox "Error No: " & Err.Number & "; Description: " & _
      Err.Description
   Resume ErrorHandlerExit

End Sub
```

You can select one or more records in the listbox by Ctrl-clicking to select noncontiguous records, or Shift-clicking to select a range of rows (as with the Windows Explorer). The Select All button lets you quickly select all the records. Figure 13.7 shows the listbox form, with several records selected for export.

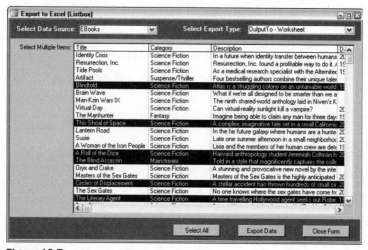

Figure 13.7

After making your selections, selecting an export type sets several public variables.

```
Private Sub cboSelectExportType_AfterUpdate()

On Error GoTo ErrorHandler

   pstrExportType = Nz(Me![cboSelectExportType].Column(2))
   pstrFileType = Nz(Me![cboSelectExportType].Column(3))
   plngExportType = Nz(Me![cboSelectExportType].Column(0))

ErrorHandlerExit:
   Exit Sub

ErrorHandler:
   MsgBox "Error No: " & Err.Number & "; Description: " & _
      Err.Description
   Resume ErrorHandlerExit

End Sub
```

Finally, clicking the Export Data command button runs a Click event procedure that checks that a data source, export type, and at least one record have been selected, and then runs the appropriate Sub procedure to do the export. This procedure is listed below, with explanatory text.

```
Private Sub cmdExportData_Click()

On Error GoTo ErrorHandler

    Dim cbo As Access.ComboBox
    Dim lngNoFields As Long
    Dim varItem As Variant
    Dim strSQL As String
    Dim dbs As DAO.Database
    Dim rst As DAO.Recordset
    Dim dflds As DAO.Fields
    Dim i As Integer
    Dim strTable As String
```

Check that a data source has been selected, and exit if not.

```
    Set cbo = Me![cboSelectDataSource]
    pstrDataSource = Nz(cbo.Column(1))
    If pstrDataSource = "" Then
        MsgBox "Please select a data source."
        cbo.SetFocus
        cbo.Dropdown
        GoTo ErrorHandlerExit
    End If
```

Check that an export type and file type have been selected, and exit if not.

```
    If plngExportType = 0 Then
        MsgBox "Please select an export type"
        Me![cboSelectExportType].SetFocus
        Me![cboSelectExportType].Dropdown
        GoTo ErrorHandlerExit
    End If
```

Print the data source and export type values to the Immediate window, for purposes of debugging.

```
    Debug.Print "Data source: " & pstrDataSource
    Debug.Print "Export type: " & plngExportType
```

Check that at least one record has been selected, and exit if not.

```
    Set lst = Me![lstSelectMultiple]
    If lst.ItemsSelected.Count = 0 Then
        MsgBox "Please select at least one record."
        lst.SetFocus
        GoTo ErrorHandlerExit
    Else
```

Set variables representing the number of columns and rows in the listbox, for use in picking up data from the listbox.

```
        intColumns = lst.ColumnCount
        intRows = lst.ItemsSelected.Count
    End If
```

Set a variable representing the table to fill with selected data, based on the selected data source. I fill a table with data for use in the export, because the OutputTo and TransferSpreadsheet methods require either a table or a query; they can't work directly with the ItemsSelected collection of a listbox as a complete entity.

```
        strTable = "tblSelected" & Mid(pstrDataSource, 4)
        Debug.Print "Selected table: " & strTable
```

Clear old data from selected table.

```
        strSQL = "DELETE * FROM " & strTable
        DoCmd.SetWarnings False
        DoCmd.RunSQL strSQL
```

Set up a recordset based on the selected table.

```
        Set dbs = CurrentDb
        Set rst = dbs.OpenRecordset(strTable, dbOpenTable)
        Set dflds = rst.Fields
```

Write data from selected listbox rows to a table for export.

```
        For Each varItem In lst.ItemsSelected
            rst.AddNew
```

Iterate through the columns; the number of columns varies according to the selected data source. Note that the Columns collection is zero-based.

```
            For i = 0 To intColumns - 1
```

Use Debug.Print statements to print data to the Immediate window for debugging purposes.

```
                Debug.Print "Field name for column " & i & " - " & dflds(i).Name
                varValue = lst.Column(i, varItem)
                Debug.Print "Field value: " & varValue
```

Check for Nulls or zero-length strings and don't attempt to save the data to the table in these cases.

```
                If IsNull(varValue) = False And varValue <> "" Then
                    dflds(i).Value = Nz(lst.Column(i, varItem))
                End If
            Next i
            rst.Update
        Next varItem
        rst.Close
```

Use a query based on the table filled with selected records because the export procedures expect a query, not a table.

```
pstrDataSource = "qrySelected" & Mid(pstrDataSource, 4)
Debug.Print "Data source: " & pstrDataSource
```

Set up a Select Case statement to call the appropriate procedure for each export type, using the Me keyword for the Access Form argument of each procedure, so that the procedure can pick up values from the calling form.

```
Select Case plngExportType

    Case 1
        Call TransferToCSV(Me)

    Case 2
        Call OutputToWKS(Me)

    Case 3
        Call OutputToTXT(Me)

    Case 4
        Call TransferToWKS(Me)

    Case 5
        Call CreateWKS(Me)

End Select

ErrorHandlerExit:
```

Remove the progress bar, in case it might be left over from one of the procedures called in the Select Case statement.

```
    varReturn = SysCmd(acSysCmdRemoveMeter)
    Exit Sub

ErrorHandler:
    MsgBox "Error No: " & Err.Number & "; Description: " & _
        Err.Description
    Resume ErrorHandlerExit

End Sub
```

The five procedures called by the above procedure follow, with commentary on the first and last (the middle ones are basically similar to the first).

```
Public Function OutputToWKS(frm As Access.Form) As Boolean

On Error GoTo ErrorHandler
```

Set variables used to create the appropriate Excel file name. The GetDocsDir function picks up the default Documents directory from tblInfo. This path can be edited as needed in the Docs Path textbox on the main menu.

```
strFileName = Nz(frm![cboSelectDataSource].Column(0))
strExtension = ".xls"
If CheckDocsDir = False Then
    GoTo ErrorHandlerExit
End If
strFilePath = GetDocsDir()
strFileAndPath = strFilePath & strFileName & strExtension
Debug.Print "File name and path: " & strFileAndPath
```

Initialize the progress bar (using an arbitrary division of three units). The progress bar is displayed in the status bar, as a way of informing users of progress of the export.

```
varReturn = SysCmd(acSysCmdInitMeter, _
    "Creating output file ...", 3)

'Update the progress bar.
varReturn = SysCmd(acSysCmdUpdateMeter, 1)
```

Delete the old Excel worksheet, if there is one.

```
Set fso = CreateObject("Scripting.FileSystemObject")
If fso.FileExists(strFileAndPath) = True Then
    fso.DeleteFile strFileAndPath
End If

'Update the progress bar.
varReturn = SysCmd(acSysCmdUpdateMeter, 2)
```

Create the new worksheet file in the \My Documents\Access Merge folder, using the OutputTo method.

```
'Create new worksheet file in Documents\Access Merge folder
If Left(pstrDataSource, 1) = "t" Then
    'Data source is a table
    DoCmd.OutputTo objecttype:=acOutputTable, _
        objectname:=pstrDataSource, _
        outputformat:=acFormatXLS, _
        outputfile:=strFileAndPath, _
        autostart:=False
ElseIf Left(pstrDataSource, 1) = "q" Then
    'Data source is a query
    DoCmd.OutputTo objecttype:=acOutputQuery, _
        objectname:=pstrDataSource, _
        outputformat:=acFormatXLS, _
        outputfile:=strFileAndPath, _
        autostart:=False
End If
```

Test for the existence of the specified worksheet file, with a loop to give it some time to create the file.

```
      Set fso = CreateObject("Scripting.FileSystemObject")
      For i = 1 To 100
         If fso.FileExists(strFileAndPath) = False Then
            i = i + 1
            GoTo TryAgain
         End If
TryAgain:
      Next i

      'Update the progress bar.
      varReturn = SysCmd(acSysCmdUpdateMeter, 3)

      OutputToWKS = True
      strTitle = "Done"
      strPrompt = "Worksheet created as " & strFileAndPath
      MsgBox strPrompt, vbOKOnly + vbInformation, strTitle

ErrorHandlerExit:
      'Remove the progress bar.
      varReturn = SysCmd(acSysCmdRemoveMeter)
      Exit Function

ErrorHandler:
      MsgBox "Error No: " & Err.Number & "; Description: " & _
         Err.Description
      OutputToWKS = False
      Resume ErrorHandlerExit

End Function

Public Function TransferToCSV(frm As Access.Form) As Boolean

On Error GoTo ErrorHandler

      strFileName = Nz(frm![cboSelectDataSource].Column(0))
      strSpec = strFileName & " Export Specification"
      strExtension = ".csv"
      If CheckDocsDir = False Then
         GoTo ErrorHandlerExit
      End If
      strFilePath = GetDocsDir()
      strFileAndPath = strFilePath & strFileName & strExtension
      Debug.Print "File name and path: " & strFileAndPath

      'Initialize the progress bar (using an arbitrary division of five units).
      varReturn = SysCmd(acSysCmdInitMeter, _
         "Creating output file ...", 5)

      'Update the progress bar.
      varReturn = SysCmd(acSysCmdUpdateMeter, 1)

      'Delete old file, if there is one
```

```
        Set fso = CreateObject("Scripting.FileSystemObject")
        If fso.FileExists(strFileAndPath) = True Then
            fso.DeleteFile strFileAndPath
        End If

        'Update the progress bar.
        varReturn = SysCmd(acSysCmdUpdateMeter, 2)
```

Create a new comma-delimited text file in \My Documents\Access Merge folder, using the TransferText method.

```
        DoCmd.TransferText transfertype:=acExportDelim, _
            specificationname:=strSpec, _
            tablename:=pstrDataSource, _
            FileName:=strFileAndPath, _
            hasfieldnames:=True

        'Update the progress bar.
        varReturn = SysCmd(acSysCmdUpdateMeter, 3)

        'Test for existence of specified comma-delimited file, with loop
        'to allow some time to create the file
        Set fso = CreateObject("Scripting.FileSystemObject")
        For i = 1 To 100
            If fso.FileExists(strFileAndPath) = False Then
                i = i + 1
                GoTo TryAgain
            End If
TryAgain:
        Next i

        'Update the progress bar.
        varReturn = SysCmd(acSysCmdUpdateMeter, 4)

        TransferToCSV = True
        strTitle = "Done"
        strPrompt = "Worksheet created as " & strFileAndPath
        MsgBox strPrompt, vbOKOnly + vbInformation, strTitle
ErrorHandlerExit:
        'Remove the progress bar.
        varReturn = SysCmd(acSysCmdRemoveMeter)
        Exit Function

ErrorHandler:
        MsgBox "Error No: " & Err.Number & "; Description: " & _
            Err.Description
        TransferToCSV = False
        Resume ErrorHandlerExit

End Function

Public Function OutputToTXT(frm As Access.Form) As Boolean
```

```
On Error GoTo ErrorHandler

    strFileName = Nz(frm![cboSelectDataSource].Column(0))
    strExtension = ".txt"
    If CheckDocsDir = False Then
        GoTo ErrorHandlerExit
    End If
    strFilePath = GetDocsDir()
    strFileAndPath = strFilePath & strFileName & strExtension
    Debug.Print "File name and path: " & strFileAndPath

    'Initialize the progress bar (using an arbitrary division of three units).
    varReturn = SysCmd(acSysCmdInitMeter, _
        "Creating output file ...", 3)

    'Update the progress bar.
    varReturn = SysCmd(acSysCmdUpdateMeter, 1)

    'Delete old file, if there is one
    Set fso = CreateObject("Scripting.FileSystemObject")
    If fso.FileExists(strFileAndPath) = True Then
        fso.DeleteFile strFileAndPath
    End If

    'Update the progress bar.
    varReturn = SysCmd(acSysCmdUpdateMeter, 2)
```

Create a new text file in the \My Documents\Access Merge folder, using the OutputTo method.

```
    If Left(pstrDataSource, 1) = "t" Then
        'Data source is a table
        DoCmd.OutputTo objecttype:=acOutputTable, _
            objectname:=pstrDataSource, _
            outputformat:=acFormatTXT, _
            outputfile:=strFileAndPath, _
            autostart:=False
    ElseIf Left(pstrDataSource, 1) = "q" Then
        'Data source is a query
        DoCmd.OutputTo objecttype:=acOutputQuery, _
            objectname:=pstrDataSource, _
            outputformat:=acFormatTXT, _
            outputfile:=strFileAndPath, _
            autostart:=False
    End If

    'Test for existence of specified text file, with loop
    'to allow some time to create the file
    Set fso = CreateObject("Scripting.FileSystemObject")
    For i = 1 To 100
        If fso.FileExists(strFileAndPath) = False Then
            i = i + 1
            GoTo TryAgain
        End If
```

```
TryAgain:
   Next i

   'Update the progress bar.
   varReturn = SysCmd(acSysCmdUpdateMeter, 3)

   OutputToTXT = True
   strTitle = "Done"
   strPrompt = "Text file created as " & strFileAndPath
   MsgBox strPrompt, vbOKOnly + vbInformation, strTitle

ErrorHandlerExit:
   'Remove the progress bar.
   varReturn = SysCmd(acSysCmdRemoveMeter)
   Exit Function

ErrorHandler:
   MsgBox "Error No: " & Err.Number & "; Description: " & _
      Err.Description
   OutputToTXT = False
   Resume ErrorHandlerExit

End Function

Public Function TransferToWKS(frm As Access.Form) As Boolean

On Error GoTo ErrorHandler

   strFileName = Nz(frm![cboSelectDataSource].Column(0))
   strSpec = strFileName & " Export Specification"
   strExtension = ".xls"
   If CheckDocsDir = False Then
      GoTo ErrorHandlerExit
   End If
   strFilePath = GetDocsDir()
   strFileAndPath = strFilePath & strFileName & strExtension
   Debug.Print "File name and path: " & strFileAndPath

   'Initialize the progress bar (using an arbitrary division of four units).
   varReturn = SysCmd(acSysCmdInitMeter, _
      "Creating output file ...", 4)

   'Update the progress bar.
   varReturn = SysCmd(acSysCmdUpdateMeter, 1)

   'Delete old file, if there is one
   Set fso = CreateObject("Scripting.FileSystemObject")
   If fso.FileExists(strFileAndPath) = True Then
      fso.DeleteFile strFileAndPath
   End If

   'Update the progress bar.
   varReturn = SysCmd(acSysCmdUpdateMeter, 2)

   Debug.Print "Data source: " & pstrDataSource
```

Create a new worksheet file in the \My Documents\Access Merge folder, using the TransferSpreadsheet method.

```
    DoCmd.TransferSpreadsheet transfertype:=acExport, _
        tablename:=pstrDataSource, _
        FileName:=strFileAndPath, _
        hasfieldnames:=True


    'Update the progress bar.
    varReturn = SysCmd(acSysCmdUpdateMeter, 3)

    'Test for existence of specified worksheet file, with loop
    'to allow some time to create the file
    Set fso = CreateObject("Scripting.FileSystemObject")
    For i = 1 To 100
        If fso.FileExists(strFileAndPath) = False Then
            i = i + 1
            GoTo TryAgain
        End If
TryAgain:
    Next i

    'Update the progress bar.
    varReturn = SysCmd(acSysCmdUpdateMeter, 4)

    TransferToWKS = True
    strTitle = "Done"
    strPrompt = "Worksheet created as " & strFileAndPath
    MsgBox strPrompt, vbOKOnly + vbInformation, strTitle

ErrorHandlerExit:
    'Remove the progress bar.
    varReturn = SysCmd(acSysCmdRemoveMeter)
    Exit Function

ErrorHandler:
    MsgBox "Error No: " & Err.Number & "; Description: " & _
        Err.Description
    TransferToWKS = False
    Resume ErrorHandlerExit

End Function

Public Function CreateWKS(frm As Access.Form) As Boolean

On Error GoTo ErrorHandler

    Dim rstData As DAO.Recordset

    strFileName = Nz(frm![cboSelectDataSource].Column(0))
    strExtension = ".xls"
    If CheckDocsDir = False Then
        GoTo ErrorHandlerExit
    End If
```

```
    strFilePath = GetDocsDir()
    strFileAndPath = strFilePath & strFileName & strExtension
    Debug.Print "File name and path: " & strFileAndPath
    'Delete old file, if there is one
    Set fso = CreateObject("Scripting.FileSystemObject")
    If fso.FileExists(strFileAndPath) = True Then
        fso.DeleteFile strFileAndPath
    End If
```

Set a global Excel application variable; if Excel is not running, the error handler defaults to CreateObject.

```
    Set gappExcel = GetObject(, "Excel.Application")
```

Create a new workbook, and set a reference to its first worksheet.

```
    Set wkb = gappExcel.Workbooks.Add
    Set wks = wkb.Worksheets(1)
    wks.Activate
    gappExcel.Application.Visible = True
```

Excel columns are lettered, so initialize a column letter variable with 64, so the first letter used will be A.

```
    lngASCII = 64
    lngStartLetter = 64
```

Initialize a row number variable with 1, to start on the first row.

```
    i = 1
```

Create a recordset based on the selected data source.

```
    Set dbs = CurrentDb
    Set rstData = dbs.OpenRecordset(pstrDataSource, dbOpenDynaset)
```

Write field names to column headings of worksheet, by iterating through the Fields collection of the recordset.

```
    Set dflds = rstData.Fields
    lngCount = dflds.Count

    For Each dfld In dflds
        lngASCII = lngASCII + 1
        strASCII = Chr(lngASCII)
        strRange = strASCII & CStr(i)
        Debug.Print "Range: " & strRange
        Set rng = wks.Range(strRange)
        Debug.Print "Field name: " & dfld.Name
        rng.Value = dfld.Name
    Next dfld
```

Save the value of the highest letter used for titles, to use in writing data to rows in the worksheet.

```
lngEndLetter = lngASCII
lngNoColumns = lngASCII - 64
Debug.Print "No. of columns: " & lngNoColumns
```

Write data from the selected query to rows of the worksheet.

```
With rstData
    Do While Not .EOF
```

Go to the next row in the worksheet, and reinitialize the column letter value with 64, to start with column A again.

```
        lngASCII = 64
```

Increment the row number.

```
        i = i + 1
```

Set up a loop for writing data from the appropriate number of fields to this row in the worksheet.

```
        For j = 0 To lngNoColumns - 1
            lngASCII = lngASCII + 1
            strASCII = Chr(lngASCII)
            strRange = strASCII & CStr(i)
            Set rng = wks.Range(strRange)
            Debug.Print "Range: " & strRange
            Debug.Print "Value: " & Nz(dflds(j).Value)
```

Turn off the error handler, to prevent errors when writing nonstandard data to the worksheet (such as dates way in the past).

```
On Error Resume Next
```

Write data from a field to a cell in the worksheet.

```
            rng.Value = Nz(dflds(j).Value)
        Next j

    .MoveNext
```

Turn the error handler back on.

```
On Error GoTo ErrorHandler
    Loop
    .Close
End With
```

Save the worksheet to the previously created name, and format the columns and rows. You can do as much formatting as you wish—use the Excel macro recorder to capture the syntax needed.

```
    wks.SaveAs strFileAndPath
    wks.Rows("1:1").Select
    gappExcel.Selection.Font.Bold = True
    With gappExcel.Selection.Borders(xlEdgeBottom)
      .LineStyle = xlContinuous
      .Weight = xlThin
      .ColorIndex = xlAutomatic
    End With

    strASCII = Chr(lngEndLetter)
    gappExcel.Columns("A:" & strASCII).Select
    gappExcel.Columns("A:" & strASCII).EntireColumn.AutoFit
    gappExcel.Rows("1:" & i).Select
    gappExcel.Selection.RowHeight = 28
```

Put up a success message indicating that the worksheet has been created.

```
    strTitle = "Done"
    strPrompt = "Worksheet created as " & strFileAndPath
    MsgBox strPrompt, vbOKOnly + vbInformation, strTitle

ErrorHandlerExit:
    'Remove the progress bar.
    varReturn = SysCmd(acSysCmdRemoveMeter)
    Exit Function

ErrorHandler:
    If Err = 429 Then
        'Excel is not running; open Excel with CreateObject.
        Set gappExcel = CreateObject("Excel.Application")
        Resume Next
    Else
        MsgBox "Error No: " & Err.Number & "; Description: " & Err.Description
        Resume ErrorHandlerExit
    End If

End Function
```

The export types produce various types of files, which are discussed below. The OutputTo method produces the worksheet shown in Figure 13.8.

The worksheet is very plain—the same font is used throughout, and all the columns and rows are the default size. If all you need is the data, this will do, but if you need a more attractively formatted worksheet, you will need to use Automation code to create the worksheet, so you can work with it in code. The TransferSpreadsheet method creates a similar, plain worksheet, and the comma-delimited method creates a comma-delimited (.csv) file, which can be opened in Excel (it looks just like the .wks file) or used for importing into many other file formats, including those that can't import directly from an Access database. It can also be opened in Notepad or another text editor.

If you select the Plain text file selection, you will get a text file that has some minimal (and ugly) formatting accomplished with ASCII characters, and wrapped to illegibility if the data source has more than a few columns. Figure 13.9 shows the plain text file created from the Employee Phones data source (which has only four columns).

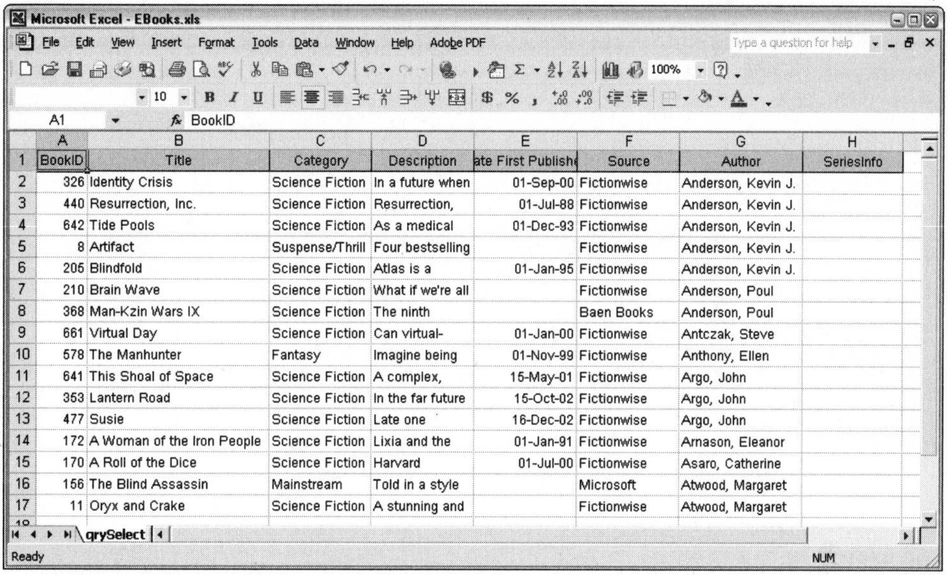

Figure 13.8

Figure 13.9

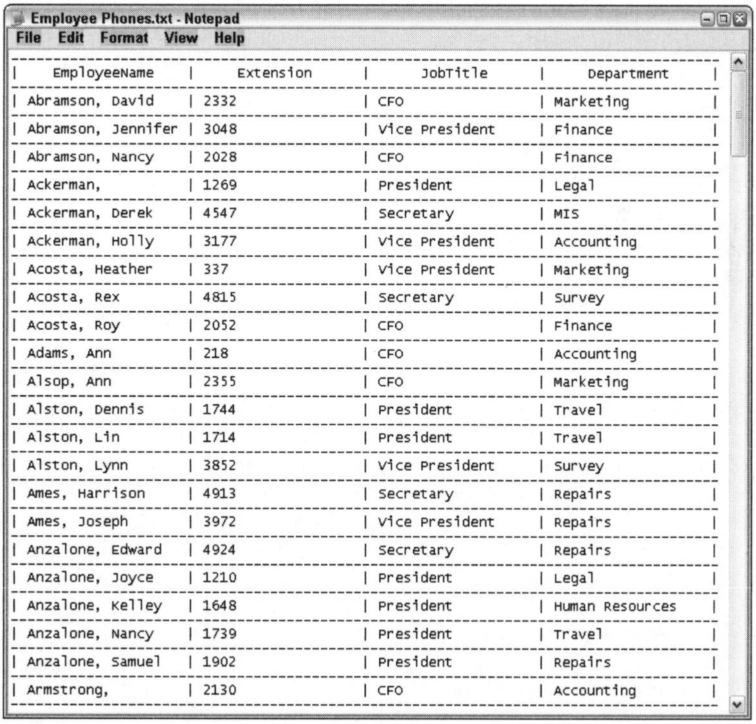

The last selection (Automation) uses VBA code that works with the newly created worksheet to do some formatting. The amount of formatting you can do with Automation code is virtually unlimited, and you can use the Excel macro recorder to help with the syntax needed for various operations. Figure 13.10 shows the formatted worksheet created by this procedure.

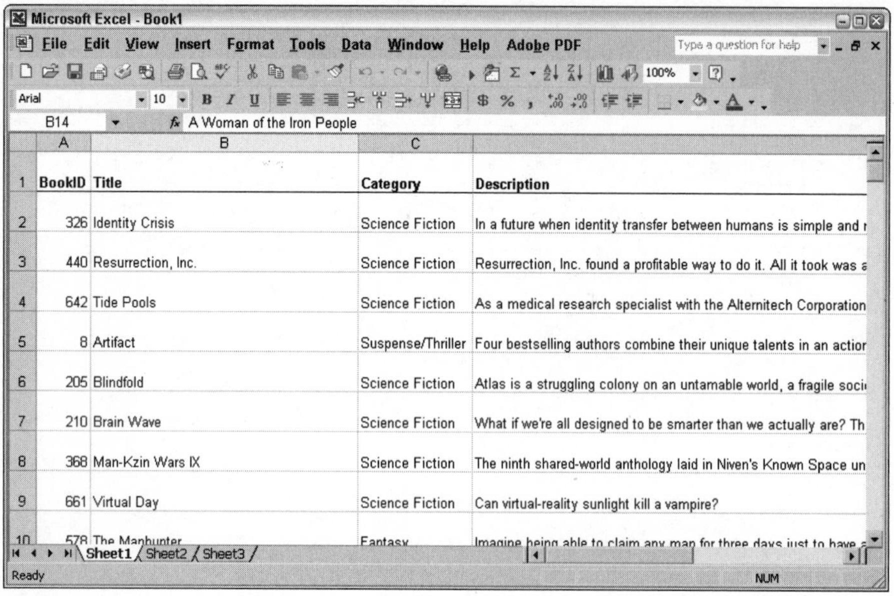

Figure 13.10

This worksheet has columns that are adjusted to fit their contents and rows that are taller than normal so that wrapped descriptions can be read. The column headings are bold, and the headings row is underlined.

Datasheet Form

The Export to Excel (Datasheet) form has two comboboxes in its header, for selecting the data source and export type, and also a set of controls for filtering the data source by a selected value. The code for cboSelectDataSource follows. It clears the txtFilterString textbox, sets several public variables for use later in the code, and then makes the appropriate subform visible, and the other subforms invisible, depending on the data source choice. After this, the cboFilterField and cboFilterValue comboboxes are cleared, and cboFilterField's row source is set to a version of the selected data source query (with the Alpha suffix) that has its columns in alphabetical order, for easier selection from the combobox's list. Finally, the fraRecords option group is enabled, so the user can select to filter the records.

```
Private Sub cboSelectDataSource_AfterUpdate()

On Error GoTo ErrorHandler

    Me![txtFilterString].Value = Null
    pstrDataSource = Me![cboSelectDataSource].Column(1)
```

```
            pstrQuery = Nz(Me![cboSelectDataSource].Column(1)) & "Alpha"

      Select Case pstrDataSource

         Case "qryContacts"
            Me![subContacts].Visible = True
            Me![subContacts].Locked = True
            Me![subEBooks].Visible = False
            Me![subEmployeePhones].Visible = False

         Case "qryEBooksAndAuthors"
            Me![subContacts].Visible = False
            Me![subEBooks].Visible = True
            Me![subEBooks].Locked = True
            Me![subEmployeePhones].Visible = False

         Case "qryEmployeePhones"
            Me![subContacts].Visible = False
            Me![subEBooks].Visible = False
            Me![subEmployeePhones].Visible = True
            Me![subEmployeePhones].Locked = True

      End Select

      Me![cboFilterField].Value = Null
      Me![cboFilterValue].Value = Null
      Me![cboFilterField].RowSource = pstrDataSource & "Alpha"
      Me![fraRecords].Enabled = True
      Me![fraRecords].Value = 1

ErrorHandlerExit:
   Exit Sub

ErrorHandler:
   MsgBox "Error No: " & Err.Number & "; Description: " & _
      Err.Description
   Resume ErrorHandlerExit

End Sub
```

The AfterUpdate event procedure on cboExportType is the same as the procedure for the corresponding control on the listbox form.

On making a selection from the Records option group, an AfterUpdate event procedure runs. It is listed below, with commentary for the first case.

```
Private Sub fraRecords_AfterUpdate()

On Error GoTo ErrorHandler

   Dim intRecords As Integer
```

521

Run a procedure to clear the source objects of the subforms, set filter comboboxes to Null, and delete old tables created by make-table queries.

```
Call ClearList
intRecords = Nz(Me![fraRecords].Value, 1)
```

Set up a Select Case statement to process each data source separately.

```
Select Case pstrDataSource

    Case "qryContacts"
```

Make the appropriate subform visible and locked, and the others invisible.

```
        Me![subContacts].Visible = True
        Me![subContacts].Locked = True
        Me![subEBooks].Visible = False
        Me![subEmployeePhones].Visible = False
        If intRecords = 1 Then
```

If All Records was selected, assign fsubContactsAll as the subContacts subform's source object, and disable the filter comboboxes.

```
            Me![subContacts].SourceObject = "fsubContactsAll"
            Me![cboFilterField].Enabled = False
            Me![cboFilterField].Value = ""
            Me![cboFilterValue].Enabled = False
        ElseIf intRecords = 2 Then
```

If Filtered Records was selected, clear subContacts subform's source object (it will be assigned after selecting a filter value), and enable the filter comboboxes.

```
            Me![subContacts].SourceObject = ""
            Me![cboFilterField].Enabled = True
            Me![cboFilterField].Value = ""
            Me![cboFilterValue].Enabled = False
        End If

    Case "qryEBooksAndAuthors"
        Me![subContacts].Visible = False
        Me![subEBooks].Visible = True
        Me![subEBooks].Locked = True
        Me![subEmployeePhones].Visible = False
        If intRecords = 1 Then
            Me![subEBooks].SourceObject = "fsubEBooksAll"
            Me![cboFilterField].Enabled = False
            Me![cboFilterField].Value = ""
            Me![cboFilterValue].Enabled = False
        ElseIf intRecords = 2 Then
            Me![subEBooks].SourceObject = ""
            Me![cboFilterField].Enabled = True
            Me![cboFilterField].Value = ""
            Me![cboFilterValue].Enabled = False
```

```
            End If

        Case "qryEmployeePhones"
            Me![subContacts].Visible = False
            Me![subEBooks].Visible = False
            Me![subEmployeePhones].Visible = True
            Me![subEmployeePhones].Locked = True
            If intRecords = 1 Then
                Me![subEmployeePhones].SourceObject = "fsubEmployeePhonesAll"
                Me![cboFilterField].Enabled = False
                Me![cboFilterField].Value = ""
                Me![cboFilterValue].Enabled = False
            ElseIf intRecords = 2 Then
                Me![subEmployeePhones].SourceObject = ""
                Me![cboFilterField].Enabled = True
                Me![cboFilterField].Value = ""
                Me![cboFilterValue].Enabled = False
            End If

    End Select

ErrorHandlerExit:
    Exit Sub

ErrorHandler:
    MsgBox "Error No: " & Err.Number & "; Description: " & _
        Err.Description
    Resume ErrorHandlerExit

End Sub
```

As with exporting to Word (see Chapter 11, *Working with Word,* for a more detailed discussion), a SQL string is constructed as a row source for cboFilterValue. cboFilterValue's AfterUpdate event procedure processes the field data type similarly to the Word procedure, but then applies the filter to the selected record source and makes a table to it. It then assigns the appropriate filtered subform as the source object of the appropriate subform, as follows:

```
Me![txtFilterString] = strFilter
strQuery = "qmakMatchingRecords"
strSQL = "SELECT " & pstrQuery & ".* INTO tmakMatchingRecords " _
    & "FROM " & pstrQuery & " WHERE " & strFilter & ";"
Debug.Print "SQL Statement: " & strSQL
Set qdf = dbs.CreateQueryDef(strQuery, strSQL)
qdf.Execute
Me![cboFilterField].Value = Null
Me![cboFilterValue].Value = Null

Debug.Print "Data source: " & pstrDataSource
Select Case pstrDataSource

    Case "qryContacts"
        Me![subContacts].SourceObject = "fsubContactsFiltered"
        Debug.Print "subContacts source object: " _
            & Me![subContacts].SourceObject
```

```
        Case "qryEBooksAndAuthors"
            Me![subEBooks].SourceObject = "fsubEBooksFiltered"
            Debug.Print "subEBooks source object: " _
                & Me![subEBooks].SourceObject

        Case "qryEmployeePhones"
            Me![subEmployeePhones].SourceObject = "fsubEmployeePhonesFiltered"
            Debug.Print "subEmployeePhones source object: " _
                & Me![subEmployeePhones].SourceObject

    End Select
```

Figure 13.11 shows the datasheet form, with the EBooks data source filtered for the Fantasy category.

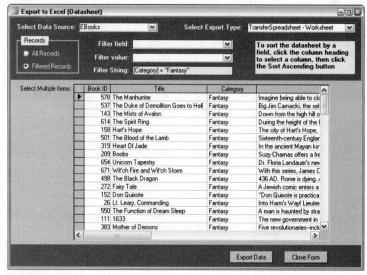

Figure 13.11

The Export Data command button's Click event procedure checks for required choices, as with the comparable procedure on the listbox form, but then uses a different technique to work with the table created by a make-table query, for filtered records.

```
Private Sub cmdExportData_Click()

On Error GoTo ErrorHandler

    'Check that a data source has been selected.
    Set cbo = Me![cboSelectDataSource]
    pstrDataSource = Nz(cbo.Column(1))
    If pstrDataSource = "" Then
        MsgBox "Please select a data source."
        cbo.SetFocus
        cbo.Dropdown
```

```
      GoTo ErrorHandlerExit
   End If

   'Check that an export type and file type have been selected.
   If plngExportType = 0 Then
      MsgBox "Please select an export type"
      Me![cboSelectExportType].SetFocus
      Me![cboSelectExportType].Dropdown
      GoTo ErrorHandlerExit
   End If

   intRecords = Me![fraRecords].Value
```

Determine what data source and export type are to be used, and whether all records or just filtered records are to be merged.

```
   If Me![fraRecords].Value = 2 Then
```

Filtered records—change data source to filtered table.

```
      pstrDataSource = "tmakMatchingRecords"
   Else
```

Keep the selection made in cboSelectDataSource.

```
   End If

   Debug.Print "Data source: " & pstrDataSource
   Debug.Print "Export type: " & plngExportType
```

Set up a Select Case statement to run the appropriate procedure for processing each export type separately.

```
   Select Case plngExportType

      Case 1
         Call TransferToCSV(Me)

      Case 2
         Call OutputToWKS(Me)

      Case 3
         Call OutputToTXT(Me)

      Case 4
         Call TransferToWKS(Me)

      Case 5
         Call CreateWKS(Me)

   End Select

ErrorHandlerExit:
   Close #1
```

```
    'Remove the progress bar.
    varReturn = SysCmd(acSysCmdRemoveMeter)
    Exit Sub

ErrorHandler:
    MsgBox "Error No: " & Err.Number & "; Description: " & _
        Err.Description
    Resume ErrorHandlerExit

End Sub
```

Importing Data from Excel

When you import data from Excel, you are working with either an entire worksheet or a range of data. Since Excel worksheets often have titles, explanatory text, and perhaps charts or other graphics, you will rarely have a worksheet to import that contains nothing but a row of headings and data, so in order to export just the data, you need to define a range and import data from the range. You can also link to an Excel worksheet, which is an option that allows you to work with an Excel worksheet whose contents may change over time.

Importing from Worksheets and Ranges

To test importing data from worksheets, first copy the sample worksheets to your \My Documents\ Access Merge folder, then, to import data from the entire Customers.xls worksheet, click the Import Data from Worksheet button on the Worksheet page of the Import from Excel form. The data is imported, and displayed in a subform, as shown in Figure 13.12.

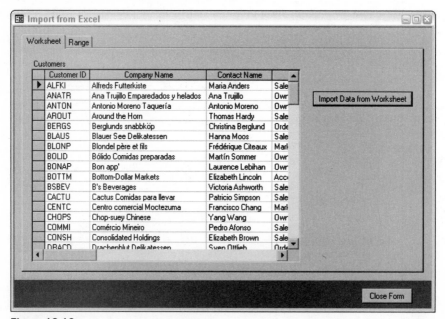

Figure 13.12

The Import Data from Worksheet's Click event procedure follow, with commentary.

```
Private Sub cmdImportDatafromWorksheet_Click()

On Error GoTo ErrorHandler
```

Set variables for the workbook and table names.

```
If CheckDocsDir = False Then
    GoTo ErrorHandlerExit
End If
strWorkbook = GetDocsDir & "Customers.xls"
strTable = "tblCustomers"
```

Clear old data from the table to be filled with data from the workbook.

```
strSQL = "DELETE * FROM " & strTable
DoCmd.SetWarnings False
DoCmd.RunSQL strSQL
```

Import data from the entire workbook into the Access table, using the TransferSpreadsheet method.

```
DoCmd.TransferSpreadsheet transfertype:=acImport, _
    spreadsheettype:=acSpreadsheetTypeExcel9, _
    tablename:=strTable, _
    FileName:=strWorkbook, _
    hasfieldnames:=True
```

Assign the fsubCustomers form as the subform's source object.

```
Me![subCustomers].SourceObject = "fsubCustomers"

ErrorHandlerExit:
    Exit Sub

ErrorHandler:
    MsgBox "Error No: " & Err.Number & "; Description: " & Err.Description
    Resume ErrorHandlerExit

End Sub
```

For the case where you need to define a data range for importing, the procedure listed below does the job. It adds the Range argument to the TransferSpreadsheet method, specifying the CategoryData range for importing data into the Access table.

```
Private Sub cmdImportDatafromRange_Click()

On Error GoTo ErrorHandler

    If CheckDocsDir = False Then
        GoTo ErrorHandlerExit
    End If
    strWorkbook = GetDocsDir & "Categories.xls"
    Debug.Print "Workbook to import: " & strWorkbook
```

```
    strTable = "tblCategories"

    'Clear old data from table
    strSQL = "DELETE * FROM " & strTable
    DoCmd.SetWarnings False
    DoCmd.RunSQL strSQL
```

Import data from the CategoryDate range in the workbook into table, using the TransferSpreadsheet method.

```
    DoCmd.TransferSpreadsheet transfertype:=acImport, _
        spreadsheettype:=acSpreadsheetTypeExcel9, _
        tablename:=strTable, _
        FileName:=strWorkbook, _
        hasfieldnames:=True, _
        Range:="CategoryData"

    Me![subCategories].SourceObject = "fsubCategories"

ErrorHandlerExit:
    Exit Sub

ErrorHandler:
    MsgBox "Error No: " & Err.Number & "; Description: " & Err.Description
    Resume ErrorHandlerExit

End Sub
```

Figure 13.13 shows the Range page of the Import from Excel form, with Northwind food category data imported from a worksheet range.

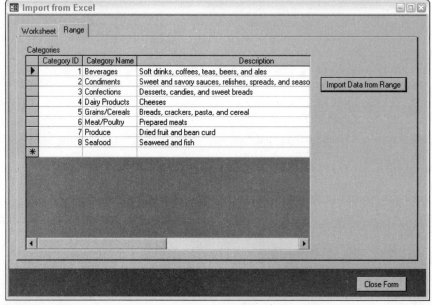

Figure 13.13

Linking to Excel Worksheets and Ranges

As well as importing data from Excel worksheets into Access tables, you can also link to worksheets. If you need to work with data in Excel worksheets that may be updated from time to time, linking can be useful, though there are limitations on what you can do with linked worksheets. To link to a worksheet in the interface, follow the steps below.

Select File | Get External Data | Link Tables, as shown in Figure 13.14.

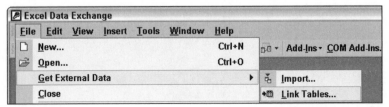

Figure 13.14

In the Link dialog (shown in Figure 13.15), select Microsoft Excel (*xls) as the file type, browse to the folder where the worksheet is stored, select the worksheet to link, and click the Link button.

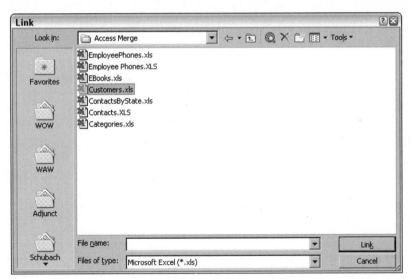

Figure 13.15

The Link Spreadsheet Wizard opens; you can generally accept the defaults. When the Wizard is done, you will have a linked table whose data source is the Excel worksheet you selected. You can't delete records in a linked Excel worksheet, but you can modify data in its cells.

I use the tag txls for linked Excel worksheet tables.

You can also link an Access table to an Excel worksheet in VBA code, using the TransferSpreadsheet method, as follows:

```
Public Function LinkToExcel()

On Error GoTo ErrorHandler

    If CheckDocsDir = False Then
        GoTo ErrorHandlerExit
    End If
    strWorkbook = GetDocsDir & "Customers.xls"
    Debug.Print "workbook to link: " & strWorkbook
    strTable = "txlsCustomers"

    'Clear old data from table, if there is one
On Error Resume Next
    strSQL = "DELETE * FROM " & strTable
    DoCmd.SetWarnings False
    DoCmd.RunSQL strSQL

On Error GoTo ErrorHandler
    'Link to the worksheet, using the TransferSpreadsheet method.
    DoCmd.TransferSpreadsheet transfertype:=acLink, _
        spreadsheettype:=acSpreadsheetTypeExcel9, _
        tablename:=strTable, _
        FileName:=strWorkbook, _
        hasfieldnames:=True

ErrorHandlerExit:
    Exit Function

ErrorHandler:
    MsgBox "Error No: " & Err.Number & "; Description: " & _
        Err.Description
    Resume ErrorHandlerExit

End Function
```

For convenience, this function can be run from the mcrLinkToExcel macro.

Summary

With the information in this chapter and the two previous chapters, you should be able to extend the functionality of your Access database to include the best features of Word, Outlook, and Excel.

Working Outside of Office

The previous three chapters discussed how to use other Office components to enhance your Access applications. There are other export options as well, beyond the bounds of Office—you can write code to send faxes via Symantec WinFax, using either the older DDE technology or Automation, and you can use the antique DOS Write method to create plain text files with information about the progress of mail merges and other procedures.

Sending Faxes with WinFax

Depending on your Windows and Office version, you may have some built-in faxing capability, but if you need more control over sending faxes, especially with attachments, WinFax Pro is an excellent solution. For many versions now, WinFax has supported DDE (Dynamic Data Exchange), an older method of data exchange. With WinFax v. 10.0 or higher, you can also use Automation code to communicate with WinFax.

> **There have been reports of compatibility problems between WinFax 10.0 and Windows XP; the 10.02 upgrade should fix these problems. On my system, WinFax 10.02 works fine with Windows XP Pro, SP 1.**

Sending a Single Fax Using DDE

The main menu of the Non-Office Data Exchange sample database (shown in Figure 14.1) lets you send a simple fax to a recipient selected from a combobox.

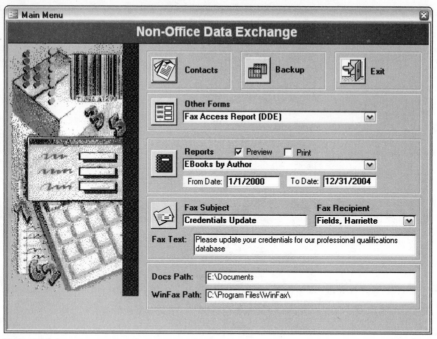

Figure 14.1

There are two textboxes at the bottom of the main menu for entering the Docs path (for creating document files to fax as attachments) and the WinFax folder. The AfterUpdate event procedures for these textboxes are listed below, together with two sets of functions that verify the paths; the functions are called from various procedures in the database.

```
Private Sub txtDocsPath_AfterUpdate()

On Error GoTo ErrorHandler

    Dim strFolderPath As String

    DoCmd.RunCommand acCmdSaveRecord

    'Test the validity of the new folder path
    strFolderPath = Nz(Me![txtDocsPath].Value)
    Debug.Print "Folder path: " & strFolderPath

    If strFolderPath = "" Then
        strTitle = "No path entered"
        strPrompt = "Please enter a Docs folder path"
        MsgBox strPrompt, vbOKOnly + vbCritical, strTitle
        GoTo ErrorHandlerExit
    Else
        'Check for trailing backslash, and add if needed
        If Right(strFolderPath, 1) <> "\" Then
            strFolderPath = strFolderPath & "\"
            Me![txtDocsPath].Value = strFolderPath
```

```
            Call SaveDocsDir(strFolderPath)
        End If

        Set fso = CreateObject("Scripting.FileSystemObject")
        If fso.FolderExists(strFolderPath) = False Then
            strTitle = "Folder path invalid"
            strPrompt = "Please enter a valid Docs folder path"
            MsgBox strPrompt, vbOKOnly + vbCritical, strTitle
            GoTo ErrorHandlerExit
        End If
    End If

ErrorHandlerExit:
    Exit Sub

ErrorHandler:
    MsgBox "Error No: " & Err.Number & "; Description: " & Err.Description
    Resume ErrorHandlerExit

End Sub

Private Sub txtWinFaxPath_AfterUpdate()

On Error GoTo ErrorHandler

    Dim strFolderPath As String

    DoCmd.RunCommand acCmdSaveRecord

    'Test the validity of the new folder path
    strFolderPath = Nz(Me![txtWinFaxPath].Value)
    Debug.Print "Folder path: " & strFolderPath

    If strFolderPath = "" Then
        strTitle = "No path entered"
        strPrompt = "Please enter a WinFax folder path"
        MsgBox strPrompt, vbOKOnly + vbCritical, strTitle
        GoTo ErrorHandlerExit
    Else
        'Check for trailing backslash, and add if needed
        If Right(strFolderPath, 1) <> "\" Then
            strFolderPath = strFolderPath & "\"
            Me![txtWinFaxPath].Value = strFolderPath
            Call SaveWinFaxDir(strFolderPath)
        End If

        Set fso = CreateObject("Scripting.FileSystemObject")
        If fso.FolderExists(strFolderPath) = False Then
            strTitle = "Folder path invalid"
            strPrompt = "Please enter a valid WinFax folder path"
            MsgBox strPrompt, vbOKOnly + vbCritical, strTitle
            GoTo ErrorHandlerExit
        End If
    End If
```

```
ErrorHandlerExit:
   Exit Sub

ErrorHandler:
   MsgBox "Error No: " & Err.Number & "; Description: " & Err.Description
   Resume ErrorHandlerExit

End Sub

Public Function CheckDocsDir() As Boolean

On Error GoTo ErrorHandler

   Set dbs = CurrentDb
   Set rst = dbs.OpenRecordset("tblInfo", dbOpenDynaset)

   With rst
      .MoveFirst
      strFolderPath = Nz(![DocsPath])
      If strFolderPath = "" Then
         strFolderPath = "C:\My Documents\"
      End If
   End With

   'Test the validity of the folder path
   Debug.Print "Folder path: " & strFolderPath

   If strFolderPath = "" Then
      strTitle = "No path entered"
      strPrompt = "Please enter a Docs folder path on the main menu"
      MsgBox strPrompt, vbOKOnly + vbCritical, strTitle
      CheckDocsDir = False
      GoTo ErrorHandlerExit
   Else
      Set fso = CreateObject("Scripting.FileSystemObject")
      If fso.FolderExists(strFolderPath) = False Then
         strTitle = "Folder path invalid"
         strPrompt = "Please enter a valid Docs folder path on the main menu"
         MsgBox strPrompt, vbOKOnly + vbCritical, strTitle
         GoTo ErrorHandlerExit
         CheckDocsDir = False
      End If
   End If

   CheckDocsDir = True

ErrorHandlerExit:
   Exit Function

ErrorHandler:
   MsgBox "Error No: " & Err.Number & "; Description: " & _
      Err.Description
   Resume ErrorHandlerExit

End Function
```

```
Public Function GetDocsDir() As String

On Error GoTo ErrorHandler

    Dim strFolderPath As String

    Set dbs = CurrentDb
    Set rst = dbs.OpenRecordset("tblInfo", dbOpenDynaset)

    With rst
        .MoveFirst
        strFolderPath = Nz(![DocsPath])
        If strFolderPath = "" Then
            strFolderPath = "C:\My Documents\"
        End If
    End With

    'Test the validity of the folder path
    Debug.Print "Folder path: " & strFolderPath

    If strFolderPath = "" Then
        strTitle = "No path entered"
        strPrompt = "Please enter a Docs folder path on the main menu"
        MsgBox strPrompt, vbOKOnly + vbCritical, strTitle
        GoTo ErrorHandlerExit
    Else
        Set fso = CreateObject("Scripting.FileSystemObject")
        If fso.FolderExists(strFolderPath) = False Then
            strTitle = "Folder path invalid"
            strPrompt = "Please enter a valid Docs folder path on the main menu"
            MsgBox strPrompt, vbOKOnly + vbCritical, strTitle
            GoTo ErrorHandlerExit
        End If
    End If

    strDocsDir = strFolderPath & "Access Merge\"
    Debug.Print "Access Merge subfolder: " & strDocsDir

    'Test for existence of Access Merge subfolder, and create
    'it if it is not found
    Set fso = CreateObject("Scripting.FileSystemObject")
    If Not fso.FolderExists(strDocsDir) Then
        'Access Merge subfolder does not exist; create it
        fso.CreateFolder strDocsDir
    End If

    GetDocsDir = strDocsDir

ErrorHandlerExit:
    Exit Function

ErrorHandler:
    MsgBox "Error No: " & Err.Number & "; Description: " & _
        Err.Description
```

```
        Resume ErrorHandlerExit

End Function

Public Function CheckWinFaxDir() As Boolean

On Error GoTo ErrorHandler

    Set dbs = CurrentDb
    Set rst = dbs.OpenRecordset("tblInfo", dbOpenDynaset)

    With rst
        .MoveFirst
        strFolderPath = Nz(![WinFaxPath])
        If strFolderPath = "" Then
            strFolderPath = "C:\My Documents\"
        End If
    End With

    'Test the validity of the folder path
    Debug.Print "Folder path: " & strFolderPath

    If strFolderPath = "" Then
        strTitle = "No path entered"
        strPrompt = "Please enter a WinFax folder path on the main menu"
        MsgBox strPrompt, vbOKOnly + vbCritical, strTitle
        CheckWinFaxDir = False
        GoTo ErrorHandlerExit
    Else
        Set fso = CreateObject("Scripting.FileSystemObject")
        If fso.FolderExists(strFolderPath) = False Then
            strTitle = "Folder path invalid"
            strPrompt = "Please enter a valid WinFax folder path on the main menu"
            MsgBox strPrompt, vbOKOnly + vbCritical, strTitle
            GoTo ErrorHandlerExit
            CheckWinFaxDir = False
        End If
    End If

    CheckWinFaxDir = True

ErrorHandlerExit:
    Exit Function

ErrorHandler:
    MsgBox "Error No: " & Err.Number & "; Description: " & _
        Err.Description
    Resume ErrorHandlerExit

End Function

Public Function GetWinFaxDir() As String
```

```
    On Error GoTo ErrorHandler

    Dim strFolderPath As String

    Set dbs = CurrentDb
    Set rst = dbs.OpenRecordset("tblInfo", dbOpenDynaset)

    With rst
        .MoveFirst
        strFolderPath = Nz(![WinFaxPath])
        If strFolderPath = "" Then
            strFolderPath = "C:\Program Files\WinFax\"
        End If
    End With

    'Test the validity of the folder path
    Debug.Print "Folder path: " & strFolderPath

    If strFolderPath = "" Then
        strTitle = "No path entered"
        strPrompt = "Please enter a WinFax folder path on the main menu"
        MsgBox strPrompt, vbOKOnly + vbCritical, strTitle
        GoTo ErrorHandlerExit
    Else
        Set fso = CreateObject("Scripting.FileSystemObject")
        If fso.FolderExists(strFolderPath) = False Then
            strTitle = "Folder path invalid"
            strPrompt = "Please enter a valid WinFax folder path on the main menu"
            MsgBox strPrompt, vbOKOnly + vbCritical, strTitle
            GoTo ErrorHandlerExit
        End If
    End If

    GetWinFaxDir = strFolderPath

ErrorHandlerExit:
    Exit Function

ErrorHandler:
    MsgBox "Error No: " & Err.Number & "; Description: " & _
        Err.Description
    Resume ErrorHandlerExit

End Function
```

After entering the fax subject and text into textboxes (bound to fields in tblInfo, so the values are preserved between Access sessions), and selecting a fax recipient from the combobox, clicking the large Fax command button runs the code listed below. This Click event procedure sets a number of variables to use when sending the fax, picking up information from the textboxes and various columns of the selected row in the combobox's list. If no subject or text was entered, a default subject ("Reminder") and a message about scheduling the next meeting is composed. Finally, a dialog form opens for inspection and possible editing of the fax text and date (the fax is sent from this form).

```
Private Sub cmdFax_Click()

On Error GoTo ErrorHandler

    Dim strFaxRecipient As String
    Dim strFaxNumber As String
    Dim dteLastMeeting As Date
    Dim strSubject As String
    Dim strMessage As String
    Dim strBody As String
    Dim strCompanyName As String
    Dim frm As Access.Form

    'Check for required fax information
    strFaxNumber = Nz(Me![cboRecipients].Column(1))
    If strFaxNumber = "" Then
        GoTo ErrorHandlerExit
    Else
        strFaxRecipient = Nz(Me![cboRecipients].Column(3))
    End If

    strCompanyName = Nz(Me![cboRecipients].Column(4))
    dteLastMeeting = CDate(Me![cboRecipients].Column(2))
    strSubject = Nz(Me![FaxSubject], "Reminder")
    strMessage = Nz(Me![FaxText])
    If strMessage <> "" Then
        strBody = strMessage
    Else
        strBody = "Your last meeting was on " & dteLastMeeting _
        & "; please call to arrange a meeting by the end of the year."
    End If

    'Open form for creating new fax
    DoCmd.OpenForm FormName:="fdlgFax"
    Set frm = Forms![fdlgFax]
    With frm
        ![txtFaxNumber] = strFaxNumber
        ![txtContactName] = strFaxRecipient
        ![txtCompanyName] = strCompanyName
        ![txtFaxDate] = Date
        ![txtSubject] = strSubject
        ![txtBody] = strBody
    End With

ErrorHandlerExit:
    Exit Sub

ErrorHandler:
    MsgBox "Error No: " & Err.Number & "; Description: " & Err.Description
    Resume ErrorHandlerExit

End Sub
```

The Edit and Send Fax dialog form is shown in Figure 14.2.

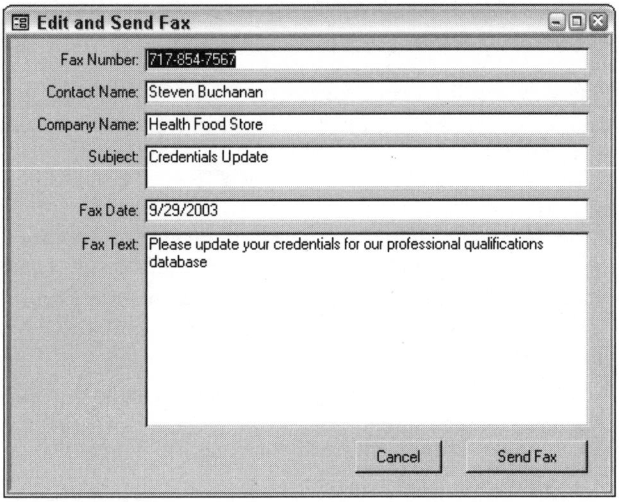

Figure 14.2

The Edit and Send Fax form's Load event calls a Sub procedure, OpenWinFax. This procedure (which follows) creates an instance of WinFax and opens the Message Manager so you can see the progress of the faxes you send. I open WinFax at this point to prevent delays when clicking the Send Fax button. If you do a lot of faxing, you could run this function from the main menu's Load event or an AutoExec macro. Once the Message Manager has been opened, it is available for any future faxes you may send from the database.

```
Public Function OpenWinFax()
'Opens an instance of WinFax (if WinFax is not open) when the
'Fax dialog is opened

On Error GoTo ErrorHandler

    Dim lngChannel As Long

    lngChannel = DDEInitiate(Application:="FAXMNG32", topic:="CONTROL")
    DDETerminate channum:=lngChannel

ErrorHandlerExit:
    Exit Function

ErrorHandler:

    If Err.Number = 282 Then
        strWinFaxDir = GetWinFaxDir & "FAXMNG32.EXE"
        Shell strWinFaxDir
        Resume ErrorHandlerExit
    Else
        MsgBox "Error No: " & Err.Number & "; Description: " & Err.Description
```

```
        Resume ErrorHandlerExit
    End If

End Function
```

The error handler of this procedure gets the WinFax directory from tblInfo, in case WinFax is not found in the default directory. The GetWinFaxDir function is one of the set of path-checking functions described earlier in this chapter.

> If you look up information about DDE communication with WinFax in WinFax Help or the Symantec Knowledge Base, the sample code is not quite right for Access (the nearest code samples I could find were for Word 95, as near as I could tell). I had to do a good deal of trial-and-error tinkering to figure out the DDE syntax that would work in Access 2000 and higher.

The Send Fax command button's Click event procedure follows, with explanatory text.

```
Private Sub cmdSendFax_Click()

On Error GoTo ErrorHandler
```

Declare variables for sending fax.

```
    Dim strFaxNumber As String
    Dim strSubject As String
    Dim strContactName As String
    Dim strCompany As String
    Dim strBody As String
    Dim dteSend As Date
    Dim frm As Access.Form
    Dim strMessage As String
    Dim strSendTime As String
    Dim strSendDate As String
    Dim strRecipient As String
    Dim lngChannel As Long
    Dim strWinFaxDir As String
    Dim strCoverSheet As String
```

Test for required information, and exit the procedure if not found.

```
        strFaxNumber = Me![txtFaxNumber].Value
        If strFaxNumber = "" Then
            MsgBox "Please enter a fax number."
            GoTo ErrorHandlerExit
        Else
            strFaxNumber = "1" & strFaxNumber
        End If

        Debug.Print "Fax: " & strFaxNumber
        strSubject = Me![txtSubject].Value
        strBody = Me![txtBody].Value
```

```
   If strBody = "" Then
      MsgBox "Please enter the fax text."
      Me![txtBody].SetFocus
      GoTo ErrorHandlerExit
   End If
```

Check whether a valid date has been entered, and exit if it has not.

```
   If IsDate(Me![txtFaxDate].Value) = False Then
      MsgBox "Please enter a send date."
      Me![txtFaxDate].SetFocus
      GoTo ErrorHandlerExit
   Else
      dteSend = Me![txtFaxDate].Value
   End If
```

All tests passed; send fax.

```
   If strFaxNumber <> "" Then
      strContactName = Nz(Me![txtContactName])
      strCompany = Nz(Me![txtCompanyName])
      If dteSend = Date Then
         strSendTime = Format(Now(), "hh:mm:ss")
      Else
         strSendTime = "08:00:00"
      End If
      strSendDate = Format(dteSend, "mm/dd/yy")

      strCoverSheet = GetWinFaxDir & "COVER\BASIC1.CVP"
      Debug.Print "Cover sheet: " & strCoverSheet
```

Start the DDE connection to WinFax.

Create the link and disable automatic reception in WinFax.

```
      lngChannel = DDEInitiate(Application:="FAXMNG32", topic:="CONTROL")
      DDEExecute channum:=lngChannel, Command:="GoIdle"
      DDETerminate channum:=lngChannel
```

Create a new link with the TRANSMIT topic.

```
      lngChannel = DDEInitiate("FAXMNG32", "TRANSMIT")
```

Start DDEPokes to control WinFax.

```
      strRecipient = "recipient(" & Chr$(34) & strFaxNumber & Chr$(34) & "," _
         & Chr$(34) & strSendTime & Chr$(34) & "," _
         & Chr$(34) & strSendDate & Chr$(34) & "," _
         & Chr$(34) & strContactName & Chr$(34) & "," _
         & Chr$(34) & strCompany & Chr$(34) & "," _
         & Chr$(34) & strSubject & Chr$(34) & ")"
      Debug.Print "Recipient string: " & strRecipient
      DDEPoke channum:=lngChannel, Item:="sendfax", Data:=strRecipient
```

Specify the cover page to use.

```
DDEPoke channum:=lngChannel, Item:="sendfax", _
    Data:="setcoverpage(" & Chr$(34) _
    & strCoverSheet & Chr$(34) & ")"
```

Send the cover sheet text.

```
DDEPoke channum:=lngChannel, Item:="sendfax", _
    Data:="fillcoverpage(" & Chr$(34) _
    & strBody & Chr$(34) & ")"
```

Show the WinFax send screen.

```
DDEPoke channum:=lngChannel, Item:="sendfax", _
    Data:="showsendscreen(" & Chr$(34) _
    & "0" & Chr$(34) & ")"
```

Set the resolution for the fax.

```
DDEPoke channum:=lngChannel, Item:="sendfax", _
    Data:="resolution(" & Chr$(34) _
    & "HIGH" & Chr$(34) & ")"
```

Send the fax.

```
        DDEPoke channum:=lngChannel, Item:="sendfax", Data:="SendfaxUI"
        DDETerminate channum:=lngChannel
        lngChannel = DDEInitiate(Application:="FAXMNG32", topic:="CONTROL")
        DDEExecute channum:=lngChannel, Command:="GoActive"
        DDETerminate channum:=lngChannel
    End If

ErrorHandlerExit:
    DoCmd.Close objecttype:=acForm, objectname:=Me.Name
    Exit Sub

ErrorHandler:
    MsgBox "Error No: " & Err.Number & "; Description: " & _
        Err.Description
    Resume ErrorHandlerExit

End Sub
```

You will see a WinFax dialog (shown in Figure 14.3) showing the progress of the fax call. If it doesn't connect the first time, WinFax will try again several times until the fax is sent.

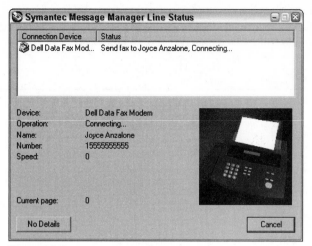

Figure 14.3

Faxing a Report Using DDE

The Main Menu faxing button only sends a fax cover page with a message. If you need to fax a report, you can use another form in the database to select a report to fax to a recipient. This dialog form is similar to the form in Chapter 12, *Working with Outlook,* but with fewer formatting choices: You have a choice of Snapshot or PDF format, or printing directly to the fax. The Snapshot and PDF format choices create a Snapshot or PDF file, which is then attached to an outgoing fax. The Print to Fax selection just prints the report directly to the fax. Printing directly to fax saves the time it takes to create the Snapshot or PDF file, but you have to enter the phone number, fax subject, and text manually, so it may not save time in the long run.

The Fax Access Report (DDE) dialog form is shown in Figure 14.4.

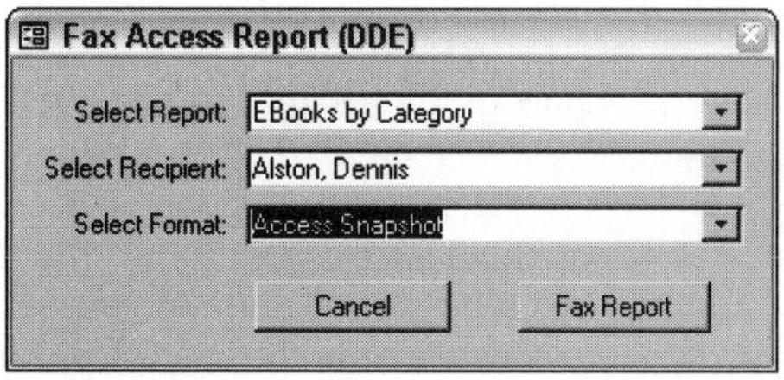

Figure 14.4

When you click the Fax Report command button, if you selected the Snapshot format, you will first get a Printing dialog; while the report is exported to Snapshot format, and then a Creating Attachment Image dialog from WinFax, while the Snapshot file is converted to an attachment, and then the fax with the selected attachment is sent.

If you selected the PDF format, you will get a Save PDF File As dialog, with the \My Documents\Access Merge folder preselected; save the document to this folder with the default file name, because that is where the code will look for it. This dialog is shown in Figure 14.5.

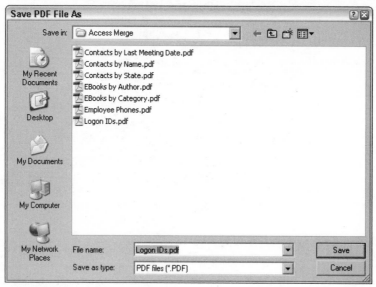

Figure 14.5

The Creating Adobe PDF dialog appears, while the PDF file is created. After the file is created, it opens in Adobe Acrobat or Acrobat Viewer. Next the Creating Attachment Image dialog appears, and finally the fax is sent with the attached report.

In Access 2003, there is a problem with converting both snapshot and PDF files to fax format for use as fax attachments; at the time of writing it is not clear whether the problem is with Access 2003 or WinFax.

Both the Snapshot and PDF selections pick up the recipient's name and fax number from the Access dialog. The last selection, Fax to Printer, does not pick up this information; you need to enter it into the WinFax Send window, as shown in Figure 14.6.

After filling in the name, fax number, and other information on this screen, and clicking the Send button, you get another WinFax screen where you can type in the text to appear on the cover sheet (if desired), and click the Send button to start sending the fax.

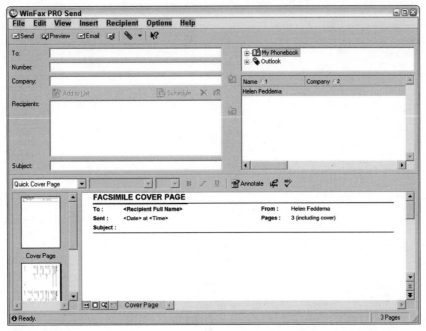

Figure 14.6

The Fax Report command button on the Fax Access Report dialog runs the Click event procedure listed below, which calls the appropriate procedure for each of the three available format types.

```
Private Sub cmdFaxReport_Click()

On Error GoTo ErrorHandler

    Dim strFormatType As String

    strFormatType = Me![cboSelectFormat].Column(0)
    Debug.Print "Selected format: " & strFormatType

    Select Case strFormatType

        Case "Access Snapshot"
            Call FaxReportSNP(Me)

        Case "Adobe PDF"
            Call FaxReportPDF(Me)

        Case "Print to Fax"
            Call FaxReport(Me)

    End Select

ErrorHandlerExit:
```

```
    Exit Sub

ErrorHandler:
    MsgBox "Error No: " & Err.Number & "; Description: " & _
        Err.Description
    Resume ErrorHandlerExit

End Sub
```

The Snapshot procedure is listed below, with commentary.

```
Sub FaxReportSNP(frm As Access.Form)

On Error GoTo ErrorHandler
```

Declare variables for fax properties, picking up information from columns of various comboboxes on the form.

```
    strReport = Nz(frm![cboSelectReport].Column(0))
    strDataSource = Nz(frm![cboSelectReport].Column(2))
    strDisplayName = Nz(frm![cboSelectReport].Column(1))
    strRecipient = Nz(frm![cboSelectRecipient].Column(1))
    strFileName = Mid(Nz(frm![cboSelectReport].Column(0)), 4)
    strExtension = Nz(frm![cboSelectFormat].Column(1))
```

Get the Documents directory from tblInfo.

```
    If CheckDocsDir = False Then
        GoTo ErrorHandlerExit
    End If
    strFilePath = GetDocsDir()
    strFileAndPath = strFilePath & strFileName & strExtension
    Debug.Print "File name and path: " & strFileAndPath
    strCompany = Nz(frm![cboSelectRecipient].Column(4))
```

Test for required information, and exit if not found.

```
    strFaxNumber = frm![cboSelectRecipient].Column(1)
    If strFaxNumber = "" Then
        MsgBox "Please enter a fax number"
        GoTo ErrorHandlerExit
    Else
        strFaxNumber = "1-" & strFaxNumber
    End If

    Debug.Print "Fax: " & strFaxNumber
    strSubject = strDisplayName & " report"
    strBody = "This file was exported from the " & strSubject _
        & " on " & Format(Date, "m/d/yyyy") & "." & vbCrLf
    strSendTime = Format(Time, "hh:mm:ss")
    strSendDate = Format(Date, "mm/dd/yy")
```

Initialize the progress bar (using an arbitrary division of four units).

```
varReturn = SysCmd(acSysCmdInitMeter, _
    "Creating output file ...", 4)
```

Update the progress bar.

```
varReturn = SysCmd(acSysCmdUpdateMeter, 1)
```

Delete the old file, if there is one.

Set fso = CreateObject("Scripting.FileSystemObject").

```
If fso.FileExists(strFileAndPath) = True Then
    fso.DeleteFile strFileAndPath
End If
```

Update the progress bar.

```
varReturn = SysCmd(acSysCmdUpdateMeter, 2)
```

Create new snapshot file in Documents\Access Merge folder.

```
DoCmd.OutputTo objecttype:=acOutputReport, _
    objectname:=strReport, _
    outputformat:=acFormatSNP, _
    outputfile:=strFileAndPath, _
    autostart:=False
```

Update the progress bar.

```
varReturn = SysCmd(acSysCmdUpdateMeter, 3)
```

Test for existence of specified report file, with a loop to prevent premature cancellation.

```
TryAgain:
    Set fso = CreateObject("Scripting.FileSystemObject")
    If fso.FileExists(strFileAndPath) = False Then
        GoTo TryAgain
    End If
```

Update the progress bar.

```
varReturn = SysCmd(acSysCmdUpdateMeter, 4)
```

Create new fax and attach snapshot file to it.

```
strCoverSheet = GetWinFaxDir & "COVER\BASIC1.CVP"
Debug.Print "Cover sheet: " & strCoverSheet
```

Start DDE connection to WinFax.

Create the link and disable automatic reception in WinFax.

```
lngChannel = DDEInitiate(Application:="FAXMNG32", topic:="CONTROL")
DDEExecute channum:=lngChannel, Command:="GoIdle"
DDETerminate channum:=lngChannel
```

Create a new link with the TRANSMIT topic.

```
lngChannel = DDEInitiate("FAXMNG32", "TRANSMIT")
```

Start DDEPokes to control WinFax.

```
strRecipient = "recipient(" & Chr$(34) & strFaxNumber & Chr$(34) & "," _
    & Chr$(34) & strSendTime & Chr$(34) & "," _
    & Chr$(34) & strSendDate & Chr$(34) & "," _
    & Chr$(34) & strContactName & Chr$(34) & "," _
    & Chr$(34) & strCompany & Chr$(34) & "," _
    & Chr$(34) & strSubject & Chr$(34) & ")"
Debug.Print "Recipient string: " & strRecipient
DDEPoke channum:=lngChannel, Item:="sendfax", Data:=strRecipient
```

Specify the cover page.

```
DDEPoke channum:=lngChannel, Item:="sendfax", _
    Data:="setcoverpage(" & Chr$(34) _
    & strCoverSheet & Chr$(34) & ")"
```

Send the cover sheet text.

```
DDEPoke channum:=lngChannel, Item:="sendfax", _
    Data:="fillcoverpage(" & Chr$(34) _
    & strBody & Chr$(34) & ")"
```

Attach the saved report snapshot file.

```
DDEPoke channum:=lngChannel, Item:="sendfax", _
    Data:="attach(" & Chr$(34) & strFileAndPath & Chr$(34) & ")"
```

Show the send screen.

```
DDEPoke channum:=lngChannel, Item:="sendfax", _
    Data:="showsendscreen(" & Chr$(34) _
    & "0" & Chr$(34) & ")"
```

Set the resolution.

```
DDEPoke channum:=lngChannel, Item:="sendfax", _
    Data:="resolution(" & Chr$(34) _
    & "HIGH" & Chr$(34) & ")"
```

Send the fax.

```
DDEPoke channum:=lngChannel, Item:="sendfax", Data:="SendfaxUI"
DDETerminate channum:=lngChannel
lngChannel = DDEInitiate(Application:="FAXMNG32", topic:="CONTROL")
DDEExecute channum:=lngChannel, Command:="GoActive"
DDETerminate channum:=lngChannel
```

Update the progress bar.

```
varReturn = SysCmd(acSysCmdUpdateMeter, 4)

ErrorHandlerExit:
```

Remove the progress bar.

```
varReturn = SysCmd(acSysCmdRemoveMeter)
Exit Sub

ErrorHandler:
    MsgBox "Error No: " & Err.Number & "; Description: " & Err.Description
    Resume ErrorHandlerExit

End Sub
```

The PDF procedure is very similar; only the different portion of this procedure is listed below.

```
Sub FaxReportPDF(frm As Access.Form)
'This code assumes that you have installed Adobe Acrobat and have assigned
'the PDF printer to a copy of each report with the PDF suffix.

On Error GoTo ErrorHandler
```

The suffix "PDF" is added to the report name, to pick up the report version with the PDF printer selected.

```
strReport = Nz(frm![cboSelectReport].Column(0)) & "PDF"
. . .
```

Print the report to the PDF printer.

```
DoCmd.OpenReport strReport, acViewNormal
```

The final procedure is very simple; it just prints the selected report (a version with "Fax" appended to its name) to the WinFax printer.

```
Sub FaxReport(frm As Access.Form)
'This code assumes that you have assigned the WinFax printer to a copy of
'each report with the Fax suffix.
```

```
On Error GoTo ErrorHandler

    strReport = Nz(frm![cboSelectReport].Column(0)) & "Fax"
```

Print the report to Fax printer.

```
    DoCmd.OpenReport strReport, acViewNormal

ErrorHandlerExit:
    Exit Sub

ErrorHandler:
    MsgBox "Error No: " & Err.Number & "; Description: " & Err.Description
    Resume ErrorHandlerExit

End Sub
```

For faxing a report, I recommend using the Snapshot format, because it is somewhat quicker than the PDF format, and doesn't require that you own Adobe Acrobat. And unlike the case with sending a file as an Outlook mail message attachment, the recipient doesn't need Access to view the report converted to Snapshot format. The Snapshot selection also lets you specify the fax information on the Access dialog form, instead of having to type it into two WinFax dialogs, as with the Print to Fax selection.

Sending Multiple Faxes Using Automation

Just as when you create Outlook items from records in an Access table, you may want to create a fax and send it to multiple recipients. This can be done using a MultiSelect listbox on an Access form. The Fax to Multiple Recipients (Automation) form also illustrates use of Automation (instead of DDE) to communicate with WinFax.

As with DDE, the syntax in the WinFax documentation (in this case, the WinFax 10.0 SDK manual) is not quite right for use in Access VBA. The closest examples are for VB 5.0, and I had to experiment with syntax variants to get the Automation code to work right.

The Fax to Multiple Recipients (Automation) form is shown in Figure 14.7.

To work with WinFax using Automation code, you need to set a reference to the WinFax Automation Server, in the References dialog opened from the Tools menu in the Visual Basic window, as shown in Figure 14.8.

The only WinFax object you need to work with when sending faxes is the Send object. I found that the CreateObject syntax given in the WinFax SDK manual did not work in Access VBA. However, I was able to create a Send object (strictly speaking, a CSDKSend object, but it is usually referred to as just the Send object) using the New keyword, as in the following line of code:

```
Dim wfxSend As New wfxctl32.CSDKSend
```

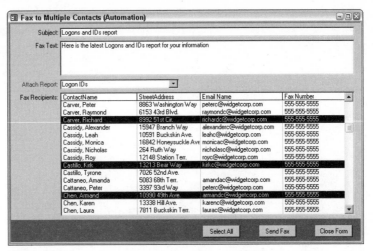

Figure 14.7

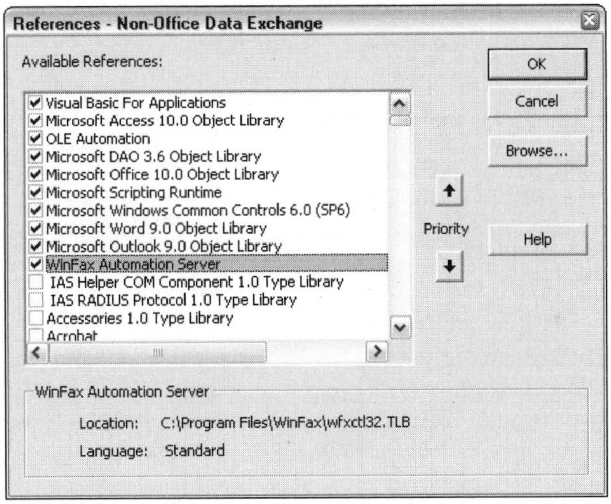

Figure 14.8

The Send object has only methods and events, no properties. They can be viewed in the Object Browser with the wfxctl32 library selected. Figure 14.9 shows some of the methods of the Send object.

Figure 14.9

More information is also available in the WinFax SDK manual, a PDF file you can print out. This manual is available on the WinFax 10.0 or higher CD, and it can also be downloaded from the Symantec Web site. However, the syntax for the VB samples (there are no VBA samples) does not always work in VBA. See the sample code that follows for some syntax that does work.

When you select a report on this form, a Snapshot file is produced for attachment to the fax, using code similar to that in the Snapshot procedure listed previously. When you click the Send Fax command button, a Click event procedure is run. This procedure follows, with commentary.

```
Private Sub cmdSendFax_Click()

On Error GoTo ErrorHandler
```

Declare variables for use in fax.

```
Dim blnSomeSkipped As Boolean
Dim i As String
Dim lngContactID As Long
Dim strBody As String
```

```
Dim strSubject As String
Dim strDate As String
Dim strTime As String
Dim strDocName As String
Dim strDocsPath As String
Dim strFaxNumber As String
Dim strFile As String
Dim strFullName As String
Dim strPrompt As String
Dim strTest As String
Dim strTestFile As String
Dim strText As String
Dim strTextFile As String
Dim strTitle As String
Dim varItem As Variant
```

Declare WinFax Send object variable. This is the only syntax that I found would work in Access VBA code.

```
Dim wfxSend As New wfxctl32.CSDKSend
```

Check that at least one record has been selected, and exit if it has not.

```
Set lst = Me![lstSelectMultiple]
If lst.ItemsSelected.Count = 0 Then
    MsgBox "Please select at least one record."
    lst.SetFocus
    GoTo ErrorHandlerExit
Else
    intColumns = lst.ColumnCount
    intRows = lst.ItemsSelected.Count
End If
```

Check that subject and fax body have been entered, and exit if they have not.

```
strSubject = Nz(Me![txtSubject])
If strSubject = "" Then
    strTitle = "Missing Subject"
    strPrompt = "Please enter fax subject."
    Me![txtSubject].SetFocus
    GoTo ErrorHandlerExit
End If

strBody = Nz(Me![txtBody])
If strBody = "" Then
    strTitle = "Missing Fax body"
    strPrompt = "Please enter fax body."
    Me![txtBody].SetFocus
    GoTo ErrorHandlerExit
End If
```

Open the text file for writing information about export progress.

```
strFile = strDocsPath & "Export Progress.txt"
Debug.Print "Text file: " & strFile
Open strFile For Output As #1
Print #1, "Information on progress faxing selected contacts"
Print #1,
Print #1,

blnSomeSkipped = False
```

Create the fax, using the methods of the WinFax Send object.

```
With wfxSend
   .SetSubject (strSubject)
   .SetCoverText (strBody)
```

Attach the report, if one has been selected.

```
Debug.Print "File attachment: " & pstrSnapshotFile
.AddAttachmentFile pstrSnapshotFile
```

Set up a For Each . . . Next structure to process all the selected records in the listbox, using the ItemsSelected collection.

```
For Each varItem In lst.ItemsSelected
```

Get the Contact ID for reference.

```
lngContactID = Nz(lst.Column(0, varItem))
Debug.Print "Contact ID: " & lngContactID
```

Check for required information, and skip any records that are missing a value in one of the required fields.

```
strTest = Nz(lst.Column(1, varItem))
Debug.Print "Contact name: " & strTest
If strTest = "" Then
   blnSomeSkipped = True
   strText = "Contact No. " & lngContactID & " skipped; no name"
   Print #1,
   Print #1, strText
   GoTo NextItemContact
Else
   strFullName = Nz(lst.Column(7, varItem))
End If

strFaxNumber = Nz(lst.Column(13, varItem))
strTest = strFaxNumber
Debug.Print "Fax number: " & strTest
If strTest = "" Then
   blnSomeSkipped = True
   strText = "Contact No. " & lngContactID & " (" _
```

```
                     & strFullName & ") skipped; no fax number"
               Print #1,
               Print #1, strText
               GoTo NextItemContact
          Else
               strFaxNumber = "1-" & strFaxNumber
          End If
```

All required information present; add recipient to fax.

```
               .SetNumber (strFaxNumber)
               .SetTo (strFullName)
               .AddRecipient
               strText = "Contact No. " & lngContactID & " (" & strFullName _
                    & ") has all required information; adding to fax"
               Print #1,
               Print #1, strText

       NextItemContact:
            Next varItem
```

Send the fax to all recipients.

```
               .Send (0)
          End With

       ErrorHandlerExit:
```

Close the text file, and set the WinFax Send object to Nothing.

```
          Close #1
          Set wfxSend = Nothing
          Exit Sub

       ErrorHandler:
          MsgBox "Error No: " & Err.Number & "; Description: " & _
               Err.Description
          Resume ErrorHandlerExit

       End Sub
```

After clicking this button, the Creating Attachment Image dialog appears as the Snapshot file is converted into a WinFax attachment, and then the fax is sent to all the selected recipients.

Writing Data to a Text File

If you don't have WinFax installed, when you open the sample database, you will see the error message shown in Figure 14.10, and the large button on the main menu will have the caption #Error, as shown in Figure 14.11.

Figure 14.10

Figure 14.11

If you open the References dialog from the Tools menu in the Visual Basic window, you will see the reference marked as "MISSING", as shown in Figure 14.12. If you uncheck this reference, you will be able to select and use the Export Contacts to Outlook form for testing text file creation, but of course you won't be able to send faxes.

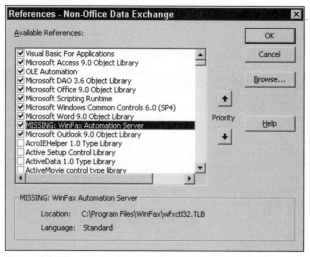

Figure 14.12

Chapter 13, *Working with Excel,* covered exporting Access data to two different text formats—comma-delimited (.csv) and plain text (.txt). However, this is not the only way you can export to a text file from Access. Fossilized in Access VBA there are some antique DOS methods that you can use to create and write to text files. I like to use these methods to write information about exports, in particular to record any problems that result in Access records being skipped. Several of the earlier chapters used the `Write` # method to write information about skipped records to a text file. In this chapter, I expand the technique to write a line to a text file about every record selected for export, to give the user a complete record of the export, including both the records that were processed and those that were skipped.

Export Contacts to Outlook

The Export Contacts to Outlook form uses this technique. This form (shown in Figure 14.13) has a command button for selecting an Outlook folder (see Chapter 12, *Working with Outlook,* for an explanation of how this button works), a listbox for selecting contacts to export, and a command button to do the export (the command button is only enabled after selecting an Outlook folder).

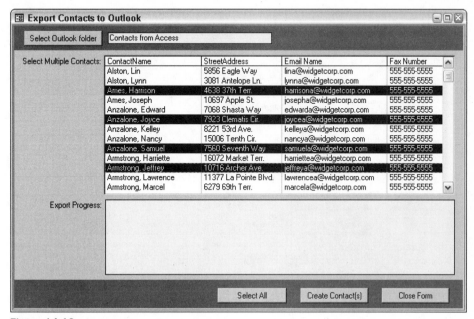

Figure 14.13

When you click the Create Contact(s) button, the Click event procedure that follows runs. It is substantially similar to the procedure for exporting data to Outlook contacts on the Export to Outlook (Listbox) form in Chapter 12. The portions of the code related to creating and writing to the text file are commented in the code listed below.

```
Private Sub cmdCreateContacts_Click()

On Error GoTo ErrorHandler
```

Declare Outlook, DAO, and text variables for use in exporting.

```
Dim blnSomeSkipped As Boolean
Dim con As Outlook.ContactItem
Dim dbs As DAO.Database
Dim fldCalendar As Outlook.MAPIFolder
Dim fldContacts As Outlook.MAPIFolder
Dim i As String
Dim itm As Object
Dim lngContactID As Long
Dim nms As Outlook.NameSpace
```

```
Dim strBody As String
Dim strCity As String
Dim strCompanyName As String
Dim strContactName As String
Dim strCountry As String
Dim strDocName As String
Dim strDocsPath As String
Dim strDocType As String
Dim strEMailRecipient As String
Dim strFile As String
Dim strFullName As String
Dim strJobTitle As String
Dim strMessage As String
Dim strName As String
Dim strNameAndJob As String
Dim strPostalCode As String
Dim strPrompt As String
Dim strSalutation As String
Dim strShortDate As String
Dim strStateProv As String
Dim strStreetAddress As String
Dim strTest As String
Dim strTestFile As String
Dim strText As String
Dim strTextFile As String
Dim strTitle As String
Dim txt As Access.TextBox
Dim varItem As Variant
```

Check that at least one record has been selected.

```
Set lst = Me![lstSelectMultiple]
If lst.ItemsSelected.Count = 0 Then
    MsgBox "Please select at least one record."
    lst.SetFocus
    GoTo ErrorHandlerExit
Else
    intColumns = lst.ColumnCount
    intRows = lst.ItemsSelected.Count
End If
```

Set Outlook application variable; if Outlook is not running, the error handler defaults to CreateObject.

```
Set gappOutlook = GetObject(, "Outlook.Application")
```

Set a reference to the textbox for writing information about exported or skipped records.

```
Set txt = Me![txtExportProgress]
If CheckDocsDir = False Then
    GoTo ErrorHandlerExit
End If
strDocsPath = GetDocsDir
```

Open a text file in the \My Documents\Access Merge folder for writing information about exported or skipped records.

```
strFile = strDocsPath & "Export Progress.txt"
Debug.Print "Text file: " & strFile
Open strFile For Output As #1
```

Write header information to the text file.

```
Print #1, "Information on progress exporting contacts to Outlook"
```

The following command creates a blank line in the text file.

```
Print #1,
```

Write the Outlook folder name to the text file.

```
Print #1, "Target folder: " & pfld.Name
Print #1,
Print #1,

blnSomeSkipped = False
strText = ""

For Each varItem In lst.ItemsSelected
    'Get Contact ID for reference
    lngContactID = Nz(lst.Column(0, varItem))
    Debug.Print "Contact ID: " & lngContactID

    'Check for required information
    strTest = Nz(lst.Column(1, varItem))
    Debug.Print "Contact name: " & strTest
    If strTest = "" Then
```

If the contact name is missing, write information on this to the textbox and the text file.

```
        blnSomeSkipped = True
        strText = "Contact No. " & lngContactID & " skipped; no name"
        Print #1,
        Print #1, strText
```

For writing to the textbox, append the new text to the existing text, and remove the leading CR + LF (Chr(10) & Chr(13)) so there won't be a blank line before the first entry.

```
        strText = txt.Value & vbCrLf & strText
        If Asc(Left(strText, 1)) = 10 Then
            strText = Mid(strText, 2)
        End If
        txt.Value = strText
        GoTo NextItemContact
    Else
        strFullName = Nz(lst.Column(7, varItem))
    End If
```

```
strEMailRecipient = Nz(lst.Column(12, varItem))
strTest = strEMailRecipient
Debug.Print "Email address: " & strTest
If strTest = "" Then
```

If the email address is missing, write information on this to the textbox and the text file.

```
    blnSomeSkipped = True
    strText = "Contact No. " & lngContactID & " (" _
        & strFullName & ") skipped; no email address"
    Print #1,
    Print #1, strText
    strText = txt.Value & vbCrLf & strText
    If Asc(Left(strText, 1)) = 10 Then
        strText = Mid(strText, 2)
    End If
    txt.Value = strText
    GoTo NextItemContact
End If

strStreetAddress = Nz(lst.Column(2, varItem))
strTest = strStreetAddress
Debug.Print "Street address: " & strTest
If strTest = "" Then
```

If the street address is missing, write information on this to the textbox and the text file.

```
    blnSomeSkipped = True
    strText = "Contact No. " & lngContactID & " (" _
        & strFullName & ") skipped; no street address"
    Print #1,
    Print #1, strText
    strText = txt.Value & vbCrLf & strText
    Debug.Print Asc(Left(strText, 1))
    If Asc(Left(strText, 1)) = 13 Then
        strText = Mid(strText, 3)
    End If
    txt.Value = strText
    GoTo NextItemContact
End If
```

All required information is present; create a contact.

Write a line about the creation of the contact to the textbox and the text file.

```
strText = "Contact No. " & lngContactID & " (" & strFullName _
    & ") has all required information; creating an Outlook contact"
Print #1,
Print #1, strText
strText = txt.Value & vbCrLf & strText
txt.Value = strText

strJobTitle = Nz(lst.Column(10, varItem))
```

```
        strCity = Nz(lst.Column(3, varItem))
        strStateProv = Nz(lst.Column(4, varItem))
        strPostalCode = Nz(lst.Column(5, varItem))
        strCountry = Nz(lst.Column(6, varItem))
        strCompanyName = Nz(lst.Column(9, varItem))
        strSalutation = Nz(lst.Column(11, varItem))
```

Create a new contact item in default local Contacts folder.

```
        Set gappOutlook = GetObject(, Outlook.Application)
        Set con = gappOutlook.CreateItem(olContactItem)
        With con
            .CustomerID = lngContactID
            .FullName = strFullName
            .JobTitle = strJobTitle
            .BusinessAddressStreet = strStreetAddress
            .BusinessAddressCity = strCity
            .BusinessAddressState = strStateProv
            .BusinessAddressPostalCode = strPostalCode
            .BusinessAddressCountry = strCountry
            .CompanyName = strCompanyName
            .NickName = strSalutation
            .Email1Address = strEMailRecipient
            .Close (olSave)
        End With

NextItemContact:
    Next varItem

ErrorHandlerExit:
```

Close the text file.

```
    Close #1
    Exit Sub

ErrorHandler:
    If Err = 429 Then
        'Outlook is not running; open Outlook with CreateObject.
        Set gappOutlook = CreateObject("Outlook.Application")
        Resume Next
    Else
        MsgBox "Error No: " & Err.Number & "; Description: " & Err.Description
        Resume ErrorHandlerExit
    End If

End Sub
```

The form also has a textbox that lists the same data that is written to the text file. You can see information about the export in the textbox in Figure 14.14.

If you are exporting only a few records, you can see all the data you need right in the textbox. However, when more than a few contacts are selected for export, you will need to refer to the text file for full information on the export. Figure 14.15 shows the text file produced by an export open in Notepad.

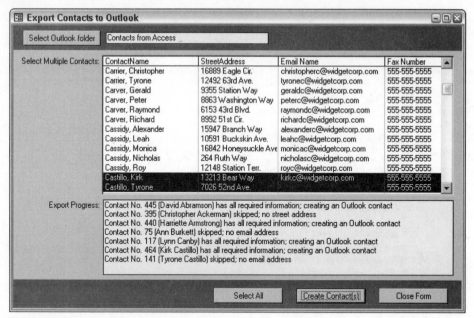

Figure 14.14

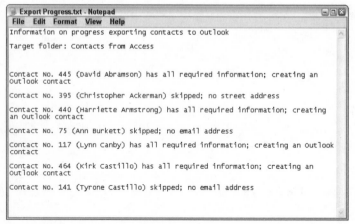

Figure 14.15

Summary

With the techniques in this chapter, you can go beyond the other components of the Office suite, exporting data to text files and creating faxes using Symantec WinFax.

Index

P